D0780532

THE
FRIENDS OF THE
ORINDA
LIBRARY

THIS BOOK IS A GIFT FROM THE FRIENDS OF THE ORINDA LIBRARY

Also by Terese Svoboda

FICTION

Pirate Talk or Mermalade
Tin God
Trailer Girl and Other Stories
A Drink Called Paradise
Cannibal
Bohemian Girl

NONFICTION

Black Glasses Like Clark Kent:
A GI's Secret from Postwar Japan

POETRY

When The Next Big War Blows Down the Valley:
Selected and New Poems
Weapons Grade
Dogs are Not Cats (chapbook)
Treason
Mere Mortals
Laughing Africa
All Aberration
Cleaned the Crocodile's Teeth: Nuer Song (translation)

WITHDRAWN

Anything That Burns You

Copyright © 2015 and 2016 by Terese Svoboda

First Hardcover Edition
Printed in the United States of America

Cover Photo: Granted by permission, courtesy Jill Quasha for the Estate of Marjorie Content

Parts of this book have appeared as excerpts in the following publications:
American Poetry Review, Boston Review

Owing to limitations of space, all acknowledgments for permission to reprint previously
published or unpublished material may be found at the end of the volume.

Library of Congress Cataloging-in-Publication Data

Names: Svoboda, Terese.
Title: Anything that burns you : a portrait of Lola Ridge, radical poet/
    Terese Svoboda.
Description: Tucson, AZ : Schaffner Press, Inc., 2016.
Identifiers: LCCN 2015037621| ISBN 9781936182961 (hardback)
    ISBN 9781936182978 (mobi/kindle) | ISBN 9781936182985 (epub)
Subjects: LCSH: Ridge, Lola, 1873-1941. | Poets, American--20th
    century--Biography. | Women poets, American--20th century--Biography. |
BISAC: BIOGRAPHY & AUTOBIOGRAPHY / Literary. |
    BIOGRAPHY & AUTOBIOGRAPHY / Women.
Classification: LCC PS3535.I436 Z65 2016 | DDC 811/.52--dc23
LC record available at http://lccn.loc.gov/2015037621

ISBN: 978-1-93618-296-1
Mobi/Kindle: 978-1-93618-297-8
Epub: 978-1-93618-298-5
PDF: 978-194618-299-2

www.schaffnerpress.com

Anything That Burns You

A Portrait of Lola Ridge, Radical Poet

Terese Svoboda

SCHAFFNER PRESS
Tucson, Arizona

"Let anything that burns you come out whether it be propaganda or not...
I write about something that I feel intensely. How can you help
writing about something you feel intensely?"

—Lola Ridge

To Lauren Cerand

Table of Contents

I

Dublin, Sydney, Hokitika, Sydney, San Francisco, 1873–1907

"One of Them"

One tall, thin figure of a woman stepped out alone, a good distance into the empty square, and when the police came down at her and the horse's hooves beat over her head, she did not move, but stood with her shoulders slightly bowed, entirely still. The charge was repeated again and again, but she was not to be driven away. A man near me said in horror, suddenly recognizing her, "That's Lola Ridge!"

In 1927 Lola Ridge was known to a huge public primarily as the author of *The Ghetto and Other Poems*, a book that portrayed the immigrant as human, struggling yes, but with hopes for the future. Sacco and Vanzetti were two such immigrants, about to be executed for crimes they most likely did not commit. Ridge too was an immigrant, having traveled across the Pacific from New Zealand. Her presence at the demonstration was announced in advance on the front page of major newspapers as an important witness to the event. She was also an anarchist when anarchy was a political possibility, especially among intellectuals and artists—and immigrants, those who had left their home country to pursue the dream of freedom in the country that promised it.

Sacco and Vanzetti were also anarchists. That alone made them suspect—and not without cause, being themselves not the leftwing radicals of Ridge's circle, the poets and painters and critics and philanthropists who picketed with her, but gun-toting subversives looking for trouble. But all their trial revealed was a blatant disregard for civil liberties by the police, and a corrupt judicial system. The presiding judge called Sacco and Vanzetti "Bolsheviki" in public, and announced to the world that he would "get them good and proper." Even after another criminal confessed to the charges, he would not consent to a re-trial. Leaders all over the world found the situation appalling. Nobel Prize-winner Anatole France, eloquent during the Dreyfus case in Europe, wrote in his "Appeal to the American People": "The death of

Sacco and Vanzetti will make martyrs of them and cover you with shame. You are a great people. You ought to be a just people." After the immigrants' execution, fifty thousand mourners attended their funeral, and film footage of the event was considered so powerful that it was destroyed.

Ridge was an outsider capitalizing on her accent, her sex—female poets were ascendant just then—and her looks. Anorexic and Virginia Woolf-ethereal, she worked as an artist's model when she first arrived in the U.S. Tiny, yet always described as tall, she stood up to the rearing horse outside the Charleston State Prison, baiting the police officer to turn her into another martyr. "All in the one beating moment, there, awaiting the falling/ Cataract of the hooves," she wrote, describing the confrontation in her last book, *Dance of Fire*.

Would we remember Ridge now if she had died under that horse? Ridge dead would have emphasized the seriousness of the situation—but the situation was already serious, people all over the world were demonstrating. Sacco and Vanzetti would, most likely, have been executed anyway, given the vehemency of the judiciary. The obligation of the artist, and especially the artist-celebrity, is to witness and record—like a journalist, yes—but also to express their feelings about what they see. Such a highly charged public event had emotional repercussions with a great number of people. Perhaps Ridge recognized that by living to write more poems, she might lessen the number of executions—but she did not step back. Did the poems she wrote in the aftermath relieve her submerged guilt, anguish and frustration and that of the public? Were the poems, in other words, counter-revolutionary? Poetry—the opiate of the people? Or does poetry do nothing, as the New Critics would have it? In Ridge's case, it kept the issue alive.

Ridge was one of the first to delineate the life of the poor in Manhattan and in particular, women's lives in New York City. The title poem of her second book, *Sun-up and Other Poems*, is a striking modernist depiction of a girl's interior life. Harriet Monroe, founder of *Poetry*, and William Rose Benét, founder of the *Saturday Review of Literature*, called Ridge a genius. Four years before Eliot's bleak and anti-Semitic "The Waste Land," her equally long poem "The Ghetto" celebrated the "otherness" of the Jewish Lower East Side and prophesied the multiethnic world of the 21st century. "An early, great chronicler of New York life," wrote three-time poet laureate Robert Pinsky in a *Slate* column about Ridge in 2011. She embraced her subject along Whitmanian lines, yet here's a small bomb of a poem likened to the poetry of H.D. and Emily Dickinson, that remains a model of imagist engagement with the world:

Debris

I love those spirits
That men stand off and point at,
Or shudder and hood up their souls—
Those ruined ones,
Where Liberty has lodged an hour
And passed like flame,
Bursting asunder the too small house. (*Ghetto* 43)

At the end of the teens and early 1920s, when Ridge was one of the editors of *Others* and then *Broom* magazine, she presided over Thursday-afternoon salons filled with modernist hotshots. Eating slices of Ridge's cake and drinking whatever Prohibition would allow (and not), William Carlos Williams and Robert McAlmon hatched plans for their magazine *Contact*, 20-year-old Hart Crane flirted with everyone in sight, Marianne Moore read early drafts of her own work, and Mayakovsky stomped on her coffee table.

In 1919, Ridge gave a speech in Chicago entitled "Woman and the Creative Will," about how sexually constructed gender roles hinder female development—ten years before Virginia Woolf wrote "A Room of One's Own." "Woman is not and never has been man's natural inferior," Ridge announced. Although she wrote little personal poetry, Ridge advocated individual liberty. She supported not only the rights of women, but laborers, blacks, Jews, immigrants, and homosexuals. She wrote about lynching, execution, race riots, and imprisonment. As a rebellious lefty, she interacted closely with the most radical women of her era, from editing Margaret Sanger's magazine on birth control in 1918, to reciting her own poems at Emma Goldman's deportation dinner. Eventually she was arrested during the demonstration against the execution of Sacco and Vanzetti and hauled off with Edna St. Vincent Millay. In 1936, watching a Mayday parade in Mexico City, she raised her fist in solidarity with the marching communists.

Despite the praise she received in her obituary in 1941, which described her as one of the leading poets of America, few have heard of her today. She died at the nadir of leftist politics, just as the U.S. was entering World War II. By then Eliot and Pound had very effectively equated "elitism" with "good" in poetry. Surely the 60s generation that rediscovered feminism and anarchy would have resurrected her. Not quite. Although her work appears in two important anthologies of the period, and her life as an anarchist should have had great appeal to the revolutionary spirit of the time, her poetry was not revived. For the last forty years, her executor has promised a biography and a collected works, contributing much to Ridge's relative obscurity and neglect. Feminist critic Louise Bernikow singled out Ridge and Genevieve Taggard as twice-neglected because they were women and radicals, part of "the buried history within the buried history." Although poetry has always addressed society's problems and recorded its cultural and political history—whatever its formal precepts—society has not always wanted to hear about these subjects. What has been lost by these omissions is the radical and political tradition in twentieth-century American poetry, and the idea that such subjects are even appropriate for poetry. An entire generation and tradition has essentially been amputated from literary consciousness. Today, the same neo-fascist threat that Ridge experienced in the earliest years of the century appeals to Americans and Europeans now in search of order and conformity. An increasing disparity between rich and poor, revived racist agendas, a re-definition of torture, seemingly ineradicable war, violence toward immigrants, and a discounting of art and culture, increasingly treated as unnecessary to society. The truncated branch of poetry that Ridge represents should remind readers that the discourse of today does not have to take the form that it does, and that many self-evident truths are actually hysterical responses to change or threats to privilege. Poets should have a continuing presence in dissent from those "truths." "I write about something that I feel intensely," Ridge told an interviewer, "how can you help writing about something you feel intensely?" The freedom she exercised came at a time when the Russians were in revolution—and a urinal was put on a pedestal by the Baronness Elsa von Freytag-Loringhoven, not Duchamp. Politics + art + free expression + women = fire, Ridge's favorite image. In 2014's *Modernist Women Poets: An Anthology* included her work, prompting *Publisher's Weekly* to note: "even sophisticates can still make discoveries here, among them Lola Ridge." Perhaps Ridge's time has come at last.

Born in Ireland, Ridge asserted that she was "a descendant on my mother's side of a very old Irish race of Princes." As unlikely as that seems, a distant contemporary relative produced a document that traced Ridge's lineage in a direct line from Hemon, king of Ireland, and Scota, the daughter of the king of Egypt, and descent from the last prince of Briefney. The report was extracted from 70 pages of genealogical detail dictated by Ridge's grandfather, John Reilly, with six critical pages verified by the Biographical Society of Ireland.

> I, John Reilly, a retired officer collector of Customs in Her Majesty's service, and eldest son of John Lazarus Reilly, claim to be the Representative Head of the Reilly family in the 8th generation, lineally descended through the elder branch from Edmond who died in 1601, being the last reigning prince of Eastern Briefney...

Ridge's branch of the family lived in Loughrea, in the county of Galway. Built around the mile-wide Loughrea Lake fed by seven springs, in 1846 the market town had 5,000 inhabitants living among the remains of a castle, a garrison, a nunnery, a monastery, a lovely promenade, two branch banks, an extensive and long-established brewery, two tanneries, six corn mills, and three hotels. Ridge's paternal grandfather, Joseph H. Ridge, worked as an attorney in Loughrea and in North Dublin where he and Ridge's maternal grandfather would move before 1867. Perhaps like many who had means, they fled to Dublin to avoid the worst of the famine that reduced County Galway's population by nearly a third, decimation that included sending boatloads of orphan girls sent off to Australia. Ridge's maternal grandmother, Maria Ormsby Reilly, died in 1868. She left behind Ridge's mother, Emma, the second to youngest, with five more sisters and three brothers.

By 1869, the widower John Reilly had retired to St. James Terrace, Dolphin's Barn in Dublin, in an area known as The Back of the Pipes, the location of a waterworks for the River Poddle for 400 years. James Joyce knew the place well, mentioning it eight times in *Ulysses*, most immortally in Molly Bloom's soliloquy: "then I wrote the night he kissed my heart at Dolphins Barn I couldn't describe." Two Dolphins Barn is where Bloom lives—the house right next to the Reillys'. The Back of the Pipes was a popular place for courting couples, and featured a "stone sofa" at St. James Walk. The Victorians were desperate for a place to get away to do their courting: later and fewer marriages were a marked characteristic of Irish society of the time. John Reilly's eldest daughter, Maria, married an attorney when she was 28. Emma may have been in her early thirties when she wed medical student Joseph Henry Ridge in 1871, presumably the son of the same-named attorney who had lived in Loughrea, where they were raised. Born two years later, on December 12, 1873, Lola Ridge was wanted and cherished as an only child tends to be, and that love was reciprocated.

Mother

Your love was like moonlight
turning harsh things to beauty,
so that little wry souls
reflecting each other obliquely
as in cracked mirrors...
beheld in your luminous spirit
their own reflection,
transfigured as in a shining stream,
and loved you for what they are not. (*Sun-up* 69)

Ridge's parents separated in Dublin when she was only a year old. Perhaps Joseph Henry Ridge had inherited his namesake's tendency to get into trouble. An 1828 newspaper ran an account of a duel held between a Mr. Skerrett and the solicitor Mr. Ridge, who had asked questions of Skerret's father in court that his son considered unnecessary. After the shots were fired, the two parties agreed that horsewhipping Mr. Ridge at the Loughrea racecourse the next day would be an amicable solution. Whatever the problem between Ridge's mother and father, divorce was anathema in Catholic Ireland, and was not recognized as a legal remedy until 1996. Emma was living with her father when Lola was born. Most likely Joseph had left or was evicted. The few letters known to exist are not hostile but suggest that "fate" is all that kept them apart. But then Ridge's grandfather died.

Grandpa, grandpa...
(Light all about you...
ginger...pouring out of green jars...)
You don't believe he has gone away and left his great
     coat...
so you pretend...you see his face up in the ceiling.
When you clap your hands and cry, grandpa, grandpa,
     grandpa,
Celia crosses herself. (*Sun-up* 4)

As customs collector, Ridge's grandfather must have afforded the services of at least one servant. Sarah Kinsella made an X on Ridge's birth certificate beside her address, 28 Cole Alley, a less than desirable street eleven years earlier "with 915 persons who sleep in 294 beds, including 170 wads of straw." In *Sun-up and Other Poems*, Celia is the servant who comforts her mother in a moment of extreme distress.

> ...mama's eyes stare out of the pillow
> as though she had gone away
> and the night had come in her place
> as it comes in empty rooms...
> you can't bear it—
> the night threshing about
> and lashing its tail on its sides
> as bold as a wolf that isn't afraid—
> and you scream at her face, that is white as a stone on a
>   grave
> and pull it around to the light,
> till the night draws backward...the night that walks
>   alone,
> and goes without end.
> Mama says, I'm cold, Betty, and shivers.
> Celia tucks the quilt about her feet,
> but I run for my little red cloak
> because red is hot like fire. (*Sun-up* 5-6)

The mother seems inconsolable. What could a separated woman do to make a living in Ireland? The nunnery was out. Prostitution? Apparently joining the household of one of her siblings in Dublin was less appealing than emigrating halfway around the world. Perhaps her father had left her enough money for overseas passage to live with her oldest sister Maria, "Mysie," who had sailed for Australia around 1876, with a second husband, Richard Alfred Penfold, "Fred." The three Penfolds in the New South Wales Directory in 1867 suggest the possibility that Fred's family might have greeted them, and on Mysie's side, the Reilly family documents show an uncle William and a Reilly cousin emigrating even earlier to Australia. In 1877 Emma and four-year-old Lola followed Mysie and Fred, boarding the *Duchess of Edinburgh* that arrived in Melbourne August 4, 1877.

Ridge kept one souvenir from the voyage: the down from the breast of an albatross "the sailor had caught and killed on the ship on our way from Dublin. He had skinned and cured it and [had] given the glossy plumage to Mama." There usually wasn't a lot of fraternizing between passengers and sailors. With or without children, unaccompanied women were kept in the locked "virgins' cage" below decks. But romance in the larger sense attended the voyage, especially in the quest of beginning again.

> I wish Celia
> could see the sea climb up on the sky
> and slide off again...
> ...*Celia saying*
> *I'd beg the world with you....*
> *Celia...holding on to the cab...*
> *hands wrenched away...*
> *wind in the masts...like Celia crying....*
> ....
> It is cool by the port hole.
> The wet rags of the wind
> flap in your face. (*Sun-Up* 6)

There would be no money for a nursemaid in Australia. Although factory and office work had just opened up for women in Sydney, Emma had a small child and needed help to even consider going to work. Logically this would have been Mysie, her big sister, but some animosity caused her to refuse to even keep them. Emma and her small daughter were forced to move to Redfern, a Sydney suburb of mostly immigrants and factories. "My mother said 'Tomorrow we shall be going away—we shall live by ourselves. Just you and I.'" In her diary, Ridge remembers their new place in detail:

> A small bare room, lit by a gas jet, a bed, two chairs, a fireplace. There, in the fireplace a few chips, yet burning. We had our supper— of bread and milkless, sugarless tea...
>
> We had been living with Aunt Mysie and Uncle Fred and my two cousins Alfred and Eddie Penfold...
>
> Well fed and taken care of, petted by my cousins, especially by Eddie, I had been very happy there (I remember the big yard, my playfellow, the gentle furred mastiff Rover)...

Emma took up sewing to support them, a trade she seemed to know nothing about, suggesting the family's upper-class status in Dublin.

> A man carried a sewing machine into the room and Mama paid him with the money she had borrowed from Aunt Mysie...
>
> A little book came with the machine and mama [sic] read it for a long time...
>
> Then she took an old nightgown out of her trunk and tore it in several pieces (she wound thread on the bobbin, she had to look in her little book many times...

Her mother caught her finger in the sewing machine and bled, and she dropped her head in her hands. "Why do you watch me, she cried, 'go away from me—go away and play.'" Ridge describes her response: "I drew back away from her and sat down on the floor and watched the blood drip from her finger on the white cloth and trickle down the back of her hand onto the white frill of her sleeve." In the silence, she retreated into her imagination: "I had often tried to hear the sunlight singing, but the air about us never seemed to be quiet enough..."

The rift between family members remained. Ridge memorialized one miserable Christmas holiday in *Sun-up and Other Poems*, and at length in her diary. On Christmas Eve they were planning to go to Paddy's Market, "an open air affair, a mixture of merry-go-rounds, sideshows, saveloy sellers, farmers with produce and animals for sale, second hand dealers, craftsmen and members of the rag trade." Instead, her mother gave most of the shillings she had saved from her work to her sister, as payment on the sewing machine. "But, dear, are you sure you do not need it," [her sister] asked. Her voice had taken on a plaintive, almost a wheedling note that I was to hear many times in future years." Judging from her sister's vindictiveness, Emma may have been the favored daughter back in Dublin, and pride compelled her to hand the money over to her sister. When Ridge discovered the money gone, the effect on her was indelible: "just under the ribs a small hot place, maybe size of a shilling, a live coal...to be with me my life long, even as my shadow."

With what little was left over, they went on to visit Paddy's. "I asked for biscuits, nice coffee biscuits with scalloped edges. So Mama had some biscuits put in a paper bag and instead of the loaf, fine slices of bread." After her mother gave most of the treat to a beggar woman and a child, Ridge managed not to cry. "My angel," her mother called her. "She held my hand tightly as we walked along. For no reason I felt very happy." The next day her mother refused her landlady's offer of Christmas dinner. Was Emma waiting for a last-minute invitation from her sister? Even Ridge's doll Janie was deprived.

> Christmas dinner was green and white
> chicken and lettuce and peas
> and drops of oil on the salad
> smiley and full of light
> like the gold on the lady's teeth.
>
> But mama said politely
> Thank you, we are dining out.
> She wouldn't let you take one pea
> to put in the hole where the whistle was
> at the back of Janie's head,
> so Janie should have some dinner
> So you went to the park with biscuits
> and black tea in a bottle. (*Sun-up* 9-10)

The day was sweltering—Christmas in Australia! A woman who seemed to be Jewish wished them a Merry Christmas. Her mother admonished Ridge: "The Jews are good people—you must always be very nice to them," an influential remark, given that the main subject of her first book is the Jewish ghetto. When a walk to the gardens in that part of Sydney proved to be too distant for Emma and her daughter, "we turned our faces to the sand hills...glancing back I saw the spire of the little church in which I sat with my mother on Sunday mornings and had to pretend not to notice the fleas." They met a well-dressed man and his son, who whined for food. Her mother gave away the rest of their tea and biscuits and again Ridge said not a word. Ridge would inherit this compulsive generosity, but it would often leave her penniless, forcing her to beg at the last possible moment. She assumed that the wealthy, whom she considered her equal, given her aristocratic heritage and her gift of poetry, would always have the same compulsion to give. She was often very lucky.

Based on the richness of detail in Ridge's poems, Emma and her daughter may have spent several years in Sydney. Although the city was home to

7,000 more men than women, Emma could not hope to wed again—her relatives would have known she was still married to the Irishman. Perhaps the solution laid out in Jane Mander's *The Story of a New Zealand River* was typical: "I took what money I had and came over to Australia...one woman, good kind soul, bought me a wedding ring and made me widow's clothes, and told me to go to New Zealand as a widow, and never to tell anybody— and to marry, if I get the chance, for the sake of the child." David Hastings in *Over the Mountains of the Sea: Life on the Migrant Ships 1870-1885* mentions a similar ruse. Add to this the tales of New Zealand gold miners finding ore the size of a man's palm, and rumors of a new gold strike, and Emma must have decided she had nothing to lose. At some point at the end of the 1870s or early in 1880, they set sail for New Zealand.

Little Lola might have enjoyed this shorter voyage, with penguins and flying fish to spot, but her mother was leaving the last of her family behind. Had her husband, the young doctor-to-be back in Dublin, died? Probably not, since what would have seemed a tragedy didn't inspire Ridge to mention him more than once in her entire oeuvre.

> Celia says my father
> will bring me a golden bowl.
> When I think of my father
> I cannot see him
> for the big yellow bowl
> like the moon with two handles
> he carries in front of him. (*Sun-up* 3-4)

Unfortunately, the gold rush in Hokitika that rivaled California's was over by the time they disembarked. Hokitika had always attracted risk-takers, not only in the laborious and often futile hunt for gold, but even in the earliest effort of the enterprise, getting ashore. As Eleanor Catton describes the situation in *The Luminaries*: "The river mouth itself was calm, a lakelet thick with masts and the fat stacks of steamers waiting for a clearer day; they knew better than to risk the bar that lay concealed beneath the water and shifted with each tide." The town saw 32 ships go down between 1865 and 1867, the height of its gold rush. Beach-rakers working together by moonlight carried off some of the goods, and sometimes there was enough insurance money left over to refit a new boat and run it aground again.

Regardless of the danger, five thousand people set up the town of Hokitika in a matter of months, with not only "sly-grog" shops of every kind, billiards rooms, a skating rink, waxworks, and a hundred hotels, but also an opera house with gas chandeliers and a cigar divan. It was the boomtown life. But fifteen years later, all the easy ore was gone, only half the hotels were still open, boys ran barefoot winter and summer to make a few pennies on errands, and the saloons, those that were left, were crowded with company miners. The goldfields had been picked over by the Chinese, a sign to others that the gold rush was finished, and the Maori, considered a dying race then, wandered through town.

Life in post-boom Hokitika was still hazardous. In September 1880 alone, a young fisherman drowned in the river, a carter cut his throat with a razor, a cook disappeared between the wharf and a vessel, and a man murdered his wife and child. This was the month that Emma declared herself a widow and married again to the Scotsman Donald MacFarlane, a seaman who took up prospecting after he deserted his ship. They moved four miles inland to the much smaller Kanieri Forks—barely a bush town—where he had a working stake. Emma at last had a man with potential, and, given Hokitika's shortage of females, MacFarlane probably felt blessed to snag even an older single mother. Whether the three-room shack they settled in was an improvement over their previous lodging, Ridge didn't say. Jane Mander's heroine moves to a new home in the bush and observes: "The first thing that struck Alice about it all was its appalling isolation."

Compounding the isolation was MacFarlane's alcoholism. The Scots and the Irish who made up the majority of the miners in Kanieri Forks tended to drink. It was hard going out every day deep into the mud in search for the glint of gold. MacFarlane had been one of the first at the goldfields and by 1880 had been at it for a decade and a half. Like the stepfather in Mander's book, who is admired for how hard he works yet disliked for what he does, Ridge's appreciation for her stepfather was conflicted. She imagined that he had some education because he knew a bit of Shakespeare :

> I remember he impersonated Macbeth with a great deal of passion and power. He used, too, to tell me stories out of Homer and be crudely kind when he was not in one of those raging drunken sprees when he would smash every stick of furniture in the three-roomed shack—until we had to rely for seats on the big wooden boxes holding

five gallon cans of kerosene we used in the tiny lamps with which we
lit its mean rooms.

Emma, so proud of her ancestry, must have been distraught over their
poverty and her drunken husband. As Ridge writes much later in a proposal
for a series of poems, the narrator's mother

> is a member of an old and very proud Irish family, now financially
> and socially ruined....totally unfitted to cope with the conditions in
> which she finds herself. Her only escape, therefore, is into a strange
> dream existence by which she moves in secret and detached from
> the lives of all about her. Realization of reality is left to the child who
> is thrown almost entirely on her own resources for amusement and
> companionship.

For Ridge, it was her stepfather, and not her mother, who inspired her
first poem. In her diary she records that while he supervised her homework,
she heard the creek murmuring and

> something stopped me like a touch on my heart. In the still...night,
> through the pressure of the silence reaching on and on through—
> the bush undulating, wave on wave—I heard the clear treble of the
> little creek, more than half a hundred feet below. The creek chirrups
> incessantly...This trickle of water—so long docile, unnoticed, less
> obtrusive than the cat, suddenly...separating itself from all the noises
> of the night, suddenly falling...for my ears alone.

She looked at her mother but "the pure pale cameo of her face
[remained] unmoved...She did not hear my waters trebling." Ridge would
have to wrestle with her perceptions alone. Then she noticed her brooding
stepfather "staring at the log fire, he heard nothing...as though I touched
him, he glanced up at me..." Ridge manages to calm the ire in her stepfather's glance by "making [her] own sweeten." This sweetening is reflected
literally in her poem "Sun-up," in what seems to be a cathartic moment,
beating her doll, but instead becomes an occasion for the speaker to use
literal sugar to obtain forgiveness.

> I beat Janie
> and beat her...
> but still she smiled...
> so I scratched her between the eyes with a pin.
> Now she doesn't love me anymore...
> she scowls...and scowls...
> though I've begged her to forgive me
> and poured sugar in the hole at the back of her head. (*Sun-up* 21)

Lola, sitting with her stepfather at the fire, remained attuned to the force of inspiration from "the whistling water...the one sound that would not deplete itself, like the small erect fire in my stepfather's eyes." "Erect" labels the struggle incestuous but Ridge decides the outcome by asserting her dominance: "My stepfather's gaze quieted *under* mine, [italics added], the blue small fire sinking. He said in a low grave voice, 'I am thinking of my dead sister Jessie.'"

> I did not answer, myself listening, waiting...yet noting his unexpected speech, as a person pondering deeply, might yet notice a white [moth?] suddenly fluttering in a doorslit. He turned back to staring in the fire.
> The door closed.
> Then, without warning, my whole being shivered. I felt as though something had struck and passed through me, leaving behind it some of its terrific power. I turned back to my copybook as one picks himself up after an earthquake that had flung him on the ground.
> But I did no more arithmetic. Instead I wrote what I believe now was my first real poem—how I wish I had kept it...

This poem erupted from her ("my whole being shivered") as soon as her stepfather was defeated ("the blue small fire sinking"). It was as if only by subduing her stepfather and asserting her own independence could she harness poetic power. When her mother looked at the "scrambled lines," she recognized them for what they were: "There is something in it dear—a poetic image." "I thought," wrote Ridge, "I am a poet, one of them."

Chapter 2

Ambition in New Zealand

Despite his alcoholism, MacFarlane cared enough for Ridge to pay for the best local education that could be had, at a Catholic girls' school in Kanieri named St. Joseph's. Ridge found the nuns lacking. "I was educated— or rather taught a few things, mostly useless—in a convent school," she writes to a friend late in life. "The tone is much superior to that of schools founded by the state," boasts the school's centenary booklet. Ridge sat at desks with four or five other children, and did all her schoolwork on slates. But local attitudes toward literature and women (and perhaps anxiety over impending New Zealand suffrage) were not encouraging, as is evident in a speech given at Ridge's convent school in the 1880s, complete with the audience's response:

> What was the use of a girl...who could play the piano most brilliantly, who could speak French, German, Italian, or even Chinese (laughter)... but could not cook a mutton chop...Very many of the great and good men that had lived, and almost every one of the great women that had lived—he did not know that there were very many great women (renewed laughter)—owed a large part of their success in life...to lessons inculcated in their father's house and at a mother's knee...
> —Mr. Richardson Rae,
> a member of the Westland Education Board

Forty years later, Ridge's depiction of the female students in this milieu is particularly telling:

> Little girls sit there
> dressed in white
> and the dolls in their arms
> all have white handkerchiefs

over their faces.
Their shadows cannot play with them...
their shadows lie down at their feet...
for the little girls sit stiff as stones
with their backs to the mouth of the cave
where a little light falls off
the wings of the silence
when it comes down out of the sun. (*Sun-up* 24-25)

Ridge's education as a radical began early. When she was 10, politician Richard Seddon (1845-1906) announced to Parliament: "It is the rich and the poor; it is the wealthy and the landowners against the middle and labouring classes. That, Sir, shows the real political position of New Zealand." By the time she was 20, Seddon was premier of the country and ruled for the next 13 years. He got his start in Hokitika, where a statue of the youthful "King Dick" still stands in front of the town's government buildings. A populist without any tie to an ideology that would check his freedom or that of the miners, he was a kind of anarchist-without-portfolio, only "partially civilised." His class-war approach appealed to the Irish and Scotch pioneers who had left countries where the wealthy controlled both the land and the capital. In the goldmines of the West Coast, theoretically at least, everyone was equal and anybody with a pick and a shovel could get rich. "There's no masters here to oppress a poor devil/But out in New Zealand we're all on the level" went the popular mining song, "London and The Digging."

Throughout Ridge's twenties, whole platforms of leftist politics were debated and passed. Seddon approved legislation for old age pensions, minimum wage, and a system for settling trade union disputes, making New Zealand at the forefront of workers' rights. Americans praised his work and proclaimed the country as an idyll of social progress. "American reformers...held up the Australiasian colonies as examples of what the United States could become if only it had the wit and the will to work along similar legislative lines," writes historian Peter J. Coleman. Seddon did not, however, support women's suffrage, although women had been clamoring for it for decades, and he had six daughters of his own. Like his friends in the liquor trade, he was afraid that women would vote in Prohibition. In 1893, suffrage supporters in Parliament wore white camellias in their buttonholes while Kate Sheppard (1847-1934), head of the Women's Christian Temperance Movement, presented the signatures of nearly a quarter of the female population, some 32,000 New Zealanders. She pasted the sheets together and rolled the petition onto a broom handle and, with great drama, had it unrolled through the center of Parliament "until it hit the end wall with a thud." Feeling cornered, Seddon ordered a Liberal Party member to change his vote to defeat the issue. His meddling so annoyed two other members that they reversed their vote. The issue passed, making New Zealand the first country in the world to allow women the vote.

Over the mountains in Christchurch, librarian Wilhemina Bain hosted the first meeting of the National Council of Women of New Zealand in 1896. The council demanded legal equality for men and women in marriage and employment, and the repeal of the Contagious Diseases Act of 1869, which required medical inspection of those women suspected of being "common prostitutes," but not men. It also called for women to be elected to Parliament, and appointed to the police and to juries, free and longer education for children, and better care and training of those orphaned or neglected, universal old age pensions, prison reform, and the abolition of capital punishment.

With such a heady heritage, Ridge's exposure to these progressive measures must have encouraged an innate belief that she could control her own destiny, and that others deserved that power too. Her first published poem, "On Zelanda," appearing in *The Canterbury Times* when she was just 18, reflected a serious interest in social justice.

> Her sons shall toil at that furnace,
>> Where the fuel is thoughts and deeds,
>> And follow the heroes of ages,
>> Where the light of their glory leads.
> Injustice shall fall by the sword of the brave.
> With the fetters of class in an honourless grave;
> O'er the ruins, let Freedom and Brotherhood wave—
>> On Zelanda!

At the time of its publication, newspapers on New Zealand's West Coast—and most of the rest of the world—carried poems side by side with national and international news. Sometimes the poems were just filler, but often they reflected the concerns of the readership, many of whom were questioning the worker's wage and his working conditions and the nascent nationalism echoed in Ridge's poem. The country would soon "assert itself in the political sphere"—New Zealand declining to join Australia in 1901—and writers were hoping to incite "a dawning of national pride." Pember Reeves, Parliament member and occasional poet, author of *The Long White Cloud* (1898), the country's first history, was part of that movement. "No art?" he wrote. "Who serve an art more great/Than we, rough architects of State." Much of Ridge's poetry of that period reflected these debates, as did her efforts as an editor decades later to find the true voice of the American people. When the nationalistic *New Zealand Illustrated* was founded in 1899, proclaiming a mission of "the Encouragement of the best Literary and Artistic Talent which we have in our midst," it began featuring Ridge's poems just three years later. In 1940, critic E.H. McCormick assessed the literary efforts of the new nation in his *Letters and Art in New Zealand*: "In all the work of the 'Young New Zealanders'...there are signs of prematurity, as of people urgently striving to say something but without adequate means of self-expression." This would best sum up Ridge's earliest poems.

By 1894 miners who stayed late at the Hokitika gold fields had become despondent. Decades spent searching for gold in the rock, and where was the wealth? The physical hardships of mining and its terrible disappointments—and drink—broke many of them. Ridge's stepfather was driven mad, diagnosed with mania, and admitted to Hokitika's Seaview Mental Hospital on December 4, 1894.

> He glanced up at me, shrewd blue glance of blue very blue, ever-ready-to-be-angry-eyes[sic]. An irascible look as of a small angry thing erecting itself before the door of its covert—of the snug hole it has industriously hollowed for itself and that it is prepared to defend at whatever cost...

Although Ridge seemed to have felt an affection for MacFarlane, her home life must have been bleak during the many years before he was admitted. Her mother may have exacerbated the tension, if Ridge's own uncompromising tendencies with regard to men later are any indication. Ridge reframed her stepfather's breakdown to her own ends, publishing "The Insane" 13 years later. The poem conflates his situation with the poet's, suggesting that the only true freedom is in the insane asylum.

> Oh! we are the merry and glad men,
>   Ye crazed, irresponsible things,

Who brand us and bind us as madmen,
   And pose as our rulers and kings.

Ye—wandering blind through the ages,
   And dazed with your schisms and schools—
Know we are the wise men and sages,
   And ye are the children and fools.

New Zealand doctors believed then that the best therapy for insanity was good food, rest, tending the kitchen gardens, and recreation. The Seaview Asylum shared grounds with the Westland Hospital and the Hokitika jail, all with a fabulous view of the ocean and "a never failing supply of ozone from the sea," according to an interview with Superintendent Mr. Downey in 1906. The asylum also had chess tables and a billiards room, a large theater, and dances every two weeks with music from instruments played by the staff. A tennis court remains on what's left of the grounds, and only one of its villas still has a cage bolted to it for unruly patients. The treatment was a far cry from what New Zealand novelist Janet Frame endured some 50 years later, when she was saved from a lobotomy only after a hospital official noticed she had received a literary prize. MacFarlane, on leave from the asylum in 1895, somehow fell 50 feet over a cliff. Emma signed a paper saying he was suicidal, and he was readmitted. Six years later, Emma reported that he was still contemplating suicide if released.

By the end of 1895, Emma and her daughter had moved to Hokitika, a big step up from living in the bush, and Ridge married Peter Webster (1870-1946) in the family home. The marriage certificate shows "painter" as her occupation, which could have been a point of pride for Webster—but it should have been a warning as to his wife's priorities. Three years older than Ridge, Webster was a handsome young man in his *Cyclopedia of New Zealand* photo, which shows off his high forehead, dark hair, thick mustache, slight dimple and large ears. He had money because the *Cyclopedia*, a six-volume series of books aiming to "place on record plain facts regarding the settlement and progress of the Colony," charged for its entries. A pioneer in the Kanieri area when he was still in his teens, he worked the same goldfield as Ridge's stepfather. Ridge was gambling on the luck her mother had hoped for: at their marriage Peter owned a share of a mine, and his father owned a nearby pub. Her dreams were not unjustified. In ten years, "precious rubies [were] found in the drift...at Kanieri Forks," and the largest chunk of gold ever discovered in New Zealand would be unearthed only 23 miles away. The newlyweds moved back to Kanieri Forks closer to his stake. At least the Forks was no longer a tent town. Its 46 souls had one store/post office that also housed visitors, but it was without regular coach service, with mail only on Mondays and Fridays, delivered by a postman who walked a four-day trail. For Ridge, claustrophobia descended.

> Radiant notes
> piercing my narrow-chested room,
> beating down through my ceiling—
> smeared with unshapen
> belly-prints of dreams
> drifted out of old smokes—
> trillions of icily
> peltering notes
> out of just one canary,
> all grown to song
> as a plant to its stalk,
> from too long craning at a sky-light
> and a square of second-hand blue.
>
> Silvery-strident throat—
> so assiduously serenading my brain,
> flinching under
> the glittering hail of your notes—
> were you not safe behind...rats know what thickness
>   of...plastered wall...
> I might fathom
> your golden delirium
> with throttle of finger and thumb
> shutting valve of bright song. (*Sun-up* 47)

The town of Kanieri is pronounced "canary," ostensibly because the neighboring bush once harbored a large number of yellow birds. If this excerpt refers to Ridge's response to life in Kanieri, her rage is palpable. The canary is throttled, its song extinguished. Or is it the canary that warns miners of imminent danger? The Hokitika Library or the local literary society would very likely have had a copy of Mary Wollstonecraft's *A Vindication of the Rights of Woman*, in which Wollstonecraft insists that women must be more than pretty canaries. A copy of George Eliot's *Daniel Deronda* would have shown a mother who marries twice for money, both times unhappily—like Ridge's mother—and a stepchild who strangles her sister's canary when it interrupts her training for a career in music. For Ridge, the strangling is a kind of self-extinguishing too, since the poet is doing the singing as well as the bird. It has even more autobiographical import with the fork of Kanieri Forks inserted in the lines immediately after: "But if...away off...on a fork of grassed earth.../Somewhere...away off..." Further on, Ridge posits that this far-off place is where a canary could "bloom" out of a cactus, a rather surreal, desperate miracle. "Cactus...why cactus?" she herself asks.

Claustrophobia-thick bush surrounds the *Cyclopedia's* photo of Peter Webster's sluicing claim. Inside this bush the photo shows a hole, and inside the hole sits a hut. A hose is positioned beside the hut, shooting jets of water "strong enough to kill a person" aimed at the gravel face, washing whatever gold-bearing gravel down through sluice boxes not included in the picture. Dynamiting from hard-rock mining shook the area at regular intervals. Smoke from the steam-powered engines of the mining apparatus lay thick to the ground on cold days, and wherever the lumber had been cleared or burned for power all that was left was the desolate vision of tree stumps.

> Like lepers, sad, forsaken
>   Of their kind,
> The pine trees' naked trunks
> Arise, & from the stagnant
>   Swamp behind,
> Bereft and bare of branches,
> Reach up their withered stumps. (*Verses* 63)

A buggy ride from the Websters' new home lies Lake Kanieri, an Ansel Adams-beautiful platter of water surrounded by the snow-capped mountains of the Southern Alps. In a period photo, visitors to the lake sit stiffly in their Victoriana: clothing buttoned to the neck and wrists and ankles, the women bound at all entrances except the bloom of the skirt. The photo's sepia has faded, the faces are indistinguishable, blending into the color of the world around them: mud. One of the wettest places on earth, Hokitika and its environs receive more than 100 inches of rain a year. When the New

Zealand Alps thaw, the hills in front of them become waterfalls, mud covers the buildings where paint dries slowly and peels quickly. Women's heavy long skirts would be always stained. Imagine Ridge scrubbing them, pulling one wet from the washtub and wringing its 30 pounds of fabric through the mangle over and over, the water finally running clear. The chill held in all that wet mud could be lethal, even in summer. In 1896 Ridge's first child, Paul Webster, was born into that world on December 9, and died two weeks later of bronchitis. His birth wasn't recorded until after his death.

Due to the difficulties of childbirth and childhood disease, dead children were a major subject of Victorian women poets. Ridge did not address the tragedy directly. In her poem "The Magic Island," immigrants mourn children lured into the sea by a wizard, but it sounds more like a cautionary tale than a personal lament, similar to the effect of her poem "The Three Little Children," about children who wander into the bush never to be seen again, and an early story, "The Returned Hero," in which a Chinese bogeyman so terrifies a child she jumps from a train. In the poem "Baby's Sick," the father or a brother is summoned from the track when a little boy falls sick at home.

> I've laid it all on shamrock—
> > Ten to one;
> The knowing ones are backing
> > Up old Sun.
> I got a wire this morning—
> > "Come home quick,
> Mumma badly wants you—
> > Baby's sick!" (*Verses* 54)

Kanieri and Hokitika held regular horse races. It is likely that Ridge's stepfather and husband would have attended. In the poem, the horse named "The Sun" wins the steeple but the man appears remorseful at the end: "The Cup may go to—pieces!/Baby's sick." In general, however, the poem paints the husband as culpable, having been gambling while the mother is coping with the sick child.

For most parents, the death of a child is an indelible loss, especially for the mother. She has failed in her most basic adult role. Some scholars feel that the high infant mortality rates in those years lessened the impact of the death of a child, but in the 17th century, with much worse rates, Ben Jonson's moving elegy "On My First Son" suggests that even fathers were devastated by such a death. New Zealand poet Robin Hyde's attempted suicide in 1933 is linked to mourning a stillborn out-of-wedlock child. Perhaps Ridge's fierce ambition to make something of herself was sublimated to that strong maternal sorrow, and eventually channeled into the intensity of the persona of Mary, the mother of Jesus, in her fourth book, *Firehead*. But in Kanieri, mortality pressed on the living. Ridge was tortured by the knowledge of the shortness of her life, trapped in a tiny town at the edge of the known world.

> I smelled the raw sweet essences of things,
> and heard spiders in the leaves
> and ticking of little feet,
> as tiny creatures came out of their doors
> To see God pouring light into his star...
>
> ...It seemed life held
> No future and no past but this... (*Ghetto* 73)

The price of gold dropped drastically, making striking it rich less likely for everyone. The miners had to work twice as hard to make the same money. Kanieri Forks organized all kinds of entertainments to counteract despair—balls, cycling clubs, carnivals, more horse races, and excursions to beautiful Lake Kanieri. In 1898 the Kanieri Dramatic Club presented "a sparkling comedietta" called "*I've Written to Browne*," which included Mrs. P. Webster [Lola] in the cast. She starred as the rich widow Mrs. Walsingham and must have done a good job since she was remembered by relatives as an actress, not a poet. At the conclusion of the entertainment, the floor was cleared and dancing kept up till the "we sma' hoors." Two years later, on January 21, 1900, Ridge bore another son, Keith, who survived despite the difficult climate.

Ridge's mother also lived in Kanieri Forks, whether with Ridge is unknown, but it was such a small community that she surely would have been near enough to help with the baby, making it possible for Ridge to write. In 1903 Ridge's poem "The Dream Man" won first prize in the *New Zealand Illustrated*, an accomplishment which must have piqued her aspirations. Its title is captioned by fanciful script most likely Ridge's own, with a tree forming the "T." The poem rattles along—"Deep are the spells he weaves,/And dark is the path he goes,"—and it ends:

And now from the distant sea
And now from a far off range
He calls to the soul of me,
And plays in an unknown key
A song in a rhythm strange! (*Verses* 38)

Ridge was being lured away—but not by another man. Consider two lines from her early poem "At Sun-Down": "Ah God: the strife for a remembered name!" and "My heart is throbbing for the roar of streets."

Ambition.

Chapter 3

"The Smoking Fuse"

A woman artist had no place in New Zealand at the turn of the century—
even if you never left like poet Jessie MacKay (1864-1938), whose political
interests resembled Ridge's. "We plowed a lonely furrow," wrote MacKay. Ten
years older than Ridge, this "thin, grey, fragile woman, with intense eyes,
low-toned speech, and a slow smile" was raised in Christchurch just across
the Southern Alps from Hokitika. She published her first book in Australia,
but like Ridge, hoped to be part of the nationalist movement that Pember
Reeves had exalted. By 1891 she was writing satirical and political poems
about Prohibition and suffrage. In poems like "The Charge at Parihaka,"
she likened driving the Maori off their lands to what had happened to her
ancestors in Scotland with the English. An article profiling MacKay in the
influential *New Zealand Railways Magazine* described her interest in the
political: "The weaker side, the little nations oppressed by the powerful, have
drawn her passionate championship." She became editor of the *Canterbury
Times* in 1906, where Ridge had published 14 years earlier. They also shared
publication in the *Otago Witness*, the conservative illustrated weekly that was
particularly popular in the rural areas of the south island. Like most of New
Zealand's female artists of the period except Ridge and Mansfield, she never
married and achieved little fame in her own country. "MacKay's place in
the history of New Zealand poetry has been considerably under-recognised,"
writes Heather Roberts in the *New Zealand Encyclopedia*.

Ridge's main competitor for "New Zealand's best woman poet of the
early 20th century" is another modernist, Ursula Bethell (1874-1945). "New
Zealand wasn't truly discovered," according to critic D'Arcy Cresswell,
"until Ursula Bethell, 'very earnestly digging', raised her head to look at
the mountains. Almost everyone had been blind before." Nearly Ridge's
exact contemporary, she lived half her peripatetic life in England where she
was born, spent her childhood in Christchurch, was educated at the Oxford
High School for Girls and a Swiss finishing school, and studied music

and painting in Europe. Just after the turn of the century, she called off a marriage and met Effie Pollen, another single woman from New Zealand. At the age of 50, after working with the poor in London for 20 years, she moved back to Christchurch with Pollen, where they set up house, cultivated an extensive garden, and explored the countryside in "a big, black Essex motor car." Perhaps Ridge would have felt differently about New Zealand if she had had the wealth of Bethell, whose house offered views of the Southern Alps, the Kaikoura Ranges and the Canterbury Plains, mountains that inspired Bethell's best work. Influenced by Gerard Manley Hopkins and the more prosaic lines of Whitman, her subjects were often the natural world or religion, confronting the tension between "religious certainty and everyday experience." Not exactly Ridge's line, although she did not hesitate to use Christian iconography when it suited her purposes. Bethell, saintly and single, fulfilled the Anglo-directed expectations for women beloved of many literary gatekeepers, but published her books under the gender-vague pseudonym Evelyn Hayes, perhaps because of her relationship with Pollen. Like Ridge, she never felt as if she belonged in New Zealand, but existed as an exile of two countries. "I don't belong anywhere in particular. I've dodged to and fro...I have not been able to settle.".

Jane Mander's *Story of a New Zealand River* portrayed the difficulties of immigrant women with such intensity that it inspired Jane Campion's Oscar-winning film, *The Piano*. Just four years younger than Ridge, Mander (1877-1949) moved 29 times growing up while her father struggled to make a living in the bush. She soon wanted to escape the "brain-benumbing, stimulus-stifling, sense-stultifying, soul-searing silence" of provincial New Zealand. To educate herself, she became what was known as a "pupil-teacher" and taught while she attended high school, then assisted her father in his election to Parliament. He, in turn, allowed her to work for two newspapers he now owned, at a time when few journalists were women. Like Ridge, she left first for Australia. There the future premier of New South Wales encouraged her writing until her mid-30s, when she traveled to America. Working to support her studies at Columbia University, she fell ill and couldn't complete the degree. World War I delayed the publication of *Story of a New Zealand River* until 1920 but it was widely praised—outside New Zealand. The depiction of an adulterous affair and women with minds of their own so shocked those at home that conservative women forbade their daughters to read the book. Mander persisted, writing five more novels in New York and London. When a Greenwich Village bookstore closed in 1925, she and Ridge were noted as being among the literati who had scrawled their names on its wall. Mander returned in 1932 to care for her elderly father, wrote very little and died seventeen years later. Until 1966, her entry in the *New Zealand Encyclopedia* read: "She was a little too enthusiastic about new social and political movements without assessing their impact on the future, a fault she attributed to an undigested diet of Bernard Shaw and Nietzsche."

Short story writer Katherine Mansfield (1888-1923) was the only contemporary New Zealander with international ambition equal to Ridge's. After having lived and studied in England with her family, Mansfield dubbed her hometown, Wellington, "Philistia itself" in 1906. Willa Cather, no stranger to the hinterland, writes about Mansfield's return to New Zealand:

> But at eighteen, after four years of London, to be thrown back into a prosperous commercial colony at the end of the world, was starvation. There is no homesickness and no hunger so unbearable. Many a young artist would sell his future, all his chances, simply to get back to the world where other people are doing the only things that, to his inexperience, seem worth doing at all.

It was only much later, in 1916, that Mansfield decided she wanted to make "her undiscovered country leap into the eyes of the Old World," an ambition that Ridge fulfilled for Australia with *Sun-up*'s publication in 1920. According to poet Robin Hyde, New Zealand responded to Mansfield's work by "mumur[ing] sympathetically if vaguely 'Katherine the Great'... But she went far from us[.] Most of her tales were written in a subtle foreign language which is not yet fully understood out here [as] the language of twentieth century art." Mansfield never returned to New Zealand. A chronic invalid suffering from venereal disease, she also contracted tuberculosis—perhaps from her friend D.H. Lawrence—but that disease proved virulent and Mansfield died at age 35. At the end she turned to the mystic Gurdjieff for help, and thought his prescription for her disease inspired: to stand on a platform above a feedlot and inhale the smell of dung.

In Hokitika, Ridge had been hedging her bets with painting, perhaps taking lessons from two very skilled landscape artists working in the neighborhood: John Peele, an important Australian painter, who completed "A Bush Track, Kanieri River" in 1892, or Joseph Wharton Hughes, a New Zealand painter who signed her keepsake album in 1902. But for New

Zealand women, the visual arts did not prove any more fulfilling than writing. Ten years younger than Ridge, Mary Margaret Butler, New Zealand's first woman sculptor, grew up in Greymouth, a town 25 miles from Hokitika. Like Ridge, she was educated by nuns. By the time Butler was 30, her work far eclipsed her teacher's, but it was another 10 years before she left New Zealand and spent a successful decade in Europe. On her return in 1935, the governor general called her "our local lady Praxiteles," but New Zealand collectors saw no value in homegrown talent. For want of commissions, Butler gave up sculpture.

Like Ridge, painter Frances Hodgkins was most famous for the work she did abroad. After her training in Europe, she returned to New Zealand only to teach. One of her pupils was Katherine Mansfield's lover, Edith Bendall. But Hodgkins became discouraged by the provincialism Ridge felt, and like fellow New Zealand visual artists Dorothy Richmond, A. H. O'Keeffe, Margaret Stoddart and Grace Joel, she returned to Europe. Settling in England, she worked alongside Henry Moore, Ben Nicholson and Barbara Hepworth, eventually becoming one of England's leading artists.

Ridge's keepsake album dates from 1900 to 1905, when she was in her mid-twenties. It contains the usual sentimental inscriptions written by friends and relatives in New Zealand and, eventually, Australia. Dr. Ebenezer Teichelmann, a famous physician-photographer-mountaineer with three peaks named after him, inscribed the album in 1900. "There was a sense of intimacy in his photographs and writing," according to his biographer Bob McKerrow, "and when he was moved by the beauty around him, would often quote from Longfellow, Stevenson or other romantic poets." He moved to Hokitika in 1897 after being named surgeon general of Westland, and his signature indicated that Ridge held the esteem of prominent Hokitikans, or at least sought it.

A schoolteacher, Evelyn MacFarlane, also left an entry in the album. MacFarlane was one of the two witnesses—both female—at Ridge's wedding. As a contemporary, she was probably a relative of Ridge's stepfather, a cousin or a niece, and her position as educator would have made her a reader with access to the more up-to-date periodicals. She chose a poem by Harriet Monroe, founder of *Poetry* magazine in Chicago and later publisher of Ridge's poetry, that concerned leaving and lost love, which suggested that MacFarlane might have known that Ridge was having marital difficulties.

A Farewell

Good-bye!—no, do not grieve that it is over,
    The perfect hour;
That the winged joy, sweet honey-loving rover,
    Flits from the flower.

Grieve not—it is the law. Love will be flying—
    Yes, love and all.
Glad was the living—blessed be the dying.
    Let the leaves fall.

Other signers of the album included a bevy of actors and actresses from the area, appropriate to Ridge's involvement in the theater, the minister who married her, various relatives by marriage, including Edith Grahame, whose brother Stanley shot seven people in 1941, and Jesse Matheson from nearby Greymouth who appeared in theater productions, an opera, and concerts. Everyone quotes Tennyson or Shakespeare or William McCall, the 19th-century hymnist, and such was the erudition at that time that they probably did not have to consult their libraries for an accurate passage.

"The Trial of Ruth," Ridge's first published short story, appeared in the 1903 New Zealand Illustrated eight years after her marriage. Early published stories are sometimes romans à clefs. "It was rather a depressing outlook over the long uneven plain, dotted with slab huts, and here and there a grey line of tailings running into the creek," she writes. The husband drinks and ignores his bride while his partner woos her with a kiss. "The world for him meant only two things—women and gold." While the husband is incapacitated by drink, the partner asks for another kiss.

> "Ruth," said the man, unsteadily, "A few weeks ago I took a kiss from you and you were angry. Will you be angry if I take one tonight? Answer me, Ruth, they will be here in a minute." "No," said the woman. "I will not be angry—"

A page later, the lover attempts to kill the husband with dynamite. The young wife puts out the fuse just in time—"Are you mad? You will be blown to atoms!"—although her husband manages to get injured. Lying in bed, he wonders where his partner has gone because they've finally struck gold. She gives him a smile, her future now assured, with the "clean white page in the Book of Love" lying open between them, ready for rewrite.

Ridge illustrates the story herself, drawing a woman on tiptoes snuffing out the dynamite. Her technique is Edward Gorey-like in detail—the dark line flaring at the bottom of her skirt as if a breeze might cause the fire to reignite, and the intricacy of the snaky tree roots crawling among the rocks at her feet. "Death hissed at her from a half inch of smoking fuse" reads the caption.

Ridge's neat solution of making the wavering wife the heroine is classic pulp, the kind of fiction that solves all the problems of their authors' lives— escapist. To her credit, Ridge escaped. She gathered her determination from the pioneer gold rush milieu and her mother's energy and example, but just as much she drew from her anger over the lack of opportunity in New Zealand, and a youth's belief in possibility anywhere else.

Three months after "The Trial of Ruth" appeared in 1903, Ridge left Hokitika and Kanieri Forks for Sydney, Australia, where she would continue her education in the arts. She and her mother and her three-year-old son Keith traveled saloon class, in style, since she had the support and consent— albeit reluctant—of her husband, whose company was touted as one of the most profitable in the district in 1901. They traveled to Wellington, where they boarded the steamer S.S. *Mokoia* for the four-day trip to Sydney.

Chapter 4

The Arts in Australia

"I am an Australian by sympathy & association," writes Ridge shortly after her arrival in 1903, beginning her disavowal of all things New Zealand: country, family, husband. Although she could have studied art at the New Zealand Academy of Fine Arts in Wellington, Sydney was the more ambitious choice. At the time, the city was one of the largest in the Western world and terribly cosmopolitan: electric trams ran on the wooden streets, Her Majesty's theater—very grand—had just reopened after a fire, and the movie playing when they arrived was "Battle of Gettysburg," a "masterpiece of Cycloramic art." The Sydney Art School, run by Julian Ashton, was considered the best in Australia. "There is no better teacher in Paris," declared the internationally known painter George Lambert, a student of Julian Ashton's until 1900. Ridge—and her mother—must have believed she had some talent for both of them to have left the security of New Zealand for her pursuit of the arts.

The day they arrived was November 11, 1903—Ned Kelly Day, auspicious for Ridge as it is named after the Australian Robin Hood. With bulletproof armor and helmets made out of farm tools, the Irishman Kelly and his gang were forced into violence by the ill-treatment of Irish Catholics, according to his famous 56-page "Jerilderie Letter." Police corruption was at the center of his protest. He not only killed three policemen, but he and his gang pulled off one heist dressed as cops. According to Australian historian Amanda Kaladelfos:

> Kelly articulated a struggle between rich and poor that resonated with many at a time when the Victorian government's land policies disadvantaged small farmers, and thereafter during a period of growing Australian nationalism and the rise of the Australian labour tradition.

On December 9, Ridge's mother inscribed her autograph book with lines from the 17th-century poet Sir Samuel Garth: "To die is landing on some silent shore/Where billows never break nor tempests roar;/Ere well we feel the friendly stroke, tis o'er." What was the message to Ridge? Comfort, in that Victorian attitude of oh-let's-all-die-and-get-it-over-with? Or did her mother feel she had died to everyone she ever knew in the 24 years she spent in New Zealand, the country and husband she had turned her back on? Or did she have premonitions of her own death four years later? At the very least, the verses show that Emma must have had an education.

By January, Ridge was asking the editor of the *Sydney Bulletin*, the most influential magazine in Australian culture and politics from 1890 to 1917, to omit her married name in her contributor's note. She had already published nine poems in the magazine, mostly as "Lola." She was setting out her terms, declaring her marital independence, and announcing her literary identity. For the last eight years, she had been Rosa Webster or Lola Webster or Mrs. Peter Webster, and before that, Rosa MacFarlane after her mother's remarriage, and before that, Rosalie Ridge and Rosa Delores Ridge. She was christened Rose Emily Ridge. Although Ridge would have three more name changes before she died, the result of marital estrangements and entanglements, from 1903 on she published as Lola Ridge.

Such a decision was not without precedent. In the 1850s the American Lucy Stone kept her family name as a protest "against all manifestations of coverture," a practice that had dictated a woman's subordinate legal status during marriage and allowed the husband almost exclusive power, and custody of the children. Perhaps Ridge's mother feared that her first husband would invoke coverture, and that's why she fled Ireland. Reflecting women's profound shift in social status at the turn of the century, Ridge's generation were notable name changers: Hilda Doolittle taking on the sobriquet H.D., her lover Bryher's choice of a single name, Willa Cather changing from Wilella Cather to William Cather, M.D., then back to Willa, Polly-turned-Caresse Crosby, and Mina Loy who omitted two letters from her father's surname Lowry. Ridge had the opportunity of immigrant rebranding, but how much did her renaming have to do with a deeper psychological need to answer to someone new—*Who am I after the century turns?*

Ridge received her only post-secondary education at the art school, and in music classes arranged under the auspices of Trinity College in Dublin, which still examines candidates for music in Australia. She passed four exams, and her education in music served her well when she met and befriended Aaron Copland many years later. Together with her son and mother, she lived at 193 West Street in North Sydney, at the center of Australia's nascent bohemia, but still a somewhat rural area. Bullock teams hauling loads of tree trunks were not uncommon, and most of the houses were only two years old. The newness was perfect for a re-examining of goals and mores, the more bohemian the better. Frank Morton, editor of the Wellington magazine *Triad*, writes in 1908, "In New Zealand there is no Bohemia, and the few Bohemians who are the salt of the colony are like wrecked mariners on a desolate coast." In contrast, according to literary historian Tony Moore, "By the turn of the century Australians had come to think that a writer or artist should be a bohemian." In North Sydney, Ridge immediately came under the influence of the two major adherents of the Australian bohemian lifestyle: her art teacher Julian Ashton (1851-1942) and her publisher A.G. Stephens (1865-1933).

Australian bohemianism had its start in Melbourne, with the *flâneur* Marcus Clarke attracting such *bons vivants* as Queen Victoria's son who visited the city's artistic haunts in 1896. Many artists and writers and illustrators moved to Sydney after the 1890's depression, partly as a result of the decision of the New South Wales Art Gallery to encourage the purchase of local art. Its chairman was Ridge's instructor, Julian Ashton. As head and founder of the Sydney Art School, Ashton taught *plein-air* techniques in the impressionist tradition, supporting and promoting Australian artists who had been damned by European critics for rendering their subjects in harsh lighting—the light they saw, not the light in France as painted by the Impressionists, nor that of the luminists working in the Hudson River Valley. A photograph of a white-haired Ashton looking much like Thomas Eakins: high forehead, thin nose, short mustache, shows him in the out-of-doors, leaning back from the easel in a suit coat, with two Victorian women alert to his critique and, amid the bristling Australian foliage, an enormous St. Bernard sitting at their feet, perhaps the subject of the painting. The son of an American and grandson of an Italian count, Ashton proclaimed the Wildean dictum: "The artist must be content to live for art and for art's sake only." He was also quoted as saying: "I think women artists have the artistic taste and the appreciation of beauty in them to a greater extent than the men," suggesting that he would be an encouraging mentor to Ridge.

He shared a penchant with Eakins for using live models, and there is a photograph of him poking a cane toward a male model clothed in briefs. Writing about the practice, contemporary George Augustus Taylor tries to be chaste with regard to the female models, but his descriptions betray him: a "dimly lit room," "draped with dark velvet," "a high priestess," in a "brilliant spotlight," "her flesh glistening." An Ashton drawing in pencil of a beseeching female nude model fills a page in Ridge's autograph book— perhaps it is Ridge? It is known that she modeled for the school, a practice she continued in America.

The Sydney Art School houses no record of Ridge's artistic output. Only a few sketches exist in her file at Smith College. They include a very nice unsigned pen-and-ink of an older woman seated with clasped hands, hair parted down the middle, her black jacket labeled "Sunday" (perhaps her mother in her Sunday best?) and what appears to be a self-portrait made much later in Mexico in the 1930s that looks very much like Ridge's photos—wide-eyed in the way that the model tends to look under self-scrutiny, cheekbones gaunt from hard travel. The close-up of an eye on the back of a sketch of a Mexican church is probably the result of a bored moment in that same journey. Also in the collection is a pen-and-ink drawing of her good friend Evelyn Scott, her hand a little too big but neatly done. All of the pictures are strictly naturalistic, she makes no experiments in perspective, color, or shape, although by the time the Scott portrait was made, Léger and Picasso and Modigliani had illustrated *Broom*, the magazine Ridge helped edit. This lack of interest in modernism is not too surprising since Julian Ashton, being more conservative than the conservative British, denigrated it in the visual arts. Ridge seemed to have mostly given up her artistic practice shortly after arriving in New York, perhaps because of the cost of art supplies. Even while writing poetry, she was sometimes reduced to writing on scraps of paper with a pencil.

Many of the Australian visual artists who signed Ridge's autograph book between 1904 and 1905 became prominent. Ruby Winkler was a cartoonist and early fantasy illustrator who eventually traveled to the U.S. and published two children's books. Henry George Julius, "Harry," a graphic designer, cartoonist, printmaker, illustrator, and animator, whose autograph is a chorus line of "characters" with bowler hats and walking sticks captioned "Friends of Julius," founded a successful ad agency with Sydney Smith, another signer. Together they also began the influential periodical, *Art in Australia*. One-eyed Mick Paul, "a renowned Kings Cross Bohemian and drunk," left Ridge a lively sketch of "a satyr," and became a professional cartoonist. Howard Ashton, Julian's son, who trained at his father's art school but took up journalism and collected the cicadas for the Australian

Museum, sketched a subtle watercolor landscape. Nelle Rodd, who "painted with a strong virility as one would not expect to find in a woman artist," became a founding member of the Society of Women Painters in 1910 but died shortly thereafter. Her sketch shows a woman in bed with covers up to her neck.

Ridge had to depend on Emma or her extended family to look after Keith while she worked, but she made good use of whatever child-free time she had, publishing more poems in Australia than she had in New Zealand. These were more gold-mining bush ballads, a few vaudevillian light poems, and poems of sad romance, both public and private, all of them written in iambic pentameter. Many of them appeared in the *Sydney Bulletin*, no mean feat since it received a thousand submissions a week as the leading journal in the country. New Zealand scholar and poet Michele Leggott writes that "Ridge's practice is as good as that of her *Bulletin* peers." Its contributors were often fellow bohemians. Christopher Brennan, for example, had shown his indifference to authority by "rolling stones down the floor when he disliked a lecturer, wearing an academic gown hung about with jam-tins and horseshoes." Using the language of the streets and the shearing sheds to mock those in authority, the *Bulletin*'s bohemian writers created a picture of romanticized bush life that appealed to the middle class and earned it a circulation of 80,000 subscribers by 1900. It also paid. "For pecuniary and other reasons, the *Bulletin* had first call on almost every Australian writer," according to critic H.M. Green.

While still living in New Zealand, Ridge collected her poems into a manuscript entitled *Verses* and then offered it to A. G. Stephens sometime between 1902 and 1905, when he was then the most important publisher of poetry in Australia. He was also editor of the "Red Page," a column featuring literature and criticism in the *Bulletin*. He would run 23 poems from Ridge's *Verses* in the magazine, over a quarter of the manuscript, before she left for America. Stephens was the man to know, he was "the strongest single force in the shaping of Australian literature." His colleague, the illustrator and novelist Norman Lindsay, said that his "head, thrown back, the jutting beard, the resolute walk and the expanded chest" concealed an artistic temperament that was extremely sensitive. He had his meat cut up before it was sent to his room so he could eat it one-handed, without taking his eyes away from his book. Solidly built, blue-eyed, and handsome, he wore an open-necked shirt with rolled up sleeves and wrote in purple ink with a confident hand. Seven years older than Ridge, he was especially fond of the wild married Louise

Mack, the only woman he ever published in his series. "It was said that all the men at the *Bulletin* were in love with her," writes Mack's biographer and niece Nancy Phelan, "she had a great deal of Irish charm." Like Ridge, Mack was also determined to break free of female convention. The heroine in her first novel, *The World is Round*, gives a devastating assessment of her best friend's writing:

> I hate your stories. Why do you always give your girls golden fluffy hair, and sweet ripe, scarlet lips? And no brains. I'd make them as bald as the woman before she used Barry's Tricopherus, and as white about the lips as if they had eaten a barrel-load of starch, but when they spoke I would make them say something smart, and to the point something worth saying, and worth listening to, not a string of empty meaningless frippery.

Lola's mentors, Stephens and Ashton, often socialized together, and both attended Mack's farewell party in 1901 when she left for Europe. Perhaps Stephens saw Ridge as her replacement. Whatever his opinion of her as a woman, he didn't have a very high regard of most New Zealand writing. "Maorilanders, [New Zealanders] when they come to do things with their heads, the things are usually tame and uninspiring," he writes in the *Bulletin* in 1900. Ridge began to mix locales in her poetry, and when she organized the poems into the collection, she deleted "Maoriland," an alternate name for New Zealand, from the title of the first poem she had published in the *Bulletin*. However, Stephens took her work seriously, and inserted revisions into her typescript of *Verses*, and included her in two lists of Australasian writers. "It is tempting to think that Stephens backed off [from publishing *Verses*] because Lola was too junior to be worth a book in 1905, rather than because her poetry was insufficiently Australian in its markings," Leggott hypothesizes. Perhaps the man was distracted. Stephens became a literary agent a year after Ridge arrived. When that occupation failed, he emigrated to "uninspiring" New Zealand and wrote for a Wellington newspaper. Ridge last submitted revisions to him in 1905. A year later he left or was pushed from his *Bulletin* column and lost much of his power.

Ridge claimed to have left behind all her early work, but a copy of her manuscript was archived at the Mitchell Library in Australia where it was bound with the work of bush balladeer John Shaw Neilson, who became one of the country's finest lyric poets. She also left a typescript with her cousin John E.M. Penfold. Sixty years later, this copy was found with his descendants in Australia but only the poems that did not appear in the Mitchell version were duplicated before the manuscript was lost again. She also republished several of the poems from the collection in America after she arrived, so she must have had her own copy and used it as a bridge between Australia and the U.S., the way she used her New Zealand work to establish herself in Australia.

The best poems in the *Verses* manuscript are Ridge's bush ballads, a genre that arose from Australian sheepherders' songs. Banjo Paterson had just published "Waltzing Matilda," the ballad that quickly became the unofficial Australian national anthem. Primarily oral, bush ballads had only been in print for around ten years, and compilations had become very popular. They promoted an idyll of preindustrialization, new nationalism, and worker's rights. Like Paterson's "Waltzing Matilda," about an itinerant worker who commits suicide after being caught stealing a sheep, Ridge's ballads frequently concern the trials of the New Zealand workers, in particular gold mining and class conflicts.

"It's the gas mates! Where's the Tommy?
Cut those moka bushes here—
Beat the air in, swirl 'em round—"
"Now let down a lighted candle:
Steady boy! The air is clear,"
And they wound him under ground. (*Verses* 58)

Class conflict and industrial exploitation, the communal feeling between workers, the coming proletariat revolution were common topics for all the bohemians who wrote for the *Bulletin* and other pro-labor publications in Australia. More than a hundred of these magazines and newspapers for the working man were established in Australia between 1870 and 1899. That the effete, city-living bohemians published these rough-and-tumble ballads must have seemed ironic, although not in the case of Ridge, who was raised in the bush with the egalitarian principles of the New Zealand miners. Other bohemians found the topics congenial to their principles and the rising feeling for social justice. The accomplished artist Emily Letitia Paul, a student of Julian Ashton and mother of one of Ridge's fellow students, gave up art for politics and became a leading speaker for the Socialist Party. One of Stephens's authors, Bernard O'Dowd—a correspondent of Whitman's—

became a political activist and a founding member of the Victorian Socialist Party, and called for "the poetry of purpose." His second wife Marie Pitt worked as a poet-activist and, according to her husband, "criticised the press, the Church and the State." In her 1911 essay, "Women in Art and Literature," she wrote that women were educated to be "a community of marionettes, a race of mental and moral geldings, spayed by the knife of Respectability." She, like Ridge, grew up in the bush.

The extremely popular working-class poet Henry Lawson (1867-1922) was a committed socialist who "contributed his talents to progressive reform groups and the wider labor movement," and wrote realistic fiction and poetry as a result of reporting jobs in the outback and other assignments that showed him "the unromantic side of the country." His rise as a writer revealed how "social art" could pull even someone like Ridge without ties to the upper class through the ranks of the radicals into wide literary recognition. Like many of the male bohemians, Lawson's progressive political sympathies had no place for women. He quarreled often with his formidable mother Louisa, who published and edited *Dawn*, a proto-feminist magazine, for seventeen years. She did, however, bring out his first book of poems. At the time, women in Australia were just beginning to find their voice in matters of gender politics, particularly of sexuality. Like the Victorian sentimentalists who used the imagery of flowers to convey a secret language of eroticism, Ridge often wrote her early poems from the point of view of an erotically inclined female, and continued the practice throughout her career, although less tied to botanical imagery. Sometimes editors removed stanzas or particularly suggestive phrases in her work. For example, the *Bulletin* published "The Bush" one stanza short, but included winds that "fondle with the maiden Bush/Who sways & quivers in their close embrace." Ridge's *Verses* manuscript contains the excised stanza:

> The rival sunbeams their fingers thrust
> Amid her guarded & most secret sweets;
> They steal & nestle on her swelling bust,
> And view unhidden all her chaste retreats. (*Verses* 8)

No romance is documented during Ridge's life in Australia. Michele Leggott calls Ridge's more autobiographical poems in *Verses* "romantic agony" with lines like:

I forgot the pride of lineage,
I forsook the hope of fame—
I'd ha' left the road to heaven
For the magic of your name. (*Verses* 13)

Such sentiments underscore a marriage made up of sacrifice, with her princely family heritage forsaken. Instead of love poems, she writes "Think of Me Not with Sadness" which begins:

Oh, think of me not with sad thoughts
bedecked in mourning grey,
But weave ye a woof about me
Of colors gold and gay;

The poem continues with a warning:

For if I were your own, love,
We might regret—some day. (*Verses* 14)

The partner in the paired poem ("The Man") answers: "I think of you—not sadly, yet with a half-regret," an idealized version of what her leaving might have cost her husband. "To an Old Playfellow" follows. The poem recalls a romance between childhood sweethearts that slowly deteriorates.

But the mistical [sic] pines lean over,
And their shadows are falling black
between one on the trampled highway,
And a chum on an old bush track. (*Verses* 15)

Her husband, Peter Webster, could have been the "old playfellow" from Ridge's youth. Ridge admitted to using real people from her life as characters for her second book of poems, *Sun-up and Other Poems*: "The small boy Jude—he was one of the real parts of 'Sun-up'—he who never grew up—'my darling' who never was…his face still clear." "The Parting," a farewell-to-love poem in *Verses*, features the well-known Hokitikan glow-worm colony in its sarcasm-touched ending.

When possums mount on moon-shine bars,

And glow-worms hidden in the mine,
Shall leave their caves to mock the stars—
Oh, then my lips shall meet with thine! (*Verses* 30)

Bitterness is the overwhelming trope of her poems about relationships, especially in "The Seed," placed near the end of the manuscript:

Oh, waste & bare & barren space!
Arise ye rank & bitter grasses,
And heal & cover o'er the place;
For pain must pass as passion passes. (*Verses* 52)

Ridge returned to New Zealand for a brief visit in 1905. Hokitika and its environs must have looked considerably smaller after Sydney's bustling streets. Was the intent of her return to parade her new cosmopolitan status before the women her character disparaged in the "Story of Ruth?" Or was she there just to collect more funds? Did she hope to drop off her son with her in-laws? Or did she return to try to persuade her husband to join her in Australia? A man did not follow a woman in that milieu. Besides, he had the gold mine to look after. A January 1905 announcement in the local New Zealand paper amounted to a public declaration of Ridge's second and final separation from Peter Webster:

Mrs. Peter Webster, of Kanieri, recently returned from Sydney, where she has been for the last twelve months studying painting in the studio of Julian Ashton, one of the most famous painters in Australia. Mrs. Webster is an artist of much higher than average talent, and the opportunity of such tuition as she has been able to get in Sydney has greatly increased her gift. It is, we understand, her intention to return to Sydney for another lengthy period to perfect herself in all branches of the art.

It took her a while to extricate herself. In February she was still in Hokitika when a local law clerk, Charles JP Sellers, signed her autograph book with Isabel Learmont, a storekeeper, perhaps his sweetheart since they signed it together. Sellers would have been someone she could have consulted about a possible legal separation. After Ridge left New Zealand for Australia for the second and last time, she never saw her husband again. He knew she had plans to leave for America at some point because he threatened to kill her if she took along their son.

Ridge's radical personal decisions paralleled her mother's, she who left her husband in Ireland to sail for Australia with their child. But Ridge must have also found inspiration as well in the unconventional mores of the bohemian artists of Australia. Julian Ashton wrestled too with the problems of convention. His wife, one of the founders of the Womanhood Suffrage League, spoke out publicly against marriage before her death in 1900, and recommended an annual review of the marriage contract. In 1901 just after A.G. Stephens published Louise Mack's book of poetry, Mack abandoned her husband of five years to work in Europe.

A few months after Ridge sailed away, Peter Webster was hauled into the magistrate's court in Hokitika on a charge of assault—for spitting in the face of one John Roberts. Such was the rough-and-ready life in the mining town. Six witnesses were called. They testified that Roberts said "Thank you" after being spat upon, but the judge found Webster guilty and fined him eight pounds. By May of that year he had their seven-room house auctioned off, a clear indication that it wasn't for lack of income she had left him, and a signal that Webster knew she was not returning. There is no record of him pursuing his wife and child to Australia. He died in 1946, just three miles south of Kanieri Forks in Rimu, the tiny town where his parents lived and died. No second wife, no other children—he never saw his son again—but fifty nephews and nieces survived him, as he was one of thirteen siblings. The Webster family remembers Ridge as "a rather wicked figure."

Chapter 5

Beyond Sydney

(Air
heavy and massed and blue
as the vapor of opium...
domes
fired in sulphurous mist...
sea
quiescent as a gray seal...
and the emerging sun
spurting up gold
over Sydney, smoke-pale, rising out of the bay...) (*Sun-up* 43)

"Where shall I pour my dream?" is the last line of "The Dream" quoted above. The poem invokes her dilemma of whether to remain in Australia this second time, or cut all ties and move to America. Fellow poet Henry Lawson traveled between New Zealand and Australia three times before he got up the nerve to find a patron to send him to England. On his return to Australia, he wrote in an 1892 *Bulletin*:

Talent goes for little here. To be aided, to be known,
You must fly to Northern cities who are juster than our own.
Oh! the critics of your country will be very proud of you,
When you're recognised in London by an editor or two.
You may write above the standard, but your work is seldom seen
Till it's noticed and reprinted in an English magazine.

At the time, Ridge was perhaps the most successful poet coming out of Australia to excel internationally. Australian women were thought to be particularly competitive. The 1888 poem "The Australian Girl" by Ethel Castilla describes the species: "Her frank, clear eyes bespeak a mind/

Old-world traditions fail to bind./She is not shy/or bold, but simply self-possessed." Women who remained in Australia, however, suffered the same struggles to write and be recognized at home as their New Zealand counterparts. "I was not born a parasite," declares Sybylla, the heroine of the bestseller *My Brilliant Career* (1901) written by Miles Franklin, who left Australia for America a year before Ridge. Sybylla refuses to be "one of the blood-suckers who loll on velvet and satin, crushed from the proceeds of human sweat and blood and souls." Instead she insists on acknowledgement as a writer, but is ambivalent about the outcome. "Ah, thou cruel fiend—Ambition! Desire!" she cries, after refusing an offer of marriage. "Why do I write?" she asks. "I am only an unnecessary, little, bush commoner. I am only a—woman." The novel ends without hope that she will have the "brilliant career" she so wants.

In 1906, Ridge was 32 years old, living with her mother and son, now six. Their address is just an eight-minute walk from her cousin Eddie's house at 69 Alexander Street in North Sydney. The neighborhood, known as "Crows Nest" for the promontory that once bore the residence of Mary Wollstonecraft's cousin, was then full of boarding houses, shanties, and several mansions, including one that housed a future premier, and one that offered a view that remains the most photographed panorama of the city. It was also home to writers and artists like Norman Lindsay, who was then working at the *Bulletin* with A.G. Stephens, and the Van Dyke-bearded Rubbo, who reportedly fought Sydney's last duel. Henry Lawson kept a room in the neighborhood at Isabella Byer's Coffee Palace and his daughter went to high school three blocks from Ridge's address. While Lawson was publishing his stories and poems in the *Bulletin*, Ridge's work appeared some thirty times. As Stephens's or Ashton's protégé, she would have frequented the Sydney events and been introduced to everyone. "Everybody was brighter [t]here than anywhere else," writes novelist Louise Mack. "People talked more brilliantly, laughed more naturally, and found themselves of more importance." The new subjects discussed were gender, race, and nationalism, and the various *isms* in art. The salons were also where the bohemians learned to preen and attract financial patronage, a talent key to Ridge's later survival. Although women attended these salons, they were rarely invited to the bohemian clubs. They could, however, now go with men to the pubs to extend their salon talk, to "Beerhemia" as coined by Lawson, whose alcoholism and bohemianism eventually killed him.

Lawson memorialized the North Sydney neighborhood with many sharply political poems that depicted the thriving but quickly changing community at the turn of the century.

The old horse ferry is a democratic boat,
For she mixes up the classes more than any craft afloat;
And the cart of Bill the Bottlo, and the sulky of his boss,
Might stand each side the motor car of Mrs Buster-Cross...

The radical freethinker William Chidley also lived in the neighborhood and used its "Speakers Corner" to deliver speeches about sex while wearing a toga. While he was no Australian Walt Whitman, his presence suggested a freethinking, open society that would also tolerate and perhaps encourage a single mother with aspirations to become an artist or a poet. She would certainly not have been regarded as a "wowser," Australian slang for the prim temperance women of the time who were thought to want to take all the fun out of life. Another freethinker in the neighborhood was Lawson's former girlfriend and *Bulletin* poet Mary Gilmore (1865-1962). After her relationship with Lawson, Gilmore traveled to Paraguay in 1896 to establish a socialist community but soon returned. Her later writing pioneered the view of the Aborigines as victims of injustice and discrimination. (In contrast, some of Ridge's early work mirrored Australasian prejudice against the Chinese). Gilmore was eventually accorded a state funeral, a postage stamp, and her face on the $10 bill inscribed with two lines of her poetry: "Our women shall walk in honour/Our children shall know no chain."

Melbourne-based Lesbia Harford (1891-1927) would be Ridge's closest Australian counterpart in poetry and politics. Contemporary poet Les Murray claims that Harford is "one of the two finest female poets so far seen in Australia," and she is deemed "a poetic sister of sorts to John Shaw Neilson," the lyric poet whose work is bound with Ridge's in the Mitchell Library. Of Irish descent, Harford even looked a bit like Ridge, with her hair pulled back in a similar style. Harford's early years may have influenced her turn to radicalism: her father went bankrupt and abandoned her and her siblings for the gold mines in Western Australia. Harford was one of the first women to graduate with a law degree from the University of Melbourne, but instead of practicing, she joined the Wobblies, organized in clothing factories, fought against conscription, and worked as a servant, despite ill health. An advocate of free love, she had affairs with both sexes, including

Guido Barrachi, one of the founders of the Australian Communist party. She wrote imagist poems, skipping the bush ballad tradition that Ridge began with, her brother having introduced her to cubism and vorticism. She felt that "poetry and fiction should not be consciously propagandised" and published little. Perhaps in response to the disastrous Gallipoli campaign in 1915, she wrote:

> I will not rush with great wings gloriously
> Against the sky
> While poor men sit in holes, unbeautiful,
> Unsouled, and die.

Harford herself died in 1927 at the age of 36 of a weak heart, leaving behind three thick exercise books of her work, and the draft of a novel.

After A.G. Stephens returned to Australia, he opened a bookstore in 1906 in order to recoup losses from his magazine, but it failed a year later. There were no other presses in Australia as interesting as Stephens's. The few that paid promulgated that women were merely the "breeders" for the newly federated "white" Australia. That alone might have persuaded Ridge to move on. But she was very fond of Sydney. "Beloved city, city I love," she writes at the very end of her life. It must have been hard to leave.

While Ridge was mulling over her prospects, her stepfather died of pneumonia in the Hokitika insane asylum, and was buried January 16, 1906. She did not return for the funeral. A year and a half later, her mother died of acute gastroenteritis and cardiac failure in Sydney's Ellis Coffee Palace. She was planning to travel with Ridge and her grandson Keith to San Francisco. Were mother and daughter just downing a quick cup of coffee while shopping for their voyage, scheduled only a month away? The area was the center of Sydney working class shopping, where all the electric trams stopped, and there's still a coffee bar today at that address at street level. Australian turn-of-the-century "coffee palaces" also provided rooms, and were considered more respectable than other lodgings because they didn't serve liquor. Ridge and her mother might have been living there.

The informant on the August 5, 1907 death certificate is Ridge's cousin Alfred. For the last three years he had been alderman in the district of Canterbury, a citizen of some standing. Was it customary to spare a woman the task of identifying the body, or was Ridge already on her way to Brisbane to buy her ticket and catch her boat? She wasn't there to correct Alfred when he misidentified Emma's father and put "tutor" in place of "customs officer" as his position. Ridge is listed on her mother's death certificate as "Rosa Webster."

Imagine Peter Webster showing up at her relatives' doorstep weeks or months later, demanding to know where his wife and child had gone. Did the aunt or her cousins feign ignorance—*Bugger off, you bastard*—or were they too kept in the dark and did they try to console him? Perhaps Webster was too demoralized to search for her. "Nil" is what Ridge put down for the names and address of nearest kin on her departure. On the manifest she identified herself as Sybill Robson, perhaps after Miles Franklin's heroine, Sybylla, "a fiercely independent girl who is rebelling at the limits imposed by circumstance on her life." While she and Keith could have sailed directly from Sydney to San Francisco, instead they traveled to Brisbane, some 450 miles away, where they waited for nearly a month before sailing to San Francisco via Melbourne. In a final bit of subterfuge, Ridge—now Mrs. Robson—gave Keith, described on the manifest as fair, with brown hair and blue eyes, the name Eric. On September 4, 1907 mother and son set sail on the *Moana* for America.

Chapter 6

Last Links with Australasia

The brochure called the *Moana* "a palatial liner." The 350 foot-long vessel was a ten-year-old mail steamship, and the largest of the Union Company's fleet. Decorated with Brussels carpet runners and sofas upholstered in blue moquette, the ship was equipped with a stage for amateur theatricals, a music saloon paneled in sycamore, 500 incandescent lamps, five electric fans "so convenient for travel in the tropics," 11 tons of refrigerated food, and last but not least, a special dining room for children.

"They who travel from Australia are the moneymakers," writes Louise Mack about her voyage to Europe in 1901, "[they are] the business people, the butchers, bakers and iron-mongers, people who don't waste time looking at the unseen but convert the visible into gold or silver as quickly as possible." Ridge was not among the moneymakers. "Remember I came steerage to America in an Australian boat," she writes in 1932. "It was not bad at all." Then she immediately contradicts herself: "though 23 years ago [it] was a ghastly nightmare beyond belief."

Ridge must have been full of grief at the loss of a mother so beloved. But she must also have been thrilled to be leaving the Antipodes at last, joining her fellow passengers in planning their conquest of a new world. She was, however, traveling with her small son, without the advantages of the "special dining room for children." In New Zealand and Australia she had her mother, and in Australia she also had the possibility of her aunt or cousins to help look after him, and he had cousins to play with in both countries. On the boat, there was only the hope of meeting playmates—and she might have been reluctant to befriend anyone in her role as a fugitive.

Their first stop was Suva for a day's refueling and perhaps taking on sugar for a Vancouver/Fijian firm, since the boat would dock in Vancouver. A shipping brochure of the period extols the native populace that collected on the Suva wharf upon the arrival of a steamship:

the ever-smiling face of the little thick-set Fijian with the carriage of a born soldier, the slender Oriental swathed in picturesque cotton garments, brightly turbaned, his womenfolk, lithe and childlike, decked with bracelets, anklets, noselets, earrings, and a wreath of bright-colored necklaces, following behind...

How would a New Zealander view the Fijians—like the Maori, a dying race? Despite a superior racial attitude, the Edwardians had little better technology than the Fijians. Clothing was still washed by hand, mangle or no mangle, and their cooking stoves burned wood. She may have seen an exhibition of fire walking—still prime tourist entertainment today—but dressed in layers and layers of cotton and wool that were popular with colonials even in that climate. Surely the Fijians thought the Edwardians crazy.

The *Moana* also docked in Honolulu for at least a day. The only hotel on Waikiki beach was also known as The Moana, which means "the sea" in Hawaiian. Built by U.S. investors immediately after the overthrow of the Hawaiian government nine years earlier, the hotel was one of the more obvious outcomes of the political maneuverings of American businessmen. It featured 75 guest rooms with telephones, bathrooms, and an electric elevator. The port at its feet was always crowded with boats steaming between one continent and the next, commerce just beginning to replace the native Aloha. Jack London, the popular novelist and committed socialist whom Ridge would meet in a few years, spent the year before surfing on a nearby beach. He describes the view: "We could see the masts and funnels of the shipping in the harbor, the hotels and bathers along the beach at Waikiki, the smoke rising from the dwelling-houses high up on the volcanic slopes of the Punch Bowl and Tantalus." Between the beach and the jagged volcanic peaks flourished large taro beds beside the earliest buildings of the University of Hawaii. Electric trolleys ran nearby.

Ridge and her son Keith must have walked the *Moana*'s gangplank to stroll along the pier where the Chinese worked as longshoreman. They would have been familiar since Ridge included a Chinese fruitseller in a poem she wrote later about her childhood in Australia, and there was a Chinese man in one of her earlier stories. The tattoos on the Hawaiians, their general demeanor, and the sound of their language must have reminded her of the Maori, a culture she knew well enough to draw an elaborate Maori fish trap as an illustration for the end of her story, "The

Trial of Ruth," and cite references to their mythology in a number of early poems. A patois had evolved on the Hawaiian docks between Maori in its many varieties: Cockney-English, the Marquesan, Hawaiian of course, as well as Portuguese, Chinese, Fijian and various kinds of American, San Francisco to New England—rich cacophony for a poet from anywhere. Perhaps Keith found a playmate or two and they ran along the sand, scaring up the gulls and throwing sticks in the water, relieved to be off the boat for a few hours. But he couldn't run entirely free—he had to remember he was Eric Robson—*Eric*, she must have called out to him. Or did he cry to go back on the boat, sensitive to the hot sun and the sand?

Why didn't Ridge leave him with his grandparents? In their *Cyclopedia* photo, James Webster is bewhiskered and balding but not unkind-looking, and Margaret, with a friendly smile and bright eyes, holds a small book open as if she had just read it aloud. By 1907 James had retired from the pub and worked as a government valuator. Most of their thirteen grown children had children who lived in the area—surely they would have welcomed Keith. But Ridge's mother was the one who acted the doting grandmother, having accompanied them on both trips to Australia. Then she died.

Ridge was fleeing a difficult history: childhood poverty, a dead baby, a bad marriage, an insane stepfather, a recently deceased mother. She must have given considerable thought to how to manage with her son by the time she reached Hawaii, halfway to San Francisco. On board her fellow passengers were remaking themselves, perhaps changing their names too, invoking new life stories. Edwardians were very mobile, and as immigrants they were making their way to America by the thousands.

> Wind rising in the alleys
> My spirit lifts in you like a banner
>   streaming free of hot walls.
> You are full of unspent dreams....
> You are laden with beginnings....
> There is hope in you...not sweet...
>   acrid as blood in the mouth.
> Come into my tossing dust
> Scattering the peace of old deaths,
> Wind rising in the alleys,
> Carrying stuff of flame. (*Sun-up* 93)

Ridge's boy Keith was her last link to her old life. He definitely inherited his father's large ears. Although he was separated from his father the first time at age three, he could have inherited his mannerisms too, a walk like his or gestures. These would be daily reminders of her husband. The boy could have missed his father or his cousins in New Zealand or Australia and let Ridge know, the way children do, how unhappy he was without them. He might have wanted to go home. He must certainly have been bewildered by all the travel, true of many travelers no matter what age en route to a new country. He might have whined on the boat, or fallen ill and had to be nursed for days. Other children might have picked on him because he didn't have a father. She may have realized on the boat that she couldn't do for him as her mother had for her. Or had her mother already suggested that she was the flower to be treasured, not to squander her talents on her grandson?

Perhaps Ridge feared that together, the two of them would starve. There were still poorhouses in the U.S. Only a few years later, the poet Marina Tsvetaeva would leave her daughters in a Russian orphanage during a famine, thinking they would survive better without her. Her two-year-old quickly died of starvation anyway. Where would Ridge find employment to feed her son? Who would care for him while she searched?

> Motherhood, for the women poets of 1915-45, was virtually compulsory, in that a childless woman was made to feel essentially a failure...no matter what else she might accomplish...The majority of woman poets who rose to prominence between the World Wars did not, however, have children, indicating the choice of an artistic identity as opposed to the threat of anonymity that motherhood represented. And those who did have children tended to be stricken with ambivalence and conflict, or highly unconventional...

writes William Drake in *The First Wave: Women Poets in America 1915-1945*. Mina Loy (1882-1966) left two children, one her lover's, the other her husband's, for several years in Italy, returning only to deposit a third by Arthur Craven. When the children's nanny suggested that leaving them again might damage them, Loy broke all the dishes. Heiress and publisher Caresse Crosby (1891-1970) housed her children in an icy toolshed so that Harry would not have to endure their company. Olga Rudge (1895-1996), Ezra Pound's mistress, deposited Mary with shepherds until she was old enough to take dictation for them in Venice. Ridge's friend, the poet Elinor

Wylie (1885-1928), told everyone she had been pregnant eight times, but never mentioned the son she had abandoned when he was very young. Although Ridge gave her assistant, the poet and novelist Kay Boyle, $100 for her first abortion, Boyle subsequently had five more children, and left the first at Isadora Duncan's brother's commune in London. While Boyle typed her work across the street and took dance classes, her daughter wore tunics and sandals all winter and was severely punished for defecation. The novelist Evelyn Scott (1893-1963), another good friend of Ridge's, had a child in the wilds of Brazil and dragged him through a ménage à trois with Thomas Merton's father. D.H. Lawrence was so jealous of Frieda (1879-1956) seeing her children, she had to wait outside their school so she could talk to them and give them presents to "keep herself fresh in their memories." The most positive of these unusual stratagems was that of the poet H.D. (1886-1961). Hilda Doolittle bore a daughter as the result of an adulterous fling with Cecil Gray, a Scottish music critic, when she was 28, and persuaded her husband, the poet Richard Aldington, to give the infant his name. A few years later she began a relationship with Bryher (1894-1983), the daughter of a British shipping magnate, who then married writer Robert McAlmon in order that, now married, she and H.D. could travel together, free of suspicion. McAlmon, initially attracted to H.D., acted as surrogate father until Bryher divorced him for Kenneth McPherson, a nascent filmmaker and critic who was also in love with H.D. H.D. then aborted McPherson's child but allowed him to give his name to her daughter. Perdita, "the lost one," had many last names but, in her case, they chronicled a history of fathers. She claimed to have been happy because she enjoyed two mothers, but she was also looked after by an extensive staff.

Ridge and her son Keith, however, were alone.

Chapter 7

"Not Without Fame in Her Own Land"

On September 26, 1907, the *Moana* docked first in Victoria, then in Vancouver, during a record dry spell not to be equaled until 2012. This meant the fjords of British Columbia were spectacular, the air and water crystal blue, the mountains, like those in Hokitika, in majestic evidence, and the bustling dockworkers in a good mood. Ridge's accent and her assumed name—Robson—would have passed unnoticed, both common in Canada, then and now. Robson Street, at the center of downtown Vancouver, was named after John Robson, the premier of British Columbia from 1889-1892, Mount Robson is the highest peak in the Canadian Rockies, and by 1911, 40 Robsons lived in Vancouver.

Ridge must have seen Canada as just another British colonial outpost unworthy of her long trip and all she had given up. Many Canadian artists felt the same way—half of all Canadian writers emigrated to New York at the turn of the century. Ridge transferred her son and their five pieces of luggage to *The City of Puebla* and sailed on to San Francisco without a break. Four days later, on September 30th, she arrived at her final destination. The front page of that day's *San Francisco Call* screamed: "Parents To Fight for Custody of Babes." A wealthy banker's brother had knocked his sister-in-law to the ground while he was trying to retrieve her child for his brother. Not such a positive sign for the runaway Ridge.

To conceal her departure from her husband, she had not only changed her name but had also declared herself 10 years younger on the ship's manifest. She had begun taking years off her age in Australia, when she gave her birth date as three years later in a note to her publisher. It was an era in which it was socially unacceptable to ask a woman's age, and official records were less detailed and accurate than they are today. This worked to Ridge's advantage, and for anyone wanting to disappear. Her mother at various times had declared herself 8 and even 14 years younger than her estimated age. Whether or not it was more of Ridge following her mother's footsteps, she must have realized that in addition to making it harder for her husband to trace her journey, she would be starting over in a new country, yet another new literary scene, and she would need more time to establish herself—and that youth more easily attracts opportunity. She hid the deceit well: no one knew about her true age until after her death.

Her third subterfuge was to declare on the manifest that she was Australian, erasing the 24 years of the youth she spent in New Zealand. She did love Australia, and perhaps claiming it as her homeland suggested less esoteric roots, while explaining what was most likely not a regulation British accent. She certainly wouldn't want to be mistaken for one of the English, who oppressed her Irish forebears. Perhaps she claimed the country as a way to express her gratitude to her cousin Eddie in Sydney—the one she refers to as "a dear cousin"—who might have helped her with their passage.

Ridge was plucky and determined to rise in the world. She had no parent to frown on her efforts, no peers from school measuring her progress or condemning her chutzpah. Given that she claimed an aristocratic past, she might have felt she was regaining her proper station by reshaping her identity. She could have revealed her true age when she arrived, and she had the option of admitting her New Zealand youth, especially after she became friends in New York with several New Zealanders, including Thomas Merton's father. She could have taken the name Reilly, for that matter, and strengthened her hold on her illustrious genealogy, or even kept her alias Sybill Robson. Pride in her literary achievements, however, made her want to claim those earlier publications, and she quickly published her first poem in America under the name Lola Ridge, the Australian. "Not without fame in her own land" read the introduction to her poem in the *Overland Monthly* of March 1908. "Miss Ridge is sure to win fame in the United States for her style is breezily strong, and, in her sentimental moods, appealingly beautiful."

The ballad she published, "Chronicles of Sandy Gully as Kept by Skiting Bill" is laden—or overladen—with the colorful language of the gold rush: "The sandy pug was risin' an the claim was duffered out/The divy of the washin wouldn't pay a three bob shout." Anyone from New Zealand would have known the locale, and anyone who knew her pen name would know the poem was hers. But even if Peter Webster had spies on the lookout, poems in a San Francisco magazine weren't going to tell him her location. Taken from her "lost" *Verses* manuscript, the poem was well worth resurrecting in her new country. Robert Service's book of ballads, *The Spell of the Yukon*, had just become a bestseller and would go on to sell three million copies. The central poem in his book, "The Shooting of Dan McGrew," drew on his gold rush experiences in the Klondike. With her poems on gold mining in the Antipodes, she was assured a positive reception.

First edited by Bret Harte in 1868, the *Overland Monthly* was deemed a "Western *Atlantic Monthly*," where Harte ran his famous "The Luck of Roaring Camp" in one of its earliest issues. Willa Cather was a contributor, as was John Neihardt. Jack London received 15 cents a word for his stories in 1907. In June 1908, the editor accepted another of Ridge's poems and writes: "Mrs. Ridge, in the "Under Song," gives us a poet's appreciation of the great australian [sic] mystery." She must have thought well of his selection: "Under Song" appears as part of "Voices of the Bush," the first poem in her *Verses* manuscript. Tucked in the *Overland Monthly* between the book reviews and the publisher's note, the poem begins evocatively enough:

> The mystical, the strong
>   Deep-throated Bush,
> Is humming in the hush
>   Low bars of song:
> Far singing in the trees
>   In tongues unknown—
> A reminiscent tone
>   On minor keys: (*Verses* 1)

The year before she arrived, San Francisco's own gold-mining era had ended in the terrible fire caused by the earthquake. The city still smelled of ash, and bubonic plague had broken out. Rats were everywhere— even in the municipal government. It had been dismissed for graft, and hearings about the mishandling of relief funds resulted in the publisher of a leading newspaper being kidnapped, a witness's house dynamited, and one of the country's most notable prosecutors shot point-blank in the courtroom by a "madman." President Theodore Roosevelt decided to hand over the relief money to the Red Cross. In May a streetcar strike resulted in "Bloody Tuesday," with the police chief ordering shoot-to-kill, the governor threatening to send in troops, and three dead and scores wounded. Some streetcar conductors were still armed when she arrived. People made homeless by the earthquake were living in horse stalls, one-room shacks, and tents. Mary Kelley, a mother of two with an invalid husband, resented having to pay the city for donated shelter and teamed up with several other women to "liberate" flour from the city's supply, accusing them of hoarding. On the other hand, the telephones were working within a few days of the quake, and saloons were closed for only two months.

Ridge was certainly not unfamiliar with the chaos caused by earthquakes. New Zealand had had at least three major quakes while she was growing up, including one as strong as the 2011 earthquake that destroyed Christchurch. In the 13 stanzas of "Two Nights," she had already commemorated a volcanic eruption, the terrifying Tarawa that killed 120 New Zealanders in 1886.

> A low, continuous, booming sound—
> Like beat of surf on the distant Sound,
>   It swelling in the rumbling east;
> The deep hill heeled on the rolling ground
>   And moaned like a waking beast. (*Verses* 65)

As a result of the San Francisco gold rush fifty years earlier, some 7,000 Australians and New Zealanders settled between Telegraph Hill and the end of Pacific and Broadway, so many that it was known as "Sydney Valley" or "Sydney Town." No Penfolds are listed in the 1907 San Francisco Directory, but there are three MacFarlane's. Given that it was unlikely that she would find refuge with her husband's relatives, perhaps Ridge knew someone through the Australian Martin Lewis (1881-1962), a student of Julian Ashton's during the early days of the art school. Born in Castlemaine, a gold-mining town in similar decline to Hokitika's, he traveled to New Zealand as a "posthole digger and a merchant seaman before settling into a Bohemian community outside of Sydney." Two of his drawings were published in the *Bulletin*. After several years of training in Sydney, he painted backdrops for the McKinley presidential campaign of 1900 in San Francisco, and was working in New York by 1909. A teacher and friend of Edward Hopper's, he eventually sold proto-social realist prints of city life to the Brooklyn Museum, the Metropolitan Museum of Art, and the Whitney. Described by his dealer as looking "like an escapee from a tramp steamer in an early Eugene O'Neill sea tale," he saw quite a lot of Ridge after she arrived in New York, and he was listed on her second husband's draft card as "one who would always know his address."

He may have already been in New York when she needed, at the very least, a babysitter so she could work. Daycare in San Francisco was five cents a day at the Holy Family Day Home, the only facility in the city at the time. Perhaps Ridge tried leaving Keith there, although with all the dislocation from the San Francisco earthquake more children would have been roaming the streets than ever. Some time after her arrival in San Francisco, she and Keith traveled to Los Angeles. Changing her name to Rosa Bernand, she posed as a widow, her mother's ruse, and a part she had played long ago in "*I've Written to Browne*" in Hokitika, gave Keith the new surname and a new birthplace—Australia—and asserted that her husband in Sydney had died in 1904. She lied in order to hide her son from her husband, or to hide her deed from posterity, or to separate herself psychologically from what she was doing, and left her son at the Boys and Girls Aid Society on February 3, 1908, two weeks after his eighth birthday.

In 1899, a Mr. Heap reported that the orphanage's sister institution in San Francisco cared for "incorrigibles," children arrested for minor offenses, abandoned children, and half-orphans. No more than 10 to 20 percent of the children were actual orphans, the balance being these "half-orphans," children with at least one parent unable, unwilling, or unfit to care for them. According to *The Encyclopedia of Children and Childhood in History and Society*, "single poor parents often regarded them [orphanages] as places they could leave their children temporarily until circumstances improved, or as places where their children could get a good education." More than 100,000 children were living in American orphanages by 1910. Before the turn of the century, labor leader Rose Scheiderman's mother put three of her children in an orphanage after the death of her husband while she cared for a newborn. Forty years later, Dorothea Lange left her five children in three different foster homes while she went off on photo shoots. One could think of Ridge's act as analogous to placing the child in boarding school at the same age as British children, as children were not regularly adopted in orphanages then but taken home after the family crisis was over. Perhaps she hoped she would return to Los Angeles or send for him after she had settled in New York. She must have had some idea about the terrible conditions that typically occur with the overcrowding of children who were supported by the state—four years earlier Keith's orphanage was home to 426 children. Like its sister organization in San Francisco, it received only $25 from the city and county for the first two months to care for each boy, and nothing thereafter. Ridge didn't have to pay anything.

Perhaps due to overcrowding, Keith was moved to the Los Angeles Orphan Home Society in 1909 and spent over a year there. A combination of orphanage and census records revealed that he returned to the Boys and Girls Aid Society in 1910. Neither Ridge's executor nor any biographical entry has ever mentioned either placement, one measure of the stigma still attached to such an act. Keith remained in the orphanage until he was 14, the age when all orphans were then turned out into the world.

Because New Zealand was a world leader in social legislation, Ridge was surely not ignorant of the possible emotional consequences of her actions. In just a few years, her soon-to-be-friend Theodore Dreiser would meet with President Roosevelt to press for the end of orphanages, arguing that families should be supported instead of torn apart. Decades would pass in America, however, before the orphanages emptied. In the 1930s, after muckrakers published the worst of the evils of the institution, orphanages were still burgeoning with Depression-era castoffs. Maybe Ridge did her son a favor, maybe she was not a good mother. A father, in the same circumstances, would not have risked social condemnation leaving his child at an orphanage. One hundred fifty years earlier, Jean-Jacques Rousseau abandoned five bastards on the doorsteps of orphanages to their probable deaths. A contemporary example is Apple founder Steve Jobs, who abandoned his daughter for many years.

Perhaps Ridge never considered keeping Keith. Perhaps after erasing ten years of her life, she wanted the freedom to truly pursue that life. On March 20, 1908, just after she would have received payment for her first publication in the *Overland Monthly*, she sailed on the S.S. *Finance* from Panama to New York, a route cheaper than traveling by train overland. She arrived at Ellis Island a week later as Lola Ridge, claiming to be single and a U.S. citizen.

II

New York City and Beyond, 1908–1917

Chapter 8

"Our Gifted Rebel Poet"

Seven months after Ridge's arrival, Emma Goldman, the most famous anarchist of the century, was writing her as "Dear Comrade." Emma shared Ridge's mother's name and her monumental status in her life.

> Emma Goldman
>
> How should they appraise you,
> who walk up close to you
> as to a mountain,
> each proclaiming his own eyeful
> against the other's eyeful.
>
> Only time
> standing off well
> will measure your circumference
>   and height. (*Sun-up* 90)

Middle-aged, bespectacled, and stout, fiery Emma Goldman (1869-1940) was in the midst of delivering a five-week Sunday afternoon Yiddish lecture series sponsored by the Free Workers Group of New York City. Her talks included "Love and Marriage," "The Revolutionary Spirit in the Modern Drama," and "The Political Circus." Perhaps the printmaker Martin Lewis introduced them, as he traveled in Goldman's circle. Ridge had just missed hearing Goldman lecture in Los Angeles April 30, and in San Francisco where a crowd of 5,000 had gathered in May. Goldman, on her part, had announced at one of her many speaking engagements that year that she was sailing in January of 1909 for Australia, hoping to live a quieter life. The wealthy Melbourne anarchist Chummy Fleming, most famous for distributing champagne to the unemployed on behalf of a retiring governor-general, promised her the funds. But Immigration informed Goldman that if she left the country, she could never return.

"Between 1890 and 1920, it is probably no exaggeration to say anarchism became the favorite doctrine of the literary and artistic avant-garde, in America as well as in Europe," writes Paul Avrich, a noted historian of anarchy. James Joyce, George Bernard Shaw and Eugene O'Neill held to anarchist principles in their youth and often later. In a sense, Avrich argues, they were the pioneers of social justice. "Every good person deep down is an anarchist," he writes. Adherents believed they were making the responsible choice by thinking for themselves, in congress with democratic ideals. Their beliefs were grounded in peace, love and brotherhood. In 1870 the Russian anarchist Bakunin defined anarchy as a daily practice: "I mean the only kind of liberty that is worthy of the name, liberty that consists in the full development of all the material, intellectual and moral powers that are latent in each person..." A glance through Paul Avrich's who's who in the back of his *Anarchist Voices*, however, shows that plenty of anarchists were plotting or practicing violence. Although Emma Goldman's lover, Alexander Berkman (1870-1936), spent months in solitude for protesting the beating of other inmates, he was serving 14 years for attempted murder of robber baron Henry Clay Frick.

The kind of anarchism adopted by many of the New York bohemians was "the red Jack London speaks of, the red of comradeship," writes Guido Bruno, a proselytizer of all things bohemian in Greenwich Village. Anarchists there "danced and laughed and were happy and if anyone would want to call a gathering of young men and women like that dangerous, it wouldn't be safe to attend an opera performance or to enter a subway train," protests Bruno.

> An elderly lady in black silk evening dress, deep décolletée, diamonds in her ears, and around her neck and on six fingers, speaking to a gentleman in evening dress. He is immaculate like his shirt front: "I went to Emma's lecture last night. Isn't she a dear? She spoke about those darling children of the Colorado miners and she really made me cry. I'm so sentimental..." At another table, two men, the one looks rather prosperous; the other fellow looks like an artist. "I say," he says, "this fellow Berkman makes me sick. Imagine a man being fourteen years in prison and living the balance of his life in telling his fellowmen of his experiences in prison." A fat Italian plays on the

harpsichord. Everybody eats roast chicken, drinks red ink and enjoys being in an anarchistic place.

For a definition from the trenches, Bruno went on to interview Hippolyte Havel, a close friend of Emma Goldman and possibly another of her lovers. Havel practiced free love with the owner of the restaurant he worked in, Polly Holladay ("Polyandrous" according to playwright George Cran Cook), who complained vociferously when he didn't commit suicide as he so often promised. They lived on 15th Street between Broadway and Fifth Avenue, very close to Union Square, a park renowned for its political orators of all stripes. "To be an anarchist means to be an individualist," says Havel in his interview. "To be an individualist means to walk your own way, do the thing you want to do in this life—do it as well as you can." When asked about throwing bombs and killing people, Hippolyte answered: "No true anarchist could destroy something that is existing. It would mean to deny his own existence, if he would not grant the right of existence to everybody and everything created."

Like most immigrants, Ridge had arrived in America with hope, then measured it against the strictures of class and money. America was in a recession. There were few jobs unless you were skilled. The unskilled went to work in sweatshops or factories where dehumanizing hours and treatment prevailed. The poor—and Ridge was one of them—lived poorly, often in situations worse than those they left behind. With her background in working-class New Zealand, and her abiding interest in labor and bohemianism, she had all the makings of an anarchist. Emma Goldman "addressed herself implicitly to all the people on the edge of leaving one thing—a marriage, a job, an identity, a town—for something else." Ridge was ripe for Goldman's influence.

Goldman's letter urges Ridge to finish an illustration for one of her pamphlets. Ridge's only surviving commercial illustration (she drew one for *Playboy* magazine but it remains lost), the drawing was taking a lot of time to complete. "I hate to hurry you dear, but I ought to take the Patriotism manuscripts to the printer, if I want the pamphlet done before I go." The published drawing depicts "Patriotism: A Menace to Liberty," showing one mythical woman crushing another—not the most supportive of feminist images. Ridge had been laboring so hard on it that Goldman admonished her to take a little time off to attend the *Mother Earth* ball. Although there is no anarchists' ball documented until May of the next year, Goldman often held such fundraisers for *Mother Earth*, her magazine "devoted to social science and literature." Admission for these balls ranged from 10 to 20 cents, plus 15 cents to check your hat. An additional 15 cents was charged if one were reporting from the "capitalist press," with socialist reporters turned away entirely because they were "false friends and that is worse than an open enemy." The *New York Times* (whose correspondent must have paid 15 cents) reported that "persons who regard the anarchists as a saturnine and dyspeptic lot will have a chance to see how they disport themselves under the influence of music and dancing when they are out for a good time." One year Goldman went as a nun and waltzed to "The Anarchists Slide." In her letter to Ridge, Goldman wants to introduce her to Voltairine de Cleyre who was planning to attend, whom Goldman believed "a greater literary talent than any other American anarchist." De Cleyre's poetry and anarchist texts would have appealed to the passionate Ridge. She spoke for those

> whose every fiber of being is vibrating with emotion as aspen leaves quiver in the breath of Storm! To those whose hearts swell with a great pity at the pitiful toil of women, the weariness of young children, the handcuffed helplessness of strong men!

De Cleyre opposed the state, marriage, and the domination of religion in sexuality and women's lives. She tried to anticipate a future in which gender was not a defining characteristic for social roles. Her 1895 lecture "Sex Slavery" wasn't just about prostitution, but also referred to marriage laws that allowed men to rape their wives without consequences. Like Ridge, she had a child whom she didn't raise, a boy who, left with his father, was unaware of de Cleyre's existence until he was 15 years old. DeCleyre—and Jean-Jacques Rousseau—had clearly defined theories about the education of children, but little love for their own. Candace Falk, a leading Emma Goldman scholar, hypothesizes that Goldman herself had a child whom she gave up for adoption sometime between 1902 and 1904. That may explain why she was highly critical of radical women who suffered too long over the loss of their children, and would have made Ridge loath to mention the existence of her son. In general, anarchists found children to be an insoluble problem. Just ten years earlier, two leading anarchist theorists argued that parents had the right to treat their offspring any way they wanted, short of murder, and that parents were not responsible for their upbringing or their support. One of them went even further:

A child upon whom its parents at great cost to themselves have conferred...life is, on reaching maturity, under an obligation...to either make good to the parents the cost incurred by its production and maintenance, or else show, by committing suicide, that there has been no value received; failing in which obligation, the child should be subjected, by all decent people, to the...boycott.

Anarchist feminists were antifamily at a time when the family was highly romanticized. Like Shulamith Firestone of second-wave feminism and Charlotte Gilman of the first, radical feminists understood that family life was at the root of gender inequality, that political and legal freedom wouldn't free them from the gender trap. Perhaps Ridge understood this best, with women's suffrage having been passed in New Zealand so many years earlier, yet producing only the appearance of change. Emma Goldman went a step further and announced that she was anti-women's suffrage. "Suffrage is an evil...it has only helped to enslave people...it has but closed their eyes that they may not see how craftily they were made to submit." She was particularly furious with suffragists who insisted that voting women would not cause any disruption in the society. For Goldman, disruption was necessary for change, and although she preferred education as a means, she espoused violence if there was no other way. De Cleyre, on her part insisted that "the ballot hasn't made man free and it won't make us free."

At the time of Goldman's letter, De Cleyre would have been traveling to the ball from Philadelphia, where she was living and teaching among poor Jewish immigrants. Anarchist Gussie Denenberg described Ridge as "fragile looking and intense and reminded me of Voltairine de Cleyre. She had the same spirit." De Cleyre suffered from similar debilitating migraines, hers connected to public appearances. According to Emma Goldman, she had "an extraordinary capacity to conquer physical disability—a trait which won for her the respect even of her enemies and the love and admiration of her friends." This trait would be one that Ridge would emulate. Whether she actually met De Cleyre is not known, but such a meeting was possible since De Cleyre visited New York more than once around that time.

Ridge was working for Goldman, but she also made money as an artist's model, something she had done before in Australia, an archetypal job for a bohemian. Walt Whitman, that anarchist, celebrator of the body, and poetic model for Ridge, also seems to have modeled at least once. Recently, seven photographs that closely resemble an elderly Walt Whitman posing in the nude have been identified as part of the collection of Thomas Eakins, a friend of Whitman's. It takes quite a bit of self-assurance—something neither Whitman nor Ridge lacked—to remove one's clothing for an artist's critical eye, and it also requires stamina if it's not for the camera, hours of posing with aching muscles in cold, drafty lofts. In the 1910s the going rate for modeling in New York was one dollar an hour, about $25 in 2014, nice money if you could get the job frequently enough.

Modeling could also lead to prominent recognition. Around this time, the Italian immigrant Tina Modotti became the most successful artist's model in America. After a stint as a Hollywood silent movie star, she modeled for the photographer Edward Weston. Later, she was Diego Rivera's model—and the lover of both artists. Trained as a photographer herself, raised as a revolutionary, Modotti published work on four covers of *New Masses*, a magazine in which Ridge published poems and acted as contributing editor. After being deported from Mexico as an insurgent, Modotti devoted herself to antifascist activities, only returning to Mexico City in 1939. She died under suspicious circumstances a year after Ridge, in 1942.

The artist model whose life unfolded in ways most similar to Ridge's was the poet, visual artist, and activist Helen West Heller. In 1892 she moved to Chicago from a farm at age 20 to support herself by modeling. She became a founding member of the Chicago No-Jury Society, a Salon des Refusés inspired by the Armory Show that had its first exhibition at the Marshall Field's department store in 1922. Her poetry, first recognized by Jane Heap, editor of *Little Review*, was published in a number of literary journals. She knew Ben Hecht, Maxwell Bodenheim, and Edna St. Vincent Millay through the Towertown studio of the radical modernist painter, Rudolph Weisenborn. When Heller led a protest against WPA job layoffs in December 1936, she was beaten unconscious by police and arrested with several hundred other strikers.

Peter Quartermain's 1987 biographical sketch of Ridge claims that she also wrote advertising copy at this time, a serious source of income for writers. Advertising was just coming into its own: mergers had consolidated many independent firms, cars extended the reach of advertising to the roads, better transportation allowed better distribution of goods, chain stores and mail order had begun to dominate the retail industry. Although women were the country's main purchasers, they were allowed to write advertising only for food, soap, fashions, and cosmetics. The most famous poet-copywriter was Hart Crane, who wrote ad copy for the J. Walter Thompson agency. "I got so I simply gagged everytime [sic] I sat before my desk to write an ad," he writes in 1923. Although there is no example of Ridge's practice, she later included ad copy in "Morning Ride," one of her most accomplished poems. Perhaps she also put her familiarity with advertising to good use when she solicited ads for *Broom* years later.

At the end of 1909, Ridge pencilled a series of desperate notes into a small gray notebook that contained her Australian cousin Eddie's address, and a few others. The notebook must have been important to her as she managed to hold onto it for her entire life, when she lost nearly every other keepsake or manuscript. At the time she may have been working in Goldman's office at 210 East 13th Street, where Goldman lived with her lover Ben Reitman and put out *Mother Earth*. Goldman was about to start on a 37-city tour in January and surely needed help. But Ridge was greatly preoccupied with other things.

> Nov. 19 '09
> This day my affairs desperate. I shall not go to the office unless for mail. To deny will offend [?]

> Nov. 30 '09
> I will never forget this desperate night. Oh to be able to see only one little hour into the future that would do it. I must act and yet action may be fatal!

> Dec 29 '09
> This is a strange morning...how will it end? Well, a week from now, all things for my immediate future will be decided—perhaps for all time!

Then Ridge quotes the opening lines of the Victorian poet William Ernest Henley's melodramatic "Invictus," her only act of invention to change "unconquerable" to "inconsolable."

> Out of the night that covers me,
> Black as the pit from hole to hole,
> I thank whatever gods that be
> For my inconsolable soul.

The entries continue:

> Dec. 30 12 a.m.
> No change

> Dec. 31 10:15 a.m.
> No change
> surely something must snap with the old year!

> 2:30 p.m.
> I put my fate to the test once more[.] will the god's turn their thumbs
> up or down?

> Jan 1st
> thumbs up.

Could she have been pregnant? She was 36. "I must act yet action may be fatal." An abortion? She would have had access to the latest in birth control from Goldman, who was smuggling contraceptives in from Europe. But Ridge's "all things for my immediate future will be decided—perhaps for all time!" sounds more like a possible career break than the gradual revelations of a changing body. Whatever religion was, it was no longer a consolation, judging from "The Martyrs of Hell" published eight months earlier in *Mother Earth*:

> Not your martyrs anointed of heaven,
>   The ages are red where they trod;
> But the hunted—the world's bitter leaven,
>   Who smote at your imbecile God:

> A being to pander and fawn to;
>   To propitiate, flatter, and dread
> As a thing that your souls are in pawn to,
>   A dealer that barters the dead;

The conviction of mind evident in this poem is echoed in the otherwise fey potboilers she was selling to pay the rent. In "Clem o' The Creek," her

1909 novella about adventure in New Zealand, the strong-willed heroine turns a gun on her lover after throwing out her husband. The *Evening Chronicle* of Charlotte said of its last installment: "through many strong climaxes [it] brings to a satisfactory conclusion an exceptionally fine novel." Some of these stories—like the poems—she had already published in Australia. She eventually sold thirteen stories in America between 1909 and 1911. Seven ran in *Gunter's Magazine* and its successor *The New Magazine*, with its full-color pulp covers, and contents containing adventure stories like Anthony Hope's "Zenda" and those by Sir Henry Rider Haggard, whose work inspired the contemporary Indiana Jones film series. "Clem o' The Creek's" 52 double-columned pages is a page shorter than her other "novel," "The Ladybird," also published in *Gunter's*. "The cities call me with a million lips" says the Ladybird, its mouthy, cross-dressing heroine who becomes a New Zealand cowhand. Couched in the pulp of "nameless dread," "deep eyes of understanding," "bosoms rising and falling tumultuously," and men "vaulting lightly into rooms," the stories' thrills, to a modern reader, are mostly transgressive although they also provide a glimpse of Australian life and mores. Perhaps she would have continued writing them—except for Goldman's letter of August 1911.

Emma was having the first vacation of her life and had had time to read Ridge's "The Undesired," her latest potboiler. Alexander Berkman disagreed with Goldman about it being better than her last. "I am glad that you let me read it," writes Goldman, "because I know now that you can write." She must have meant "write fiction," because she had already featured two of Ridge's poems in *Mother Earth*. "Our gifted rebel poet," Goldman described her later in her autobiography. Ridge must have discarded or retitled the story because it doesn't show up in the list of her publications, and in December of that year she publishes her last. Was she derailed by Goldman's final comment on her prose? "There is one thing I meant to ask you, why do you choose such remote and rather conventional themes? Surely you are sufficiently part of the great pulse of our time to convey something of that."

Goldman promised they would discuss her work further after she returned from her meeting in Mexico. Her next remarks suggest that Ridge was working directly for the anarchist cause. "What is being done about the Unions?" "Have you succeeded last Sunday?" and "Are the boys working on the Union Square meeting?" Because Goldman was traveling as Miss Ida Crossman, one of her many assumed names—Ridge must have been sympathetic with the problems of an alias—Goldman ends the letter by saying she wanted David Lawson to forward a note that she'd enclosed. Lawson was Ridge's new sweetheart.

Chapter 9

David Lawson and the
Ferrer Center

Ridge met the Glasgow-born David Lawson in 1910 at the Ferrer Center, an anarchist organization on St. Mark's Place where Goldman was a prime mover. Five years earlier, Ridge left her husband in New Zealand without divorcing him, and two years earlier had declared herself "single" on the S.S. *Finance* manifest. Close in height to Ridge—around five-four—gentle and soft-spoken and "always shabbily dressed, [with] an air of dryness and fatigue about him," Lawson dropped in on the Ferrer Center almost every night. "The Ferrer Center has certainly done one thing, it has attracted quite a few young Americans very willing and eager to work like…Lawson," writes Emma Goldman in 1911. According to the anarchist Gussie Denenberg,

> Visitors [to the Ferrer Center] included Jack London…and Lola Ridge, the poet, came every Sunday evening…There was a nice young man who always accompanied her. Without him, she couldn't do much. He was right by her side all the time.

David—or Davy as he was best known—Lawson was a direct descendant of a signer of the Declaration of Independence, Captain William Whipple, whose signature is the second after Hancock's, but his immediate forebears had returned to Scotland. Throughout his early life, Lawson suffered a confusion of names. His parents were already separated when he was born and his mother named him Charles M. Howie (her last name), but his father registered him as John Whipple. When he was four, he and his mother immigrated to New York in 1890, a journey that parallels Ridge's from Ireland across the Pacific at the same age, and a few years later he was christened with a compromise—Charles Whipple. His mother remarried, becoming Helen Lawson. He took the name Charles W. Lawson. Some time later, after having been both Charles and John, he settled on David. Only 24 when they met (to Ridge's secret age of 36), Lawson had just moved to New York. Short, red-headed, and tight-lipped, and with a gold tooth in the front of his smile until 1931, he wrote endless letters to Ridge whenever they were separated that were always sensible and supportive. "[His] rather prosaic personality, his steadiness and durability, were an effective foil for Ridge's mercurial, driving, excitable force," writes William Drake. In a 1925 census, Lawson identifies himself as a 39-year-old artist (and Ridge says she's 28! and both say they're head of the household) but for decades he found work in New York and New Jersey as a low-paid engineer. In 1918 he was a toolmaker, a machine designer in 1924, and in 1929, a consulting engineer in the employ of the New Jersey State Highway Commission.

By the late 1920s he had become interested in building bridges and took exams for assistant engineer in structural steel design but never found a job in that field. Instead he worked for the Board of Water Supply until the middle of the Depression. In 1940, he was making $2,400 a year working as a civil engineer for New York City ($69,914.70 in today's money). When the two of them met, industry was pouring its energies into building and rebuilding cities, making engineering one of the most exciting occupations of the time. However, like many other contemporary writers, Ridge's critique of all this industrial activity was not always positive.

Brooklyn Bridge

Pythoness body—arching
Over the night like an ecstasy—
I feel your coils tightening...
And the world's lessening breath. (*Ghetto* 70)

Ridge worked as the first manager of the Ferrer Center. Francisco Ferrer was a Spaniard much hated by the Catholics for founding "Modern Schools" at the turn of the century, institutions that educated children without the coercion of state or religion. When someone connected to one of his schools threw a bomb at King Alfonso XIII and Queen Victoria of Spain in 1906, Ferrer was charged with complicity. Released, he was imprisoned again for instigating a general strike against the war in Morocco and shot in 1909. Ferrer's last words were "Long live the Modern School!" Internationally prominent figures Sir Arthur Conan Doyle, H.G. Wells, Anatole France, and

George Bernard Shaw mourned Ferrer's death. The response of the Catholic Church was to send a gold-handled sword engraved with the pope's good wishes to the prosecutor who sentenced Ferrer. Instead of discouraging the movement, his martyrdom very quickly inspired the founding of Modern Schools in 15 countries, with 200 more in Spain, and 20 in the U.S. Forty of his Modern Schools operated in Barcelona alone. The Ferrer Center in New York did not have a Modern School when it first opened in June of 1910, less than a year after his execution, but acted instead as a community center for anarchists and freedom-loving writers and artists. The Rand School for Social Science had opened two years earlier a few blocks away, with the aim of educating socialists for the trade union movements. They shared a founder with the Ferrer Center, Leonard Abbott (1878-1953), but not much in the way of dogma. At the Ferrer Center, "Tolstoyans and pacifists who spurned revolutionary activity rubbed shoulders with tough labor activists, Nietzschean supermen, and apostles of terrorism and dynamite...to learn the English language, to study French or Spanish or Esperanto, to dance, drink tea, and talk for hours on end," according to Avrich. The Center was a "seething ocean of thought and activity." Ridge "organized educational (paying) classes for every night of the week" and "carried almost the entire work of an association of three hundred members for eight months—the longest period for which any person hung on to that terrific job." Leonard remembered "her vivid personality and her tireless energy." In a letter she wrote a decade later, Ridge describes her trials as manager: "every new measure had to be put to the vote, and I had to fight hostile forces inside that mob...mostly foreigners and all wild unkempt spirits, haling from one another by its hair that new, wonderful doll, Liberty." Anarchism had a special appeal to the previously oppressed and now disillusioned immigrant, and the Center welcomed Eastern European Jews, Frenchmen, Germans, Italians, Spanish, English, Irish, Russians, Rumanians and others. Together with a near-aristocratic group of Harvard and Columbia anarchists, they argued their political beliefs and learned about new ones. Ridge's poetry shows that she observed the immigrants closely at such meetings:

> Little squat tailors with unkempt faces,
> Pale as lard,
> Fur-makers, factory-hands, shop-workers,
> News-boys with battling eyes
> And bodies yet vibrant with the momentum of long runs,

Here and there a woman...

Words, words, words,
Pattering like hail,
Like hail falling without aim...
Egos rampant,
Screaming each other down.
One motions perpetually,
Waving arms like overgrowths.
He has burning eyes and a cough
And a thin voice piping
Like a flute among trombones.

One, red-bearded, rearing
A welter of maimed face bashed in from some old wound,
Garbles Max Stirner.
His words knock each other like little wooden blocks.
No one heeds him,
And a lank boy with hair over his eyes
Pounds upon the table.
—He is chairman. (*Ghetto* 23-24)

The Center held a fundraiser one night and David Lawson went out on the Bowery, a major skid row at the time, to find hungry men to finish up the leftover food. In a photo taken on the street the same year, men are lined into the far perspective for bread. Another photo from that year shows eight homeless men sleeping sitting up on a crowded park bench, straw boaters tipped low over their faces. Vagrancy had increased by 50 percent from 1907 to 1911.

Deadly uniformity
Of eyes and windows
Alike devoid of light...
Holes wherein life scratches—
Mangy life
Nosing to the gutter's end...(*Ghetto* 38)

Robert Henri, founder of the Ashcan School of painting, gave free art lessons at the Center three times a week alongside his student, the urban realist painter George Bellows. Henri emphasized the gritty realism of the streets and insisted both his male and female students develop their "personalities" in the slums of New York, paralleling Ridge's evolving interest in the ghetto. Among those who attended Henri's classes were John Sloan, Rockwell Kent, Man Ray, Max Weber—most of the leading artists in America for the next decade. Arthur B. Davies trained with Henri and organized the Armory Show a few years later. Even Leon Trotsky attended his classes in 1917 before he returned to Russia. Henri believed that art would "keep government straight, end wars and strife, [and] do away with material greed." He too began life with a different name: Robert Earl Cozad. His father had to flee Cozad, the little Nebraska town he had founded, after he shot another rancher. Henri was 17 at the time. Not only did his father change his last name to Henri but he insisted that Robert and his brother pretend to be adopted. Such extreme measures to hide their identities from the state must have increased Henri's interest in anarchism.

"Sees Artists Hope in Anarchist Ideas" reads the *New York Times* headline regarding the exhibit Robert Henri organized at the Ferrer Center. It quotes from a review by Bayard Boyesen, an academic who had recently lost his job at Columbia as a result of his anarchist beliefs: "Because all genuinely inspired artists have stood for absolute freedom of consciousness they have recently stood exactly where the philosophic anarchists stand." Whether Ridge took Robert Henri's class is unknown—she was probably too busy with managing the Center—but, given her training with the Australian bohemians Julian Ashton and A.G. Stephens, his mixing of radical politics with creativity was not unfamiliar.

Besides Robert Henri, Ridge would have heard lectures or helped organize talks with a host of other activists, artists, and writers. These included Margaret Sanger, Upton Sinclair, Clarence Darrow, Ben Reitman, Bill Haywood and Elizabeth Gurley Flynn. They spoke on topics ranging from "The Limitation of Offspring" to "The Syndicalism and Woman." The attorney Theodore Schroeder who founded the Free Speech League had advanced ideas on anthropology, psychology, and sociology, and lectured on sex. He talked so often about the obscenity of religion that Lincoln Steffens commented: "I believe in Free Speech for everybody except Schroeder." Emma Goldman lectured about new literature and drama. According to Will Durant, the most eclectic of lecturers, audiences were "delighted to hear that almost every symbol in religious history, from the serpent of paradise to the steeples of churches in nearby Fifth Avenue, had a phallic origin."

Among the famous poets who visited was Edwin Markham (1852-1940). He most probably gave the Center a recitation and a lecture about his wildly popular poem, "The Man with the Hoe," inspired by Millet's painting, *L'homme à la houe.*

> Bowed by the weight of centuries he leans
> Upon his hoe and gazes on the ground,
> The emptiness of ages in his face,
> And on his back the burden of the world.
> Who made him dead to rapture and despair,
> A thing that grieves not and that never hopes,
> Stolid and stunned, a brother to the ox?
> Who loosened and let down this brutal jaw?
> Whose was the hand that slanted back this brow?
> Whose breath blew out the light within this brain?

According to critic Edward B. Payne:

> Clergy made the poem their text; platform orators dilated upon it; college professors lectured upon it; debating societies discussed it; schools took it up for study in their literary courses; and it was the subject of conversation in social circles and on the streets.

"The Man with the Hoe" was reprinted literally thousands of times in dozens of languages. "I am myself in a limited sense one of the 'Hoemanry,'" wrote Markham, once "a workingman under hard and incorrigible conditions." Anxious to undermine the socialist taint of this popular poem, railroad magnate Collis Huntington offered $5,000 for a poem countering Markham's claims. No one came forward.

Leonard Abbott, president of the Ferrer Center, wrote a piece for *The Comrade* entitled "Edwin Markham: Laureate of Labor," but the closest Markham came to any real political activism was working with Robert Frost and William Rose Benét for the Poets Guild in 1919, an organization that read poems to poor children on the Lower East Side. Pulitzer Prize winner Margaret Widdemer's parody *A Tree with a Bird on it* depicts Markham as much the professional poet: "Edwin Markham (who, though he had to lay a cornerstone, unveil a bust of somebody, give two lectures and write encouraging introductions to the works of five young poets before catching the three-ten for Staten Island, offered his reaction in a benevolent and unhurried manner.)" The parody is of course entitled: "The Bird with the Woe."

The "hobo poet" from Ohio, Harry Kemp (1883-1960) lectured and read his poems at the Center and published them in *Mother Earth*, Hippolyte Havel's *Revolt*, and elsewhere. Like Hart Crane, he was the son of a candy maker, but without the good fortune to invent Lifesavers. As a student, Kemp invited Emma Goldman to speak at the University of Kansas. A very traditional poet, he was known for his less than traditional ways with women: he absconded with Upton Sinclair's wife when he was still in his twenties. Eventually he became known as "the poet of the dunes" in Provincetown where a road is now named after him. "When an abscessed tooth nagged him, he removed it himself with a screwdriver. He scratched out his verses with a seagull feather, wore beach rose garlands in his light colored hair, and fancied wearing capes," according to the *Eugene O'Neill Newsletter* that remembered his part as a seaman in one of O'Neill's plays, opposite the revolutionist John Reed and Eugene O'Neill himself.

Signing his letters: "Yours for the Revolution," Eugene O'Neill (1888-1953) spent time at the Ferrer Center as a result of rooming with the painter George Bellows (1888-1953). Emma Goldman published 23-year-old O'Neill's first poem in 1911, a dreadful workers' parody of the *Rubaiyat*, in the issue before Ridge's second poem appeared. O'Neill helped produce the first issue of Havel's weekly, *Revolt*, until a police raid forced them to move out, and they were raided again three months later. A character based on Havel, famous for calling the patrons of Polly's "bourgeois pigs," opens O'Neill's play *The Ice Man Cometh* with those words. Havel also worked on the scenery for O'Neill at the Ferrer Center's Free Theater, out of which emerged the Provincetown Theater. Just a few years after his association with Havel and the Ferrer Center, O'Neill won the Pulitzer Prize.

John Reed (1887-1920) shared his wife, Louise Bryant, with O'Neill one summer in Provincetown, and wrote mostly poetry during his involvement with the Center. Ferrer Center regulars helped him put on the "Paterson Strike Pageant" at Madison Square Garden with a cast of thousands when he was only 24. Using Margaret Sanger's apartment as headquarters and his lover Mabel Dodge's money, he persuaded John Sloan to paint a 90-foot backdrop that dramatized the plight of many strikers who were also the actors, and Hutchins Hapgood, Lincoln Steffens, and Upton Sinclair to play the parts of cops and scabs. After Wobbly leader Bill Haywood gave the last speech, the entire audience of 15,000 and its huge cast sang "The Internationale." Reed became most famous for publishing a firsthand account of the Russian Revolution, *Ten Days that Shook the World*, in 1919. Ridge must have been envious of his achievement. She repeatedly tried to scrounge up enough money to travel to Russia to see the revolution herself.

Reed wrote the introduction to *Crimes of Charity*, the first book by Ferrer Center habitué Konrad Bercovici (1882-1961). It concerned the controversial practices of New York's private charitable organizations. Penniless and knowing very little English when he arrived from Rumania, Bercovici supported his family of five as a streetcar conductor, a house wrecker, a painter, a stone cutter, an organist for nickelodeons, a sweatshop worker, a piano teacher, and a tour guide for the Lower East Side. His children— Free Love, Gorky, and Liberty—attended the Ferrer school. The first story Bercovici wrote in English was published a week after he submitted it, and he won a prize for his first story in Yiddish, a language he picked up in the neighborhood. In 1921, he wrote a study that accused doctors of using orphans as guinea pigs for the medical study of rickets, but he was most famous for his gypsy novels, and eventually published 42 books. In Paris, he made friends with Hemingway and Fitzgerald, and when he worked in Hollywood he associated with Fairbanks, Pickford, and Chaplin. He sued Chaplin for plagiarizing *The Great Dictator*—and settled. Later a lawyer proved that Chaplin had used Bercovici's story.

Ridge met Jack London (1876-1916) in the winter of 1911-12. He was visiting New York and the Ferrer Center, reciprocating Emma Goldman's recent visit to him in California. He wrote the introduction to Alexander Berkman's *Prison Memoirs of an Anarchist* that year, but was critical of Berkman's methods—and may have been put off by his sympathetic treatment of homosexuality. Berkman did not use the introduction. A short man, London weighed nearly 200 pounds by 1913, and was too burnt out to find the Mexican Revolution when he went down as a reporter a year later.

Another writer frequenting the Center was Manuel Komroff (1890-1974) who, like Ridge, drew illustrations that Goldman published. He wrote plays while involved at the Ferrer Center, began a class in music appreciation, became an art critic, and traveled to Russia to cover the revolution like John Reed. On his return, he edited *The Modern Library* and wrote fifty novels. His most successful book was an edition of the travels of Marco Polo.

The many books by Will Durant (1885-1981) popularizing philosophy and history, especially the Pulitzer Prize-winning multi-volumed *The Story of Civilization* written with his wife, Ariel, began as a series of lectures at the Center. President Ford awarded the two of them the Presidential Medal of Freedom in 1977, the highest civilian honor in the country, an honor surely much disparaged by the anarchists. Durant never claimed, however, to be an anarchist, but was always sympathetic to their cause. He was pleasantly surprised by his first encounter with them at the Center.

> I looked for long whiskers, disheveled hair, flowing ties, unwashed necks, and unpaid debts. I had been led to believe that most of these men and women were criminals, enemies of all social order, given to punctuating their arguments with dynamite. I was amazed to find myself, for the most part, among philosophers and saints."

Hutchins Hapgood (1869-1944), author of *The Spirit of the Ghetto* in 1902, was also part of the Ferrer Center group. Influenced by William James and Santayana at Harvard, Hapgood also published *The Spirit of Labor* in 1907, about the intellectual and political life of radicals in Chicago, and in 1909, *The Anarchist Woman*. This third book concerns, in part, a couple who holds a salon attended by Goldman and Berkman, where everyone ends up kissing one another. In describing Marie, the anarchist, Hapgood could have been writing about Ridge: "The intensity of her nature showed in her anaemic body and her large eyes, dark and glowing, but more than all in the way she had of making everything her own, no matter from what source it came." In 1919 he published *The Story of a Lover*, about his open marriage. Called "varietism" at the time, the arrangement produced a series of provocative letters between Emma Goldman, her lover Ben Reitman, a lesbian interested in Goldman, and Hapgood, who had his eye on Ben. Hapgood was on the bill with Ridge in the 1918-1919 season of the Provincetown Players.

As soon as Ridge had the Ferrer Center functioning, the anarchists wanted to get a Modern School going. Instead of training children for society, they wanted them to learn values that would transcend that society, and at most, encourage them to rebel against it. One hundred sixty-three people attended a banquet at Tenth Street and Second Avenue on June 30, 1911, to contribute to the financing of the school, with fundraising speeches by Goldman and others, including Henrietta Rodman, who was then campaigning against the firing of pregnant teachers in public schools. John Coryell, the author of the Nick Carter detective series who had trained wild Manchurian ponies in China and worked as a journalist, was appointed the Modern School's first teacher, along with his wife Abby. They lasted only a few weeks in the chaotic atmosphere of children and anarchy.

David Lawson traveled to New Jersey to invite 26-year-old Will Durant—only a year older than Lawson—to take over the Modern School. As Durant described it:

> It was Dawson [Lawson]—red-haired, brown-eyed, bare-headed, open-hearted Dawson—one of those who through thick and thin remained loyal to their faith in a free world. He embraced me in the most passionate French style.
>
> 'What luck! He cried. Do you know I've been hunting all over Arlington and Newark for you?'

Ridge met them at the Center. His description of her is the first of many that emphasize her intensity. "I stood in amazement before this strange and fascinating woman."

> She was so frail that her energy made me uncomfortable; at any moment it seemed that her physical resources would be exhausted, and she would fall to the floor consumed in the fire of her own spirit. Every word she spoke dripped with feeling. Her large dark eyes looked out on the world with a mixture of passionate resoluteness and brooding love; she would remake this sorry scheme of things whether it consented or rebelled. I found later that she was a poetess, whose lines trembled with the ardor of the soul that made them. It was fitting that a poetess should be the head of a group of splendid dreamers; but it was extraordinary that this sensitive plant should be the director of any association whatever. I liked her so much, after a few minutes with her, that I was prejudiced in favor of anything she might ask.

It was love at first sight, according to Paul Avrich. Durant writes:

> 'We are organizing the Freedom [sic] Modern School,' [Lola] said...
> 'To give a libertarian education to ten or fifteen children. It will be a

glorious experiment; and if it succeeds, it will affect the practice of every school in America. We want you to take charge of it. We can't pay you well; and if you come to us you will be losing something in security and worldly position. But we thought you were the kind of man who would dare to make the sacrifice.'

How could I escape this inveigling compliment? I wanted to say yes; it would be an exciting game, this trial of teaching without compulsion or authority; many times I had felt the absurdity and the inhumanity of the discipline which I had been forced to impose upon my pupils in the public schools. But was I ready to associate myself with the exponents of the most extreme of all movements in the world of politics and industry?

'You see,' I said, 'I'm not an anarchist.'

'Never mind,' she smiled, confidently; 'you will be.'

Durant came very close to converting to anarchism, just as Ridge had predicted. Rewording Oscar Wilde, he ponders: "What if the best school, like the best government, was that which governed least?" and also: "We would try education by happiness."

This philosophy of educational anarchy was sorely tried by the students. There were nine of them at the start. Bercovici's son mentions in his memoir that he, along with the other students, would chase Durant around a fire in the back yard and whoever caught him would have the privilege of burning his clothes. Durant bought them off with "bribes of bananas." "Lola Ridge," writes Bercovici, "fulfilled the specialized functions of frying [the] bananas and telling charming stories." She was also managing the day-to-day business of keeping the school together. When one of the students decided not to return, she wrote a letter to his father, asserting that the child was a sort of anchor to the school. In keeping with anarchist principles, the children raised funds for the Mexican revolution and protested in January 1911 against the "execution of Denjiro Kotoku and a group of Japanese anarchists in Tokyo." Emphasizing intellectual freedom rather than rote learning, Durant lectured on anything that came into his mind, including "the facts of sex psychology," and surprised everyone by marrying his 15-year-old pupil. The judge at the wedding told Durant he couldn't sleep with her until she was 16. Bercovici's son remembered the public school he attended after the Modern School with great disgust: "No discussions on sex and the revolution, no rioting, no excitement."

Let men be free!
All violence is but the agony
Of caged things fighting blindly for the right
To be and breathe and burn their little hour.

Ridge's poem "Freedom" was published in the June 1911 issue of *Mother Earth*, six months after the Modern School opened its doors. The issue also contained a notice of the first anniversary of the Ferrer Association, the banquet celebrating the founding of the Modern School, Leonard Abbott's article "The Ideals of Libertarian Education" that cites Dewey as an influence, and a piece by Alexander Berkman on teaching economics to children. Freedom at any cost was Ridge's credo and, free of husband and child in the land of the free, under the tutelage of the country's most famous anarchist, she wanted to further extend freedom's reach. On top of her duties at the Ferrer Center and the Modern School, she proposed to publish a magazine. Goldman's *Mother Earth* would do for the Ferrer Center and the anarchists, but what about the Modern School? After a year at 6 St. Mark's Place in the East Village, the Center and the school moved to East 12th Street where Ridge "started, edited, made up and saw to the printing, circulating and distributing of a magazine, the MODERN SCHOOL." The magazine's masthead read, "To Retain the World for the Masters They Cripple the Souls of the Children." David Lawson designed the cover for its premiere issue in 1911. It shows a photograph of Durant and the students, two of them with black masks pulled over their faces, and one child throwing a punch. Durant looks a bit dismayed. Like many of the influential magazines of the period, *The Modern School* contained fiction and poetry as well as essays promulgating its political views. Eventually it became "one of the most beautiful cultural journals ever published in America, rich alike in content and design," according to Avrich. Although the early issues were more like a school bulletin, they gave Ridge her first experience as an editor.

In 1914, three anarchists who frequented the Ferrer Center died on Lexington Avenue in an explosion of bombs intended for John D. Rockefeller. The soft-spoken Ferrer president Lawrence Abbott addressed a crowd of 15,000 New Yorkers anxious for explanation but told them "the real danger lies always in suppression, not expression." As a result of the bad publicity around the bombing, Alden Freeman, the son of a Standard Oil millionaire and a homosexual attracted by the movement's support of all sexual expression, withdrew his funds from the Center and school. Although the school had moved uptown, it was forced then to relocate in New Jersey where it persevered for another 40 years, becoming "one of the most radical experiments ever to take place in the history of American education." The Center itself soon closed.

By then Ridge was long gone. After the second issue of *The Modern School* in 1912, she and Lawson abruptly left New York to travel around the country for five years. Was her leaving a result of a disagreement with Goldman? "There was something of the stern authoritarian in her [Goldman] which made a strident discord with her paeans to liberty," writes Will Durant. "Where she could not dominate she could not work." As Ridge wrote in her 1940 diary: "We parted spiritually—in silence—neither speaking of that which had parted us. It was only that she could brook no independence of action in any associate—indeed she did not want associates but disciples—and I realized sadly I was no disciple."

Perhaps Ridge was also uncomfortable about working at the Modern School. How did she feel, surrounded by children every day, debating how their education should proceed, while her son was living in California, being taught—or not—at the orphanage? Her soon-to-be best friend, the novelist Evelyn Scott, gave her own son very little schooling, and when he became an adult he blamed his mother for the extreme difficulty he had finding work without an education. Perhaps Ridge's son was lucky to have had at least some schooling at the orphanage. Surely Ridge wouldn't have wanted him taught formally after her exposure to the Modern School precepts. In 1914 she published an essay criticizing public school education that was either hypocritical or filled with buried guilt:

> In the first place, no gardener would think of giving each plant the same amount of air and sun, and the same quality of soil. Yet this is exactly what you are doing to your children, and there are as many different kinds of children as there are different kinds of flowers. Why pay more attention to the cultivation of a vegetable than to the development of a human being? Each child requires individual attention, individual understanding, and individual mental food.

Why didn't she send for Keith in 1911 when the Modern School first opened? Davy was working, and she had a job. It wasn't until 1914 that she

saw him again. "In New Orleans," Lawson remembers in his interview for
Anarchist Voices, "we sent for her son who was living out West."

Chapter 10

"Small Towns Crawling Out of Their Green Shirts"

Do you remember
Honey-melon moon
Dripping thick sweet light
Where Canal Street saunters off by herself
   among quiet trees?
And the faint decayed patchouli—
Fragrance of New Orleans
Like a dead tube rose
Upheld in the warm air...
Miraculously whole. (*Sun-up* 65)

When Keith arrived in New Orleans sometime after January 21, 1914, he was 14. Ridge must have kept in contact with him, despite all the business with assumed names, and somehow money was found to transport him to her. The suitor he met, David Lawson, was only 28. He and Ridge had already been traveling the countryside together for two years. Did the boy Keith argue with Lawson as Gladys Bernand-Wehner, Keith's daughter, born two decades later, suggested? Time had not stopped for him, he was nearly an adult with six years of loss behind him. But even in the grow-up-fast era of 1914, it is hard to believe that a 14-year-old would want to alienate the only family he'd ever known. Did Ridge refuse to split her allegiance? The poem she published in the *Bookman Anthology* eight years later puts a child in a curiously fatal Ben Franklin-like situation, and the kite he's holding is hers.

Child and Wind

Wind tramping among the clouds
That scatter like sheep—
Wind blowing out the stars
Like lights in open windows—
Wind doubling up your fists at the tall trees
And haling fields by the grass—
Keep away from the telegraph wires
With my kite in your hand!

In New Orleans, the family lived together, perhaps in "a small house on a side street/off Canal Street in New Orleans/near the Catholic churchyard," a location that Ridge mentions in a poem written much later. They then traveled to upper New York State, Pennsylvania, Ohio, Missouri, Tennessee, and Detroit. Were they helping Goldman on her tour? In 1915 Goldman spoke three times in Detroit on such topics as "Frederick Nietzsche, the Intellectual Storm Center of the European War," "The Philosophy of Atheism," and "The Right of the Child Not to Be Born." She also lectured 18 times in Missouri between 1912 and 1915, spoke 13 times in Albany in 1915, spoke 26 times in Ohio between 1912 and 1917, and 32 times in Pennsylvania. Is it a mere coincidence that these are many of the same locations that Ridge visited? Whatever they were doing, it wasn't easy. "I know we've done it together before—when I was able to scrub, wash and work my hands off, [but I] can't do these things now," Ridge writes years later to Lawson.

Surely they traveled by train.

Train Window

Small towns
Crawling out of their green shirts...
Tubercular towns
Coughing a little in the dawn...
And the church...
There is always a church
With its natty spire

And the vestibule—
That's where they whisper:
Tzz-tzz...tzz-tzz...tzz-tzz...
How many codes for a wireless whisper—
And corn flatter than it should be
And those chits of leaves
Gadding with every wind?
Small towns
From Connecticut to Maine:
Tzz-tzz...tzz-tzz...tzz-tzz... (*Sun-up* 52)

When they settled in Detroit sometime in 1917, it was a beautiful Midwestern city in the midst of tripling its population, with musicians playing on steamers that took city-dwellers to island parks, and wide avenues lined with striking hotels and office buildings. Ford proclaimed the $5 day in 1914, upping his laborers' wages dramatically, and a year later, the one-millionth car came off the assembly line. In the face of America's involvement with the approaching war, Ford became a "fighting pacifist," and chartered an ocean liner to cross the dangerous Atlantic to try to help prevent the conflict. Perhaps Ridge became a "fighting anarchist," and assisted at the Detroit Ferrer School, which was then at the height of its anarchist presence.

In 1917 she and Davy left Keith in a Detroit boardinghouse, never to see him again. According to his daughter Gladys, Keith wrote to Ridge while at vocational school, but those letters have not been shared. Gladys said they were full of declarations of love. Keith was by then seventeen, old enough to stay behind and get a job. Perhaps he went to Cass Tech High School, a progressive trade school located in the middle of the city, with brand new facilities in 1912. Employees actually paid students to attend, which would have relieved Ridge of providing for him. Keith was an avid reader of the "Electrical Experimenter" that ran an ad for the New York Electrical School whose "graduates...have proved themselves to be the only men that are fully qualified to satisfy EVERY demand of the Electrical Profession," and asked his mother if he could attend. Its address was 39 West 17th Street, not far from where Ridge eventually settled. She must have discouraged him.

Although Ridge intended to visit Detroit en route to Chicago in 1919, "staying with people I know," there is no indication that she visited him. Later in her life, she avoided traveling to Los Angeles and San Francisco because going there would be "too painful." She alludes to her son only twice in the letters held at Smith. In the first, he is mentioned by her friend Evelyn Scott in response to something (*he wouldn't even care if I were dead?*) Ridge had written in 1930:

> I don't want you [Ridge] to dream of being dead, even with the pain smoothed from your dear forehead, though I think Keith may be looking at you even now in a way to smooth some of it out. I'm afraid he has your own rather demoniacal pride and would keep at long range even so, but I can't but believe he is old enough now to have read and realized something of what is in you and has been so wonderfully expressed. I think your child would have to recognize his mother in beauty.

Scott tried to console Ridge by suggesting he would be proud of her, how she hoped her own son would feel. It must have been easier for Ridge to think that Keith was dead than to have him hate her. In a letter to David Lawson six years later, Ridge herself writes:

> I remember the night of August 4th 1914...a warm, fragrant, sultry night in New Orleans...the doors and windows open...my little boy... my dead boy (yes I know now that he is dead; it is one of the things I have not told you; the knowledge came to me here in Mexico, last November) ran out on his always willing feet and brought in the paper...I remember the great black headlines "Ghosts"...as Ibson's [sic] Helen muttered.

It doesn't sound like a letter you'd send to someone who had rejected your son. Ridge was writing out of maternal guilt, having been the one to reject him. In the first place, he was not a little boy in New Orleans, he was a teenager who had lived with them for three years, long years if the adolescent was not happy with the arrangement. But Ridge persisted with a fantasy of the small boy she had abandoned in California. He may as well have been dead to her after such a separation, he was a child she could never recover. Why was she fabricating this dramatic scenario for Lawson?

Secrets

Secrets,
infesting my half-sleep...
did you enter my wound from another wound
brushing mine in a crowd...
or did I snare you on my sharper edges
as a bird flying through cobwebbed trees at sun-up
carries off spiders on its wings?

Secrets,
running over my soul without a sound,
only when dawn comes tip-toeing
ushered by a suave wind,
and dreams disintegrate
like breath shapes on frosty air,
I shall overhear you, bare-foot,
scatting off into the darkness...
I shall know you, secrets
by the litter you have left
and by your bloody foot-prints. (*Sun-up* 64)

Many of the political events Ridge wrote about throughout her career occurred in 1917: the lynching of labor leader Frank Little ("Frank Little at Calvary"), the terrible riots in East St. Louis ("Lullaby,"), the first electrocutions—there were 45 in that first year of operation—("Electrocution"), and the passing of the draft law for World War I ("The Fire").

The Fire

The old men of the world have made a fire
To warm their trembling hands.
They poke the young men in.
The young men burn like withes.

If one runs a little way,
The old men are wrath.
They catch him and bind him and throw him again to the flames.

Green withes burn slow...
And the smoke of the young men's torment
Rises round and sheer as the trunk of a pillared oak,
And the darkness thereof spreads over the sky....

Green withes burn slow...
And the old men of the world sit round the fire
And rub their hands....
But the smoke of the young men's torment
Ascends up for ever and ever. (*Ghetto* 71)

Political activist Tom Mooney, tried for alleged participation in a bombing in San Francisco in 1916, began serving his 22 years of jail in 1917. Ridge's poem on his incarceration written many years later helped free him. The Russian Revolution had at last begun in 1917, the inspiration for a number of her poems in her third book, *Red Flag*, and the revolution in Mexico, where she would spend several years writing, was then in full swing. In addition, "some 50,000 lumber workers in the Northwest and 40,000 copper miners in Montana, Arizona, and New Mexico were on strike at one time during 1917," according to Elizabeth Gurley Flynn. Ridge often wrote about labor.

Most importantly, the Espionage Act was passed in 1917. This law made it a crime to interfere with the operation or success of the military. America's first Red Scare ensued, with the Alien Immigration Act passed shortly thereafter, so the government could deport those who were not citizens. The Sedition Act passed the following year forbade Americans to use "disloyal, profane, scurrilous, or abusive language" about the government, the flag, or its army. Perhaps Goldman inspired this last bit of legislation. In June of 1917, Emma Goldman and Alexander Berkman spoke against the draft. 15,000 radicals waited outside, surrounded by mounted police armed with clubs and revolvers, with another 5,000 inside, standing cheek-to-jowl with agitators. Bottles and bricks thrown by these agitators broke the speaker's table and a stage light during Berkman's speech, and catcalls constantly interrupted him. Eventually soldiers tried to storm the podium, and fighting broke out. Goldman took the stage and called them to order.

'I am an anarchist,' she said, 'and do not believe in force morally or otherwise to induce you to do anything against your conscience, and that is why I tell you to use your own judgement and rely upon your own conscience...If that is a crime, if that is treason, I am willing to be shot.'

Goldman and Berkman were arrested and imprisoned for trying to "induce persons not to register" for the new draft. Others, according to Elizabeth Gurley Flynn, "who made chance remarks on war, conscription or sale of bonds, were tarred and feathered, beaten sometimes to insensibility, forced to kiss the flag, driven out of town, forced to buy bonds, threatened with lynching." Historian Lilian Symes describes German farmers whipped to make them subscribe to the Red Cross, religious pacificists beaten and tortured, an I.W.W. organizer hung from a tree by the chief of police until unconscious. She writes that when "the war fever was at its height, radicalism or pacificism in the smaller towns and rural communities was almost suicidal."

Perhaps Ridge, wandering these small towns as an anarchist without proper papers, felt the authorities closing in. Or did she just run out of money? She returned alone to New York City in August 1917. Lawson returned in December.

III

Modernism in New York
1918–1928

Chapter 11

The Ghetto
and Other Poems

The revolution for Ridge during her five years of exile was primarily aesthetic. What was she reading those crucial years? Her library at Bryn Mawr—culled by Lawson—contains only two literary works published before 1920: *The World We Live In* by Helen Keller and *Children of the Frost* by Jack London. Lawson may have sold the first editions of poetry that inspired her. In those years, "Rockets of poetry went up and burst in the sky over the heads of an amazed people," according to poet James Oppenheim. A few months after Ridge left New York in 1912, Harriet Monroe, at the urging of Pound, began publishing modernist work in her new magazine, *Poetry*. As an ambitious poet traveling the Midwest, Ridge would have read the magazine, followed the uproar over the new free verse, and assimilated its tenets. *Others* magazine too had been launched and lauded, and she must have closely followed its trajectory as well since Ferrer colleagues like Man Ray published in it.

Soon after she settled with Lawson in Manhattan, she published thirteen modernist poems in the best magazines: five in *Poetry*, two in *Current Opinion*, one in *Dial*, one in *Literary Digest*, one in *The International*, two in *Others*, and three in the *New Republic* that April, including "The Ghetto," which was then reprinted in *Playboy*, a serious avant-garde magazine with a full-page spread and a glamorous headshot taken by Esta Verez, the concert singer, pianist, and the companion of Ridge's friend, Martin Lewis.

The son of a rabbi, publisher B.W. Huebsch (1876-1974) would have been interested in her subject matter, the Jewish immigrant, and he was known to only choose work that "appealed personally" to him. He had already published Joyce's *A Portrait of the Artist as a Young Man* and D.H. Lawrence's *The Rainbow*. Hart Crane always wanted to be published by him. Francis Hackett, founder and editor at the *New Republic* and a journalist who wrote on the subordination of women and immigrants, made the connection to Huebsch for Ridge early that spring, and her manuscript was accepted May 4. Although Huebsch "refused to degrade literature by dragging it into the same marketplace with toothpaste and movies," when he brought out *The Ghetto and Other Poems* that September, it created an immediate sensation.

> Cool, inaccessible air
> Is floating in velvety blackness shot with steel-blue lights,
> But no breath stirs the heat
> Leaning its ponderous bulk upon the Ghetto
> And most on Hester Street...
>
> The heat...
> Nosing in the body's overflow,
> Like a beast pressing its great steaming belly close,
> Covering all avenues of air...
>
> The heat in Hester Street,
> Heaped like a dray
> With the garbage of the world. (*Ghetto* 8)

The *New Republic*, only four years old, emphasized the importance of Ridge's *The Ghetto and Other Poems* by advertising the book on its cover alongside a notice for work by H.G. Wells. In preparation, Ridge published four very good reviews in the magazine from May to October. Hackett himself reviewed her book. "Miss Lola Ridge is capable of that powerful exaltation on the wings of real feeling which brings a new world into vision...["The Ghetto"] is beyond doubt the most vivid and sensitive and lovely embodiment that exists in American literature of that many-sided transplantation of Jewish city-dwellers which vulgarity dismisses with a laugh or a jeer." Conrad Aiken at *The Dial* gave her the left-handed compliment of "masculine": "She arranges her figures for us with a muscular force which seems masculine; it is singular to come upon a book written by a woman in which vigor is so clearly a more natural quality than grace." Although there were many instances at the time in all the arts when critics evoked the masculine to praise a woman's work, in this case such an evocation was particularly paradoxical since the nine-part title poem situates the ghetto within the "cramped ova" of the female body. Consider the image of parturition put forward in these early lines:

> The street crawls undulant,
> Like a river addled
> With its hot tide of flesh
> That ever thickens.
> Heavy surges of flesh
> Break over the pavements,
> Clavering like a surf—
> Flesh of this abiding
> Brood of those ancient mothers who saw the dawn break over Egypt...
> And turned their cakes upon the hot dry stones (*Ghetto* 9)

"Miss Ridge is a trifle obsessed with the concern of being powerful," Aiken added. His criticism contains the kernel of what would condemn her later—she evinced a literary power that threatened men. Other reviewers were more generous. Babette Deutsch in *The Little Review* wrote, "To read Lola Ridge is to shudder with the throb of unrelenting engines and the hammer on the pavement of numberless nervous feet." Poet and anthologist and eventually U.S. poet laureate Louis Untermeyer announced that it was the discovery of the year, and for the *New York Post* he wrote, "Nothing is forced or artificialized in her energetic volume, which contains some of the most vibrant utterances heard in America since Arturo Giovannitti's surprisingly neglected 'Arrows in the Gale.'" Untermeyer also recognized her unique frame of reference: "Her early life in Australia has doubtless enabled her to draw the American city with such an unusual sense of perspective." Then he conflates the poet with the poetry: "the still small voice of the poet makes itself heard—a strangely attenuated voice with a tense accent, a fineness that, seeming fragile, is like the delicacy of a thin steel spring." Emma Goldman, who knew Ridge better than the others, wrote to her niece about the publication: "New Republic...contain[ed] a masterly poem by Lola on the mob—the finest thing she has written...she really is a poet, Stella dear—and what is more important, she is close to the people." Alfred Kreymborg went further in *Poetry*: "She is a prototype of the artist rebels of Russia, Germany, and Austro-Hungary who were the forerunners of the present regime over there—men like Dostoievsky, Gorky, Moussorgsky, Beethoven, Heine, Hauptmann, Schnitzler." He likened her work to Emily Dickinson, Adelaide Crapsey and H.D. When Ridge read excerpts years later to an admittedly captive audience at a sanatorium, "girls [who] had lived in the ghetto...were hurt and [had] tears behind their eyes because they were reminded of something they wished above all to forget." She had captured something true.

In an early 20th-century photograph, an almost impassable Hester Street is filled with pushcarts and vendors and street hawkers and shoppers and vagrants and people who had no place to go other than the street. Known as "Pig Market" because the street vendors sold everything except pork, the street had one of the densest populations in the world. Roaches were stacked inches high in the apartments photographed by Lewis Hine, and garbage of all kinds was pitched out the windows: bones, feces, dead rats. People ate raw oysters from the carts, rented their dinner plates, and hung out their clothes between buildings, despite an ever-present rain of soot from the chimneys. The clomping of iron-shod horses, the occasional roadster, and the hawking and yelling of the immigrants kept the streets noisy. Children were left in nearby Seward Park to fend for themselves while their mothers worked. After a day in the sweatshops, these mothers came home to washing and ironing and cooking until 2 a.m. Instead of portraying them as victims or as subhuman, "snarling a weird Yiddish," as Henry James had termed them, or the Jew squatting on the windowsill in Eliot's "Gerontion," or beneath the rats in his "Burbank with a Baedeker: Bleistein with a Cigar," Ridge found the possibility of renewal in their difficult lives.

Nights, she reads
Those books that have most unset thought,
New-poured and malleable,
To which her thought
Leaps fusing at white heat,
Or spits her fire out in some dim manger of a hall,
Or at a protest meeting on the Square,
Her lit eyes kindling the mob...

....

She reads without bias—
Doubting clamorously—
Psychology, plays, science, philosophies—
Those giant flowers that have bloomed and withered, scattering their seed...

—And out of this young forcing soil what growth may come—
what amazing blossomings. (*Ghetto* 11-12, 13)

An interview in 1919 revealed that she lived "in a five by seven room in an East Side tenement" when she first came to New York City, although Lawson maintained that she saw Jews for the first time only on a tour given by Konrad Bercovici around 1911. However, *The Ghetto and Other Poems*, published five years after she last lived in New York, displays an intimate knowledge of life on Hester Street. Working terms in the sweatshops would have been rough: nine hours a day on weekdays plus seven hours on Saturdays, with women earning between $7 and $12 a week. Her fellow workers would have been the Italians or Eastern European girls who ruled the neighborhood. She knew them well:

> Bodies dangle from the fire escapes
> Or sprawl over the stoops...
> Upturned faces glimmer pallidly—
> Herring-yellow faces, spotted as with a mold,
> And moist faces of girls
> Like dank white lilies,
> And infants' faces with open parched mouths that suck at the air
> as at empty teats. (*Ghetto* 8)

Just fifteen blocks from Hester Street stood the Triangle Shirtwaist Factory, which employed hundreds of female garment workers. In 1909, after a wave of strikes when women "announced to the world women's wage-earning presence," the factory received notice from a fire-prevention expert, suggesting safety measures. The letter was ignored. "Let 'em burn. They're a lot of cattle, anyway," said another factory owner, reflecting the prevailing attitude. The shirtwaist factory had no fire escapes for the upper floors, unfortunately a common situation, and tiny bits of fabric floated through the air, ready to act as tinder. Within a year of the notice, the Triangle Shirtwaist Factory fire killed 146 garment workers, mostly women from the ages of 16 to 23, making it the deadliest industrial disaster in the history of New York City. Even the technology was against them. Although some of the women had been warned about the fire by telephone, they couldn't get down, and when help arrived it was only a horse-drawn fire engine, although motorized equipment had been in use for several years. So many of the workers were driven to jump that it took an hour to find two survivors under a pile of 40 bodies. A few years later, one of the owners was fined $20 for locking the doors of the same factory again.

> Sadie dresses in black.
> She has black-wet hair full of cold lights
> And a fine-drawn face, too white.
> All day the power machines
> Drone in her ears...
> All day the fine dust flies
> Till throats are parched and itch
> And the heat—like a kept corpse—
> Fouls to the last corner. (*Ghetto* 11)

Using the ghetto and its immigrants as subjects was at the time not so remarkable. Jacob Riis's bestselling book of photographs, *How the Other Half Lives*, had been in circulation for a decade, and silent movies like Chaplin's *The Immigrant* (1917) were popular. Israel Zangwill's 1909 play *The Melting Pot*, based on his novel *The Children of the Ghetto*, earned accolades from former president Theodore Roosevelt, who leaned out of his box to shout, "That's a great play, Mr. Zangwill, that's a great play." Morris Rosenfeld, the "pants presser poet," had published *Songs from the Ghetto* in a Yiddish/ English edition by 1898. Maudlin and Victorian in style, the book showed the reality of life in the sweatshop at the turn of the century as the inverse of Whitman's *Song of Myself*: "My self is destroyed, I become a machine." Ridge owned Hutchins Hapgood's novel, *The Spirit of the Ghetto*, which was "an attempt made by a 'Gentile' to report sympathetically on the character, lives and pursuits of certain east-side Jews with whom he has been in relations of considerable intimacy." The book is a series of prose sociological portraits that ends with Levitzky, an anarchist and young poet, declaring:

> "I have written a poem on liberty which I intend to read at the meeting. Do you wish to hear it?" He drew a manuscript from his pocket and read enthusiastically a poem in which a turbulent love for man and nature, for social equality and foaming cataracts was expressed in rich imagery.

That certainly sounds like a prescription for Ridge.

"To The American People," the epigraph to *The Ghetto and Other Poems*, immediately depicts the exuberant but bitter spirit of the disillusioned immigrant:

To The American People

Will you feast with me, American People?
But what have I that shall seem good to you!

On my board are bitter apples
And honey served on thorns,
And in my flagons fluid iron,
Hot from the crucibles.

How should such fare entice you! (*Ghetto* [7])

Unlike Emma Lazarus, a comfortable middle-class Jew whose ancestors emigrated during the colonial period, whose "Give me your tired, your poor,/Your huddled masses yearning to breathe free" is engraved on the Statue of Liberty, Lola Ridge knew the miseries and disappointments of the immigrants firsthand, as one of them. The persona driving "The Ghetto" rooms with a Jewish family, the Sodos, on the fifth floor of a tenement "in the little green room that was Bennie's/with Sadie," a room

Bare,
Save for bed and chair,
And coppery stains
Left by seeping rains
On the low ceiling
And green plaster walls,
Where when night falls
Golden lady-bugs
Come out of their holes,
And roaches, sepia-brown, consort... (*Ghetto* 20)

The father, an old saddlemaker, dovens: "I hear his lifted praise,/Like a broken whinnying/Before the Lord's shut gate." His young wife is making a new and more secular life for herself without wearing the traditional wig. The daughter, Sadie, a pieceworker, twice injured to the bone by her sewing machine, reads radical politics by night and entertains a Gentile lover. Two young women live above them, Sarah whose "mind is hard and brilliant and cutting"—an idealist who works in a pants factory (the speaker finds this "droll") and Anna with "the appeal of a folk-song." A parrot screams "Vorwaerts...Vorwaerts" across the courtyard, the name of the most popular radical newspaper in Europe. Translated from German and Yiddish, *vorwaerts* means "forward." Headquarters for the Yiddish newspaper "The Forward" was located only a few blocks from Hester Street. The speaker of "The Ghetto" observes the parade of immigrant life below her fifth-floor window, the buying and selling, the courting, and the children adapting to their new lives:

> The sturdy Ghetto children
> March by the parade,
> Waving their toy flags,
> Prancing to the bugles,
> Lusty, unafraid.
> But I see a white frock
> And eyes like hooded lights
> Out of the shadow of pogroms
> Watching...watching... (*Ghetto* 15)

Part of the power of the poem is not only due to Ridge's perspective of faraway New Zealand bush towns but also from the small towns in the U.S. where she must have lived during its composition. As Raymond Williams points out in his *Politics of Modernism*: "The most important general element of the innovations in [modernist] form is the fact of immigration to the metropolis, and it cannot too often be emphasized how many of the major innovators were, in this precise sense, immigrants."

"Let anything that burns you come out whether it be propaganda or not," Ridge told an interviewer in the 1930s when writing poems about politics was especially prevalent. It was Ridge's gift to feel so deeply about the situation in America, and a stance she would not relinquish. The trick was to transcend propaganda, and that she learned from Shelley.

England in 1819

An old, mad, blind, despised, and dying King;
Princes, the dregs of their dull race, who flow
Through public scorn, mud from a muddy spring;
Rulers who neither see nor feel nor know,
But leechlike to their fainting country cling
Till they drop, blind in blood, without a blow.
A people starved and stabbed in the untilled field;
An army, whom liberticide and prey
Makes as a two-edged sword to all who wield;
Golden and sanguine laws which tempt and slay;
Religion Christless, Godless—a book sealed;
A senate, Time's worst statute, unrepealed—
Are graves from which a glorious Phantom may
Burst, to illumine our tempestuous day.

Ridge loved Shelley's work, as did quite a number of her contemporaries. Fellow poet Elinor Wylie wrote many essays, four novels, and two books of poetry about him—and swore she actually saw his ghost. Novelist Evelyn Scott packed a volume of Shelley's poetry as one of the six books she took with her when she ran off with someone else's husband to Brazil. Like Ridge, Edna St. Vincent Millay wrote many sonnets after Shelley—not Shakespeare—in particular, her homage to geometry, "Euclid alone has looked on Beauty bare." Oscar Wilde, Karl Marx, George Bernard Shaw, and Upton Sinclair loved Shelley too, for his uncompromising idealism and for his enthusiastic practice of free love (two ménages à trois, a ménage à quatre, and various communal endeavors). Shelley also publicly sympathized with the Irish. "The Tidings," the last poem in Ridge's book, pays homage to her ancient forebears with a poem about the Irish Easter Rebellion in 1916.

My heart is like a lover foiled
By a broken stair—
They are fighting to-night in Sackville Street,
And I am not there! (*Ghetto* 79)

An even greater influence on Ridge is Whitman. All the modernists embraced the freeness of his style, even Eurocentric Ezra Pound who wrote "A Pact" with him, declaring him "the best America has produced." Ridge retained Whitman's headlong and expansive line, sharing with Whitman the second enormous wave of immigration that engulfed New York decades after he witnessed the first. Ridge particularized the multitudes that Whitman "contained."

> They are covering up the pushcarts...
> Now all have gone save an old man with mirrors—
> Little oval mirrors like tiny pools.
> He shuffles up a darkened street
> And the moon burnishes his mirrors till they shine like phosphorus...
> The moon like a skull,
> Staring out of eyeless sockets at the old men trundling home the
>   pushcarts. (*Ghetto* 27-28)

And she includes the sex:

> Nude glory of the moon!
> That leaps like an athlete on the bosoms of the young girls stripped
>   of their linens;
> Stroking their breasts that are smooth and cool as mother-of-pearl
> Till the nipples tingle and burn as though those little lips plucked at
>   them.
> They shudder and go faint. (*Ghetto* 26-27)

Whitman's appeal to radicals runs deep. He liberated poetry with his unrhymed, ragged lines, he sang freely of the body, he wrote about the workman and his troubles, he entreated the American youth to "resist much, obey little." He showed the way in poetry 50 years earlier, about the same time bohemianism and its anarchical view on life began to take hold in Australia. "Bohemia comes but once in one's life. Let's treasure even its memory," he exclaimed, recalling the many hours he spent at Pfaff's beer cellar at the table of "The King of Bohemia" Henry Clapp, Jr, who "nursed controversies and kept Whitman in the public eye as a radical new voice" during a low point in Whitman's career. Clapp also frequently published Whitman in his *Saturday Press*, a countercultural answer to the *Atlantic*

Monthly that featured poetry, stories, and radical politics with an enthusiastic spirit of individual freedom and sexual openness. Whitman was grateful, and promulgated this spirit in his poetry, which continued to gain adherents by the year. "Not songs of loyalty alone are these," he writes, "But songs of insurrection also,/For I am the sworn/poet of every dauntless rebel, the world over." There were consequences, however. In 1897 three editors of *The Firebrand* were tried and convicted by Anthony Comstock's laws for sending Whitman's "A Woman Waits for me" through the mails, and one of them, aged 74, served four months in prison.

In a 1907 *New York Times* article announcing the translation of *Leaves of Grass* into Russian, Whitman is referred to as the "Poet-Anarchist." By the time the Ferrer Center was in operation in 1910, the radicals there revered him as a comrade, "uncouth, elemental, Anarchistic." Manuel Komroff and Ferrer organizer William Thurston Brown wrote pamphlets about Whitman's work, Voltairine de Cleyre called him a "supremely Anarchist" writer. Emma Goldman and other devotees discussed his work at the Hotel Brevoort once a year. Theodore Dreiser delivered a speech at the Center about Whitman. Whitman's literary executor Horace Traubel, who published nine volumes of his conversations with Whitman in his old age, contributed to *The Modern School* magazine. Sadakichi Hartmann, one of the more flamboyant Center characters, lunched with Whitman, discussing literature and art. Half Japanese, Hartmann freed genre with Whitman-like flourishes, putting on finger dances, shadow pictures, perfume concerts, and pantomimes, as well as being one of the best critics of photography in America, and the first to write haiku in English.

Louis Untermeyer's review of *The Ghetto and Other Poems* mentions Ridge's little-known contemporary Arturo Giovannitti (1884-1959) as a rival. Published five years earlier, Giovannitti's *Arrows in the Gale* also uses Whitman's proselike line to very similar advantage, but where Ridge declaimed the integrity of those in the ghetto, he did so for the striker. Educated at McGill and Columbia, Giovannitti became an ordained minister, but was later radicalized by his work in the coal mines. A fearsome orator, he spoke four languages fluently, and the authorities wanted him kept quiet. Falsely accused of starting a riot during the Lawrence mill strike, he spent ten months in jail fearing the death penalty, where he composed his best poetry, conflating Christian beliefs with proletarian morality. The following is an excerpt from his poem "The Walker."

I have heard the moans of him who bewails a thing that is dead and the sighs of him who tries to smother a thing that will not die;

I have heard the stifled sobs of the one who weeps with his head under the coarse blanket, and the whisperings of the one who prays with his forehead on the hard, cold stone of the floor;

I have heard him who laughs the shrill, sinister laugh of folly at the horror rampant on the yellow wall and at the red eyes of the nightmare glaring through the iron bars;

I have heard in the sudden icy silence him who coughs a dry, ringing cough, and wished madly that his throat would not rattle so and that he would not spit on the floor, for no sound was more atrocious than that of his sputum upon the floor;

I have heard him who swears fearsome oaths which I listen to in reverence and awe, for they are holier than the virgin's prayer,

And I have heard, most terrible of all, the silence of two hundred brains all possessed by one single, relentless, unforgiving, desperate thought.

Arrows in the Gale was introduced by Helen Keller, then deeply interested in socialist causes. She wrote: "Giovannitti is, like Shelley, a poet of revolt against the cruelty, the poverty, the ignorance which too many of us accept." Workers paid to have Giovannitti's book read to them while they slaved away in sweatshops. He resembled Pound in his youth, with a Van Dyck beard, flowing tie and Lord Byron collar, but his situation was the very opposite of Pound's so many years later. While Pound was tried for broadcasting treasonous speeches against America from Italy, the Italian Giovannitti was tried for inciting immigrants in America. But, like Pound, he spent weeks in a cage, incarcerated during his trial in 1912.

The Cage

All was old, and cold and mournful...
and their faces were drawn and white and lifeless...

> For of naught they knew, but of what was written in the old, yellow books. And all the joys and the pains and the loves and hatreds and furies and labors and strifes of man, all the fierce and divine passions that battle and rage in the heart of man, never entered into the great greenish room but to sit in the green iron cage.

His prosecutors rightly feared his ability with rhetoric—he gave such a stirring defense of himself that he was acquitted.

> But I say that you cannot be half free and half slave...the man that owns the tool wherewith another man works, the man that owns the house where this man lives, the man that owns the factory... that man owns and controls the bread that man eats and therefore owns and controls his mind, his body, his heart and his soul...it may be that we are fanatics...we are fanatics...And so was a fanatic the Saviour Jesus Christ.

Giovannitti's particular contribution to modernism was in pressing Whitman's long lines toward the construction of the modern prose poem. Like Ridge, his ellipses—sometimes known as "suspension periods"— signal a bigger pause than a comma, rather than indicating something left out. Like Ridge, he too wrote a poem commemorating the lynching of labor activist Frank Little, his called "When the Cock Crows," and both invoke Christian ideology. As soon as Giovannitti was acquitted in 1913, he visited the Ferrer Center but by that time Ridge had already begun her travels.

A young wunderkind poet of Ridge's time, Charles Reznikoff (1894-1976), wrote about the Jewish ghetto of his childhood in Brooklyn, using very plain, long prosy lines like Ridge.

> The shopgirls leave their work
> quietly.
>
> Machines are still, tables and chairs
> darken.
> The silent rounds of mice and roaches begin.

Unlike Ridge, Reznikoff shunned publication and avoided recognition. His family supported him for many years. Reviewing his work in the twenties, W.R.B. (most likely Ridge's friend William Rose Benét) says that Reznikoff showed that "seared and disillusioned humanity which, rightly or not, we associate with the ghetto," but complained that the poems often lack development: "Most poets do not know when to leave off; by contrast, Mr. Reznikoff does not know when to go on!" In the 1930s, Reznikoff, along with fellow Lower East Sider Louis Zukofsky (1904-1978), identified with objectivism, a movement derived from imagism that focused compressed lines on everyday life and language, emphasizing sincerity and clarity. In "Flotsam," a two-part poem in free verse, Ridge depicts a couple on a bench in compressed, simple language that could be called proto-objectivist:

> This old man's head
> Has found a woman's shoulder.
> The wind juggles with her shawl
> That flaps about them like a sail,
> And splashes her red faded hair
> Over the salt stubble of his chin. (*Ghetto* 35)

The imagists were the first modernists in poetry. In 1909, while Ridge was showing her stories to Goldman, trying to make money publishing pot-boilers, Englishman T.E. Hulme originated the theories of imagism. Its maxims were concision, the isolation of a single image to reveal its essence, "a new cadence means a new idea," and emphasis on a poetry that was hard and clear. Initially inspired by Japanese forms of haiku and tanka as a result of the craze for all things Asian, including Gilbert and Sullivan's "The Mikado" and the poems by Ridge's Modern School acquaintance Sadakichi Hartmann, imagism was soon taken up by Ezra Pound. In London at the time, he introduced imagism to his ex-flame H.D. and promoted her as a central figure in the movement. By March of 1913 *Poetry* had published imagism's "A Few Don'ts" as elucidated by Pound. The next month *Poetry* ran his "In a Station of the Metro," the defining poem of the movement. In 1914 Ridge's soon-to-be colleague Alfred Kreymborg published Pound's *Des Imagistes* in his literary magazine *The Glebe*, which included imagist work by other soon-to-be friends William Carlos Williams and Amy Lowell, as well as James Joyce and Ford Maddox Ford. In 1915, 1916, and 1917, Amy Lowell published three volumes of imagist verse in London. She had the financial means to take over the movement from Pound, who then mocked it, calling it "amygism." She believed imagism to be derived from Keats. Short-lived in its purest state, imagism has had a long influence. Amy Lowell's first tenet of the movement—"To use the language of common speech, but to employ always the exact word, not the nearly-exact, nor the merely decorative word"—could apply to the practice of most of the poets writing today.

Imagism often produced very condensed shorter poems, the inverse of Whitman's long prosy lines; however, some of the inspiration may have come from Whitman too.

A Farm Picture

Through the ample open door of the peaceful country barn,
A sun-lit pasture field with cattle and horses feeding,
And haze and vista, and the far horizon fading away.

Ridge abjured the imagist's interest in the classical as subject matter. Perhaps she found Kreymborg's hesitations about the movement apt: "[imagism] was too remote from our lives among the lonely streets and byways of this mysterious land...We craved a more direct cultural expression, however crude, hard and blundering." As Untermeyer writes in his review: "In this poem ["The Ghetto"] Miss Ridge achieves a sharp line, the arresting and fixing of motion, the condensed clarity advertised by the imagists with far more human passion than they ever betrayed." "The Ghetto" could be considered a long sequence of imagist poems, especially sections one through six where Ridge packs concise language into nearly every line, as specific as "And mothers take home their babies,/Waxen and delicately curled,/like little potted flowers closed under the stars." or

But a small girl
Cowers apart.
Her braided head,
Shiny as a black-bird's
In the gleam of the torch-light,
Is poised as for flight.
Her eyes have the glow
Of darkened lights. (*Ghetto* 14)

"The Ghetto" is also a poem of the *flâneur*. The speaker of the poem observes the parade of immigrant life below her fifth-floor window, and she also walks the streets of the city, seeing it up close. "Lemons in a greenish broth/And a huge earthen bowl/By a bronzed merchant..." As Whitman sauntered through Brooklyn 63 years earlier, Carl Sandburg celebrated immigrant labor in "Chicago Poems" four years earlier, and T.S. Eliot would bemoan the decay of London in "The Wasteland" four years later, Ridge saw the urban landscape in passing as a woman and an immigrant, an entirely new perspective. As critic Nancy Berke says: "[Ridge] records her reflections on a new life of art and freedom, as well as an understanding of the social dislocation created by the abrupt changes of "a new century" and "a new city.""

While Ridge was traveling and writing her first book, women burst onto the literary scene as writers and prominent editors. Harriet Monroe founded *Poetry* in 1912, Margaret Anderson began editing *The Little Review* in 1914, to be joined by her lover Jane Heap two years later, and Amy Lowell took over imagism with her three-volume anthology in 1917. In England, Dora Marsden edited the *New Freewoman* under the credo that "The intense satisfaction of self is for the individual the one goal in life." The *New Freewoman* soon became the *Egoist* in 1914 under the direction of Harriet Shaw Weaver who published much modernist poetry. Ida Purnell edited *Palms* from Guadalajara. Forty percent of the poets published in *Others* were women, a number unequaled even today in most literary magazines. According to cultural critic Christine Stansell:

> It is safe to say that in the 1910s, the vogue for writing free verse—
> poetry that was unrhymed and unmetered—became what landscape
> painting had been for young people, especially young women, in the
> 1890s, a way to define oneself as an artist and to distinguish oneself
> from a family background seen as philistine or soulless.

Publishers rushed to discover and issue women's poetry in runs of thousands. Critic Edmund Wilson wrote in the early 20s: "I find [the women poets] more rewarding than the men. Their emotion is likely to be more genuine and their literary instinct surer." The entire modernist movement was seen as a woman's attack on men in a 1920 editorial of the *Philadelphia Record*:

> The vigorous male note [is] now seldom heard in the land, and
> almost never at all in the pages of *Poetry...Poetry* is edited by a
> woman; its policy is largely dominated by another woman with

radical and perverse notions of the high art of singing, and most of
its contributors are feminine by accident of birth, while the majority
of the male minority are but thin tenors.

William Drake asserts that "Most of the women poets...did not think
of themselves as rebels, however, but simply aimed at achieving the same
kind of success as men." Likewise, Ridge's approach was not particularly
feminist, she tended not to weigh in on either gender. Although she
makes many references that derive from a female perspective, referring
to women at least as often as men in her poems, and she twice organized
books around the nine-month gestation period, she strove for equality in
this perspective, and such equality can seem, in this masculine-weighted
world, a focus on the feminine.

> Mothers waddling in and out,
> Making all things right—
> Picking up the slipped threads
> In Grand Street at night—(*Ghetto* 16)

is balanced by:

> What if they tweak his beard—
> These raw young seed of Israel
> Who have no backward vision in their eyes—
> And mock him as he sways
> About the sunken arches of his feet—
> They find no peg to hang their taunts upon.
> His soul is like a rock (*Ghetto* 18)

A number of critics have labeled Ridge's approach maternal. Drake
writes: "Ridge's poetry is marked both by rage at injustice and by a fiercely
maternal urgency, as if the disorder of the world arose out of a separation
from the spiritual center the mother represents." Donna Allego, author of
*The Construction and Role of Community in Political Long Poems by Twentieth-
Century American Women Poets*, which often focuses on Ridge, writes:

> [Ridge] uses the maternal role to support laborers in the work force,
> and thereby redefines an American notion of liberty so that it is

consistent with the intrinsic value of labor, labor's contribution to society, and violent and destructive confrontations between labor and management.

"Maternal" isn't the word used when men support social causes in their poetry, and designating her point of view as "maternal" denigrates her work with the taint of the 19th century "sentimental." Given Ridge's behavior with her own child—consigning him to an orphanage—she must not have had many overt maternal feelings, and those she had were complex.

Caroline Maun, author of *Mosaic of Fire*, a study about Lola Ridge and her friends Evelyn Scott and Charlotte Wilder, suggests that Ridge had "maternal" feelings toward them. The exchanges in their letters, however, seem rather quid pro quo and not particularly maternal. Ridge writes letters to publishers and editors for Scott and Wilder—but she also writes these for the Armenian poet Leon Srabian Herald and Mitchell Dawson. If anything, Evelyn Scott seems the more maternal, perhaps because she raised her son herself and expresses her concerns about Ridge in the same breath that she worries about him. She frets over Ridge's health, offers to take her in, arranges for a new publisher for Ridge, gives her all her contacts, and worries about her output. Ridge's letters to the editor/poet Idella Stone were more solicitous but they stopped after Ridge returned from visiting Stone's father in Mexico, suggesting that Ridge's concern was more to secure introductions for herself. Rather than the maternal urge, Ridge was more interested in sex.

Chapter 12

"Sex Permeates Everything"

"Sex permeates everything" is scrawled across Ridge's little gray notebook from 1909. "All over the city...candlelit tea-rooms echoed with discussions of erogenous zones and similar intimate matters," crows one history of the time. Free verse was free in subject matter as well as line—even from a woman's point of view, surely one reason poetry began to fly off the shelves. Even dour, stout, 45-year-old Amy Lowell was publishing suggestive material by 1919:

> The Weather-Cock Points South
>
> I put your leaves aside,
> One by one;
> The stiff, broad outer leaves,
> The smaller ones,
> Pleasant to touch, veined with purple,
> The glazed inner leaves,
> One by one
> I parted you from your leaves,
> Until you stood up like a white flower.

Not far from licentious Greenwich Village, the Tenderloin district supported some 2,000 brothels, and judging from the number of abortions performed at the turn of the century on the Lower East Side (about 100,000), nearly everyone in the ghetto was having sex. At the Ferrer Center, sex enthusiasts included Goldman and her acolyte Margaret Sanger, Will Durant who spoke on sex psychology—he who had fled the seminary shortly before teaching at the Modern School—and Theodore Schroeder, who talked up free speech in "Obscene Literature." Leonard Abbott, the Ferrer Center's leader, professed bisexual encounters, and the gay Englishman poet/philosopher

Edward Carpenter influenced Goldman in her talk, "The Unjust Treatment of Homosexuals."

> But a pale pink dream
> Trembles about this young girl's body,
> Draping it like a glowing aura.
>
> She gloats in a mirror
> Over her gaudy hat,
> With its flower God never thought of...
>
> And the dream, unrestrained,
> Floats about the loins of a soldier,
> Where it quivers a moment,
> Warming to a crimson
> Like the scarf of a toreador...(*Ghetto* 38)

Sexuality was a central force in Ridge's work, celebrated but not separated from the rest. To isolate it was to vulgarize and trivialize it. She was primarily a sensualist, following Baudelaire's declaration of "modernité," with art acting as a vessel for aesthetic values that embody "the transitory, the fleeting, the contingent." She simply did not forget the rest of the world in those sensual glimpses.

Birth control was the corollary of all this interest in sex. Goldman worked as a nurse on the Lower East Side 30 years before Margaret Sanger (1879-1966) and smuggled contraceptives into the U.S. for those in need. Goldman had also lectured on the subject of birth control since 1908, six years before Sanger's single-issue campaign began with the publication of her newsletter *The Woman Rebel*. "No Gods, No Masters" emblazoned Sanger's cover, a slogan that was pure anarchist. "Women were subjugated," Sanger proclaimed, "by the machine, by wage slavery, by bourgeois morality, by customs, laws and superstitions." Goldman supported and encouraged Sanger, selling copies of Sanger's journal on her lecture tours.

Sanger described Ridge at the Center as that "intense rebel from Australia" and as its "organizing secretary." Ridge would have met Sanger soon after the Ferrer Center opened. As a nurse working on the Lower East Side in 1911, Sanger had the authority to lecture on "The Limitation of Offspring," and to give talks on birth control at the Ferrer's mothers meetings. Like

Ridge, Sanger had little formal education, and the Ferrer Center acted as a sort of university of the liberal arts for her, providing lectures and debates by leading thinkers on many areas of the humanities, as well as anarchist tips on rallying the masses. The Ferrer Center was most likely where Sanger met the Greek anarchist and dentist John Rompapas, who may have given her money to launch *The Woman Rebel* in 1914, since they were having an affair and he had already funded Hippolyte Havel's journal *Revolutionary Almanac*. Although Sanger and her husband professed an open marriage, her relationship with Rompapas may have increased their estrangement and brought her closer to the Ferrer community of anarchists.

Sanger's eldest son Stuart was one of the first pupils at the Modern School. Sanger donated the many-volumed *Book of Knowledge* to the classroom after Will Durant asked: "What do I teach them?" The books must have served as inspiration—Sanger later judged his teaching as "extraordinarily effective." She certainly knew Ridge's work as editor of the magazine *The Modern School.*

After Sanger fled the country (under the name "Bertha Watson") following her 1914 arrest by anti-obscenity officers, Goldman mustered support for her from the anarchist community. Ferrer Center art student Rockwell Kent had already designed Sanger's logo and Bill Shatoff printed her publication "Family Limitation" that landed Sanger's husband in jail in the U.S. around the same time. Abbott acted on behalf of the Free Speech League by helping her and her husband with strategy. Abbott warned Sanger: "If you do return, you will get a long prison sentence," and then, more encouragingly, "There is undoubtedly growing interest in the whole issue of birth control." She was fighting the charge of obscenity and for "inciting murder and assassination" because she had published "In Defense of Assassination" about birth control. From Europe, she criticized Goldman for not doing enough for her, but Goldman and her magazine *Mother Earth* continually brought her case to their reader's attention, collected funds for her, and distributed her pamphlets. She took up the birth control issue for her again in 1915 and was arrested twice trying to publicize it. Goldman was so certain that she would be incarcerated the second time that she took a book with her to read in jail. Her 15-day sentence was eclipsed by Sanger's trial, which was conducted around the same time.

While exiled in England, Sanger began an affair with the martyred Ferrer's close associate, Lorenzo Portet, and traveled with him to London, Wales, Paris, and Spain. She was planning to resettle with him and the children in Paris when she received the news that her five-year-old daughter

Peggy was ill. Peggy had been left with her older brother in the care of the Modern School, which now offered only very spartan living conditions in its new location in New Jersey. Eva Bein, who slept next to Margaret Sanger's children, describes the school facilities: "We had only one stove in the middle of the dormitory. The Sanger girl came down with pneumonia, and Mother feared that I would catch it too." She continues: "In the morning, when we went to wash, there was ice. The toilet was outside." Another child remembered waking up with her hair frozen to her pillow, and that children stayed warm by exercising beside bonfires.

Sanger became haunted by a series of dreams about Peggy in which she pleaded for her mother to come home. But Sanger delayed. Within days of her arrival, Peggy was transferred to a New York hospital, where she lingered for a few more days and died. Sanger had returned to face trial, and sympathy for the loss of her daughter was part of the reason the prosecution dropped the charges. Sanger dreamt of little girls for years afterwards and believed she actually saw and spoke to Peggy during then fashionable Rosicrucian rituals. Ever alert to the implications of guilt, by 1953 Sanger suggested that her use of the word "guilt" in a letter to Emma Goldman was more similar to "regret." But she finishes this letter to Goldman by using the word "leave" three times: "As to leaving the children I knew it was a necessary sacrifice to leave them to prepare my defense in order to leave them a clear record of their mother's work." The Modern School and the Ferrer Center were blamed for the death, but Sanger did not desert the radical cause right away, and wrote "To My Friends and Comrades" a year later in Havel's magazine, *Revolt*.

Sanger's involvement with the Modern School and the Ferrer Center lasted a total of five years, and her experiences and education there were formative. They also provided support and strategies to achieve radical reform—not to mention several love affairs and mentoring by Emma Goldman. In 1918 Sanger and Ridge rekindled their acquaintance, despite both being away from New York. By then Sanger had repudiated Goldman, and cut ties with her entirely, and so had Ridge. Sanger hired her to be one of six literary editors of her newly reorganized magazine, *The Birth Control Review*. Sanger's former managing editor had absconded with everything in the office, including the furniture, in an effort to oust control of the movement. Sanger had gone to the district attorney for help, which alienated the radicals. She had already recognized that she needed the support of upper-class women more than theirs, and organized the New York Women's Publishing Company to finance the new review from wealthy benefactors.

Perhaps Ridge saw her association with Sanger and editing her magazine as a way of finding her own wealthy supporters.

"ASIDE, DARE NOT retard my passage!" begins the poem that opens an essay by the art editor Gertrude Boyle in the May 1918 issue. Magazines like Sanger's and *The Modern School* were meant to be not only an outlet for polemic but "a place of expression for the young idealists in arts and letters" like Goldman's *Mother Earth*. Editors then believed that all people, not just idle wealthy men, deserved contact with the arts, and that the arts, in this case, might also attract an audience of women who would contribute to the cause. In June the magazine published two more poems of Boyle's, "To the Little Unfortunates," about babies born in the tenements, and "Woman of the Street," about prostitutes, which begins: "I stretch my hand to thee—." In the July issue, Maude Durand Edgren asks "What is there between the deep sea of celibacy and the devil of sex gluttony?" Almost in answer, Ida Wright Mudgett writes in another article: "The bitter injustice [of] the women of the poor, who are compelled to be the mothers of enormous families." Ridge must have been partial to these women since she included a multitude of ghetto babies, both at home and at work, in her first book.

> And ah, the little babies—
> Shiny black-eyed babies—
> (Half a million pink toes
> Wriggling altogether.)
> Baskets full of babies
> Like grapes on a vine. (*Ghetto* 16)

Immigrant women were often the subject of *The Birth Control Review* articles. Many must have subscribed, since circulation jumped from 2,000 in 1917 to 10,000 by 1922. Like Ridge, they had made the decision to emigrate, survived the passage, found a way to support themselves—in many cases without any system of welfare or relatives—and now knew they needed access to Sanger's information. Although Ridge was at the time 45 years old, a decade earlier, when she was a newly arrived immigrant, she may have had some contraceptive worries. After all, she and David Lawson lived together throughout that period.

In the eyes of those who knew Ridge in New York, by living with Lawson she was committing the sin of fornication, not adultery, because it was unlikely anyone knew about her marriage in New Zealand. She did not suffer the terrible scandal that the poet Elinor Wylie had when she left her husband and their three-year-old for another man and fled to England. At the time President Taft sent a note of consolation to Wylie's mother and offered to use his diplomats to negotiate her return. Few had the financial resources to so brazenly affront public morality. Those without such social ties or money had to somehow support themselves if they were then rejected. Ridge understood their plight too.

A Worn Rose

Where to-day would a dainty buyer
Imbibe your scented juice,
Pale ruin with a heart of fire;
....
What favour could she do you more?
Yet, of all who drink therein,
None know it is the warm
Odorous heart of a ravished flower
Tingles so in her mouth's red core... (*Ghetto* 76)

Most probably Ridge's life of sin increased her cachet. It was, after all, the Roaring Twenties.

Chapter 13

Others and Its Editors

Alfred Kreymborg (1883-1966), a chess master and the son of a cigar-store owner, was very good at discovering and promoting avant-garde writing, a sort of American Pound, but without the bluster. Poet Orrick Johns said Kreymborg "had the gift...of leading up to the point where you said the thing he wanted said." Along with his remarkable editorial skills, Kreymborg published 40 books of poetry, plays, and prose, was elected a member of the American Academy of Arts and Letters, made president of the Poetry Society of America, and was considered for the Pulitzer Prize. In the 1940s Archibald MacLeish called him "the great granddaddy of American literature." A convivial yet discerning man about town, Kreymborg was the first writer to be accepted into the Stieglitz circle, a group that formed around the photographer/entrepreneur Alfred Stieglitz and his avant-garde 291 Gallery on Fifth Avenue. Like Ridge, Kreymborg wrote poems in both free and formal styles, with political and imagistic subjects, making him as hard to classify as Ridge. His editorial ventures included a magazine on music, the ten-issue literary magazine *The Globe: Songs, Sighs, and Curses* (with Man Ray), which ran Pound's anthology *Des Imagistes*, and the two rather more famous modernist magazines that Ridge was involved with, *Others* and *Broom*.

He may have met Ridge through their mutual association with Man Ray at the Ferrer Center. Ridge was already out of town in 1913 when Kreymborg and 23-year-old Man Ray were friends enough to move from New York across the Hudson to Ridgefield, New Jersey, and live in shacks that over the next few years became a sort of artist colony. "On one memorable afternoon there, Man Ray and Marcel Duchamp played a game of tennis without a net—the first Dada sports event," writes historian Ross Wetzsteon. *Others* began after Ezra Pound suggested in a letter that Kreymborg contact William Carlos Williams, who then drove down to their enclave and became friends. They planned the first issue of *Others* with Wallace Stevens and another of

Williams's friends, the poet Skipwith Cannell. Picnicking on Sundays, they would play a little ball, and talk, writes Kreymborg in his reminiscences of the period, *Troubadour*. They met with "the purpose of working together and of condemning the world at large." Many of the visual artists who frequented the colony contributed both their artwork and their writing to *Others*, and these included Picabia and Marsden Hartley as well as Man Ray. Poet, avant-garde art collector, and *salonnière* Walter Arensberg provided the funds to launch the first issue, dated July 1915. By March 1916, the monthly had also published an annual for collectors. At a time when "everybody is reading poetry; yes, and nearly everyone, from the hotel porter to the overseas veteran, is writing at it," when as Harriet Monroe noted, poetry was stacked high at the front of bookstores, and "crowds of people, three and four deep, were reaching over each other to buy it." the appearance of *Others* made headlines. The most graphic of its many reviews was "This Summer's Style in Poetry, or the Elimination of Corsets in Versifying" in the *New York Call*. "It is with this magazine [*Others*] and the group that grew up around it that modernism in American poetry really begins," according to critic and poet Kenneth Rexroth.

When Kreymborg married his second wife, Dorothy, in the fall of 1918, he was "accompanied by a new and devoted pair of friends, Lola Ridge, the Australian poet and now one of the editors of *Others*, and her husband, David Lawson, an electrician from Wales." Judging from Kreymborg's description of the couple, his acquaintance with them never went very deep. Lawson was not yet her husband, and he certainly was not an electrician from Wales. That Kreymborg should not know the first is understandable, although odd at a wedding when such experiences are often shared (Ridge did not invite Kreymborg to their wedding a year later or Kreymborg, writing this memoir in 1925, would have been better informed). That he still didn't know Lawson's true nationality or occupation suggests their friendship was based more on the silence of the chess matches they must have had rather than the confidences between friends. Or does it suggest that Lawson had colluded with the "Australian" Ridge in presenting himself with less-than-truthful information?

Kreymborg had tired of his editorial duties by the time of his marriage, and the magazine was falling apart. Ridge alone "kept the movement going," according to his memoir. Although he states that she was already working as an editor in the fall of 1918, Ridge first appeared on the *Others* masthead December 1918. For three issues Ridge shared the associate editorship with the poet/illustrator William Saphier and Dorothy Kreymborg, and with poet Orrick Johns and art editor William Zorach for one and two issues, respectively.

Presumably Ridge too picnicked with the boys—the back of her apartment at 21 East 15th Street joined the Kreymborgs' backyard at 17 East 14th Street for almost a year. Off the masthead of *The Birth Control Review* since September 1918, Ridge published two poems in Kreymborg's *Others* December 1918 issue, which included Wallace Stevens' "Le Monocle de Mon Oncle," Mina Loy's "The Black Virginity," and Carl Sandburg's "I Tried the Door." (This was around the time that Sandburg first read Ridge's work. Two years later, Ridge would assert in the *Double Dealer* that Sandburg's recent devaluation as a poet was due to critics who "fear to be identified with the crowd," the crowd being his enormous number of readers.) "The Woman with Jewels" opens the issue. It had already appeared in *The Ghetto and Other Poems*, and concerns an "obscenely beautiful" woman covered in jewels who visits a bohemian basement event. On exit, "the mountainous breasts tremble," her gems agitate and "quiver incessantly, emitting trillions of fiery rays...every step is an adventure." Given that Ridge depended on wealthy women for support most of her life, the poem is oddly derisive, but she often framed political critiques with a sarcasm that mocked sentimentality, exposing the poem to a modernist self-consciousness. Her second poem, "Blossoms," found in her book as part of "Song of Iron," is an extended metaphor between molten ore and its similarity to the bloom of a flower. Kreymborg liked this poem so much he included it in the 1919 *Others* anthology.

> Put by your rod, comrade,
> And look with me, shading your eyes...
> Do you not see—
> Through the lucent haze
> Out of the converter rising—
> In the spirals of fire
> Smiting and blinding,
> A shadowy shape
> White as a flame of sacrifice,
> Like a lily swaying? (*Ghetto* 46-47)

Later Ridge said she wished she had pulled out that lily by the roots.

"*Others* is as important as *Poetry* to the development of free verse in America and better represents the insurgent, heterodox character of many modernist little magazines," writes Suzanne Churchill in *The Little Magazine, Others, and the Renovation of Modern American Poetry*. "[*Poetry*] was less committed to formal innovation...and more intrusive in its editorial practices than *Others*." Fiercely experimental, *Others* was uninterested in courting an audience and the magazine's subscription base never rose above 300. Its motto revealed a casual approach to its eclecticism: "The old expressions are with us always, and there are always others." Adolf Wolff and Carl Sandburg, anarchist, communist, or at least socialist writers, were published beside avant-garde poets Mina Loy, T.S. Eliot, Man Ray, and Marsden Hartley, as well as popular poets Sherwood Anderson, Louise Bogan, and Vachel Lindsay. Robert Frost wrote Ridge to apologize for not having a poem ready that he could offer—"Taking a poem out of me now would be like taking out a swallowed fish hook"—but sent a check and eventually three poems for its anthology. This collision of aesthetics— avant-garde, popular, and political—is what kept *Others* in the vanguard. Kreymborg's refusal to produce a manifesto "should be considered a significant modernist choice," according to John Timberman Newcomb in *How Did Poetry Survive?: The Making of Modern Verse*. In response, *Poetry* magazine derided *Others*. Instead of "the outworn conventions of the I-ambic school, we now have the I-am-it school." (NOTE: *Les-I-am-its* are not to be confused with *Les I'm-a-gists*, who are already out-classed and démodé.)" A critic from the *Kansas City Star* wrote: "Poetry is, shall we say, cutting its 'I' teeth," in an article entitled "I-sores is the Modern Substitute for Poetry." In the magazine's defense, Williams responded that *Others* was "a free running sewer."

According to Newcomb in *How Did Poetry Survive?*, *Others* opened at least one new door for poetry, years before "The Waste Land" appeared, suggesting that long-form lyric verse was encouraged because it mirrored the experience of contemporary life:

> *Others* contributed to the expansion of modern poetic form by cultivating...the verse libre variation sequence which was premised upon an understanding of twentieth-century experience as perceptually disjunct and socially heterogeneous.

Wallace Stevens's "Thirteen Ways of Looking at a Blackbird" and Mina Loy's "Love Songs" were the two most famous "variation sequences" to appear in the magazine. Ridge, as the author of the 22-page poem "The Ghetto," with its long, multifaceted parts, would have been sympathetic to the longer poem's ambitions as an editor, but she did not publish any more of her own in *Others*.

Belinda Wheeler writes in "At the Center of American Modernism: Lola Ridge's Politics, Poetics, and Publishing," that Ridge's "enthusiasm for supporting American modernism, regardless of the form or the varying aesthetics used, broadened the purview of *Others*." After Ridge was added to the masthead, *Others* had art on its cover, and other genres in its pages. Her influence as a promoter of freedom in all its aspects can be seen as early as January in this notice: "[T]he feeling is simply that everything of individual quality, whether poem, play, prose, or painting, should have equal chance of coming out in the magazine." That included gender. Along with 40% of the contents being written by women, the sixth issue had been solely devoted to women's work, guest-edited by Helen Hoyt, aunt of the poet Elinor Wylie. "At present most of what we know, or think we know, of women has been found out by men," Hoyt writes in her introduction. "We have yet to hear what woman will tell of herself, and where can she tell more intimately than in poetry?"

Ridge dedicated her poem "Jaguar" to Evelyn Scott in the March 1919 issue. She had wowed Ridge as "a mystery woman in far off Brazil," and when they met sometime in 1919, the feeling was mutual. "I had thoroughly made up my mind," writes Scott afterwards, "that it was impossible for two women to be honest in the same room." She had just arrived in New York after a harrowing year of near starvation in South America with an unemployed husband, a crazy mother and a new baby. She sent Ridge a present and Ridge answered with a mash note: "your action is the greater gift, that I would not return if I could but shall keep always like a flower..." and "My thought reaches out to you and when it returns without touching you, I am as surprised as though a light had gone out" and, finally, "May [I] not know your name?" There is no evidence of them as lovers, although their ensuing 20-year correspondence is replete with over-the-top endearments like "Lola, I never think of you but with the taste of metal in my mouth as if the gods were moulding you with fire." Scott was as straightforward about sex as a man, her affairs legion, including attempted or successful seductions of Kreymborg, Sinclair Lewis, Waldo Frank, and year-long affair with Williams. Very shortly after they met, Ridge agreed to come to Rio with Scott and her husband Cyril Kay-Scott (whether or not with Lawson is unclear) but the plan must have fallen through because it was never mentioned again. To Ridge her vision was "an electric ray, that seems to focus—almost lovingly—upon decay and death" with "a ruthless eye which sees through rosy and gracious contours to the putrescence."

Jaguar

Nasal intonations of light
and clicking tongues...
publicity of windows
stoning me with pent-up cries...
smells of abbatoirs...
smells of long-dead meat.

Some day-end—
while the sand is yet cozy as a blanket
off the warm body of a squaw,
and the jaguars are out to kill...
with a blue-black night coming on
and a painted cloud
stalking the first star—
I shall go alone into the Silence...
the coiled Silence...
where a cry can run only a little way
and waver and dwindle
and be lost.

And there...
where tiny antlers clinch and strain
as life grapples in a million avid points,
and threshing things
strike and die,
letting their hate live on
in the spreading purple of a wound...
I too
will make covert of a crevice in the night,

and turn and watch...
nose at the cleft's edge. (*Sun-up* 39-40)

Writing for *The Little Review*, John Rodker, whose work had taken up most of the entire fourth issue of *Others*, and who was not included in the 1919 anthology, dismissed many of the women who were with just a series of exclamation marks. "Lola Ridge!!'; M.A. [Marjorie Allen] Seiffert and Evelyn Scott!!!" He also noted in Marianne Moore's work that "bits of the plaster are sadly trivial." He skewered Mina Loy as well: "It is painful to notice that since the last 'Others' [Mina Loy] appears to have lost [her] grip." Loy responded for them all in an article entitled "John Rodker's Frog." She begins by quoting from one of his poems: "I'd have loved you as you deserved had we been frogs," and asserts that "perhaps to be loved like a frog is the best way to be loved by Mr. Rodker." Loy insists that women be given full critical consideration and ends her riposte with: "Note. For information on the love of frogs the reader may purchase Margaret Sanger's book, which will help boost the Birth Control Movement, aiming to suppress the only indulgence of frogs." Her article was accompanied by a photo of Loy by Man Ray, and the poem "Lion's Jaws" that ends with "impotent neurotics [wincing] at the dusk." Married three times, Rodker may have had problems with women—here is an excerpt from his "Hymn of Hymns":

God damn
woman
mushroomy flaccid
and smelling of old clothes woman.

Rodker would reappear as the unofficial English editor of *Broom* while Ridge was working as the American editor in New York. For some reason, a manuscript of his forwarded to Ridge to secure a publisher was permanently mislaid.

Chapter 14

Soirées for *Others*

Ridge hosted weekly soirées for *Others* in her one-room apartment at 21 East 15th Street. "She was older than most of the young writers," Flossie Williams recalled, reminiscing about the varied guest list for one of Ridge's parties. "There was John Reed, who wrote *Ten Days That Shook the World*; and Louise Bryant—they were all in that group." Famous and not-so-famous writers and artists and activists poured into her apartment to discuss the future of art in America and its various freedoms: literary, sexual, and political. In his *Autobiography*, Williams writes: "It doesn't sound exciting, but it was. Our parties were cheap—a few drinks, a sandwich or so, coffee—but the yeast of new work in the realm of the poem was tremendously stirring." Kreymborg writes in his autobiography a few years later: "The printed page was not enough; one wanted to greet the other fellow, and failing such a meeting, wished to hear about him, read about him, talk about him." Using her own money, which was very little, Ridge sent out invitations, arranged the refreshments, and made the introductions, becoming a major force behind the continuing publication of the magazine. "She was charismatic," writes Cyril Kay-Scott,

> and Evelyn was not alone in falling under her spell. Few left her salon with anything but good words for their hostess. In a subtle way her influence on American letters was greater than many polemicists and clique leaders for, by virtue of her radiant, dedicated spirit, she made things happen.

Regarding the very real achievements of the women who held these salons, Cecily Swanson writes in "A Circle is a Necessity: American Women Modernists and the Aesthetics of Sociability":

These women...have been difficult to "read" as important figures
of literary modernism because their contribution was less *literature*
as we are accustomed to perceiving it than a new conception of the
literary, which championed the aesthetic merits of salon conversation.

In *Sinbad*, Cyril Kay-Scott's novel about Evelyn's affair with William
Carlos Williams, he recalls the guests at Ridge's famous soirées with some
sarcasm: "Little Celia St. John,"—surely Edna St. Vincent Millay—"ever the
center of a group of men...recalled a wax lily." He quotes her: "'Well, tired
little boy, if it's too far to your place, you might spend the night with me,
only one flight down in this same building...' No one laughed." He mentions
Ridge wearing pendant earrings and speaking with an almost too perfectly
modulated low-pitched voice, "her enunciation theatrically distinct, and her
manner well-bred to the point of discomfort." Overcompensation for a less
than advantageous upbringing? Scott was never close enough to Ridge to
discover why she worked so hard to disguise her origins: "[she] remembered
with despair the bourgeois home from which she had escaped." But he did
acknowledge Ridge's complexity: "[She] had a code of worldliness, and her
vanity made her demand some sexual recognition from most of the men she
met. But unknown to herself her tendency was toward a morally beautiful
idealism." On the same page, Scott has her admit: "I am a bitter female."

Literary soirées had flourished in lower Manhattan since the 1910s.
They were used to solicit money to publish magazines, to celebrate a
writer's publication, and, most often, to talk over new ideas in politics and
literature and art. Margaret Sanger held such soirées. From 1913 to 1916
Mabel Dodge invited guests on Wednesdays to her luxurious apartment just
off Washington Square, salons launched in imitation of those of her friend
Gertrude Stein in Paris. Willa Cather held hers on Fridays at 5 Bank Street in
1917. As soon as Margaret Anderson and Jane Heap brought the *Little Review*
from Chicago to New York, they entertained in an apartment with lacquered
black walls and a magenta floor "the color of the inside of a stomach." Black
chains supported a big divan. Jean Toomer also attended Ridge's parties,
and later founded the Harlem Gurdjieff reading group, which minutely
recorded not only their discussion, but also the affect of each participant.
Edna St. Vincent Millay made enough money writing potboilers in 1919 that
she held soirées at 25 Charlton Street. According to critic Jeffry Kondritzer,
"Of the many social and literary gatherings in Manhattan, those held at Lola

Ridge's tried most fervently to keep the flame of literature alive." Kreymborg remembered that

> [Ridge] kept the movement going by giving a party nearly every time she sold a poem or an article, though editors sent her sums hardly ample enough to be converted into the refreshments gracing her dark room on Fifteenth Street....Some of the older members hob-nobbed about Lola's room with some of the newer: Evelyn Scott, a green-eyed person with a satiric languor, Emanuel Carnevali, a young Italian with a tempestuous vocabulary that promised to usher new cadences into American poetry...Waldo Frank, one of the moving spirits of the now defunct *Seven Arts*...and entering the room late in the evening, Scofield Thayer, who had recently bought out *The Dial* from Martyn Johnson.

"We had arguments over cubism that would fill an afternoon," William Carlos Williams recounts in his *Autobiography*. His father had died at the end of 1919, and that "may have intensified his quest for place and belonging," writes one critic. Williams had begun to write about his love of America in both his fiction and poetry but he was also working hard to "make it new." One result was *Kora in Hell: Improvisations*, a work so new few understood it. Ridge, however, appreciated his talent for experimentation: "The words of William Carlos Williams either rend and pull apart or set about erecting a new building," she writes a few years later, reviewing *In The American Grain* in the *New Republic*. Williams called Ridge a "Vestal of the Arts," to denote her dedication to the world of poetry. His relationships with other female poets varied wildly, ranging from punching performance artist/poet Baroness Elsa von Freytag-Loringhoven in the face ("I flattened her with a stiff punch to the mouth") to the canonization of Moore ("Marianne was our saint").

Marianne Moore (1887-1972) enjoyed Ridge's parties, and her comments about them reveal their playful yet serious tone, for example: "I am interested in Marsden Hartley's 'exposition' of the American quality in poetry. I am not just ready myself to say what I think that quality is." Moore was no ingenue to the group. She had visited Kreymborg during her first trip to New York in December 1915, and picnicked with Kreymborg and Williams at the Ridgefield shacks. *Others* was among the several magazines that first published her work that year. "He [Kreymborg] thought I might pass as a novelty." Moore "talked as she wrote and wrote as she talked, and the consummate ease of the performance either way reminded one of the rapids of an intelligent stream," Kreymborg wrote in admiration.

Although Moore never embraced anarchism, she did espouse socialism and supported suffrage. "Of course we all are Socialists," Moore writes in a letter from college in 1909, "in so far as we know economics and are halfway moral, and want clean politics." While Ridge was an editor of *Others* in 1919, she printed Moore's poem "Radical."

Tapering
to a point, conserving everything,
   this carrot is predestined to be thick.
    The world is
     but a circumstance, a mis-
erable corn patch for its feet. With ambition, imagination, outgrowth,
nutriment,
with everything crammed belligerent-
   ly inside itself, its fibres breed monopoly—
   a tail-like, wedge-shaped engine with the
   secret of expansion, fused with intensive heat
   to the color of the set-
ting sun and
stiff.

Contemporary critic Stephen Burt points out that roots are also radicals, therefore carrots are radical vegetables with possibly political overtones, and the orange carrots are "the color of the set-/ting sun," not quite red. Moore's continuing interest in the political world is indicated in a few of her titles: "To Statecraft Embalmed to Disraeli," "To Disraeli on Conservatism," "To Military Progress," and her various anti-German poems, most importantly "You Say You Said," with its uncharacteristically vehement lines: "I hate/You less than you must hate/Yourselves," published in 1918. Wallace Stevens called her "a moral force in light blue." Moore's poem, "Spencer's Ireland," published in 1941, addressed her need to speak on Irish issues that Ridge shared. Found amongst Moore and Ridge's correspondence are lines from the Moore poem, "Sojourn in the Whale," written around 1915, which refer to Ireland's political situation as well as the difficulties of gaining a literary reputation. The poem was written while Ridge was traveling and probably before they met, but it suggests the bond of asceticism between them.

> You have lived and lived on every kind of shortage.
>   You have been compelled by hags to spin
>   gold threads from straw and have heard men say:
> "There is a feminine temperament in direct contrast to ours,
>
> which makes her do these things.["]

Although Ridge eventually exchanged only a dozen or so letters with Moore and Mary, her mother, they considered themselves good friends. Judging from the number of entries in Moore's "Daily Diary" from 1920, Ridge and Padraic Colum, another poet, were her main social contacts that year. "They are practically recluses," writes Ridge. Like Ridge's stepfather, Moore's father was institutionalized for religious mania. Moore never met him, although she knew he had chopped off his right hand. Like Ridge, she too considered herself a visual artist and "did a little painting for fun." According to critic Betsy Erkkilla, Moore believed that female identity could transform the world, and she, like Ridge, sought an Americanness that recalled a national, moral, and spritual destiny.

A reading at one of Ridge's parties marked the beginning of Moore's famous association with *The Dial*. Recasting poetry from a fireside recitation into a more public occasion, Ridge encouraged guest participation by having them read from their work. Moore gave a command performance of her poem "England" at 2 a.m. one night after a number of other readings. "Even Stevens was inspired to try something," writes Kreymborg,

> but Wallace waited for conversation to reach a fairly confused height before he drew forth a paper that looked like a poem but sounded like a tête-à-tête with himself. Orrick Johns, Krimmie [Kreymborg], Williams and the rest took their turn and finally Marianne Moore joined them...A beautiful poem few of the guests could hear distinctly, but which the mystery man from the *Dial* [Scofield Thayer] heard so well, he stole over to her and, after a whispered consultation, induced her to part with it.

Scofield Thayer had previously rejected the poem. He then invited Moore to tea at his office, and walked her home. She wrote the angry, conflicted poem "Marriage" after he proposed to her a year later. Even before his resignation from *The Dial* as a result of mental instability, she replaced him as editor-in-chief in 1925.

Hart Crane came to many of Ridge's parties, and he may have been in attendance when Thayer "discovered" Moore. "My dear Hart Crane," Ridge writes the 20-year-old in April 1919. "We will print one perhaps two of the three poems you submitted though I cannot use them this month—or even say just when they will appear." Her tone is sternly editorial but he was a veteran of submitting to magazines, having had his first poem published at 16. He must have been happy to get even the suggestion of publication, since in 1918 Pound did not like his work and had ordered *The Little Review* never to publish him again. (Crane rented a room over their offices hoping to persuade them otherwise.) Williams accepted several of Crane's poems for *Others* in 1916 but never printed them, possibly out of jealousy. At the time of Ridge's first parties, Crane was reading all of Swinburne, making money as a shipping clerk, and about to return to Ohio to work in his father's candy factory. Ridge's writing and introductions proved to be very important for his poetic development. His copy of *The Ghetto and Other Poems* naturally falls open to her "Brooklyn Bridge," where it is stained at the seam.

One of the very few reviews Crane wrote was for *The Ghetto and Other Poems*. He conveyed much enthusiasm for the book, particularly for its imagery of the city:

> Over the black bridge
> The line of lighted cars
> Creeps like a monstrous serpent
> Spooring gold... (*Ghetto* 51)

He insisted that Ridge's sincerity was "the essential to all real poetry" and admired the book because it seemed "so widely and minutely reflective of its time." He added, however, that her metaphoric technique sometimes devolved into a "barren cleverness." Still, he would not forget her work when he came to write his "To Brooklyn Bridge."

Ridge introduced Mina Loy and her wild poetry to traditional poets such as Louise Bogan. At this juncture, the two of them had poetry and emotional upheaval in common. The 22-year old widowed Bogan had recently moved to the city and was getting over an affair with a Robin Hood who shoplifted furs in order to call attention to the needs of the poor, and Loy was in New York after giving birth to the baby of the boxer/artist Arthur Cravan, who had disappeared mysteriously off the coast of Mexico in a sailboat. Louise Bogan's two poems, "Betrothed" and "Young Wife" appeared in the 1917 *Others* before Ridge's tenure, when Bogan was living in Panama with her still-living husband and a new baby. Both poems are in free verse, a form she would later repudiate, and both concerned the difficulties of marriage. Mina Loy's poems "The Dead" and "The Black Virginity" had been included in the *Others* 1919 anthology. Her "Summer Night in a Florentine Slum," written in 1920 two years after Ridge's *The Ghetto and Other Poems* appeared, echoed the style and subject of Ridge's title poem. Although only two pages in length—compared with Ridge's 22—its long prose lines concern watch-ing the neighborhood poor from a window on a hot summer night.

> I leaned out of the window—looking at the summer strewn street
> late in heat—lit with lamps, and mixed my breath with the tired dust.

Loy's *flâneuserie* includes a legless woman on a board, a suicidal husband, and a madwoman with a knife. "Is the game fair?" asks the speaker. "Nature umpires!" In the window across from hers, a carpenter "stretched a lean arm across the table and pawed his young wife's breast," the same table he'd beaten her with that morning. She would return to the topic of the poor and oppressed in the 1940s with poems like "On Third Avenue" and "Mass Production on 14th Street."

Jean Toomer (1894-1967) attended a Ridge party in May 1920. Introduced by a mutual friend, Ridge was nearly the first person to recognize Toomer as a writer, telling him his work would be "talked about and studied twenty years hence." She mentored him for a number of years, and he did indeed become an important figure, straddling the modernists and the Harlem Renaissance movement. She wrote her first response to his poetry in 1920:

> Your poems are delicately impressionistic—surfacey so and they show much whimsical fancy and a sense of form (unity) as well as of cadence—but most of them are *weightless*. They are surface impressions, light as petal blown delicately upward by a breeze.... They seem to be poems of concealment rather than of revealment—a placing of flowers and ferns before closed shutters and drawn blinds

rather than the spirit singing or saying aloud its lonely questioning through open windows."

Toomer was poor gentility like Ridge. Although described by Ridge as "a young Indian boy," his grandfather had been the first African American governor in the country, serving in the state of Louisiana for a month and a half. Toomer liked to use the phrase "First American" to describe his racial heritage and to suggest that he represented a new America unhindered by racial polarity. Extremely handsome, he dedicated himself to poetry—and to finding women to support him.

Painter-poet Marsden Hartley was part of the *Others* circle from the beginning. When he was fourteen, his family left him in Maine to work in a shoe factory for a year, an experience that mirrored Ridge's son's. Shattered by it, he once described the New England accent to Stieglitz as "a sad recollection [that] rushed into my very flesh like sharpened knives." As described by Kreymborg: "He wrapped his coat like a toga about his spare form, held his extraordinary nose in the air, used his aristocratic cough as a warning not to come too close." Although now remembered mostly as a modernist painter, Hartley published in *Poetry, The Dial, The Little Review,* and five poems in the *Others* anthology in 1919, including "The Fishmongers," which begins: "I have taken scales from off/The cheeks of the moon./I have made fins from bluejay's wings."

Emmanuel Carnevali, mentioned as a guest by Kreymborg, was 22. An Italian immigrant who worked at menial labor in New York, he had won an important prize in *Poetry* that year. A chapter in his only book, *A Hurried Man,* chronicled the spirit of a Ridge party. Robert McAlmon, who convinced Williams to start *Contact* at a gathering in 1920, also immortalized her parties in several chapters of his novel *Post-Adolescence.* Marianne Moore took vivid notes of the parties verbatim. Her *Conversation Notebooks,* little bigger than postage stamps, are filled with quotes caught at the soirée, some of them annotated years later. Moore quotes William Saphier as saying: "Marsden Hartley—He's always so bored. He's so much above everything and some so much below it. I don't see how we are ever to meet." Someone answered: "If you don't stop I'll die." Robert McAlmon—or "Piggy" as Moore liked to call him—insulted Harriet Monroe: "[She] can't read. What she does...I don't know what she tries to read. She's chiefly concerned with the cross and the crown." The next comments appear to be the critic Paul Rosenfeld's: "cummings' poem sounds like him he talks just that way when he has had a little more to drink so I like it better." She attributed half of the following dialogue to Bryher:

> Isn't Ezra married? Where is Mrs. Pound? She's there in the flat usually. People come over from America and say poor Mrs. Pound. I assure you it's quite the other way. She is one of those languid people without a spark of life that you couldn't strike fire (then how do they get on?) Oh, occasionally Ezra forgets to wash the frying pan and she strolls off to her mother's for a week and then she comes back.

The camaraderie and community that these quotes reveal about these poets-in-action underscore the rivalry as well as the exchange of energies—if not always ideas—that went on at the gatherings. That Ridge was able to attract and hold the attentions of so many first-rate writers attests further to her position as a major influence on the modernist movement.

> But you do not yet see me,
> Who am a torch blown along the wind,
> Flickering to a spark
> But never out. (*Ghetto* 62)

Chapter 15

"Woman and the Creative Will"

"They say there never has been, there is not, and there never will be a really great woman artist," Ridge begins her speech "Woman and the Creative Will" 52 years before Linda Nochlin asks, "Why have there been no great women artists?" and ten years before Virginia Woolf published "A Room of One's Own." Ridge's choice of title may have been influenced by *Woman and Labor*, an important book by the South African Olive Shreiner that outlined the social changes caused by technological progress and advocated new and expanded roles for women. A 1911 essay by the Australian Mary Pitt, "Women in Art and Literature," advocated for gender neutrality in art, and the American Charlotte Perkins Gilman's 1911 essay, "Our Androcentric Culture; Or, The Man-Made World" contained such stirring phrases as: "Neither the masculine nor the feminine has any place in art— Art is Human." Feminist and *Masses* editor Floyd Dell published *Woman as World Builders* in 1913, which proclaimed equal opportunity for women in all things.

In advance of Ridge's arrival in Chicago where she was to give her speech for the *Others* Speakers Bureau, she writes to Mitchell Dawson, one of the organizers: "I would like...to be as quiet as possible and see as few people as possible before my talk on Tuesday night...I'm [in] a little nervous mood...."

She had two speeches prepared. She kept changing the title of a speech on individualism, one that might have mentioned Nietzsche, Stirner and Ibsen, the triumvirate that stressed independence and self-reliance over social expectations. Or she could have taken a less political stance on the subject. According to contemporary anarchist Murray Bookchin, "individualist anarchism remained largely a bohemian lifestyle, most conspicuous in its demands for sexual freedom and enamored of innovations in art, behavior, and clothing." Right before her arrival, Ridge decided to give the second speech, "Woman and the Creative Will." "I shall try to show that woman has not only a creative will, but a very great future in creative art," Ridge declares at the onset of her speech.

> Genius...is composed of the male and female principles of mental order and intuition vitalized by spiritual energy....And a work of creative art requires a union of these principles, just as the act of physical creation requires them....And for this reason—the dual sexuality of genius—men and women so gifted usually show characteristics of both sexes...

She doesn't deem any woman artist great. "There have been many gifted [women]," and lists Sappho, Bronte, Dickinson, and the 1914 Nobel Prize winner, the novelist Selma Lagerlof. Ridge had just written a very positive notice of Lagerlof's work in the *American-Scandanavian Review*. No one in poetry is judged equal to Sappho until Dickinson, and she "belongs in spirit to the period upon which we are now entering." No women novelists rival Flaubert, Ibsen, Balzac, or Dostoevski in psychological insight, and only Dostoevski and Turgenev understand women.

The biological explanation of woman's inferior status, she says, is only half true. "Even Nietzsche, Schopenhauer and Strindberg—three of women's most hostile critics—have agreed...in granting her [woman] the largest share of intuition." Positing that intuition is the "first requisite of what we call genius," she divides intuition into male and female principles which "must be united in one individual before we can have that perfect expression that results in a work of great creative art." The male principle is "the power of correlating thought" and the female's is "the ability of the mind to grasp truth with a minimum of effort." These two principles must be "coupled with an intense urge to expression" which is "easily squandered" in the "arduous years of child-bearing."

There is no separating the body from the mind. "Genius is a quality of the spirit rather than of the brain, and spirit is as much permeated with sex as the flesh." Ridge asserts as popular belief that if a woman should create something of genius, she is not a woman. "In order to prove that no woman ever has been or ever could be a creative artist, [philosophers and critics generally] have said that...all the women of genius are...men." But— and this is Ridge paraphrasing sexologist Havelock Ellis—homosexuality "is found in a greater proportion of male geniuses but no woman has yet made herself ridiculous by asserting that men of genius are women." She sees that "the [male] artist is naturally predatory. His soul sits like a patient spider, throwing out infinite antennae, clutching and drawing within," and writes that he allows women in the salons solely for his own stimulation.

Her most vivid example of the opportunities withheld from women is illustrated in a reversal of genders. The Baroque painter Murillo leaves a canvas unfinished and his "mulatto" works on it without permission but is freed after showing great talent. Ridge postulates that "a girl slave who had the temerity to dream of painting a white Virgin would probably have been raped." Transgressive creativity in a woman is not tolerated. "Sex antagonism has been expressed in every age," and Ridge speaks of Athens, with its "strange spectacle of artists and philosophers on one side and stunted illiterate, cow-like women on the other" that is saved only by "the so-called courtesans." She then turns to politics and notes that the "present occupation by women of men's places in industry" was occurring only because of the war. If it had continued, the women would be once again at the "task of providing fodder for still more deadly cannons." She doesn't believe in the promotion of women's rights "as much as a human rights movement." She claims that "the aspirations of women and the aims of labor are two things that can no longer be dictated by governments" and that fear is the only thing holding them back. When women have realized "that art must transcend fear, and that thought is a spiritual substance to be molded like clay—they too will be the masters of dreams." She refuses even to acknowledge the still current argument cultural critic Vance Thompson made twenty years earlier: "When with simian—the feminine is nearer the simian than the masculine—ease they imitate the gestures of an artist one must always look in the background for a man." She sees "a great future for women in creative art."

She does not waste time blaming men for suppressing women's creativity, but proposes an androgynous blending between what Drake calls "the male/intellect-female/intuition polarity" that will enable "real equality and an end to sexual antagonism between men and women." She puts it succinctly: "Woman is not and never has been man's natural inferior."

What she wants is for women to work "not merely toward reorganization and reform, but toward the construction of a completely new social and economic fabric"—an insight that De Cleyre and Goldman would have agreed with, if not inspired. She is tremendously moved by the Russian Revolution and sees it as the place where feminism will result in liberty for both sexes, part of the "Woman Renaissance" that she feels is taking place.

Her contention is that if men and women can work together, America will finally overtake Europe as the intellectual and artistic world leader.

Ridge's landmark presentation on February 25, 1919 was the first of five lectures by poets from the *Others* Speakers Bureau. Although Kreymborg claimed to have thought up the Bureau, it could well have been Ridge's idea since her friend Emma Goldman had been doing such tours for decades. Other historians said it was conceived by William Saphier, funded by *salonnière* Margery Currey and directed by Dawson, but Ridge certainly helped organize the tour from the New York end. In correspondence with Carl Sandburg's lawyer, Mitchell Dawson, "a red-headed poet at heart and a red-headed lawyer by avocation," Ridge promised "lecture/readings" with Conrad Aiken, Kreymborg, Williams, Orrick Johns, and herself. Conrad Aiken, who reviewed her first book, is now best remembered primarily for his short story, "Silent Snow, Secret Snow," but eventually won every poetry award available including becoming the first two-term U.S. poet laureate. One-legged Orrick Johns won the 1912 *Lyric Year* contest that made the loser, Edna St. Vincent Millay, famous. After her poem narrowly failed to win, it received such extravagant praise that Orrick Johns felt too humiliated to show up in person to claim the prize. For some unknown reason, he was not included in the final Chicago schedule. Robert Frost originally declined an invitation to speak for the Bureau, and by the time he changed his mind, it was too late to accommodate him.

"Respectable, high-minded persons are given to classifying writers of *vers libre* with dog stealers, ticket scalpers, wife deserters, and the Bolshevikii" begins "Miss Ridge to the Rescue," the newspaper announcement of Ridge's talk as the first of the series. The poets delivered their speeches up the elegant glass-doored elevator, past the panels of dark wood and pre-Raphaelite murals into the drama school of the Anna Morgan Studios in Chicago's Fine Arts Building, the epicenter of Chicago's bohemian art scene. For his part, Williams spoke on the 15th of April, describing poets as "rebels who took calculated chances," in a speech entitled "A Provisional Scheme of the Universe." He very much enjoyed the whole experience. "You could hear them breathe," he wrote, describing his rapt audience. A 15-column review in the *Chicago Daily Tribune* of his lecture was subtitled: "Women Do Not Like His Poems, but They Seem to Like Him." That weekend he slept with Marion Stroebel, the associate editor of *Poetry*, and proclaimed in a letter: "I had never before had the opportunity to be just a poet, the one thing I wanted to be."

Chicago was hot, at least in terms of poetry. The Jackson Park Art Colony of writers at the time—Pulitzer Prize-winner Carl Sandburg, Harriet Monroe, Sherwood Anderson, Edgar Lee Masters, Ben Hecht and soon-to-be New Yorker Margaret Anderson—circled around critic Floyd Dell who had moved with his wife into the old concession stands of the Columbian Exposition. Kreymborg himself had lived in the city two years earlier while editing a Chicago number of *Others*, which included four of Mitchell Dawson's poems. Dawson and Kreymborg had met during the war when Dawson relocated to New York as a soldier. Spending all his evenings in the Village with artists and writers, Dawson—like Kreymborg—became caught up in starting his own magazine. Kreymborg knew just the man to collaborate with: Man Ray, fresh from their adventures with *The Glebe* three years earlier and Man Ray's own *Ridgefield Gazook*, a single-issue four-page Dadaist magazine he published in 1915 before Dada was claimed by Europe. Man Ray, Dawson and the anarchist/sculptor Adolf Wolff put out one issue of the magazine *TNT* in March 1919, with assistance from the wealthy Henry S. Reynolds. *TNT* featured a preliminary drawing of "The Bride Stripped Bare by Her Bachelors, Even" by Marcel Duchamp, a sound poem by Adon Lacroix (Man Ray's lover at the time), and a poem by Philippe Soupault, one of the founders of surrealism in France, among other contributors. On Dawson's return to Chicago, he met the writer/illustrator/machinist William Saphier, "a stocky Roumanian with dancing eyes," perhaps through Saphier's involvement in *The Little Review*, and the two of them set to work, collaborating with Ridge on setting up the lecture series. Also credited in the collaboration were the poets Marion Stroebel and Elma P. Taylor.

Envisioned as a sort of sideshow for this new strange practice of modernism, the *Others* Speakers Bureau was to have toured other Midwestern cities, according to the March 1919 issue of the magazine. Ridge was the only one to have spoken in St. Louis where she delivered her "The Growth of Individualism in American Poetry" to a good crowd. Frost, Lindsay, Sandburg, and Stevens were to have lectured in Chicago in the fall and winter. But the first season of the lecture series was its last— no reason given. Nonetheless, William Saphier reported in the next *Others* issue that "the result [of the tour] was that Lola Ridge, Conrad Aiken, Alfred Kreymborg and William Carlos Williams visited Chicago, addressed hundreds of people, made a great many friends and sold lots of books."

Ridge's speech received enough praise (although no reviews) that she repaired to Montreal with unsolicited money given to "individuals working for society along radical lines," to expand her speech to book-length, with chapters on "Woman's Creative Past, The Nature of Aesthetic Emotion, Man's Conception of Womanhood as the Rib, Puritanism and Art, The Bisexual Nature of Genius, The Inner Room, Sex Antagonism, Motherhood and the Creative Will, and Woman's Future in Creative Art." But she sensed that the project wasn't going to be popular. "People hate to mistake you for a lamb and then catch the glint of teeth," she writes after her trip to Chicago. She never completed the book and finally discarded it nine years later when Viking, then her publisher, withdrew its support on the grounds that she would have no readers.

Ridge revealed the debt she owed Dawson with regard to setting up the *Others* Speakers Bureau when she wrote to him a year later about setting up something similar for D.H. Lawrence:

> Huebsch [her publisher] asked me to speak to you about H. D. (sic) Lawrence. He is fetching him over here to lecture and wants some one interested really in poetry to help this matter along in Chicago and so that he gets a hearing[.] (I)f agreeable he wishes you to write to him. I hope you will—this time you'll get the credit. I don't mean that you didn't get it before though—only its success was really *all* due to you....

Dawson must have been very gentlemanly about who was due the credit—or Ridge was being modest. She very much valued the friendship, and they exchanged work and loaned each other books. "Send me what new stuff you have so that I can criticize fiercely [?] and perhaps you'll do the same for me. Be sure to let me have "Antonia" back." (Willa Cather had published *My Antonia* the year before.) "I could write to you standing in a trolley," she exclaims, and later astutely evaluated her own approach to poetry with his: "I want to deny or destroy something and you want to...make affirmation." She also held the wider view with regard to poetry's squabbles: "Oh there's nothing in the world that's any good—after our work—but love and courage."

In May, 1919, fresh from the *Others'* Chicago success, Dawson attended one of Ridge's soirées. He had a wonderful time. "A tremendous party at Lola's...Talk and talk till the room turned around." Ridge's Australian friend Martin Lewis came—"a brilliant conversationalist"—Marianne Moore,

William Carlos Williams, Kreymborg, and the very young Emmanuel Carnevali who imagined Dawson doing "phallic dances in solitude."

This was the party that ended *Others*. Carnevali staged a filibuster about getting rid of the old guard—Williams, Ridge, Kreymborg—accusing them of having forgotten their youth. Carnevali began his rant with praise. His estimation of Ridge recalls the "bisexual" nature of her *Others* speech in Chicago, as well as Untermeyer's reception to her first book:

> Virile?—it may be an insult to use that adjective since Lola Ridge has begun an era in which for a woman to be virile, i.e., masculine, might mean to be weaker. I think she is one of the most beautiful signs we have of woman's emancipation and independence. Let her be a socialist; this rebellion of hers is pure beauty, it is sanctified, it is nothing less than burning human blood. It is no longer that particular fact of the revolt against actual social conditions, which is, unfortunately, what affects today's socialists and anarchists. It is an eternal thing, the thing that caused Prometheus to be bound. It is the fire of heaven burning in this wonderful woman's blood.

"My Speech at Lola's," later recounted in a chapter of Carnevali's book, *A Hurried Man*, quickly turned into an attack on the poets for "their preoccupation with technique instead of the 'soul of poetry'." The diatribe is described by Paul Mariani in Williams's biography as "shrill, half-crazed." Carnevali sets the scene:

> the suggestive violentism and the heavy scented drunken whirlwind that is Williams; the sweet simplicism and the capering bitterness that is Kreymborg; the voracious hunger of Lola Ridge—flashlights searching a battlefield, slicing a thick foul night, breaking one another to be drawn together into pools of swarming gold over corpses...How could I put them together?

Then he damns them:

> My friends, Kreymborg, Bodenheim, Saphier, Williams and Ridge, I hate you...The fight you had started in the beginning has you exhausted....Who the hell are you, judging us and laughing and

sneering at us, at me, out of what unknown unsaid miracles have you earned your right to write?

He takes on some of the responsibility for his disillusionment himself:

The dear sufferer Lola Ridge has spoken of a wind in such a way that I saw the hand of a god bringing clean stillness to man—and I was ashamed, I, the restlessness that has no direction....

He unflatteringly compares the group's theorizing to Pound's:

I am disgusted with your little review talk of technique and technicians. Easier than everything, commoner than everything is to have a technique, to talk like Ezra Pound does in his "Subdivisions of the Poetical Department Store with Antiques for Sale only to those Who Know how the Oriental Pooh-Pooh-Chink wore his Slippers.

Then he rejects the whole enterprise, sounding as young as he was:

If you are poets, as they say, I don't want to be a poet....If you say nothing, then I'll shout into your ears, the world expects a formal surrender from you....I'm ready...to knock you down and step over your bodies.

With such an incitement, not even Ridge's energies could stop William Carlos Williams, very prickly about being thought old guard, from pulling *Others* apart. He was already worried about the freshness of his experimental quest when he announced *Others'* death in *The Egoist* three years earlier in an article entitled "The Great Opportunity." Kreymborg had put him in charge of the July and August issues but Williams decided to declare it dead in July. Although *Others* had launched his career, he didn't like where the gadfly Kreymborg was steering the magazine's success, proposing a club house, a stock company and a bookstore—and he was moved by Carnevali's speech. In the final issue, Williams praised Carnevali for being "wide, wide, WIDE open." He announced that the magazine "has grown inevitably to be a lie, like everything else that has been a truth at one time." His eight page essay "Belly Music," appended like an encore at the end of the magazine, insisted that *Others'* end was "the BEGINNING of artistic criticism."

Williams, Dawson, and Ridge may have already been planning another magazine. Eventually referred to as "the Compromise/New Moon project," Ridge's role in it was never specified. At the time, she wrote a number of letters to Dawson from the hospital where she was having tests. She also sent Williams a letter with some reservation about the project—"IF" as Williams quotes her—and it seems to have had something to do with money, because Williams then suggested that Dawson give him money to forward to her. "I will hold myself ready to act as a kind of intermediary," writes Williams, then he goes on: "I will write to her at once telling her I know nothing as yet but as soon as I hear definitely—No. No. I'll tell her nothing at all." He then mentions Evelyn Scott as "a good ally," that "the lady in question has more stuff packed away in her blond bean than any other of her sex I have so far poetically encountered," but whether he was considering her as a possible collaborator is not clear. Their affair is still in the future. Dawson did end up sending a number of checks to Ridge, but he didn't have the kind of money that was necessary for a magazine launch. "We need that sort of an acetylene torch to bore thru the steel that surrounds the money-boys," he writes his mother. He and Williams were also supporting Carnevali who had abandoned his wife and children for a six-month stint as associate editor at *Poetry*, where Carnevali was known as "my dear boy" to Harriet Monroe.

Marianne Moore's "Poetry" begins the last *Others* issue, with "I, too, dislike it," setting the tone for Williams's renunciation of the poetry at hand, although she had no idea he would use it that way and did not appreciate its placement. Mitchell Dawson had a poem in the issue, as well as Marion Stroebel, Williams's paramour. The upstart Carnevali's poems appear twice, and of course there's a Kreymborg poem. William Saphier, who helped so much in Chicago, also merits a poem. Alva N. Turner, who published three poems, was "an amateur poet" encouraged by Williams. "Never have I seen such ROTTEN work which gives such hope—such failure mixed with such an intangible something that is down in the ROCKS at the center of the world," Williams writes to him. After Wallace Stevens's two poems comes Ridge's uncollected "Easter Dawn." In her poem, the spring light runs over Grace Church across from her apartment, coming to rest on the "Winged Victory" above her bed.

> Dawn at my window...
> Dawn, a spent runner resting on white stones,
> stones of Grace Church,

stones of Fifth Avenue,
stones of the arch at Washington Square—
touching now with a gaunt pallor
    the winged Victory above my bed.

World War I had just ended, but victory for the late-coming Americans was hollow, given the number of casualties they suffered in such a short time. A photo of Ridge's studio shows a three-foot-tall copy of *Winged Victory* looming in the background. Did she admire the sculpture in defiance of the futurist manifesto by Mina Loy's boyfriend Filippo Marinetti: "a race-automobile which seems to rush over exploding powder is more beautiful than the 'Victory of Samothrace'"? Or was the feminist statement—the headless yet powerful woman—the greater attraction? In her case, even the wings could be removed. "The winged Victory of Samothrace is greater as pure Victory without its wings. I only knew this after the wings of our cast of it were broken in moving," she writes at the end of her life.

Chapter 16

Red Summer

July 1919 marked the end of *Others* but also the middle of the violent "Red Summer." Activist-poet James Weldon Johnson coined the term. Primarily remembered as a leader of the NAACP, Johnson published eight of his poems alongside Ridge's in the 1919 *Others* anthology. His use of "Red Summer" described the wave of violence that engulfed the country as a result of friction between returning soldiers, white and black, who needed jobs. For the first time in America's history of racial violence, blacks fought back. Red Summer resulted in 70 lynchings and serious rioting in more than 30 American cities, with hundreds killed and thousands left homeless between May and October of that year. Some of the worst violence occurred in Chicago, where a black teenager accidentally floated into the unofficially segregated part of Lake Michigan and drowned after a white man stoned him. Police refused to arrest the man.

A particularly vicious prequel to Red Summer occurred in East St. Louis in 1917, when 10,000 white men rioted, seeking revenge on the blacks who acted as strikebreakers and kept their jobs. Josephine Baker was eleven at the time and remembered her brother asking: *Is that a storm coming?* and their mother answering: *It's the whites.* The result was over 100 dead African Americans. Ida B. Wells, a famous black journalist whose report was kept secret for the next 69 years, writes:

> During the East St. Louis riots, white women stabbed black women in the eyes with their hatpins while on a trolley, whites took potshots at blacks attempting to swim to safety across the Missouri, and the few blacks who managed to cross were then stoned by children waiting for them.

Refugees were turned out of houses owned by whites, to be torn apart by the mob. W.B. DuBois and Martha Gruening reported that a Mrs. Cox saw a "baby snatched from its mother's arms and thrown into the flames, to be followed afterwards by the mother." Ridge commemorates this last with her searing "Lullaby." "It is in the lyric of the East St. Louis burning of a Negro baby, that Ridge...fuses her emotion into her expression and becomes a full poet," notes the *New Republic*.

Lullaby

Rock-a-by baby, woolly and brown...
(There's a shout at the door an' a big red light...)
Lil' coon baby, mammy is down...
Han's that hold yuh are steady an' white...

Look piccaninny—such a gran' blaze
Lickin' up the roof an' the sticks of home—
Ever see the like in all yo' days!
—Cain't yuh sleep, mah bit-of-honey-comb?

Rock-a-by baby, up to the sky!
Look at the cherries driftin' by—
Bright red cherries spilled on the groun'—
Piping-hot cherries at nuthin' a poun'!

Hush, mah lil' black-bug—doan yuh weep.
Daddy's run away an' mammy's in a heap
By her own fron' door in the blazin' heat
Outah the shacks like warts on the street...

An' the singin' flame an' the gleeful crowd
Circlin' aroun'...won't mammy be proud!
With a stone at her hade an' a stone on her heart,
An' her mouth like a red plum, broken apart...

See where the blue an' khaki prance,
Adding brave colors to the dance
About the big bonfire white folks make—
Such gran' doin's fo' a lil' coon's sake!

Hear all the eagah feet runnin' in town—
See all the willin' han's reach outah night—
Han's that are wonderful, steady an' white!
To toss up a lil' babe, blinkin' an' brown...

Rock-a-by baby—higher an' higher!
Mammy is sleepin' an' daddy's run lame...
(Soun' may yuh sleep in yo' cradle o' fire!)
Rock-a-by baby, hushed in the flame...

(An incident of the East St. Louis Race Riots, when some white
women flung a living colored baby into the heart of a blazing fire.)
(*Ghetto* 65-66)

In modernist terms, Ridge's ironic tone inverts the lullaby into anything but a calming song, and her derisive stance works to destabilize the ballad tradition from within, a technique she had already used in 1904 with "Sleep, Dolores," in which the child remains unconsoled while "the grey wolves ride thee down." Black poets like Sterling Brown and Claude McKay used similar strategies to invert traditional forms. In Ridge's poem, the white woman mocks the baby, its parents, and all African Americans with her "blackface" language of minstrelsy, while at the same time failing the basic precept of motherhood—to protect infants. How much of this impulse was buried in Ridge, who tossed her own child away in an orphanage?

The government was searching for ways to pin all this upheaval on the anarchists. Attorney General Palmer wanted to suppress all political dissent ever since an anarchist's bomb blew up on his own doorstep, one of 10 that exploded in American cities at the end of 1919. He decided that blacks were susceptible to anarchism because of their subservient status, and that Red Summer was solely a result of radical foment. President Wilson laid the groundwork for this belief in a statement he made earlier that year: "The American Negro returning from abroad would be our greatest medium in conveying Bolshevism to America."

Whether or not she knew it, Ridge had already been mentioned in the subcommittee of the Judiciary Committee on January 23, 1919. Ostensibly investigating "Brewing and Liquor Interests and German Propaganda," but in reality investigating German and Bolshevik influence in America, it was a predecessor of the House Un-American Activities Committee of the McCarthy era, with the express purpose of "repression carried on by and with the consent of the vast majority in the interests of that majority." Attorney Archibald E. Stevenson discussed the politics of the Modern School with a Senator Overman and mentioned that Lola Ridge had lectured there on the unlikely titled "The anarchist's relation to the law," and that others were giving similar speeches in New York.

> "Are any of these people educated people?" asked Overman.
> "One is Hutchins Hapgood, who is the brother of Norman Hapgood."

Norman Hapgood would be appointed American ambassador to Denmark a month later, so his black sheep brother's political connections did not compromise his rising career. Stevenson suggested that "It was through their influences [the anarchists'] that the German Spartacus group, headed by Liebkneicht and Rosa Luxembourg got their start...We have several avowed agents of the Bolsheviki government here—avowed propagandists."

> A Senator Nelson asked: "In this country, operating here?"
> "Yes," answered Stevenson. "Two of them are American citizens. One is John Reed, a graduate of Harvard University...who is a descendant of Patrick Henry."

The investigator certainly had his man there—John Reed's *Ten Days That Shook The World* would soon become a bestseller. The Senate shortly summoned him for interrogation.

"I'm again trying to get to Russia," Ridge writes Mitchell Dawson on July 16, 1919. Although an anarchist, not a communist, she was anxious to see the revolution for herself. Her Ferrer literary comrade, Manuel Komroff, was already there, having taken advantage of free passage from the provisional government in May, 1917, sailing via Siberia and publishing a newspaper, staging plays and lecturing onboard. Komroff reported for the *Russian Daily News*, took the Trans-Siberian railroad to China, and got a job working for the *China Press*. Ridge's acquaintance, Lincoln Steffens, also reported from Russia and pronounced: "I have been over into the future and it works." But 1919 was also the year that union leader—and presidential candidate—Eugene Debs went to jail for sedition, for calling Lenin and Trotsky the "foremost statesmen of the age." Socialism, that close cousin of communism, had become a political threat, with Debs garnering nearly a million votes for president in 1920, despite being incarcerated at the time.

In July 1919 Ridge published "To Alexander Berkman In Solitary" in *The Modern School*. Berkman had spent the last seven and a half months of his two-year sentence in solitary confinement for protesting the treatment of fellow prisoners.

> The prison squats
> with granite haunches
> on the young spring,
> battened under with its twisting green...
>
> ....
>
> and the silence shuffles heavy dice of feet in iron corridors...
> until the day...that has soiled herself in this black hole
> to caress the pale mask of your face...
> withdraws the last wizened ray
> to wash in the infinite
> her discolored hands.
> Can you hear me, Sasha,
> in your surrounded darkness? (*Sun-up* 89)

Berkman was not a U.S. citizen, a situation that made him eligible for deportation under the new sedition laws, but Emma Goldman, held in a Missouri prison, assumed that she was a citizen, as she had twice married Jacob Kershner, who had been naturalized. Palmer's assistant, 24-year-old J. Edgar Hoover, managed to convince the court to deny her citizenship rights in order to deport her.

A going-away party was held for Goldman and Berkman in October at the Hotel Brevoort, where Ridge read her poem to Berkman. Leonard Abbott spoke, objecting to the wave of arrests and deportations of radicals that had occurred all over the country: "The Constitution of America, so far as it relates to free speech and free press, is a dead letter." Assistant Secretary of Labor Louis F. Post, a friend of Goldman's who had dined with her and invited her as a guest to his home, "who had insisted that even Leon Czolgosz [President McKinley's assassin] should be safeguarded in his constitutional rights," signed the order for Goldman's deportation. When

Goldman and Berkman sailed past the Statue of Liberty, Goldman said to reporters: "It may be only the beginning."

When the couple was arrested, all lists and ledgers on the premises were confiscated, including a complete registry of the anarchists' friends in the United States. On November 7, 1919, as many as 10,000 suspected Communists and anarchists were arrested in twenty-three states. An FBI official declared, "I believe that with these raids the backbone of the radical movement in America is broken."

Ridge's political sympathies were already well known, and although passports were not required when she entered the country under an assumed name, she had asserted when she landed at Ellis Island 11 years earlier that she was a citizen. Perhaps the threat of deportation forced her into her second marriage. Although she was not divorced from her first husband, nor had he died, she married David Lawson five days before the Berkman/Goldman going-away party, the wedding having taken place after almost ten years of living together.

Chapter 17

"We Who Touched Liberty"

"You can't let anyone rock *Little Review*, and E.P. has for some time needed just such a cool and unperturbed hand to press him back into his seat," writes Ridge to the *The Little Review* editors Margaret Anderson and Jane Heap in January 1919. At the time, the magazine's collaborative effort was between Anderson, a "finishing school-educated lesbian leftist," Jane Heap, "the dour art school-educated transvestite," and E.P. (Ezra Pound), "a University of Pennsylvania-educated womanizing totalitarian," and it was this last character that Ridge was objecting to. Pound's power game of manipulating literary reputations was the antithesis of a free and democratic endeavor that Ridge espoused. In an earlier issue, Heap herself had written that "Pound has appeared always as some Pied Piper, luring his swarm of literary rodents out of their conventional stables to their doom."

But by October, the editors of *The Little Review* had gone too far. Madness was touted as art, in the form of the work of Baroness Freytag-Loringhoven, which began the issue. "Are you hypnotized, or what, that you open the *Little Review* with such a retching assault upon Art...?" Ridge writes. Jane Heap dodges the question: "No one has yet done much about the Art of Madness." Ridge, along with others, had vehemently objected to the nine page long "Cast-Iron-Lover."

> Mine body—thou maketh me sad—thou VERILY hast made sad—
> thine soul—!
> Mine body—alas!—I bid thee—GO!
>
> THOU—mine soul?!
> I—mine body.
> .....
> SQUATING IN SHADOW DARKNESS UPON CENTER
> OF CRIMSON THRONE—SQUATING CON-

TENTEDLY—FEEDING SWIFTLY—EYES CLOSING IN
PASSION—OPENING NOT KNOWING PASSION—BOWELS
DANCING—EYES STONY JEWELS IN ITS HEAD!
TOADKING!
("Mineself——Minesoul——and——Mine——Cast-Iron Lover.")

Freytag-Loringhoven wandered the Village with a pack of big dogs, her head shaved and half of it painted red, wearing black lipstick, a bra made of two tin cans tied together, and an electric tail light winking on her derriere. She was a German émigré who sent her lover Marcel Duchamp the urinal to be exhibited in the Independents Exhibition ("No judge, no prize" was its motto), an artwork that was famously turned down as his own. She met him through Man Ray at the Ferrer Center, where she modeled. The three of them made a movie of her shaving her pubis, but she was not necessarily heterosexual—one of her more successful affairs was with Djuna Barnes. Williams was awed and attracted to her, until she stalked him, which is when he punched her in the mouth. He called her "America personified in the filth of its own imagination." She in turn reviewed his book, *Kora in Hell* for the *The Little Review* in an anti-Semitic diatribe so long it ran in two issues. She replied to Ridge and the many who objected to her work that "in the nations of high culture [madness] was a public custom, as it still is—for instance in the mardi gras—or 'Fasching'—and in old Greece in the feast of Dionysus."

For Freytag-Loringhoven, making art meant expressing what was most shocking and therefore most authentic, in particular, her unorthodox and outrageous views on gender and sex. She should have appealed to Ridge on both those counts, but Ridge had too much experience dealing with her dead stepfather's mental illness. "You know how the thought of insanity scares me after my experience with the crazy," she writes her husband years later. In Freytag-Loringhoven's defense, Amelia Jones writes in *Irrational Modernism* that she represented:

> the cacophonous clash of races, sexes, sexualities, and classes of people which made up New York City between the wars, and this allowed her to embody the "irrational effects...the seedy and seamy underside of modernism that discourses of high art and architecture have labored to contain through their dominant models of rational practice.

"She's not a futurist," said Marcel Duchamp, "she is the future." Whether her practice was literary was what provoked questions from Ridge and others, and one that Ridge confronted head-on later with the work of Gertrude Stein. Now contemporary curators of the avant-garde have created the category of "outsider art" and "performance" to categorize work like Freytag-Loringhoven's. Recent critical analysis stresses her use of many voices, channelling the schizophrenic chorus that drove her into institutions. Much to Ridge's credit, however, she recognized the extremes of freedom that the Baroness practiced, and reversed her stance on her work—at least compared to Gertrude Stein's—during her Broom editorship.

In 1920, Ridge published twelve poems in *Poetry, Current Opinion, Ainslee's, New Republic* and *The Modern School.* In this last appeared "To the Free Children." At a February 1920 Modern School dinner celebrating its new buildings in New Jersey, she read "Will Shakespeare Sees the Children of the Ferrer Modern School Playing A Midsummer Night's Dream" and "To the Free Children." This second poem is particularly revealing of her attitude toward the school's anarchist principles.

To The Free Children

We of our generation
who touched liberty
had to leap for it.
—Not as over a chasm
aided by the momentum of running feet;
but up in the air...one glimpse...
lash-breadth of glory
        white as flame on snow...
then shock of falling backward...
...you
we hold up high above our heads. (*Red Flag* 71)

She also read "To Alexander Berkman In Solitary," although a number of the guests would have heard it at Goldman and Berkman's going-away party the year before. By now the two anarchists were settled in Petrograd. They had been welcomed by William Shatoff, the Russian-born linotype operator who managed the Ferrer Center for a time, acted as their bodyguard, organized in the I.W.W., and now worked as Commissar of Railroads—"the greatest railway builder of Russia"—but who would disappear around 1935 in the Great Purge. John Reed also met them and quarreled with Goldman about the realities of Russian politics. In a few weeks Goldman and Berkman would voice their disillusionment with the Revolution and with Lenin himself.

By early 1920, Ridge, Dawson, Kreymborg, and Williams had collected a number of manuscripts for their launch of *Compromise* or *New Moon* or *Glue*, the various titles of the magazine that was to replace *Others*, but they were stalled. Timidity was the reason McAlmon put forward in a "June some date" letter to Dawson. He starts off by declaring, "In spite of your letter, I shall now try to get out a magazine," suggesting that acrimony lay thick between them. For the next two years, Dawson corresponded with Ridge about his attempts to get a literary magazine of his own started. Ridge responded to one of them with a potential submission. "I was going to send you my long poem 'Sun-up,'" she writes, "though perhaps it would have been impossibly long [at] 41 x pages. And I won't have it cut." Although she encouraged his work and ambitions for a press, she began a habit of asking for money. She was a bit coy. "One should never take from anyone who has—I think it spoils the friendship..." In September, 1920 she writes: "I'll pay back that cheque but can't just now." When Ridge didn't ask for money outright, she hinted: "The Scotts want to take me back with them to Rio de Janeiro for a visit. I'd love to go. The doctor says sea and a change of climate might do a lot." She mentions trying to get to Russia but not having the funds. She was about to be admitted to St. John's Hospital in Yonkers when she writes: "Sorry I couldn't pay back that money, but it has been quite impossible. Please pay it for me and to [?]...will pay you back later on. I'm going in above hospital in half an hour." He sent her more money in light of her hospitalization.

> I know the gentle and humanly loving spirit in which it was sent and shall accept it in that way. This is a crisis and I know it would be foolish not to let my friends help me through it. Please don't send any more. I shall not accept it.

What she was suffering from isn't clear. A Doctor Carrington wants to put her under electrical treatment, "especially as he says nothing wrong but stomach troubles and nerves."

Perhaps it is a kind of nervous breakdown. She has been working awfully hard: editorships of *The Birth Control Review* and *Others*, editing and throwing parties for *Others*, scheming with Dawson and Williams to put together yet another magazine, publishing so many poems everywhere, writing five reviews of other books, getting married, finishing another book of poems, giving and expanding her Chicago speech for book publication, all in 1919.

> For the last two weeks I've had to stop work on my book Woman and the Creative Will owing to the monstrous ever present financial pressure and do work on reviews—how I hate them! I don't want to criticize. I'm afraid the truth is I don't want to work any more than Emmanuel does.

Carnevali was about to be committed to an insane asylum in the Midwest, where he had followed Dawson, abandoning his wife and children in New York. At the time Carnevali believed he was God—"although we both decided that it was undesirable to become God," writes Dawson, "without also remaining human."

Ridge's timing with regard to another handout was bad: Carnevali was writing the same kind of letter: "I can't leave the hospital until you send some dough." Eventually he was diagnosed with encephalitis lethargica, a disease that caused him to shake uncontrollably. He returned to Italy in 1922, to die slowly and very painfully twenty years later.

Chapter 18

Sun-up and Other Poems

The New York Times gave Ridge's second book, *Sun-up and Other Poems*, a rave review, saying that Ridge "takes a foremost place of any American woman writing poetry." *The Bookman* echoed this with "among the very best of women poets." Published in the fall of 1920, again by Huebsch, its 34-page, three-part title poem "Sun-up," set in a melded New Zealand/ Australia, is particularly striking for the precision of the child Betty's nightmarish vision. After declaring that the book "will inevitably be judged by the pioneer work of James Joyce," *The Dial* called it "acidly translated truth." *The Nation* said with "Freud rather than Plato...read back into the infant mind," it had an "honesty so quick as to be diabolical." The poem has a particularly contemporary appeal.

> The girl with the black eyes holds you tight,
> and you run... and run
> past the wild, wild towers ...
> and trees in the gardens tugging at their feet
> and little frightened dolls
> shut up in the shops
> crying...and crying...because no one stops...
> you spin like a penny thrown out in the street.
> Then a man clutches her by the hair...
> He always clutches her by the hair...
> His eyes stick out like spears.
> You see her pulled-back face
> and her black, black eyes
> lit up by the glare...(*Sun-up* 4-5)

It's not Blake and it's not naïve. It is also not the distanced childhood of the reminiscences of the boy in "Birches" by Frost, nor the cloying nostalgia of Longfellow remembering "My Lost Youth." Such a searing voice would not be heard again in the persona of a child for another fifty years, with the bad boys in "A Child's Christmas In Wales" by Dylan Thomas, and not from a woman until perhaps May Swenson's mild "The Centaur" in 1955. Ridge's little girl Betty pulls off the legs of flies, and her mama admonishes: "When Nero was a little boy/he caught flies on his mama's window/...and nobody loved him." But Betty likes "the picture of the Flood/and the little babies getting drowned." When a boy exposes himself to her, Betty is not at all cowed and certainly not impressed: "You wonder/if God has spoiled Jimmy." She is told not to play with the children in the alley:

> But you must be very polite—
> so you pass them and say good day
> and when they fling banana skins
> you fling them back again. (*Sun-up* 8)

The *New York Call* reviewer said of Betty that "She is not to be patted on the head or bought with candy."

> Celia never minded if you slapped her
> when the comb made your hairs ache,
> but though you rub your cheek against mama's hand
> she has not said darling since....
> Now I will slap her again....
> I will bite her hand till it bleeds. (*Sun-up* 6)

Janie, the doll Betty receives for Christmas, is much abused and then discarded.

> Yesterday
> I took Janie out
> and tied my handkerchief over her face
> and put sand in it
> and threw her into the ditch
> down in the black water
> under the dock leaves...
> and when mama asked me where Janie was
> I said I had lost her. (*Sun-up* 22)

Joyce published *A Portrait of the Artist as a Young Man* six years earlier, with its opening story immersed in a child's point of view that prefigured the stream of consciousness of his *Ulysses,* but his protagonist is not nearly as complex as Betty. Remember all those Barbies with their heads torn off, scalped, with arms missing? These are the poems of the interior mind of a girl who is unfettered by gender expectations. The tone is dreamy in the way that events present to someone with little experience in the world, and paradoxically matter-of-fact. After Betty discovers beauty from her mother's appreciation of a cabbage, they eat it the next day.

> The greens-man gave her a cabbage
> and she held it against her black bodice
> and said what a beautiful green it was
> and put it on the table
> as though it had been a flower.
> But the next day we boiled and ate it with salt.
> It was our dinner. (*Sun-up* 9)

When her mother leaves her in the care of neighbors, Betty fears she'll never return.

> But suppose
> that day after day
> you were to watch for her face
> and it didn't come back?
> Suppose
> it were to drop out of the string of white faces
> like the pearl out of my chain
> I never found again? (*Sun-up* 10)

"Sun-up" also contains the eerie re-telling of the lullaby, "O for the light of thine eyes Dolores."(Another of Ridge's nicknames is Dolores). In it

> ...the sea roars like lions.
> It leaps at the castle
> and the cliff knocks it down
> but always the sea

shakes its flattened head
and gets up again. (*Sun-up* 14)

The "castle has no roof/so the rain spins silver webs in it" and Dolores'
face "floats dim and beautiful/the way flowers do when they are drowned,"
and when she tries to walk up the castle stairs "the stair goes up into the sky/
and the sky keeps going up too,/so none of them ever get there." Although
the poem is framed in a child's perception, the frustration running beneath
its fairytale-like narrative is adult.

Not long after Betty abandons her doll, Ridge prefigures Williams's "No
ideas except in things," written seven years later in *Paterson*, by recognizing
a shadow for itself:

But there is a shadow
that is not the shadow of a thing...
it is a thing itself.
When you meet this shadow
you must not look at it too long...
it grows with your looking at it...
till you are all alone
with nothing around you...
nothing...nothing...nothing...
but a shadow
with its eyes full of black light. (*Sun-up* 27)

In the final section of the poem, Betty adopts an imaginary playmate
named Jude. "Mama peeps out the window and smiles./She thinks/I am
playing with myself...." Jude is her antithesis: "Jude isn't afraid of shadows—/
not even of the ones that have eyes in them..." But the section is more about
Betty's ambivalence with her mother's expectations than the imaginary Jude.

When you tell mama
you are going to do something great
she looks at you
as though you were a window
she were trying to see through,
and says she hopes you will be good
instead of great. (*Sun-up* 29)

Was the mother hoping to shield the child from disappointment by lowering the bar? Or did she mean "good" in terms of "good behavior?" Betty sounds extremely challenging to parent. Twenty-five lines after the admonition to do something "great," Ridge writes about the slim rewards of such greatness:

> ...When you do something great
> people give you a stone face,
> so you do not care any more
> when the sun throws gold on you
> through leaf-holes the wind makes
> in green bushes....(*Sun-up* 30)

Bitterness has been learned. All that ambition, all those years of writing draft after draft, hoping for recognition—Ridge is now 47 years old. She has retreated into her pre-adult psyche. Like fellow New Zealander Mansfield's poetic prose in "Prelude," "At the Bay," and "The Doll's House," Ursula Bethell's sequence of poems, "By the River Ashley," and Robin Hyde's sequence, "Houses by the Sea," Ridge's "Sun-up" holds up to the light what had been forgotten or considered trivial about her childhood, where the self of consequence is hidden. While Bethell's work sought to escape Victorian constraints, Mansfield's shone with emotive detail, and Hyde's revealed a world full of difficulty, Ridge's poem allows Betty to reveal her own method for maintaining courage and perseverance:

> Sometimes...before rain...
> when the stars have gone inside...
> the night comes close to your window
> and sniffs at the light....
> But you must not run away—
> you must keep your face to the night
> and walk backward. (*Sun-up* 17-18)

"You can love people very much/and never, never, never forgive them" is the piece of advice the alter-ego Jude tells Betty. Betty encounters a boy more wicked then herself, a boy who strikes her to the ground with a whip. "He is the kind of boy you knew when you had Celia.../with nice clothes on and curls," she writes, describing her loss of socio-economic status. The speaker then plots to burn the boy alive.

> I know now
> what I shall do....
> I will set fire to him
> and he will burn up into a tall flame—
> he will scream into the sky
> and sparks will fly out of him—
> he will burn and burn...
> and his blazing hair
> shall light up the world. (*Sun-up* 36)

Betty anticipates that her mother will begin to question whether her friend Jude is real, since "the grass didn't fall down under his feet." But Jude is more than imaginary by now, he is her male id. As the book began with an invocation to the mother whose "hand throws something in the fire," this poems ends with full acknowledgement of her influence over Betty's aberrant, albeit unconscious, bisexual nature.

> [Jude] is fading now...
> He is just lines...like a drawing....
> You can see mama in between.
> When she moves
> she rubs some of him out. (*Sun-up* 36)

The second half of the book is an extended reverie on sex and its secrets. The first section is entitled "Monologues," which suggests that the speaker is Ridge herself. "Jaguar," dedicated to Scott, has this speaker noting the "publicity of windows/stoning me with pent-up cries" and predicts that she too will hide "in a crevice in the night." "Wild Duck" is an aubade in which the speaker is "singing a hot sweet song to the super-stars," and then nonchalantly brushes off the lover—"Twas a great night..." "The Dream" follows, with its invocation to Sydney, so perhaps the aubade referred to a failed romance in Australia. "Altitude" opens with: "I wonder/how it would be here with you" with "pain" as "the remote hunger of droning things, and with anger "but a little silence/sinking into the great silence." Another boyfriend is rejected in "Nocturne:" "What are you to me, boy," she writes, then finishes him off with a creepy metaphor: "That I, who have passed so many nights,/Should carry your eyes/Like swinging lanterns?" "Cactus Seed," which ends the section, continues her theme of surveillance with the line: "And only the wind scandal-mongers with gum trees." In the next section, "Time-Stone" has the moon breaking a date with the City, "Playing virgin after all her encounters." In "Train Window" she asks: "how many codes for a wireless whisper" followed naturally by "Scandal," and then "Electricity" in which

> the charged phalluses of iron leaping
> Female and male,
> Complete, indivisible, one,
> Fused into light.

The final lines of "Skyscrapers" are "I know your secrets...better than all the policemen/like fat blue mullet along the avenues."

In the last two poems of the section, Ridge returns to her dark take on the metropolis. Most of Ridge's contemporaries—very much including Hart Crane—have been publishing poems about the excitement of the city, its skyscrapers and bridges and night life. Ridge's poems view its industrialization like a steampunk sci-fi video game with great computer-generated graphics, but rarely positively. The imagist "East River" and its pounding guttural last line is a particularly graphic example.

> East River
>
> Dour river
> Jaded with monotony of lights
> Diving off mast heads...
> Lights mad with creating in a river...turning its sullen back...
> Heave up, river...
> Vomit back into the darkness your spawn of light...
> The night will gut what you give her. (*Sun-up* 57)

"Wall Street at Night" obliquely renders Ridge's distaste of capitalism with the evocation of light and shadow—and dead bodies.

Wall Street at Night

Long vast shapes...cooled and flushed through with darkness...
Lidless windows
Glazed with a flashy luster
From some little pert café chirping up like a sparrow.
And down among iron guts
Piled silver
Throwing gray spatter of light...pale without heat...
Like the pallor of dead bodies. (*Sun-up* 56)

The fourth section of the book is actually titled "Secrets." It contains "After Storm," which ends with "Silence/builds her wall/about a dream impaled." Is this a blatantly Freudian flaunting of a secret? Freud was all the rage at the time, and Ridge owned his *Group Psychology and the Analysis of the Ego*, new that year. The third poem in the section takes the title "Secrets," and begins in dream with something sexual going on: "did you enter my wound from another wound/brushing mine in a crowd..."

"One thing I am sure of always is my love for you—your man size courage and woman size understanding and your complex bi-sexual brain," writes Evelyn Scott to Ridge in 1920, the year of *Sun-up*'s publication. Such compliments were reciprocated. Along with "Jaguar," Ridge included a second poem dedicated to her. Like "Jaguar," "To E.S." is not the usual positive paean to friendship. Scott's first book, *Precipitations*, published that year, has lines like: "She is Death enjoying Life,/Innocently,/Lasciviously."

Or you kissing and picking over fresh deaths...
Filth...worms...flowers...
Green and succulent pods...

....

Nothing buried or thrown away.
Only the moon like a white sheet
Spread over the dead you carry. (*Sun-up* 70)

The mob is the subject of Ridge's four-part "Sons of Belial, a poem that aims to force the reader to recognize his complicity with group violence. "Belial" is a Hebrew word for devil. Her first example of mob violence—"We beat at a door/In Gilead"—refers to the story of the Levite who offered his concubine to the mob instead of himself. The mob had wanted to rape him, but settled for her. The poem mentions the Alexandrian Hypatia, the first female mathematician. According to Gibbon, a Christian mob flayed her alive with oyster shells for exacerbating a conflict with the Jews. Was Ridge experiencing criticism over her *Ghetto* book? The poem's mob nails Christ to a tree and Rosa Luxemburg makes an appearance. The most memorable lines occur toward the end, where the poem refers to the KKK, then on the rise—"Mad nights when we make ritual"—and their lynchings: "We make rope do rigadoons/with copper feet that jig on air...."

"In Harness" begins the last section. About the singing of the French national anthem in a sweatshop, its details, so precise, suggest Ridge's employment there, one of which is the mention of orgasms. "The girl with adenoids/rocks on her hams..../Her feet beat a wild tattoo—," and graphically: "head flung back and pelvis lifting to the white body of the sun." Climax happened frequently to women who pressed their thighs together while using the treadle for so many hours, and foremen were told to listen for runaway sewing machines. The poem ends brilliantly, with French and American moneygrubbers going off to lunch while the anthem plays and the speaker equates "a racing mare" hitched to a grocer's cart to all those strong women at their sewing machines. Putting this forbidden sexual act before the next poem, "Reveille," which aimed to rouse the masses to action—"they think they have tamed you"—confirms that the revolution Ridge wanted was not only political.

"To Larkin," the second to last poem in the book, is dedicated to the Irish activist Jim Larkin, a very successful trade unionist who was arrested in the Palmer raids on an extended visit to the U.S., and jailed in Sing Sing for anarchism. According to historian Lillian Symes, "Larkin...combined Marxism with Catholicism, Irish patriotism with internationalism, irrational prejudices with economic logic." As Ridge writes: "One hundred million men and women go inevitably about their affairs..."

> They do not see you go by their windows, Jim Larkin,
> with your eyes bloody as the sunset
> And your shadow gaunt upon the sky...
> You, and the like of you, that life
> Is crushing for their frantic wines. (*Sun-up* 92)

In addition to this paean to labor activism, the book also contains her poems to Berkman and Goldman. Given the recent deportation of the two anarchists under the Espionage Act of 1917 and the Sedition Act the following year, and the Senate Committee investigations in which Ridge is named, Huebsch, in publishing this book, risked being indicted. Despite such political forthrightness, even the mild Marianne Moore admired the work. In a note after its publication, Mary Moore, Marianne's mother, included her daughter's praise: "Marianne takes great pride in the achievement you have made in your precious book." Ridge was delighted by *Sun-up*'s reception. She wrote her publisher that "three different people have told me that I am the greatest poet in America." Based on hearsay, these included Philip Moiller, a Yiddish theater producer, Edward Arlington Robinson, by way of her friend and editor of *Outlook*, Otto Theis, and Willa Cather who was said to have told another friend that Ridge "was doing better work than any of the modern Americans."

Ridge must have finished *Sun Up and Other Poems* during the summer of 1920, while staying at the MacDowell Colony, an artist's retreat in New Hampshire. For over a decade, the colony had been hosting composers, painters, and writers in rustic studios scattered throughout its 450 pine-and-birch strewn acres. The play *Our Town* would be written there a few years later, and the opera *Porgy and Bess*. "A disconcerting place for loafers" wrote the *New York Times* in 1922, emphasizing the amazing industry and concentration of the colonists. Ridge received her lunch in a picnic basket left in front of her studio, and enjoyed dinner in the camaraderie of all the other artists. She could have worked in a deck chair on her porch or strolled the grounds with pen and paper. MacDowell was especially welcoming to the artist who is "young but has made little money but who yet has given distinctive promise and shown unplumbed potentialities." All but "young" certainly fit Ridge's career arc at this point. Despite being fed and housed and coddled, however, she was ill during her stay, a situation she would repeat during visits to another artist colony years later. For admission to this one she needed two endorsements or else a personal invitation from Mrs. MacDowell herself. Certainly Edward Arlington Robinson would have written one for her, if Ridge's friend Otto Theis was right about his enthusiasm for her work. Robinson was a great supporter of MacDowell. When he first arrived there, he brought along a fake emergency telegram in case he needed to escape—and then returned every summer for the next

24 years. Ridge knew many other poets from her editorship of *Others* who might have sent a second endorsement.

In 1920 Ridge was featured in two satires of leading American poets, the insiders' index of fame, or at least notoriety. That year Witter Bynner, best known for his translations from the Chinese and a bitchy book about D.H. Lawrence, wrote *Pins for Wings*, under the pseudonym Emmanuel Morgan. William Saphier, Ridge's associate on *Others* and co-organizer for the *Others* Lecture Bureau, provided caricatures. The work of Eliot is described as "The wedding cake/of two tired cultures," cummings: "Much ado/about the alphabet," H.D.: "The Winged Victory/hopping," Wallace Stevens: "The shine of a match/in an empty pipe," and William Butler Yeats: "A pot of mould/at the foot of the rainbow." Ridge's entry is "grapes/on a ragged corsage," that Saphier illustrates with her preferred profile: sharp-nosed, with her hair arranged on her head like a nun's wimple.

Such satire did not alienate the important poets. Witter Bynner was made president of the Poetry Society two years later. He was also a chief instigator of the Spectra Hoax, a group of poets who mocked the literary *isms* popular at the time. As a participant in the hoax, Ridge's friend Marjorie Allen Seiffert wrote as a male. William Carlos Williams, as editor for an issue of *Others*, commended Seiffert for not taking the Spectra movement too seriously—in contrast to women. After the hoax was unmasked by Bynner himself, Seiffert wrote: "I have found my own emotions are not feminine." Shades of Ridge's "Woman and the Creative Will!"

Margaret Widdemer, vice president of the Poetry Society, was responsible for the second satire: *A Tree with a Bird in it: a symposium of contemporary american poets on being shown a pear-tree on which sat a grackle*, published in 1921 under her own name. She dedicated it "with my forgiveness in advance to the poets parodied in this book and the poets not parodied in this book," which implied the importance of being included. Invoking Ridge's poetry that condemns industrialization and machines, Widdemer skewered her for being a confirmed city-dweller, her use of ellipses, the size of her ego, and her reputation as a poet who often wrote about intimacy, a point never discussed in her reviews.

Lola Ridge
(Who apparently did not care for the suburbs.)

Preenings

I preen myself....
I...
Always do...
My ego expanding encompasses...
Everything, naturally....

This bird preens himself...
It is our only likeness....

Ah, God, I want a Ghetto
And a Freud and an alley and some Immigrants
calling names...
God, you know
How awful it is....
Here are trees and birds and clouds
And picturesquely neat children across the way
on the grass
Not doing anything
Improper...
(Poor little fools, I mustn't blame them for that
Perhaps they never
Knew How....)

But oh, God, take me to the nearest trolley line!
This is a country landscape—
I can't stand it!

God, take me away—
There is no Sex here
And no Smell!

Chapter 19

Sunwise Turn and Ridge's *Broom*

Two women—Madge Jenison, a journalist, and Mary Mowbray Clarke, a lecturer on art at Columbia and the author of an art history textbook—started the Sunwise Turn bookstore in 1916. "A Modern Bookshop" emblazoned its storefront like a book title, prescient in how its existence "coincided with the rise, triumph and assimilation of modernism." A signboard painted with the words "The sunwise turn is the lucky one" hung beside the door, referring to Scottish folklore in which "sunwise" is the propitious direction, a turn toward the sun. The two proprietors almost rented the back of Alfred Stieglitz's 291 Gallery a few doors down on West 31st Street and Fifth Avenue, but Stieglitz was about to pursue Georgia O'Keeffe and distracted, and he would instead close the gallery within months. His strategy of hanging photographs with paintings and sculpture in order to link them with the fine arts was similar to their own with regard to books. The bookstore's décor was by Ferrer-trained Arthur Davies, the principal organizer of the Armory Show three years earlier. The store displayed batiks, Peruvian textiles, Rajput miniatures, Greek masks, batik hangings, Hopi bowls, African tiles, embroidery, and reproductions of Gauguin, Cezanne, and Matisse against burnt-orange walls. In their midst stood modernist sculpture and tables of rare books with signed editions, not to mention bookcases crammed with poetry, books on Gurdjieff and handwriting analysis, and advice on interior decoration. "Some of the artists who worked on the[book] designs made them so deliriously lovely that it was difficult to make up one's mind to ever open them," recounts Clarke. The partners quickly discovered that the ancillary material supported the store, not rare editions and esoteric books.

But profit was not their main concern. They took a peculiarly anarchist stance with regard to sales, perhaps influenced by Clarke's husband John. Also instrumental in mounting the Armory Show, he was deemed "Sculptor of Revolt" in a review by Upton Sinclair who wrote that he had never encountered so much anticlericalism "packed into a bit of plaster."

Ferrer Center regulars such as Eugene O'Neill and the art dealer Carl Zigrosser, Ridge's successor as editor of *The Modern School*, frequented the bookshop. In 1918, the bookshop hosted a five-part conference on "libertarian education." Copies of *The Modern School* and other anarchist magazines were shelved alongside first editions of *Ulysses* when it appeared four years later. Eventually the partners created a book club for their typical book buyer: "a recent college graduate just starting a missionary career in China." Clarke boasted that "We read all the books before we sell them," an impressive feat even then. Customers appreciated the bookstore's avant-garde stock and decor, and its fireplace. But the store's anti-capitalist approach did not bode well for its finances. Three years after their founding, they sold half the store to the wealthy Harold Loeb, and relocated in the Yale Club building across from the recently erected Grand Central Station.

Harold Loeb's first cousin, a very young Peggy Guggenheim, received her modernist education at the store as one of its eight unpaid apprentices, going out for "electric light bulbs and tacks dressed in a moleskin coat to her heels and lined with pink chiffon." Her aunts came in to buy books for decorative purposes. Such customers also attended readings such as the one given by Ridge on May 4, 1920 just before she went off to MacDowell, probably sharing drafts she would include in *Sun-up*. The bookstore acted as another fulcrum for Ridge's career, introducing her to possible patrons and a supportive audience. Sunwise Turn perhaps even influenced Ridge's choice of title. Each voyage in Ridge's history turned east toward the sunrise, with all its implied optimism and hope: as a child, she and her mother sailing to Australia, and then further, to New Zealand, and as an adult setting off again with Keith across the Pacific.

Other readers at Sunwise Turn included Kreymborg, Robert Frost, Thornstein Veblen, Lytton Strachey, and Amy Lowell. The bookstore put on an early performance of Kreymborg's play *Lima Beans* in 1916 before he cast Williams and Millay in the main parts. After both the self-proclaimed founder of cubism Albert Gleizes and Stieglitz himself suggested to Kreymborg that Europe might be more interested in his theatrical experiments, Kreymborg was not ill-disposed when Loeb asked him if he'd like to sail off to Rome to launch a magazine he had started calling *Broom*. After all, *Others* had folded only two years earlier.

Hemingway modeled the "offensive cad" and "Jewish bounder" Robert Cohn in *The Sun Also Rises* after Harold Loeb. Loeb's friend Malcolm Cowley drew a less caustic portrait in his sketch "Young Man with Spectacles" that Loeb liked. In the story he's

> a squat young man of thirty-four [who dreams of]...A broad leisurely America without machines and Methodism; Sunday baseball in Pittsburgh (or better, Sunday cricket;) open urinals and racetrack gambling; the works of Freud and Boccaccio and D. H. Lawrence sold at newsstands openly.

Loeb went to Princeton, then laid concrete for the Canadian railroad before moving to New York post-war, falling in with the artists and writers congregating at The Brocken, the Clarke home in Rockland County, and eventually buying into the bookshop. He felt America was hounded on every side by Puritanism and that its art was underdeveloped. Using the proceeds of the share of his sale of the bookshop back to Clarke, some $9,000, he launched *Broom*. Like a number of other ex-pat magazines published abroad, he envisioned the magazine showcasing European work for Americans and introducing contemporary American literature to Europeans. As Michael North emphasizes in his address "Transatlantic Transfer," Loeb's impulse sounded a lot like another Henry James sailing off for England, hardly an avant-garde move. Loeb justified having his offices abroad by claiming that it would be cheaper to publish a magazine there as lavish as the one he envisioned. Leaving with Kreymborg for Rome in 1921 also allowed Loeb to escape "my mother's family and its industrial achievements"—the Guggenheims—and coincided with his separation from his wife, Marjorie Content. Marjorie would not starve, as she too came from one of the wealthiest families in New York. Her brother, New York Assistant District Attorney Harold Content, helped deport Emma Goldman to Russia and was the attorney assigned to prosecute Margaret Sanger. Of a different political persuasion, Marjorie stayed in New York and worked alongside the bookstore's radical women owners.

Publishing from Rome turned out to be more difficult than Loeb had anticipated, both financially and logistically. While preparing the third issue for January 1922, Loeb and Kreymborg argued over financial and editing issues, and Loeb had to contradict suppositions that Kreymborg was founder. Loeb then dismissed Kreymborg, bought him out of his share in the magazine, and announced Kreymborg's resignation due to "ill health" in the February issue. Loeb's brother and his wife Marjorie suggested Ridge as the American editor to replace an incompetent Nathaniel Shaw, but really it was Kreymborg she would replace in terms of contacts and experience. Shaw generously gave her an excellent recommendation: "a very self-reliant young woman."

She had been living in Montreal for the last eight months—in "this ghastly country"—where her husband was looking for work as a draftsman. Funded to turn her 1919 speech, "Woman and the Creative Will" into a book, she was suffering from a "Russian paralysis of the will that [is] always with me [and] accompanies mental depression," although she boasted that she had written two poems more than 400 lines in length. A number of her friends went off to Montreal occasionally to work: Evelyn Scott, Konrad Bercovici, Horace Traubel. In her exile, Ridge managed to stay in contact with Kreymborg. A few months after she arrived, she published "Hospital Nights" in *Broom*'s first issue. Elsewhere she hadn't been doing too badly either. "I sold $60 of poems the last ten days," she boasted to Mitchell Dawson, probably to *Poetry*.

Dawson was still trying to get out another magazine. "Let me know when you are preparing for the first number and if you want anything of mine," Ridge writes. By 1921 he had managed to put together two issues of a magazine he called *Musterbook*, the first issue with illustrations from the renowned German artist George Grosz, and the second with poems by Yvor Winters called "The Magpie's Shadow." "I like *Musterbook*, some of Winters 8," writes Ridge, "single lines such as of "Spring: I walk out the world door," but some fearfully trite: "The tented autumn gone." Dawson asked Williams, his ex-partner, for enough work to fill another issue, but by then Williams was scheming to publish his own magazine, *Contact*.

When Loeb asked Ridge to be his American editor at the beginning of February 1922, it was for a salary of $100 a month—$1,233.06 in 2014 dollars—an amount she often had to forgo, given the difficulties of the magazine. But she was very happy to be involved, and to leave Montreal. "All this has come about so suddenly...I'm full of enthusiasm for BROOM." After detailing a direct mail campaign, and several other publicity ideas, she pledged her loyalty: "If after a reasonable try out we find I'm doing no good—well I'll get from under without waiting to be pushed, but I will not ever leave you in the lurch." She went to work at *Broom*'s New York offices, which operated out of Marjorie Loeb's basement storeroom at 3 East 9th Street, right off Fifth Avenue.

With Ridge onboard, *Broom* quickly became one of the "most widely circulated privately owned literary magazines of its time." But before Ridge would agree to the position, she listed three conditions under which she would take the job:

> My name on BROOM as American editor.
> Full authority and power of veto on this side.
> All American MS. drawings etc. to come to this office.

She also wanted to "separate what I consider very good from the doubtful and send sorted sheaves of both," conditions which Loeb found "quite acceptable" but which sounded like a diminution of her second condition. Just after she took the job in February 1922, Shaw wrote Loeb to caution him: "Miss Ridge is extremely enthusiastic. She is getting the magazine talked about much more than I would ever have been able to do..." He adds : "There are matters in which she will appear headstrong. Be a good fellow and meet her half way."

From the very beginning, she plumped for an American number, to which Loeb responded: "I sympathize with the project of an all-American number, but let us wait a while and see what comes in." He also conceded veto power—"Veto power is willingly conceded"—then reversed his stand in the same letter: "I shall value your obtaining of material but feel I must reserve full veto power." He justified his waffling and offered conciliation: "You will run into difficulties as a refusal of a solicited manuscript is pregnant with trouble....I will of course give every consideration to your judgement that I can."

The magazine by then had published an impressive number of European writers and other "wide-ranging and often discordant contributions." But Ridge had her own ideas.

> I think the French influence on the whole bad for American art—bad that is in the sense that we pay too much for what ever surface elegance we acquire. Anderson's work or better comparison Sandburg's of enormously greater importance to art than Pound's for instance. Spiritually America makes me think of the dawn of

creation—all the essentials are there—great sprawling oceans and uninhabited prairies waiting for the faintly stirring life that must take form and come up out of those deeps and none other...I should love to see *Broom* be—the early visible symbol of this new birth. The French an influence—and the fact that they lead the world's fashion in (mental or bodily) clothes is bad for this—what real growth shall we foster if we squeeze the feet of this giant child into a French shoe?

But first she had to discourage Loeb from quitting. "For heaven's sake don't talk of quitting!...we should be able to make BROOM self-supporting." Discovering that *Broom* had only $95 in the bank.

Last night had a two [hour] talk with your mother who was most kind and sympathetic. She has promised five thousand dollars that I asked for this. The money will be available in fall. I am going to ask others. Don't ever think of quitting. *Broom* will be safe.

Loeb was astonished.

Your influence on my mother has been admirable; you must be a fire of enthusiasm to carry away such a confirmed believer in money as the standard of success. I am deeply grateful for the five thousand [and] hope you will be equally successful elsewhere.

Ridge responded by asserting her editorial opinion of the forthcoming machine-oriented issue:

The machine age of America should by all means be represented but *interpreted not reported*. The artist has not yet arisen who has even sincerely tried to do it...Of course I agree with you [that] it 'takes an artist to reproduce a locomotive and preserve the emotion' but there is only a faint chance that you can get that artist by calling for him.

Ridge was, in Loeb's eyes, "one of the moaners whom machines were tearing apart," and not an enthusiast for the industrialized world. As Loeb put it: "To her, capitalism was corrosive, its products corrupt. I felt that capitalism was impersonal, its products magnificent." But she wasn't against the depiction of the machine, if depicted critically. What she opposed was the attitude promulgated by Matthew Josephson who echoed Loeb in the June *Broom*: "The machine is our magnificent slave, our fraternal genius." Edmund Wilson's essay in *Vanity Fair* astutely criticized Josephson's attitude and its Dadaist frame:

> The buildings are flattening us out; the machines are tearing us to pieces...The electric signs in Times Square make the Dadaists look timid; it is the masterpiece of Dadaism, produced naturally by our race, and without premeditation.

Ridge was right that *Broom*'s essays had been omitting the effects of such sudden and worldwide change. Even Matthew Josephson in his memoir *Life Among the Surrealists* eventually admitted that "Critics assailed us [justly, I now perceive] for unconsidered and over-optimistic pronouncements on the culture of the Machine Age, which ignored its human costs."

Ridge had ideas about the artists who might best be able to depict the issue:

> I think Stieglitz could do it—if he could form emotional contact with the machine...I shall go and see him and see if he will be interested. But perhaps you have already communicated with Paul Strand?

She had already communicated with Strand herself, and he was willing. Trained by Lewis Hine, the photographer who took such striking pictures of the ghetto at the turn of the century, Paul Strand's abstract photographs were the perfect choice to interpret the machine aesthetically. With regard to Stieglitz, Loeb discouraged her from approaching him, but still he hoped she might persuade him to contribute. "We seem nearly in total agreement—especially with regard to Stieglitz' work," writes Loeb. She would not be dissuaded and pursued Stieglitz on her own. She reported that he was "quite indifferent to *Broom* when I first went in. Said the February number was dead and that the others only here and there made signs of life—life—life, that was his insistent cry." She followed up with a note to Stieglitz. "I know that Harold would be as proud as I to this [possibly 'means'] of introducing your work to Europe." Stieglitz refused to be featured in the machine issue, but did want to be included in her American number. Eventually she secured the reproduction rights of both Stieglitz's and Strand's work for *Broom*.

"It will be a big thing to reproduce photographs of Stieglitz," writes Loeb. "Europe is exceedingly anxious to see them and also I think he is probably the most important American Artist."

By May she had been so successful at stabilizing the magazine that Loeb was asking her to send him money in Rome. He wanted to forgo soliciting ads altogether and live on his mother's gift. While he neglected to do anything much on publicity in Europe, she had mimeographed 10,000 campaign letters for the magazine's support in America. In the letter she touts the Pirandello play, *Six Characters in Search of an Author*, that they were running serially, and work by Cocteau and Wallace Stevens whose publication she had overseen. The subscription rate was offered at the cost of an ordinary monthly, although the magazine was published in color and printed on handmade paper and weighed a full pound. She would send a sample copy if an interested party mailed her ten cents in stamps. She also compiled a mailing list and handed fliers out on street corners. Subscriptions flooded in from Japan, Hawaii, Philippines, Australia, India, and China. She asked Mitchell Dawson to take *Broom* circulars around Chicago to solicit advertising, since the anthologist-to-be Oscar Williams had quit. She also wanted Dawson to provide her with the names and addresses of modern art shops in Chicago that might be willing to carry *Broom*, and for him to inform her of anybody who needed a subscription at a discount (and he would get commission of a dollar). "Glad to do anything I can for *Musterbook* on this side if you will let me know," she writes. Soon he was helping her sell subscriptions. "Bless your heart for sympathy... delighted to send subscription blanks," she writes, and adds: "Yes please send me photographs of your brother's work. We may be able to use some of them in *Broom*." They did not run. Neither did Dawson's poems. After Dawson married in 1921 and had his first child in 1925, the intensity of his relationship with poetry and Ridge waned.

Ridge wrote Williams in April to "send something good." Among other things, he sent "Red Eric," the first chapter from *In The American Grain* of the six that were to appear in *Broom*, the single most significant American work published in the magazine, according to critic Michael North. Loeb immediately accepted two of Williams's poems that Ridge had put forward, and a poem each by Louise Bogan and Elinor Wylie. Although these were not new authors, Ridge was very clear about her intentions: "What I'd like is to have *Broom* discover, lead not follow." Loeb admitted that "without New York...[*Broom*] is only fulfilling a fraction of its function..." Although

Ridge had set the magazine back on its feet, Loeb was uneasy, suspecting that Ridge's interest was primarily editorial. The preferred female editor archetype was Maria Jolas, who supported *Transition* with her inheritance, doing the translation and the administration while her husband Eugene took most of the credit. Ridge, on her part, wished that she "could let up a little on the financial end as its [sic] not at all the one I'm interested in." By September she reiterated she was not so enamored of running bad work by "good" authors, she wanted to publish "the great unknowns who will be acknowledged ten years or five hence...."

Chapter 20

Broom's Parties
and the Making of an
American Idiom

The knowns and the unknowns flocked to Ridge's new round of parties. These events were so influential that even Pound noted their impact as late as 1928, while listing new publicity strategies for Louis Zukovsky. Cummings apologized profusely for missing one of her parties, enclosed six poems, and wrote:

> I know you know the ropes which I do not and do not pretend to know, but I don't know whether or no[t] you have the time to introduce these sensual integers of mine to people who would like to publish them—supposing that any such exist in These United States—nor Am I sure, perfectly, that you have what is vulgarly called "the inclination"! But if you haven't, I shan't be the least offended.

In view of the importance of her gatherings, she added one night a month in addition to her Thursday afternoons. American modernism was the topic, but also the importance of multiple aesthetics, and how to make a mix of genres and sensibilities interesting. Gone or deported were most of the anarchists that had harangued and declaimed at earlier festivities. The new mix of partygoers often came in evening dress, despite the place being unheated and bare to the point of bleakness. Between the wars, the atmosphere was serious yet buoyant, and Prohibition made parties necessary— and raucous. Harold Loeb sounded grateful:

> Lola gave a party and nearly everyone in the city interested in the magazine came in late or early. The two rooms in the basement

were jammed with writers, painters, musicians, dilettanti and old copies of the magazine. Joseph Stella turned up, as well as Maxwell Bodenheim, whose work, up to till then, had not been accepted. I did not know many of the faces. Eyes shining above her scimitar nose, Kay Boyle helped Lola make the guests welcome.

Nineteen-year-old Boyle had replaced Ridge's friend, the poet Laura Benét, as Ridge's third assistant. Kay Boyle (1902-1992) would become a noted short-story writer, novelist, and European correspondent for the *New Yorker*. "I naively took some of my poems to the *Broom* office, found Lola Ridge alone there trying to handle all the work, and we loved each other instantly," Boyle recalled. Ridge wrote at once to Loeb to give her a salary of $18 a week. Boyle claimed Ridge as a mother figure—a very positive association, since Boyle was close to her mother: "I had the more satisfactory of childhoods because Mother, small, delicate-boned, witty, and articulate, turned out to be exactly my age." Although uneducated, her mother managed to give Boyle a taste for the avant-garde and an appreciation for the proletariat. But "it was Lola who spoke the vocabulary I wanted to hear," writes Boyle. Ridge "expressed a fiery awareness of social injustice" in "a woman's savage voice." Ridge gave her money for her first abortion, and according to Boyle's biographer, the two of them danced together at the parties, with Boyle as the lead. Boyle's first book, a volume of poetry, reflected Ridge's political concerns and was structured in long Whitmanic lines. Ridge would publish a poem of Boyle's in *Broom*. "She is always for me one of the rarest and most beautiful persons alive," writes Boyle. "I cherished and protected her as tenderly if she were a small, bright flame I held cupped in my hand." An excellent typist, Boyle lasted three months as an assistant, long enough for Ridge to encourage Evelyn Scott and Marianne Moore to read her work. "I sometimes feel that I am too pleasant to be great," Boyle gushed later in a letter to Ridge. But she would be pleasant to Ridge's guests, which included John Dos Passos, Marianne Moore, Elinor Wylie, Jean Toomer, Waldo Frank, Babette Deutsch, Edward Arlington Robinson, Bryher, H.D., William Carlos Williams, and Glenway Wescott. After selling *Brooms* in the lobby of a theater—"some forty-eight dollars' worth during a Saturday matinee and evening showing"—Boyle would cut the cake that Ridge had scraped up the money to buy, wash all the cups and glasses in the apartment, spread a tablecloth, all the while asking Ridge who was coming and why, and would she introduce her?

It was at one of Ridge's parties in 1922 that Jean Toomer caught his first glimpse of Waldo Frank (1889-1967), an important mentor, as "a light in that room of smoke and many faces and literary talk." Frank, a slightly older Jewish pacifist and one of the associate editors of *Seven Arts*, had just published *Our America*, which saw the country's culture as "an untracked wilderness but dimly blazed by the heroic ax of Whitman." Instead of the cynicism of disengagement espoused by the "lost generation," Frank's book urged cultural and social involvement. *Our America* was well received and went through three editions in six months. During an inspirational trip to the South with Toomer, Frank passed for black while Toomer maintained his "racial composition" was of no concern to anyone but himself. Toomer's *Cane*, a modernist classic, and Frank's *Holiday*, a white man's account of a Southern lynching, were published a year later, in 1922. They had hoped to have their books published together, but only managed to publish on the same day. Both were written in a fragmented modernist style, and Toomer wrote the dialogue for *Holiday*. Toomer was also good friends with Hart Crane, and the three of them would later explore Gurdjieff's teachings together, whose influence some critics say ruined their writing.

When Frank suggested that Toomer try submitting work to *Broom*, he acknowledged Ridge's influence on him by writing: "I do not know it; I do know the calibre of Lola Ridge." The relationship between Frank and Toomer suffered after Toomer began an affair with Frank's wife soon after they were introduced, and Toomer resented being identified as black in Frank's introduction to *Cane*. After a romance with Georgia O'Keeffe in the 1930s, Toomer married the photographer Marjorie Content, O'Keeffe's friend and Harold Loeb's estranged wife, whose basement, being the *Broom* office, was the location for many of Ridge's parties. Ridge tried to introduce Toomer to the "madonna-faced" Content at a party in 1920, but since she was just then separated and not yet divorced from Loeb, she stayed upstairs.

Marianne Moore continued to be a faithful partygoer. "Perhaps even you do not know how much you have given to me in your gentle solicitude," she writes Ridge in 1927, long after the parties were over. They made sure they kept up with each other's work. Ridge had already published twice in *The Dial* before Moore took over as editor, one a labor poem on the page facing Thorstein Veblen's "Industry and The Captains of Industry." Moore accepted a total of three of Ridge's poems as editor. Her suggestion for a change in one of them was quite solicitous: "But should you rather not, I shall accept your decision understandingly and bear the disappointment with what patience I can summon." (Ridge made the change.) Moore's rejection of Ridge's poem about Adelaide Crapsey was equally delicate: "A diminution of intensity at certain points which impairs the symmetry?" After the publication of Ridge's third book in 1927, she writes: "Be sure your own book is sent to the *Dial*." Ridge published Moore's poetry and reviews in both *Others* and *Broom* and recommended her work to the editors of the *New Republic*. Moore (and sometimes her mother) even typed up Ridge's manuscripts. As critic William Drake remarked on Moore's generosity, "Imagine Frost typing up a long poem of Stevens."

A Paris Review interview of Moore reveals her enthusiasm for Ridge's frequent guest Hart Crane. "You remember *Broom*?" she asks,

> Toward the beginning of that magazine, in 1921, Lola Ridge was very hospitable, and she invited me to a party—previous to my work on the Dial—Kay Boyle and her husband, a French soldier, and Hart Crane, Elinor Wylie and some others. I took a great liking to Hart Crane. We talked about French bindings, and he was diffident and modest and seemed to have so much intuition, such a feeling for things, for books—really a bibliophile—that I took a special interest in him.

Crane knew just how to entrance Moore. But when the interviewer mentioned that Crane complained of her changing a title of one of his poems and of making what he considered extreme revisions, she replied: "He was in dire need of funds," then she equivocated: "Really I am not used to having people in that bemused state."

A childhood friend of Marianne Moore's was the poet Laura Benét (1884-1979), an early assistant of Ridge at *Broom* and a long time friend of both. Laura and her brother William Rose Benét (1886-1950), a classmate of Moore's brother at Yale, were frequent guests. Laura became assistant editor for book reviews at the *New York Evening Post* and the *New York Evening Sun*, and substitute review editor for the *New York Times* in the late 20s and early 30s. Her first book of poetry, *Fair Bred*, had just come out in February 1921. Bill Benét, as he was known, cofounded the *Saturday Review of Literature* in 1924 and won the Pulitzer Prize in poetry in 1942. Their brother, Stephen Vincent Benét, winner of two Pulitzer Prizes, was also a friend, and reviewed Ridge's fourth book, *Red Flag*, when he was the most widely read poet in the country.

The poet Elinor Wylie (1885-1928) would soon appear at Ridge's parties as Bill Benét's wife. She both wrote and spoke with "a lovely, amused formality," according to critic Carl Van Doren, but she never pleased her sister-in-law Laura. Wylie wore slinky silver dresses with a chain-link weave, and Louis Untermeyer wrote admiringly of Wylie's "imperious brows; the high cheekbones...the long smooth column of the throat." "Her likeness could appear without identification in magazines like the *New Yorker*, one of many where her work appeared; readers were expected to recognize the "queen of poets." She wrote highly detailed, short formal poetry. Edna St. Vincent Millay, who wrote her own share of formal poetry, reviewed only one book in her life, Wylie's first, and said it was an important one. Wylie published three more books of poetry and four highly ornate novels between 1921-1928. When her first novel was published in 1923, Van Doren organized a torchlight parade in New York to celebrate its publication. He also claimed that her obsession with Shelley was so great that "he stood between her and living men." Indeed, Sara Teasdale teased Wylie with lines illustrating the rivalry:

> Elinor Wylie, Elinor Wylie
> What did I hear you say?
> I wish it were Shelley
> astride my belly
> instead of poor Mr. Benét.

Wylie and Benét spent four summers at MacDowell and Wylie is said to still haunt it. Extremely sensitive to the artist rivalries, she was not always comfortable at the artist colony:

> Did you see how they hate me, how they all hate me? They are all trying to down me, to injure me, to keep me from working. But I won't be downed! I have a typewriter and a better brain than any of them, and they won't succeed. I'll beat them all yet! Did you see how they asked me to recite so they could laugh at me? Did you see how they left the door open on purpose so that the mosquitoes would get in and bite me tomorrow when I'm trying to write? The mosquitoes—I tell you they will stop at nothing—

Wylie may have influenced Ridge's later turn to mysticism. She was intensely interested in witchcraft because she had a distant relative who was convicted as a witch in 17th-century Massachusetts. After Wylie died of a stroke at age 43, Ridge had a vision of the "beautiful and great poet Elinor." She "stood with crimson roses in her hands—in my high room in Thirteenth Street—three days after she died. Thank you, Lovely."

Among the visual artists at Ridge's parties was Gaston Lachaise, termed "the greatest American sculptor of his time," whose most compelling works commemorated his wife's body. "You are the Goddess I am seeking to express in all things," he said of her. He was the only artist among them who didn't consider also consider himself a poet.

Beat poet Allen Ginsberg's father, Louis Ginsberg, also attended the Ridge parties. A socialist, he published traditional poetry and his first wife—and Allen's mother—was a radical Communist and nudist.

When Ridge was ill in September 1925, the poet Babette Deutsch substituted for her as hostess at a party where Vladimir Mayakovsky declaimed in Russian. Deutsch wrote Ridge that she liked how Mayakovsky "thundered out his tremendous strophes." Williams remembered the Russian's feet on the coffee table. Mayakovsky started writing futurist poems in 1912, and published his most famous book, *Cloud in Trousers*, in 1915. A handsome man, Mayakovsky was already a silent film star by 1918. In 1930, after having satirized Stalin in two plays, he died a suspicious suicide. Williams particularly appreciated his use of the demotic as the poems were translated at the party and stole from him the idea of long-fragmented lines.

Deutsch was the perfect choice to host the event. *Banners*, her first book of poetry, celebrated the Russian Revolution with precise imagist detail. In "Petrograd," she writes: "Hunger and empty death and puny war:/The red hour loomed. The lunging city knew." Ridge would have appreciated Deutsch's poetry in that first book—and her first novel, *A Brittle Heaven*, which critically viewed the life of a writer, wife, and mother. Deutsch praised both *The Ghetto and Other Poems* and Ridge's third book, *Firehead*, in major reviews.

The drunken, bisexual, pretty party-boy Robert McAlmon, a self-described Michelangelo, had a reputation for bitchiness that moved F. Scott Fitzgerald to remark: "God will forgive everybody—even Robert McAlmon." Hemingway called McAlmon "that disappointed half-assed fairy English jew ass-licking stage husband," and Joyce, offended because McAlmon depicted him as more of a drinker than a writer in his memoir,

Being Geniuses Together, dismissed his work as "the office boy's revenge." McAlmon published Fitzgerald, Hemingway, and Joyce as well as Gertrude Stein's huge *Making of Americans* in his *Contact Editions*. The cost of the last ruined him.

Born the youngest of ten children in Kansas, McAlmon wandered to California as an itinerant farmhand and cowpuncher. In 1920 he dropped out of USC after publishing six poems in *Poetry*, and traveled to Chicago to consort with the poet Emmanuel Carnevali, who was unfortunately already in the insane asylum. Marsden Hartley discovered McAlmon on a garbage scow on the East River a few months later, where he was living on wages he earned from modeling. Hartley tried to seduce him but ended up kissing his hand. Or so the story went. McAlmon fell for the poet H.D. but married her friend, the 26-year-old Bryher, perhaps to play a part in a ménage à trois. Bryher's father was one of the wealthiest men in the world, another attraction. He wrote a firsthand account of the gay subculture in *Germany in Distinguished Air: Grim Fairy Tales*, and *The Scarlet Pansy*, a gay classic. Kay Boyle inserted her own autobiography into McAlmon's memoir, *Being Geniuses Together*, and wrote that she had slept with McAlmon who'd slept with Lord Alfred who'd slept with Oscar Wilde. He was primarily the reason Mitchell Dawson had to publish his own magazine and not the one Williams was planning to found to replace *Others*. In all, McAlmon co-published five issues of *Contact* with Williams, whom he'd met at Ridge's party that night he arrived with Hartley.

The party must have been in the early summer of 1920, after *Others*, but before *Broom*, when Marsden Hartley was still around. He read "On the Hills of Caledonia," and Marianne Moore read "Those Various Scalpels," a taunt to Mina Loy. Perhaps Ridge read a poem as well. According to Williams's biography, McAlmon "distrusted people like Ridge for their liberal championing of the oppressed masses without themselves ever having experienced firsthand the lives of the poor." Ridge obviously had not made public her humble beginnings in New Zealand, her dire financial straits as an immigrant in America, or her own experience as an artist's model, nor was he familiar with her views on bisexuality. His novel *Post-Adolescence* satirizing her party was published in 1923, just a few years after he made his important connection with Williams. It is unusually bitter and angry toward women, especially those of power.

The book opens with a woman accidentally spitting in the narrator's face. He thinks "O well, have to take her as she was—too bad there wasn't somebody else to go out with nights to dance..." Later, he is not "unwilling to kiss her." By page 24, one of the female characters suggests: "We'll have to form a union of women to show the men up, and make ourselves exhibits A and B of horrible examples." Three pages later, even the coffee tastes like vinegar. The narrator notes on page 31 that most of the faces on the subway are Semitic, and there's a dead horse on a curb when he emerges.

"Dora"—Ridge—has invited him to a party by page 50. "She sent me a note saying she was having a number of people at her studio in honour of— think who—that lady poetess Vere St. Vitus—the jumpy cooey little thing..." he tells his friend Jimmy—William Carlos Williams. Vere St. Vitus must be Edna St. Vincent Millay, whom the narrator later seduces. "But lordy," the narrator exclaims, "if Nora [sic] gets up and starts to evangelize any of that verse of hers! Ouch!." He goes on: "She begins swaying and spouting with a super trance look in her eyes at the perspiring moon or the hot belly of that illegitimate child of industrialization, the city..."

Nevertheless, he and his friend arrive at Dora's address and start up three flights of stairs to a blue door. Sometimes Ridge moved her parties out of *Broom*'s headquarters to her own apartment at 793 Broadway, where revelers had to climb several flights up to a blue door at the top. "He saw that Dora's glance evaded his," writes McAlmon, "and helped her in the evasion." He continues: "Darned little she and he had to say to each other, poor old thing, pretending to be revolutionary and flaming with passion when a few good meals would change all of that perhaps, except that she had still been pathetic." Then another partygoer says: "We fête all these English novelists and poets...but never do we fête our own worker" which reflected Ridge's interest in a truly American literature. Oddly enough, after McAlmon founded *Contact* with Williams, that was his interest too. He wanted to be "writing about one's own place in one's own idiom straightforwardly, without obeisance to European models." Later McAlmon admits in the novel that

> the evening was not actively painful however until Reginald Crackeye read an extract from his play "The Mummy"...and became dramatic about it [,] much worked up apparently over his inability to keep his long hair out of his eyes...'Are these my eyes looking at me in the mirror. Am I then that matter of a man?'...Torture me not thus... Everyone applauded the reading, enthusiastic at all costs...Verses were read by several ladies, and by one young man whose verses were, according to Dora, "'very sensitive.'"

Could that last reader have been Hart Crane?

"God...isn't this modern poetry movement awful?" asks the narrator. "Lemon water, anguish, sand and sweat." Another character says "I'd like to take art and drown it in the river." The narrator decides that "Jimmy [Williams] needed to be rescued from a woman [Ridge?] who was sure that he'd be a greater poet if he would put more social content into his work." Williams was no longer the faun-eared young man as described by Matthew Josephson and had a "spinsterly aversion" to Marianne Moore, thought H.D. "an utterly narrow-minded she-bard," and called Harriet Monroe a "she-ass." Under McAlmon's pen, his equivocal evaluation of Ridge is: "I used to think she had a sense of what not to do once...I used to like Dora, and thought I liked some of her things. What's there to say anyway?" He and the narrator escape from the party, walking down the street while continuing to trash the evening. They order at a cafe and the narrator makes the mistake of quoting his own poetry: "What does one do? What does one do?" and doesn't pay for his coffee, betraying the shallowness of his own social conscience by remarking: "It's only ten cents, they can stand it."

By the 17th chapter, the narrator has slept with the Millay character, only McAlmon skips the sex, she's making him breakfast the morning after, while "he wondered why more moments of tenderness such as they'd felt for each other in intercourse did not occur in life."

An autographed copy of McAlmon's self-published 1929 book, *North America: Continent of Conjecture*, is part of Ridge's library housed at Bryn Mawr. It is inscribed "To Lola Ridge with fond memories of some of her good and often gaga gatherings." The poem inside—"unfinished"—satirizes every modernist topic: Wall Street, race riots, Native Americans, advertising on the subway, the ghetto, the mechanized city, and the sex-obsessed.

Machine Dance Blues

O O O the lovely gushing
of oiled machines rushing.
Love, love, love, lovely machinery.
Dream pistons slushing,
super-lubricated pushing,
machine's sex dream.

Perhaps Ridge hadn't read his novel *Post-Adolescence*, or perhaps she managed to admire his talent despite his attitude. Or did she pity him and his envy of women and his situation with Bryher? Perhaps she agreed with Marianne Moore, who "questioned both the stability of his sentences and his poor choice of vocabulary." He'd sent one of the first books of the run to Ridge—it is the fifth copy out of only 305 copies. She had been writing reviews. Perhaps he valued her opinion.

Chapter 21

Broom and Its Demise

Broom was gorgeous. Oversize, 11 by 13 inches, it came printed on handmade paper with its artwork tipped in. "I hoped that the glamor of *Broom*'s format would carry us over till our ideas crystallized," writes Loeb. On the back cover, a sailor danced with a broom over a quote from Melville that suggests (perhaps tongue-in-cheek like Melville) that editors are slaves to their readers.

> What of it, if some old hunks of a sea-captain orders me to get a broom and sweep down the decks? What does that indignity amount to, weighed, I mean, in the scales of the New Testament? Do you think the archangel Gabriel thinks anything the less of me, because I promptly and respectfully obey that old hunks in that particular instance? Who ain't a slave?

In June 1922, the month Ridge's name first appears on the masthead, *Broom*'s cover by the Hungarian stage designer Ladislas Medgyes (misspelled in the credits), was strikingly cubist/futurist. Among the issue's offerings were the first half of Nobel Prize-winner Pirandello's *Six Characters in Search of An Author*, and an essay by Cocteau about a bust made by Lipchitz: "The critics have never been able to remove a hair from my head, but Lipchitz has decapitated me," writes Cocteau. Wallace Stevens's poetry began the magazine with "Hymn from a Watermelon Pavilion," and a second poem, "Stars at Tallapoosa," appeared later in the issue. Ridge's poem "Waste"—later renamed "Debris"—was printed after Gertrude Stein's serialized "If You Had Three Husbands." The essay "Made in America" by Matthew Josephson also appeared. Then an editor of a rival magazine *Secession*, Josephson fancied himself an American Dadaist but eventually wrote mostly biographies and a book of economic history. His essay in the June issue satirized "Foreign Exchange," an article Loeb had written for the previous issue. In Josephson's piece, the editor of a "pretentious magazine" discovers that America is "all the rage" in Europe. Although the argument about money and art is confused, with cheeky Josephson both identifying with it and mocking its contradictions, Michael North calls it "an elaborately odd job application," and Josephson's name eventually appeared on the masthead as associate editor.

In July, Ridge writes Loeb: "I am further hindered from getting the best work in either art, poetry or prose, because the bigger artists refuse to have their work accepted by me and returned—after a delay of weeks— from Europe by you." Loeb had rejected most of what she had put forward, and still complained that he had no American material. But he wanted her support: "If you are still a comrade I shall be happy." Loeb asked her to find a publisher for a manuscript by her old nemesis, John Rodker, the critic who had made fun of her work in *Others*, and ended the letter with: "One cannot express gratitude for assistance such as yours, one can only be thankful that you exist."

The first feature of the July issue was a poem by e.e. cummings that faced a Picasso drawing. Another three e. e. cummings poems appeared later. There were more drawings by Picasso and one by Modigliani. Elinor Wylie's poem preceded Evelyn Scott's. Matthew Josephson translated several poems by Paul Eluard, and his article "After and Beyond Dada" also ran. Pirandello's play was continued. Blaise Cendrars gave a negative review of the movie "The Cabinet of Doctor Caligari," and there were more new ads from art galleries in New York. The cover was by Léger.

The Bookman Anthology of Verse for 1922 noted that "With her wiry energy and her frail determination...[Lola Ridge] has now settled as head of the American offices of "Broom." But Loeb's relationship with Lola Ridge deteriorated steadily. He criticized Ridge's stubbornness: "anyone who failed to agree with her felt that she pitied his inability to see or feel the obvious." He argued that "*Broom* is no longer a forum...It is becoming an organ with a strongly held point of view...But because of it I must cling to veto power. I do hope you can follow me far enough to continue with the glorious energy and enthusiasm with which you have revived *Broom*." Ridge replied:

> In regard to the American number; you say in your letter of May 1st, "I have every sympathy with the project!" And then, "can you get together such a number efficiently even though the material is subject to veto on this side?" My answer is: "*I can not.*

He did not respond.

A few weeks later, they tangled over an article on "American Esthetics" by Evelyn Scott. "I like [her] poetry...but I dislike intensely her criticisms. They seem to me hollow, erudite obscurity." He promptly lost her manuscript. Scott, for her part, admonished Ridge: "for GODS SAKE don't get onto [sic] any arguments with Harold Loeb re the Scott family." Three years later, Scott remembered Ridge's *Broom* days:

> I could just see you at the kitchen table laden with everything you ought not to eat dispensing a lunch that had, besides some flavors commonly recognized as approved, a psychic seasoning which made it the most delicious you ever ate. There would be a sofa with a few hundred of rejected or approved mss and something by an unknown author that you wanted to show me but had maybe mislaid in the coal bin, and there would be a dressing table sink and a chiffonier on which hairpins intermingled with the ingredients for salad, etc. etc. and Davy would come in with every determination to resist affection and couldn't quite and I would have that sadistic masochistic attraction to his hair which I always want to pull because it is most exceptionally lovely, and we would have a long, long talk...then the world, if it would listen, would know just exactly all about modern art and people in general.

The cover of the August issue was by the Polish cubist Louis Macoussis who later illustrated Apollonaire's *Alcools*. The work of his wife, the painter Alice Halicke, who was collected by Gertrude Stein, was also featured in a later issue of *Broom*. Reproductions of their work can be found in Ridge's papers. Max Weber, whom Ridge knew from the Ferrer Center, provided several woodcuts, Yvor Winters contributed a poem from Marianne Moore, there was more Pirandello, the Williams poem "Hula-Hula," many translations from the Russian, German, and French, a big announcement of the works of George Moore by Boni and Liveright, and an ad for a Robert Henri monograph on Nietzsche, most probably solicited by Ridge since she knew him from her Ferrer days. The full-page ad at the end provides an interesting effort in cross promotion:

The *Smart Set* readers of *Broom* will find it a natural complement and the two magazines together will furnish an intellectual diet that contains the proper proportions of proteins, vitamins, and other properties essential to perfect intellectual and spiritual nourishment.

August was the month that Ridge suggested Loeb contact his mother. "Why don't you write your mother, Harold? She is anxious about you." The promised $5,000 was scheduled to arrive in the fall. Ridge reported that she was now hoping to interest the wealthy widow of poet and playwright Vaughn Moody in funding the magazine, who was hosting Ridge in her Massachusetts home. Moody, whose husband had written anti-war poems about the Spanish American War, invited many writers for visits, including Robert Frost. Ridge told Loeb that she proposed that Moody give her the names of a hundred wealthy patrons who also had an interest in modern art who might contribute $100 yearly. In the same letter to Loeb, Ridge captures the excitement around the magazine by describing the *Broom* office activity, with the radical millionaire philanthropist Charles Garland pitching in:

> Vachel Lindsay also here the other day, [Gorham] Munson, Ridgley Torrence, Bill Williams, [Maxwell] Bodenhiem [sic], Benéts, Stephen and Bill, Marie Garland—mother of too famous Charles (whom I'm asking for a fund) Evelyn Scott, Waldo. The strangely unlike drift in and out. If there is anything doing, they sit around Davy's wonderful table—brought for me from his old studio on 14th—and lick stamps, close or address envelopes—sometimes—but how they hate this!... Charles Garland wrapped up and tied nearly one whole issue of BROOM.

Unfortunately, that was the extend of Garland's contribution.

Juan Gris illustrated the September cover. D.H. Lawrence's books were advertised just inside. "Little Birds and Old Men," a poem by Lawrence Vail, who had married Peggy Guggenheim that year, appeared opposite a very phallic sculpture. There was an essay on Buddhism and a number of South Indian illustrations, a translation by John Rodker who was now the unofficial English editor for *Broom*, a prose poem by Pierre Reverdy translated by Josephson, and a poem by Ridge's friend William Rose Benét. Josephson appeared again with "One Thousand and One Nights in a Barroom or the Irish Odysseus," an essay on Joyce that would have annoyed him. Loeb's essay, "The Mysticism of Money," suggested that if you lived in America you couldn't appreciate American art. Only by being an expatriate could you come to understand its value. In the advertising, Ridge, along with Hart Crane, Babette Deutsch, and Sherwood Anderson, was listed as one of the authors featured in *The Double Dealer*, "the only honest literary magazine in the U.S." There were also two new bookstore ads, and an ad for "The Forum," whose speakers include sexologist Havelock Ellis, philosopher George Santayana, and philanthropist Otto Kahn.

"You do so much, nearly all the disagreeable work and get such scanty thanks or help from this office," writes Loeb that month. "Your working without pay over the summer is the devil..." Why hadn't he paid her? Was she supposed to take her salary out of the receipts? Such denial was an indication of her dedication to the magazine. Under the influence of Matthew Josephson, Loeb had decided to move to Berlin, but didn't give her the new address for another six weeks. In the meantime, the magazine was a month late in delivery, losing publicity, customers, and ads. Although Ridge had increased the subscription base from 600 to 2,500 in less than a year, (and eventually to 4,000) the magazine could ill afford such mishandling.

Cubist-rendered big machines appeared on the October cover. Although it lacked Strand's photographs—he had not turned them in on time—it was known as the "machine issue." It contained an advertisement for the New York production of Pirandello's play, noting that *Broom* had first published it. Ridge had spent a month straightening out its copyright situation so it could run. The Ridge-solicited translation of new chapters from *The Possessed* translated by Babette Deutsch's husband, Avhram Yarmolinsky, chief of the Slavonic Division of the New York Public Library, also appeared. According to his introduction, these were found among Dostoevsky's papers in a tin box inside the Central Archives in Moscow. A reclining nude by Matisse, a translation of science fiction prose poems by Blaise Cendrars, a Francis Picabia poem, more Matisse, an essay on Constructivist art in Russia, and an essay by the futurist Enrico Prampolini on the aesthetics of the machine followed. Ridge's friend, the *New York Evening Post* editor Henry Seidel Canby, advertised its "Literary Review."

Although Loeb had not been interested in any American art other than images by Strand, Stieglitz, and Man Ray, Ridge put forward a cover done by "MC" that he liked—and it turned out to be the work of his ex-wife, Marjorie Content. But subterfuge was not confined to the New York office. That October, the same month *Broom* moved to Berlin, Matthew Josephson came forward to admit his part in the editing of *Broom*, "a confession of faith:"

> I was all set to go back to America and work in a bank, [but] I find myself here in Berlin helping edit *Broom*, plotting and scheming with HL for campaigns and programs months ahead. Personally I think being an editor is a disagreeable and ungrateful task. But the conditions of this outfit are far too good, offered too much chance for fun and experimenting...[speaking of Loeb] we can trust each other perfectly when our backs are turned....As for me, no doubt a surprising development in the *Broom* staff, there is no use investigating my past record. You will only hear bad things said of me.

He exclaimed over the American issue in terms that suggested he was claiming it: "here is something we have both been dreaming of," and in his memoir, *Life Among the Surrealists*, written 25 years later, he further asserted his editorship over the issue. The memoir also shows him claiming the Dostoevsky publication Ridge had found "as our pièce de résistance." He ends his October letter to Ridge by name-dropping Williams, admonishing her to give his regards to him. The next issue features Josephson as associate editor. By mid-November Josephson had asked Ridge to use his essay "The Great American Billposter" to promote the magazine. She had already set in motion the idea, thinking that Josephson was on her side. That was not the case. "Since becoming associate editor of the magazine," Josephson writes in his memoir, "we had been at loggerheads with Lola Ridge, the American editor, an excellent woman who wrote rather dull free verse." Loeb's correspondence with Ridge, however, acknowledged her contribution thus far: "We have a good fund of American poetry now, most of which you have sent," he writes on November 4, 1922.

Broom's November issue was organized around Strand's tardy photographs, a Malcolm Cowley poem, another Ivor Winters poem, a Hans Arp illustration, and Josephson's most notorious essay, "The Great American Billposter," in which he dismissed European influence on American writing but suggested that only in Europe can one appreciate American work, a slight refinement on Loeb's essay in the September issue. As confusing as their argument was, it related to the conflict that was soon to evolve between Loeb and Ridge that led to Ridge's resignation: the inclusion of work by the expatriate Gertrude Stein in Ridge's American issue.

The December issue featured dance, beginning with Halicke's cover of ballerinas. Its literary component started with a piece by Ridge's protégé, Jean Toomer, "Seventh Avenue," that breaks into prose and back again into poetry. Containing the line: "God would not dare to suck black red blood," the poem would soon appear in his masterpiece *Cane*. Despite Loeb's stated intentions, he was never very excited about publishing new American writers, but Ridge had pressed for inclusion of Toomer's work: "Jean Toomer, almost unknown...Stuff has rhythm color flavor of smoke-acrid like the burning of green roots." By then she had been critiquing Toomer's poetry for several years.

Toomer had written Ridge to tell her he could blend "the rhythm of peasantry [sic] with the rhythm of machines. A syncopation, a slow jazz, a sharp intense motion, subtilized [sic], fused to a terse lyricism." Corresponding with him over the editing of "Seventh Avenue," she suggested numerous cuts. With regard to his "Kabnis," which would be published in *Broom* after Ridge was gone, she told Loeb, "I sent the story back to Jean and asked him to hurry with it. Asked him to take out Louis [sic], cut out first four pages and sharpen and condense the whole." To Toomer she writes: "Lewis in the poem is "not convincing...he seems to have been yanked into your story from some other source entirely without your own experience and therefore he is not authentic—he has not been felt by you." Toomer revised it twice more before the piece ran. Although Waldo Frank has most often been credited with mentoring Toomer, critic Jeffry B. Kondritzer writes, "the brilliance of his [Toomer's] contributions is apparent in both 'Karintha' and 'Kabnis,' neither of which would have found their way into *Broom* had it not been for Lola Ridge's diligent championing of the young Toomer." Critic Bryce Conrad identifies *Broom*'s influence as one of the "major forces working on [him] as he composed *Cane*." Toomer was not without gratitude: "I thank you Lola Ridge for pushing me to the work."

Toomer heard that Loeb was planning "a Negro number." He didn't hesitate to identify as black if that opened up a venue. He heard the rumor

> through a friend of mine here who is in touch with several people out in Hollywood. It seems as if they've been reading me out that way. On learning that this fellow knew me, they wrote him asking about me, and expressing the hope that I would be well represented in the Negro number which *Broom* was planning. When do you expect to run it?

Loeb referred to the issue as the "nigger" number, one that would carry "the great negro sculpture also origined [sic] poetry and prose...[James Weldon] Johnson should be able to help." Johnson had just published *The Book of American Negro Poetry*. Loeb had great hopes for this issue, wanting to push it forward to May. "Should be our star number." Karl Einstein in Berlin was the "world authority" and he was providing assistance. Nephew of Albert, Einstein's theories about African art were central to the European discovery of its aesthetics. Loeb already had photos of "very wonderful" sculpture, never before published, on hand. "We also have an unlimited stock of African prose and poetry, epic, religions [sic] and narrative, I wish to complete the number with an assortment of American Negroe [sic] English writing. Can you get it?...Has Toomer any negroe [sic] blood[?]" These and other enthusiasms, including a plan for a Mongolian number, did not materialize.

Pablo Picasso's lithographs of ballerinas also appeared in the December issue alongside an "Instant Note on Waldo Frank." Josephson was the author. He reviewed Frank's *Rahab*, a modernist novel about a woman who struggles to overcome sin. Ranting against the Puritanism of earlier times in America, Josephson writes: "The shocking sex-repression of the nineteenth century has reaped the shocking sex-outletting of the twentieth in our unhappy land." The magazine ended with a full page announcement of Mayan sculpture and architecture in the January *Broom*, alongside contemporary American prose and poetry:

> BROOM from old Europe will present in the JANUARY number an array of AMERICAN writings such as no magazine in America has yet ventured...BROOM has never lacked faith in the Artistic future of America...The January number of BROOM is a challenge to America to recognize a national art as profoundly American...

In response to a contemporary enthusiasm for all things Mexican, the announcement goes on to tout Mayan art as central to this American-ness, perhaps also preparing its readers for Williams's forthcoming essay on Mesoamerica, "The Destruction of Tenochtitlán."

> Conceived some ten centuries ago, it [Mayan art] remains the magnificent expression of one of the noblest races which inhabited

America. Since then, many races, many cultures have come and gone. All but the topography of North America has ever altered. But the new races which populate the transformed continent are also creating a new art which mirrors as faithfully the astonishing environment they have made for themselves. Why not read them now?

There's also a contest with a first prize subscription to *Broom* for life! Ridge had won her battle for an American number.

When the issue finally appeared in January 1923, Loeb had already admitted that 90 percent of it was due to Ridge. To start, Ridge published another excerpt, Toomer's "Karintha," "to be read accompanied by the humming of a Negro folk-song." Ridge also introduced Hart Crane's work to Europe in this issue. He had been fearful of publishing in *Broom*, but she pushed him, playing a major role in encouraging him to submit "The Springs of Guilty Song." As Belinda Wheeler points out in *At the Center of American Modernism: Lola Ridge's Politics, Poetics, and Publishing*, "Though Crane had published a couple of poems around 1916 and 1917, it was not until he wrote and published ['The Springs of Guilty Song'] in *Broom* that he began reaching a wider audience." The poem would become part of his famous "The Marriage of Helen and Faustus." "No one else writing in the magazine captured the spirit as lyrically as did Crane," writes Kondritzer, "and Ridge, once more, was the person who endorsed Crane's work for the magazine." As a result of Ridge's friendship with Marianne Moore, "it was Ridge who brokered Moore's post-Kreymborg contributors to *Broom*," according to critic Robin G. Schultze. Ridge had to encourage Loeb to publish Williams' essays: "He has the fine idea of writing an American history in a *different* way." In all, the issue "pushed its readers to forgo colonial histories of triumph, consider the authentic history of violence and loss, and ponder America's present and future," writes Wheeler. Josephson crows over its contents in his memoir as his own, admits on the next page that Ridge selected most of the material, then states that "her literary taste was retrograde." She had no idea of his animosity, responding to his "confession" the month before by writing to him: "I have been much encouraged by your cooperation."

The issue contained essays on baseball, the jazz band, the cinema, and the dizzying skyscraper, all chosen to be "fundamentally in harmony with the Art of the ancient Mayans," as the magazine proposed. Kenneth Burke's story, Williams's essay, and Marianne Moore's review of H.D.'s "Hymen," her last contribution to *Broom* as a result of the insults administered by Matthew

Josephson later in the issue, were featured. Kay Boyle's poem begins "Morning creeps in across his hair." There was fiction by Josephson—he couldn't be left out—concerning "Ribald libidinous lickerish Mr. Excrement!," a shaped poem "Circle" by the Baroness Elsa von Freitag-Loringhoven, and "Wear" by Gertrude Stein. The final article was Josephson's unflattering review of Marianne Moore's work. He begins by condemning American women: "Let us admit to begin with that the great shortcoming of American women is their brutality, their coarseness, as seen in manners, gowns, habits, books, dew-daws." Moore herself is "a rebuke to our heedless womanhood: the humility that goes with knowledge—the pride that goes with sensibility. Emotion in her is calcined to a thin ash."

An ad for *Broom* on the last page asks: "Is *Broom* too Conservative?" and mentions that a Philadelphia bank director had "revoked his subscription on the grounds that the work of a noted American poetess was unfit to be read by his daughter, aged sixteen." But it was not the Josephson insults nor the lascivious content that brought down the magazine, but the small Stein poem.

Six months earlier, Loeb had asked Ridge: "Is there any general interest in Stein?" Ridge responded with her opinion: "mostly blah! Blah!...In a few years her work will be on the rubbish heap with the rest of the literary tinsel that has fluttered its little day and grown too shabby even for the columns of a daily." To feature Stein, the expatriate, as representative of the best new American writing was a slap in the face. Ridge sent Loeb a telegram on November 15, 1922, saying "RESIGN ON INCLUSION OF GERTRUDE STEIN IN AMERICAN NUMBER." But Loeb wrote that he felt that Stein's influence on American literature was so pervasive that any review that left her out would be flawed. Ridge gave him another chance on November 23: "Am rushing everything in case you should refuse to keep G. Stein out of American number." *Broom* in New York was in an uproar. Even Marianne Moore had heard about it. Her letter November 27 to Ridge thanking her for *Broom*'s check includes her sympathy: "You amaze me—by your exertion on my behalf—in the midst of so much calamity."

A week after Ridge's resignation by cable, Josephson wrote unofficially to Gorham Munson, his co-editor on *Secession*, with "a proposition." He outlined Ridge's involvement with *Broom* by stating that she "has been our New York office for some time, rather than American Editor." He called her resignation "hysterical," and that what *Broom* needed was "a man, a *man* this time to get right in and drive it along...In such a pinch, I think he [Loeb] would agree to replace L.R. with you as American Editor." Josephson called *Secession* a "sporadic group magazine...with a wholly different aim" than *Broom*'s which was "For the present...trying the slant of presenting a form of 'American culture'"—primarily Ridge's idea. He tried to suggest that the job would be a snap, but inadvertently revealed his lack of commitment: "I don't know how many hours Lola puts in. Sometimes she calimes [claims] to stay up till morning. But we never spend more than five or six hours here." He boasted about how many ads they had (most of which Ridge had secured) and that "this could considerably round out your income, as well as the possibility of contributing steadily." He suggested mismanagement on Ridge's part: "From what I know of the BROOM accounts, it would immediately be on its feet, if some honest American low common 'efficiency' were applied." But like Loeb, he did not relinquish power and offered him the same deal that Ridge had been given: "Final responsibility stays in Europe." Anticipating that an American magazine might best be edited from America, he writes: "Ultimately BROOM may come to America and establish itself permanently." Then he couldn't help but damn *Secession* with this admission: "I am the last one to want *Secession* to die off." At the end of the letter he contradicted his earlier statement that Loeb knew nothing about the letter, by saying that Loeb had already approved his making the offer. Defending himself, Loeb, in his aptly-titled memoir, *The Way It Was*, flatly denied knowing the letter's contents. "Josephson refused to send it to me on the plea that it was personal." Munson, for his part, was infuriated— he could see that his magazine was being dumped and himself demoted. His relationship with Josephson ended a year later with a wrestling match in the mud in upstate New York. According to Josephson's memoir, Munson eventually showed Ridge the letter, but she didn't sound as if she had seen it in the contemporary correspondence. Along with her polite reply to Josephson's "confession of faith" in December, she writes in January that "The co-operation of Josephson since last September has been one of the things that made me feel that I might be able to continue some time longer with BROOM."

Ridge resigned again in her 2 January 1923 letter to Loeb. This time she must have sensed that Loeb wasn't being difficult all on his own, but thought that he'd been swayed by Sherwood Anderson's recent review of Stein's work in the *New Republic*.

I see that you advance his slushy sentimentalities about her in the *New Republic* as an argument in support of your opinion of her importance. I object to her work in BROOM, not because of the missing substance in her work, not because she merely plays with words, but because she does not do it well enough. If you must play with words, as such, with no impetus or passion behind, then you must do it skillfully as a swordsman plays with rapiers—as Marsden Hartley, Amy Lowell, Wallace Stevens have done it. G. Stein's words— house-wifes [sic] canning plums—peanuts rattling in a straw hat—at best, corn popping in a skillet.

Then Ridge went over the top.

Personally, I have nothing against Miss Stein. I do not know her, but she is doubtless a lady of charm. Witness her power thereof in her literary reputation—a bladder blown up by many breaths. Well, my breath will not help to fill this particular bladder.

In this case, even the Baroness was a genius when set against the work of Gertrude Stein:

The Baroness writes a great welter of words, lit with an occasional flash of something that is near genius...One is a crazy artist, the other a tricky craftsman whose highest attainment is an occasional flippant cleverness of presentation.

No less a personage than T.S. Eliot found Stein's work more than challenging:

It is not amusing, it is not interesting, it is not good for one's mind... IF this is the future, then the future is, as it very likely is, of the barbarians. But this is the future in which we ought not be interested.

Much earlier, Kreymborg had published a negative review in the *Morning Telegraph* titled "Gertrude Stein—Hoax and Hoaxtress: A Study of the Woman Whose 'Tender Buttons' Has Furnished New York with a New Kind of Amusement." Even Matthew Josephson dithered in the American issue of *Broom* alongside her poem: "The din of Gertrude Stein's barbarous chants rises relentlessly: one may succeed in being indifferent to it with taut muscles." But it was most likely not so much the *New Republic* review that swayed Loeb as Josephson. Twenty-five years later Josephson admitted that he knew that "Miss Ridge...had no liking for the work of Gertrude Stein, whom I found so intriguing and whose publication I strongly favored." He also claimed that "Loeb and I insisted on publishing more of Gertrude Stein....over Miss Ridge's protests..."

Whether Stein was aware of the furor over her work isn't known, but her poem "Wear" wasn't high enough on her list of favorites to be collected in any future Stein volume. Loeb had not yet met Ridge and couldn't believe that she was so upset: "the effect is entirely disproportionate to the cause." But Ridge found Stein's nihilistic doctrine of art for art's sake polar opposite to her commitment to the world at large. She had other reasons too and set them out.

> I took hold of BROOM early last March for the purpose of saving a failing venture in which I felt strongly interested. But I did not propose to do this either as your agent or as your mss. reader, but as the American editor....I should not have greatly objected to it [Stein's poem] in any other [issue]...you are right in believing that the Stein poem was not the sole cause of my resignation, but merely the last jerk that snapped the string.

She had found herself circumvented and frustrated.

> Contributors in New York and abroad have sent their work to you, sometimes after I had returned it. It has happened that I have opened a new BROOM to see some shivering bit of mediocrity that I had rejected cheeping feebly out of the pages.

It also wasn't as if Loeb had been the ideal business partner. Not only was he thousands of miles away, he lost letters, misplaced work, shipped the magazine late. He would agree to publish material Ridge put forward and then he wouldn't, he didn't proof paid advertisements—the funniest mistake was "Practical Home Study Course of Inferior Decoration"—he printed Strand's work upside down, he mixed up contributor's names, he would write that he was finished with the magazine and then wire that he was not.

In her January 2 letter, Ridge still hoped that she might convince Loeb of Stein's obsolescence:

> Ten years ago, when Kay Boyle was a child of ten, Gertrude Stein was quite the rage in her mother's literary set in Cincinnati...I mention the fact to show the incongruity of the inclusion of Stein—a woman who reached the height of her noteriety [sic] a decade ago—in the group of unknown or little known moderns mentioned in your ad.

Loeb, writing later in his memoir, lays part of the blame for the rift between them to Kreymborg, and then reinterprets the whole Stein incident:

> Lola did not approve of Gertrude Stein's work. I didn't either. But I had been persuaded by Alfred Kreymborg to run several bits of it in early numbers. It didn't seem to make any difference. Nobody read it anyway. Now I proposed to run another small piece of Gertrude's meaningless prose (she had formerly written meaningful prose such as 'The Lives' in the American number which Lola had suggested. My thought was that regardless of the worth of Gertrude's contribution, her prose had influenced several important writers, especially by its effective use of repetition...

By January 2nd, Ridge was once again accusing Loeb of being unable to think on his own—"I knew that I should always be struggling with obscure forces—the invisible rather than the visible editor." Instead of suspecting Josephson's intrigues, she thought that Boni [of Boni and Liveright] was complicating the situation, as he and Loeb had been discussing publishing books under the Broom imprint.

Loeb visited New York a few weeks later, when the reception of the American number was at its height, and met Ridge for the first time. Marianne Moore remembered a *Broom* party with both Ridge and Loeb present:

> Dinner at the Broom Tuesday was very enjoyable. Dr. Williams, Harold Loeb, Lola Ridge and Mr. Lawson on a wooden table in the kitchen. Mole [Moore's mother] gave me a chicken to take which was greatly praised and enjoyed grapefruit (first), peas, sliced ham, roquefort cheese, 3 kinds of bread, sherry wine, fruit jelly and cake

(coffee and tea). Harold battled nobly but less as Glenway Wescott said of Mrs. Monroe "his intellect didn't sustain him." We laughed a great deal, belabored Louis Untermeyer and various upstarts.

Loeb did not find it too hard to come to terms with Ridge. As he remembers it:

> At first there was a watchfulness between Lola Ridge and me. But she had a warmth that was hard to resist. Quickly we became friends. Although Lola did not withdraw her resignation, she agreed to carry on until we heard from my uncles."

Loeb was too much of a coward to meet his uncles in person to ask for money and sailed before they could convene, preferring to negotiate by mail. Ridge had warned Loeb earlier to be more businesslike, counseling him to at least show that he had done some publicity on his side. "These big businessmen may think it strange that more of this has not been done in Europe." The Guggenheim uncles were not impressed. They deemed *Broom* a "magazine for a rich man with a hobby."

Ridge and Boyle worked on the magazine for nothing for another month. Ridge asked that Loeb print a poem he had held for a year and eight months, and gave editorial comments to Toomer. By the end of February, Boni had withdrawn his offer because the German mark had gone up, and another backer pulled out after being told he should put his money "into a vacuum cleaner rather than into BROOM," and Loeb's mother now refused to meet with Ridge at all. Ridge telegrammed an offer to buy *Broom* herself, a detail that has never been mentioned in any previous history of this altercation:

> I offer you one thousand in monthly payments for complete owner-ship BROOM beginning April. Debts included. Willard approves offer. If you agree I will distribute March. Cable yes or no.

Willard was Loeb's brother. She reiterated her offer by letter:

> If you accept my offer I shall fight along to keep BROOM going ahead. I shall try to raise enough money from friends to bring out the April number in America. I only thought of this at 4:00 o'clock

yesterday. Went up immediately and talked it over with Willard, who was quite in favor of the offer."

Where she was going to get $1,000 when she had drawn no salary since June remains a mystery. Nonetheless it sounded like a serious offer to Loeb. On March 1st, he accepted by cabling back "Yes." After all, she was the obvious person to take over—she had been very successful arranging publicity, soliciting advertising, befriending patrons, securing manuscripts, and negotiating with lawyers. She had proved herself quite competent—indeed, Loeb admitted that "probably you can edit a review better than I can; I mean this sincerely." That she would care enough to take over after all the abuse and trouble she had had with him was testament to her admiration for what the magazine had become, and its potential.

Thirty hours later, she received a second cable from him: "Second thought, no." She then quickly sent her own cable: "Returning subscriptions. Closing office. Cable if other plans." She received no answer for nine days. In the meantime Willard suggested that she sign over the subscribers to *The Dial*, a common practice to finish out a subscription when a magazine had failed. Hearing nothing from Loeb, she turned the lists over to *The Dial*, notified dealers, and returned subscriptions. Josephson, in his memoir, asserted that he was the one who insisted the lists be returned. "About the time that I received your [Loeb's] March 12th cable asking me to hold subscriptions," writes Ridge on April 7, "I was informed from outside sources that Mr. Josephson's father had bought *Broom* for Matthew Josephson." Josephson and Cowley had bought 2/3 share of the magazine, leaving Loeb with 1/3. Whether this was a better deal than Ridge offered, is not clear. She was never allowed to negotiate. She ended her letter reiterating this, and by refusing to honor his request to destroy the letter in which she stated why she had resigned: "No, I will not withdraw carbon of my letter setting forth the true reasons for my resignation from the files."

Loeb forwarded a letter he'd written in March dated February to (very clumsily) cover his tracks. "Your offer to distribute March was made contingent on my selling *Broom* to you and I had thought that it was your health that prevented you from closing up." As Josephson put it: "At the New York office [Loeb] had found things in a state of confusion...chiefly because Miss Ridge was ill and tired and was merely waiting for someone to supplant her." Loeb apparently never seriously considered her taking over *Broom*, or was persuaded not to consider it by Josephson who was planning to take over with his friend Malcolm Lowry and remake it as a Dada magazine. Lowry, then in Paris, was described by Hemingway as "that American poet with a pile of saucers in front of him and a stupid look on his potato face talking about the Dada movement." Of course a publisher has every right to sell a magazine to anyone he pleases but by Loeb never mentioning her offer to anyone, and by suggesting to others that she had disappeared from the masthead because of reasons of health, he insulted her initiative. Perhaps he feared she would succeed. He could not resist an elaborate self-justification and re-interpretation:

> If you look it up you will find that I reserved absolute veto power to myself. Within two months you were much put out because I stuck to this reservation and would not permit an American number assembled by you. I am still puzzled how you could have expected this.

"Then a letter from Lola Ridge reached us," writes Loeb in his memoir. "This is to inform you that after March 25th no mail will be opened, no order attended to, or any other business transacted by us." As Ridge wrote novelist Mary Austin years later: "Ridge and Loeb quarreled (expensively) by cable and Ridge resigned, also by cable, and thereafter with regularity every month, but was not permitted to let go until April-May 1923."

He asked that she deny that she "sacrificed herself" for *Broom* without pay. "The small salary balance still owing you I consider a personal debt and hope to forward it to you next autumn." He went into much more self-justification in an unsent letter, stating that her quibble about his consulting "a third trained intellect" when differing with the opinion of a poetess of "at least ten years older connection with the arts, with a reputation and prestige greater than one's own...would be laughed out of any business, army, or governmental office." On her part, she made the mistake of not telling him the whole truth about his finances, apparently so as not to discourage him. He should, of course, have intuited that the magazine had financial problems from her repeatedly forgoing her salary.

Because issues are put together months in advance, Ridge's resignation still meant that *Broom* would feature much of the material she had already assembled. The inclusion of George Grosz's work in February is probably a result of her correspondence with Mitchell Dawson, who had recently put out his issue of *Musterbook* on Grosz. Toomer had another poem in the magazine that she had had a hand in, Williams published another piece from *In The American Grain* that he'd read at one of Ridge's parties. Ads began to drop. Man Ray did the cover of the March issue, which included a Carnevali poem she had sent Loeb.

In all, Ridge's tenure at *Broom* spanned 13 out of 21 issues, quite a number for an editor whose work is today seldom even mentioned. She solicited and shepherded the publication of Crane, Toomer, Strand, Stieglitz, Wylie, Boyle, Moore, Bogan, and Williams, obtained Yarmolinsky's translation of Dostoyevsky's *The Possessed*, and negotiated the copyright issues for the first appearance in America of *Six Characters in Search of an Author*, most of which accounts for *Broom*'s posthumous fame. "One of the most important collaborators [for Loeb] was Lola Ridge," writes Kondritzer. At the time when Loeb finally made her resignation public, he allowed her some credit:

> It is with deep regret that we announce the resignation of Miss Lola Ridge. Much of the progress which BROOM has made toward establishing itself in America can be ascribed to Miss Ridge's whole-hearted and unselfish labors.—THE EDITORS.

Josephson and Cowley at last had a shot at the magazine. Josephson was given "an equal voice in editorial matters" by Loeb. Then Loeb was pushed out. By September, he complained that he had received no books, magazines, manuscripts or letters from the new editors at all. Although 50 years later Malcolm Cowley would retire as one of the eminent editors of Viking Press, in 1924, he and Josephson ran *Broom* into the ground within four numbers, shrinking it precipitously issue by issue, discovering that money was indeed a problem, no matter how many essays were written about how little it mattered to art, and ironically confirming the Dada tenet that a magazine should destroy itself. As Cowley put it:

> In the life of any magazine [the editors] decide whether to struggle on...They search for new benefactors with thousands to give, for those with hundreds, for any kind soul, at last, who will contribute five or ten dollars toward the printer's bill. They begin subscription campaigns that are doomed to failure; successful campaigns cost money.

All these "doomed" efforts had been successful under Ridge. As Wheeler points out, the magazine's failure so soon after her resignation emphasized Ridge's power and influence at the height of its importance. When Ridge met Josephson in 1923 in the midst of all this wrangling, he condescendingly recorded Ridge's aesthetic: "[Her] idea of the poem is a snowflake sparkling and melting in the sun" and accused her of promulgating "the snowflake school" of poetry—she, the author of poems on labor, riots, murder, lynchings, Wall Street, and political executions. Gorham Munson, his partner on the magazine *Secession* that also failed, rated Josephson a "dishonest, treacherous, irresponsible, self-seeking, and an intellectual faker." Language failed Marianne Moore entirely after a long conversation with him at a party around the same time: "Words couldn't do justice to the revolting inanities of it & as I said to Mole [her mother], the many limitations [of his] which should enlist one's pity merely alienate me."

Loeb worked for the government in administrative positions for the rest of his life. Embittered, when he saw Evelyn Scott's name on a hotel register years later, he avoided her. "For Evelyn had caused unwittingly nearly as much trouble between Lola and myself as Gertrude Stein...I no longer wanted to meet ES or anyone else." As editor, Ridge twice sent him Scott's article on American aesthetics, and pushed to include the review of Scott's first novel, *Escapade*. The book was not only outrageous in its treatment of sex but it also tore apart form. But Ridge was not wrong about her importance and influence. When Scott was briefly a bestselling author, her enthusiastic support of *The Sound and The Fury* catapulted Faulkner to fame. He never thanked her. In 1940, when Faulkner was asked if there were any talented women writers, he said: "Well, Evelyn Scott was pretty good, for a woman...."

Michael North cites Loeb's reversal of the aesthetic aims of the magazine at the root of the problem between Ridge and Loeb. Loeb was hamstrung either way: American writers were either valued because they published in Europe (which made the writing European) or because they were wholly American and refused to. The mostly confused satires in *Broom* written by Cowley and Josephson highlighted this conundrum. Belinda Wheeler, on the other hand, reviewed the argument between Ridge and Loeb from a feminist viewpoint. She writes: "Ridge's pivotal role at *Broom* is noteworthy because the disagreements she had with Loeb highlight prescribed roles female editors encountered." That is, a woman editor was expected to stick to the administrative tasks, not the editorial.

Ridge was as important to this period of American modernism as Pound was to the European. She had edited two important modernist magazines, she wrote books of modernist poetry to excellent reviews, she recommended other modernists' work be taken. Rather than pit American writing against European like Pound, she wanted Americans to recognize and be recognized for what was American about their work. She set contemporary American writing in the context of avant-garde art and photography, she used ancient cultures as a way to explore the contemporary, and she requested essays on new directions in American writing. The best writers and intellectuals in the country convened at her apartment to consider the question of American art, which made her a fulcrum for modernism when the whole venture could have collapsed or retreated to Europe like surrealism. Even the placement of work in the magazine emphasized its Americanness: Toomer's "Karintha" against the Mayan sculptures, for example. Moore offers the best illustration of Ridge's goals at the end of the issue with her famous dictum that her poems were "written not in Spanish, not in Greek, not in Latin, not in shorthand but in plain American which cats and dogs can read!"

Chapter 22

Finding the Means:
Marie Garland and
Louise Adams Floyd

Twenty-year-old Kay Boyle went off to Europe in 1923 with her French husband, and soon took it upon herself to confront Loeb in Paris on behalf of Ridge. Rousing him in Paris from his bed with his mistress, she "told him with heat and bitterness what I thought he had made of *Broom*, and he apologized for almost everything in it and excused his part of it by saying:

> 'You see, I'm practically out of it. The main reason why I let my name appear on it is because I get paid a salary.' How Harold! Richard [her husband] detests him—I think men do—but I finished by liking him, without having the slightest respect for him.

Loeb apologized: "I should never have sent that first cable," then said he had no idea they worked for nothing through March. But Kay had in her possession his letter thanking her for just that sacrifice. But while she may have condemned Loeb, she didn't hesitate to send him a poem for Josephson to consider in the next *Broom*.

Boyle's husband did not yet have a job. She persuaded Ridge to try to get her a grant from the Garland Fund that funded liberal and radical causes. Despite Garland having helped send off an issue of *Broom*, and having been on the committee that funded her work on "Woman and the Creative Will," Boyle's few days dropping off Eugene Debs leaflets in Chicago did not seem radical enough, nor did the fund see how her modernist poetry would further working class causes. She was much disappointed. Ridge's response was to send $100 to Boyle's mother, who had sold her carpets in order to join her daughter in Europe. Boyle then insisted that Ridge read the book of fiction she had written. "I want you to see it and write me all you think of it."

Boyle was also thinking of starting her own magazine without Ridge, using her health as an excuse. "You are not strong, [and] that prevents me from suggesting any sort of cooperation." But then Boyle asks Ridge to send anything she found, and Boyle would publish it, listing Ridge as associate editor, with Boyle as publisher. In 1924, she suggested that Ridge take her (unread) novel to her publisher. By 1925, Boyle was demanding that Ridge re-read her novel after she had given her comments—and to send her the name of an agent. Ridge introduced her to Evelyn Scott, a relationship that proved more enduring than theirs. The two had much in common: both began as poets, lived abroad for very long stretches, praised Faulkner and Joyce, wrote experimental prose, and pursued unconventional lives.

The next year Boyle abandoned her husband for the poet Ernest Walsh, who had his own magazine, *This Quarter*—and T.B. She casually mentioned his hemorrhaging in a letter to Ridge, but since she was now running *This Quarter*, to please send the subscription lists for *Dial* and *Broom*. Toward the end of their correspondence in 1927, after she returned to her husband with Walsh's baby and *This Quarter*, she writes: "I wish you were near by so that you could edit and stimulate me." Boyle asked for more money in nearly every letter, although early on she crowed that the quickly employed Richard had "had a fine raise."

Evelyn Scott was another friend who always asked for money. She begins nearly every one of her single-spaced, often several paged, letters (she wrote at least once a week for years) with sympathy for Ridge's many illnesses, a catalogue of illnesses of her own, and an illustration of her current state of poverty. To her credit, she introduced Ridge to at least one patron. It wasn't as if Ridge had the means to be a reliable patron herself. Her bank balance tended to hover at $100 but often sank below $10, and she often had to borrow from Lawson, who kept his accounts separate because she thought he couldn't manage money. Between 1921-22, Scott was living on a monthly stipend from Marie Garland, the mother of Charles who managed the fund for social justice that rejected Boyle. Along with the stipend, Garland gave Scott a house in Bermuda with a cook, and had promised her a piece of land of her own. Scott invited Ridge to visit Bermuda and later France in nearly every letter, as did Boyle, but Ridge turned them both down. Perhaps in Scott's case, the chaos of her ménage à trois with Thomas Merton's father, the bisexual New Zealander Owen Merton, and Scott's husband Cyril, along with

Scott and Evelyn's son Jig and Thomas Merton, both boys still quite young, might have been too much for her, all of them packed in a small Bermuda bungalow. Her stated reason was her new employment with *Broom*. With regard to Boyle, she had a new baby that was not her husband's and was living as a guest of the Princess of Sarawak in Paris. Besides, Ridge had no money to travel, having no income from any editing position after the *Broom* debacle, and giving what little she earned on her poems to Boyle and Scott.

One source of income was the $100 Ridge won for the Guarantor Prize in *Poetry* with "Fifth Floor Window" in 1923. Other recipients of this prize included W.B. Yeats, H.D., Robert Frost, Edna St. Vincent Millay, Vachel Lindsay, and William Carlos Williams. *Poetry*'s editor, Harriet Monroe, had been Ridge's supporter from her first book. Monroe began her own poetry career with an audience of 5,000 for a commemorative ode she'd written on the 400th anniversary of Columbus's discovery of America. After the poem was published without her consent, she collected a $5,000 settlement, using it, together with 100 $50-a-year-for-five-years subscriptions from Chicago businessmen, to begin *Poetry* in 1912—and always paid poets for their work thereafter. A year after the magazine's founding, her contributor Rabindranath Tagore won a Nobel Prize. This was also the year Monroe published "In a Station of the Metro," written by Ezra Pound, her overseas editor, who also brought her T.S. Eliot's "The Lovesong of J. Alfred Prufrock." In the first two years of the magazine she featured Robert Frost, H.D, Amy Lowell, Vachel Lindsay, William Carlos Williams, and D.H. Lawrence. James Joyce appeared soon after. But Monroe did not confine herself to the literary elite. She also published African Americans, Midwesterners, unknowns—like Lola Ridge and Wallace Stevens—just starting out.

Monroe published five poems from Ridge's first book in 1918, and 12 more in subsequent years, the last poem right before Monroe's death in 1936. All of Ridge's books were reviewed in her magazine, two of them by Monroe. A woman with exquisite and catholic taste, she set a fine example for Ridge in her own editing. "The greatest poet is not always the noisiest," she writes in a 1923 *Poetry*, the same issue that carried Ridge's prize-winning "The Fifth Floor Window."

Ridge's poem implicates a man in the death of his child who has fallen out a window, but the crowd of "shawled women" in the poem excuses him: "It's hard on a man out of work/an' the other gone out of his door/with a younger lover..." They look up at the window

where the little girl used to cry all day
with a feeble and goading cry.
Her father, with his eyes at bay
before the vague question of the light,
says that she fell... (*Red Flag* 23)

Ridge conflates the wind with the "shawled women" and their voyeurism.

Now the wind
down the valley of the tenements
sweeps in weakened rushes
and meddles with the clothes-lines
where little white pinafores sway stiffly
like dead geese. (*Red Flag* 24)

Ridge's response to the horror of the dead child is restrained modernism, not documentary. The burning cigarette found in the lines "Between his twitching lips/a stump of cigarette/smoulders, like a burning root" and the suspicions—and sympathy—of the shawled women assert the husband's guilt, but without the suggestion that he will be punished. The speaker of "The Ghetto" also lived on the fifth floor—but whether "The Fifth Floor Window" was originally written as part of that poem is unknown.

Evelyn Scott and Ridge stayed at Marie Garland's compound in Buzzard's Bay, Massachusetts, Scott in 1921, and Ridge some time later. Twenty-two acres with a dance hall, pool, tennis courts, and nearby beaches, the grounds were quite adequate for inspiration. Kahlil Gilbran drafted *The Prophet* on the estate in 1918-19. "Angel of the South Shore," Marie Garland founded Home Colony Union, a school for arts and crafts on Cape Cod. She was also the mother of eight adopted children as well as two of her own, a confirmed suffragist, having attended an international convention in Switzerland, a supporter of the socialist La Follette, and a member of the Committee of 48 alongside her second husband, Swinburne Hale, who acted as counsel for the radicals held at Ellis Island during the Red Scare. The Committee of 48 was organized after Jack London's 1906 speech at Yale where he asserted that a million workers "who begin their letters with 'Dear Comrade' were about to take over America." Yale was so frightened that it banned speakers from Woolsey Hall for the next ten years. Originally headed by Upton Sinclair, the committee included Theodore

Dreiser, Jack London, Will Durant, and Sinclair Lewis—all Ridge's acquaintances—and B.W. Huebsch, her publisher. Their aim was to form a third party by reaching "the home folks on Main Street" with their socialist propaganda.

Marie's son Charles must have absorbed some of the committee's beliefs because in 1922, at the age of 21, he announced that he was refusing his Boston inheritance because he would not accept money from "a system which starves thousands while hundreds are stuffed." A friend of John Reed, he said he acted not as a socialist but as a follower of Tolstoy, Christ, and H.G. Wells. Eventually Upton Sinclair convinced him to use the money for social change. As a result, Garland founded utopian communities in Massachusetts and Pennsylvania, and gave away $2 million in grants to such radical organizations as a summer school for women workers, Sacco and Vanzetti's Defense Fund, the N.A.A.C.P., and the Brotherhood of Sleeping Car Porters. Although he did not fund Kay Boyle, his family had a serious interest in supporting literature, especially poetry. His mother was the author of three books of poetry: *The Winged Spirit, Marriage Feast,* and *The Potter's Clay,* the last which included a poem published in *Poetry* magazine. The title poem of her third book considers her young son's dilemma of what to do with the family money:

> If we could take the world and "shatter it to bits"
>
> And "mold it nearer to the heart's desire,"
> What would we make of it?

Garland's poem, "Because I am a Woman" does not approach the feminist: "If you were not the brute you seem/The tenderness you now show me/Would lose all meaning." But there's also a poem in *The Potter's Clay* entitled: "We Women Who Have Lost a Child," one that might have elicited Ridge's sympathy or at least a buried sisterliness, assuming that Ridge did not reveal her own history in that regard.

Scott left Garland's Bermuda villa in 1923, after her relationship with Marie soured. Marie paid for Ridge's passage on the *Arcadian* to visit Bermuda a year later, on April 28, 1924. Ridge was provided with a bungalow for a month, where other artists, including Georgia O'Keeffe, would also stay.

Ridge wrote sonnets every morning. Not everyone thought that was a good idea. On hearing the news, Scott wrote:

Lola dear, will you think I am an uncomprehending idiot insulting
you by a misapprehension that could not be appropriate if I say that I
pray you will not give up free forms? You are too completely creative
in temperament to ever realize yourself completely in a predestined
mould, and I don't care how many sonnets you are writing.

While Scott's assessment was quite accurate, the only regret Ridge
expressed was not dedicating the five sonnets to Marie Garland when she
published her next book. While composing them, she befriended a very
large spider she named Marcus Aurelius, after the Roman emperor and
Stoic philosopher. "I wouldn't let them touch him. His den was over the
ledge of the only door that opened outward to the sea. There he ate his
cockroaches and dropped their bodies over the precipice of the door ledge."
But the vivid island flowers, not the spider, inspired her better sonnets. "The
flowers there burned almost as intensely as the flowers one sees in one's
thought..."

Not yet shall pansies, darker than a bruise,
By torn-out scarlets of hibiscus lie
In gaudy deaths, festooning the bleak ground,
Nor faded pinks that have no more to lose:
Petunias will be the first to die
And go down quietly without a sound.(*Red Flag* 60)

Ridge was home from Bermuda only a few months when she and
Lawson applied for passports. The handwriting on Lawson's forms looks
very excited. He states they will leave the country by the yacht *Blue Moon*
in five days, heading out from New Bedford to England, France, Egypt,
Italy, Australia, Brazil, and China, and that they will be away for two years.
Headlines all over the country announced the trip: "*Blue Moon* Schooner
Yacht to Sail on Adventure Quest in South Seas" and "Romance Awaits
the *Blue Moon*" and "Marie Garland Plans Two Year Tropical Cruise."
The yacht—"one of the finest of her kind"—was 106 feet long with
accommodations for eight and a crew of nine, two dining saloons, and an
elaborate refrigeration unit specially made for the tropics. Marie, one of
the few female members of the New York Yacht Club, did not know exactly
where they were going, but had invited

Lola Ridge, whose book, *Sun-up*, is just published, and her husband David Lawson who will serve as one of the crew. Mrs. Lawson is a frequent contributor to the Dial...and will share my stateroom which has a skylight, affording good working light. I plan to do a good deal of writing myself..."

Garland had also invited the young filmmaker/anthropologist Henwar Rodakiewicz, since they were not only making the trip as "inspiration for literary achievement" but also "to contribute to geographical information... and adventure." The (envious?) poet Eda Lou Walton, Martin Lewis, Lawson, and Ridge were photographed on the yacht, with Ridge standing a bit away from Lawson, looking askance. She wears a beautiful coat with geometric designs on the sleeve, in keeping with the modernist taste she showed in photographs of her apartment, and perhaps Garland's wardrobe.

By the end of October, the newspapers and Ridge had announced that the trip around the world was off. Marie Garland, said to be a descendant of Henry the VIII, had suddenly decided to marry a fifth time. Described as "very, very sexy" by Roger Baldwin, founder of the ACLU and friend of the Garland family, she was 55 and Henwar Rodakiewicz, the young filmmaker, was 22. Rodakiewicz later worked with Paul Strand on *Redes*, his lyrical Mexican documentary, and made a noted fiction film about Georgia O'Keeffe.

Of course the trip is off. So is Marie—on a winter trip to California and New Mexico—she's put a lot into it and been done always on all sides by everyone concerned in the building, provisioning and everything else as far as I can make out, all those fine honest New Englanders made a good thing out of it. Of course Davy and I have been up in the air and no bottom in sight all summer and fall. He's now hunting a job (he gave one up twice to make ready [to] join *Blue Moon*) when the end fell out of things. Marie gave us some money. We were roofless eatless and jobless—this enabled us to get our things out of storage and take this old studio and left Davy breathing space to look round for a job...

Ridge had already met another supporter, Louise Adams Groat, at a 1921 Civic Club party celebrating the work of Zona Gale, the first woman to win the Pulitzer Prize in Drama. Groat had come in third for secretary of state in Massachusetts on the Socialist ticket in 1916. She had already visited Ridge's neighborhood by 1918 as secretary of the Intercollegiate Socialist Society that met at the Washington Square Restaurant, discussing such topics as "Socialist Theory; Should It Be Revised?" *Masses* illustrator Art Young listed her along with Margaret Sanger, Genevieve Taggard, and Helen Keller as one of the "beautiful women I have met who were active in progressive or radical affairs." Like Marie Garland, Groat served on the Committee of 48. She also organized the School of Social Science in Boston, one of the first workers' schools in America.

Groat would soon marry William Floyd, a direct descendant of a signer of the Declaration of Independence. She herself was a member of the ultraconservative Daughters of the American Revolution. Given her leftist tendencies, however, the D.A.R. listed her as a "doubtful speaker" and blacklisted her in their membership book. Her husband declared himself a war resister during World War I, and published and distributed radical pamphlets like "War Resistance: What Each Individual Can Do For War Prevention." He was also the director of the Peace Patriots, "the effort to make civilized people ashamed of war" and conducted walks with Louise's "antiwar" St. Bernard. He wrote:

> It is difficult for capitalists to understand how a descendent of a signer of the Declaration of Independence and of William Bradford of the Mayflower can be a Red. To the Reds I am a bourgeois, the Socialists being the middle ground people hated by all.

Charlotte Perkins Gilman, most famous as the author of the strikingly feminist short story, "The Yellow Wallpaper," also served on the Committee of 48. "There is no female mind. The brain is not an organ of sex. Might as well speak of a female liver," she writes in *Women and Economics*. In the same book, she asserts that marriage is primarily an economic arrangement. (For Ridge, it didn't work that way!). Gilman, like Ridge, was often invited to stay at the Floyd estate with her on Long Island, "Old Mastic House," with its 25 rooms, 12 outbuildings, a family cemetery, and 613 acres of forest, fields, marsh, and five miles of beach, but their visits did not overlap.

Ridge's stays at the Floyd estate were frequent throughout the 10-year period beginning in 1923. She also corresponded with Louise throughout that decade, and revealed parts of her life that she told no one else. Addressing her as "Elai," Ridge became one among a number of radicals that Louise supported and entertained. Sometimes Ridge would bring

Lawson to Long Island, and they would each inscribe a poem or a reflection in Floyd's guestbook. Ridge thought well enough of the following inscription to include it in her next book. "Pine Needles" is the nickname for William Floyd.

Portrait of Mine Host
    (To W.F.)

Testy
Pine needles
Bristling on end
And soothing velvet-soft under the touch...
Out of the sharp grass
Two hands
Holding a rose...so gently. (*Red Flag* 99)

It was at the Floyd estate that Ridge is captured in a 1925 photo wearing a black model's smock. She must have been sitting for Louise, an amateur sculptor, who worked on a bust of Ridge until 1931. "The mouth bad," says the note on the back of the photo of the finished piece. In a photo which includes Floyd and several friends, Ridge is turned to profile while everyone else faces the camera. Her expression is solemn, as if sunk inside herself, two stanzas deep. She left the following epigram that year: "For a perfect peace as for a quarrel there must be two. Lola Ridge."

Chapter 23

Politics and *Red Flag*

"I am...an individualist, and I know individuals will always rule, no matter what the society," writes Ridge in 1932. With beliefs derived from 19th-century romanticism, she followed the precepts of the anarchist Benjamin Tucker who held that "if the individual has the right to govern himself, all external government is tyranny." Ridge would use her position in American literature to fight its encroachment. Although she refused the job of managing editor of the radical *New Masses*, she became one of its first contributing editors in 1926. The magazine replaced *The Masses*, a radical magazine started by an eccentric socialist Dutch immigrant in 1911. According to poet James Oppenheim, *The Masses* was interested in "socialism, sex, poetry, conversation, dawn-greeting, anything so long as it was taboo in the Middle West." Max Eastman held open editorial meetings with John Reed, Louis Untermeyer, and others voting on its essays, fictions, illustrations, and poetry. Hippolyte Havel once interrupted with "Poetry is something from the soul! You can't vote on poetry!" It attracted illustrators John Sloan from the Ferrer Center, Art Young and his bracing political cartoons, including his famous wanted poster for Jesus Christ, and even Picasso. The magazine shut down after the government put the editors on trial for conspiring to obstruct conscription at the beginning of World War I.

After a trip to Moscow in 1925, the novelist/critic Mike Gold became convinced a new magazine was necessary. He had been a past contributor to *The Masses*, and had once before tried to revive it with the short-lived magazine *The Liberator*. After Ridge and other potential editors turned down the job, it fell to him to lead the way. Charles Garland's fund contributed half the launch costs and *New Masses* became "the principal organ of the American cultural left from 1926 onwards." Poems, short stories, journalistic pieces and "sketches" predominated at the beginning "to make the 'worker-writer' a reality in the American radical press." Gold declared in a 1926 article "that poetry must become dangerous again. Let's have poems thundering like 10-ton trucks and aeroplanes," sounding like an old futurist but still attracting new blood like Langston Hughes to the masthead. One of Gold's most famous articles was "Gertrude Stein: A Literary Idiot." According to him, her works "resemble the monotonous gibberings of paranoiacs in the private wards of asylums...The literary idiocy of Gertrude Stein only reflects the madness of the whole system of capitalist values."

Early issues of *New Masses* featured articles on feminism, poetry by Robinson Jeffers and William Carlos Williams, a short story by D.H. Lawrence, essays by Leon Trotsky and John Dos Passos, and artwork by Stuart Davis, as well as writing by Theodore Dreiser, Eugene O'Neill, Ernest Hemingway, and Ralph Ellison. By 1928, Gold was pressing for proletarian literature rather than writing by literary leftists, and the magazine's political view shifted from liberal to Stalinist/Trotskyist. He hoped to replace the *New Masses* board of contributing editors—"vague, rootless people known as writers"—with "a staff of industrial correspondents." Joining Ridge as one of the "rootless" were Claude McKay, Eugene O'Neill, Carl Sandburg, Upton Sinclair, Jean Toomer, Edmund Wilson, and Genevieve Taggard. By 1930, Gold had published his bestselling memoir, *Jews Without Money*, and was considered the preeminent author and editor of U.S. proletarian literature. His magazine's popularity rose during the Depression, when leftist soothsayers appeared to have predicted the collapse of capitalism. After becoming a weekly in the late 1930s, the magazine struggled with ideological upheaval and ceased publication in 1948.

Ridge contributed five poems to the magazine in 1926-27 just after its launch. The poem "Kelvin Barry" concerns the death of an Irish radical: "And your bare throat warm to the wishful rope." "Re-Birth" begins: "Though your wild dreams/May die perhaps on the cemented stone/That they have cracked asunder..." "Russian Women" subtly charges politics with the suggestion of bisexuality: "You swing of necessity into male rhythms/that at once become female rhythms" and notes: "Yet in you there is no peace,/ but infinite collisions,/impact of charged atoms/in ceaseless vibration." In "Moscow Bells 1917" the bells ring "Loose/over the caught air that trembles like love-flesh/Songs of all wild boys who ride forth/to love and death..." The title of "Histrionics" must refer to the last words of its subject, the radical editor Albert Parsons who was hung because he merely talked about violence at the Haymarket gathering: "There will be a time when our silence will be more powerful than the voices you strangle today." All of these poems would appear in Ridge's 1927 book, *Red Flag*. They did not, however, represent a strengthened commitment on her part to any political party. Like Elsa Gidlow, an anarchist poet who published the first explicitly lesbian poetry in the U.S. in 1923 and discovered she "could not see salvation in any brand of politics," Ridge's beliefs were rooted in a more inward looking anarchy. As early as 1920 she writes to Modern School director Leonard Abbott: "I'm beginning to realize I'm 'without dogma' except what I painfully construct for myself."

Red Flag is the book that came closest to being overtly political. Published in the wake of the Red Scare, when 28 states banned the public display of red flags, it benefited from well-publicized radical backlash. Isadora Duncan wore only a red flag when she appeared onstage in Boston in 1922, exposing her breasts to declare: "This is red, and so am I."

Despite the book's radical appearance and title, *Red Flag* was well received. It was published with bright red covers by Viking two years after its founding, Huebsch having joined them. Harriet Monroe reviewed it for *Poetry*: "On the whole one finds in this book [*Red Flag*] a possibility of reconciliation with life, such as there was no hint of through the bitter fires of "The Ghetto." Babette Deutsch, now a critic for the *New York Herald Tribune*, disagreed with Monroe: "The fire, the earnestness, the bitter and honey savors are here as in her earlier work. She has been wrought upon by the years on their passing, but she has not been changed by them." Conrad Aiken, for his part, was not so positive in *The Dial*: "Miss Ridge's free voice is oddly devoid of instinctive rhythm—one hardly ever feels under the shape a reason for the shape...One wonders, indeed whether she is not an excellent short-story writer gone astray." But Aiken may have fallen into a reviewer's solipsism by echoing his own fear, since he himself was in the throes of switching from writing very formal poetry to the short story form for which he is considerably better known.

Evelyn Scott objected to the book's title: "Bad because it misleads the average mind to accept the symbol as one of specific rebellion." Scott did admire "Mo-ti," the first poem in the book, perhaps because it shows Ridge's political beliefs to be more complex than strictly those of the Russian Revolution. The placement of "Mo-ti" contextualizes and opens all the poems in the book to a reading broader than those of current ideologies. A Chinese philosopher from the fourth century B.C., Mo-ti believed in an agrarian communism brought about by benevolent rulers.

> You pitted your words against the words of princes,
> but softly, in even tones, and few listened...

so that you were not nailed on four boards
nor smeared with honey and left naked
where sands crawl living under the sun. (*Red Flag* 11)

The world that Mo-ti tried to change also contained women, a point usually overlooked by poets and politicians alike. "Did women...catch a garbled word or so/and mutely/quiver along the margins of their silence?" Ridge notes

Only your
words have floated out of the night
...words still seeking in vain noise
for some green hush to rest upon...

Harriet Monroe read the book's second poem, "Death Ray," as one that concerned "the beauty of a city dawn." This was the year when "death rays" were widely discussed, as a result of Englishman Harry Grindell-Matthews trying to sell one to the British Air Ministry. Two days later, the *New York Times* ran "The Death Ray Rivals," about the competition worldwide to develop such a weapon, which included quotes from the chief militarist of the German Army who had invented "a device that will bring down airplanes, stop tank engines, and 'spread a curtain of death.'" By September 1924, Americans claimed to have built one, the same month Winston Churchill speculated about such a device in the essay: "Shall we all commit suicide?" "Might not a bomb no bigger than an orange be found to possess a secret power to destroy a whole block of buildings—nay to concentrate the force of a thousand tons of cordite and blast a township at a stroke?"

The setting of "Death Ray," a part-sonnet series of four poems, offers a "glamorous dim light" and "a joy [that] floats in the morning..." and "spires, swarming up the mauve mist" but in that innocent landscape: "There is that in the air, an imminence/Of things that hold the breath still and heart pale." Christian iconography contextualizes the threat: "Jesus...Washed, as a white goat before the slaughter..." By the second section the poem turns with

a stirring at the quick
of some white palpitating core
of such intensity as might
burn up Manhattan like a reed.

At this point, the poem becomes the first verse prescient of the nuclear threat, perhaps the first such poem in the world unless the excerpt from the Bhagavad-Gita as quoted by Oppenheimer during the first detonation counts. Indeed, a reference to the Hindi is appropriate, since the first section of the poem was published as "Om" in the *New Republic* in 1924.

It is very unlikely that Ridge knew much about the nascent development of nuclear fission, although what little was known fascinated the public. Ridge might have read *Among the Reeds*, a 1913 novel by Australian Alice Musgrave in which her bohemian heroine peers into a Cooke's spinthariscope, a device to view nuclear disintegration, "the Key of Life and Death." The last section of Ridge's poem describes the atomic bomb in eerie metaphor.

> This nuclear
> Period set against the rushing hour
> That holds there, motionless, the leaning sheer
> Stalk of its unfathomable flower.

Was this Ridge's intuition, that her favorite subjects, light and fire, might ignite some terrible weapon? The poem ends by implicating Christianity in the development of this weapon: "Yet know that there shall cleave forever there/A golden nailhead, burning in your palm." But Ridge was no Christian Marxist. Her religious tropes gesture toward the most familiar of Western religions' to stand in for the spiritual, the way in "Mo-ti," Chinese philosophy frames agrarian communism. Her belief in Christianity was the same as her Marxism: nonexistent. But she does salute the flag:

> Red flag over the domes of Moscow...
> There gleaming like a youth's shed blood on gold
> Red flag kerchief of the sun—
> Over devastation I salute you. (*Red Flag* 40)

Lawson remembered that "we rejoiced over the Russian Revolution... It looked as if the world would open up," echoing the beliefs of many other artists and intellectuals of the time. That year, Ridge spoke to the Irish Women's Council on the third anniversary of the execution of Patrick Pearse, an Irish poet who helped lead the Easter Rebellion. Instead of bemoaning the situation of the Irish, she extolled the coming revolution in America in the wake of the Russian.

Following "Death Ray" is the prize-winning poem "Fifth Street Window," with its speaker witnessing the aftermath of the possible murder of a child in the ghetto. In a later section, "Morning Ride" is an equally stunning modernist depiction of violence. Written after Ridge resigned from *Broom*, the poem concerns the 1910 lynching of a young Jewish pencil factory manager in the South. Alternating between newspaper headlines about the man's innocence and the commuter's distractions on an open-air bus, the poem renders cubist the two intersecting worlds. The poem even uses the kerning type that Dos Passos employed in his books a few years later.

Morning Ride

Headlines chanting—
y o u t h
l y n c h e d t e n y e a r s a g o
                    c l e a r e d—
Skyscrapers
seeming still
whirling on their concrete
bases,
windows
fanged—
l e o f r a n k
l y n c h e d t e n
    s a y i t w i t h f l o w e r s
w r i g l e y ' s s p e a r m i n t g u m
  c a r t e r ' s l i t t l e l i v e r—
lean
to the soft blarney of the wind
fooling with your hair,
look
milk-clouds oozing over the blue
    Step Lively Please
    Let 'Em Out First Let 'Em Out
did he too feel it on his forehead,
the gentle raillery of the wind,
as the rope pulled taut over the tree
in the cool dawn? (*Red Flag* 67)

Anticipating the breeziness of a future Frank O'Hara invoking the distractions of the New York subway rider, the poem insists that the reader identify with the lynched man with the proffered intimacy of "your hair." The cubist collage technique underscores the pathos of learning about a man's wrongful death so casually. "The soft blarney of the wind" suggests the Ireland of her infancy, the country her mother fled for a better world, the same impulse Ridge acted upon 20 years later with her own child. But what a disappointment! In America she found lynchings, homelessness, senseless murders, epidemics, oppression of all kinds.

Other modernists made similar formal innovations to pit the experience of traveling through a city's right angles at great speed against the inherent inhumanity of advertising. Influenced by visual artists who used advertising in their work, Williams published "Rapid Transit" in 1923, two years before Ridge's poem, with the lines: "Somebody dies every four minutes/ in New York state—" and "AXIOMS//Don't get killed//Careful Crossings Campaign/ and "Take the Pelham Bay Parkway Branch/of the Lexington Ave. (East side)/Line and you are there in a few..." The poem ended with a subway ad. Jean Toomer's "Gum," written around the same time, uses two flashing billboards to illuminate the "gum-chewing missionaries" working the crowds on Seventh Avenue.

> STAR
>   J E S U S
> The Light of the World
>
>   . . .
>
>   WRIGLEYS
>   eat it
>   after
>   every meal
>   It Does You Good
>   Intermittently, their lights flash
>   Down upon the streets of Washington,

Red Flag is sprinkled with poems either dedicated to various contemporaries, including Amy Lowell and Adelaide Crapsey, or poems with the dedicatee's initials in the title. For example, "After the Recital" is addressed to Roland Hayes, "Him black doll of the world," the African American tenor who gave a command performance for King George V and Queen Mary of England in 1921. But unless the poems are elegies, they usually come off as closed and personal, the opposite of their intent to immortalize. Ridge had second thoughts about this practice. A few years after *Red Flag*'s publication she writes to Lawson: "I enclose the poem from Laura. It is very beautiful, but seeing my name on it in this way gives me a psychic shock—I shall never again even initial a poem to anyone in a book."

Two imagist-built poems are situated toward the end of the book. "Fame" with its reference to Aldebaran, a red star found in the constellation Taurus, the zodiac sign of the Bull, gives achievement its perspective—an interesting one, given Ridge's great ambition.

Fame

The dewdrop on the sorrel-blade
Is a tiny silver mirror
Held to the high stars:
Not the august eye
Of Aldebaran
Can miss the sorrel-blade
On this dark night. (*Red Flag* 95)

"Obliteration" offers the flip side of "Fame," describing a sea of "wrinkled silence" that "holds in its blue vacuum/No bleached white evidence," the absolute erasure of any struggle for recognition.

Obliteration

The sea is a wrinkled silence
Moving darkly
Under the audacious lustre of the air...
The emptily effacing air,
That has closed upon so many cries...
Yet holds in its blue vacuum
No bleached white evidence. (*Red Flag* 97)

Ridge wrote Louise Adams Floyd that she had sent a copy of *Red Flag* to Trotsky. Had Ridge met him at the Ferrer Center in late 1917, when he was studying with Robert Henri? Or did she get his address from Max Eastman, the former *Masses* editor who was now Trotsky's quasi-literary agent and translator? Her patron Corinne Wagner was delivering the book to Russia while traveling with a "Dr. Goldwater," most probably Walter Goldwater, an iconoclastic Village bookseller who traveled to Russia in 1931, the likely date of the letter. Perhaps Ridge knew him through Lawson's interest in chess, since Goldwater was an avid player. However, Trotsky probably did not receive the book since by 1931 he was living in exile in Turkey, working on his own book, *History of the Russian Revolution.*

Ridge remained alert to the political landscape to the end of her life. Known—if she is known at all—as a Communist poet, she never embraced the dogma any more than Williams did with his poem "Russia" and its lines "O Russia! Russia! Must we begin to call/you idiot of the world."

Chapter 24

"Brunhilda of the Sick Bed"

While the reception of *Red Flag* was very good, Ridge appeared to be in trouble personally, at least to her friends. In July 1927, Williams heard that Ridge "was separated from her husband and was ill and in need of funds." The poets and writers who attended her parties rallied. Williams's mutual friend Marjorie Allen Seiffert sent Ridge $50 that Williams claimed to have supplemented. He wrote her a note a few days later, and perhaps that was when he enclosed his contribution, saying "I think I have a special privilege to ask you to lay aside delicate feelings in these matters for once, and to take freely what is freely given since I love and highly value the poetry you have given us all." There's a tally that survives of other contributors to what became Ridge's fund, including $100 from Louise Adams Floyd, $15 from Louise Bryant (John Reed's widow), and $50 in three installments from Evelyn Scott, who had just published her fourth novel—altogether some twenty or so contributions for a total of $620 (this is $8,225 in 2015 dollars). But everyone knew it wasn't going to be easy to convince Ridge to take the money. Marianne Moore's mother tried to persuade her: "I do feel that one who checks and throttles generous love, stultifies the life of another." Then she went so far as to threaten: "To deny me would be to deny love, which from Marianne and me you have." A few years earlier, when Mary Moore had sent Ridge a check, she described it as being "just in the rough my roses, or big loaf of brown bread." This time she left a chicken at Ridge's door. "I hope it gave whichever of my neighbors annexed it indigestion, but fear it was too well cooked," writes Ridge to Floyd after the incident.

As soon as Ridge got wind of the fund, she insisted on paying all the money back—"virtually throwing what's left in the bank in the faces of the donors"—as Scott writes to Ridge's husband. "Lola is showing us all what she thinks of the unheralded nerve and extreme vulgarity of said E. Scott." Scott was especially sensitive. Always broke, always cadging for loans, she shared a similar disdain with Ridge for financial matters: "Money's a nuisance, and I'm afraid I'm like that—incorrigibly improvident and quite unable to save." A year later, she tried to explain to Ridge how the fund came about: "I went one night with Becky [Strand? Paul's wife]

> to Romany Marie's and was there introduced to large quantities of young and old poets. The question of poetry came up and your name. Someone mentioned that they had heard you were ill and seemed to wonder that your health did not improve. This went on to various discussions of your work and some very congenial praise of it, with some remarks to the effect that you did not seem to write as frequently...as a while back. I said I thought too much of your energy had to go in other things than writing. Somebody else said...that it was hell to make a living out of poetry, and that poets ought to be subsidized. That led to my saying good poets ought to be subsidized, and, finally, that you ought to be subsidized. Says someone, Well aren't there any rich people who know Lola Ridge's work who would subsidize her until she got back her health? Says I, I suppose there are but I don't know any likely to do it in a tactful enough way to be acceptable to her.

Was it her infirmities in addition to her poverty that stood in the way of her progress? Ridge's friend, the writer and art dealer Harry Salpeter, described her as "blood-drained, ravaged by illness." Newspapers too noted her continued illness: "Lola Ridge...happens also to be one of our bravest and most invincible personalities, since she has been an invalid most of her life and wrote much of her material propped up in bed," according to the *Syracuse Herald*.

"Pain," writes critic Elaine Scarry, "is that which cannot be denied and that which cannot be confirmed." All her adult life Ridge complained of migraines, "blind attacks," and "stomach troubles," but other than an occasional infection of the foot or tooth, and bad colds, she contracted nothing that might warrant the life of an invalid. She boasted that she was never seasick, did not fall ill "in that Lu. [Louisiana] swamp," and took no precautions regarding food or drink in Mexico or Baghdad, where she later traveled. Yet she was hospitalized in 1919, 1920, 1926, 1929, 1936, and 1937, with an alleged surgery in 1924. "Again, seized with the old spasm," Ridge writes in her poem "Ward X." There was another element in play with her apparent ill health: "This pretense of being younger than her years would later increase the perception of sickliness and fragility that she inspired by making her worn appearance seem due to illness rather than age," writes critic Emily Vicary.

Ridge was also too thin. In a send-up titled "The Lady Poets With Foot Notes," Ernest Hemingway satirized the leading ladies in poetry, with Edna St. Vincent Millay as "One lady poet was a nymphomaniac and wrote for Vanity Fair" and Amy Lowell as "One lady poet was big and fat and no fool," and Lola Ridge as "one lady poet who didn't have enough to eat" and "It showed in her work." In 1928 the five-foot-tall Ridge weighed less than 77 pounds. A year later she was down to 72. Although being a skinny "new woman" was an expression of sexual liberation and a rejection of the buxom Victorian female's traditional role, Ridge was unusually thin. Perhaps this thinness was what caused contemporary observers to describe her as "tall" when in photographs standing beside her husband or Edna St. Vincent Millay, both known to be barely five feet, she matches them in height. Kay Boyle describes her as "fragile enough to be blown away like a leaf whenever a gust of wind came through the door." In 1928 Marianne Moore exclaims: "The poor Lola looks as if she were about to die—though her face is animated and she is full of gratitude and humor but she weighs 70 pounds and is nearer to a skeleton physically than anything." Moore should talk— her weight dropped at times to 75 pounds. Wylie was also extremely thin, and Woolf appears so gaunt in a photo with T.S. Eliot in 1932 that she looks barely able to stand. When Ridge's weight dropped to below 70 pounds in August 1935, the doctors were baffled.

Was she so poor that she was starving to death? According to many of her biographers, she lived in "voluntary poverty," such a state considered not as a moral flaw but one that was environmentally produced by society, in her case, by the lack of enough generous patrons. Suffering such extreme self-denial, Ridge radiated a saintly quality. She was "a devout believer in the humanity of letters," according to Williams. "She made a religion of it." Saints fasted and fainted and finally gave everything away until they had nothing but their lives to be rid of. Ridge borrowed considerably more than she gave away, but she did radiate an "unworldly presence," as "a slender, tall, [!!] softly-speaking, thin-featured woman in a dark dress," wrote Horace Gregory shortly after her death. "Even as one rereads her books one gains the impression that she regarded her social convictions and the writing of poetry in the same spirit in which an Irish girl invokes the will of God by entering a convent."

The nuns had taught her well, or at least steeled her for the deprivations of her chosen lifestyle. After making a living writing potboilers, modeling, illustrating, and working in a factory, she decided around the end of her thirties that she would survive on only what she could make from writing. It was not as suicidal a gesture as it might seem today. The small magazines in the teens and the twenties paid relatively well, and often very quickly. In 1917 *Smart Set* sent a check for stories and poems in just four days. As earlier noted, in 1921 she boasted to Dawson that she had sold $60 worth of poems in ten days (almost $1,000 in today's money). But it didn't help her finances that she gave a party every time she sold her work.

Ridge was almost alone among the Modernists with regard to her lack of inherited wealth, spousal wealth, or the earned wealth of Willa Cather's bestsellers. Ezra Pound married well and his mistress had money. Mina Loy began well with wealthy parents. H.D. came from a well-off family, and her partner Bryher inherited an enormous fortune. Elinor Wylie and Marjorie Seiffert were members of the wealthiest families in America. Millay married money. Although Ridge's husband managed to pay his college tuition and professional licensing fees, he seldom held a well-paying job. A comment between two women in a 1915 *Masses* cartoon by Cornelia Barns illustrated the attitude of the emancipated woman of the time: "My Dear, I'll be economically independent if I have to borrow every cent." Ridge kept her own bank account but her husband had to give her money on many desperate occasions, and she was not immune to hoping that he would become a more reliable patron—she was always asking when could he pass his exams and get a better job. Were they separated in 1927, as Williams suggested? She liked to keep a studio in addition to their living quarters, which may have started the rumor. But how could she have afforded the second rent? Money was found to support her writing, more money than she could have made herself.

Ridge secured patrons in the manner of Isadora Duncan, who "held that it was the duty of rich people, and rich people's hotels, to support geniuses." The 1920s was the first (and the last?) time since the Renaissance in which artists expected to be supported by the more fortunate. Ridge's decision was also inspired by the anarchists. Like artists, they also had to depend on handouts for their sustenance, although even Emma Goldman worked as a midwife and a masseuse when money was low. Later in life, Ridge would not accept (much) money from close friends like Mary Moore, only from her patrons Mitchell Dawson, Marie Garland, Jeannette Marks, and later

Louise Adams Floyd, Corinne Wagner, Mrs. Mary Pratt Richter, Josephine Boardman Crane, and Lenore Marshall. It must have been at the Australian soirées that she learned the first lesson in patronage: to attract money from the wealthy you have to move among them, inviting contradiction, especially anarchist beliefs. But Ridge had her alleged descent from Irish royalty to bolster her confidence.

She attended Bryher and Robert McAlmon's lavish wedding party in 1921. Bryher's father was the only Englishman whose wealth rivaled the robber barons of America, as he was heavily invested in shipping, coal, newspapers, and property. Coal was especially subject to strikes at that time, the very topic Ridge often vilified. She certainly did not turn down Marie Garland's *Blue Moon* round-the-world yacht trip. When she solicited funds, she felt entitled, like Isadora Duncan. "But is it not queer that people who have money to give should have to be coaxed by offering them something in exchange," she writes her patron Louise Adams Floyd. Certainly male poets of the same era received sinecures: Edward Arlington Robinson secured his from none other than Theodore Roosevelt, Ezra Pound from the lawyer John Quinn, Hart Crane from financier Otto Kahn, and Robert Frost from Amherst, Dartmouth and Harvard, who competed for the honor. By the end of Ridge's life, she was finished with patronizing liberal sympathy: "To hell with all their pity" she writes her husband—then she writes another letter for money. Two poems in her very first book illustrate her ambivalence: "Woman with Jewels" with its sneering description, and "Spires" that turns Grace Church, New York's most fashionable house of worship, into a shameful icon of exploitation:

Spires

Spires of Grace Church,
For you the workers of the world
Travailed with the mountains...
Aborting their own dreams
Till the dream of you arose—
Beautiful, swaddled in stone—
Scorning their hands. (*Ghetto* 53)

"To be married or buried within its [the Grace Church] walls has been ever considered the height of felicity," according to Matthew Hale Smith in

1869. Ridge was not unaware of its snob appeal, and before she left it for one of her hospital stays in 1928-9, she described her apartment that faced it with a fillip of class-consciousness:

> It is spacious, sunlight streaming through [the] entire length from [the] front windows looking out on the spires of Grace Church, opposite, and its mystic rise embalmed in stone....My bed pulled up next [to a] big coal fire...This—if one *has* to be ill—[is] a good place... in touch at one end with [the] life of [the] roaring city, at [the] other, the contemptuous silence of brick and stone.

Ridge's patrons supported her hospitalizations and convalescence— sometimes even her doctor paid for her stays. Mitchell Dawson helped pay for a hospitalization in 1920, Jeannette Marks in 1924. In 1929, Ridge checked into the hospital compliments of *Saturday Review of Literature* editor Henry Seidel Canby and philanthropist Josephine Crane. Lenore Marshall paid for a workup after Ridge returned from Mexico in 1937. Ridge was determined to keep herself free from material concerns, even if it meant she suffered physically. In 1935, Ridge wrote Lawson in response to why she wouldn't fill out an important questionnaire: "Sorry but I'm constitutionally unable to consider things which would advance me materially."

But lack of means did not completely explain her dangerous thinness. Yaddo, the artists' colony she visited twice, offered copious amounts of food.

> The German chef—the best of her kind—was appal[l]ed at my turning down her gorgeous lunch—she came up to see me about it—I had an awful job explaining & it was as though I had said—'It's no use—I can't stand your poems!'

Her behavior parallels many characteristics of the anorexic, including "the unusual handling of food, in particular the selection of low-calorie food and/or avoidance of regular meals." Anticipating returning home from Yaddo, she writes Lawson: "I'm eating well and hope I shan't worry you by playing with an inch of toast while you eat your dinner." Five years later, a waitress brings her four pieces of toast and she "carefully picked out an occasional buttered part..." When she was served three meals a day at the Bent Hotel in Santa Fe, so much food made her sick. Or she could have had ulcerative colitis, a lifelong disease that causes erratic fever, weight loss, and stomach pain. She wrote once that the lining of her bowel was coming away. But those who suffer from this disease are fatigued. In comparison, anorexics present themselves as energetic, tireless, and impervious with "a striking physical and often intellectual hyperactivity (a strange endurance despite emaciation)." All that party-giving took a lot of stamina! Ridge also boasted at various times that she had written 127 lines before lunch, 400 as a prelude, 900 lines in bed—and she completed the 218 page *Firehead* after only six weeks at Yaddo while complaining in nearly every letter about severe illness. Among her papers at Smith is a reproduction of one of the paintings of Edward Middleton Manigault, whose work was not featured in *Broom*, indicating that Ridge had taken a personal interest in him. In 1922 he starved himself to death in Los Angeles trying to "see colors not perceptible to the physical eye." He was only 35.

Severe anorexia often ends in heart disorders. Ridge tried nitroglycerin injections for her heart in New Mexico and complained of heart problems to Mitchell Dawson. Her friend Elinor Wylie was extremely thin and died at a young age of heart failure. Ridge herself died of "myocardial degeneration," a heart condition that occurs with anorexia. The death certificate also lists pulmonary T.B., date of onset, 1929.

"I look pale," said Byron, looking into the mirror. "I should like to die of a consumption." "Why?" asked his tubercular friend Tom Moore. "Because the ladies would all say, "Look at that poor Byron, how interesting he looks in dying." Also known as the unpronounceable phthsis, T.B.'s reputation as the sensitive young artist's disease was still being touted in 1941 with O'Neill's play, *Long Day's Journey into Night*. Susan Sontag notes that T.B. made its victims interesting, romantic, and ethereal. Having T.B. was presumed to be a form of protest or rebellion, part of the myth of the bohemian who, while living in extreme poverty, celebrated a life of the spirit instead of the body. The disease has also been associated with youth and purity, with genius, with heightened sensibility, and with increased sexual appetite. According to Montaigne in 1583, girls swallowed sand to ruin their stomach lining to develop a tubercular pallor. Victorian women took arsenic to make their skin as pale as a tubercular, slowly poisoning themselves to death. Because patients often lose weight with T.B., it was imagined to be a disease of malnutrition, linking it to anorexia. Byron himself struggled with his appetite and took the "vinegar cure," laxatives, and other diets to remain thin. Out of Ridge's extensive experience in sanatoriums, she describes an enervated hospital patient—perhaps herself—in several lines of "Ward X":

> Her hands monotonously
> scoop up the shallow moonlight,
> pale as weak lemonade,
> that spills through her fingers
> over the white sheet. (*Red Flag* 90)

The archetypal bohemian died of T.B. Many Irish died of T.B.—"our great reservoir of consumption"—according to the British Home Office, and Ridge could have contracted the disease on one of her long voyages. Or the dust, dirt, rags, and dried sputum in any sweatshop she visited or worked in could have infected her. But it is unlikely the disease would have lain dormant for so many decades. In more than half of untreated cases it is fatal within five years. In the same era, tuberculars Katherine Mansfield and D.H. Lawrence died very quickly. One puzzled doctor in 1929 told her that the spot on her lungs was "in fact so large that if it was active you would be having night sweats, a short dry cough, and higher temperatures than you are having." Several doctors were about to consult each other that day, but their final diagnosis was never mentioned in her letters. She does write a few nights later that she was

> awake all night with pains in my legs—very severe—and very heavy night sweats. The nurse had to change my sheets and all my underwear at 2 a.m. I do not think it had anything whatever to do with my insides—it is either the other thing I'm supposed to have or something else.

Perhaps the doctors too decided it was menopause—the "other thing"— its onset unusually early since everyone thought she was ten years younger. She had no cough or chest pain. They treated her with castor oil for a pain in her side that had vexed her for ten years, but castor oil is also a laxative abused by anorexics. She had Davy smuggle in hard candy while she was a patient in a convalescent home, another way anorexics quell thirst and hunger. She was also prescribed both codeine and veronal, addictive barbiturates that keep you thin. At least she was grateful for the care. "Davy [,] [you] have been a beautiful and loyal person...I wanted to tell you...thank you," she writes from the hospital in 1929. She also bemoans her incapacity to cure the suffering of others: "I seem always taking and seem unable to help anyone, even the [?] girl recovering from a wound in the head, who is my roommate." When she was hospitalized in 1933, she went to a private sanatorium simply to gain weight, paid for by her doctor, who "liked her sonnets." Over the years, her illnesses became less serious, albeit not her weight. Her hospitalization in the late 1930s for weighing less than 70 pounds gave her a clean bill of health despite nearly two years living in Mexico. By 1938, Evelyn Scott writes: "You darling Brunhilda of the sick bed, Jean d'Arc of the germs."

Being ill allowed her to prioritize her needs over all others—and to pursue them in ways that a healthier woman couldn't. No housework, for one thing, and much sympathy from her patrons. Being sick meant she didn't have to be economically productive. She was free and encouraged to write. She didn't have to answer letters or come to the door or entertain when she was ill, allowing her more time to concentrate on her poetry. The archetypal T.B. sufferer was believed to suffer some passionate feeling that caused the illness and which she must express—often love, but also possibly political or moral beliefs. Having an illness similar to T.B. enabled Ridge to speak out. It was also a useful tool in asserting her gentility and rectifying her inferior social status—all that bed rest implied wealth.

A preponderance of her acquaintances spent enormous amounts of time in bed: Louise Adams Floyd, her patron, retired to her room for years, Evelyn Scott underwent numerous operations, botched and otherwise, Kay Boyle began nearly every letter with a listing of complaints, Elinor Wylie fell down the stairs in a faint and severely injured her back and suffered from chronic inflammatory disease of the kidneys. Perhaps all Ridge's correspondents mentioned their ailments because they were trying to create a sympathetic bond. In contrast, William Carlos Williams didn't ever seem to get sick, although he was always being exposed to disease as a doctor, and Amy Lowell, suffering from high blood pressure, retina deterioration, sporadic gastritis, heart trouble, obesity, and an umbilical hernia that made it difficult for her to climb stairs, seldom mentioned any illness. Would Ridge's problem be a female complaint, a relative to 19th century hysteria? Critic Carroll Smith-Rosenberg in *Disorderly Conduct: Visions of Gender in Victorian America* states that hysteria sometimes mimics T.B., heart attacks, blindness, hip disease, while a woman is in perfect health.

Whenever Ridge saw an opportunity to go abroad—or protest, in the case of Sacco and Vanzetti—she miraculously recovered. She traveled solo in her 50s and early 60s to the Middle East, to Paris, to Mexico. Evelyn Scott knew Ridge well, and after Ridge couldn't get a diagnosis out of her doctor, Scott writes to Lawson: "I feel that it maybe would take a genius equal, in his way, to Ridge herself, to really grasp and understand completely the problem of her health." Ridge began to resort to the latest health cures. Scott asked if the osteopath was coming regularly and whether the "sun machine" was working, and in another letter she hoped Ridge was wearing her radioactive belt. Poet Leon Srabian congratulated Ridge on her new "catalyzing belt." Ridge also suffered from chronic depression, what she called "the Russian intellectual sickness."

The psychological forces that might have borne down on Ridge's unconscious and produced such sub-acute, chronic ill health might include the stress from her struggles for freedom. "My side...never bothers me unless I am very much irritated or in some way emotionally upset," she confessed to Lawson in 1932. After all, she was not only a woman artist, a difficult situation she well described in "Woman and the Creative Will," but also a poor immigrant poet without a suitable American background. Her unconscious surely housed Victorian mores that insisted she stay bound to the home and to strictly feminine roles. Less embedded in the unconscious were the new flapper codes that emphasized a youth she didn't have, even after subtracting ten years from her age. As Paul Bennet writes in *My Life a Loaded Gun: Female Creativity and Feminist Poetics*: "The woman writer's principal antagonists are not the strong male or female poets who may have preceded her within the tradition, but the inhibiting voices that live within herself."

If she couldn't be forever young like Edna St. Vincent Millay whose tininess, long red hair, and penchant for clothes that made her look like a child well into her fifties, she would be ill. As an invalid, Ridge turned being female, an immigrant, poor, and a poet into assets. Were her posings worse than Pound the impresario with his cape and beard? Or Moore's celibacy, her tricornered virgin's hat like a nun's flaring headpiece? Or Williams's constant philandering? Or Scott's ménage à trois? They were all branding themselves in the contemporary sense, flaunting their eccentricities while enduring the searing hot poker of the collective psyche bent on condemning the artist's way of life. At least Ridge turned some portion of her personal powerlessness into compassion and indignation over the suffering of others. She left a legacy of poetry attuned to social justice that others could draw on, themes her poetic counterparts for the most part left unexplored.

One of Evelyn Scott's biographers, D. A. Callard, and Ridge's composer friend Henrietta Glick suggested that Ridge committed suicide. Ridge mentions eating only one meal a day for nine days in her diary at the end of her life. Her ambition, combined with her various ailments, imagined or real, could have taken her body—and her spirit—too far.

Chapter 25

Sacco and Vanzetti

A month after Williams wrote to Ridge so movingly about her illness and poverty, Ridge was standing vigil in a protest against the execution of Sacco and Vanzetti. Some hidden reserves of strength and money must have allowed her to travel to Boston to the prison and witness the uproar that surrounded the last-minute pleas for the anarchists' lives. Perhaps Ridge's good friend, the Mount Holyoke scholar and writer Jeannette Marks, arranged her trip. She mentions Ridge in her personal account of the execution and its preparation in her book *Thirteen Days*.

A fan of Ridge's dating from the publication of *The Ghetto and Other Poems*, Marks had offered extravagant praise immediately: "I considered your poem the most brilliant piece of work I had seen in modern poetry." She invited Ridge to speak on campus as part of her "Poetry Shop Talks," a series which already included Robert Frost and Amy Lowell. Marks and Ridge began a decade-long correspondence that included Ridge's last mention of "Woman and the Creative Will": "I have not touched my woman book since July...." Ridge was about to take over *Broom* as American editor at the time, and asked in the same letter if Kreymborg had accepted anything of Marks's. A poem by Marks appears in a later issue. After Ridge's resignation, they continued to correspond in frank letters like the one Ridge writes Dec 23, 1923:

> Louis Untermeyer—I don't care for him either. He was good about
> my work. But I can't help it. He always makes me think of a spurious
> diamond stud. Are there two D's in studd? It seems as though to me
> it ought to be, in Louis['s] studd anyhow. I've had a hell of a summer
> which is why you haven't heard from me for so long.

Part of that hell might have referred to an illness that required a procedure that Marks will help pay for a few months later. Ensconced in the hospital,

Ridge enjoyed "Sappho...I wish I could read Greek. What damn rot to call it a "dead language" when it is the container of living and eternal beauty..." Marks's partner was Mount Holyoke president Mary Woolley, who was also an officer in William Floyd's Peace Patriots.

Marks had served on the Sacco and Vanzetti Defense Committee since their trial in 1920. The case was a showdown between American patriotism and the radicalism that founded the country. Arrested a few days after anarchist Andrea Salsedo "fell" 14 stories out of a New York Department of Justice building, Sacco and Vanzetti were accused of murdering two men during an armed robbery of a shoe factory. They were not even at the scene of the crime, but suffered from "a dubious place in society, an unpopular nationality, erroneous political beliefs, the wrong religion socially, poverty, low social standing," as Marks put it. Court appeals went on for six years. The handling of the case was so controversial that it is still open. According to historian Arthur Schlesinger, the trial and execution of Sacco and Vanzetti ignited worldwide public feeling comparable to the Haymarket bombing in the 1880s, or the Dreyfus case in Europe, or even Pearl Harbor. George Bernard Shaw, Anatole France, and Albert Einstein wrote letters on behalf of the anarchists who said they had emigrated because the country promised them freedom. "I was crazy to come to this country," Sacco said in broken English during the trial, "because I was liked (sic) a free country." But Paul Avrich puts their presumed innocence in perspective:

> Both men...were social militants who advocated relentless warfare against government and capital. Far from being the innocent dreamers so often depicted by their supporters, they belonged to a branch of the movement that preached insurrectionary violence and armed retaliation, including the use of dynamite in an assassination.

What the execution of the two Italians with so little evidence revealed was the true extent of the buried hate for new immigrants, an issue Ridge had been exposing her entire career in America: whose freedom is it? The newspapers announced that Lola Ridge would be one of "an imposing number of liberals" supporting Sacco and Vanzetti in silent protest outside the prison in Charlestown, Massachusetts. As Upton Sinclair observed: "The case worked upon the consciences of persons who were cursed with artistic temperaments." Although a good number of poets and prominent intellectuals were protesting, Amy Lowell's brother, president of Harvard, headed the commission that denied Sacco and Vanzetti a retrial, "earning [for] Harvard the name of Hangman's Hall" among radicals.

Ridge was arrested on August 8, 1927, along with 44 men and women, including John Dos Passos, Dorothy Parker, Babette Deutsch, Hutchins Hapgood, Polly Halladay, and Mike Gold. Jeannette Marks described Dorothy Parker's experience: "[She] was roughly handled by officers who bruised her neck and arms, marching her in the middle of the street up three cobblestone blocks...The mob watching the arrest started shouting "Hang her! Hang them all! Hang the anarchists!" White-gloved Parker, best known for her *bon mots* at the Algonquin Round Table and her writing in the *New Yorker*, was so struck by her bad treatment at the vigil that she became politically active, and eventually left her estate to Martin Luther King. Marks saw her crying later, badly shaken by the mob's frenzy. "She was not an anarchist; she was not a Communist; she was not, so far as I knew, even that constitutional radical known as Socialist."

Marks spent most of her time at Defense headquarters in the North End's poor Italian neighborhood. Most shocking to her was the manipulation of Sacco and Vanzetti's situation by the Communist supporters. Short-story writer Katherine Anne Porter, who had covered the Mexican Revolution a few years earlier, reported it: "Rosa Baron...snapped at me when I expressed the wish that we might save the lives of Sacco and Vanzetti: 'Alive—what for? They are no earthly good to us alive.'"

On the picket line Edna St. Vincent Millay held a sign that read: "If these men are executed, justice is dead in Massachusetts." Ridge and Millay were filmed and photographed being marched away by a policeman between them. The two poets had the same demeanor—determined. Those who defended Millay and a few others in a sort of "show trial" included three-fourths of the Harvard Law School graduating class, Felix Frankfurter, Albert Einstein, G.B. Shaw, H.G. Wells, and Jane Addams. But for the rest of the 172 arrested, Porter writes:

> The judge, not just with a straight face but portentously, as if pronouncing another death sentence, found us guilty of loitering and obstructing traffic, fined us five dollars each, and the tragic farce took its place in history....A busy, abstracted woman wearing pinch-nose spectacles, whom I never saw before or since, pushed her way among us, pressing five dollars into every hand, instructing us one and all to pay our fines, then and there, which we did.

The money was provided by Edward James, nephew of Henry.

On the day the execution was scheduled, martial law was declared in Boston. Planes circled overhead, as if expecting a full-scale invasion from the Red Menace. The protesters did not leave. They waited under great tension for the final verdict and possible stay of execution at midnight. Meanwhile, the handsome Dos Passos flitted around, covering the situation for *The Worker*. He would later write *The Big Money*, using the Sacco-Vanzetti case to represent America's growing corruption, commercialism, exploitation, and injustice. Somehow Dorothy Parker made her way into the prison where the prisoners were chanting, "Let them out! Let them out!" Jeannette Marks stayed hopeful.

> As we sat on, quiet in the tense office, messages coming and going, now and then a cup of coffee being poured or a sandwich eaten, in my thoughts were lines from Lola Ridge's "Two in the Death House" which, repeated to me the week before, she was now chanting over in Salem Street.

> You have endured those moments, you
> Close to the rough nap of earth, and knowing her
>   perennial ways.
> And when, on some one of your counted mornings,
>   light
> That pulls at the caught root of things
> Has pierced you with a touch, or leavened air,
> You too have hoped—with the ardor of young shoots,
>   renascent under concrete,
> And with them have gone down to defeat again.

The railroad yards were lined with machine guns, and searchlights were placed in clusters of three at 20-yard intervals with 500 police officers on alert, 20 of them armed with riot guns. The remainder of the police had pistols and tear gas. Boats patrolled the river. A thousand cars blocked traffic, horns blaring. According to the *New York Times*, "motion picture photographers held aloft flaming calcium torches, lighting up a passing detail of mounted State police with a ghastly flicker and silhouetting their silent figures against the grim gray of the prison walls."

At 11 o'clock, without any directive from Defense Headquarters, Lola Ridge led a group of 50 demonstrators on the walk from the courthouse to the prison. They were met by mounted police armed with pistols, grenades and tear gas. Porter provided an eyewitness account of the assault 50 years later:

> They galloped about, bearing down upon anybody who ventured out beyond the edge of the crowd, charging and then pulling their horses up short violently so that they reared and their forehoofs [sic] beat in the air over a human head, but always swerving sharply and coming down on one side. They were trained, probably, to this spectacular, dangerous-looking performance, but still, I know it is very hard to force a good horse to step on any living thing....Most of the people moved back passively before the police, almost as if they ignored their presence; yet there were faces fixed in agonized disbelief, their eyes followed the rushing horses as if this was not a sight they had expected to see in their lives.

Most of the people—but not Lola Ridge. Jeannette Marks recounts Ridge's response to the police presence:

> With a young Scotchman [probably Lawson] and another girl, Lola Ridge slipped under the ropes and started straight for the cordon of mounted police and the prison doors. A young mounted guard, a boy, rode down upon her. As he reined in his horse fairly over her, she heard him whispering in a frightened voice, "What do you want?"

Katherine Anne Porter gives another perspective to the confrontation. After describing the horse beating its hooves over her head and a bystander recognizing her, the man

> dashed into the empty space toward her. Without any words or a moment's pause, he simply seized her by the shoulders and walked her in front of him back to the edge of the crowd, where she stood as if she were half-conscious. I came near her and said, "Oh no, don't let them hurt you! They've done enough damage already." And she said, "This is the beginning of the end—we have lost something we shan't find again." I remember her bitter hot breath and her deathlike face.

Porter sat in a hotel room with other protesters after the midnight execution. "In my whole life I have never felt such a weight of pure bitterness, helpless anger in utter defeat, outraged love and hope as hung over us in that room." Outside, others wept or fell silent, and went their separate ways, and many of them "marched the streets alone," according to Malcolm Cowley. "Just as the fight for a common cause had brought the intellectuals together, so the defeat drove them apart, each into his personal isolation." Ten thousand people had gathered in New York's Union Square awaiting the verdict.

> They responded [to news of the execution] with a great sob. Women fainted in fifteen or twenty places. Others, too overcome, dropped to the curbs and buried their heads in their hands. Men leaned on one another's shoulders and wept. There was a sudden movement to the east of Union Square. Men began to run around aimlessly, tearing at their clothes and ripping their straw hats, and women ripped their dresses in anguish.

Emotional reactions to the execution swept the world. Forty people were injured when foot police charged 12,000 British sympathizers in London, Buenos Aires boycotted American goods, and an American flag was burned on the steps of Johannesburg's Town Hall. Sweden, Denmark, Finland, Sydney, and at least two cities in France reported rioting. Even the peaceful Swiss mobbed the American consulate and the League of Nations Palace.

A procession of 50,000 people marked the anarchists' funerals. "One of the most tremendous funerals of modern times," reported the *Boston Globe*, but all footage was destroyed by order of Will H. Hays, head of the movie industry's umbrella organization. At the head of the coffin marched Mother Bloor, a veteran organizer, carrying a placard quoting Judge Webster Thayer: "*Did you see what I did to those Anarchistic Bastards?*" She was arrested for "distributing anarchistic literature." The crowd marched arm-in-arm until it was charged by mounted police and a car filled with officers holding drawn guns, who diverted traffic into the cortège and clubbed onlookers.

As Caroline Maun says in her *Mosaic of Fire*:

> [Lola Ridge] was prepared to martyr herself at a decisive moment in American history, where the future of a political movement

she had been involved with for two decades hung in the balance, demonstrating that for her art and activism were one.

Like some kind of doting Red mother, Emma Goldman, writing from exile to Evelyn Scott, noted her bravery: "I was glad to see that our dear Lola Ridge has taken such an active part in the Sacco Vanzetti protests."

IV

Yaddo, Firehead, *Baghdad,*
Dance of Fire, *Taos,*
1929–35

Chapter 26

Yaddo and the Writing
of *Firehead*

The artists' colony Yaddo doesn't share the bucolic spirit of the woodsy cabins at the MacDowell Colony that Ridge visited in 1920. With the ground's Victorian 55-room mansion and its two-story-tall Tiffany windows, Yaddo is more "Henry James to MacDowell's Henry David Thoreau," according to one visitor of both. Yaddo's main house boasts a massive staircase that a drunken John Cheever supposedly rode down on an 18th-century ice sleigh usually parked in the reception area. The mansion is situated next to the racetrack in Saratoga Springs, New York, and is said to be haunted by the founder's wife, Katrina Trask, the housemaid, and her children—unless you favor the novelist Allan Gurganus's theory that these visions have been reports of Cheever (or someone similar) caught flitting naked in the hallway between trysts.

The first time Ridge arrived at the colony was June 1929, a few months after she left the hospital with her possible diagnosis of T.B. She would leave Yaddo just a month before the stock market crashed. Yaddo's benefactor, Spencer Trask, founded the very successful Wall Street firm that still bears his name, backed Thomas Edison and Marconi, and saved the *New York Times*. He and Katrina built Yaddo together and had four children. But the children died, three of diphtheria within seven days of each other—and the original Yaddo mansion burned down in 1900. With the precedent of visiting artists—Edgar Allan Poe was said to have written part of "The Raven" there fifty years earlier—the Trasks decided to turn the property into an artists' colony. Katrina Trask had visions of generations of those yet unborn strolling the lawns, "creating, creating, creating," but before the guests began pouring in, Spencer Trask died in a train wreck. Katrina, writing poetry, survived him another 13 years, until 1922.

Mrs. Elizabeth Ames, daughter of the president of the Yaddo corporation, was hired to administer the premises in 1926. Three years later she invited Ridge for a stay of the customary month. Ridge was offered another month in June when she arrived, and then perhaps more time if she wanted it. Ames particularly enjoyed the company of radical writers, and Yaddo's policy included "the support of artists at political risk." Thirteen years later Yaddo became the site of "The Lowell Affair," when a paranoid Robert Lowell broke down and had a six-year visitor Agnes Smedley extracted by the FBI as a suspected Communist.

Ridge may have been recommended to Mrs. Ames by her friend Alfred Kreymborg and Lewis Mumford, who recommended others. Their own work as editors and contributors to the influential *American Caravan* Ridge was in the process of severely criticizing for the *Saturday Review of Literature*. She held strong views and believed others could benefit from hearing them. "Americans are the most malleable of people," she wrote in a review eight years earlier: "With a child-like confidence, amounting to hero worship with their leaders and hypocritically open to suggestion, they are a people whose art sense could be developed by intelligent direction."

She must have been in an especially self-destructive mood with regard to the *American Caravan* review:

> Heaven[s] what a job. I have now disposed of 37 writers, ignored 7, have 18 more to read and write about. I am saying exactly what I think of friend and foe and stranger. It is the first time I have done so without any reservations whatever.

The review wouldn't come out until the end of the month.

She herself had just been reviewed positively in the *New York Times* along with Eliot, cummings, Moore, Williams, and others in *Prize Poems 1913-1929*. The review she was really worried about was that of Mrs. Ames, who might think that she was "too sure of myself and perhaps [I] give her a wrong impression." Mrs. Ames warmed to few women and especially did not tolerate any foolishness. One female guest, known to have been entertaining a number of partners, returned from her breakfast one morning to find a single bed had replaced her double. But Ridge needn't have worried. Mrs. Ames ended her 25 June note by saying, "I admire you with all my heart."

Ridge was given one of the best rooms in the mansion, with a spectacular view of the Green Mountains of Vermont. She didn't stay long. "I do not however find this grand room ideal. It is too large. I like to be shut in and feel secret and hidden," she writes Louise Adams Floyd. Five days passed and she wasn't able to work. She became desperate, she wanted to leave. Mrs. Ames persuaded her to stay, moved her, and arranged to have her breakfast brought to the new room. "I seem to feel Mrs. Trask's gentle presence in this room and she must have had a tender, innocent and [?] kind personality to judge from the distressingly bad full-length painting of her downstairs," wrote Ridge.

Ridge brought along a copy of T. Sturge Moore's *Judas* she received from critic Llewellyn Jones in 1928. Jones would review all Ridge's work glowingly in the Chicago newspapers, and was deemed by John Cowper Powys to have "the most comprehensive and the most scholarly knowledge of modern poetry of any man in America." He had edited the *Judas* he sent, a book of poems that contained an unusual conception of the traitor's character that may have influenced Ridge's decision to choose the Crucifixion as her next subject, or shaped her own vision of Judas. Two weeks after she arrived at Yaddo, her husband mailed her a book on the historical Jesus, along with the Bible, her friend Laura Benét's third book of poetry, *Macabre Danse*, and Robinson Jeffers's *Roan Stallion*. This last is a long narrative poem that uses mythic characters to express mystical experiences. By then she herself happened to be writing a long narrative poem about the Crucifixion from a psychological vantage. Kahlil Gilbran's koan-like book, *Jesus, the Son of Man*, came out the year before. Although she worried that people would think she "begged his idea," she knew "Gilbran is more formalized, therefore more predictable than I." Later in another letter she wrote to Floyd, "Note the poor little circumscribed, temperate, and slightly runish (?) Jesus of Kahlil Gilbran!"

Her real competition was Jeffers. She had read most of his work, starting with *Tamar* in 1927, and she very much admired it. Perhaps she appreciated his acknowledgement of Australia—a rare literary nod—in his early "Eucalyptus Trees": "Thankful...to him who first/Brought hither from Australia oversea/Sapling or seed of the undeciduous tree," and his mention of the "long white southern road" that provided ecological and racial links between Australia and America.

She withheld her assessment of Jeffers until the very end of her *Saturday Review* roasting. She starts off by condemning Sherwood Anderson, whose "shoddy monologue" opens the collection. About Hemingway she writes: "That which is called classicism is really the male principle functioning in art." She talks of a "glass ceiling" in which Hemingway's "exterior perfection" exists, using "boundaries individual talents may freely express themselves, but whose limitations they may not transcend." She posits that the opposing female principle appeared during the Italian Renaissance, and puts forward Evelyn Scott's story about a gunman as a contemporary example. She prefers Scott's story to Hemingway's because it is "life in flux" and not deterministic. Her comments on Gertrude Stein are interesting, given it had been six years since her resignation from *Broom* over Stein's work: her "jazz is in the way of becoming the folklore of American intellectuals" and "has in it the mysticism of a child, who, twirling dizzily on its heels, isolates itself by staring blankly at the sky of which it does not even see the light." Her criticism is not gender-biased. The remainder of the stories, particularly the women's, "bear hysterical witness to that arch-romanticist, Freud." H.D.'s story is "a jumbled litter of things and people, shaken to scintillance in a bright memory, throw[ing] off lustrous dust...her thoughts flutter like butterflies excited by a magpie." She brings down the rod hard on her acolyte, Jean Toomer, and her colleague Alfred Kreymborg, declaring that they have not "produced at their former levels." "Mr. Toomer rambles on like one who has learned a few words of a strange language and repeats them endlessly" and "Mr. Kreymborg's failure is due partly to a slovenly presentation." (*American Caravan* will be the last magazine he will work on.) She does praise Frost, Van Doren, Winters, and Babette Deutsch. She does not fully approve of Aiken's contribution. "Whatever of creative utterance is his [Conrad Aiken] will be found embedded, still-born, in some lovely phrase." And finally, she writes: "These plaintive murmurs make me crave, perversely, for the disturbing voice—how many eagle cries above—of that great death-carrier, Robinson Jeffers." But by the end of the residency Jeffers and his forthcoming *Dear Judas* will nearly undo her.

All of Ridge's letters speak of a difficult time at Yaddo, despite the coddling atmosphere. She had "blind" attacks—migraines—and a debilitating pain in her side, terrible headaches, problems with her teeth, and insomnia. "One hour's sleep at night will not keep you going," writes her husband by August. In letter after letter she begs him to send Gynergen, an amphetamine prescribed for one of her many maladies. The addictive narcotic had side effects which could have caused the headaches, the sleeplessness, and possibly the pain in her side she complained of—and it certainly enabled her to finish all 200 plus pages of her poem *Firehead* in just fifteen weeks. Her husband was leery of sending her so many bottles at once, but neither he nor Ridge seemed concerned that it was habit-forming, nor that its side effects might be contributing to her feeling unwell. She also took Corax intermittently, also known as librium, to calm herself. Its side effects are similar to Gynergen's and it is also addictive. Withdrawal causes constipation and hallucinations. In addition to her constant use of castor oil, she has visions: "The trouble has been I could not concentrate—even on reading a book—for five minutes at a time and I could not keep my thoughts from flying back to things that had distressed me. Now I am quite calm...but with a bad headache....have had strange dreams and apparitions."

In addition to the drugs she was prescribed, she may have been taking any one of the many medications that were still sold over-the-counter that caused addiction, or using contemporary products that contained narcotics such as cough syrup, Coca-Cola, and toothache powder. Even 7-Up contained the mood-stabilizing drug lithium citrate until 1950. Since Prohibition was in effect, drugs were legally easier to obtain than booze. Her friend Jeannette Marks published *Genius and Disaster: Studies in Drugs and Genius* in 1925. "Do not assert, as if there were some demoniacal logic in it, that Coleridge and DeQuincey were geniuses and ate opium. Chaucer, Milton and Wordsworth, Blake, George Eliot, and Robert Browning, were geniuses and they did not take opium," she writes. Later in the book, Marks presents an idea that Ridge might have approved—that illness helps creativity:

> The biographical study of Stevenson's life shows that when he was in an improved condition, his literary output was least. Emily Brontë's life may have been shortened by consumption but in her poems power and passion were made greater by tuberculosis.

In the last chapter Marks puts a positive spin on addiction, writing that "Opium taken within bounds lessens gastric secretions. Men who starve... find in it a blessing." Ridge's copy is inscribed: "For Lola from Jeannette."

Ridge also owned *Dope: The Story of the Living Dead* by "Annie Laurie," the pseudonym for Winifred Black, who wrote human-interest stories for Hearst, and Fitz Hugh Ludlow's classic *The Hashish Eater* with its resounding endorsement:

> My own personal acquaintance with this drug, covering as it did a considerable extent of time, and almost every possible variety of

phenomena, both physical and psychological, proper to its operation, not only empowers, but for a long time has been impelling me to give it a publicity which may bring it in contact with a larger number of minds interested in such researches than it could otherwise hope to meet.

Her husband sent drugs and money. He also acted as her reader and chief critic while she was so furiously writing. "You have a good sense of form and economy of words and often make many good suggestions," she writes to him June 7, 1929. Eleven days later, she proposed that he join her somewhere near Yaddo to go over her work. He responded the next day: "I'm already looking forward to coming up and having you away with me for a few days." They sounded like young lovers but she was a real 56 by now, to his 43. Three days later, she rescinded her offer, and he counteroffered to visit in another two weeks. Back and forth they went, Ridge expressing hope that he would come, but whenever he arranged the travel, she had an attack of illness or the work was too much, or there wouldn't be room for him at Yaddo. This was a pattern they continued throughout their 20-year relationship: she invites him to wherever she's retreated, then changes her mind when he tries to make plans, then she stays away months longer. It must have kept the relationship vital. "I'd like to have a whole week with you," her husband begged by June 21st. He suggested he comfort her while she had her teeth worked on, he bought a suit for $28 so he'd look better when he saw her—maybe instead of his coming to Yaddo, she could come down to New York? But by mid-July she was in full swing with her writing. Her letters were filled with requests: Send me more paper, a book, what do you think of these sonnets? "I worked til 3 am. This morning slept 3 hours started again worked till 4 pm." Finally, she took two days off and met him in Saratoga Springs, where they discussed her latest efforts together. "Our little holiday didn't turn out much but I was glad to see you and read your poem," writes her husband. As a way to lure her home, he began to fix up her studio at 220 West 14th Street, painting and repairing it, but she had already decided to stay the extra month of August. "This morning am starting the Bondman!" she writes Louise Adams Floyd. "So you see how well I am— beaten the last attack and mean it...I feel like a race horse getting the whip on the last lap." By August 8th her husband writes: "I'm very pleased you've got so much done...I am sending you Gynergen....I hope you will be here Sept. 1st before going to Floyd's." Apparently she was already planning to retreat to the Long Island estate instead of returning to New York. He ends his letter with: "You are creating great literature." She took that to heart, and four days later she reported: "I wrote 378 lines in two days but I had to work on them two days more."

She was in a hurry. Viking wasn't taking another book, but Bill Benét had found her a new publisher, Payson & Clarke, who promised they would feature a book whenever she could produce it. Benét was to be her editor. She worked hard and seldom went down for dinner. Another resident, Emanuel Eisenberg, analyzed her proclivity for seclusion in the horoscope he cast, producing an accurate character sketch, one similar to many an ambitious artist:

> Yours is a nature of intense idealism. It is almost completely uninterested in the literal substance of human beings or in the constructional aspect of individuals. People are attractive and meaningful to you only insofar as they present ideas of themselves or symbols of their ideational significance. This provides you with the strength for solitude; you have no essential need for actual persons, having the ideas of them within you; it is your surest focus of existence.

His insight is reinforced by Kay Boyle's comment about Ridge made years earlier: "She is made for everyone to worship—and she doesn't really give herself to or actually NEED anyone." In Ridge's extreme concentration she interacted with few of the other forty Yaddo guests. Nineteen-year-old Paul Bowles was in attendance. Eventually a composer, translator, and famed short-story writer, his works are now part of the Library of America. Ridge would enjoy meeting his lover/teacher Aaron Copland during her next Yaddo stay. Edward Dahlberg had just published *Bottom Dogs*, his book about being orphaned in America, with an introduction by D.H. Lawrence. She already admired Gerald Sykes, then a poet, later a critic, whose work she had complimented in her *Saturday Review* piece. "The one I like best is Gerald Sykes, one of the young writers in the last Caravan I picked in that benighted article." Her friend Laura Benét arrived mid-July for two weeks, but Ridge found she couldn't write after talking to her. Twenty-six year old Dudley Fitts, just a few years out of Harvard, was just then taking up the task of translating literary works from Latin that would occupy most of the rest of his career. Her good friend Evelyn Scott came for two weeks in July with her new husband, the Englishman John Metcalfe, who stayed on until the end of August. Scott had dedicated her bestselling and most critically approved book *The Wave* to Ridge that year. Ridge met Eda Lou Walton for the first time in June, the Navajo scholar, poet, anthologist, and critic who later became Henry Roth's lover and helped him write and publish *Call It Sleep* in 1934. Even for the wild 20s, Walton's sexual embrace was wide. Her friend, the-less-than-prudish Margaret Mead, found herself disapproving of Walton bedding both Mead's brother and her husband. Like Ridge, Walton had a soft spot for "card-carrying communists, avowed or clandestine, fellow travelers, russophiles and voyeurs of the 'liberal' persuasion, zealots committed to the utopias of Trotsky and Marx or Franklin Delano Roosevelt." Walton appeared on a Congressional list along with Rockwell Kent for UnAmerican Propaganda Activities in the 40s. She and Ridge published in *Poetry* together in 1920, and Walton would review Ridge's last book in the *New York Tribune*.

Like Walton, Ridge was not a believer in sexual exclusivity. She wanted the monogamous Lawson to loosen up while she was away, judging from his dismissive comment by mid-August: "I'm seeing no one and it wouldn't help if I was." But she needed his support desperately. On August 20th, she writes: "I must have more Gynergen....to help me through this ordeal," but five days later she admits: "The Gynergen is failing me—my system is establishing a tolerance for it. I now take seven and eight before I can get an effect." Two days later she writes that she was more ill than before she went to the hospital in the spring, but then finishes the letter with her signature fierceness: "I'll do it. I'll get out the poem and have it to them in first few days of September. Only death will stop me." Davy responded the next day by pointing out that "The most important thing is not that your book should appear Nov. 1st instead of Dec. 1st...in your present condition you can do more damage to yourself in two weeks work than can be undone in six months, and it isn't worth it." The next day he proposed that he come up to collect her. "What I really had in mind was that we would take the boat at Albany and have the nice ride down, and we would have a state-room." When she didn't respond, he writes: "Of course you must decide how long you stay there. Only your personal condition and work should decide." The next day she became extremely distraught by the news that

> Robinson Jeffers is this fall bring[ing] out a book on my theme! He calls his *Dear Judas*. His will *appear before mine two months*....Jeffers'

theme is like mine on the crucifixion and his will foil any chance of mine selling.

She finished *Firehead* anyway, and Davy met her at the train with roses.

Chapter 27

Firehead's Success

Firehead was a smashing success, published in time for Christmas giving, with 25 copies on handmade paper, 225 copies on rag paper, and a trade edition. It received 60 or so reviews across the country, almost twice as many as any of Ridge's previous three books. Daumier's woodcut *Ecce Homo* illustrated her full page *New York Times* review. Society pages talked about her book alongside new work by Countee Cullen and Edna St. Vincent Millay. "Poet Has Perfect Command of a Most Treasured Theme," "New Poetic Heights are Attained in *Firehead*," and "Fighting Pain and Death, Lola Ridge Writes Mighty Poem of Crucifixion" are a sampling of the headlines. She was "one of possibly three woman poets who hold first rank in this country," according to the *Helena Independent* of January 12, 1930. In the *Chicago Daily Tribune,* her friend Stephen Vincent Benét wrote "This is magnificent work...In this long narrative poem of the crucifixion, her mature gift has come to unique fruition." Louis Untermeyer, long a supporter, wrote in the *Saturday Review of Literature* that *Firehead* was "one of the most impressive creations of any American poet."

"To Yaddo" read the dedication. Thanking Ridge, Mrs. Ames wrote: "That you in your high estate in literature should pay this tribute to us with your magnum opus makes us proud indeed—and very humble." Ridge herself did not shrink from acknowledging the book's greatness. She wrote her husband: "It was ordained that I am to do this work. I was born for it when I was an infant in my cradle, this work that I am to do was already forecast." She proclaimed: "*Firehead* was the first—all before that goes for next to nothing, it was only a preparation." She celebrated and "had lunch with all my publishers on Monday the day my book came out. Tomorrow go to a tea Mrs. Kahn [perhaps the wife of philanthropist Otto Kahn who supported Hart Crane?] is giving for me."

Firehead is a retelling of Christ's crucifixion from the point of view of Magdelene, Judas, John, Peter, and Mary, this last character narrating a substantial portion of the poem. With its emphasis on the female, and in this instance, the maternal, it is divided into nine sections, like *The Ghetto and Other Poems*. Irregular blank verse, the book-long poem with its almost Shakespearean dramatic monologues is touched with Elizabethan "thous" and "thees," sometimes uses end rhyme, and some sections of the book end in couplets. In style, it falls between the (mostly) free verse of *Red Flag* and the contortions of her sonnets in her last book, *Dance of Fire*, transforming her ever-present concern with world politics into a growing metaphysics.

Jesus is depicted as an anarchist. "He was a man dangerous to governments, a despiser/of rules, making a mockery of ordinance..." As critic Julie Lisella notes, every character carries some form of inner violence, in particular, jealousy—Magdalene for the disciple John, Mary for Jesus's followers, and Judas for Magdalene's pure love of Jesus. Jesus is the great seducer, "the searing fire of that glance," who, like a committed Communist or one of those wild anarchists of Ridge's youth, feels more for the masses than his mother. "Only a multitude could fan his eyes /To that deep blaze of tenderness." At the end of the poem, Mary mourns his dead body with a simple nursery rhyme.

Then—as now—a poet had to make her own publicity efforts. "Josiah Tits[z]ell went three times to the New York Times and talked me up to the editor in chief—when he managed to see at last [i]t was all this that sold out first edition of *Firehead* on the first day," writes Ridge to her husband. Titzell was an occasional poet, lyricist, novelist, critic, and as associate editor of *Publisher's Weekly*, the man-in-the-know. When the *Times*'s laudatory review appeared, Ridge had mixed feelings: "Percy Hutchison's review in the Times was founded on a complete misconception of the poem and it was favourable of course...." He likened the poetry to Dante's, and wrote:

> Those whose senses have been dulled with the paucity of imagination and emotion that brings so much of contemporary verse to a monotonous level of attainment will find themselves stung tinglingly awake by Miss Ridge's multiplicity of images, drawn impartially from religious or secular sources, and the vibrant quality of her lines...It is forceful and beautiful, a work in which imagination and intelligence fuse in a white flame.

Many critics—and Ridge herself—said the book was written in direct response to the Sacco and Vanzetti trial and execution. Ridge asserted that she began writing it after two nights without sleep a week after their deaths. According to Nancy Berke in *Women Poets on the Left*, the book "reconfigures Christ as our most famous victim of institutionalized murder" as a protest to the country's obsession with capital punishment. Certainly the idea is in the air. *America Arraigned*, an anthology of poetry sent to Governor Fuller in an effort to stop the execution, was divided into sections like "After the Intercession was Refused but Before the Crucifixion." William Closson called Governor Fuller another Pontius Pilate in his poem selected for the anthology, and "Two Crucified" was the title of Jeannette Marks's contribution. Ridge's own poem "Two in the Death House," referred not to the parallels of the execution to Christ's but to immigrant labor:

> Shall we "make heroes" of you—when all you ruminate,
> Of songs, books, art, or the world's thought,
> Hard-learned, meagerly fitting, like worker's clothes,
> Askew upon you, might be talked out in one evening?
> Of you—not having any bright possession, or good hope of it,
> Save what lies in two hands—hands cognizant
> Of the cool feel of fish and of the grains of leathers.
> Hands made stiff
> In such plain service as men live by, yet despise the servers.

While it must be true that the execution was of tremendous importance to Ridge, given that a few years later she writes "Via Ignis," twenty-eight very abstract sonnets on the subject, the psychological impetus in *Firehead* seems to be much more about her guilt over the abandonment of her son Keith. Mary, the mother of Christ, reminisces in page after page:

> I gave
> To his small frantic lips, the one
> Deep need of his that I could ever fill
> And wrapped him in a finer linen than I wore
> > But that was all (*Firehead* 131)

"He was but eleven then...and this/Was almost the last time he looked on me./As one half-pleased to know that I was there" (133) and Mary's acknowledgement: "I did not love him as a mother./Should have loved such a son. I know this now..." (136). The son too speaks:

Has my small ghost
That stumbled after thee so many years
So pressed its image on thy heart, that now
I am a stranger with a beard? 'Tis true
My bones were smaller when thou sawest me last,
My head a silken thistle for thy hand
To stroke and start away as from a sting (*Firehead* 93)

Ridge did not know whether her son was alive or dead after his letters stopped coming from Detroit 15 years earlier. As mentioned, Evelyn Scott responded to some lament Ridge had made about him around the time of *Firehead*'s publication with: "I can't but believe he is old enough now to have read and realized something of what is in you and has been so wonderfully expressed." Ridge's hurried composition methods—aided by a literal fever, drugs, and anorexic visions—without time for revision—stripped bare a preoccupation different from the religious or the executed immigrants, despite cloaking the narrative with archaic language. The *Yale Review* came closest to such an evaluation:

Miss Ridge has attempted too much; she has ventured on a theme which many greater poets have wisely declined. She has treated this theme with force, but as we read we feel that this force is not the force of a poetic sensibility, but some darker power of neurotic violence.

Here the maternal emerges, incestuous yet divided, both burning and cold. William Drake remarks on Ridge's whole oeuvre: "Ridge's poetry is marked both by rage at injustice and by a fiercely maternal urgency, as if the disorder of the world arose out of a separation from the spiritual center the mother represents." Ridge went transgressive. Amongst her "tirelessly extended metaphors" writes Lisella, lies "an anachronistic poetess-like lyric style in the service of clearly un-lady-like material." "Let thy trumpeting mountains urinate upon her their scalding lavas." "Dance, dance with thy legs agape—call on hills to enter thee!/Ravish her, O hills!"

The far-off mutter of the desert, licking her dry parts...
Her sands
Lolling in the darkness...tufts of grass on the bare hills...the stretched

Sinews between mountains. (*Firehead*, 47)

Finally, after it seems that Christ has raped his mother, he begs to return to her: "Thou wound of time that gangrenes now, thou mud of ages,/open and take back thy son."

"*Nice* is the one adjective in the world that is laughable applied to any single thing I have ever written," Ridge writes two years later. Such outrageousness did not prevent the radical preacher John Haynes Holmes, founding member of both the N.A.A.C.P. and A.C.L.U. and friend of William Floyd, from having her read from *Firehead* at the Community Church on Park Avenue.

It was hardly the first time she used sex as a shock tactic. Among other examples, there is "Brooklyn Bridge" in her first book, with its sadomasochistic overtones:

> Pythoness body—arching
> Over the night like an ecstasy—
> I feel your coils tightening...
> And the world's lessening breath. (*Ghetto* 70)

and "After the Recital" in *Red Flag*, with its suggestion of interracial sex when anti-miscegenation laws were in effect nationwide until 1967, and violations might result in mob punishment or lynchings. As previously mentioned, Roland Hayes was the internationally famous black tenor to whom the poem is dedicated.

> Who cared...amid the suave-shoed, white-skinned day
> That scanned his body...if beneath her fires
> Yet throbbing like five wounds, unhealed, he lay
> Back turned...as one not caring over much
> To see her golden head upon the spires
> And all the windows flower at the touch. (*Red Flag* 79)

Those put on the spot by Ridge did not know what to say about *Firehead*. "Criticism of it is quite beyond me," wrote the poet Gerald Sykes, who had been at Yaddo with her. He had motive for circumspection: she supported his Guggenheim application a year later. Evelyn Scott provided a promotional insert for the book but mentioned *Firehead* only in the last two lines and then rather offhandedly: "In her new book, 'Firehead,' Miss Ridge, superlatively rational, superlatively modern, has defied the cowardice of an age which, in the fear of making itself laughed at, has made itself paltry." Moore must have annoyed Ridge with the Christian focus of her interpretation: "There are triumphs of technique: flame-touched attributes of sanctity emerge; we are led to deliberate upon Christ's mystic power." Only Horace Gregory, with his vantage of a decade later, writes in *A History of American Poetry*, that her "reiterated images of light within the poem, effective as they were upon first reading, dazzled rather than enlightened the understanding of her sympathetic critics."

That Robinson Jeffers's *Dear Judas* came out at the same time probably helped her sales. Certainly the two books were often reviewed together. The treatment of their Crucifixions was close, although Jeffers was influenced by Noh plays rather than Ridge's Elizabethan models. Like Ridge, Jeffers wasn't interested in Christianity except as a means of using the most familiar story of Western civilization as a frame for poetic drama. This review from the magazine *Bozart* is a good example of how the books were seen side-by-side.

> Necessarily the conception of Jeffers is more subtle and more sophisticated than that of his less mysterious opponent...Lola Ridge...offering her glitter and golden intensity of descriptive epithet, victoriously in the manner of a pageant, as contrasted with the agonizing dumbshow of Jeffers....[Judas] is to Jeffers the lover of Christ; he is to Ridge the lover of Magdalene. To Jeffers he is possibly the hero of the tragedy; to Ridge he is not the impossible villain... Lola Ridge's poem is one of the most firmly marrowed long poems by a woman to come from our generation; and Robinson Jeffers's another link to that iron chain whereby the great prison themselves to the eternal.

Tambour, a magazine that published Williams, Shaw, and Dreiser, carried this evaluation: "I believe Miss Ridge's book is in all manners more momentous than that of Jeffers, no mean achievement either." In the end Jeffers received far fewer reviews and perhaps that is why he refused to give Ridge an award from *Poetry* two years later. "I have been thinking seriously about our selection," he writes Harriet Monroe, and I've talked to a few friends, two of whom suggested Lola Ridge. I am not an enthusiast for her work, but "Firehead" was much admired. I believe she was ill and poor when it was being written, and no doubt she is still in need. What do you think of her?...if the casting vote is left to me I'll vote for MacLeish...who is probably in need or he wouldn't be working for "Fortune" magazine.

Ridge had no idea of his antipathy. "Jeffers was for me," she writes Louise Adams Floyd, "but could not convince the others, especially Monroe and each of the other judges had a choice...Finally they all compromised on Alexander McLeish [sic]." In another letter, Ridge revealed a more competitive stance: "A great puritan poet," she writes, "but I did not think so much of [Dear Judas.]" Still she dedicated an admiring poem to him in her last book, recommended him to others, and often shared copies of his work. In 1932, he appeared on the cover of *Time* magazine, but his politically aloof, really anarchist leanings—"boys will hang Hitler and Roosevelt in one tree"—caused him to fall out of favor, just as Ridge did.

Originally *Firehead* was to be a book set in New York, but Ridge eventually decided it was the first of what was to be a five-volume poetry series entitled *Lightwheel*. The series title is perhaps a re-visioning of the huge 50-foot waterwheels that turned in Kanieri Township, and her preoccupation with light and fire born from the ever-present threat of fire in Hokitika. But, in the case of the book *Firehead*, there's just the scorched earth of ambition. While *The Ghetto and Other Poems* and *Sun-up and Other Poems* and parts of *Red Flag* have an immediacy of image and voice that is contemporary, in *Firehead*, Ridge's vision outpaces the material, and the work sounds dated and wrought. It's not the religious theme that proves difficult. Eliot's "Prufrock" and Pound's *Cantos* deal with religion. It's not that other poets didn't have grand ambitions—there's the *Cantos*, the already published "Prufrock," Williams working on *Paterson*, H.D. 10 years from beginning her *Trilogy*—they were all ambitious. Ridge's hubris, the flip side of ambition, was her downfall. If Shelley could write "The Mask of Anarchy" in six days, she could write *Firehead* in six weeks. Only Davy saw drafts and he didn't offer her anything other than encouragement. Perhaps he understood all her obscure allusions and followed the logic of her lines. In any case, she gave herself hardly any time at all to improve the first 53 pages. "Of *Firehead*...it is not to go to printer for 10 days—in case I want to make alterations."

Ridge uses "twixt" on the third page of the poem, ringing a death knell for modernism. Or rather, like cummings re-thinking how words move on the page or Williams admitting the demotic, Ridge is asking the reader to admit that "twixt" and dense illusion and archaic forms like inversion are techniques that will enliven the modernist poem. After all, other modernists were insisting on similar tactics. Edna St. Vincent Millay wrote ten sonnets for breakfast and did not shrink from "thees" and "thous," and of course Crane used heightened language and many inversions in "To Brooklyn Bridge," parts of which Ridge had published while editing *Broom*. Her dizzying metaphorical leaps anticipated or followed or at least paralleled Crane's dictum in 1926: "The nuances of feeling and observation in a poem may well call for certain liberties which you claim the poet has no right to take. I am simply making the claim that the poet does have that authority, and that to deny it is to limit the scope of the medium so considerably as to outlaw some of the richest genius of the past." Deutsch explains it: "The modern poet moves from the style of one period...with unexampled freedom...Pope might translate Shakespeare into 18th-century verse, while the modern can draw on both." Where Ridge's *The Ghetto and Other Poems* heralded proletarian modernism, *Firehead* forged a way into its Elizabethan form. To some extent the strategy of such borrowings are the same as Jeffers appropriating the Noh plays or Pound the troubadours' voices.

"To Brooklyn Bridge" was published a year after *Firehead*, in 1930. Crane begins it with a very ornate Elizabethan inversion:

> How many dawns, chill from his rippling rest
> The seagull's wings shall dip and pivot him,

By the fourth stanza he uses "thee" and "thou" just as freely as Ridge, to refer to the bridge as if it were a deity.

> And Thee, across the harbor, silver-paced
> As though the sun took step of thee, yet left
> Some motion ever unspent in thy stride,—
> Implicitly thy freedom staying thee!

Several stanzas later there's the addition of the antique "guerdon," "dost," and "bestow"

And obscure as that heaven of the Jews,
Thy guerdon...Accolade thou dost bestow
Of anonymity time cannot raise:
Vibrant reprieve and pardon thou dost show

Randall Jarrell wrote: "*The Bridge* does not succeed as a unified work of art, partly because some of its poems are bad or mediocre." Tennessee Williams, a big fan of Crane, writes that he could

> hardly understand a single line—of course the individual lines aren't supposed to be intelligible. The message, if there actually is one, comes from the total effect...it is a lot of raw material, all significant and moving but not chiseled into any communicative shape.

But the big critics adored Crane: "The only poet of the twentieth century that I could secretly set above Yeats and Stevens," writes critic Harold Bloom. Harvard critic Helen Vendler deemed "Crane's 'Voyages' the greatest contemporary American love poem." Critic David Yezzi suggests that:

> his very purpose in writing the poem was to arrive at non-rational, connotative connections that could not be fully elucidated in logical terms. In a sense, what disturbed Crane's editors most about his poetry was its resistance to paraphrase, or as Harrison Smith said, an irritation with "the denseness of one's own intellect."

Although a childhood friend of Crane's, the publisher Harrison Smith refused to bring out his books. He preferred Lola Ridge.

Among today's poets, Crane's reputation appears, *pace* Bloom and Vendler, a case of the "Emperor's New Clothes." In a *Field* magazine symposium on his work, the introduction outlines how his work is evaluated by contemporary poets:

> From the time of Crane's death until the mid-1970s, there seemed to be a concerted effort to promote him as a major poet. That effort, essentially, has failed. There are simply too many problems of diction, syntax, prosody, structure, and vision in Crane's work to validate that kind of claim.

Pulitzer Prize winner Charles Wright admits that "mostly I've loved lines." David Young finds Crane's work "overly sweeping and mythic, too grandiose and unanchored for its own good..." Marianne Boruch laments "his sentimentality, his predictable cadence and mannered language, his boosterism for America, for the 'Machine Age,' his fondness for bombast and excess and prophecy." A queer studies critic from another symposium comments on what he believes is at the root of Crane's difficulty, but he could also be referring to Ridge's secret shame of abandoning her child:

> The intensity responsible for Crane's particular form of difficulty involves not only linguistic considerations but also culturally subjective concerns. This intensity produces a kind of privacy that is comprehensible in terms of the cultural construction of homosexuality and its attendant institutions of privacy.

Of course there is also the possibility that Crane and Ridge have accomplished an aesthetic leap that surpasses contemporary appreciation. As critic Catherine Daly suggests with regard to "Via Ignis," a later poem of Ridge's:

> The thees and thous, the verbs ending in "eth,"and the stilted diction may now seem ridiculous, but the archaism and spirituality expressed in these poems has a purpose: it subverts both the modernism and the Marxism Ridge held in complex and difficult relationship.

Occasionally, *Firehead* breaks into intelligibility:

> I do remember how the old blue sea
> Shuffled in glistening coils about the day
> That cast thy shadow on our street and how
> From out the passing litters, in which bared
> White jeweled arms moved languidly their fans
> And topaz glimmered in the small pink ears
> That curled about thy voice, shrewd eyes outstared
> Outdiamonding the twinkling of the sands. (*Firehead* 69)

Except for the "small pink ears" suddenly coming to life and curling, the lines follow grammatically and graphically, there is an identifiable speaker doing the reminiscing, and Ridge coins "outdiamonding" acceptably, if excessively, as a verb to describe glittering eyes.

What becomes admired depends so much on taste and timing, as well as the proper publicity, the right psychological mix in the Zeitgeist that allows a poet to step into the light just when the hands of the audience are coming together—and not just the text, as New Critics would have readers believe. The value of poetry is always changing. As Cary Nelson writes:

> We tend to ignore evidence that promotion by oneself or others plays
> a role in building careers, preferring to assume it is the best poets,
> not necessarily those who are the most ambitious or most widely
> publicized, who retain long-term visibility.

One example contemporary with Crane and Ridge's technical rivalry is Hope Mirrlees, whose very modernist book-long poem *Paris: A Poem* perhaps outdoes Eliot's "The Waste Land," but was published three years earlier. Her volume was surely something he had seen since their mutual friend Virginia Woolf published it right after his *Poems*. However, Mirrlees never discussed it with him. "I am unaware whether he ever saw it," she said. "We were not yet acquainted in 1919." From a wealthy Scottish family, she grew up partially in South Africa, and was living with her former Cambridge tutor in Paris at the time the book was written. Although Mirrlee's book focuses on the female and aberrant sex, "The Waste Land" echoes it, particularly in emotional resonance. Beautifully bound in a fleur-de-lis print, the handset volume in the Mortimer Rare Book Room at Smith College contains Woolf's penciled-in corrections. Woolf did not rewrite her poem as Pound did Eliot's, and Pound also did not use his considerable skill in promotion that the new modernist work required and that Eliot embraced.

> Verlaine's bed-time...Alchemy
> Absynthe,
> Algerian tobacco,
> Talk, talk, talk,
> Manuring the white violets of the moon.

Mirrlees published her next book of poetry more than 40 years later.

As for Joyce, his doppelgänger could be considered his friend Abraham Lincoln Gillespie, "Link," who somewhat resembled him. Like Pound who was also a friend, Link was groomed for bourgeois life via the Quakers, and he too attended college in Pennsylvania. Also a friend of Stein's, Gillespie published work in *Transition* in the late 1920s that outdid Stein and Joyce and Pound in typographical innovation.

Sweettrustmisery-Eyed hurtbyherMan-Woman
motherready-responsewarmth
cashregisterAnnote dissemINFO...

In Europe, Gillespie lived in a stone house that had one room with all the furniture fixed to the ceiling. After his return to the U.S. in the 1930s, Gillespie disappeared into dense sound experiments, speaking just the way he wrote, making sonic performances that brought down the house at New York's Village Vanguard. His literary achievements went largely unrecognized, and his death certificate in 1950 listed his occupation as "none."

Chapter 28

Return to Yaddo:
Taggard and Copland

Only ten months after leaving Yaddo, Ridge settled back in her old room. Her husband must have been relieved to have her gone. As she admitted to her friend Louise Adams Floyd in the spring of 1930:

> I'm in a beastly temper. Davy started it off this morning by an *optimistic* remark. He was crossing the room and my snarled retort caught him half way. He stood as though stuck fast staring at me with sharp bewildered eyes and hair standing up straight—he looked like the ram caught in the thicket.

George Peabody, Katrina Trask's second husband, and Mrs. Pardee, the nanny and eventually the Trask secretary, had invited her for this second stay, beginning July 9th, even though artists were then only allowed to visit once. Ridge began her work by reading Babylonian history, hoping this visit to capture the rise of culture in all humanity. Again too preoccupied to come down for dinner, she entertained visitors in her room.

Her first was the radical poet and fellow guest Genevieve Taggard, who sent Ridge a note the day she arrived requesting to see her, the grand dame, reclusive, and ailing. Ridge had been featured in four anthologies in 1930, including *Best Poems of 1929*, and *Firehead* was a national hit. "At last you are here," Taggard writes.

They had much to share. The child of missionaries, Taggard spent her formative years immersed in the multicultural polyglot of the Pacific in Hawaii, which shaped her strong views on race and class. She helped publicize *Sun-up* when she worked for Huebsch, Ridge's publisher in the 20s, and co-founded *The Measure*, a poetry journal, editing it the same time Ridge was editing *Broom*. Ridge's poem "The Ailanthus Tree" was published in its second issue. While Ridge cited Dickinson as one of the few women geniuses in literature, Taggard had just published an adoring and prescient biography of Dickinson that year which suggested, among other claims, that Dickinson had had a fairly ordinary love life. Taggard and Ridge were also both contributing editors to *New Masses* that published many of Taggard's poems, reviews, and articles during the 1930s. Taggard also shared Ridge's "bisexual" belief in the source of creativity. In her preface to her collected works, she argued that her poems "hold a wider consciousness than that colored by the feminine half of the race. I hope they were not written by a poetess, but a poet." She rephrased Ridge's ideas on male and female creativity in her 1935 essay "Equal Rights": "There is one impulse for control and its antagonistic impulse for abandon; one pushing inward, the other exploding at the Center." The two of them also held similar views on the Russian Revolution, although Taggard professed an ideological fascination that Ridge, in the end, did not. While Taggard would visit Russia in 1936, Ridge decided that traveling to Baghdad was more important to her work, revealing once again that her political agenda was not doctrinaire. According to William Drake, Taggard's aim in her most proletarian book of poetry, *Calling Western Union*, published in 1936, was "to transform the isolated line into a script for collective chants," something Ridge had already done in her work on Sacco and Vanzettti, chanting them at the demonstration before the execution. Taggard's later interest in the African American lyric tradition intersected with Ridge's work "Lullaby," the ballad written in dialect on the St. Louis riots. As white women, they both had had to develop an appropriate strategy for speaking about another race.

Fiercely liberal, Taggard would later be grouped with Kenneth Fearing and Muriel Rukeyser as one of the "Dynamo Poets," who, with Ridge as a kind of foremother, took labor as a serious topic for poetry, but saw imagism as too static to convey the dynamic drive for social justice. Sol Funaroff's magazine, *Dynamo*, celebrated this aesthetic. It appeared sporadically between 1934 and 1936, until its editor died from the deprivations of poverty. Rukeyser's famous lines "Not Sappho, Sacco," were first printed in *Dynamo*.

Like Ridge, Taggard had developed a great interest in metaphysical poetry, especially Donne, perhaps sparked by Eliot's influential essay "The Metaphysical Poets" in 1921, and his various writings afterwards. "Metaphysical poetry," Taggard writes, "has been inspired by a philosophical conception of the universe and the role assigned to the human spirit in the great drama of existence." This statement appeared in the introduction to

Circumference, her anthology of metaphysical poetry, in which Ridge was not included. "Emotion, as a source of art forms, is in disrepute—it is more decorous to assume the mind, as well as incubating the egg, supplies the germs," writes Ridge in her mostly positive review of the book. Perhaps during their meeting at Yaddo, Taggard thanked Ridge for the notice which appeared in the *New York Evening Post* that April.

Aaron Copland was Ridge's next guest. He arrived at Yaddo after Taggard had already left, but would later set Taggard's poem "Lark" to music. With socialist and pro-Communist leanings, the 30-year-old composer was then defining what was American in music, a topic in literature very dear to Ridge. Her first impressions were good: "He is a lovely person. Everyone up here likes him. He mentioned some of his several hundred intimates whom he'd like me to meet—I think he's the most friendful man in America." He was working on "Piano Variations," and also re-writing the rhythms of "Symphonic Ode," a piece that he finally approved only in 1955. By September, he was inviting Ridge to his studio to listen to his drafts. She writes:

> I've only got to work today. I think I owe the fact that I have been going to Aaron Copland's studio yesterday...he played...an adaptation of his Symphonique ode—the theme is The Creation. I guessed it at once before the first of the 5 movements were played. I asked him if it wasn't that afterwards and he said yes. But this ode is the greatest music—in fact the only music...promise of greatness—that I have so far heard from any American composer. He has so far played it before only three or four people.

Ridge had finally found a use for her study of music theory long ago in Australia. In addition, Henrietta Glick, a 27-year-old graduate of Chicago Musical College, had begun an oratorio based on *Firehead* in January. Glick, also a friend of Stein and Moore, composed symphonies that were performed in Italy and Rochester, New York. Ridge was collaborating: "I [am] reading aloud to her, describing musical themes that came to me during the writing of it." In April, Ridge had also begun collaborating on a choral piece with the Chicago composer Dr. Wesley LaViolette.

Copland visited her studio several more times. In contrast to Stravinsky, Schoenberg, Hindemith, and perhaps Glick, Ridge had faith in him as the future of composing: "I've heard enough of your music now to feel you belong definitely with the coming group of yea-sayers. You have experienced something of what the late dead that are yet alive have passed through, but you are already past it, with a perspective on it."

He was thoughtful in a response to her a year later: "I feel sure that there is a certain essence of contemporary reality which is expressed in the Variations which I was too young to grasp at the writing of the Ode."

Her opinion of his work had changed by the end of her life:

Nov. 10. Last night we listened to Aaron Copland's Billy the Kid—the arrangement from music of the Ballet which I didn't see. I didn't want to listen—because the cowboy phase of America does not interest me—or rather the persistence of the theme disturbs me.

Nov 11. The exuberance of the frontier man still in the American blood, the glorious energy, lacking direction, turned inward in the weak, the emotionally immature, making a vicious circle in the unit of being...that breast to breast grapple with nature the forefathers so intrepidly met meant too the barefisted grapple with our fellow man—here too the howling will to power—and all thrown on the dice for the moment of tawdry [?] glory. And how soon the guns for those who had had target practice on the Indians—gun to gun—I'll beat them on the draw—and this yet in our alleys....There is a new race forming in America. Billy the Kid belonged and yet belongs in the childhood of that race.

Her acquaintance Paul Strand also spent a month at Yaddo. He and Copland had been friends since 1927, sharing an interest of Stieglitz's work and ideals. She doesn't mention Strand at all in her letters, busy instead reading "Myths of the Origin of Fire," an essay by Sir James George Frazer, and working on the sonnets that would fill much of her last book, *Dance of Fire*. In August, Bill Benét wrote to her from the MacDowell Colony, where he was reading Catullus and consorting with Edgar Arlington Robinson and Thornton Wilder: "Most certainly we will publish a book for you next year! We regard you as our 'white hope'—though it's a lot more than hope, naturally. We regard you as one of our stars."

Her need for Gynergen had not abated. She worked long hours under its influence and suffered all its side effects. On July 24, she writes: "I've opened my second bottle of Gynergen and in about ten or twelve days will need another..." She was asking for another bottle August 9. "A bottle of Gynergen goes to you tonight," Lawson writes back on August 11. Ridge returned to New York for a few days so the requests were interrupted. "We'll have some time together," she had promised her husband. But the trip home would be for research purposes. "You'll take me to [the] Museum of art [sic] [where] they have Babylonian things I want to see." Davy wished she could stay a week "but I suppose you won't want to." By September 7, Lawson was sending her a clock and more Gynergen. Four days later she writes ominously: "I want more Gynergen soon," and by the 22nd she ends her letter by underlining: "Don't forget the Gynergen." In her druggy intensity, she must have looked wild. Eloise Gard Wright, the Yaddo secretary remembered her vividly: "You are called up to me in white fire with only the black band of your hair to make my mind call you woman." When Ridge came down with a cold, her room was flooded with flowers—eight vases. Sympathy she knew how to get.

She sent her husband copies of what she produced and then chastised him for not answering her sooner. "Perhaps if you had more interest in my work." She writes to him: "Sept. will not be possible [for you to come up] because Gorham Munson and a crowd of 'humanists' or near-humanists are coming up here for a powwow on the trend of American Letters." Did a letter from a "Stan" dated September 9 have anything to do with her stalling? Addressed to "Darling, " and signed "all my love," the letter is replete with compliments regarding her work and statements like "I...dare talk to you as an equal." From the contents of the letter, however, it seems that Stan was an acquaintance from other than Yaddo, and not on the premises. Perhaps it was an affair, but rarely did she deflect her time or energy on anyone else. In "Woman and the Creative Will," she established that women owed it to themselves and the world to recognize and use their expressive talents, but she had no answers to how they might fulfill their obligations to an intimate relationship or family.

Although Mrs. Ames asked to meet Lawson at the beginning of Ridge's stay, Lawson began to sound resigned to Ridge's ambivalence about his visit:

> I am pleased that Mrs. Ames should have asked me up, but as I said
> in my last letter it won't be possible for me to come up on account of
> my surveying work which will keep me extra busy for some time but
> I thank her very much, and hope to see her some other time

In rather formal language, he made it clear he wasn't as upset with her illness as she was. "The care and attention you are receiving should help you out of your present poor condition."

Ridge received another note from her publisher and deduced that "they seem quite eager to have my next book and indicate they will publish anything I write." But in October Bill Benét lost his job and she had to find another publisher, perhaps ruining her plan to produce a book as quickly as she had the year before. She carried on, however. "Last night, when I knocked off after eleven hours of work, I was too tired....went to bed with a frightful headache and ready to scream with nervous strain but I woke up again at 5:30 a.m." She managed to borrow money to have her teeth fixed but still needed her Gynergen. She became frantic for the drug, and once wrote her husband twice in one day asking for it. Her urgent requests continued until the very end of her stay: "I'm afraid I must (underlined twice) have Gynergen when I go down."

Fall at Yaddo is pronounced: the studios are surrounded by huge trees that respond vividly to the changing season. Perhaps Ridge was beginning to feel her true age—57—when she wrote:

> From my window I can see the gorgeous woodline of the trees like evening fountains of gold that look as though they had been struck still in the act of flowing and left miraculously in mid air. Others are going up like scarlet flames in between all the colors—royal browns shading into purples—that wonderful color you find in some eyes— deep burning oranges and sultry red—the tree I call Evelyn, still of a lovely green. Why can't human old age be like that?

After this second stay, Elizabeth Ames invited her to become part of a group of artists who might suggest new guests every year. Ridge put forward several. But she was already planning travel to another retreat, a trip to ancient Babylon.

Chapter 29

Europe on Patronage

Undaunted by lack of funds or the challenges of an exotic culture, Lola Ridge set sail alone for Babylon on the *Tuscania* in mid-May 1931. The Near East had been an interest of Ridge's for some time, judging from the poems "Palestine" and "Babel" in *The Ghetto*. Perhaps she had seen her friend Martin Lewis's 1929 print, *Building a Babylon*, a cityscape with a ziggurat skyscraper. She certainly had the support of her friends. "Joe [Brewer, her co-publisher] brought me books and a big packet [of] more letters of introduction," she writes in her first onboard letter to Louise Adams Floyd.

> Warren [the other co-publisher] [brought] a box of magnificent flowers that nearly fills a table in the dining room. It, the box, was as big as himself...Martin Lewis also came and Martin, Davie, Laura Benét, and Eda Lou Walton waited to see me off and watched until I lost their dear faces in the dark.

Mrs. Mary Pratt Richter gave her the funds to launch her trip. "Mrs. Richter (of the friends of music) has also sent me a hundred dollars....it was she who gave me the money to come to Europe this summer." Two years earlier at Yaddo she had longed for a patron to fund travel to the Middle East while working on *Firehead*. "O Davy if only someone would have sent me to Palestine to write my poem!...everyone but me has been able to go to the location of their creative work and do it." But Mrs. Richter hadn't given her enough money to get all the way to Baghdad, and Ridge began asking around for additional funding a month into the trip. Gone were Ridge's qualms about borrowing that resulted in the return of the kitty Scott had collected for her in 1927.

Of course she traveled alone—Davy would just be another expense and distraction and apparently she still hoped he would move on. "Do not be lonely for me dear, make friends with other women," she admonishes him just a week after sailing. He sent her $50 in July and said he would do the same in August, and she writes to Louise Adams Floyd: "I'm afraid this means he's having a dreadful time, for he won't have money to take any other woman around. This thought troubles me very much—but what can I do about it?" Yet her very first letter home points to her acute need for him and his assistance: "If only I had not forgotten the Babylonian notes and my *slippers!*"

Traveling third class, she made one of her few references to her Australasian past in a letter to Lawson: "The sea...for years I lived within the compelling sound of it. Its thunderous song mixes up with so many of my memories." Ridge prided herself on never getting seasick, and even managed to smoke during the voyage. "Needing a light for my cigarette, [I] said 'got a match?'" In response, she received a lecture on smoking from an Englishwoman who was a missionary to India. The woman said she had been "'astounded' to see how many American women smoked. Ridge was a New Woman, so certainly she smoked, and an American New Woman, only now learning America's place in the world from the point of view of Europeans. "Our table steward said to me as I said goodbye to him: "When America is [depressed] it hits the whole world. We've been depending on America."

She stayed in London two months, losing her purse, taking notes at the British Museum, waiting for her Babylonian notes to arrive. A friend of her publisher's invited her to spend several weekends at a 17th century country house. "I'm enchanted with the English countryside," she wrote. "[I]t is beautiful[,] rolling wild downs—no one told me how beautiful. I heard a cookoo [sic] sing at daybreak yesterday morning. I'm feeling better than I've felt for years and think the slower tempo of London responsible." She had dinner with Evelyn Scott and "drank half a bottle of Algerian claret between us...they [Evelyn and Jack Metcalfe, her husband] had quarreled early in the day and she [Evelyn] was unhappy." By June 8th, Ridge was frantic about her Babylonian notes, and accused Lawson's mother of having taken them during a visit. "She hates me with the ruthless female hate of jealousy." But Ridge received the notes two days later so they were obviously en route. She visited the publisher Jonathan Cape who told her he would have brought out *Firehead* in London, "only that times were so bad for books...He's an old satyr, I did not like him." She arranged a tête-à-tête with the novelist Richard Hughes, whose famous pirate novel *High Wind in Jamaica* had been published the year before. He had also edited *Oxford*

Poetry with Robert Graves in 1921, making him an important contact. They had quite a visit, and he seemed to have had to concoct an elaborate escape. They began by dining at a little out of the way Italian place

> where we sat and talked for two hours, drinking delicious dry white Chianti, then he drove me along the Thames embankment and other parts of the city until four in the afternoon...He had promised to visit a child in hospital who had an operation, and read to her at three thirty, and after leaving me at my door rushed off, troubled that he was late and that she would be anxiously waiting.

She left London by boat for Corsica, thinking it cheaper than overland. Five hundred people had drowned off the coast of France just before she left, when a ship capsized in high seas near Pointe Saint-Gildas. She managed to lose all her baggage en route, including her Gynergen, and immediately came down with a terrible headache, probably the result of withdrawal. Isolated in her illness and by distance, she recognized what a trial she could be to her husband: "To-day I remember with what contrition that it is your rare holiday, that you will be away at camp and that it [her letter] will worry you so...I cannot forgive myself for my stupid self-absorption."

Ajaccio, the Corsican capital, reminded her of New Zealand. Paintings of the time show a bay with an idyllic row of sailboats, edged by snow-topped mountains. Long a British vacation spot, it was (and still is) renowned as the center of organized crime in Europe. Ridge's contact tried to reassure her about how secure the city was: "He [Thomson] says I'm as safe here as I would be in the middle of New York—I asked him if this were irony." A couple of months after she left, the French army invaded the island to make arrests, the subject of the newsreel "Ajaccio. 'Cleaning up Corsica!'" in which French troops launched a miniature war against Corsican bandits, "the curse of the famous Isle of Beauty," complete with shots of soldiers enjoying the local cuisine.

Ridge admitted the island had beauty, and had trouble getting down to work. But she still had ambition. When she received news that Evelyn Scott's paramour, Owen Merton, had died, she writes: "Let him rest, poor chap, with his futile hunger to paint great pictures and attain fame—how many o lord, how many...well perhaps me too..."

By the middle of July she had no money to buy bread, and she spent her last sous on a cable to her husband. It was as if the Depression and its deprivations didn't exist for her. Penniless at its beginning, she could not have been much affected by the sinking economy of the world. The Depression did, however, affect her friends. In response to her request of $200 from her friend Ellen Kennan, she received only $50. "Well god knows," Ridge writes, "I do not wish to take advantage of her or anyone. Simply the artist whose work is not accepted by his generation is pushed into the position of a parasite." Kennan was a Denver schoolteacher who had befriended Emma Goldman on one of her tours, lost her job because of antiwar activism, and later became the lover of Cyril Kay-Scott, Evelyn Scott's first husband. Ridge had had a falling out with Kennan in 1928—"malicious behavior"—a few years after Kennan traveled with Scott's entourage of lovers and children to Europe. They must have patched it up for Ridge to have asked for such a large sum. Ridge tried to borrow money from other friends to pay Kennan back right away, but was always too poor by the time the money arrived to return it. She kept hoping Davy would have the money. "Did you get your expected raise?" she asked him, who was about to be fired, along with thousands of other workers. Or maybe the raise he said he was getting was a fabrication all along, invented to reassure her. Eventually she turned to all her previous backers, including Josephine Boardman Crane. "Now as to ways and means [of getting on with her travels]: I shall write to Mrs. W. Murray Crane who was so kind before when I was ill." Mrs. Crane was the widow of a governor and senator who established the famous stationery business. She helped found the Metropolitan Museum of Art and held a weekly salon that Marianne Moore frequented. She had been sending Ridge checks since 1928.

A month after Ridge's arrival in Corsica, she noted that Ajaccio had "some epidemic on...It must be playing havoc with the children from the number of little coffins I see." Writing to her husband, she tried to brush off the danger, she who was nearly always ill:

> "The sickness here killing so many is a bad form of malaria. Thomson
> is very afraid of it—I not at all. I don't believe I catch anything...there
> is also light typhoid in the town. T[Thomson] would not accompany
> his friends to the movies the other night for fear he'd pick up a germ.

She sounds as if she is whistling in the dark, trying to be brave. The next day's letter began with her saying that she wasn't well and hinted at another peril: "the water, which I drank (though only a little at a time, after medicine) unboiled for the first month." This was the year that the British writer Arnold Bennett died in Paris after drinking a glass of French water to prove how safe it was.

By the beginning of August, her Corsican landlord was asking for the rent in advance. She suspected Thomson had spread a rumor about her being broke. In the same letter that she begs Davy not to raise money for her trip to Mesopotamia, she mentions "the cost of traveling in Arabia enormous." She wasn't deterred. The day before she writes Louise Adams Floyd: "Planning when it cools to decrease by train the distance between me and Baghdad and the site of Babylon." By August 3, she was very anxious to leave Ajaccio: "I'll die with hatred of this city if I don't get out." She planned to go to Nice. After being harassed by a crazy person in the hotel, she reflects: "I feel more and more my place is with the outlaws and outcasts of the world. The thing is I've got soft. I shrink from dirt and poverty. But I'm not going to give in to it." She vows to "try and harden myself more at Nice, I'll try to get a studio[,] fix my own meals[,] and go out to dinner at night." Ridge's idea of roughing it with the "outlaws and outcasts" had not yet been tried by the squalor of the Middle East. Still in Ajaccio, she changed seats in the dining room to get away from a poor old Frenchman. He had moved with her, in seeming sympathy—and then lusted after her food scraps, she the anorexic!

Trying to spare her husband, she wrote him not to send her $60 but the next day she wrote she might need money quickly because she feared her face would become disfigured by dental problems. She would send him a telegram so he could solicit their friends without her having to beg for money in separate telegrams. A few days later, she gladly accepted his $60, but chided him for withholding Paul Strand's address since she hoped to write a paying article on Strand.

"I learned to live cheaply and comfortably in Ajaccio—just two days before I left!" she boasted to her publisher. Soon after she arrived in Nice, she resettled in a cheaper motel, happy to be away from "all those bourgeois people," a routine she maintained in every town. Evelyn Scott was impressed: "I have never been in Nice, because fearful of its cosmopolitan expensiveness." It was the very fashionable French Riviera, and the climate both in sensibility and weather was perfect for art. The year before, Marlene Dietrich had starred in *Blue Angel* as Lola Lola, cavorting in the local nightclubs. Nabokov worked in a Riviera vineyard in 1924, Ernest Hemingway and Scott Fitzgerald spent much time at Cap d'Antibes only 12 miles from Nice in the 30s. Art stars like Matisse worked in studios in the area. Ridge exclaimed that the wine was cheap.

At the end of the month, she writes her husband: "No dear, do not think I am starving myself. I'm having fresh eggs and plenty of fresh figs and good wine. This last seems to help me very much." Her face, with its possibly disfiguring dental problems, was better. In order to reassure him of her safety she writes: "I have seen only *one* policeman since I have been in Nice—and how different he looked beside my memories of the brutalized [ing?] new york cops." But to Louise Adams Floyd she writes more seriously:

> I have little doubt but that communism will sweep the entire world....I do believe in communism...but I do not think America is ready for it....America is not yet a people in the large sense of this word. She is not only distracted...by the infected and as yet unassimilated bloods, but these bloods, or most of them, have suffered a loss of certain massing elements in their transfusion.

The "massing elements" would seem to have gathered: unemployment in the U.S. was then at 16 percent and climbing. Her husband was refusing to reveal his job status to her. "I must not let my work spoil yours," she wrote him. "Do not send me any money October. At least start in on your classes. If I can raise enough to cover the journey it will give you breathing space." She writes him that she had started her long poem about Babylon. By October 3rd she mentions not so very reassuringly that she read in a French paper that "the plague has appeared in the valley of the Euphrates (it would, you know!)...it's a big valley." This was alongside reports that she had been successful in gathering funds to travel there: $50 from Mrs. Floyd, $100 from Mrs. Crane. She also explained the modernist movement by conflating rage and beauty, her own two sources of inspirations:

> The extremes of what we call modernism in music, poetry, particularly painting and sculpture is the expression, the symptom of a secret and frustrated rage of the mass-consciousness—a universal resentment that vents itself in a deliberate negation of beauty, that in itself (because it is perfectly sincere, at least at its beginnings in the deeps) achieves a new, a sort of hunch-backed beauty.

Her husband sent only $7 on Oct 7. It was a bad year to send money anywhere abroad, with markets falling and the exchanges less than advantageous. She responds to the small amount with: "Yes, I know things very bad all over the world, everywhere whispers of revolution or war." Six days later she writes: "Try and save a little so that you will not be penniless.... For me, I'm not afraid. If I'm stuck somewhere I may be able to get some kind of a job." She had not had a job since editing *Broom* eight years earlier, let alone a job in Europe or in the Middle East. She was brave—or foolhardy?

She chose the last cheap boat to Beirut and sailed via Alexandria. "Tonight I saw the most gorgeous sunset I've seen since leaving Australia." But the view at her feet was different. "Huge rats are running about the deck to-night[,] I wonder why I have not seen them before." She went ashore with an Austrian woman and admitted: "It's very hard on me to live now in close proximity to others. I can't think." On the road to Damascus—for she had accumulated just enough money to cross the desert—the driver of the Buick she was traveling in discovered

> that someone had been murdered a few minutes before ahead of us on the road. He stopped the car by standing in the middle of the road, directly in its path, and wildly waving his arms. However we went on and saw no sign of either the dead man or his assailants. Perhaps, unlike New Yorkers they call one killing a day and go home.

Ridge wasn't the intrepid Isabel Bird, that 19th-century adventurer, traveling to Baghdad armed with her revolver and "tea-making apparatus," or Gertrude Bell, the female Lawrence of Arabia, sometime spy and archaeologist who traveled there in the 1920s with a tin bath, a full Wedgwood dinner service, and a formal dinner dress for evening wear. Ridge did, however, travel with one of Bell's books. Described by a male colleague as a "conceited, gushing, flat-chested, man-woman, globe-trotting, rumpwagging, blethering ass," Bell was also a linguist and the greatest female mountaineer of her age. She became so powerful in Iraq that it was she who drew its boundaries. "I had a well-spent morning at the office making out the southern desert frontier of the Iraq," she wrote her father in 1921. She died of an apparent overdose of sleeping pills three years before Ridge arrived and Bell appeared as a ghost to Ridge, entreating her to disregard her own illness and continue her work. Ridge would hold her own. "I'm in the old mood, the one in which I landed in New York[,] with two dollars, all the money I had in the world." She sat bolt upright for 28 hours across the desert, a feat that would put many contemporary travelers to bed on arrival. "Look, here is the Baghdad we heard about when we were little girls," she writes.

> I opened my eyes on [the] toll bridge over a muddy winding channel which the blond cried out was the Euphrates[.] I saw dazedly clumps of green, a few palms, savage looking Arabs, one of whom out of whose fierce eyes hate streamed like a deadly fire, pointed a shaking and menacing finger at our driver.

Chapter 30

Babylon and Back

Babylon, once the largest city in the world, is the ancient "Gate of the Gods," the city of every evil, the name of a whore riding on a seven-headed beast who rules over all the kings of the earth, the city that produced the world's first wheel, first agriculture, first code of law, first base-60 number system, and possibly the first writing. It's the home of Hammurabi, whose principles of justice are still recognized today, where Sir Leonard Woolley in Ridge's day uncovered scores of priceless artifacts and claimed it was the site of the ancient flood and Abraham's birthplace. Nebuchadnezzar did not maintain his Hanging Gardens in Babylon but Fritz Lang shot his 1927 film *Metropolis* there, and the workers constructing the Tower of Babel destroyed it for better working conditions. It is also the location of Saddam Hussein's $5 million "Disney for a Despot," an elaborate re-creation of a single Babylonian palace the size of the Louvre. It is a city brought down by babble and trumpets, a meme for the incessant noise of technology today, and the name of extremely popular translation software. The Babylon a/k/a Camp Alpha occupied by the U.S. Army in 2003 and 2004 resulted in the wholesale destruction of much of the city's 5,000-year history.

Ridge arrived at the end of October 1931 and claimed to have moved into Baghdad's cheapest hotel. But like the hotel in Damascus, the stationery she used bore the Ritz heading, and the price included three meals, afternoon and early-morning tea. She even indulged in breakfast in bed, "on special request so suppose it is more"—with all the imported luxuries: sausage, bread and butter, jam, and bananas. She met another American poet who was writing his own poem about Babylon, but she didn't mention his name. "These things are in the air," she writes. But the air was also "filled with sand that has been ground to a fine dust by innumerable feet and wheels. This dust is filled with appalling filth, it blows in one's face [,] fills one's mouth nose and eyes." Still she was thrilled with her arrival and feeling up to its challenges, not the least of which was once again, a lack of funds. "It's true

I've lost my figure and my looks and can't pose as a model now, but I'll make out somehow, or someone will come to the rescue." But she had certainly pushed her luck. In the same letter she confesses: "I did not stop at Beirut to use my letters of introduction, I'm without reliable information of any kind." The next day she negotiated a lower hotel rate so she wouldn't have to move. She says she had become fearful of relocating to a cheaper place because she and another woman were stoned by the locals while touring the neighborhood. "I asked the woman born in Baghdad before I left the ship, why Americans were hated in Alexandria. She said in innocent surprise, 'Are they not hated everywhere?'"

Ridge had four days of good health in Baghdad before coming down with a fever. A doctor attended to her twice a day, an Indian practitioner who in the end charged her nothing. He told her that her "old lung trouble [was] stirred up now." She had two servants to tend to her. Again she reassured her husband by listing the epidemics raging "at present—pneumonia (Baghdad very bad for chest) cholera—not epidemic—always on—and typhoid fever. Malaria also, the Baghdadese have always with them. It's possibly the worst climate or one of the worst in the world." She was wrong about the cholera— it was an epidemic. Newspapers at the time reported that hundreds refused to be treated and died, with the death toll at 415 out of 787 cases. She wrote Louise Adams Floyd about the sickness too, justifying the danger with: "But the last two weeks has given me more for my poem than a year's research. I'm glad I've come."

Everyone told her that Hillah, where ancient Babylon is seated, was a terrible place for tourists. "Hilla[h] very bad town, very dirty town, much sick, bad Arabs in Hilla[h]," mimics Ridge. Those with whom she consulted, taking one look at her genteel shabbiness, urged her to spend her money in Baghdad. Ignoring their advice, she wrote her husband about her plans:

> I think I will have enough money left after I pay my hotel bill here to go to Hillah, and back, for a couple of days then I'll come back here to the same hotel, where, if necessary I can stay for 2 weeks without paying my bill...Yes, dear, it's a bit like living on my wits, I know, but it seems I haven't much else to live on.

Then she broke down and became, in her bravado, downright maudlin: "We ought to get together soon. I think the world is going to break into war or bust up in revolution and it may then be impossible....America dearest country in world to live in...." She may have sensed the Arabs' growing sympathy for the newly elected Hitler. One-third of Baghdad's population was Jewish in the early 1930s. Animosity toward them had increased, and it would eventually result in Iraq's own Kristallnacht in 1941. Arab boys were already being sent to be educated in Germany to organize paramilitary groups modeled after the Nazis'. Of particular concern would have been the Iraqis' wish to be rid of the British and democracy, and to return to Islamic values.

Ridge ended her letter to her husband with: "I'll get out my book [,] only death will stop me." Although she had written the same thing to him while at Yaddo while she was working on *Firehead,* this time she must have felt that death was more of a reality. But she still enjoyed the comforts, both psychological and physical, of the British rule, even if she couldn't tolerate the narrow-mindedness of her fellow travelers. An Englishwoman derided Ghandi

> stirring up the poor Indians, deceiving and lying to them. It was too much for me and I descended on her. You should have seen how she looked! Like an out-raged turkey-hen who has confidentially approached what she looked on as another lady-turkey hen, feeling indisposed...

Ridge arrived in Hillah by train on November 15th. In 1924, when Gertrude Bell visited Hillah, she found a taxi at the train station to take her 12 miles farther to the digs at Kish. When the taxi fell into a canal and eventually broke down and no car arrived in rescue, she climbed a ziggurat and hailed four horsemen and commandeered two of their horses. Ridge didn't mention any transportation problems during her six-day visit, but touring the town must have been memorable. Thick mists often surround the canals and channels of the river Euphrates, which runs right through Hillah, and the city is dotted with palms planted to reduce the effect of the desert's aridity. Excavations had been taking place on the site since 1875, with the Iraqis continuously selling antiquities to the British from three huge mounds. Of the sights in ancient Babylon Ridge writes: "There is little left, portions of walls[,] arches, the great stone lion intact but for the head which the Germans hacked off and brought to Berlin." She began to enjoy the local people: "The Arab peoples are beautiful....they wait on one with a chieftain-like air, as though they were the hosts [which they were] and it was their pleasure to make you comfortable." Her maternal role, however, was tried:

> They dragged out a mattress and cushions upon which I sat with some misgivings, and made me tea—which willy-nilly I had to drink. They set the baby on my lap—it seemed I had to hold her—it was some kind of a ritual—she peed copiously before I could give her up. She had sore eyes and a bad cold.

She needn't have interacted with the Iraqis at all. "A very nice Irishman, a Mr. Halbert and his wife are [,] it seems, in control here." They and other ex-pats provided the logistical support she needed for her solo adventures. But she needed more money. She calculated that she would be penniless on her return to Baghdad and asked for a $100 advance from her publishers. "You are dear persons and angel-publishers...I shall try to have the mss. in your hands by June but at this stage cannot promise this for certain." She writes her husband that "They [her press] seemed to be wondering how they are going to get through the winter. I suppose its the same with most everyone." Then she hit him up too. "If you could send me fifty dollars a month it would keep me." Still she was charitable toward his own dilemma. "Yet if you are to be out of work and in trouble, then I want to be in New York and help you to bear it, even in the winter." She also casually mentioned that "Cholera was in Baghdad [,] Dr. Lewes told me (not yet official) [,] and they have 6 cases of Bubonic plague" [,] which is confirmed by contemporary newspaper accounts. Although she admitted she was down to three rupees for her return trip, she bought two trinkets for a rupee and a half apiece from the Irishman Halbert. If this was not hair-raising enough for her husband, she adds:

> I killed a scorpion tonight. I hated to do it, but he was running up the wall and into my coat, which I put on the bed at night...I had only a shoe...However I felt it some inadequacy in my development that I had to kill him...everything responds to love. Well...I have no time to tame scorpions.

She went on to Kish, an archaeological site 12 miles from Hillah, an ancient city of Sumer brimming with ancient bricks and pottery. On her return to Baghdad, a car was waiting for her at the train station. Imagine her two servants securing her bags in the car, with Ridge secretly terrified, knowing, with counter-intuitive exhilaration, that she was again only a few coins away from destitution. This time poverty would be a bit different than New York's—the Baghdad streets had its beggars in rags, its hungry rats, and the desert just outside the city gates.

Ridge did not dwell on her problems. Once back in her hotel, she wrote that she preferred to move to Beirut or Jerusalem to work on her poem in a better climate. But first she needed to see more. Her husband had sent her $38 out of his final paycheck, which she promptly decided would be best traveling going to Ur

> if I can get any concession. Writers and all professionals, who are going to places for their work and not for pleasure, get this but I could not—I think because I have a husband in New York; at least after this fact came out I could not get any reduction.

Obviously any woman wandering the Near East and staying at the Baghdad Ritz had a husband with money, and Davy, bless his heart, had done his best. She was not as grateful as she could have been.

The Royal Tombs at Ur were well worth the trip. Just two years earlier, Woolley had discovered "The Great Death Pit," containing "six armed guards and 68 serving women." A complex set of streets with houses, a school, shops, shrines—even a fast food restaurant—had been uncovered as well. Ridge viewed the ruins of Ur's great Sumerian ziggurat from 21 century B.C. that Jacob-ladders about 50 feet up. With her interest in female achievements, she might have been drawn to the temple of the goddess Ningal, situated immediately southwest of the ziggurat. The Sumerian goddesses were extremely important from Neolithic times until the old Babylonian period when they were married off to the gods. Woolley himself gave Ridge the tour.

Close to penury on her return from Ur, Ridge expressed gratitude toward her publishers and friends for sending her funds. "My wonderful friends—as with *Firehead* it's they that are writing my book as well as me... in reality no one ever does anything alone." Her generous Indian doctor was returning home and had invited her to visit. Nonplussed by her hand-to-mouth existence, she schemed with ever more abandon: "I'd love to make India." She had already begun a campaign to drum up sympathy for her trip out of Baghdad by mentioning that all the tourists had fled. "Perhaps...

the cholera, of which everyone seems terrified, has kept them away...from Baghdad." By Dec. 8 she had received another $50 donation from Louise Adams Floyd, enough to cross the desert again. Her doctor wanted her to go to the hospital instead. Although the trials of the desert journey had increased—"There's snow in a neighboring town[. I]t will be close to zero now in the desert at night and I have inadequate covers"—she didn't seem to even remotely consider the hospital. Ridge did, however, have a personal revelation, a moment of clarity, with regard to her temperament in contrast to Davy's:

> Your brave clear spirit is like crystal water with none of the dark tinctures that are in mine. I who fling snarls and curses at everything that abrades or even obstructs me [,] feel respect for your endurance but that you should have to endure hurts me. You never pity, never dramatize yourself. I do both—although my self-pity is always of the dramatic order, therefore never quite real.

She barely endured the long difficult desert crossing, her head pounding against the roof of the car so hard it brought on an attack of vomiting, and she almost missed her bus to the docks because the mist over the snow-capped mountains en route to Beirut turned into sheets of ice. The driver understandably ignored her urgings for speed. Within hours she was happy be in a storm at sea en route for Trieste. "The sky ahead of us is black and like another and darker sea. The two seem about to join and rush madly into one. As usual the approach of danger has put me into high spirits." She wasn't in the least seasick.

Before leaving the boat, she decided to stay in Paris. An Englishman told her fortune, advising her that she should wait there before going on to New York. She often consulted fortune tellers at important junctures of her life, and they always told her what she wanted to hear. Docking in Marseilles, she discovered that the patron who sent her the $100 that enabled her to finally leave Baghdad was her Park Avenue doctor in New York.

After sunny Trieste, Rue Arago in Paris must have been quite gloomy. The neighborhood featured the high walls of the Broca hospital and the Paris Observatory, the nearby entrance to the Catacombs, and worst of all, the Prison de la Sante. President Doumer would be assassinated by a Russian patriot that May while talking to an author at a book fair, and the assassin guillotined in the prison by September. The Depression made the city even gloomier. As one French journalist put it:

> On street benches and at métro entrances, groups of exhausted and starving young men would be trying not to die. I don't know how many never came round. I can only say what I saw. In the rue Madame one day I saw a child drop a sweet which someone trod on, then the man behind bent down and picked it up, wiped it and ate it.

Ridge moved to Rue Arago after two weeks at the fancy Hotel Slavia. The thrills of her sea voyage and arrival in Paris had worn off by Christmas Day 1931, when she grumbled to her husband that he hadn't written for three weeks. "I'm surprised at your silence...I'm praying to be well enough to start work tomorrow." She announced then that she couldn't possibly return to New York until April. "It would be practically suicide." A few days later, faced with the prospect of starting work, she began to complain of her side. She wasn't, however, suffering from symptoms of T.B. She credited Baghdad with having "some mysterious force—rays of some kind possibly—[that] acted on my weak chest and eliminated all the bad germs." She then changed the wallpaper in her room, ordered breakfast in bed, and chose to stay there until noon in order to conserve heat. She reported on the rest of her day: "Then I get up, go out and buy a roll and a slice of ham and return and make myself hot tea. Then I sit down and type what I wrote in bed longhand."

To Louise Adams Floyd, she writes: "Hitler will make Paris—unless he dies on the way...The earth-crust has worn thin and the fire about to break through." Hitler had a half-million recruits and many more in the wings, with six million hungry unemployed in Germany. His followers kept the country in continuous turmoil. Like many other Germans, Hitler saw France as the archenemy, being rankled, in particular, by the French occupation of the Ruhr in the 1920s. Dispelling various gloomy scenarios, Ridge wished William Floyd "a good fighting year of peace."

Out in the cold drizzly streets of Paris, Ridge caught sight of Emma Goldman, who must have been there consulting her editor on *Living My Life*, the autobiography she was then writing.

> No, she did not see me. I turned and walked a few steps, observing her. She looks much older and smaller. I had forgotten what a short woman she is. No, I made no move to speak to her. Our ways have

long since parted and to get now into a group of Paris anarchists, which I should have to do if I met Emma, would deflect my thought from my work....Well, Emma has had a difficult, yet a rich and varied life. She has seldom been bored. She is not to be pitied but envied by countless women of drab and colorless lives. If I had the means I would aid her in any way I could but I feel no desire to take up a lapsed friendship. There are many who mean much more to me and even for them I have not time or energy. My work, my work...

But Ridge wasn't working. Despite repeated reassurances, she finally confessed to her husband: "I haven't really done any work on my poem since I left! I got a start on [it] in Nice, but couldn't go on." Goldman, on the other hand, was still fighting for the cause—the pursuit of personal freedom—and writing the summary of her life to inspire others. Although Ridge had taken an equally grand stance in her plan to capture the fire of life through all of history, it was still just a plan. Her failure was not too surprising, given that the plan was daunting, even without completing a grueling nearly yearlong itinerary over difficult terrain. Still, a meeting with Goldman might have been humiliating.

Typical of Ridge to have cast Goldman's triumph in feminist terms, comparing her life to those "countless women of drab and colorless lives," and not a man's. Goldman's influence on her must have been great, either directly, through her example and rhetoric, or indirectly, through all the contacts she provided in grooming Ridge to organize the Ferrer Center. Certainly Goldman's support and the publication of Ridge's poetry came at a critical time for Ridge and her emergence in America as an artist. Goldman always noted her work when it came to light, both poetic and political, and expressed her approval in letters to her niece Stella Ballantine or Evelyn Scott. In a letter to Louise Adams Floyd, Ridge put their loss of contact to differences in temperament and politics.

[We] had not corresponded for years. Ever since *Red Flag*—of which I sent her an inscribed copy which she did not acknowledge—I have never heard from or received any message from her. She did not like me much though she was very kind to me always, but she was very fond of Davy. I think her silence after *Red Flag* was because at the time she was very much against communism. Then she is against

violence of all kinds and there is much incipient violence in me that
I think she felt.

"I have not forgotten you, dear Lola," wrote Goldman's lover Alexander
Berkman on Christmas Day of 1927 four years earlier. But Ridge seemed to
have forgotten him. She didn't visit him in St. Tropez, where he was living
when she was twice in Nice 65 miles away. It would be only another nine
years before he killed himself, suffering from cancer, still in exile.

> I cannot reach my hands to you...
> would not if I could,
> though I know how warmly yours would close about them.
> Why?
> I do not know...
> I have a sense of shame. (*Sun-up* 88)

Ridge found it hard to imagine returning to the U.S. "Although I have
dear friends in New York [,] the only thing I am going back for is you," she
writes Davy. However, she had no other choice. She couldn't get a job in
Paris because she couldn't speak French well enough, and her supporters'
donations could not be counted on forever. She made certain, however, of
the terms under which she was returning, no trivial matter with the press
of gender expectations: "I'll be able to cook cheaply for us both, and you'll
have to help me with the cleaning up of the big room—I can't scrub or
sweep but can wash up, cook and dust and other light things." For now, she
had to focus her energies on finding "some way to help raise my passage
money. I wish I wasn't so rotten bad at asking for help." But that was a
task she had performed splendidly, having financed nearly the whole of her
trip from donations solicited $50 to $100 at a time. In less than a month
she obtained a down payment for her ticket home. "I'm puzzled as to how
to raise the rest," writes Ridge. "If Mary Marquis [artist and photographer]
will loan us fifty [,] I can perhaps borrow a little elsewhere." She deflected
Davy's suggestion to ask her doctor for more. "No, I won't take advantage of
[Dr.] Hyman's generosity for I feel assured that everyone else does." But she
had complete confidence in some patron coming through with the money
because she went on in the next paragraph to tell Davy not to worry if he
didn't see her right away—U.S. immigration would take a while. She was
a bit like Isadora Duncan who bought all the lilies in New York for a single

performance, partied all night with the remainder of her money, then sat on the dock with her dance troupe the next morning until someone—a schoolteacher—arrived with her life savings and bought them return tickets to Europe.

Paris was freezing in mid-March when she admitted that "you know I am strangely hardy." Indeed she was, having accomplished her goal of traveling to Baghdad and back with a minimum of illness, really not much more than any other traveler, now or then. She also told her husband that she finally had "one of the scenes in the first part of *Lightwheel* finished" and that "The stately and rather weighty content seems to demand the sonnet form." She describes the narrative: a pregnant Babylonian woman is watching for her husband from the roof of her house when she goes into labor and "she cannot get back. The exact thing I've done here and the forces at work in the woman have not been done before. I think it's good." No poem with those lines has been found, and perhaps at this point her husband suspected that all she had on the section were just notes. A few weeks before her departure, she begged him not to have her publisher meet her boat. "I'd have to go at once into explanations of [the] book's delay. I think I should die right there." Her ambivalence about returning to New York evidenced itself materially when she lost her passport on March 24. She had no identification number, she knew no one who could help her, and she was nearly out of money. Somehow she sailed.

Chapter 31

The Radical Left
in the 1930s

By May 1932, Ridge was again living in her apartment at the top of 793 Broadway across from Grace Church. Just a block away was the office of the Emergency Committee for Southern Political Prisoners, of which she was a member. Founded in 1930 by the John Reed Club and the International Labor Defense Committee, the legal arm of the Communist party, it began its mission by assisting six workers who faced the death penalty for holding protest meetings on unemployment in Atlanta and, in the next year, by defending the Scottsboro Boys in Alabama. Its chairman was Theodore Dreiser. Dos Passos was treasurer, and 16 writers along with Ridge served as committee members, including Josephine Herbst, Edmund Wilson, Carl Van Doren, Alfred Kreymborg, Louis Untermeyer, Scott Nearing, and Upton Sinclair. Dos Passos wanted to appeal to middle class liberals to see past Communist propaganda toward a more fair treatment of fellow citizens. "We can't affect the class war much, but we might possibly make it more humane." In the *New Republic*, Edmund Wilson hoped the Committee would "take Communism away from the Communists" and realign it more with the American democracy. When the organization became the National Defense of Political Prisoners a year later, a precursor to PEN, its committee had been expanded to include (among others) Langston Hughes, Edna St. Vincent Millay, and, interestingly, the Australianist C. Hartley Grattan who was, like Ridge, also a member of the Writers League against Lynching.

Radical poets in the 1930s rejected the idea that poetry occupied a separate sphere in the national life and promoted conscious participation. The work was not all party cant. According to critic M.L. Rosenthal, the style was "anarcho-individualistic, Freudian," and written as much "in the image of D.H. Lawrence" as of Lenin. Contrary to critiques made in the ultraconservative 1950s, jargon and lockstep demagoguery were abhorred, and experimentation à la the 1920s flourished. Indeed, Gertrude Stein was still being reviewed positively by radicals. Critic Alan Filreis notes that poet-lumberman "Joe Kalar...agreed that "revolutionary poetry written in conventional rhythm and meter often enough seems naïve, sentimental and hackneyed." Ridge's friend and critic Babette Deutsch, whose early work, *Banners*, venerated the Russian Revolution, wrote that the new generation had many issues in common with the modernists, among them "disgust for institutionalized religion and for a facile idealism." Still, she omitted nearly all leftists poets of the 1930s, including Ridge, in her important anthology, *Poetry in our Time*, and even tried to discredit W.H. Auden by likening him to "some wild incomprehensible 'modernist' like [Tristan] Tzara," according to Kenneth Rexroth. Even *The Left: A Quarterly Review of Radical and Experimental Art* neglected radical women in 1931, as Ridge was the only female contributor out of 32.

"Just the other day I discovered that the John Reed Club plans to hold another Red Poets Night in the near future," Edwin Rolfe wrote Ridge a month after her return from Europe, asking her to read at a venue that was enthusiastically Communist. Rolfe would become poet laureate of the Abraham Lincoln Battalion after his experiences in Spain. For leftist poets, it was a heady time since their agenda seemed almost prophetic— the Depression calling out for the revolution they had envisioned. It is unclear whether Ridge accepted his invitation or not. She may not have felt recovered from her European travel or felt that her political views were not Red enough, even though she was still a contributing editor to *New Masses*. Surely it was important to her standing as a poet that on her return she would so soon be invited to read. She had plans to finish her manuscript, and within the month she abandoned the city to work on her writing in seclusion.

Marianne Moore and her mother met Davy on the streets of New York just after she left.

> Outside Schulte's we were joined by David Lawson, Lola Ridge's husband. He was very kind, said he would urge us to come to his rooms to tea but he didn't want to have us climb the stairs on a hot day and so on. He said Lola had been in Mesopotamia but was now visiting Mrs. Floyd, and was going later to Yaddo.

Ridge got to work at the estate in July 1932. She composed a strong draft of a poem about Tom Mooney, the activist who had been wrongly convicted of a bombing in San Francisco 16 years earlier and was now serving time in San Quentin. Like the Sacco and Vanzetti case, protest against Mooney's incarceration was seen by the right as a "money-making agitation for the Communist Party and the excuse for countless riots, strikes, demonstrations and profitable collections." During the 1932 LA Olympics, the defense committee sent six members of the Young Communist League onto the track shouting, "Free Tom Mooney" with the words printed across their chests and backs. While Mooney remained in prison, James Rolph, the governor who could have pardoned him, condoned a California lynching. Ridge published "Stone Face" in *The Nation* of September 14, 1932.

The first line of "Stone Face": "They have carved you into a stone face, Tom Mooney," echoes and complicates a line from the title poem in her 1920 book, *Sun-Up and Other Poems*: "when you do something great/people give you a stone face." But all bear responsibility for his imprisonment: "disparate signatures are scrawled on your stone face/that all/Have set some finger on..." Then she immortalizes his face like a president on Mt. Rushmore: "set up in full sight under the long/Gaze of the generations—" The poem was nearly the last of her political efforts, only the long "Three Men Die," a poem truly about Sacco and Vanzetti, was still to be written.

Louise Adams Floyd, who was involved in the Mooney defense, may have worked on Ridge's bust while she was visiting. Ridge writes later: "I'm very proud of that bust you have—the first one. I recognize in it something [that] is essentially me." When Ridge worried out loud to Louise about her husband's loss of pay, she gave Ridge $25 to cover her fare to Saratoga Springs. After nearly three weeks, she traveled upstate to stay near, but not at Yaddo itself, with Elizabeth Ames footing the bill. She had found Ridge a "quiet little home on the outskirts of Saratoga where there is light and air and silence and only two grown persons who are mouselike in all their habits."

Ridge reported on her new work location to Floyd and commented rather optimistically on how the locals were faring the economic downturn:

> There is no noise except the honking of an occasional Ford. (All the farmers have autos now). Fields of cabbages and corn, carrots, squash, peppers, cucumbers are growing outside the windows. The biggest cauliflowers I've ever seen...These people here in Saratoga

seem less hit by the depression than any I've seen anywhere....Miss A. tells me no man has come to the house and asked for anything in years....

The mother of her friend Laura Benét sent a note from Europe, where she and Laura were touring: "It is bad in America now...and we don't know what we shall have to live on when we get back." If the wealthy Benéts were feeling the deprivations of the Depression, times were quite serious for everyone. A few days later, Ridge wrote Floyd with her not-so-red view of the political situation:

> Just now I think the communists are more fit to rule than any other group, but I tremble to think of the result once the greater part of the world has become communist. When Ibsen said "the majority is always wrong" it stood for then, to-day and a hundred years hence.

Still, Ridge wanted to visit a factory where there was a strike on, or go to a Communist or a socialist meeting and take notes. But she had fallen into despair. She told her husband that she had a "dream of Keith which always results in a couple of days intense depression," indicating that she still had strong feelings about his abandonment, and then went on to describe yet another change in writing tactics, perhaps as a result of the dream:

> I want to take my own life as a theme only not in the sense of strict or obvious autobiography—and do that in a long poem. I'd begin with childhood, picking it up about where I left off in *Sun Up*. No[,] the Babylonian poem is by no means given up, but it will have to initiate its own expulsion. I do not think it is quite ready.

Then she went three nights without sleep and asked again for her Gynergen.

The pressure of producing another book took its toll. She was home by the end of August when she wrote Louise Adams Floyd: "I was so weak Davy had to take me to the [doctor's] office. Dr. H. thought I should go at once to the hospital but I protested so much he agreed that I should wait a few days." At the same time her ambitions grew. She promised her publisher that she would "have [a book] next fall. I'm writing very much the way I did at *Firehead*—circling and going from place to place except that now, instead of having one book, I have a whole series—a cycle."

She stayed out of the hospital as long as she could, attending a party given by her friend Eda Lou Walton at the end of January, 1933—"so you can't be sick all the time" writes Evelyn Scott to Davy because he had taken over her correspondence. But by July Ridge weighed only 72 pounds. She was admitted to Mt. Sinai Hospital under the care of her beloved Dr. Hyman, then moved to the Loeb Home for Convalescence in East View, New York. "It is a little like Yaddo in general surroundings. Sixty-nine women in the place of all types. A lot of young girls—five or six..." The rules were strict: "one has to rest and do absolutely nothing from 11:30 until 2:30—a big hole in the day. Lights out at 8:30 p.m." Her codeine was stopped. She had written most of her 25 sonnet sequence, "Via Ignis" before she arrived so perhaps it was overwork on top of weight loss that caused the crisis. Ridge reported to Louise Adams Floyd on August 1st that she was fighting for her life, and her weight had dropped below 70 pounds. By August 5, she had given up lipstick, but she was still asking Lawson to send her things: "I must have my white silk slip. My black sweater with white stripes—Mary will find it if you cannot...(no darling this is not being sarcastic...) Isn't anything international happening?" She may well have been concerned about the Simele massacre on the border between Iraq and Syria that had just taken place, with 300 Assyrian men killed, a number that would increase to 3,000 several days later, the slaughter truly Old Testament, Babylonian.

The grim political and economic situation wore on in the States. In 1933 DuPont and J.P. Morgan united with other millionaires—including President George W. Bush's grandfather—to overthrow Roosevelt and install a fascist government. They tried to recruit General Smedly Butler, offering him a half million war veterans and unlimited funds to finance a military coup, but he revealed the plot to Congress. No one was prosecuted, according to a BBC report released decades later.

Meanwhile, Evelyn Scott had befriended Emma Goldman to the extent that Goldman helped her arrange an abortion. Scott's letter to Ridge in July 1933 reveals the depth of their relationship, and Goldman's continued interest in Ridge:

> I know Emma can make the most brutal and unperspicacious gestures and has probably been insulting to many people whose mental-spiritual plans she couldn't reach. She has been a very

good friend to me, but that is a matter of getting off with the foot which happened not to step on her corns. I would have been more remembering about you except that I always mention you and she always asked after you as if all were o.k.

That November Scott asked Ridge to sign a petition to allow Goldman into the United States for a brief tour. It isn't clear whether Ridge signed it. Goldman subsequently spent 90 days speaking across the country, confined to the subjects of literature and drama. Thousands were turned away although sometimes the audiences were disappointing. Old radicals, now referred to as the "lyrical left," stayed away, including Ridge, although Goldman spoke in New York several times. "Today the Anarchists are a scattered handful of survivors, and the extreme left is divided among the various communist groups...Emma Goldman is not a symbol of freedom in a world of tyrants; she is merely a wrong-headed old woman," wrote *The Nation*.

By August 20, Lawson had his pay reduced again on his new job. "It's too bad about your cut, but we'll manage somehow—as long as you let me handle the money." Given Ridge's ineptitude at finances, perhaps Lawson bridled at her suggestion, although this was unlikely; he seems so even-tempered in his letters.

"I gained 14 pounds [at the hospital]," she writes Floyd by September. Plump and full of ambition, she left for the Jersey Shore as soon as she could. Henrietta Glick had returned from Rome with most of the music for the *Firehead* oratorio finished. Glick anticipated "a performance there next Easter...she wants me to write an opera, she to compose the music and I'm thinking of this—or will try to work out an American theme as soon as I have the present book out of my hands."

Chapter 32

Shelley Awards,
a Poets Guild Prize,
and a Guggenheim

Evidence of Ridge's secure place in poetry in the early 30s was a request from her previous editor and close friend, Bill Benét, to contribute to his *Fifty Poets: An American Auto-Anthology*. Marianne Moore, Louise Bogan, Frost, cummings, Stevens, Eliot and Jeffers were also to be anthologized. Each poet was to pick one "briefer" poem that he would want to be remembered for. "Bill...has asked me for the poem of mine (published) I consider my best—Jiggered if I know," she writes Floyd. She selected "Light Song," a section of *Firehead*.

> Light omnivorous and without mercy
> Consuming all things for fuel—
> Denying no toad beast man fowl worm,
> Seizing, transfixing the mean norm,
> Leaving it starrily, as it left Peter
> Pierced with the white crow of dawn
> In the arrested moment, like a spear,
> To remain without falling and without flight,
> A cynosure to burn forever there
> Impaled on the implacable light. (*Firehead* 52-53)

The poem's irregular rhythm and rhyme make it neither free nor formal. The structural ambiguity reflects the subject matter: Peter impaled on his disbelief, in stasis until, one assumes, Christ, as the light, frees him after his repentance.

Two years in a row, in 1934 and 1935, Ridge's colleagues at the Poetry Society of America honored her with the Shelley Memorial Award. "I wish we could bring you the world you don't need on a platter and you could chuck away all but the rare best part your divine intuition would unerringly select," congratulates Evelyn Scott the first time. Named after one of Ridge's most revered poets, the prize was endowed by the wealthy poetry-lover Mary Pratt Sears four years earlier. The award is still given to an American poet every year, "selected with reference to his or her genius and need, by a jury of three poets—one appointed by the president of Radcliffe, (now Harvard), one by the president of the University of California at Berkeley, and one by the Poetry Society of America's board of governors." The first winner was Conrad Aiken, the poet, short story writer and critic who was on the bill of the *Other*'s Speakers Bureau with Ridge. When he won the Shelley, he had just been awarded the Pulitzer Prize, but two years later he attempted suicide.

Although the amount of the Shelley award is now between $6,000-9,000, it was $1,750 during the Depression, nearly the same as a Guggenheim, equivalent to about $30,000 in 2014 currency. Ridge shared the prize with Frances Frost in 1934. Splitting the award has been a common occurrence throughout its history, here perhaps because of the Depression's difficulties, especially with regard to women's finances. Frances Frost, best known as the mother of the poet Paul Blackburn, wrote verse in traditional form and meter, like the other Frost in Vermont. Published nine years after "The Road Not Taken," her poem "Dare" begins: "The wood's-edge thicket holds a path/Twisty enough for any seeker" and ends "best go the long way round/ Or find another road to take."

A New Woman with bobbed hair, cigarette in hand, a divorcée with many affairs, and just then a lesbian in the Village, 28-year-old Frost was someone Ridge might have admired: "Arrogance and defiance were not negative terms to her," writes Frost's biographer, Margaret Edwards. "Nothing could comfort her." Frost left Paul and his sister with their grandparents while she produced many children's books, seven books of poetry, and four novels, including one bestseller.

In 1935 Ridge's co-winner was Marya Zaturenska, who won the Pulitzer Prize four years later. She was married to the anthologist Horace Gregory, and together they wrote *A History of American Poetry 1900-1940*, making them an extremely powerful couple within poetry circles. At 32, she was Ridge's first rival as poet for the Lower East Side, being the only female

Jewish poet from the neighborhood to publish in English, but her subjects usually veered into fantasy.

> Imperceptibly the world became haunted by her white dress.
> Walking in forest or garden, he would start to see
> Her flying form; sudden, swift, brief as a caress
> The flash of her white dress against a darkening tree.

The publishing firm Brewer and Warren that advanced Ridge money in Baghdad, had by then brought out books by Cocteau, Dorothy Sayers, Rockwell Kent, Le Corbusier, and Ridge's friend from the Ferrer days, Konrad Bercovici. After *Firehead* was published under the Brewer imprint of Payson & Clarke, the firm fell into difficulties. They were rescued by Putnam in 1931, just after its publisher G. P. Putnam married Amelia Earhart. Ridge was not brought along.

In 1934 Evelyn Scott introduced her to the publisher Harrison Smith, who was also her editor for four of her novels. Known as "Hal" Smith, he and his partner Robert K. Haas published William Faulkner, Isak Dinesen, Robert Graves, and André Malraux, and eventually completed a merger with Random House in 1936. They took on Ridge and Lenore Marshall, one of the press's literary advisors and editor of *As I Lay Dying*, became one of her patrons and sent baskets of food and checks. A wealthy woman, she was treasurer for the Writers League Against Lynching. She also helped found S.A.N.E., an organization that worked for the passage of the 1963 partial nuclear test-ban treaty. Her writing appeared in the *New Yorker*, the *Saturday Review of Literature*, and *Partisan Review*, and she eventually became the author of three novels, three books of poetry, a collection of short stories, and selections from her notebooks. She is remembered today for endowing the $25,000 Lenore Marshall Poetry Prize, administered by the Academy of American Poets for the most outstanding poetry book of the year.

The Academy was founded in 1934 by Marie Bullock, assisted by Edward Arlington Robinson. Although Robinson had been very active in the Poetry Society—attending annual dinners, judging and collecting prizes, he wanted an alternative to its "notoriously quarrelsome" meetings. Anything named "the Academy" must certainly be less lively. In the 1980s, Betty Kray, its first director, held soirées in folding chairs encircling poet celebrities like Margaret Atwood in order to liven it up, and eventually founded a much more open institution, Poets House, in 1985. This organization was originally headed by Stanley Kunitz, who, under the pseudonym of Dilly Tante, interviewed Lola Ridge in the 1930s for a book on living poets.

In 1934 there was also a downtown organization known as Poets House—more frequently referred to as the Poets Guild—that awarded Ridge a prize for a poem "lofty in thought and universal in feeling...it should not be patriotic in a war like sense." Such constraints reflected the changing political climate of poetry. As critic Joan Shelley Rubin writes:

> At first glance, that directive appears to epitomize everything of which modernists accused their genteel predecessors: the exclusion of genuine emotion, the emphasis on uplift, the feminine sensibility (here symbolized by the condemnation of war)...Yet the purpose behind them was not to keep poetry on the safe ground of disengagement with the troubling aspects of reality; it was, rather, to make the genre serviceable for the attainment of social ends by untried means...

The Poets Guild met at the Christadora, a 17-story settlement house on the Lower East Side with a swimming pool, a gym, and an arts program for underprivileged children. Organized by the poet Anna Hepstead Branch in 1921, its original members included (once again) Edward Arlington Robinson, Robert Frost, Sara Teasdale, and Edwin Markham. When Ridge received her $500 on October 30, 1934, Countee Cullen and Babette Deutsch were listed among poetry readers for the Christadora children.

With the first Shelley Award and the Poets Guild money, Ridge had funds to travel again. But she still had to turn in her manuscript. To finish it, she contemplated leaving for Montauk in June for the home of her patron Corinne Wagner, but also suggested another plan: "have the telephone taken out, feed Davy on fried eggs and apples, say I'm out of town and see no one. I think it will work." Ridge always demanded a great deal of isolation for her composition. In 1931 she elucidated its importance in her review of Paul Strand's photography:

> The act of creation is an emotional as well as an intellectual process and calls for a concentration of the forces of the entire being on one glowing point of purpose. For that moment...the self must isolate itself from its familiar world and the litter that personality has accumulated must be continently shed.

By the end of June she had left Davy to his own fried eggs and apples and spent the summer in Montauk and Mastic. "If only Davy could get a job," she bemoans to Floyd in July. That remark would ring true for most of the American populace that summer. Davy was kept busy reading her work and writes: "It is not important people may not understand them [the poems] at first or tenth reading, nor will they all get the same meaning." But he was not pleased when she returned in September. "I was very disappointed about your work and concerned about yourself." Nevertheless, by the beginning of November 1934, she had added a hundred lines to her manuscript when Hal Smith climbed three flights to visit her frozen aerie on Broadway, a "little Klondike," where she typed away with one finger. By the end of the month she was apologizing for her lateness to Smith: "Yes, I understand about the spring list and I am sorry not to have sent it in before." She finally turned the manuscript in a week later. Haas hired her friend Bill Benét as either reader or editor but she was surprised by Benét's response. He must have echoed Davy's comment about the poem's intelligibility. In a letter to Floyd she writes:

> his remarks are on the margins—very honest, very interesting [but] sometimes quite perturbing, because he apparently has no idea as to the actual meaning of some of the sonnets. He consequently thinks them "incoherent"—the last thing in the world they are. He has written on the margin of one: "I know she means something profound but I haven't the faintest idea as to what it is.

To Hal Smith, she writes: "Interested in Bill Benét's reactions...but I do not think any of my sonnets are incoherent. But I'll read them all over." Smith writes back in Benét's defense: "if there is too great a gap between the intelligence of the reader and the thought of the artist, the spark cannot flash between these two poles." This being the first time her contemporaries have really ever criticized her work, she must have been devastated. Whether Ridge changed much of the material is unknown. Smith tried to smooth over the criticism with the news that "I saw an admirer of yours this weekend in the person of Archibald MacLeish."

But MacLeish was not someone she could depend on either, even if he were a friend of Kay Boyle's in France. Early in his triple-Pulitzer career, MacLeish coined the motto for her arch-enemy, the New Critics, in his "Ars

Poetica:" "A poem should not mean/but be." He later rescinded that stance, slowly becoming convinced that poets could indeed mix the world and its politics with aesthetics. But he was neither an anarchist nor even a pacifist: he wrote war propaganda during World War I and became the first Librarian of Congress. Described by the left as an "unconscious fascist," in 1933 he published "Background with Revolutionaries," a poem that in his own words, "is pretty completely negative, not with the revolutionaries but with the little New York Marxists." The poem begins with the epigraph: "And the corn singing Millennium!/Lenin! Millennium! Lennium!" and mentions a Ridge:

> Also Comrade Edward Remington Ridge
> Who has prayed God since the April of 'Seventeen
> To replace in his life his lost (M.E.) religion

Ridge assumed that he was referring to her. She didn't bridle at being cast as a revolutionary, it was the accusation of any religious affiliation that aggrieved her. "Did you see the jibe at me?" she writes Lawson.

> [it] would perhaps surprise him...by telling him I "lost religion" in
> his sense of the word at twelve years old and having a larger one have
> never felt the need of searching for it—in or out of Red meetings as
> he suggests "since 1917." Twas long before that alack!

After walking across Mexico in 1931, MacLeish won his first Pulitzer Prize for *Conquistador*, which recognized the common man's contribution to history, but also denied the rights of the Aztecs to their own country. Perhaps the book inspired Ridge's trip to Mexico in 1935 to research the female equivalent. But first she would win a Guggenheim.

Her friend Lenore Marshall called Mr. Moe, the director of the John Simon Guggenheim Fund, to suggest that he invite Ridge to apply. Ridge's friends Aaron Copland and Stephen Vincent Benét were the first composer and first writer, respectively, to win. By 1926 the Foundation was receiving 900 applications a year, awarding only 39. "Miss Millay says her poetry is first rate and so does everybody else whom we consulted," according to Ridge's Guggenheim documentation. Such a positive endorsement from Edna St. Vincent Millay, the reigning queen of poetry, would certainly have cinched the award. Ridge won the sole poetry fellowship in 1935, with

Langston Hughes one of the three fiction fellows. Only four women out of 60 recipients received fellowships that year but Ridge was optimistic: "This is very significant of something coming."

Ridge's project was "The Passage of Theresa," an extension of "Sun-up," her second book's long title poem. The Australasian girl is older in this proposed project and more cognizant of having a mother who is unable to cope, but both of them live dream lives. If only she had pursued the project! It might have led her back to the clarity and emotional freshness of those earlier poems.

Ridge's grant, along with her other three awards, would support her for the next two years, give or take various handouts. Travel was the way Guggenheims are most commonly spent, so much so there is a genre of "Guggenheim poems" written by recipients contemplating Europe's beauties. Ridge told the Guggenheim Foundation she would be traveling to Ireland, but instead she headed south.

Chapter 33

Dance of Fire
from New Mexico

Similar to her peregrinations through Europe en route to Baghdad, as soon as Ridge set her sights on Mexico, she made certain that she missed none of the important literary stops in between. First would be the art colony at Taos. According to Ridge, the town was "without street names or numbers" and, at every turn, there were mountains that reminded her of the New Zealand Alps. Its population of Native Americans and Hispanics ensured that her stay would be both exotic and inexpensive. By 1935 Taos had been a destination for artists for 20 years, and this was the year that Dorothea Lange came through, taking pictures of the migrant poor struggling through the Depression.

By March 29th, Ridge had moved into a room at Bent House, home of the first territorial governor. "I am here in horribly inconvenient but most attractive little studio—white adobe walls, woodwork green and rose, which I, if I stay[,] shall change to blue and dark red," she writes Lenore Marshall. She might have regretted leaving New York so soon after the publication of *Dance of Fire*, or did she fear its reception, still smarting from Benét's criticism? Its first reviews were beginning to appear. Horace Gregory in the *Saturday Review of Literature* best described the book's genesis: "It was as though the wind in the alleys of 'The Ghetto,' 'carrying flame,' had discovered tinder and then transformed itself to larger meaning."

> ...Fire, of which our grain
> Is cored, in very nature treacherous,
> Fulfills itself in fire. (*Dance of Fire* 16)

Her publisher was not at all happy about her going to Taos just then. She excused herself by saying that she was in a hurry to get to the Southwest for her chest and her ostensible T.B., but March was early for her annual exodus from New York. She acknowledged once she was settled that she should have stayed in the city, yet she accused Hal Smith of letting the publicity for her book go cold. "No ads, no reviews," she lamented, although her friend Eda Lou Walton had just published a long review in the *New York Herald Tribune*. "I'll bet it is as dumb as usual, though I understand it's complimentary," writes Evelyn Scott. It was indeed complimentary, and more importantly, it presented Ridge to a new generation. "Today, perhaps twenty years after [Ridge] knew her own loyalties," writes Walton, "this poem finds a world of young writers and poets becoming convinced of all that she stated long ago."

Dance of Fire was no casualty of Depression frugality, having been published in a gleaming, metallic, copper-colored jacket with a Julian Wehr Art Deco cover image of a red Oscar-like figure holding the sun. Wehr had been trained by John Sloan and Max Weber, both of whom worked with Robert Henri at the Ferrer Center. Wehr sought to convey values of racial and social justice in his art. The cover image was appropriate, for the world was, according to Ridge's note on the flap, "living in a dynasty of fire." Hitler had just opened the first concentration camps, socialists battled Communists in a Madison Square Garden rally, and workers were striking all over the country—"in the midst of the fire-dance," writes Ridge. She only hopes that "we may come forth, for a period, into the time of light." Stephen Vincent Benét blurbed the book: "It is magnificent. There are some few books that bear the unmistakable stigmata of genius—this is one of them. I know of nothing like it in American letters."

But Ridge was not satisfied. By the end of the month Ridge complained to her husband that

> Harrison S. has determined to ruin me and kill my books. Well, I know only one thing and that is that he will someday suffer for it. I will never give him another book. As he has them all in his hands this means no more books will come out til after my death—but I'll strike from my dust… Even if he destroys every book in his possession some one of them will escape to be discovered by future historians.

Alas, no further books have been discovered, at least not in Smith College's archives. She was always losing her luggage, her pens and souvenirs, her passport, her permits, and her manuscripts—if she actually wrote them. She published only two more poems, the first, "Lyric" in the

1935 summer *Fantasy*, a serious journal of genteel and formally conservative verse that had gradually become more radical in both politics and form. Her last published poem appeared in *Poetry* that October, the sonnet "This is to bear, with cleavage and in pain" collected in *Dance of Fire*.

Her belief in *Dance of Fire*'s neglect was unfounded. That July, Marion Stroebel, the associate editor of *Poetry* whom Ridge met in 1919, covered an entire page of the *Chicago Tribune* with her review of the book: "This is major poetry...this is a fearless spirit of sexless energy...Whether or not the reader agrees with this concept he cannot fail to be scorched by Miss Ridge's presentation." Louis Untermeyer called it her best book and said her sonnets were "more deeply impassioned than Elinor Wylie's or Edna St. Vincent Millay's," and proclaimed her "a revolutionary in a technical as well as a spiritual sense." This was exactly the position she aspired to in the work. While writing the sonnets, she told her husband that they were "revolutionary and metaphysical." The August review in the *New York Times* was written by P.H., most likely the Percy Hutchison who had written the rave review of *Firehead* in 1930. He harkened back to the accomplishments of her earlier books:

> Long before most of our proletarian writers became self-conscious in their art, long before they began to analyze the evils of the day and explain the class basis of injustice, Lola Ridge, Irish and intense, was writing poems describing social injustices, poems about people living in the slums, poems in praise of that great labor.

The Nation critic Philip Blair Rice wrote: "In "Dance of Fire" Miss Ridge has written more mature poetry than any other American who is motivated by sympathy with the workers' cause." He compared her to German symbolist Stefan George, with imagery and manner that suggested that of Dante's "Vita Nuova" and even the work of "that other Dante, Rossetti."

> The workers of all lands that day
> Looked toward the death house where the two
> Lay with a thief between
> ....
>   ...These shall not die,
> Fell back upon them where they stood,
> Went round and round as men will go

When they are lost in some deep wood
And circle the same spot. (*Dance of Fire* 61)

By the time the year was out, there would be 30 reviews appearing in newspapers across the country, from Alabama to Oklahoma to New Orleans, most of them very positive. Although not the sixty Ridge garnered for her previous book, this was still a substantial number, and in all the right places. Critics unanimously praised "Stone Face," her poem on Tom Mooney, and "Three Men Die," the irregularly rhymed long poem on the execution of Sacco, Vanzetti, and a third man convicted of thievery. "She presents them unforgettably but without bitterness," writes Stroebel. "Her "[political poems] are remarkable for their restraint and lack of special pleading," comments Rice. "She presents even the former Governor of Massachusetts as a human being."

And there did stir (for this I know)
Some thing...there in the twilight zone
Within the hollow of his spirit
A thing...afraid and very lone...
It darted back into his soul
And closed the narrow opening. (*Dance of Fire* 67)

The Sacco and Vanzetti trial continued to inspire many writers and artists. In September 1935, Ridge's acquaintance Maxwell Anderson opened "Winterset," a sentimental play on Broadway in blank verse about the case, receiving the first New York Drama Critics Circle Award. Ben Shahn had been working on a suite of twenty-three paintings on the executions that were finally exhibited in 1932. He also used the Crucifixion as a trope, the way Ridge had with *Firehead*. "Ever since I could remember I'd wished that I'd been lucky enough to be alive at a great time—when something big was going on, like the Crucifixion. And suddenly I realized I was! Here I was living through another crucifixion."

In *The Legacy of Sacco and Vanzetti*, a book written in 1948 examining the literary work written in response to the execution, critic Louis Joungin and lawyer Edmund M. Morgan studied 144 poems generated by the event and determined that "the longest and in many ways the most significant of the Sacco-Vanzetti poems is Ridge's 'Three Men Die.'" Ridge's poem was judged better than the work of John Dos Passos, Amy Lowell, Babette Deutsch,

Malcolm Cowley, and Edna St. Vincent Millay, whose poem "Justice Denied: Massachusetts" was published the day before the execution in the New York Times. "Lola Ridge's verses most certainly deserve a permanent place among the chief American poems," write the authors. "Her several volumes of verse are not widely known to the general public, [just seven years after her death, she had already been forgotten] but it is difficult to believe that this relative obscurity can continue indefinitely."

"Three Men Die" is much clearer and less metaphorical than the book-long *Firehead*. The third man executed with Sacco and Vanzetti was Celestine Madeiros, a young man who killed a bank cashier and had confessed that he, and not the other two, was connected with the robbery and murders for which they were all going to die. Ridge uses the Christian story as ethical and chronological framework and at one point, justifies this by acknowledging Eliot's concern with tradition: "old myth/Renews its tenure of the blood/Recurrently." Her description of her confrontation with the mounted policeman at the demonstration is the most striking part of the poem: "Drumbeats of the hooves...so close, so close," she writes, "feeling the wet foam on his mouth, glimpsed spread/nostrils and the white/Fire of the eye, rolling as in agony."

Dance of Fire was not the Babylonian epic she had gone to Baghdad to write, nor the sequel to *Sun-up* that she had proposed in her Guggenheim application, nor part of the trilogy *Lightwheel* she had so grandly envisioned when she published *Firehead*. It was in-between, a portion of it politically minded, but an even greater measure of it inclined toward the metaphysical. "Via Ignis," its very long sonnet sequence, received mixed reviews.

> This is to bear, with cleavage and in pain,
> Adhesions wrenched at and to suffer thrust;
> This is to feel the slip of the world's crust
> And rage of forces, ages over-lain;
> To know in the whelmed spirit heavily
> The self's eclipse, yet in each plighted grain
> Endure this radiant energy of dust. (*Dance of Fire* 44)

Louise Bogan, then poetry editor for the *New Yorker*, lauded Ridge's extended foray into the formal: "Three sonnets in the sequence "Via Ignis" of the present volume stand equal to the best modern work." She condemned Ridge's previous efforts in free verse by suggesting that they were old-fashioned: "[Ridge's] early work—written in the free-verse form now so obsolete that it might be the product of the century before last..." Bogan, still valued today as a poet and critic, was being very short-sighted here, no doubt because of her own bias as a converted formalist. She ended the review with "Miss Ridge's endowment is of the sort to celebrate the noblest and the bravest, and to cast over them some reflection from her inner and her symbolic fire." Despite the praise, Ridge was not happy with the review. "As to the suggestion I should celebrate only the 'noblest' it merely makes me sick." She would celebrate every man, the proletariat, anyone she liked.

As early as 1924, Evelyn Scott reminded Ridge that it was not her sonnets but her free verse "by which posterity is going to judge you." Ridge knew well enough of the dangers of the sonnet when she wrote in a review of Babette Deutsch's work in 1925: "I hope, however, that she [Deutsch] will not become ensnared by the sonnet form—whose beguiling rhythms are as destructive as a happiness that arrests the artist's growth by stroking him to sleep." Nonetheless, Ridge began publishing sonnets in *Red Flag* in 1927. Even her friend Alfred Kreymborg disliked them. "The sonnets of Miss Ridge are not the equal of her poems in free verse," he writes in *Our Singing Strength*, his history of American poetry. But by then Pound and Eliot had, for the most part, abandoned free verse for formal. Frost, of course, never really practiced free verse. Form's commercial popularity was evident with Edna St. Vincent Millay's triumphant sonnet sequence, *Fatal Interview*, a book that sold 66,000 copies in just a few months in 1931, a bad year in the Depression. Millay's well-received *Wine from These Grapes*, published in 1934, contained the 18-sonnet sequence, "Epitaph for the Race of Man," that prophesied the end of the human race, a subject equal in ambition to Ridge's proposed *Lightwheel*.

Other critics did not quite echo Bogan's assessment of Ridge's sonnets. *The Nation* critic writes in his bemused review "Not Easily Labeled":

> The language of the sonnets is in the tradition, and occasionally even archaic, but it is not hackneyed...Miss Ridge is able to bring out the poetry latent in abstractions. When she errs, it is often because of inability to evoke a sense of immediacy.

The *New York Times* notice ends with:"But in *Dance of Fire* she allowed herself to be enticed into unfortunate poetic paths." Louise Adams Floyd, to whom the book is dedicated, forwarded a mostly positive review by a

"Miriam," probably Miriam Allen deFord, a leftist poet who wrote formal poetry.

> In spite of things which repel me—archaism, halting metre which is apparently deliberate but which offends me in a fixed verse form, such atrocities as dividing "anonymous" to rhyme with "anon"—it is authentic and fine poetry of the cerebral sort.

In the otherwise sympathetic entry in *A History of American Poetry* 1900-1940, Horace Gregory writes that the sonnets of *Dance of Fire* "remained disembodied and curiously abstract." Was Ridge's advance into formal abstraction related to what was happening in the world of abstract expressionism? As Maurice Tuchman hypothesizes in *The Spiritual in Art*, "the genesis and development of abstract art is inextricably tied...to a desire to express spiritual, utopian, or metaphysical ideals that cannot be expressed in traditional pictorial terms." She could, like Hart Crane, also be interested in what Crane called "the so-called illogical impingements of words on the consciousness" that provide "fresh concepts, more inclusive evaluation" than can be arrived at through reasoning. Horace Gregory noted in his anthology entry that

> In *Dance of Fire* Lola Ridge's poetic maturity began, and it was evident that in the sonnet sequence, "Via Ignis," which opened her last volume, Hart Crane's revival of Christopher Marlowe's diction left its impression upon her imagination. The poems were written at a time when many of those who had read Hart Crane's *The Bridge* felt the implied force of Crane's improvisations in archaic diction.

Had Gregory forgotten that she used the same diction in *Firehead*, a year before *The Bridge* was published? Contemporary poet Robert Pinsky called her work a "premonitory echo" of Crane's. As editor of *Others* and *Broom*, Ridge had seen a lot of Crane's work before it appeared in book form, but couldn't he have been equally as inspired by her poetry, with her "Brooklyn Bridge" opening so neatly in his copy of her book? Why couldn't Crane be copying Ridge? Ridge didn't hesitate to commemorate him. As Horace Gregory points out, she specifically recalled Crane's suicide in *Dance of Fire*:

The sea enfolds him; we shall not retrieve,
Though we should drag the waters to their mire,
Either for earth or acquisitive fire
His bones as we did Shelley's...

....

Balanced on high arc precariously
He saw the fire on all lands; the flame-
Encircled waters drew him sweetly down... (*Dance of Fire* 35)

Brian M. Reed, in his *Phenomenal Reading: Essays on Modern and Contemporary Poetics* notes the striking similarity to Ridge's work in Crane's lines "again the traffic lights...Skim thy swift/Unfractioned idiom...Beading thy path" in his long and most famous poem, "To Brooklyn Bridge." Like Ridge, Crane also used "spoor" as a verb in "Cape Hatteras," where "spouting pillars spoor the evening sky." In *A Life: Hart Crane*, biographer Clive Fisher notes that Ridge's "description of a sparkling traffic-burdened bridge at night would haunt him when he came to evoke a similar scene of his own." According to critic John Unterecker, the lines Crane quoted from Ridge in his review that he later mimicked so closely reveals "his habit of adapting other people's imagery and other people's themes to his own purposes." Unterecker goes on to write: "No critic could fail to see the relationship between Miss Ridge's lines about the serpentine cars that cross the black bridge and Crane's adaptation of the image in the brilliant 'Proem' he was to write years later for "The Bridge." Yet Unterecker quickly qualifies this by writing that "no critic could honestly describe Crane's lines as in any way 'derivative' from Miss Ridge...Crane barely echoed—certainly not borrowed." However, Crane also borrowed very heavily from the less well-known poet Samuel Greenberg, in particular his early poem "Emblems of Conduct." When Ridge reviewed Crane's *Key West and Collected Poems* after his death in 1932, she began with the statement: "Like most men of creative power, Hart Crane lacked the ability to invent; he could only discover."

Abstraction—even "mysticism"—in poetry, was not unappreciated at the time. Wallace Stevens, the most abstract of poets, had just published his second book, *Ideas of Order*, with Knopf, and it was well received. But even Stevens, in his own way, injected politics into his work. "Who can think of the sun costuming clouds/When all people are shaken." In absolution of some critics' harsh evaluation of his abstractions, he writes:

If they throw stones upon the roof
while you practice arpeggios,
It is because they carry down the stairs
A body in rags.

In addition to the publication of *Dance of Fire* in 1935, Ridge's poem about Tom Mooney, "Stone Face," was republished as a broadside. Printed on both sides so it could hang in midair, and big enough that its text was visible ten feet away, it was designed to be used at "Labor Day, May Day, Working Class and Mooney parades and demonstrations, Mass meetings, Union halls, and Workers headquarters" and sold to support Mooney's defense committee. Distributed by the thousands all over the nation, the poem became an extremely powerful tool in keeping his face and the fact of his incarceration before the public. A survey published that year revealed that Tom Mooney was one of the four best-known Americans in Europe, after FDR, Lindbergh and Henry Ford. Although Mooney's biographer, Richard H. Frost, wrote that "Mooney often called for a Zola but a Zola never came," critic Nancy Berke suggests that, on the contrary, Ridge fulfilled that role well. New Zealanders now claim that Ridge's poem remains perhaps the best circulated of any New Zealander's poems in the U.S. Mooney was eventually released in 1939 but his health was broken and he died a few years later.

Local politics in New Mexico drew Ridge only a month after she arrived, in particular, the miners who had been on strike in Gallup since 1933. Because its leaders had initially been effective, the miners were blacklisted and evicted from their homes, then charged with breaking and entering when they tried to return. After the police tear-gassed and open-fired on a crowd gathered after the trial, scores were wounded, hundreds were gassed, and an officer killed, most likely in friendly fire. Ten men were arrested under a statute that held all those present at the scene of the killing of an officer of the law were guilty of murder. The lawyer defending them was Daniel Levinson, who also defended Marinas Van Der Lubbe for the burning of the German Reichstag in 1933. Ridge's *Dance of Fire* ends with "Fire Boy," a poem on 24-year old Lubbe's execution for protesting the Nazi's encroachment, an event that Hitler called "a sign from heaven" and was used to establish his dictatorship.

...There had been anger, valid, a bright

point; shivering at impact; now
There was no more rage in him against those who had
    denied him—*let them*
Deny this! (*Dance of Fire* 99)

"[Levinson] spent an evening in my studio with Carl Howes[,] strike leader last year against the American Coal Company," Ridge writes Lenore Marshall.

> General Wood's son and his hired thugs knocked all Carl's teeth out last year, beat him up and threw him across the state line—he calmly walked back...it is dominated and terrorized by the Am. Legion...the artists who gave in Taos were actually afraid to sign their names to the fifty cents or dollar or so they gave.

Ridge writes her husband and Louise Adams Floyd for money to support the cause. "This [underlined three times] is the revolution I expect since I have come here, and it is I believe now being plotted," she writes Marshall.

Two days later, David Levinson and political organizer Robert Minor met with one of the wives of the accused in a car parked in the plaza. Minor was a famous illustrator for *The Masses* before going into organizing, and had trained at the Ferrer Center while Ridge was in charge. Three men shoved revolvers inside the rendezvous car. Leaving the woman behind, the men drove Levinson and Minor into the desert and beat them brutally. "I lost consciousness and when I came to was again beaten," writes Levinson.

> I was dragged out [of the car] and thrown on the ground, bleeding profusely, kicked on the knees and left again. "I heard Minor asking for his fountain pen. 'You won't need it in hell, they told him. I could not see him. A hood was placed over my head. I was sure they were going to hang us. I was dragged into an upright position and asked if I had anything to say.

They were left to walk 12 hours through the desert.

Ridge reported that some Greek hoteliers asked her friend the artist Ofer [Walter Ufer] how he could associate with Jews—the lawyer Daniel Levinson, defending for free the Mexicans falsely charged with murder in the strike. Ofer answered that "this was only one of the many signs of a worldwide pogrom against the Jews [in] which they will again be slaughtered and outraged."

Ridge didn't mention any further involvement with politics in New Mexico. Writing to Louise Adams Floyd at the end of the summer, she admitted that she had become discouraged. When she asked "Ted Stevenson a communist writer here about the chances of my going there and getting down into the mine," he told her she would never get by the guard. Both he and his wife had been warned they would be killed if they attempted to enter Gallup.

Chapter 34

Poetry in the Southwest

Mabel Dodge presided over the arts in Taos, the peyote-taking 1910s *salonnière* whose lavish Fifth Avenue apartment was just a few blocks from Ridge's studio on 14th Street. Brought to Taos by her third husband in 1917, Dodge fell in love and married a fourth, the Tewa Indian Tony Luhan. She then pushed D.H. Lawrence to visit her in Taos. After he arrived, waves of artists came to stay with or near her, some 250 between the wars. These included Ridge's friends Marsden Hartley, Jean Toomer, Alfred Stieglitz, and Paul Strand. Around the time of Ridge's 1935 trip to Taos, composer Leopold Stokowski was staying with Dodge—now Mabel Dodge Luhan—and was soon to collaborate on scoring *Fantasia* with Disney.

Through an introduction given by Evelyn Scott, Ridge met Dodge's son, the novelist and later government official John Evans and his novelist wife, Claire Spencer. Spencer had been married to Ridge's current publisher, Hal Smith. Ridge had certainly not been happy with Hal and the two of them might have found a shared sympathy. Ridge wrote that she also met Evans's first wife, Alice Oliver Henderson Evans, who had married at age fifteen, and whose mother was the assistant editor at *Poetry* and now literary doyenne of Santa Fe opposite Mabel. Alice is "the devoted wife of John Evans," according to Ridge, although Alice and John had already been divorced for a number of years. Perhaps Alice was trying to play the devoted ex-wife hanging around Taos with their three children? She hosted Jean Toomer while Ridge was in Taos.

Toomer had reasons for keeping his distance from Mabel, since he may have had an affair with her during an earlier visit. Luhan's biographer, Lois Palken Rudnick, references an uncharacteristic Langston Hughes poem "A House in Taos" to suggest such an entanglement was known to at least a few of his friends. Luhan certainly lent him $14,000 in 1926 that he hadn't repaid. One of the characters in his unpublished play, "A Drama of the Southwest," reveals a fear of New Mexico's "female fascism—[the] strong resourceful women who like the starkness and isolation of this country...It's they, these women, who are claiming this land which used to be thought of as man's country." He was traveling with his second wife Marjorie Content, previously married to *Broom* publisher Harold Loeb, the woman who was Ridge's friend and landlord while she edited the magazine. Content had become a very accomplished photographer since her Sunwise Turn days, and a portrait of Ridge taken in 1935 was purchased by the National Gallery of Art. Her marriage to Toomer, who wrote that "women want men genuinely to be their lords and masters," was not easy—he later slugged her for suggesting that he was a fake—and was based on having access to her money.

Around the time of his visit, Taos endured a three day "drizzle" that is known historically as "The Great Flood of 1935." "I sat up all night in a chair by the fire in my little room, an umbrella over my head to catch the drips and falling plaster," writes Ridge. Toomer's play immortalizes it with a description of Ridge (as Riva Lentin).

> You know how other-worldly Riva is, much here mentally but as if her body were absent-minded...The rain came down and the house leaked...Water was streaming down the walls. The floor was a puddle. Riva, on a chair in the middle of the room, had rubbers on! Over her head she held an umbrella and with her free hand she was writing poetry!

Ridge also met the poet Spud Johnson, Mabel's sometime secretary. Ridge and Johnson quarreled, but made up by the end of April, when he promised to review her new book. Ridge may not have wanted to get any closer to Luhan than Johnson, given Luhan's propensity for manipulation. According to Mabel's frequent visitor, Ansel Adams, the famous hostess would "insult, confuse and reject people," and he described her as having "talons for talent." Luhan's mercurial personality resulted in her being "imagined dead in a greater variety of ways than any other woman in American literary history," according to Louise Palken Rudnick, Luhan's biographer. D.H. Lawrence was first on the list of those with that kind of imagination. While Ridge was visiting Taos, Lawrence's wife, Frieda, ended a final tug-of-war with Luhan over Lawrence by cementing his ashes into a monument, rather than allowing Mabel to scatter them over New Mexico.

Ridge reported on the feminine rivalry in Taos:

There is here among the women suspicion and jealousy [and a] love of power (social power alas!!) to an extent which I have not met before—at least not since the New England small town's...They twist and torture some perfectly harmless word into malefic [sic] meaning—and then carry it and there is something added from every fresh simmer of the spirit through which it passes.

That was a fairly accurate portrait of Mabel Dodge Luhan's behavior, but Ridge may have also been referring to Rebecca Strand's. The ex-wife of Ridge's friend, Paul Strand, "Beck" arrived in Taos with Georgia O'Keeffe, perhaps as her lover. The daughter of the manager of Buffalo Bill in Europe, she had inherited his strong ways and personality. "I've not come all this way to watch Becky Strand striding in front of the mountains," writes Ridge. "She's been awfully kind, but I cannot have her morning noon and night." By the end of May she reports: "Rebecca...has stopped trying to dominate me," but went on with an *arte della furia*:

Why does everyone who becomes at all fond of me at once begin to lay out my life—try to manage me? I tell you I'd rather live in a treetop or a cave and sleep on stones even if they did collide with my thin spine and that frightened constriction of the spirit I suffer when others try to put their will on me is so terrible that I can imagine how people drift into murder of their nearest and supposed-to-be-dearest who have striven to dominate them for years. It is what I suppose an eagle would feel if some ground-loving, flat- footed garden fowls, that had somehow got hold of it by a wounded foot, held on to keep it off the crags because "crags" are dangerous. (yes I know I'm ungrateful).

In the same letter, she notes that one of her supporters, Mrs. Murray Crane, was sending her a warm coat for Mexico.

Ridge always saw herself embroiled in a fierce battle for freedom, emotionally, financially, politically, and aesthetically, including most importantly, her choice of subjects for poetry. In late May she wrote a stirring letter about this to a Miss Bartlett, most probably Alice Hunt Bartlett, American associate editor of the *Poetry Review*, the magazine of the English Poetry Society. Bartlett solicited many American writers for their views on poetry around this time, including Willa Cather, Robert Hillyer, and Robinson Jeffers. Ridge's response justified her continued interest in things not conventionally "poetic," in subjects political as well as personal, elucidating a modernist stance of inclusiveness that would be thoroughly assaulted by conservatives in the 1950s: "All life is the domain of poetry; not only the ancient rituals of love and birth and death, but all vast happenings, from wars, strikes, the endless crucifixions of labor to the being of the smallest flower."

In June, Ridge moved to Santa Fe, into "a beastly room" in Hotel Fidella, but didn't stay in the hotel long, citing food poisoning. Rafael Alfredo (or Alfonso?—she used both names interchangeably), helped her find new lodgings in the historic and fashionable La Fonda in Santa Fe. He also located a doctor for her, made social contacts, arranged her excursions, and tutored her in Spanish, insisting that she not pay him. He was, according to Ridge, the son of one of the governors of Mexico, and "one of the loveliest spirits I have ever known." They had met at least as early as April, having wine together, although most likely he was also the "Alfau" mentioned in a telegram who missed her when she first arrived in New Mexico at the end of March, and the "lovely "Alfon" who helped her April 2. He was working on a novel. Left in her correspondence with Lenore Marshall around that date was a slip of gold-orange paper with a note written in Ridge's hand:

> that has nothing to do with the emotional attractions of one being for another in which while it lasts anyhow—dignity is pretty generally forced to abdicate—and most every other attribute of the ego that is likely to obstruct that very exclusive jealous and single urge...

Alfredo was ten years younger than the 62-year-old Ridge although she, like many other contemporary women, tended to refer to him—and all men—as "boy." That she became involved with someone who, as it became evident, was even more impecunious than herself is testament to her lack of calculation, her clinging to the notion of freedom in all exchanges even though it might mean disaster. It quickly became apparent in her letters that they had a growing intimacy. To her husband she writes: "The south west is infinitely more bigoted on the negro question than the East. And every one in Taos looks on Jean [Toomer] as a man of blood...Raffael [Alfredo] and I have discussed this together...." By the end of July, Alfredo was walking all the way to the doctor's office to make sure she had gone. Perhaps to assuage her guilt, she tried to set up her husband by suggesting that Lenore Marshall call Davy "sometime...I think he's mis-mated with the industrial world. He loves art in all its forms..."

Becky Strand offered to help find Davy a job so he might join her, but Ridge, now embroiled with Alfredo, discouraged that possibility. Regardless of Ridge's outrage with Strand's manipulation, she continued to meet with her. Strand was then making striking modernist paintings on glass. Often symbolic, one of these paintings was a portrait of Ridge but it did not satisfy Strand and she destroyed it.

Ridge threw herself into socializing. "I'm very popular—too darn popular, yet I cannot very well refuse to meet fellow artists and writers who wish to meet me." She continues justifying herself: "I did need to see the country with the type of the idle rich who have taken me around." She spent time with Witter Bynner, the gay fixture of Santa Fe, satirist of poets and novelists, past president of the Poetry Society, and translator of Chinese poetry. He writes of the aftermath of some wild evening: "I shall never forget your ecstatic soul-slumber on my library floor with the elfin smile... What a girl you are!" Mrs. Hoover from Chicago's *Jewish League Magazine* recognized Ridge from Marjorie Content's photo and invited her for dinner. They both had tea with Alice Corbin Henderson who had already scheduled a review of *Dance of Fire* by Hildegarde Flanner for October's *Poetry*.

Ridge struggled to keep up appearances. Her New York clothing was out of place. She wanted a black coat embroidered with silver, and was having a dressmaker make her a new dress. She had to "give up" a $27 dollar woven dress—worth $324 in today's dollars—due to lack of funds. This in the face of the Depression, and her dwindling cache of awards and handouts. In the same letter she boasted that she had drafted the "Mexican sequence" and the "one carrying on my childhood from SunUp on." Perhaps her husband was skeptical since she had written of similar feats throughout her year in Europe, yet returned home with nothing. By August 5 she writes that she gave herself an exhausting social schedule in order to have a "blind attack" come on so her new doctor could test a shot of nitroglycerin on her. He thought she had low blood pressure.

Poetry warfare broke out in August. Willa Cather's friend and correspondent, Elizabeth Shipley Sergeant, invited Ridge to a reading by Robert Frost in Santa Fe. Ridge was anxious to reacquaint herself. They had exchanged letters in 1919 after her talk in Chicago, when she asked him for a poem for *Others*. She had made quite an impression with her speech because after his polite refusal to send her anything, he writes: "You of all people won't want me to behave as anything else after what you said in Chicago." She had also praised him lavishly and perceptively in a 1920 *New Republic* review. After his reading in Santa Fe to an audience of 200, Ridge "had a talk with Frost for the first time for years."

> They wanted (a poem) from me and as I couldn't remember I went away and wrote from memory the opening sonnet of Via Ignis. I had to read it twice as the first time only Frost and Bynner got it or seemed to (you know its rather complex)[.] I said [,] when I'd finished now you can all criticize (they'd criticized all the others)[.] Robert Frost said "No they can't, this is different, it's superb." I was sorry—it would have been much more amusing to get reactions! Of course no one said a word after that. I'm giving Frost my book *Dance*. As for the next day, I went to a lunch Bynner was giving for Frost—Davy [,] it would take pages to describe the comedy of errors that ensued... Frost, in the first place, was two hours late (he'd been held up by a flood it turned out. He looked like a defiant rock and Hal like a playful weasel [?] with its tail between its legs....Bynner and Frost had an argument. Frost called Hal a Williams Lyon Phelps [a popularizer of lit]—and Hal emptied a glass of beer over Frost's head.

The argument was recounted differently in the official biography published by Lawrance Thompson and R.H. Winnick in 1981. Frost's tardiness was one-upmanship for Witter Bynner's late arrival as his introducer the day before. When Frost finally appeared for lunch, Bynner praised a book of poetry containing references to homosexuality, and Frost went along with him until Bynner challenged Frost to read his favorite. Frost read one of the more erotic poems but said that the 54-year-old Bynner was "too young and innocent to understand such verse." That's when the beer was poured over Frost's head.

In early July, Ridge asked Lawson to send her black kimono, and nearly two months later she asked for it again, mentioning in passing that she hadn't seen Alfredo for ten days, and railing at Lawson, for being "rather uncommunicative." He finally sent the kimono at the end of September. Perhaps he could read between the lines—or he read all the lines that suggested that Alfredo had replaced him. Her behavior towards Lawson was, as usual, ambivalent and, if anything, worse, given that she had a lover: she wanted him there, she didn't, she didn't want to come home, she would go to Mexico, she delayed leaving for Mexico by herself, insisting that the doctor wanted her to stay in Santa Fe until at least October.

Although she had declared in April that she "want[ed] to do Cortez," she kept returning to the possible Australasian poem. In May an astrologer guessed that she felt strongly drawn to travel to Antipodes-Australia, and by August Ridge admitted that she had "a great urge to go to Australia now for a long time...[The astrologer] startled me for it really was true." In the same letter, Ridge talked of going to China. She had to get some writing done either way. A few days later she announced that she had written 255 lines of a poem—but not whether it is the Australasian one or another. She said she had added 340 lines to her "magnificent Prologue" by the end of August, and ten more by September 10.

By early September she decided that the Prelude she had written would work for either poem, and began to study Cortez at the American School of Research. Lawson must have proposed that she return to New York before her money ran out, or travel again to France—at last he knows the language, having, on her urging, studied it for at least a year—for, in response, she became quite adamant about not returning:

> I can't work there [New York] much and cook clean and all the petty details of housekeeping that litter the mind more than a straight day's office work...Also *I would not think* of going to France now. France and its atmosphere fatal for [the] kind [of] book I'm writing—I want wild country...Everything depends on the book dear [.] I must [underlined twice] get it out. Meanwhile do *not* [also underlined twice] consider me in any way[,] do only what you wish."

She had already made arrangements to drive to Albuquerque to the Mexican consul for a permit to cross the border.

> I think best I start for Mexico alone...I could not pay your fare here and our *two* to Mexico to save my life...I do not expect to stay there more than two or three weeks...*If* you lose *your job*, telegraph me at once and I'll telegraph enough if I can raise it, as I think I can by *drawing ahead on Guggenheim*, enough for you to join me....I may come back to Calif for winter...perhaps you could join me then in Calif?

Two weeks later she wrote that someone had offered to put her on the train to Mexico. She asked Lawson to forward her blue dressing gown—now that she finally had the black kimono—then broke into recrimination: "you are a self-centered person who has besides a great deal too much to do for himself and I'm not blaming you for a combination of character and circumstance." But she did blame him, the devoted husband who had been sending her books and money and sleepwear and medication for at least the last 10 years of her wanderings. Perhaps she was feeling guilty about Alfredo. As if justifying her trip, she reported to Lawson that an Ouija board urged her to travel to Mexico, even "spelling out Nahutl [sic] repeated several times—we kept losing words the glass went so fast—we had to separate letters later."

V

Mexico, California,
New York City,
1935–1941

Chapter 35

Mexico and Romance

In the 1930s a trip to Mexico for artists was as sought-after as a stay in Europe. According to Tina Patricia Albers, Tina Modotti's biographer:

> Mexico City teemed with fanatics, bohemians, idealists, radicals, and visionaries. Intellectuals who had once looked to Europe for cultural revelation now turned their backs upon the old continent, embracing instead the genius of peasants and indigenous peoples whose inclusion in the Mexican community promised to bring forth the "regeneration and exaltation of the national spirit."

Mina Loy spent her brief romance with Arthur Cravan in Mexico City in 1918, William Carlos Williams sojourned over the border in a wild train ride even earlier, Mexico was where D.H. Lawrence began writing *The Plumed Serpent* in 1923, Archibald MacLeish wrote his epic *Conquistador* after his walk through Mexico in 1928, Katherine Anne Porter shuttled between Mexico City and Greenwich Village from 1920-1931 as a journalist, and Hart Crane committed suicide on his Guggenheim voyage returning from Mexico in 1931. In one of his last letters he wrote: "I do know...how emphatically I love [Mexico]—population, customs, climate, landscape and all." During Ridge's editorship of *Broom*, the magazine had championed pre-Columbian art as quintessentially American. Although very popular, travel to Mexico was just one destination for the modernists' wanderings.

"It is mainly poets, novelists, and a few painters who have lived this tortured spiritual impulse, [homelessness] in willed derangement and in self-imposed exile and in compulsive travel," writes Susan Sontag about the modernists' search for identity. As the critic Raymond Williams writes:

> They were exiles one of another...but without the organization and promotion of group and city—simultaneously located and divided.

The [emigre's] self-referentiality, their propinquity and mutual isolation all served to represent the artist as necessarily estranged, and
to ratify as canonical the works of radical estrangement.

Ridge's friend, the moody and inconsolable painter/poet Marsden
Hartley, was never able to find a home. Born in Maine, educated in Ohio and
New York, he lived and worked in France, Austria, Italy, Germany, Mexico,
Rhode Island, Bermuda, Massachusetts, New Hampshire, Maine, New
Mexico, California, and Nova Scotia. Ridge was no better. Her hegira began
in Ireland, Australia, New Zealand, San Francisco, Montreal, New York—
five years wandering the Midwest—then back to New York again, where she
kept changing apartments. She always included a return address when she
wrote *Poetry* editor Harriet Monroe, making it easy to track her movements
beginning in 1918: 18 Vannest Place (demolished that year), 21 East 15th
Street, 17 West 8th Street, 469 West 22nd Street, 114 East 121st Street, 3 East
9th Street, 252 West 12th Street, 793 Broadway, and 296 West 11th Street.
Their correspondence ends in 1933, so it doesn't include 47 Morton Street,
or the two additional addresses at the end of her life in Brooklyn. During
those years she also spent long stretches outside the city, in Long Island or
Saratoga Springs or Montauk or Bermuda or Massachusetts, as well as a
year wandering through Europe that ended in Baghdad, five months in Taos
and Santa Fe, where she moved seemingly every few weeks, all over Mexico
for a year, back to California again, then across the country to New York. She
recognized her peripatetic nature. "I could never live in Santa Fe as a steady
thing—my personality is too strong—that is, I could never live in it and
be myself...I need a wilderness or a city big enough..." As a solo wanderer
through the most exotic of ports, she was indefatigably ambitious in her
travel, and seemed to relish her homelessness. "I feel always in 'a room for
the night,'" she writes from Mexico.

Long before crossing its border, she listed all the difficulties of travel
to the country—"the mosquitoes, the hygiene" but she trumped every
objection with "but I've been to Baghdad!" Her trip, however, did not start
off smoothly. "Curious holdup[,] something gone wrong," she writes in
a short note to her husband just before she crossed the border, and then
elaborated later:

I overheard one woman on the train ask a newly arrived passenger
(the one who gave me this hotel address) what was to be done about

a person who had been preaching sedition against Am. Government and had now gone to Mexico to stir up seditions and rouse!!! revolution against *that* government. She was Californian and they may be stirred up about my poem on Mooney.

Ridge's radicalism would have been seen as positively conservative in Mexico. Although officially the Mexico Revolution had been over for ten years, the Cristeros war between the Catholic church and the government continued until 1934, the year socialist Lazaro Cardenas became president. In order to quell the effects of the Depression in his country, he had nationalized much of the land, the oil, and the railroad, and empowered the peasants to run collective farms in the south. It worked. At the time, Mexico City had a million inhabitants whose cars flooded the main avenues, their terrible pollution still a few decades off, who enjoyed parks equipped with "outdoor radios" and whose nightclubs celebrated the latest in jazz in the Zócalo, although the women, always the last to feel any improvement, still carried water on their heads in the suburbs.

Ridge stayed three days at the Imperial, one of the most expensive hotels in Mexico City, then moved to "a most comfortable Spanish-German home." She crowed that she was drinking the "water[,] eating all foods[,] vegetables[,] and fruits[,] which I was particularly warned against...feel fine[,] no medication since I was here. I've felt this from the first—accepted by Mexico," and she wasn't ill for another two months. She was delighted with the country and "amazed about D.H. Lawrence—he was simply terrified of Mexico—frightened every moment he was here." But the hotel took all her funds, and it would be another three weeks before the Guggenheim Foundation would send her another installment of her fellowship. When it came, she had quite a bit of trouble cashing the check, even with the intervention of the American consul. "The Mexicans are...against the very idea of the Guggenheims being permitted to amass their vast fortunes," she writes her husband. The Chase Bank manager was incredulous about her trials getting the money. "The idea of a poet hatching a plot!" In the end, the chief postmaster of Mexico endorsed her check. However, more trouble loomed: her travel permit was lost.

But Ridge had less tedious concerns. The first was, happily, recognition. "My book must be becoming known for I've received so many letters from strangers...It is somehow getting harder for me to remain obscure." She still hadn't sent her husband a copy of her new pages. "You spoke of my poem—

my not sending you carbon[s] of the Prelude. Why dear, with all this bother I can't even get my mind serene enough to work." An undated note showed that she had at last sent a copy of the thirteen-page "Prelude" to Lawson just before she left for a trip to Guadalajara. "My mind has been too divided in copying it—which I did in great haste to do any revision." Her "Prelude" has all the grandiloquent posture and ambition of a Jeffers narrative, and begins with a mathematical creation myth:

> ...What if mind, busily com-
> puting that
> Which is numbered and the final sum set down irrefutably,
> Take tally of the heart, endlessly rocking, or of the
> teeming
> Atoms of this stone;

There is the cosmic sexual awakening:

> You, omnipresent, witness of the bright births, knew
> The long shudder; the upheaving
> Spin of the continent; the tender
> Thrust of the rock, yet barely
> Set in its too hot mold,
> Lifted and wrenched apart...

When man appears many lines later, his instincts are not so innocent:

> —He who had coerced all harmless things,
> stone and fishbone and the innocent woods, to
> Take on malign life... And from his hand, that menaced all things,
>   leap
> Forth fanged and lightninged. He climbed high cliffs and the great
>   thighs of hills, till from a thousand
> Times his little height his small eyes roved over the world.
>   He saw
> His stone-arm twitching, the vast herds, grazing and
>   the desert wrinkled in the winds, her sands
> Taking again the wild postures of the sea (he smelled (no
>   flagrant

Tang of empire yet on the sea's breath, a salt, sweet smell...

In preparing to take the first woman, man makes a sacrifice:

> Plucked the hearts from out live things and with bloody
> and propitiate hands, arms flung out like two stakes (the Cross
> implicit in that gesture) upheld them bleeding to the light.

The final lines move toward mourning humanity's eventual subjugation:

> Who shall attest
> Scanning bronze slab or a chipped cone, how oft and in
> what ages the anonymous
> Swarming out of the galleys and the black pits
> Struck without vizor; taking the down-stroke...Nebuchadnezzor
> Drove us on the wall; into the great moat... harried us
> as we
> Lifted up the gate of Ishtar, as we cast out of our burning
> The silver serpents and winged bulls.

Whatever poem "Prelude" was to proceed, it would have to equal or surpass this introduction.

Guadalajara was a 400-year-old city, where Miguel Hildago abolished slavery in 1810 and initiated the country's independence movement. The Independent University of Guadalajara was founded there in 1935 as a rebuke to the socialist education put forward by President Cardenas. With its spring climate and wide avenues of baroque and neoclassical colonial buildings, the city has always been very appealing and now hosts the largest colony of foreigners of any city in the world.

Ridge's friend Idella Stone lived there with her father, a dentist, and published *Palms* between 1923-1930. An influential magazine, it included the work of Stone's former writing professor, Witter Bynner. D.H. Lawrence, a friend of her father's, helped design several of the magazine's covers and also offered poems. Pound deemed it the best poetry magazine of its time. Its poems were published without authors so they could be judged on their own merit, the names revealed in the next issue. Ridge contributed "Pain" to one of its last issues in 1930. Retitled "Drunk with Old Youth" in *Dance of*

Fire, the speaker plunges deep into the ocean, as if framing Crane's suicide: "Shall I—bootlessly turning...evade,/In bubble-eyed waters...a sword-blue streak,/Turning on its back."

Stone had visited Ridge earlier in New York, and ran a Mexican gold mine for two years after Ridge visited Guadalajara. She then taught creative writing in Los Angeles, became a riveter during World War II, directed a Scientology center, and contributed twice to books on D.H. Lawrence. She remembered him as being pursued by women everywhere, and "petulant, cranky, rude and inconsiderate." Like Ridge, her first baby died soon after birth. She went on to write many children's books but is chiefly remembered as the author of *Thirty Classic Mexican Menus in Spanish and English*, *14 Tales of ESP*, and *Never in this World,* a sci-fi anthology she edited which contained stories by Poul Anderson and Isaac Asimov, and received the Fawcett Gold Medal. Her pop fame rests on adapting Felix Salten's *Bambi* for Walt Disney. Her father, Dr. George Edward Purnell, "a most kind gentle, honorable and utterly impractical old man," introduced Ridge to several people, including Fred Leighton who imported Mexican pottery and handicrafts. He and his wife offered to take her around to the small towns and villages. "I have never been more interested and excited anywhere in my life, so above all do not worry about me," she writes Lawson.

> I have crossed the country states from Mexico City to Guadalajara and back, stopping at each town by the way, making detours to villages and pueblos and following trails to their ends in mountains where tourists do not go. From the Town of Singing Instruments to silver mines and factories and to the poor homes in which the Indians weave their fabrics very much as they did in pre-Cortez days.

But it wasn't all tourist stops and trading opportunities. On December 23 they

> took a taxi and visited a silver mine where there was a strike on. The men were receiving two pesos (64 cents) per day and had struck for time.We found a committee of strikers guarding the mine—and this is one very fine thing the present government has done for the workers...the miners themselves and none else may guard the mine during a strike. They can prevent all from entering—even the mine-

owners themselves dare not pass the gates. I thought—how different from *our* mine strikes!

They also visited the small town of Salvo, where they "saw parades of workers marching and wearing the red-and-black strike flag in favor of the present government." She writes Marjorie Content: "I've never—not even in the old days of the Ferrer School or around America at election time—seen anything like the confusion [,] the intrigue [,] and the warring within parties that apparently exists in Mexico."

She delayed her return to Mexico City for six weeks. On her arrival, she received Lawson's letters—"depressing" she reported—and didn't accept his Christmas gift because she refused to pay the duty. Besides, she "cannot wear that hard, glittering type of jewelry—like glass or diamonds. It is too unbecoming to me." He must have asked to join her in the new year because she writes back:

> It will take me at least a year to do my book—maybe more if you come [and] you will have to help and not hinder me—it is my last book and I'm desperate. To do this you will have to learn Spanish— had you been interested in coming you would have started Spanish long ago, when I asked you last September....of course you will not be able to get any kind of a job here—

The admission that she thought it would be her last book must have rattled him. She also admitted in this letter that she was not working on the Australasian poem. "In comparison, a record of personal experiences, enclosed in the slight segment of a life seems not worth while...." By February 5, she writes that the Prelude—for some poem—was now 22 typed pages.

On January 21, 1936, she went with the Leighton's to visit Diego Rivera, at the time Mexico's most celebrated artist. "Like him; he has the reality I need," writes Ridge, "but can't agree with all his opinions. He's a Trotskyite— believing in a world uprising and I think that at the present time this would result in a race of Fascist dictators."

Rivera had been back from Moscow for two years and was repainting his destroyed Rockefeller Center masterpiece at the Palace of Fine Arts in Mexico City, inserting a likeness of abstemious John D. Rockefeller, Jr. drinking with a woman in a nightclub. A plate of syphilis bacteria wafts over their heads. Married to Frida Kahlo, Rivera was having an affair with her sister that prompted one of Frida's most graphic paintings, "A Few Small Nips," showing a blood-covered nude woman and her attacker. When Ridge met Rivera again in July, he was accompanied by Frida, who "looks like a Persian—and dresses for the part." The next year Frida would seduce Trotsky when he came to live with them in exile.

Ridge never wrote that she was homesick nor that she missed her husband, her mother, her friends, or anyone else. She did remember her son in March, but only in false conjecture, as previously mentioned. She did not elaborate as to how she might have discovered his imagined death—perhaps through a crystal gazer or fortuneteller. In the same letter that she mentioned Keith's presumed death, she accused Lawson of being "strangely secretive," and confessed to having already lost the fountain pen Lawson had sent her to replace the jewelry she refused during the holidays. She had received the pen from him just a day earlier. Had Alfredo followed her to Mexico? All the rejection is suggestive of her own secret.

She travelled from Mexico City to Oaxaca—"frightfully expensive"—but with mariachis "playing guitars in the park near by...The strolling German bands used to live in the same precarious way in Sydney." A few days later she was back at the pricey Hotel Regis in Mexico City. The Guggenheim turned down her request for an extension. "I put my arms around you and tell you to have faith in me and in my power to achieve against all obstacles," she writes Lawson. As part of her research, she talked and took photos for two hours with Dr. Alfonso Caso, who had unearthed carved stones from the Monte Albán archaeological ruins of "a civilization that existed long before the Toltecs," writes Ridge. It would be the Olmecs'.

A few days later she told Lawson to apply at once for an engineer's license in California because that's where she was going as soon as she received her last check. She hypothesized that Monterrey "or somewhere along the coast line where Carmel is" would be "stimulating and creative." She felt certain that she could "rely on Lenore Marshall to pay my fare to California when you are ready to come." In the meantime, she applied to renew her permit to remain in Mexico for another three months. The officials waived the fee after she showed them a copy of *Dance of Fire*.

Ridge ran into the noted folklorist Frances Toor on a Mexico City street. Toor was, at the time, editor of *Mexican Folkways*, the first bilingual literary magazine in Mexico. With covers by Diego Rivera, the magazine "touched upon art, music, archaeology, and the Indian himself as part of the new social trends, thus presenting him as a complete human being"—an effort that resonated with Ridge's work on *Broom*. Ridge told her about planning to move to Tepoztlán, a town about 45 minutes away by car. "O Lola, you may not even get a *bed*!" warned Toor. On the lookout for solitude, Ridge's comment was droll. "Well[,] the idea of a cell for a room does tempt me." Idella Stone had offered Ridge a job caring for her new baby in Guadalajara, but she refused, thinking Tepoztlán a better location for getting down to work.

Tepoztlán was the birthplace of Quetzalcoatl, the feathered serpent god of ancient Mexico. By the 10th-century it was inhabited by the Toltecs. Centuries later, it was razed by Cortez when the villagers refused to meet him. Situated in a lush valley surrounding by strange mountains, then undiscovered by weekenders from Mexico City, it was fiercely proud and independent. In 1994, the townspeople ran the city government out of town, sealed the city, occupied government offices, and repelled state military until developers backed out of a deal to build a golf course, a development on communally held lands, and a funicular to the top of one of their pyramids.

Just the kind of community spirit Ridge might admire. In terms of her own housing, however, she managed to get more of a cell than she had perhaps wanted: no mattress, only a trough to wash in, no vegetables, very little fruit, no cheese but her landlord did provide a table for her typewriter, and removed the junk in the convent room—all for 15 pesos a month, the price she paid in a day for her room, meals, massaging, taxis, and beggars in Mexico City! She made do and even met "a major poet," Carlos Pellicer Cámara, who stayed in town for a couple of days. A contemporary of Octavio Paz, and founder of the "Solidarity Group of the Workers' Movement" with Rivera, Orozco and others, Carlos Pellicer Cámara was one of the first Mexican modernist poets. At the time he was exploring the historical and spiritual implications of his experience with nature, with ambitions similar to Ridge's. She left a book of his in her library at Bryn Mawr, and there is now a museum in his name in Tabasco, where he served as a senator, which specializes in Olmec and Mayan art. His poetry verges on the surreal, his "Desires" beginning with the lines: "Tropics, why have you given me/hands full of color?"

"I fear Tepoztlán and its discomforts too much for me," Ridge writes her husband. "I've lost almost every trinket in my possession." Nevertheless, she announced that she had received her permit to stay in Mexico until October, and she asked him to send a copy of a chapter from a book he's translated. This little chore, along with mailing her many additional books on Mexican history she couldn't find or that she had already lost in Mexico, must have been a challenge for Lawson with a full-time engineering job. Ridge expected her husband to match her in energy. Although dangerously thin and always ailing, she climbed one of Tepotzlán's pyramids, then made her way back to Mexico City in time for huge May Day parades and strikes:

> The great strike starts tomorrow...Lenore sent me $100...Did I tell you also I was down to forty centavos—and still walking with my head held high...I actually went without one meal. No[,] these things do not crush me and deflate my spirit as they do some others.

She maintained a tone of superiority even about her poverty. But how poor had she ever been if going without a single meal merits a mention? Nonetheless, she felt a great deal of solidarity for the strikers. It was the first time since organizing for Goldman that she had had such an intimate experience with crowds of revolutionaries. She reported:

> all shops in the nation shut—including bakeries, etc. no food permitted to be sold; no hotel service—all servants in the hotels and private houses out for the day; no street cars running or automobiles or buses—only the thousands upon thousands of workers marching. I was greatly cheered by the spectacle... Suddenly I heard a familiar yelling—a tremendous noise—roaring battle cries...I thought the Communists!—and so they were. Along they came, their heads up, their eyes alight, smiles on their faces—the eyes burning with ardor and intelligence. I felt my drooping spirits lift, and the conviction came to me: here is the hope of the world. A handsome young Communist, a standard bearer, passing me. I smiled at him and clapped my hands. He smiled or rather beamed back and stuck out his clenched fist in the Communist salute. I returned the salute...

The closest Ridge came to affiliation with the Communist Party was putting her name on the 1936 "call" for the formation of the League of American Writers, somehow accomplished while she was in Mexico. Founded as a support for the Communist Party's Popular Front agenda, the League was devoted to promoting the collapse of capitalism and pressed writers to speed its demise as participants in the class struggle. "Many famous anti-fascist writers were rescued from concentration camps in

Europe by [its] Exiled Writers Committee; thousands of dollars were collected for medical aid to the Spanish Loyalists; violations of civil liberties and instances of illiberalism in the United States were publicized and protested," according to the library that holds its papers. Those who joined the "call" with Ridge included Thomas Mann, John Steinbeck, Ernest Hemingway, Theodore Dreiser, James Farrell, and Archibald MacLeish. A number of her friends were among those who served on the first executive council: Alfred Kreymborg, Waldo Frank, Joseph Freeman, and Genevieve Taggard. Waldo Frank stepped down as president in 1937, when he questioned Stalinist tactics, the same year that Ernest Hemingway gave the keynote speech. Just back from the Spanish Civil War, Hemingway spoke of fascism as "a lie told by bullies," and stated that "a writer who will not lie cannot live or work under fascism." In the keynote address two years later, Langston Hughes likened the situation of the blacks in America to that of the Jews in Europe. By 1943, after several reversals of policy including moving from antiwar to pro-war, the League was dissolved.

Describing her search for a better place in Tepoztlán, Ridge "looked at innumerable hovels, and I finally agreed to take two rooms, standing by themselves, a tiny house, in fact...*6 pesos a month.*" She must not have been down to her last peso yet as she decided to cut off the top of the second door and put in glass.

> I hope some drunk with tequila will not take it into his head to shy a stone through it...the witchie is three or four doors down across the street. There are three little holes in a row...I forgot to ask where the well was...the door of my back room opens on a gorgeous view of the mountains...despite the horrible inconveniences it seems to me to offer a wonderful peace. Of course no light in town save candles.

Ridge mentions that she had received a letter "from the Guggenheim, asking me to send them a sketch of my work and say how far it has advanced. I think that under the circumstances they have a great deal of nerve." By then Ridge had "big rats running over me in bed at night, the hundreds of bulldog ants that walk over the floor, the scorpions, the food, the awful lack of hygiene... I also killed a black widow... Alfredo says they—the black widows—kill scorpions."

This was the first mention of Alfredo in Mexico. Had the two of them been traveling together all along, choosing Tepoztlán to work on his novel? Or did they rendezvous in Mexico City? She was back there on June 19 for the general strike, staying once again at the Hotel Moritz. This time she adopted the air of a seasoned revolutionary.

> There is a strange air of silence in the city. All over Mexico no light burns beyond the gleam of a candle. Here no wheel turns. The bread is already mouldy. Internationalist that I am, I believe I am now more Mexican than anything else.

She added: "Davy, I may have something to say that you will not like."

Chapter 36

Retreat from Mexico

Some letter, now lost—burned?—revealed the particulars of the secret she had to tell her husband. In another letter she avoided coming to the point: "I'm trying hard to see a way out of the innumerable problems that are besetting me." Perhaps the rigors of Tepoztlán ended her honeymoon with Alfredo, and she felt duty-bound to confess. She writes Marjorie Content in October that she had already told Davy about her lover, and that—surprise!— he was downcast. "At first I think he deceived himself and wrote me a fine letter...It hurts me terribly to hurt him, but I cannot help it."

By June 2nd, she had returned from the strike in Mexico City to Tepoztlán, "living practically on beans." Her progress was slow learning Spanish "because it does not really interest me to learn a foreign language." This certainly sounds as if her tutor, Alfredo, was doing all the translating. In an earlier letter to Content, she feared a Jo Vollmer would spread news of their affair around since she had seen them together in Mexico City. Ridge had "had hot words" with her while defending her patron Fred Leighton, the merchant who drove her around Mexico and introduced her to Diego Rivera. But everyone she saw in New Mexico must have known or suspected the relationship. In a July 22, 1936, letter, she gives Lawson an out: "Perhaps you do not feel like writing to me and would like me to discontinue writing to you?" By then she had left Tepoztlán for good, and returned to Mexico City. To Lenore Marshall she writes: One million thanks for telegraphed money...I'd gone down to 40 centavas [sic]—about 12 cents—when it arrived..." She sketches the situation in the city. "Electric strike; no light in city save candles, for three days...Last night I walked for hours with a flashlight through the darkened city...I'm still in the throes of emotional conflict, which I've attempted to resolve in one direction" It is as if the flashlight were searching through her conscience.

She continued to write Lawson, but the letters were not especially reassuring, especially with regard to the entanglement of political violence with her romantic life:

> Two days after I left Tepoztlán I have since heard there was a gun fight between the military stationed there and the revolutionaries in the town; these are the type of fanatic catholics, called here "Cristos"[.] They would kill their own parents. (and have)...they [say] the "revolutionaries" hacked off the ears of one of the school teachers, a man, with a small pair of scissors [much crossed out.] No, the young school teacher had already gone—the one who hated me. She was not liked in the town and might have suffered the same fate...Me? I do not know...Alfred was always begging me to leave (he lived in an a[d]joining town, 30 [Ridge crossed out 60] miles away) and it was really through him I left when I did...The young school mistress hated me on account of Alfred. Though married she saw and wanted him at once. He was politely indifferent...I was more afraid of her than I was of all the rest of the town.

She ended the letter saying that she would write to Beck Strand— "though she too hurt me by her jealousy—strangely a jealousy *for*[,] not of me." Perhaps Strand too had a romantic interest in Ridge.

Several weeks later, she told Lawson not to send her any more money. At the beginning of August, she was ebullient because she believed he had taken up with someone else. "I'm so glad to see from it or infer from what you say, that you are now interested in someone else... For the first time in my life I'm being secret with [much crossed out] writing (creative) and with everything else." She had also been given—at last—a small extension of her Guggenheim fellowship, which meant she wasn't about to return home until it was spent. She ends the letter with a triumphant flourish: "Give my love to whoever wants it and bless my friends...I am sick, torn to pieces with conflicting emotions—but feel strangely full of power. Bless you, dear Davy, wishing you success and happiness."

But Lawson "did not or would not see," she wrote in a letter to Marjorie Content.

It hurts me terribly to hurt him, but I cannot help it. I've a right to
live completely, however brief the interval may be—and I had not
lived for years, because I feel the pain of others I'm fond of as my
own.

She writhed, trying to cast off her chains. For a woman to "take up" with a
younger man at her age, now 63, with someone outside her culture, required
courage—or romantic foolishness. She had been married to Lawson for 17
years, albeit much of the time separated. But she was adamant. "My life with
Davy is broken, Marjorie, and will not be taken up again by me—I mean
though I hope for and will be proud of his friendship, I cannot live with him
again." She and Alfredo were working on his novel together, "which I think
will turn out to be a Mexican epic."

No, not a poem, a novel, though it will have a poem running through
it. He has no money and has tramped the streets of Mexico looking
for work as well as other cities. Now he has gone off to take a
miserably paying job in Taxco—so as I do not like Taxco and it is very
expensive and full of tourists, we shall have to work as best we may
by correspondence.

But there was more to his out-of-town job search than she could admit.

Something utterly crushed his childhood and I've been trying to
straighten this out for months. There is much to him if he can only
bring his own will to bear on himself and use all his undirected
power. However I think it best for Alfredo and I to be apart for a
while. There is a cloud over him that will not allow him to take help
from his father.

She pointedly didn't tell Evelyn Scott about him. "I have never known
what it was all about. Don't you want to tell me?" writes Scott a year later,
trying to fathom what had gone on. Considering that Scott confided all of
her complicated love life to Ridge, even her sixteen-year-old son's elopement,
Ridge's silence showed how estranged they were. Or had Ridge wanted to
maintain her saintly reputation?

Alfredo certainly didn't seem to be sending her any of his wages. In
Ridge's next letter to Content she expressed gratitude for her loan of money

when she had only "a peso (28 cents) enough to pay for two meals." She added that "Random House seems to take kindly to the idea of the Mexican book (the novel)," and that she had received "a strange letter from Davy; it is on the defensive, but sad."

Lawson had moved to a heated basement apartment in the Village in order to save money. Ridge used a visit to a crystal gazer to try to force the truth out of him about his romantic life, presumably so she would feel less guilty about hers.

> This woman, a handsome Spaniard, asked me if it were not true that I had two husbands. I told her yes, I'd been married twice, but had left long ago one and that one was in America. She told me about it and described him, even to his right eye, also told me of his dual character...she said about you, among other things[,] that you were very blonde, that you had had a woman in your life, but that she was common and that you had parted. Now is this true?... She asked me had I one or two sons; she said she saw two, but no other children. Again I told her the truth—one dead in childhood[,] other disappeared...Well, this woman said that Keith was not dead, described him as fair—he would be called fair in dark Mexico—tall, with broad square shoulders. That he was alive, had married and had a fortune by the sea in some very hot place (also that he had changed his name) but she could not say where...

The fortuneteller was appropriately prescient: Keith was at the time living in Chile, married to the German-Chilean Margarete Wehner, with two children, about to have a third. Ridge could not have known any of this, but she uses the crystal gazer's guesses as leverage on Lawson.

> Now if you tell me that what she said about you was true—that you have had an affair—or something of the sort with a woman who ("but she's common—nothing like you") and that this is broken, I might believe there is something in what she says of Keith. So please tell me the truth.

Lawson's response is not in the Smith Collection. The end of November finds her again begging him for money. "I hope to be able to give it back some day when you need it." She writes Lenore Marshall as well: "If I do not now conserve what you may give me[,] I shall be utterly stranded." Ten days later she had an advance on her lodging with her American hotelkeeper but she was down to borrowing "forty centavos for a stamp." Still she was not suffering too seriously: "I have a room with the door opening on the beautiful garden and extensive grounds, full of tall trees, palms and flowers and cut off from the street by one of those high, mysterious Mexican walls."

Lawson sent her $50, and she received another $35 from Lenore Marshall and paid another month's rent and her debts. Then a large part of a letter to Lawson was x'ed out, followed by:

> I am too fierce and imperious, there is too much capacity for destruction in me, too little tolerance...too much pride. I notice that if I have a flower in my hand, I tear it to pieces—and that is what I do with life.

She admitted to him she had had a break with Alfredo. She went on to write:

> From now on I must try to go on alone. I have not seen Alfredo for over two weeks. The conditions of his life and temperament are such, something may easily have happened—as it had done before. The entire book is done in a kind of very rough draft; the bulk of this is only notes from which whole chapters have been made. Yet I believe it will go quickly. I am writing a poem of the strange story of his grandmother, which I shall weave throughout the book. The first third of this is written. The story is told in the first person. But I am putting in interludes in the third person as well as the poem.

What is more seductive than working in tandem with another writer on the secrets of his life? Of course the manuscript has disappeared. She had titled it *Tiger Way* and hoped it might be published as a play after its publication as a novel.

> But I have not mentioned this even to Alfredo. Anyhow, I'm going to try and make money this year. I must, if ever I'm going to write any more. I believe the book will make money, though it is psychological, tragic, somber. But—*quien sabe.*

She mentioned that she had heard that Henrietta Glick tried to place *Firehead* in Hollywood. She was "very interested" but wondered "what the dickens does she mean? To put it on the screen and have the music accompany it?" She mailed Lawson a Christmas card. He sent her five dollars. He must have suggested again she return home, and she responded with a dramatic feint: "If I were to return to N.Y. now[,] Davy[,] I'd die. [The doctor] told Pat [her hotelkeeper] [the] bronchitis had, he feared, stirred up my so long sleeping T.B. I feel this is true." Immediately after this statement she notes that a small black monkey was chained outside her window— as if it were the objective correlative to the disease. "You say you wish me happiness 'more important than work.' No—it is much less important and the nearest approach to happiness I ever expect is to be (temporarily) free of conflict!"

By mid-January, she was "much better as regards my chest." Someone had paid her doctor. She explained that "the lowest price on which one may live in the cities (for board and room) is three pesos a day. This is all I pay... for my room, three very good melals [sic] a day, use of telephone and so on..." She complimented her American hotelier's food—*very good*—so she must have been eating it. Although she was down to 20 pesos (about $30 in 2014), she managed to see Paul Strand and his famous film, *Redes*, about a fishing community overcoming exploitation. Strand's screenwriter was Henwar Rodakiewicz, who was now divorced from Marie Garland, Ridge's 1920s supporter.

Lawson continued sending money, and she was grateful: "It was corking of you to send me that check." She owed $350 to her publisher Hal Smith, whose press had been taken over by Random House. "I'm only hoping to God I'm free of Smith."

> The Book has been held up since late November, partly through my severe illness in December. Partly through Alfredo's failure to help me. I saw him January 1st and he suggested taking it up with me again, but I refused to work with him any longer. I'll do it alone now. But I felt a temporary disgust with the whole thing. I know, however, the only way to make money is through a novel—poems will never do it and if I am to do the really important work I have in mind (and which may not bring me a cent) I must have money to live on. I feel angry about everything.

She had wanted to write a serious novel since 1928. It was an obvious move, although the last of her 15 potboilers had been published in 1911. "Great poetry is no more self-indulgent than martyrdom," Evelyn Scott told her in flip consolation. Although Ridge's romance had ended, she was determined to continue writing. Ridge wrote a letter to Lenore Marshall, enclosing edits to Marshall's poems, and making her romantic situation even clearer:

> I believe all this upheaval [sic], we have both gone through, necessary. Our own walls even must burn and dissolve to be re-cast anew and give the growing consciousness space in which to expand. The being happy or not happy is relatively unimportant. I've broken with Alfredo for good [and] must go on with my work alone. His inner being is poisoned and in turn poisons the life around it, so that one who strives to help him is in danger of spiritual infection. I do not know if the last word between us has been spoken. But I cannot think of another to speak.

Three weeks later, she writes Marshall that she was "far too close to my subject matter...the emotional strain involving both my work and life has made it [working on the novel] all very difficult." She writes to Lawson from Cuernavaca with the news that she was writing poetry instead of the novel, along with a final assessment of her lover.

> Well, I'll try [to] re-start the blasted thing again...I have, as you might suspect, broken with Alfredo. In fact, the only reason I dislike being in Cuernavaca (which I love) is that it's his home town...Alas, I have not met him and I hope I won't—though he has my camera which he borrowed. I believe, Davy, that he is *or will be* insane—a pathological case like Jack Metcalfe. Like Jack too there is a streak of genius.

She left for the U.S. via San Antonio March 6th, staying in one of the 200 air-conditioned rooms of the Robert E. Lee Hotel. "As I told you in letter... impossible for me to go to N.Y. now," she continued to insist. After a wide detour to the Carlsbad Caverns, she settled in Laguna Beach, borrowing money from Norris, the man who drove her cross-country. She needed it to pay for her apartment where she intended to "cook my own food, do my own house work and try go on with my writing." She complained that it was "beastly cold" but the low in Laguna Beach for the month of March, 1937 was 43 degrees, the high 86.

At the turn of the century, the coastline around Laguna Beach had inspired a group of San Francisco artists to take up plein-air painting. Although it had only 300 inhabitants in 1918, the town founded its first art gallery that year. By the late 1930s, Laguna's summers were filled with art exhibitions, community plays, a parade, outdoor street market, tours of artists' studios, and a *tableaux vivant* of famous paintings, "Pageant of the Masters." The town had become glamorous: the area was a playground for Hollywood stars, with Mary Pickford, Bette Davis, Judy Garland, Charlie Chaplin, and Mickey Rooney owning property nearby. Humphrey Bogart and Errol Flynn stayed weekends at the Hotel Laguna in the 30s. Hildegarde Hawthorne, the granddaughter of Nathaniel Hawthorne, described Laguna "as a child of that deathless search, particularly by persons who devote their lives to painting or writing, or for some place where beauty and cheapness and a trifle of remoteness hobnob together in a delightful companionship." Another perfect location for Ridge.

But she had to have money. She writes Lenore Marshall that "I do not for a moment expect you to go on helping me—and if you cannot give me the remainder of the sum I asked for, please dearest Lenore do not worry about it." She was puzzled about what to do next. "Davy wants me to return to him and live with him. Though I'm very fond of him, I do not wish to do this...Alfredo did more for me than he knew." The politics of free love she espoused—indeed, had practiced if her bigamist union counted—had tangled with her emotions. She cared about Davy and he, in turn, refused to relinquish her. It wasn't just the money. Over and over in her letters she apologized for abandoning him, she wished he could be with her. It couldn't have all been ingenuous. She told Lawson that she didn't want to borrow any more from Norris, who wanted "to be an artist photographer like Strand" and who intended to make some portrait studies of her. Had Norris been sleeping with her? It was the "free" part of "free love" she needed more than anything to do what she wanted, or, inversely, someone to support her. She didn't want to return to New York and stalled, saying she couldn't return until after April, but then she had to ask Davy for a loan. "The truth is T.B. is on me again. I've coughed heartbreakingly for six months"—except that five months earlier she wrote that the doctor said that her chest was fine. She was not optimistic about their inevitable reunion.

It was very good of you [,] Davy [,] to ask me to live in your place—
but I think we'll both be much happier if I do not. And as for doing
housework, it is out of the question...But I should love to be in the
same town with you and this tempts me to N.Y.

By the end of March, she said she had only two dollars left in the world.
Lenore Marshall and Mary Marquis ("who has so little") sent her money but
it was only enough to stay alive, not enough to leave. She refused to have
Lawson approach Dr. Hyman again, who was so generous when she was
stuck in Baghdad. Lawson suggested that she contact the California poet
Sara Bard Field for help. As the current expert in long poems on biblical
themes, Ridge had written a mostly positive review of Field's dramatic
narrative, *Barabbas*, in 1932. Field and her wealthy lover, the satirist C.E.S.
Wood, patronized the arts and supported political causes, defending Emma
Goldman and Margaret Sanger, and working on the pardon of Tom Mooney.
They were also friends with William Rose Benét. But Ridge replied that
C.E.S. Wood had been

pronounced radical and most unpopular with capital in Fascist Calif.
They'd have *no* influence whatever. Also the gap between artists and
industrialists too complete to allow one to influence the other. The
only way art can approach industry is cap in hand.

By May 3 she had deduced that most Californians were "downright...
reactionaries." Her friend Agnes "handed *Dance of Fire* to one of her friends
to read. The friend opened it at the Mooney poem[,] read it and hurled the
book from her, saying she'd never read another word of mine." As for Ridge's
penetration of Hollywood: "No, H. Glick did not write to me. She won't
sell...*Firehead* in Hollywood in 20 years—and especially not Henrietta!"
Victor Hugo Point in Laguna featured a long pier that shot out into the
Pacific. Facing the ocean she left behind, Ridge would have seen its waves
plied by the enthusiastic surfers of the '30s. Bodies were worshipped in
California. She had just left her Mexican lover, he who "did more for me
than he knew"—that Hollywood phrase. What if she left the relationship
and its debris—the unfinished novel—behind, and started over in Laguna?
Turning back to a shoreline dotted with easels, she might have thought
of painting again, and then dismissed the idea—where would she get the
money for that? Even anorexic poets have to eat. Here she had no one she

could really rely on—just one new friend, Agnes. No one loved her enough to support her, no one remembered her power in the literary world, how she slew thirty-seven poets in one review. Books curled in the salt air. And if she should really fall sick, who would arrange her stay in a nice sanatorium?

All she had left of her Mexican sojourn was a trunk that contained a broken plastic calendar stone, a serape, and her volumes of the Sagun history of Mexico—and this was being held up at customs. "I'm utterly no good in looking after any practical matters. Heavens only knows how I've got around the world. However [,] it has been the help I've got from others of course." Then on May 4, Louise Adams Floyd sent her $100 for her return fare to New York. Traveling by bus—and considering stopping at the Grand Canyon—she lost her glasses, her recently retrieved trunk (which also contained her manuscript), and the pills Lawson had sent her. She wandered through Chicago "to 17 restaurants" looking for a meal. Instead of staying with a poet friend, she put up at the Midland Club Hotel, a sleek Art Deco skyscraper in downtown Chicago. By May 10 she was back in New York.

Chapter 37

Anti-Woman,
Anti-Experiment,
Anti-Radical

Ridge probably didn't stay long in Lawson's basement apartment. Summer was coming and she hated spending the season in New York. In previous years she had always found some supporter with a spare room to house her through the worst of the heat. In August 1937 she spent a week at a sanatorium, the "House of Rest," where doctors thought she had something wrong with her spine, but she had definitely returned to the city by October when Thornton Wilder's sister, Charlotte, offered to bring cookies and cake to a meeting. Ridge had been introduced to Wilder by Evelyn Scott, and she had supported Wilder's application in an unsuccessful bid for a Guggenheim in 1936. Wilder won the Shelley Award in 1937, two years after Ridge's second award, sharing it with Ben Belitt. Two years later, Wilder apologized for having some kind of breakdown in Evelyn Scott's apartment.

> Ever since I left Evelyn's so abruptly, on that unfortunate afternoon, I have wanted to write you, and apologize for the performance, always so disturbing to a social group; and so humiliating to the one who hasn't the will power to avert it.

Wilder was eventually locked up in a sanitarium and given a lobotomy. She had been living with Scott. Despite insinuations that Scott and Wilder were lovers, Scott had repeatedly tried to get her released from the sanatorium, although she too had begun to suffer her own severe psychiatric symptoms. The October 1937 cake-and-tea meeting with Wilder may not have taken place since Ridge was back in the hospital by November, being treated with injections of sugar. Physically Ridge was not in good shape, and psychically, forces at the end of the 30s tried her feminism, her politics, and her poetry.

Two students of the proto-New Critic John Crowe Ransom—Allen Tate and Cleanth Brooks—led the assault on women and poetry by targeting their criticism on the most successful and famous of them all, Edna St. Vincent Millay. Tate complained in 1931 that she was a second-rate poet with merely "a sensibility, not an intellect." He was perhaps responding with envy: *Fatal Interview* had sold an amazing number of copies that year. Four years later Cleanth Brooks wrote: "Miss Millay has not grown up" because he felt she lacked irony, but overlooked her brilliant use of irony in "Justice Denied in Massachusetts," insisting that her "preoccupation with social justice" had produced "disappointing" results. The execution? Brooks also conflated the poet with the speaker of the poem and wrote that Millay had the "attitude... of a child whose latest and favorite project has been smashed," equating all women—at least women writers—with children.

John Crowe Ransom published his notorious essay, "The Woman as Poet" in 1939. In it he attributed Millay's and all women's poetry to "personal moods" concerning "natural objects which call up love and pity." He suggested that women were close to "the world of the simple senses," which left them "indifferent to intellectuality" and that their minds were "not strict enough or expert enough to manage" complex poetic forms. He wrote that women threatened 20th-century poetry with immature emotionalism and obsolete formalism. "A woman lives for love," he wrote, particularly referencing Edna St. Vincent Millay. "Miss Millay is rarely and barely very intellectual, and I think everybody knows it." The New Critics and their followers effectively blotted out politics or the personal as subjects for decades for both genders, and along with that, the careers of many accomplished poets. As William Drake writes in *First Wave*: "So thorough was the denigration of the women poets who flourished between 1915 and 1945 that their continuity with a later generation of women poets has effectively been destroyed." Even Adrienne Rich, educated at Radcliffe in the 40s, struggled with the strictures between feeling and form, then believing that "a too-compassionate art is half an art." By insisting that poetry about politics could not also be beautiful, the art form was emasculated and emptied of an important source of inspiration for another thirty years.

Joining the New Critics' virulent antifeminist attacks was the burgeoning movement against radical poetry of all kinds, to the point that by the 50s, critics had recanted nearly all the work of the 1930s. "A sordid decade of liberal hypocrisy and self-deception," was how the fifties saw the 30s, according to critic Alan Filreis. The 1950s' critic Murray Kempton accused poets of the 1930s of having "felt a kind of literary contempt for their craft... and [were] devoid of education." That, of course, was blatantly untrue. The modernists' penchant for experimentation was looked upon hand-in-hand with its radical politics and perceived as threateningly chaotic, with Communist taint, echoing the *New York Times'* reception of free verse in 1913 of "poets who defy syntax and decency." The militarism that went along with the World War II did not tolerate the least whiff of socialism except for those measures necessary for men to band together to fight. The political reforms lauded and indeed heralded by the poets of the 30s had to be put down. Ridge would have been just beginning to feel the vise of this anti-Communist witch-hunt that silenced or exiled many poets of the 1930s. Her friend Eda Lou Walton nearly lost her job at NYU on account of her radical interests. Alfred Kreymborg discovered even "his old friend Tom Eliot" wouldn't publish his work because of its "embattled pacifism." Louis Untermeyer was named before the House UnAmerican Activities Committee and was so unmoored he did not leave his apartment for a year and a half, according to Arthur Miller. FBI surveillance of Muriel Rukeyser began in 1936, and she was followed by an FBI agent almost daily during the Cold War. Before Genevieve Taggard died in 1949, she told a Sarah Lawrence colleague that "they destroyed me," referring to a red-baiter—another poet—whose undermining forced her to resign her position. William Carlos Williams did not escape the political turmoil: red-baiting prevented him from serving as U.S. poet laureate. By 1955 even the anarchist revolutionary poet Walt Whitman had been deradicalized, he who was thought to put "the average man on a pedestal" but in fact, according to archconservative David Daiches, "had no such idea in his head." Alan Filreis in *Counter-Revolution of the Word* coined the term "immaculate modernism" as a ploy critics of the 50s invented in order to skip the 30s poets altogether, and put canonical figures like Pound and Eliot in a "direct unsullied continuity from the 1910s and 1920s."

On November 22nd, 1937, Ridge thanked Lenore Marshall for sending roses to her hospital room, where she was undergoing a neurological exam and X-ray of the stomach. Marshall paid for the stay. "T.B. dead, not active, no germs," Ridge reports. "I received all kinds of tests...nothing wrong with me at all except the migraine." The next day she wrote Marjorie Content: "Lenore Marshall and Dr. Lipkin interested a migraine specialist Dr.

Brickner in me. As we thought[,] nothing wrong with me except arrested T.B. germless now."

Ridge and Lawson moved from the basement of 9 East 12th Street to the seventh floor of 47 Morton Street. On the fourth of July, 1939, Ridge wrote Beck Strand for the first time since she had returned to New York, explaining the lapse in her correspondence amid the fireworks:

> I'm writing by the windows of a high apartment in Greenwich Village...already the explosions are beginning—it's half past nine. I've just been listening to a MacDowell concerto over the air. Strange to remember he composed in this century. What has his tuneful and charming tinkle to do with us who willy-nilly are grappling atoms of our time...After I reached New York from Mexico, via California, I went down ill and with brief respites of half well or better, stayed so for two years....

She told Strand that she had seen her ex-husband Paul once in '37 (probably at the Mexican *Redes* screening) and that she had hung a picture of hers "on the wall of our tiny crowded apartment." She gave it an oblique critique by quoting Davy: "too much yellow in the red" and another visitor's comment: "I don't care for it, it's like a phallus."

The phallus was a continuing preoccupation of the Ridge/Lawson household. Lawson wrote his name inside four of the eight books on phallic worship he left in Ridge's library, two of them heavily illustrated compendiums. In the context of the times and Freud's impact, such an interest is not so surprising. Will Durant discussed the phallus in art and religion at the Ferrer Center, and D.H. Lawrence found its symbolism quite important, according to Kate Millett. All the books study the cross cultural and religious beliefs that surround the phallus—in particular, the practices in India, Japan, China, Mexico, Ceylon, and the ancients. *Ophiolatreia*, with its drugstore-sounding name, begins "O, the worship of the serpent, next to the adoration of the phallus, is one of the most remarkable, and, on first sight, unaccountable forms of religion the world has ever known." Ridge noted of the author of Volume 2 of *Sex Symbolism in Religion* that "This man is too biased and undeveloped." *Phallicism in Ancient Worship* shows lots of pictures of pillars and columns, and *The Story of Phallisms* devotes a large number of pages on prostitution in Rome and all the various categories and subcategories of women who were for sale. Ridge's statements on bisexual creativity are affirmed in *Sex and Sex Worship*, published a year after her speech in Chicago. Philo, a Jewish philosopher contemporaneous with Jesus, says that Adam was a double, androgynous, or hermaphroditic being "in the likeness of God." Surely Ridge knew Plato was the first to note the androgyny of humans. The book states he "explained the amatory instincts and inclinations of men and women... Zeus separated them into uni-sexual halves, and they seek to become reunited."

She and Lawson seemed to be managing in their own uxorial style. "Davy is looking for a new place... [He] is very trustful of others and rushes into things. Against my advice he was about to sign a two-year lease. The money of course is a dead loss." She commented that "I think women are more determined to live and the vital urge in them, not to be denied." By November 1939 the two of them managed to move again, this time to Brooklyn Heights. The neighborhood was a bit down-in-the-mouth with the Depression still on, probably more so than when Whitman or even Hart Crane had lived there. Their new apartment, however, was located at 165 Columbia Heights, in a carriage house with beautiful arched windows situated very close to the Esplanade, with a magnificent view of Manhattan. Complaining about the housekeeping that she shared with a woman who came once a week, she writes: "Much work in this large apartment which [we] must have for Davy's book," indicating that Lawson had begun serious work on his biography of Paul Morphy.

New Orleans chess genius Morphy was the world champion in the mid-19th century, and stopped playing after beating everyone of note. Lawson may have become interested in the man when they lived in New Orleans. Throughout his life, Lawson played excellent chess, taking on Marcel Duchamp and Alfred Kreymborg, as well as prominent chess professionals. His study of French became useful not in chasing after Ridge in Europe but in reading Morphy's original documents. All those years that Ridge had promised to do her writing in exotic locales—now it was his turn.

Answering the 1940 census from Brooklyn, she used Lawson's name, and declared herself 59 years old. She was 67. Such fabrications were common throughout their census reports: in 1925 she said she was 25 (she was 52) and Lawson 35, and that both were born in the U.S. In the 1930 census she was both the wife and head of household, 45-years-old, and not naturalized, although by then she had held an American passport for at least a year. What's particularly striking in her 1940 reply was that, for the first time, she didn't declare herself a poet.

Chapter 38

"The Fire of the World is Running Through Me"

In January 1940, Ridge started a diary, writing as "Rose Emily Ridge," a name she hadn't used since her childhood. It would be "a record of life as it passed, obstructed or attracted me...by turns absorbed, enraged, tender, amazed, but never hated...under the deepest hell is another hell." She tore out all the pages from January to March 2—"through the most intense darkness the self can know." An early March entry chronicles a fight with Davy, and much about her struggle to maintain a separate relationship while being so dependent on him. She writes that she

> talked in bed this morning with Davy, tried to help him deal with a family problem—his family. As usual when we talk we flew apart. I irritated and made him nervous...disturbed me...to no good purpose. We simply cannot meet...Partly, perhaps, all my fault. We move at different tempos. Not that I fail in understanding, but in adjusting the movements of my spirit, swift, impetuous, moving strongly like a wind (perhaps—too—like a wind unpredictably, flying off at tangents) to his—the slower pace. Talking with him sometimes like dragging a heavy or resisting child (by the hair of the head!) through new-ploughed ground. Thinking this makes me laugh—laughter the great restorer of upset equilibriums—I feel all right...but could not pass the funny little image on to Davy...He'd become dour...reduced to resentful silence. Yet he is good, very good—not from any mental concept of goodness pressed like a straitjacket upon an unwilling spirit...but in the very substance of the self.

The rest of the entry reveals that she was suffering from a migraine, and down to only one meal a day, waiting for Lawson's paycheck to fill the larder.

I note with concern I'm getting addicted to self-pity—something I've always despised. How I've condescended to others when I've noticed its manifestation in them...

I don't think I can work at my poem, throat sore but temper sorer. I'd like to knock things over and smash them up.

Male artists have often forged careers as hypocritical egomaniacs, demanding enormous fealty and support of their mates and everyone else around them. Ridge's rage might have been generated out of her frustration with the double standard, and the waning of her opportunities. Her male modernist equivalent might be considered Rainer Marie Rilke. Like Ridge, the Czech poet had a reputation as a saint, who instead of writing poems about the proletariat, wrote brilliantly of angels. But his reputed sainthood is contradicted on almost any page of Ralph Freeman's *Life of a Poet: Rainer Marie Rilke*. "He was a seducer of other men's wives, a pampered intellectual gigolo, and a virtual parody of the soulful *artiste* who deems himself superior to ordinary people because he is so tenderly sensitive, a delicate blossom easily punished by a passing breeze or sudden frost," writes critic Michael Dirda, reviewing the biography. "He was a jerk," declared John Berryman in his third "Dream Song." Rilke began his life pandering to a mostly absent mother who imagined herself nobility, like Ridge's. Throughout his childhood and indeed, throughout "the long convalescence which is my life," he fell ill when confronted by any anxiety. Like Ridge too, he began writing in the vernacular, in his case, Bohemian folk songs, but he soon found his way to modernism. One of his first career moves was to take all his girlfriend's savings to publish his first book, dedicate it to a baroness, and abandon the fiancée. Having the opportunity to write several of the world's most important poems relied on handouts from the very wealthy whose money he spent profligately while ignoring his only child. Wittgenstein gave him nearly a half million dollars, and when that was gone, other patrons awarded him more, all of which he squandered in the most expensive hotels in Europe. After six months in Berlin's very fashionable Hôtel Continental, Rilke repeatedly sent begging notes to his patron Karl von der Heydt, asking for additional funding. "The question, L.R. [lieber Rilke], 'don't you need something?' has, to be honest, not entered my mind," writes back von der Heydt. Just a year older than Ridge, Rilke's work was probably known to her. Sunrise Turn published Rilke's monograph on Rodin in 1919 after he married Rodin's student, became his secretary, then moved in with him. "You must change your life," he wrote most famously. He and Ridge made few adjustments.

Although in her March entries to her diary Ridge claimed to be poverty-stricken, she invited Leonard Abbott over for dinner, her old friend from the Ferrer days. Perhaps they discussed her insight the day before in her diary that "capitalism is one of the great obstacles to a final disarmament..." When Evelyn Scott discovered through Laura Benét that Ridge entertained Leonard Abbott and not herself, she was angry. She wrote Ridge

> restrainedly but unmistakably in that inflamed, injured mood I know so well...
>
> As a matter of truth her friends are very loyal—we've all guarded her from the consequences of her reckless tongue.
>
> How can such a creative person with a mind so brilliant and profound be a prey to so many mean suspicions.

To which Scott replied in a letter: "Well, I just don't see how anyone can become angry at so old a friend and never say how or why." Ridge didn't know until that letter that Scott's mother had just died. Nor did she know that Scott's mental state was slowly disintegrating, and that Evelyn wouldn't publish another book as a result of her increasing paranoia. Evelyn continued to write her despite such difficulties, after years of burdening Ridge or Lawson with her publication problems, her housing problems, her romantic problems, her parental problems, her health problems, and even her storage problems. Ridge was not immune to Scott's demands. "I am upset over a letter from Evelyn," writes Ridge in her diary, then nonchalantly mentions that on the day she asked Laura Benét over for dinner, Ridge thought she had had a heart attack. As a woman so concerned with her health, it is strange that she doesn't mention her condition ever again in her diary. She could have been referring to one of her rages instead.

"One rage leads to another," she writes. "Once I've been made really angry as I was by Davy yesterday morning, I remain in a state of, not irritability, but of slow dark anger, smolder and any breath fans the half consumed embers of fury again to flame." Later on she analyzed her rush of feeling: "I believe rage is simply the frenetic desire for equilibrium, or for the restoration of a disrupted harmony...and what is harmony but a type of beauty?"

But beauty was waning. The next day she observed the pussy willow not as a harbinger of spring but as "pale green shoots, wavering outward, fragile, thin like the wasted arms of babies whose mothers have been starved...." Her next comment about the desert critiques her own isolation: "I love the desert... No green fraternities in the desert, each hardy growth fighting for its root hold..." Her insights were tending toward effacement, a withering away.

On April 8th she notes: "Morning, I am not well. Blood last night." She does not say where or why, she mentions the blood just as casually as the heart attack. It had been two and a half years since the doctors had given her a clean bill of health. Ridge went on with her forebodings in the same entry, imagining her death, and the light inside a stone singing:

> the imperishable light to perish for all alive and for me soon...soon... into that bluish twilight the other modes of being...is not this, too renascent? As the light[?]
>
> I love the light...That dim light what ever [lies] after being, must be like the dimness at the heart of stone. But the stone too, it basking in the strong sun, may admit the light, light filtering in through the stone's pores into the wheeling communities of its silence that may be filled with infinite noises and even high singing.

Reading Jung for the first time on April 14th, she was "amazed and delighted." Certainly Jung's theories on the shadow representing the dark side, aspects of the psyche that exist unacknowledged, would have appealed to her. In her speech, "Woman and the Creative Will," she writes: "We must turn an even bolder front to the shadows," and in her poem "Sun-up" she had written: "nothing...nothing...nothing.../but a shadow/with its eyes full of black light."

She had also been reading Santayana and a book about behaviorists. "Romanticism is spirituality in a state of immaturity," she asserts in her diary. There was nothing romantic about the world situation that she was hearing about over the radio.. The U.S. was just then leading straight into war, the Nazis having conquered France, Norway, and Denmark, the Dutch were under siege, a U.S. admiral declaring that war with Japan was inevitable, and 22,000 Polish soldiers had been secretly slaughtered by Stalin—all this in April, 1940. Ten days later, in a letter to Louise Adams Floyd, she set out her objections to the current Communist practice: "I am *appalled* by the rigidity of contours already taking place in Marxian Communism—a mass religion—as though some essential essence had fled and a *rigor mortis* were setting in..."

She continued by discussing what seemed to refer to the debate over the passing of the Smith Act just then in the process of being revived by the Senate Judiciary Committee. Very similar to the 1918 Alien Act that deported Emma Goldman, the Smith Act was being used against Australian-born union leader Harry Bridges who vocally opposed the coming war. The most famous trade unionist at the time, Bridges had appeared on the cover of Time magazine in 1937, and ran for president against FDR. Ridge writes:

> The constitution must not be expanded to meet the altered conditions and changing lines of force—as it was in the beginning so let it be unto the end, Amen!...they could not have possibly foreseen the rise of Industrial Capitalism nor the Dragon's form it was destined to become so that now all they think they can do is keep it from further swelling.

The Smith Act became law that June, and Bridges was arrested but not ultimately deported although the government made four attempts. He became head of the ILWU and made it a pillar of U.S. trade unionism.

Ridge couldn't persuade Lawson of the seriousness of the political situation. She commented: "There is in him a refusal to face things. A stubbornness—he will not see that which he does not wish to see. He does not so much evade reality as ignore it." Her assessment of this tendency tallies with the executor's discovery in the 1970s that Lawson refused to admit that Ridge was ever ill, poor, or radical despite Ridge's mention of all three in nearly every letter of the hundreds she wrote.

Ridge was not deluded about the state of her own health. She tried to be brave, at least to herself. "As a matter of truth, I'm making a paltry showing— we must get together on this—me, the crowd of me." It wasn't easy. "I must... if necessary continue on one meal a day[,] endure the headaches and ward off the migraine, that everlasting curse, and the colitis..." This is the only time in her life she gives her possible ailment a name.

Fragments of poetry begin to crop up in the diary, as on May 5:

> Again shall reappear
> The bloodied perennial;

By each appointed wall.
In each more inclement year,
The white stalk bearing
Again the flower.

Revelatory prose follows the poetry, with violent, almost Jungian imagery:

> After washing up, I was tired and lay down...As I lay waking, twilight
> soft at the windows, light streaming in through the open door from
> Davy's study, this: I became aware of a terrible explosion from some
> deep deep place, a burning glow through which some shattered
> substance shot up and out as though [the] earth vomited. Separate
> flames tongued but *downward* in a vast angle; converged, the point of
> the angle in the center of the crater's cup disappeared in this cup. A
> column of smoke pillared skyward...

On May 11th, she recorded that she suffered a sharp pain on her left
side, yet she "managed to get meals ready...Stress of news from Europe
made me worse. I cannot help my violent reaction." Two days later Lawson
and Ridge had "no money even to buy papers until after 15th—and that will
go in debts." Such deprivation dug deep into her relationship with Lawson,
for a week later she notes:

> I said something cruel. It was true, but how cruel the truth can be.
> I am cruel. Davy says I would destroy anyone near enough to be
> hurt by me. He said further my attitude toward the race was large
> and 'all right' but that I am destructive in my relationships with
> individuals—that I haven't destroyed him but I would destroy most
> people...I'm glad Davy spoke—any speech to me more satisfactory
> because more clarifying, than a sullen and glowering silence.

A second set of entries, these between May 28 and June 9, were torn out.
"A record of problems, illness, angers," she called them in her next entry.
Then she mentioned that Lenore Marshall had visited.

> I felt better for her coming. For all her nervousness she has stability
> and pride...a year ago when an ex-ray showed [a] cyst in [my] jaw...
> she said she would pay the bill...I've tried to hang on—but pain in

my ear scares me and I can hardly eat...Until Davy comes back on Thursday or Friday [he had gone to to his stepfather's funeral in Massachusetts] I have only a nickel."

Leonard Abbott passed on the news of Emma Goldman's death, and she responds: "the bravest woman I have ever known...Nothing daunted her. Leonard Abbott told me that to the last she was fighting and working for loyalist Spain." Scott had asked Ridge for money to assist Goldman in her last illness, and she regretted not being able to help her.

She continued reading. Spengler's *The Decline of the West* was her most recent book, one that suggested that the Western world was witnessing its "winter time," or last season of its culture. It also hypothesized that democracy, driven by money, was easily corruptible and that fascism always followed, and that the first of man's "high cultures" was the Babylonian.

She was also reading Sandburg's biography of Lincoln, most likely *The War Years*, the volume that had been published the year before. A bestseller, it became the source of most of what Americans knew about Lincoln for decades. "A stupendous achievement...I met him [Sandburg] once—twenty-two years ago," she writes, no doubt making his acquaintance during the *Others* Chicago tour in 1919. Now America would be about to face a darker crisis than any Lincoln knew in his war years

> but with vastly more terrible implications. The menace is of the same quality involving as it does the forcible subjection and enslavement of parts of the race by some part or parts that have outgrown themselves like a giant cell in the body of the race that becomes malignant in the larger and fairer life about them.
>
> But it is more terrible because it implies a spiritual, even more than a physical enslavement—blackout of the mind's light.

She had mixed feelings in her diary about the American Fourth of July celebration, although she was happy to celebrate the French Revolution. She analyzed the current American warmongering through a distinctly feminist filter: "The ancient primal *Male Dance*—from which woman is shut out same as a chattel, a breeder of warriors for the industrial handmaiden of warriors...Beware...there may be a Woman Dance..."

On July 10 she decided that she couldn't accompany Lawson to the funeral of her dear friend Laura Benét's mother.

I tried to dress to go with him to the service at the Little Church around the Corner in Manhattan but so sick I could not even finish dressing. We were so broke I could not even buy flowers to lay upon her gentle hands that will never clasp mine with warmth again...

She began to suffer once more from ulcerated teeth. She was afraid of incurring debt with a dentist but Lawson insisted on borrowing money, if not for her teeth, at least for his university classes. "He feels he needs to finish—and this will be too late for me... I am even without underwear." But Lawson must have felt guilty—or angry that she wouldn't take his money. "Davy sullen all day, will not speak unless spoken to—and not then unless an answer is absolutely necessary. How depressing to sit at dinner with a person who will not speak. There seems to be no light in him."

She had been consoling herself by reading Peter Kropotkin's *Memoirs*, "a simple and sweet book wholesome as daily bread[,] a goodwill toward men." Kropotkin was the mensch of anarchy, to such an extent that even the *Atlantic Monthly* approved of him and commissioned his memoirs in 1898-99, publishing them in serial form as "An Autobiography of a Revolutionist." Emma Goldman delivered one of the eulogies at his funeral, which was also the last public demonstration of the Russian anarchists.

Ridge concurred in the diary with Goldman's 1920s condemnation of the Russian Communists, at least on aesthetic grounds:

> I think of those awful paintings at the Soviet building in the World's
> Fair [New York's]—the mindless grimace of assumed joy on the faces
> of the people depicted...this tawdry decoration of a smile stamped
> upon the faces of a people—the Smile, not only officially approved
> but officially imposed."

But she had a scarcely better opinion of capitalism in the U.S. Writing about "the glamor boy" Wendell Wilkie, who was then Republican candidate for president against Roosevelt, she deemed Wilkie

> an intelligent businessman, a shrewd advocate of capitalism...
> he implies a society of *good* capitalists—no more believable than a
> plague of good locusts—who out of their self-imposed self control

should devour only selected crops—leaving a residue for the grateful croppers.

In August she was ruminating over Sir Leonard Woolley's excavations at Ur and his suggestion that it was the home of Abraham in early Jewish history.

> Abraham the first concept of the male, the mateless god, who was to topple from their pedestals so many goddesses...long before it was evolved in the working spirit of Abraham...it must have been a persistent though unidentified hunger in the males of the Jewish race.

She fell on a recently washed floor and was now confined to bed. "To go forward, without fear toward the new," Ridge insists in the diary. She writes that Lawson had to "cook all meals Saturday and Sunday. This he did sweetly, nervously and most incompetently. It took him fifty minutes to wash the spinach." She had considerably less fortitude by the end of the month.

> I cried yesterday afternoon for a long time, very rare for me, once in a great while, in years. When I do my heart rocks itself for a long while...bound by the load it is dragging. The load is a part of itself that has fallen out and down but is held by its leg...so the heart cannot shake itself free.

But she didn't capitulate to the solace of religion. "I wish," she writes, "that, like Lincoln,

> I could pray to a personal God, but I cannot. Because I cannot [,] L's [Lincoln's] contaminous appeals to the Almighty irritate, sometimes disgust me. His god was the god of battles, the mateless one, ruthless in shining to whom both sides in all battles (each of course believing in its absolute rightness) make a like appeal...

Her old friend Hanna Astrup Larsen visited her. A Norwegian raised in Iowa who became an anthropologist, she wrote a book on the Zulu, focusing on the Zulu's domestic, rather than warlike attributes. Larsen also wrote the biography of Selma Lagerlof, the first woman to win the Nobel Prize in literature. Ridge had championed Lagerlof in "Woman and the Creative Will," and reviewed *The Holy City,* her novel about Jerusalem. Certainly they must have discussed the recent Nazi invasion of Norway.

At the end of September, Ridge and Lawson moved for the last time, from Columbia Heights to III Montague Street, into a building with an elevator. Five stories, it is still garlanded on the interior with bas-reliefs of bowers and quite respectable, with a beautiful twist of interior stairs. Just a few blocks away, W.H. Auden, composer Benjamin Britten, Carson McCullers, and Gypsy Rose Lee, and eventually, Paul and Jane Bowles lived together as a group around the same time, attempting to re-create the excitement of the early years of the literary 1920s. What would Ridge have thought of that? Thomas Wolfe lived a few doors down five years earlier.

Reading Edna St. Vincent Millay's new *Make Bright the Arrows,* Ridge notes in her diary, "She is too complacent. If she realized her limitations she might transcend them." Millay's poems, instead of continuing her antiwar stance, propagandized now against isolationism and encouraged U.S. entry into war. "Acres of bad poetry" was how Millay herself described them later.

At the end of October, Ridge had 13 teeth removed and still lisped for the want of front teeth by the end of November. "Can't very well go out. Look droll." She felt she was being shunted aside anyway:

> I note that for some time now the friend tries always to arrange a tea date for Saturday or Sunday, when Davy may be expected to be present [,] also that at these times the friend converses almost wholly with Davy—even rushing to get in words when I begin to speak...

And even when she did speak:

> When I talk with the very few people I am now able to see it is as though we were trying to communicate over some bridgeless space, the winds whirling between, blowing away our words so that we do not hear each other or only imperfectly understand what we do hear...

How difficult for Ridge, the hostess whose parties were once so important to the literary scene! She had leveraged every avenue of power a poet could: her own poetry, of course, but also as reviewer, hostess, and editor—and now she felt shunned. She retreated into her own fierce world.

My thought is now a strong current rushing against seemingly insurmountable obstacles, sometimes making a clear path through these, more often held up, but fighting to penetrate, to blaze its way—never evading or going around, or leaving that obstruction for the one who comes after to tunnel through.

Ridge writes to Marshall that "The fire of the world is running through me."

Lawson attended a party for Richard Wright, a noted Communist writer at the time, and Ridge's colleague as a fellow *New Masses* contributing editor. Wright had just published *Native Son*, the first bestselling novel by a black American, which would also open soon as a play on Broadway, directed by Orson Welles. Dental troubles prevented Ridge from attending.

On her birthday December 12, she wrote:

Vibrations from Europe and Asia streaming through the air...The peoples moving against each other, shattered and shattering. The armies, the men who are doing the killing and maiming and getting killed and maimed seem to be moving in some kind of a frightful trance, the fleeing people, crawling into caves and holes in the earth as they did long ago in the early mornings. The radios on all sides bruiting the bare facts or segments of the facts.

A few days later, she had her teeth fixed again and refocused her radical politics on her own body:

Our bodies must be swarming with this life, beautiful, benign and destructive life.

How many worlds within us, civilizations, groups, entities, cooperative worlds repairing their little houses in our dust. Little workers, you too loving, hoping, hating, cherishing. I'm sorry not to have considered you enough, not to have considered you at all.

Ridge's body, neglected and starved for so long, contracted rheumatoid arthritis from her periodontal problems. She tried to raise her spirits with the fire of her ambition: "Through this drying reed of me...Well, I believe I can write this book, the first novel dealing with my childhood concurrently with my poems." So much ambition! Two books at once! She was not totally deluded about her ability to write prose since she had published very competent long form prose thirty years before. But she became frustrated with poetry. "When I am angry and disturbed as I so often am, I cannot write poetry." A few days earlier, she completed a lengthy entry in her diary about a Christmas Day in Australia in which her mother ignored her and gave away all their money. How did she deal with that frustration? She took after her mother. She often distributed what little money she accumulated to friends or beggars on the streets of Mexico or Baghdad. Surely this habit annoyed Ridge's husband and her benefactors.

She dealt with her frustration with writing by writing:

> O splendid obituary the will rampant unleashed to
> devour, there, emblazoned
> in the bare
> grandeur of whatever fire...

No snowflakes in this excerpt, the image that Matthew Josephson attributed to her aesthetic. Throughout March she put down poem after poem in her diary, often returning to the Whitmanesque vision of the working man that she celebrated decades earlier, but with great detachment, viewing the worker as another of her beloved insects. The following excerpt of "Red Ants" suggests that she had been once employed in a bag factory in New Orleans.

> The factories had emptied.
>   Workers
> Adrift from toil and the moist heat, trickled in alleys and back streets,
>   shedding their dank smells. (In the small, high windows of
>   the bag factory, these too glorified,
> Fluming sunlight in the long room, the tough
> Rough-fibered bags, hard to pull inside out,
> Mended, folded and laid away
>
> ....
>   The workers
> Left a quiet in their wake, an all but hush
> As New Orleans had spent her breath and
> Lay sweet as the newly dead, a city
> In the sight embalmed.

> The hard too
> Bestilled in shadow, Pharaoh's ants,
> Like the workers, had gone back into the mounds, no more than a
>   thumbnail high, the scanty
> Soil at the roots of the sunflowers sent up a faint scent—earth
> Smelling on her sweet pits, her native
> Odor mingling with the man smells.

She hadn't given up on sonnets but seemed to have discovered that free verse was truly her métier. She recorded another poem in free verse:

> Heart
>
> Knowing, as if it were in them, the still core
> Of hurricanes, holding without bruise such things
> As the dragonfly, the over-hovering wings,
> The dove, the hawk in the old return
> Of flight, pursuit, pursuit and flight again...
>   Oh, heart.

By March 28, she had named the new book of poetry, *Hymn for Liberty*. "If I were only well enough to work all the time." She exchanged poems with Dr. Rena Sabin, the first woman to hold a full professorship at Johns Hopkins, the first woman elected to the National Academy of Science, and the first woman to head a department at Rockefeller Institute. Now a retired T.B. researcher, perhaps Sabin would have donated her services to treating Ridge, had there been time, in a barter relationship like the one Ridge had with Dr. Hyman. But it was her old friend, Louise Adams Floyd, that Ridge thanked for giving her money to pay the bill for her teeth.

Ridge awoke on April 8th with a cry. She had a premonition that Greece had been taken by the Nazis—and it had. Fear about her own end might have been mingled with those for Greece. Three days later she writes: "Davy will have to get his own breakfast which he so hates....With all my sickness he's not had to get his own breakfast—or any other meal once in nineteen months." But she was on fire with the terrors of beauty and death and wrote her last sonnet—to beauty. She begins in prayer: "Show me thy way. Though I have held thy name,/That tremulously now my lips let fall" and then invokes the deity directly: "Beauty, beyond all./Be with me in this hour...In thy high company—/Whereof all things are free."

The last entry in her diary, dated Easter morning, April 14th, reads:

> Have not been able to get the doctor as he's not yet paid for last time. Anyway he could do nothing—the last time he said I should stay in bed—but I went on working until a few days ago. Davy gave breakfast in bed again this morning."

Her husband had at last brought her toast and tea in bed, her favorite luxury—such a poignant recognition of her state, *The End* writ in uxorial service.

Ridge died on May 19, 1941, five months after Joyce, two after Woolf.

Chapter 39

Legacy: Fire and Smoke

[Ridge] had proven that women bore in them a capacity to shatter the patriarchal mold and penetrate to the heart of sacred power, claiming it as their own. For this, she stands at the center of women's development in the twentieth century.

—William Drake

For all her faults, Ridge behaved as if poetry were worth her life, a dedication that few achieve. "Poor Lola, she deserved far greater recognition than she received, but we still starve poets, don't we?" writes Ridge's Ferrer School friend, Harry Kelly.

Ridge's death certificate reports that she died of a heart attack, myocardial failure. The rheumatoid arthritis she contracted can cause inflammation of scarred lungs and death by heart failure. The certificate also mentions, secondarily, her supposed tuberculosis. It also has her age at 57—she's 68. Twenty-two years of marriage, and Lawson still didn't know her true age. Neither did he know her mother's maiden name, nor her father's given name. He wrote "Ridge" for the mother, her first husband's surname, not MacFarlane, her second, and Robert Ridge as her father—it was Joseph Henry Ridge. Although she had never mentioned Lawson in her work as "husband," she was buried as Lola Ridge Lawson. He was a good foil for Ridge's flights, literal and metaphoric. He mailed her the black kimono, he found the books she needed. Were the genders reversed, his place in her life would have been devoted wife, just what any working writer requires. Ridge dedicated the sonnet "Still Water" to D.L. with its opening "I know you flower darkly," but her poem "Two" is more tender:

Two

He would have breasted space,

Moved wing to wing,
Struck stars,
Met hurricanes...instead
He was the hangar
Where ungratefully
She rested after flight. (*Red Flag* 100)

None of her patrons attended the funeral, as chronicled by Marianne Moore:

> Yesterday afternoon, since I had been specially notified—I went to Lola Ridge's funeral—here in Brooklyn. A clergyman who seemed somewhat like a layman, conducted the service and nothing more real or exalted at a funeral—have I known at all. Many passages of scripture that we don't associate with sadness were read, there was a prayer, and William Benét read three poems by Lola Ridge. The room was full of laurel and summer flowers and all present were somewhat acquainted—or if not, spoke together afterward without introduction—Ridgely Torrence, Aaron Copland, Paul Strand, Mrs. Canby, Martin Lewis, Stephen, Laura [who nursed Ridge at the end] and Rosemary Benét [Stephen Vincent Benét's wife].

Emma Goldman's niece, Stella Ballantine attended, as did Hanna Astrup Larsen, who had visited Ridge so recently, and Nancy Cox-McCormack Cushman, who lived a few doors down from Ridge in Brooklyn. McCormack, sculptor of the heads of Frank Lloyd Wright, the Benéts, Gandhi, and Harriet Monroe, had cast Ridge's life mask. Torrence was the poetry editor for the *New Republic* between 1920-33, when Ridge published nine poems and seven reviews in the magazine, and good friends with William Vaughn Moody, whose widow had hosted Ridge in Massachusetts. The restaurateur gypsy Romany Marie was also at the funeral. Queen of the tearoom craze that began in the 1910s, Romany Marie had known Ridge since the Ferrer Center days. Her sister married Lola's friend, Leonard Abbott. Millay wrote about her candle burning at both ends at Romany Marie's, probably at the poets' table, and it was there that Evelyn Scott took up the collection for Ridge that she summarily refused—and then, bit by bit, borrowed back.

Keith Bernand, Ridge's son, is not mentioned in the obituary. After Ridge left him in Detroit, he studied electrical engineering. He was working as a radio operator and engineer for the *Detroit News* by the time he was 22, sending messages into the void as he perhaps had been doing all along in the orphanage. It was as a radio operator on merchant ships that he arrived in Santiago, Chile, where he married a German immigrant, Margarete Wehner, in 1927 and had three children: Gloria, Herbert, and Gladys. He kept a subscription to the *Saturday Review of Literature* and must have received notice of his mother's death via William Rose Benét's appreciation and farewell in that magazine. "He was affected by a big depression," wrote his daughter. He was probably unaware that Ridge had written several poems that might have been addressed to him: "The Mother to Son," "The Compress" ("Very well, son...you are free") and "Son to Mother." They remain unpublished (and unseen), the manuscripts held by the executor.

Given that poets are artists who capitalize on their sensitivity, and that the children of poets might be more sensitive than others, these children might be prone to problems resulting from that sensitivity at birth, even if their parent's history isn't fraught with poverty or abuse. Out of Robert Frost's six children, three died very young, one was institutionalized, and one committed suicide. "I took the wrong way with him. I tried many ways and every single one of them was wrong," wrote Frost. Elinor Wylie's abandoned son reappeared only at her funeral, and committed suicide eight years later. She never acknowledged him. Three of Kay Boyle's daughters attempted suicide. Anthologist Louis Untermeyer's son hung himself at age 19, after his father left his mother to put himself "in a class with the greater artists of his time." As for an evaluation of Evelyn Scott's mothering, her son felt that her monstrous ego had a cruel innocence "such as a shark or a crocodile may be said to have." In the next generation, Sylvia Plath's son, a fisheries biologist, hanged himself in 2010. "Welcome to hell," wrote James Wright upon learning that Franz, his abandoned son but eventually a Pulitzer Prize-winner like his father, had published his first poem.

Keith committed suicide on December 9th, 1942. Keith's father, blind when he died, outlived his son by four years, although his obituary mentions one living son. According to Keith's daughter Gladys, Keith didn't even know his father's name, nor that he had been born in New Zealand. That Ridge never publicly acknowledged her son, and no biographical piece in her lifetime and for a long time afterwards mentioned that she had a child is odd. As a free thinker and advocate of open marriage, she wouldn't have been castigated for having had a child.

Five months after Ridge died, the poet/politician Samuel A. DeWitt endowed a Lola Ridge Memorial Prize for the Poetry Society of America with money he made in a tool company, "House of a Thousand Bargains." *Idylls of the Ghetto and Other Poems*, the first of his eight books of poetry, was published in 1927. It details in the tenements Ridge had extolled. He was most famous for being expelled from the New York State Assembly in 1920, along with four other assemblymen, for being a member of the Socialist Party. DeWitt's friend, Upton Sinclair, based a character on him in *The Jungle*. Aaron Kramer, a fellow poet/socialist, remembered him putting the Poetry Society in its place:

> One month I found the whole group beyond endurance for its aridity and egocentrism, but was not yet entrenched enough to dare say so. But Samuel DeWitt of Yonkers, a down-to-earther respected by the bluebloods surrounding him only for the wealth with which he endowed the Lola Ridge and other awards, got up to his full six-and-a-half feet, waved the pages of sterile verses we had just heard, and declared: "There are three kinds of poetry: epic, lyric, and pupik. These are perfect examples of pupik poetry!" The silence that greeted him was one of tolerance—they knew the word was Yiddish but could not guess that it meant "belly-button." I, however, broke the silence with a bellow of laughter as rough as his comment, and rushed from my seat to shake his hand.

The Lola Ridge Memorial Prize of $100-$150 was awarded for ten years, between 1942-1952. "The general theme should be to find some meaning in our own time and an attempt to interpret the forces of our day...the type of poetry which should be energized with ideas and visions," reads its call-for-entries. Louis Zukofsky and Louis Simpson were among its ten winners. Jeremy Ingalls won twice, an erudite poet who also won two Guggenheims, a Rockefeller Foundation grant, the Yale Younger Poets Prize, a prize from the Ford Foundation and the Shelley Memorial Award—and whose work, like Ridge's, is now unread. When McCarthyism asserted itself in the 50s, it made even the mention of Ridge's third book, *Red Flag*, a red flag.

Thirty-six years after her death, in an interview with the executor, David Lawson said her son was killed in a car accident. Perhaps that's what Ridge told him. A smokescreen around Ridge's life began to rise almost immediately after she died. In William Rose Benét's final piece in the *Saturday Review of Literature*, he described her as "harassed by bodily infirmity which she scorned to have mentioned because she despised the thought that it might win suffrage for her work on extraneous grounds." As one of the editors of *Firehead*, Benét would have remembered its flap copy, which began: "For years Miss Ridge has devoted herself wholly to her art, handicapped by persistent ill-health," and which went on to mention her health a second time: "impeded as she has been by dangerous illness..." A number of her reviews mentioned her health as if her sick, saintly persona sold the poems, for example: "Fighting Pain and Death, Lola Ridge Writes Mighty Poem of Crucifixion." Even Alfred Kreymborg, who knew her longest, could not resist dramatizing her fragility: "She lived on intimate terms with death... when her friends who saw her when she first arrived at the age of twenty-seven, it seemed as if she could not survive beyond that year."

Sainthood was also put forward. Horace Gregory and Marya Zaturenska canonize her a year after her death in their anthology. "[Ridge's] devotion was one that can be described only in terms of a saintliness..." Even Evelyn Scott wrote: "Going up your stairs is like mounting Jacob's ladder with the angels." Ridge makes her "feel as people would feel in a church if religion weren't fear worship and god really divine intelligent love." Alfred Kreymborg was perhaps closest to the truth of her supposed sainthood: "The Ghetto was felt by a saint who wasn't afraid to mix with the earth."

Ridge had husbands—for most of her life, two at once. She couldn't endure her child, she lived through the trials of a crazy stepfather, and was too close to a distant embattled mother. She wrote of the world, unlike her friend Marianne Moore with her quaint "habit" of the three-cornered hat and cape, whose poetry was often devoid of human connection. She was not a political saint like Simone Weil, starving for her beliefs—Ridge starved to have money for time to write, or as an affectation, or to avoid upsetting a delicate constitution. Nor did Ridge reflect the portrait Emma Goldman and others painted of the radical Voltairine de Cleyre as an ineffectual saint cut down in her prime. Although Ridge's look-alike was also taught by nuns, her disinterest in mothering mirrored Ridge's, and she lived a life full of contradiction. Ridge's presumed sainthood was a front for a woman whose writing against injustice in the home and the world was useful for her great ambitions. Did she give away her things to the poor, feed the hungry, shelter the homeless? Her political fervor seldom extended to personal activism but she chronicled lynching and murderous parenting with sophistication and subtlety that is still appreciated today.

Some thought Ridge was a Jew. Two years after she died, imagist-turned-fugitive poet John Gould Fletcher wrote of persuading

> Scott Greer to take an interest in Lola Ridge, the only really good "proletariat" poet I have seen. Her work, especially *Firehead* (written after Sacco and Vanzetti were done to death) is very extraordinary; and I have spent years wondering why she is so neglected. *As she, like Miss Rukeyser, was a Jewess,* [his ital.] there is a similar intensity to her work—and her themes, of suffering and martyrdom and rebellion, are more humanly handled than Miss Rukeyser's generally are.

Rukeyser was indeed Jewish, but not Ridge. Ridge chose the immigrants she immortalized, and her triumph was in establishing a common ground between Jews and Americans, without compromising Jewish identity. Rukeyser, however, captured the aesthetic-political moment in the month of Ridge's death with her poem "June 1941." June was the month that Germany, Italy, Romania, and Finland declared war on Russia, Germany invaded Russia, the Jews were rounded up in Amsterdam, 11,000 Estonians deported to Siberia, 2,000 Jews massacred in Lithuania, 61 U-boats were sunk, Germany took the Ukraine, and the British occupied Baghdad. Rukeyser begins the poem, "Who in one lifetime sees all causes lost,/Herself dismayed and helpless, cities down." A modernist Petrarchan sonnet, but with jumbled syntax and a final rhymeless couplet, expressed in both form and content the despair many Americans felt about winning a war that they hadn't yet entered. Rukeyser's many Whitman-inflected poems feature politicized labor as well as war, women in the city, and other subjects Ridge pioneered. Rukeyser's motto: "Not Sappho, Sacco" concerning aesthetics and Sacco and Vanzetti's execution, mirrored Ridge's prioritizing of the human predicament. Ridge's friend, Stephen Vincent Benét, editor of the Yale Series of Younger Poets, wrote the foreword for Rukeyser's first book, *Theory of Flight*. His brother, William Rose Benét, wrote in the *Saturday Review of Literature*: "[Rukeyser] is a radical politically, but she writes as a poet not a propagandist." Five poems from Rukeyser's first book appear in the same issue of *Poetry* a page before a review of Ridge's *Dance of Fire*, but there is no evidence of a personal meeting between them.

Although Ridge mentored many poets, including Hart Crane and Jean Toomer, they did not champion her. In the mid-20s, Kenneth Rexroth recited Ridge's poetry while hanging out at the Dill Pickle Club, Chicago's avant-garde cabaret, and later bemoaned the erasure of her work and other proletarian modernists in an argument with Robert Lowell. "You have left out the whole populist period," said Rexroth during their discussion of the history of American poetry that ignored Sandburg, Oppenheim, Lindsay, Moody, and Ridge. "With an expression of utmost contempt on his face "Cal" Lowell said, "well, of course, in the West, Rexroth, you haven't learned that these poor people aren't poets at all."

Robert Hayden, the prominent black Chicago poet, traced his early influences through the early Langston Hughes, the Dynamo poets and Lola Ridge—"though not the Lola Ridge of *Firehead*." As critic Alan Wald writes of Hayden's choices:

> Of course, one may hold the categorical view that the kinds of language and strategies promoted by a Funaroff [founder of the Dynamo school and magazine] are themselves less worthy than those of a Yeats or Eliot; but here one runs the risk of legislating the "proper" duties for a poet to carry out, a dubious theme in Western culture from Plato to Stalin.

By 1941, traditional forms were ascendant, and flowers and the seasons better subjects than anything remotely political. This movement away from the hard-won freedoms of the 1920s reached its nadir in the 1950s with the castigation of all modernist experiment as well as any poetics embracing radical politics. It would take Allen Ginsberg to blast away at this critical shield, the son of a Communist but an aficionado of John Clare, Adrienne Rich throwing off the glittering meter and rhyme of her first collection to write *Diving into the Wreck*, a masterpiece of political free verse, Phil Levine publishing his many poems about workers in Detroit during the 70s and 80s, and Galway Kinnell writing his most famous poem, "The Avenue Bearing the Initial of Christ into the New World," extolling nearly the same neighborhood and issues as Ridge.

But Ridge did not only write about the proletariat. She wrote most strikingly about her childhood in the Pacific. In aesthetics she embraced both formal and free verse. Her wide taste distinguished the contents of *Others* and *Broom*, but in her own poetry it made it difficult for critics to label her, especially the New Critics, with their emphasis on the poem as self-contained and self-referential. It didn't help that she used arcane language and obtuse rhetoric like Crane in her last two books. In 1947 Kenneth

Rexroth condemned her for "over-reaching ambition," but mentioned this in the company of Whitman, Sandburg, and Ford Madox Ford. It was her guilt and drug-taking and the boasting about how many hundreds of lines she wrote in how short a time that drowned her in incoherence. Even Pound felt that need for coherence. A *Selected* will do; overpraise will not.

Ridge's opera has never been produced. The score remains with Ridge's papers at Smith, and Glick's obituary in 1994 rated the depressing headline of "Henrietta Glick, Secretary, Composer." Painter-composer Charles Howard Marsh left behind a signed autograph score of music dated 1934 based on Ridge's poem "Dawn," Mildred Gardner, a fellow guest at Yaddo in 1930, set her work to music, Ned Rorem, "the world's best composer of art songs," set her poem "Electrocution" to music and recorded it twice, Edie Hill set "Thaw" for women's voices in 2011, and the Parallel Octave Chorus convened September 9, 2012 to record "Sun-Up," "Wall Street At Night," and "Celia" with musical accompaniment. Interest has been picking up. In 2014, Frederick Frahm, commissioned by the London Festival of Contemporary Church Music, composed and performed a *Firehead*-inspired organ piece, Melissa Dunphy wrote two pieces from excerpts of "Sun-up", and in Ireland, Sean Doherty won the Feis Ceoil choral composition and the Mornington Singers Composition Competition awards for his settings of Ridge's "Dreams" and "Undersong." Ron Wray's compositions "Dreams" and "I Have Been Dreaming" were launched on *YouTube* in 2015.

"She was all fire and spirit. The throat chokes, O she was/insatiable candor in a vase too frail," writes her friend William Rose Benét in the poem "Of Lola Ridge" that appeared in the 1947 book he wrote after he won the Pulitzer. "Wild honey fed her, and the unwithering gourd/of the baptist crying in the wilderness/in the desert." She had fire that he prophesized would last. "It is certain that her poem 'Firehead,' concerning the Crucifixion, will stand as one of the most remarkable long poems written by man or woman in our time," according to a *Saturday Review of Literature* editorial, most probably written by Benét.

"But for now, given the restless—and ephemeral—jostling for position among the living inhabitants of American poetry," writes Don Share, the current editor of the now over 100-year-old *Poetry* magazine, "it's no surprise that worthwhile poets have been temporarily discredited, disappeared, set aside for re-education, or forgotten." Ridge's executor allowed her books to go out of print, so few readers know of her existence and fewer poems anthologized. The executor also did not allow full access to her papers, making it difficult for her influence to be assessed. "People felt the necessity of either defending or abusing [Ridge] whenever her name came up," wrote Kay Boyle. The abuse seems to have won. Those few who have heard of Ridge now, think of her as a writer of bad propaganda poems.

Communism, with its belief in the forced sharing wealth, is the opposite of anarchy, but the two are alike in their theories having been besmirched by the violence and terror done in their names over the last century. (The violence and terror done in the name of democracy is another subject.) Anarchists are always present in a free society because they epitomize true freedom. Ridge learned her own *every man for himself* at the miner's knee in New Zealand. In Australia the drunken Henry Lawson proved that anyone was free to rise up in the poetic ranks. In America her practice in personal freedom led her to abandon her son, to bigamy, to an open marriage, to poverty relieved only by patrons, and to politics that led her to celebrate the Russian Revolution and then to rebuke it. She traveled to remote parts of the world without itinerary, alone, to be free to experience the world around her. She saw that anarchy presented an "opportunity for more complete self-expression for all." But she understood its limits. "Anarchy is the philosophy I feel closest to and shall always be, but I no longer believe in the possibility of its application to modern society."

Freedom was always her goal. "I have then the first requisite for a great book—the freedom of my own spirit, my own citadel and command of its gates," Ridge writes in her diary a few months before she died. Freedom for Ridge as a woman meant changing the terms. No motherhood, no housework, no fidelity, if it came to that. But even that struggle she saw within a larger framework. As she put it in "Woman and the Creative Will": "This is not—in its purely political and least significant aspect—a woman's right as much as a human rights movement, that stands squarely linked with the rise and fall of the proletariat of the world." She would see the world through a woman's vision but illuminate all of it; she would have men's strength too, not just a woman's. When the flame such a vision engendered grew too bright, men, who felt its heat most, had to quench it. The quintessential picture of her arrest with Edna St. Vincent Millay, hustled off by a policeman—it may as well have been John Crowe Ransom muscling them away, condemning Edna as nonintellectual and a "little girl," and Lola Ridge a saint and a Communist.

Nearly 100 years after Ridge's avowal of anarchy, philosopher Simon Critchley redefined it for the Occupy generation:

One might say that contemporary anarchism is about responsibility, whether sexual, ecological or socio-economic; it flows from an experience of conscience about the manifold ways in which the West ravages the rest; it is an ethical outrage at the yawning inequality, impoverishment and disenfranchisement that is so palpable locally and globally.

The Occupy generation that cites a continuous lineage from Whitman should be asking why today's students read Fascist Pound or Eliot and think there's no political bias in literature—and condemn the writing of proletariat modernism for being leftist. Why too are the futurists' background in fascism always mentioned in literary histories but not an individual poet's penchant for anarchism, the total freedom that Americans have historically espoused in art of all kinds? Women who focused on what shapes human consciousness rather than the individual psyche have been particularly neglected, as if that stance is a male prerogative. When Ridge wrote, modernism was open to politics as an unexplored subject, especially a woman and, for that matter, anyone else in subjugation. The question was how to freely represent their suffering and struggle. The activist-writers of the Occupy generation now have the opportunity to reoccupy that question.

Lawson would send Marianne Moore an invitation to a celebration of Ridge's birthday every year until 1971. She attended three times, in 1944, 1951, and 1960. He married a second time but divorced while having an intense relationship with chessmaster Mary Bain, then he married again. By the 1950s he was known as an established chess authority, and made friends with the master chess player Norman Tweed Whitaker, who was part of the confidence scheme around the kidnapping of Lindbergh's baby. Lawson took Bobby Fischer out to dinner after his "Match of the Century," and purchased the original score sheet for $50, now worth $100,000. He was Scotch. Frank Brady, as the 21-year-old editor of the newly launched *Chess Life*, remembers that Lawson always made him pay for dinner and refused to hand over the illustrations for the magazine's first cover story until Brady paid him twice what they had agreed. Lawson's third wife helped him with his Morphy book, which was finally published when he was 89 years old and sold very few copies before he died four years later. Now it has been reissued and is recognized as a classic. Lawson left a vast library, according to Brady, and only a portion of it was delivered to Bryn Mawr as Ridge's.

Ridge's collection is suitable for any 60s hippie. Along with the eight volumes on sex and the phallus, the library includes a collection of black plays, books by Kahlil Gibran, *Lady Chatterly's Lover*, Engels, Lenin, Bakunin, and Marx, a book on yoga breathing, "Phantasmagoria" by Lewis Carroll, poetry translations from the Spanish, German, Russian, and Norwegian, a collection of Navajo and Blackfeet songs, a number of books with antiwar titles, three books on drugs, four books on black magic, three books on "other dimensions," and *Ulysses*—but nothing by Shakespeare or Marianne Moore. Lawson's decisions about which titles to include was another way of controlling Ridge's legacy.

Photographs of Ridge taken after she arrived in New York show how deliberate she was in creating her image, just as she determined that she would always be 10 years younger than her actual age, and an ex-pat from Australia rather than New Zealand or Ireland. In nearly all her photos her eyes are cast down or show only one side of her face. She always parted her hair down the middle and wore a chignon at the nape of her neck. No bob for her. Many bohemian Village women wore the same hairstyle. Saintly would be the adjective for her expression, abetted by her extreme thinness. In the photo taken at the Floyd estate, Ridge stands out from the other visitors because she's turned to one side for the camera, while everyone else smiles into it. Even a snapshot of Ridge in her apartment on West 14th Street shows her posed, her head turned again toward the window, her hair drawn against her cheek. There's only one photo of her smiling in the archive at Smith, and it was taken during her student years in Australia, before she assumed her American mask. All the dental problems mentioned in her letters may have contributed to her decision never to smile. Or maybe she wanted a pose that always implied seriousness, the way Emma Goldman portraits always show a scowl.

Ridge was always serious. Evelyn Scott's blurb for *Firehead* reveals how well her best friend understood her: "[Ridge] came to America seeking freedom—not the licentiousness that may go by that name—but the freedom of an artist, whose passion for form, for symmetry, was the passion for the most perfect justice—freedom with responsibility and the opportunity to create." Gladys Grant, a poet and friend of Ridge's, describes wandering into Ridge's bedroom during the wake: "Here the austere simplicity and something of the windows open and looking far out over the roofs gave a sense of Lola. Everything was bare except for the winged victory by her bed..."

Ridge saw very clearly where freedom's repression could lead. Her brilliant sonnet "Electrocution," written before Sacco and Vanzetti were executed, the only poem that matches her acute social conscience with her wavering ability with form, captures the way democracy deals, finally, with its people.

Electrocution

He shudders...feeling on the shaved spot
The probing wind, that stabs him to a thought
Of storm-drenched fields in a white foam of light,
And roads of his hill-town that leap to sight
Like threads of tortured silver...while the guards—
Monstrous deft dolls that move as on a string,
In wonted haste to finish with this thing,
Turn faces blanker than asphalted yards.

They heard the shriek that tore out of its sheath
But as a feeble moan...yet dared not breathe,
Who stared there at him, arching—like a tree
When the winds wrench it and the earth holds tight—
Whose soul, expanding in white agony,
Had fused in flaming circuit with the night. (*Red Flag* 65)

Author's Note

I would first and foremost like to thank the Money for Women/ Barbara Deming Memorial Fund which gave me a small grant and large encouragement, and for the John Simon Guggenheim fellowship which, although awarded in fiction, allowed me to complete work on this book. I'm deeply indebted to poet and critic Michele Leggott at the University of Aukland who encouraged me at many critical junctures and read drafts. Gladys Bernand-Wehner, Ridge's granddaughter who bears the alias Ridge gave her son, provided details about Keith's life. Alison Clarke and Eliza McLennan revealed much about the Webster and Penfold sides of the family. Foremost among so many amazing librarians is Karen V. Kukil, Associate Curator of Special Collections at Smith College whose brilliance and enthusiasm were crucial to my progress. Catherine Daly's transcription of Ridge's books on Gutenberg was crucial.Craig Howes at the Center for Biographical Research at the University of Hawaii provided wry wisdom about both academics and biography. Simon Turkel's help, especially overseeing the footnotes and generating the bibliography, was invaluable.

At the very beginning of my research, Frances Flanagan and Brian Ward at Teichelman's Bed and Breakfast oriented my husband and I historically and geographically to Hokitika—and showed off its glow worms. I was delighted to discover Dr. Ebenezer Teichelman's signature in Lola Ridge's album. Esther Bruns gave us a fabulous tour of the gold mining district. Mary Rooney, now retired but once archivist for the Hokitika Museum, ran down her hunches for me. Jan Harbison of the Australian National Maritime Miuseum Library knew everything about period boats and shipping in the Pacific. Poppy Johnson at the Floyd Memorial Library materialized "lost" books from Australia when Columbia University couldn't find them.

Critical research assistance was given by Dr. Francesca Galligan at the Bodleian, June Can at the Beineke Rare Book and Manuscript Library at Yale, Elizabeth Fuller at the Rosenbach Museum and Library, Fernanda

Perrone at Rutgers University, Nancy Stout at Fordham University, Sue Asplin and Julia Bradshaw at the Hokitika Museum. Of course I am in love with Interlibrary loan at the New York Public Library, the University of Hawaii, Columbia University, and the National Library of Australia.

Archives and libraries that contributed material include: Sophia Smith Collection, Smith College Special Collections; Special Collections Department at Syracuse University; Columbia University Archives; Kislak Center for Special Collections Rare Books and Manuscripts, University of Pennsylvania; Special Collections, University of California, Berkeley; Tamiment Library & Robert F. Wagner Labor Archives; Bancroft Library, Berkeley; Marianne Moore Collection, Rosenbach Museum and Library; Special Collections and Archives, Kent State University; Special Collections Bryn Mawr; Mt. Holyoke; Special Collections, Harry Ransom Humanities Research Center, University of Texas at Austin; Library of Congress, Manuscripts Division; William Floyd Estate; Houghton Library, Harvard University; The Mitchell Dawson Papers, Library; Williams (William Carlos) Collection, State University of New York at Buffalo; John Simon Guggenheim Foundation; The Corporation of Yaddo; Hokitika Museum; University/Archives, Kenneth Spencer Research Library, University of Kansas; Special Collections Research Center at the University of Chicago Library; Manuscripts and Archive Division of the New York Public Library; Department of Rare Books and Special Collections, Albert and Shirley Small Special Collections Library at the University of Virginia; Department of Rare Books; Mitchell Library at Sydney, Australia; Beinecke Rare Book and Manuscript Library, Yale University; and Special Collections, Princeton University Library.

I would also like to thank critic Nancy Berke, Craig Howes, and poet Neil Shepherd for reading my first draft and providing important insights, Molly Giles and Laurie Stone for their patience with reading excerpts, the brilliant biographers Nancy Milford, Nancy Stout, and Nancy Schoenberger for professional tips, Dinah Lenney at the *L.A. Review of Books*, Ander Monson at *Diagram*, Scott Cheshire at *The Scofield*, and David Bonnano at *American Poetry Review* for publishing excerpts and essays, Clarence Coo at Columbia for extending my library privileges, Frank Brady for his candid recollection of David Lawson, Andre Bernard for locating the Guggenheim archive, Nancy Berke, Candace Falk, Suzanne Churchill, Linda Leavell, Carolyn Burke, Denise Scott-Fears, and Karen Avrich who shared their scholarship, Thomas Aiello at Valdosta State University who shared copies of documents from his work on David Lawson, National Park Service staffmember Denise Steinmacher at the William Floyd Estate for her guidance, archeologist Rick Hauser who told me what Gertrude Bell had for breakfast, Katherine Gibson, genius human geographer who oriented me in Sydney, the Australian scholars Susan Sheridan, Drusilla Modjeska, and Martin Edmond for answering my queries. Robert Polito for his early encouragement, Eleanor Wilner for her power, Janelle Cornwell for her fine hospitality and critical mind, Stevie Fitzgerald at the Authors Guild and Timothy J. DeBaets and his associate Jeffrey Lawhorn for legal advice, Steve Bull who not only read drafts but forced the computer to print them and held my hand when it crashed, my sons Felix and Frank who withheld judgment, and my dear publisher and once agent, Tim Schaffner, whose idea it was in the first place. To those I have forgotten, I quote Ridge: "My wonderful friends...in reality no one ever does anything alone."

Jill Quasha and The Estate of Marjorie Content were particularly generous with permitting me to use Content's photograph for the cover. Executor Elaine Sproat gave me lists of Ridge's publications and reviews. After Ridge's death in 1941, Ridge's papers were held by her husband, David Lawson who gave them to Elaine Sproat. She, in turn, deposited half of them at Smith College. I was denied permission to examine the remainder of the papers although copyright on all the material expired 2011. Lacking access to primary material, I am doubly grateful for the work of scholars whose writing on Ridge had been approved by Sproat.

—Terese Svoboda
November 2015

Bibliography

LETTERS/ARCHIVAL MATERIAL

Beinecke Rare Book and Manuscript Library, Yale University, New Haven, CT.
    Crane, Hart. Letter to Lorna Dietz. Hart Crane Collection.
    Hemingway, Ernest. Letter to Ezra Pound. Ezra Pound Papers.
    Josephson, Matthew. Correspondence. Matthew Josephson Papers.
    Ridge, Lola. Letter to Alfred Stieglitz. Collection of American Literature.
    ---. Letter to Henry Seidel Canby. Henry Seidel Canby Papers.
    ---. Letters to Jean Toomer. Jean Toomer Papers.
    ---. Letter to Joseph H. Brewer. Joseph Brewer Papers.
    ---. Letters to Josephine Crane. Josephine Boardman Crane Papers.
    ---. Letter to Llewellyn Jones. Collection of American Literature.
    ---. Letter to Louise Morgan. Louise Morgan and Otto Theis Papers.
    ---. Letters to Marjorie Content. Marjorie Content Papers.
    ---. Letter to Otto Theis. Louise Morgan and Otto Theis Papers.
    ---. Letter to Rebecca Strand. Rebecca Salsbury James Papers.
    Sproat, Elaine. Letters to Carolyn Burke. Carolyn Burke Papers.

Broom Correspondence of Harold Loeb, Princeton University, Princeton, NJ.
    Josephson, Matthew. Letter to Gorham Munson.
    Loeb, Harold. Letters to Lola Ridge.
    Ridge, Lola. Letters to Harold Loeb.
    ---. Letter to Matthew Josephson.

Columbia University Archives, Special Collections, New York, NY.
    Ridge, Lola. Letters to Harrison Smith.
    ---. Letter to Hart Crane. Hart Crane Papers.
    ---. Letters to Lenore Marshall. Lenore Marshall Papers.
    Smith, Hal. Letters to Lola Ridge.

John Simon Guggenheim Fund, New York.
    Guggenheim application. 1935.

Harry Ransom Humanities Research Center, University of Texas at Austin.
    Ridge, Lola. Letters to Evelyn Scott. Evelyn Scott Collection.
    ---. Letter to Idella Purnell. Idella Purnell Stone Personal Papers.
    Scott, Creighton. Unpublished Mss.

Hokitika Museum, Hokitika, NZ.
    Sproat, Elaine. Letter to J. Engles.

Houghton Library, Harvard University, Cambridge, MA.
    Bynner, Witter. Letter to Lola Ridge. Witter Bynner Papers.
    Cummings, E.E. Letter to Lola Ridge. E. E. Cummings Additional Papers.
    Ridge, Lola. Letter to Rose Freeman-Ishill. Joseph Ishill Correspondence.

Jeannette Augustus Marks Papers. Mt. Holyoke College, Special Collections, South Hadley, MA.
    Marks, Jeannette. Letter to Lola Ridge.
    Ridge, Lola. Letters to Jeannette Marks.

Kenneth Spencer Research Library, University of Kansas, Lawrence, KS.
    Ridge, Lola. Letter to Mary Austin.

Kent State University, Special Collections and Archives, Kent, OH.
    Crane, Hart. Letter to Charles Harris. Hart Crane Papers.

Kislak Center for Special Collections Rare Books and Manuscripts, University of Pennsylvania, Philadelphia, PA.
    Ridge, Lola. Letter to Carl Zigrosser.
    ---. Letter to Leonard Abbott.

Library of Congress, Manuscripts Division, Washington, DC.
    Abbott, Leonard. Letter to Margaret Sanger.
    Huebsch, B. W. Letter to Lola Ridge.
    Ridge, Lola. Letters to B. W. Huebsch.
    ---. Letter to Francis Hackett.
    ---. Letter to Marian MacDowell.

Lola Ridge Papers, Sophia Smith Collection, Smith College, Northampton, MA.
    Benét, Frances Rose. Letter to Lola Ridge.
    ---. Letters to Lola Ridge.
    Floyd, Louise Adams. Letter to Lola Ridge [enclosure from "Miriam"].
    Lawson, David. Letters to Lola Ridge.
    Ridge, Lola. Autograph book.
    ---. Diary.
    ---. Drawings.
    ---. Letter to Miss Bartlett.
    ---. Letters to David Lawson.
    ---. Letter to Florence Rena Sabin.
    ---. Letters to Louise Adams Floyd.
    ---. Letter to Mr. Small.
    ---. Letter to William Floyd.
    Scott, Evelyn. Letters to David Lawson.
    ---. Letters to Lola Ridge.
    Srabian, Leon. Letter to Lola Ridge.
    "Stan." Letter to Lola Ridge. [Sept. 1930].
    Sykes, Gerald. Letter to Lola Ridge.
    Wilder, Charlotte. Letters to Lola Ridge.

Marianne Moore Collection, Rosenbach Museum and Library, Philadelphia, PA.
    Moore, Marianne. Conversation Notebooks.
    ---. Letter from college. 1909.
    ---. Letters to David Lawson.
    ---. Letters to John Warner Moore.
    ---. Letters to Lola Ridge.
    Moore, Mary Warner. Letters to Lola Ridge.

Mitchell Dawson Papers, Newberry Library, Chicago, IL.
Dawson, Mitchell. Letters to Eva Dawson.
---. Letter to George Dawson.
---. Letter to Max Bodenheim.
Johns, Orrick. Letter to Mitchell Dawson.
Ridge, Lola. Letters to Mitchell Dawson.
Williams, William Carlos. Letter to Mitchell Dawson.

Mitchell Library, SLNSW, Sydney, Australia.
Ridge, Lola. Letter to A.G. Stephens.

New York Public Library, Manuscripts and Archives Division, New York, NY.
Ridge, Lola. Letter to Martin Becker. American Fund for Public Service Records.
Ames, Elizabeth. Letters to Lola Ridge.
Robinson, Edgar Arlington. Letter to Mr. Small. Edgar Arlington Robinson Papers.
Mr. Small, letter to Edgar Arlington Robinson. Edgar Arlington Robinson Papers.
Ridge, Lola. Letters to Elizabeth Ames.
Ridge, Lola. Letters to Genevieve Taggard.

Tamiment Library and Robert F. Wagner Labor Archives. New York University.
Masses Archive.
Printed Ephemera.

University of California, Berkeley.
Goldman, Emma. Letters to Lola Ridge. Emma Goldman Papers.
---. Letter to Stella Ballantine. Emma Goldman Papers.
---. Letters to Evelyn Scott. Emma Goldman Papers.
Seiffert, Marjorie. Letter to Helen Hoyt. Lyman Family Papers, The Bancroft Library.

University of Chicago Library, Chicago, IL.
Kreymborg, Alfred. Letter to Henry Rago. Poetry Magazine Papers.
Ridge, Lola. Letters to Harriet Monroe. Harriet Monroe Papers.

University of Virginia Libraries, Charlottesville, VA.
Frost, Robert. Letter to Lola Ridge. Albert and Shirley Small Special Collections Library.
MacLeish, Archibald. Letter to Alfred Kreymborg. Albert and Shirley Small Special Collections Library.
Ridge, Lola. Letters to Alfred Kreymborg. Albert and Shirley Small Special Collections Library.

Kislak Center for Special Collections Rare Books and Manuscripts, University of Pennsylvania, Philadelphia PA.
Ridge, Lola. Letter to Carl Zigrosser.
---. Letter to Leonard Abbott.

William Floyd Estate. Fire Island National Seashore, NY.
Floyd, William. William Floyd Estate
Historic Furnishings Report.
Floyd, Louise Adams. Guestbook.

Williams (William Carlos) Collection, State University of New York at Buffalo, NY.
Dawson, Mitchell. Letter to William Carlos Williams.
Ridge, Lola. Letter to William Carlos Williams.

PRINT SOURCES

Abbott, Leonard. "An Anarchist Poet." *The Modern School* Vol. 6, No. 1 (1919): 12.

---. "Edwin Markham: Laureate of Labor." *Comrade* 1.4 (1902): 74-75.

Abbott, Leonard, ed. *Francisco Ferrer: His Life, Work and Martyrdom.* New York: Francisco Ferrer Assn., 1910.

Adams, Ansel. *Conversations with Ansel Adams.* Berkeley: Regents of the University of California, 1978.

Adams, Katherine H. *A Group of Their Own: College Writing Courses and American Women Writers.* Albany: SUNY UP, 2001.

Adrian, Lynn M. "Emma Goldman and the Spirit of Artful Living: Philosophy and Politics in the Classical American Period." *Feminist Interpretations of Emma Goldman.* Eds. Penny A. Weiss and Loretta Kensinger. University Park, PA: Penn State UP, 2007.

Ahearn, Barry, ed. Pound/Zukofsky: *Selected Letters of Ezra Pound and Louis Zukofsky.* New York: New Directions, 1987.

Aiken, Conrad. "The Literary Abbozzo." Rev. of *The Ghetto and Other Poems,* by Lola Ridge. *The Dial* 25 Jan. 1919: 83–84.

---. "Speak as You Must." *The Dial* July 1927: 63.

Albers, Patricia. *Shadows, Fire, Snow: The Life of Tina Modotti.* Oakland: U of California P, 2002.

Aldington, Richard. *An Imagist at War: The Complete War Poems of Richard Aldington.* Madison, NJ: Fairleigh Dickinson UP, 2002.

Alexander, Doris. *Eugene O'Neill's Last Plays: Separating Art from Autobiography.* Athens, GA: U of Georgia P, 2005.

Alkon, Paul Kent. *Winston Churchill's Imagination.* Cranbury, NJ: Rosemont, 2006.

Allego, Donna. *The Construction and Role of Community in Political Long Poems by Twentieth-Century American Women Poets.* Diss. Southern Illinois University at Carbondale, 1997. Ann Arbor: UMI, 1997.

Als, Hilton. "No Place Like Home." *New Yorker* 11 May 2009.

Anonymous. *Ophiolatreia.* Privately printed, 1889.

Antliff, Allan. *Anarchist Modernism: Art, Politics, and the First American Avant-Garde.* Chicago: U of Chicago P, 2007.

Applegate, Frank G. "Enchanted Gold." *Native Tales of New Mexico.* Philadelphia: J. B. Lippincott, 1932.

Arneson, Eric. "Red Summer: The Summer of 1919 and the Awakening of Black America." *Chicago Tribune* 11 Nov. 2011.

Astbury, L. "Cash Buyers Welcome: Australian Artists and Bohemians in the 1890s." *Journal of Australian Studies* May 1987: 23-37.

Austin, Mary Hunter. *Literary America, 1903-1934: The Mary Austin Letters*. Ed. Thomas Matthews Pearce. Santa Barbara: Greenwood, 1979.

Avrich, Paul. *An American Anarchist: The Life of Voltairine de Cleyre*. Princeton: Princeton UP, 1978.

---. *Anarchist Voices: An Oral History of Anarchism in America*. Princeton: Princeton UP, 1995.

---. *The Modern School Movement: Anarchism and Education in the United States*. Oakland: AK Press, 2005.

Avrich, Karen and Paul Avrich. *Sasha and Emma: The Anarchist Odyssey of Alexander Berkman and Emma Goldman*. Cambridge: Belknap, 2012.

Baer, Ulrich. "f for Frogs." *The Rilke Alphabet*. New York: Fordham UP, 2014.

Baker, Jean H. *Margaret Sanger: A Life of Passion*. New York: Macmillan, 2011.

Bakunin, Mikhail. *Marxism, Freedom, and the State*. c.1870. London: Freedom, 1950.

Baldwin, Neil. *To All Gentleness: William Carlos Williams, the Doctor Poet*. Baltimore: Black Classic, 2008.

---. *Man Ray: American Artist*. Cambridge, MA: Da Capo, 2000.

Barnes, Harper. *Never Been a Time: The 1917 Race Riot That Sparked the Civil Rights Movement*. New York: Walker, 2008.

Barnet, Andrea. *All-Night Party: The Women of Bohemian Greenwich Village and Harlem, 1913–1930*. Chapel Hill, NC: Algonquin Books, 2004.

Bartlett, Alice Hunt. "The Dynamics of American Poetry." *Poetry Review* 16 (1925).

---. "The Dynamics of American Poetry." *Poetry Review* 48 (May/June 1934).

Bates, Stephen. "Son of Sylvia Plath and Ted Hughes Kills Himself." *New York Times* 23 Mar. 2009.

Baudelaire, Charles. "The Painter of Modern Life." *Baudelaire: Selected Writings on Art and Artists*. Trans. Patrick E. Charvet. Cambridge: Cambridge UP, 1981.

Beffel, John Nicholas. "Miss Ridge to the Rescue." *Chicago Sun Times* 23 Feb. 1919.

---. "William Carlos Williams Coming to Tell How Would Poet Operate Universe." *Chicago Sun Tribune* 12 Apr. 1919.

Bell, Gertrude. *The Letters of Gertrude Bell*. Vol. 2. Ed. Lady Bell, D. B. E. New York: Boni and Liveright, 1927.

Bell, James Macintosh. *The Geology of the Hokitika Sheet*, North Westland Quadrangle. Wellington, New Zealand: Government Printer, 1906.

Bendixen, Alfred and Steven R. Serafin, eds. "A Brittle Heaven." *The Continuum Encyclopedia of American Literature*. London: Bloomsbury Academic, 2003.

Benét, Stephen Vincent. "Vincent Praises Poetic Story of Christ." *Chicago Daily Tribune* 14 Dec. 1929: 13.

Benét, William Rose. *Fifty Poets: An American Auto-Anthology*. Duffield and Green, 1933.

---. "Lola Ridge, 1883-1941." *Saturday Review of Literature* 31 May 1941: 8.
---. "The Phoenix Nest." *Saturday Review of Literature* 7 Dec. 1935: 46-47.

---. *The Stairway of Surprise*. New York: A. A. Knopf, 1947.

Benjamin, Paul Lyman. "The Poetry of Existence." *The Survey: Social, Charitable, Civic: A Journal of Constructive Philanthropy* 29 Nov. 1919.

Bennett, Paul A. *My Life a Loaded Gun: Female Creativity and Feminist Poetics*. Boston: Beacon, 1986.

---. *Poetry in the Public Sphere: The Emancipatory Project of American Women's Poetry, 1800–1900*. Princeton: Princeton UP, 2003.

Bennett, Scott H. *Radical Pacifism: The War Resisters League and Gandhian Nonviolence in America, 1915–1963*. Syracuse: Syracuse UP, 2003.

Bercovici, Konrad. *It's the Gypsy in Me*. New York: Prentice Hall, 1941.

---. "Orphans as Guinea Pigs." *The Nation* 29 June 1921: 911-13.

Bercovici, Rion. "Life in the United States: A Radical Childhood." *Scribner's Magazine* Aug. 1932.

Bercovitch, Sacvan. *The Cambridge History of American Literature*. Vol. 5. Cambridge: Cambridge UP, 2003.

Berke, Nancy. "Anything That Burns You: The Social Poetry of Lola Ridge, Genevieve Taggard, and Margaret Walker." *Revista Canaria de Estudios Ingleses* 37 (Nov. 1998): 39–53.

---. "'Electric Currents of Life:' Lola Ridge's Immigrant Flaneuserie." *American Studies* 51.1/2 (Spring/Summer 2010): 27–47.

---. "Lola Ridge." *American Women Writers 1900-1945: A Bio-Bibliographical Critical Sourcebook*. Ed. Laura Champion. Westport, CT: Greenwood, 2000.

---. *Women Poets on the Left: Lola Ridge, Genevieve Taggard, Margaret Walker*. Gainesville: UP of Florida, 2001.

Bernikow, Louise. *The World Split Open: Five Centuries of Women Poetry in England and America*. New York: Random House, 1974.

Bernstein, Charles, ed. *Close Listening: Poetry and the Performed Word*. Oxford: Oxford UP, 1998.

Berry, Faith. *Langston Hughes: Before and Beyond Harlem*. New York: Citadel, 2000.

Berryman, John. *The Dream Songs*. New York: Farrar, Straus and Giroux. 2007.

Bethell, Ursula. *Vibrant With Words: The Letters of Ursula Bethell*. Ed. Peter Whiteford. Wellington, New Zealand: Victoria UP, 2005.

Bingham, Edwin R. *Charles Erskine Scott Wood*. Boise: Boise State University Western Writers Series, 1990.

Bird, Isabella L. *Journeys in Persia and Kurdistan: Including a Summer in the Upper Karun Region and a Visit to the Nestorian Rayahs*. New York: G. P. Putnam's Sons, 1891.

Bloom, Alexander. *Prodigal Sons: The New York Intellectuals and Their World*. New York: Oxford UP, 1987.

Bloom, Harold. "The Art of Criticism No. 1." *The Paris Review* Spring 1991.

Bogan, Louise. "Lyric Prophet." Rev. of Dance of Fire, by Lola Ridge. *New Republic* 10 July 1935: 258.

Bone, Robert and Richard A. Courage. *The Muse in Bronzeville: African American Creative Expression in Chicago, 1932-1950*. New Brunswick, NJ: Rutgers UP, 2011.

Bonner, Amy, ed. *Poetry Society of America Anthology*. New York: Fine Editions, 1946.

Bookchin, Murray. "Individualist Anarchism and Reaction." *Social Anarchism or Lifestyle Anarchism: An Unbridgeable Chasm*. Oakland: AK Press, 2001.

Boutilier, Beverly and Alison Prentice. *Creating Historical Memory: English-Canadian Women and the Work of History*. Vancouver: UBC P, 1997.

Boyle, Gertrude. "From a Scrapbook." *The Birth Control Review* May 1918: 11.

---. "To the Unfortunates." *The Birth Control Review* June 1918: 6+.

Braddock, Jeremy. *Collecting as Modernist Practice*. Baltimore: Johns Hopkins UP, 2013.

Bradley, Edward S. "Fighting Pain and Death, Lola Ridge Writes Mighty Poem of Crucifixion." *The Philadelphia Record* 14 Dec. 1929.

Bradshaw, Melissa and Adrienne Munich. *Amy Lowell, American Modern*. Newark: Rutgers UP, 2004.

Brady, Frank. *Endgame: Bobby Fischer's Remarkable Rise and Fall—from America's Brightest Prodigy to the Edge of Madness*. New York: Random House, 2011.

Brevda, William. *Harry Kemp, The Last Bohemian*. Lewisburg, PA: Bucknell UP, 1986

Brewer, Isaac W. "City life in relation to tuberculosis: a plea for better surroundings for factories and better homes for the working classes." *American Journal of Public Health* 3.9 (1913): 903–914.

Bridges, H.L. "Queries That a Few May Not be Able to Answer." *The Mixer and Server* 15 July 1920: 31.

Bromwich, David. "The Bleakest of Lords." *New York Times* 16 Jan. 1977.

Brooker, Peter and Andrew Thacker, eds. *The Oxford Critical and Cultural History of Modernist Magazines*. Vol. 2. Oxford UP, 2012.

Brooks, Cleanth. "Miss Millay's Maturity." *Southwest Review* 20 (1935): 1–5.

Brooks, Marshall. "Harry Kemp: Lest We Forget." *The Eugene O'Neill Newsletter* May/Sept. 1980.

Browning, Michael. "The Eternal Flame." *Miami Herald* 18 Aug. 1996: 12.

Bruccoli, Matthew J., ed. *F. Scott Fitzgerald: A Life in Letters*. New York: Simon and Schuster, 1995.

Bruno, Guido. "Anarchists in Our Village." *Fragments from Greenwich Village*. New York: Published privately by the author, 1921.

Buchan, Perdita. *Utopia, New Jersey: Travels in the Nearest Eden*. New Brunswick, NJ: Rutgers UP, 2007.

Burckhardt, Jackie M. "The Perils of Cohabitation: The Unmarried Father's Struggle for Rights in Ireland." *Washington University Global Studies Law Review* 9.3 (2010).

Burke, Carolyn. *Becoming Modern: The Life of Mina Loy*. New York: Macmillan, 1996.

Bynner, Witter. *Journey with Genius: Recollections and Reflections Concerning the D.H. Lawrences*. New York: J. Day, 1951.

---. *Pins for Wings*. New York: Sunwise Turn, 1920.

Byrd, Rudolph P. and Henry Louis Gates Jr. "Jean Toomer's Conflicted Racial Identity." *The Chronicle Review*, 6 Feb. 2011.

Byrne, Katherine. *Tuberculosis and the Victorian Literary Imagination*. Cambridge: Cambridge UP, 2011.

California. State Board of Charities and Corrections. *Biennial Report*. Vol. 8. 1889.

California. State Board of Examiners. *Aid Granted Orphan Asylums from July 1, 1904, to June 30, 1906*. 1907.

Callard, D. A. "Pretty Good for a Woman": *The Enigmas of Evelyn Scott*. New York: W.W. Norton, 1986.

Capper, Charles, Cristina Giorcelli, and Lester Little, eds. *Margaret Fuller: Transatlantic Crossings in a Revolutionary Age*. Madison: U of Wisconsin P, 2008.

Carnevali, Emanuel. *A Hurried Man*. Paris: Contact Editions/Three Mountains, 1925.

Carr, Virginia Spencer. *Dos Passos: A Life*. Evanston, IL: Northwestern UP, 2004.

Casillo, Robert. Rev. of *The Selected Letters of Ezra Pound to John Quinn*, ed. by Timothy Materer. The Modern Language Review 88.4 (Oct. 1993): 959–961.

Castellanos, J. "Influence of Sewing Machines upon the Health and Morality of the Females Using Them." *Southern Journal of Medical Science* 1 (1886/87): 495–496.

Castilla, Ethel. "An Australian Girl." *Australian Town and Country Journal* 22 Sept. 1888: 600.

Cather, Willa. "Katherine Mansfield." *Not Under Forty*. 1936. Lincoln: U of Nebraska P, 1988.

Cather, Willa. *Willa Cather in Person: Interviews, Speeches, and Letters*. Ed. L. Brent Bohlke. Lincoln and London: U of Nebraska P, 1986.

Catton, Eleanor. *The Luminaries*. New York: Little, Brown, and Co., 2013.

Charman, Janet. "My Ursula Bethell." *Women's Studies Journal* 14.2 (Spring 1998): 91–108.

Chertoff, Emily. "The Strange Story of New York's Anarchist School." *The Atlantic* 11 Jan. 2013.

Chesler, Ellen. *Woman of Valor: Margaret Sanger and the Birth Control Movement in America*. New York: Simon and Schuster, 2007.

Chevalier, Tracy, ed. *Encyclopedia of the Essay*. London: Routledge, 1997.

Chielens, Edward E., ed. *American Literary Magazines: The Twentieth Century*. Westport, CT: Greenwood, 1992.

Churchill, Suzanne. *The Little Magazine Others and the Renovation of Modern American Poetry*. Burlington: Ashgate Publishing Co., 2006.

---. "The lying game: Others and the great spectra hoax of 1917." *American Periodicals: A Journal of History, Criticism, and Bibliography*. 15.1 (2005): 23–41.

Clark, David G. *Route 66 in Chicago*. Chicago: Arcadia Publishing, 2007.

Clement, Tanya E. "The Makings of Digital Modernism: Rereading Gertrude Stein's *The Making of Americans* and Poetry by Elsa Von Freytag-Loringhoven." Diss. University of Maryland College Park, 2009.

Cluck, J. "Elinor Wylie's Shelley Obsession." *PMLA* 56.3 (Sept. 1941).

Coate, Douglas. *Disaster and Recovery: The Public and Private Sectors in the Aftermath of the 1906 Earthquake in San Francisco*. Newark: Rutgers University Working Papers, 2010.

Cohen, Joseph J. and Alexis C. Ferm. *The Modern School of Stelton: A Sketch*. Berkeley: Factory School, 2006.

Cohen, Milton A. *Beleaguered Poets and Leftist Critics: Stevens, Cummings, Frost, and Williams in the 1930s*. Tuscaloosa: U of Alabama P, 2011.

Coleborne, Catharine. *Madness in the Family: Insanity and Institutions in the Australasian Colonial World, 1860–1914*. New York: Palgrave Macmillan, 2009.

Coleman, Louis. *Night Riders in Gallup*. New York: International Labor Defense, 1935.

Coleman, Peter J. *Progressivism and the World of Reform: New Zealand and the Origins of the American Welfare State*. Lawrence: UP of Kansas, 1987.

The Committee of Forty-Eight: For a Conference of Americans Who Are Equally Opposed to Reaction and Violent Revolution: Its Purposes—And the Reasons for It. New York: Committee of Forty-Eight, 1919.

Conover, Anne. *Olga Rudge and Ezra Pound: What Thou Lovest Well.* New Haven: Yale UP, 2001.

Coodley, Lauren. *Upton Sinclair: California Socialist, Celebrity Intellectual.* Lincoln: U of Nebraska P, 2013.

Cooter, Roger, ed. *In the Name of the Child: Health and Welfare, 1880-1940.* London: Routledge, 1992.

Copland, Aaron and Vivian Perlis. *Copland 1900 through 1942.* New York: St. Martin's, 1984.

Cott, Nancy. *The Grounding of Modern Feminism.* New Haven: Yale UP, 1989.

Cowan, James. "Famous New Zealanders: No. 46: Jessie Mackay: Poet, Idealist, and Celtic Patriot." *The New Zealand Railways Magazine* 1 Jan. 1937.

Cowley, Malcolm. *Exile's Return: A Literary Odyssey of the 1920s.* 1951. New York: Penguin, 1994.

---. "Young Man with Spectacles." *Broom* Oct. 1922.

Crane, Hart. *The Complete Poems and Selected Letters and Prose of Hart Crane.* Ed. Brom Weber. Newcastle upon Tyne: Bloodaxe Books, 1987.

---. *The Letters of Hart Crane.* Ed. Brom Weber. Berkeley: U of California P, 1965.

---. "Lola Ridge's Ghetto." Rev. of *The Ghetto and Other Poems,* by Lola Ridge. *The Pagan* Jan. 1919.

Crawford, John. "Lola Ridge's 'Sun-Up.'" *The New York Call Magazine* 15 May 1921: 11–15.

Cresswell, D'Arcy. "Ursula Bethell: Some Personal Memories." *Landfall* Dec. 1948: 283.

Crist, Elizabeth Bergman. "The Compositional History of Aaron Copland's Symphonic Ode." *American Music* 18.3 (Autumn 2000).

Critchley, Simon. *Infinitely Demanding: Ethics of Commitment, Politics of Resistance.* New York: Verso, 2007.

Curwood, Anastasia Carol. *Stormy Weather: Middle-Class African American Marriages between the Two World Wars.* Chapel Hill: U of North Carolina P, 2010.

The Cyclopedia of New Zealand [Nelson, Marlborough and Westland Provincial Districts]. Christchurch: The Cyclopedia Company, Ltd., 1906.

Dabbagh, Maureen. *Parental Kidnapping in America: An Historical and Cultural Analysis.* Jefferson, NC: McFarland and Company, 2011.

Daggy, Robert E. "Question and Revelation: Thomas Merton's Recovery of the Ground of Birth." *Thomas Merton Society of Great Britain and Ireland.* Southampton, England. May 1996. Speech.

Daiches, David. "Walt Whitman's Philosophy." *Literary Essays.* Chicago: U of Chicago P, 1956.

Dalley, Stephanie. *The Mystery of the Hanging Garden of Babylon: An Elusive World Wonder Traced.* Oxford: Oxford UP, 2013.

Daly, Catherine. "Lola Ridge's Dance of Fire." *How2* 1.8 (Fall 2002).

Damrosch, Leo. *Jean-Jaques Rousseau: Restless Genius*. New York: First Mariner, 2007.

D'Attilio, Robert. "Sacco-Vanzetti Case." *Encyclopedia of the American Left*. Eds. Mari Jo Buhle, Paul Buhle, and Dan Georgakas. New York: Oxford UP, 1998.

Davidson, Gustav. *In Fealty to Apollo: Poetry Society of America, 1910–1950*. New York: Fine Editions, 1950.

Davies, Andrea Rees. *Saving San Francisco: Relief and Recovery after the 1906 Disaster*. Philadelphia: Temple UP, 2011.

Davin, Eric Leif. *Partners in Wonder: Women and the Birth of Science Fiction*. Lanham, MD: Lexington Books, 2005.

Davis, Alex and Lee M. Jenkins. ed. *A History of Modernist Poetry*. Cambridge: Cambridge UP, 2015.

Davis, James. *Eric Walrond: A Life in the Harlem Renaissance and the Transatlantic Caribbean*. New York: Columbia UP, 2015.

Davis, John H. *The Guggenheims: An American Epic*. New York: Morrow, 1978.

Dean, Tim. "Hart Crane's Poetics of Privacy." *American Literary History* 8.1 (1996).

Dearborn, Mary V. *Mistress of Modernism: The Life of Peggy Guggenheim*. Boston: Houghton Mifflin, 2004.

De Cleyre, Voltairine. "The Case of Woman vs. Orthodoxy." *Boston Investigator* 18 Sept. 1896.

---. "The Gates of Freedom." *Lucifer* [1891]. Joseph Ishill Collection, Houghton Library, Harvard University.

---. "They Who Marry Do Ill." *Mother Earth* Jan. 1908: 501+.

De Cleyre, Voltairine, Alexander Berkman and Hippolyte Havel. *Selected Works of Voltairine de Cleyre, 1866–1912*. New York: Mother Earth, 1914.

Denman, William and Appointed Committee. *Report on the Causes of Municipal Corruption in San Francisco*. San Francisco: Rincon, 1910.

Dennis, Oliver, ed. *Collected Poems: Lesbia Harford*. UWA Publishing, 2014.

Densmore-John, Jean. "Nutritional Characteristics and Consequences of Anorexia Nervosa and Bulimia." *The Eating Disorders*. Eds. B. J. Blinder, B. F. Chaitin, and R. Goldstein. New York: PMA, 1988.

Dettmar, Kevin J.H. and Stephen Myers Watt, eds. *Marketing Modernisms: Self-Promotion, Canonization, Rereading*. Ann Arbor: U of Michigan P, 1997.

Deutsch, Babette. "Poet of the White Bird." *New York Herald Tribune* 5 June 1927.

---. *This Modern Poetry*. NY: Norton, 1935.

---. "Two First Books." Rev. of *The Ghetto and Other Poems*, by Lola Ridge. *The Little Review* May 1919: 65–68.

Dickinson, Donald C. *Dictionary of American Antiquarian Bookdealers*. Santa Barbara: Greenwood, 1998.

Dilling, Elizabeth. *The Red Network: A "Who's Who" and Handbook of Radicalism for Patriots*. Kenilworth, IL: published by the author, 1934.

Dirda, Michael. "Devil or Angel." *Washington Post* 31 Mar. 1996.

Donaldson, Thomas. *Walt Whitman the Man*. New York: Francis P. Harper, 1896.

Dormandy, Thomas. *The White Death: A History of Tuberculosis*. New York: NYU P, 2000.

Drake, William. *First Wave: Women Poets in America 1915–1945*. New York: Macmillan, 1987.

Dreiser, Theodore. "The Child-Rescue League: The Delineator Starts a New and Aggressive Campaign for Doing Away with the Old-Fashioned Orphan Asylum." *The Delineator* Jan. 1909: 102.

DuBois, Ellen Carol. *Woman Suffrage and Women's Rights*. New York: NYU P, 1998.

DuBois, W. E. B. and Martha Gruening. "Massacre at East St. Louis." *The Crisis* Sept. 1917: 219–238.

Dunbar, Olivia Howard. *A House in Chicago*. Chicago: U of Chicago P, 1948.

Dunn, Susan E. "Fashion Victims: Mina Loy's Travesties." *Stanford Humanities Review* 7.1 (1999).

Durant, Will. *Socialism and Anarchism*. New York: A. and C. Boni, 1914.

---. *Transition: A Sentimental Story of One Mind and One Era*. New York: Touchstone, 1978.

Eastman, Max. *Einstein, Trotsky, Hemingway, Freud and Other Great Companions*. New York: Collier Books, 1962.

Edgren, Maude Durand. "Regeneration Through Sex." *The Birth Control Review* July 1918: 3.

Edmond, Martin. "Pearson's Lawson: The Subterranean Homesick Trans-Tasman Blues." University of Sydney. John Woolley Building, Camperdown Campus, New South Wales. 12 July 2014. Lecture.

Edwards, Margaret. "Frances Frost, 1905-1959: Sketch of a Vermont Poet." *Vermont History* 56.2 (Spring 1988): 102–111.

Eglington, Laura. Exhibition Review. *ArtNews* 9 Feb. 1935: 3–4.

EMF Electrical Year Book, Vol. 1, ed. Frank H. Bernhard. Chicago: Electrical Trade Publishing Co. 1921. 240.

"Emma Goldman." *The American Experience*. PBS. 12 Apr. 2004. Television.

Erkkila, Betsy. *The Wicked Sisters: Women Poets, Literary History, and Discord*. New York: Oxford UP, 1992.

Ettor and Giovannitti Before the Jury at Salem Massachusetts, November 23, 1919. Chicago: The Industrial Workers of the World, 1941.

Falk, Candace, ed. *Emma Goldman: A Documentary History of the American Years*. Vol. 2. Berkeley: U of California P, 2005.

---. *Emma Goldman: A Documentary History of the American Years*. Vol. 3. Stanford: Stanford UP, 2012.

---. *Love, Anarchy and Emma Goldman: A Biography*. New Brunswick: Rutgers UP, 1990.

Farrar, John, ed. *The Bookman Anthology of Verse*. New York: George H. Doran Company, 1922.

Fedirka, Sarah. *Toward a Locational Modernism: Little Magazines and the Modernist Geographical Imagination*. Ann Arbor: ProQuest, 2008.

Felix, David. *Protest: Sacco-Vanzetti and the Intellectuals*. Bloomington: Indiana UP, 1965.

Fellner, Gene, ed. Introduction. *Life of an Anarchist: The Alexander Berkman Reader*. New York: Seven Stories, 2005.

Ferguson, Kathy E. *Emma Goldman: Political Thinking in the Streets*. Lanham, MD: Rowman and Littlefield, 2011.

Ferrari, Arthur C. "Proletarian Literature: A Case of Convergence of Political and Literary Radicalism." *Cultural Politics: Radical Movements in Modern History*. Ed. Jerold M. Starr. New York: Praeger, 1985.

Filreis, Alan. *Counter-revolution of the Word: The Conservative Attack on Modern Poetry, 1945-1960*. Chapel Hill: U of North Carolina P, 2008.

Finkelstein, Sidney. *Art and Society*. New York: International Publishers, 1947.

Fisher, Clive. *Hart Crane: A Life*. New Haven: Yale UP, 2002.

Flanner, Janet. "Isadora Duncan's Return." *New Yorker* 1 Jan. 1927.

Floyd, William. Autobiographical MS. William Floyd (1871-1943) Papers. Fire Island National Seashore, NY.

---. *War Resistance: What Each Individual Can Do for War Prevention*. New York: The Arbitrator, 1931/2.

Floyd, Louise Adams Floyd. *Guestbook*. William Floyd Estate. Fire Island National Seashore, NY.

Flynn, Elizabeth Gurley. *The Rebel Girl: An Autobiography, My First Life (1906-1926)*. New York: International Publishers, 1973.

Foley, Barbara. *Radical Representations: Politics and Form in U.S. Proletarian Fiction, 1929-1941*. Durham: Duke UP, 1993.

Folsom, Franklin. *Days of Anger, Days of Hope: A Memoir of the League of American Writers, 1937-1942.* Boulder: UP of Colorado, 1994.

Ford, Julia Ellsworth, Mary E. Woolley, William Floyd, Laura Puffer Morgan, John Dewey, and Upton Sinclair. *Love of Country: Opposition to War.* New York: Peace Patriots, 1930.

Ford, Lillian C. "Two Poets Interpret Judas." *The Los Angeles Times* 29 Dec. 1929.

Fordham, Michael. *Explorations Into the Self.* Vol. 7. London: Karnac Books, 1985.

Fox, Clifton, R. "The Burden of the Mexican Past: The Mexican Revolution." *Raleigh Tavern Philosophical Society.* Tomball, TX. 7 Nov. 2002. Lecture.

Franciosi, Robert. "Hart Crane, Lola Ridge, and Charles Reznikoff: A Note on the Early Conception of The Bridge." *Essays in Literature* 11.2 (Sept. 1984): 305.

Frank, Elizabeth. *Louise Bogan: A Portrait.* New York: Columbia UP, 1986.

Frank, Waldo David. *Our America.* New York: Boni and Liveright, 1919.

Frazer, Winifred. "A Lost Poem by Eugene O'Neill." *The Eugene O'Neill Newsletter* May 1979.

Friedman, Lester D., ed. *Cultural Sutures: Medicine and Media.* Durham: Duke UP, 2004.

Fromm, Gloria. G. "The Remains of Katherine Mansfield." Rev. of *Katherine Mansfield: A Secret Life,* by Claire Tomalin. *The New Criterion* June 1988: 78.

Frost, Frances. *Hemlock Wall.* New Haven: Yale UP, 1929.

Frost, Richard H. *The Mooney Case.* Stanford: Stanford: Stanford UP. 1968.

Gale, Marion Perham. "Two Souls in Fire and Frost." *Poetry World* Jan. 1931: 26.

Gammel, Irene. *Baroness Elsa: Gender, Dada, and Everyday Modernity – A Cultural Biography.* Cambridge, MA: MIT P, 2003.

Gammel, Irene and Suzanne Zelazo. "'Harpsichords Metallic Howl—': The Baroness Elsa von Freytag-Loringhoven's Sound Poetry." *Modernism/modernity* 18.2 (2011): 224-5.

Garland, Marie. *The Potter's Clay.* New York: G. P. Putnam's Sons, 1917.

Georgakas, Dan. "About Tom Mooney." *Encyclopedia of the American Left.* 2nd ed. Eds., Mary Jo Buhle, Paul Buhle, and Dan Georgakas. New York: Oxford UP, 1998.

George, A. R. *Babylonian Topographical Texts.* Leuven, Belgium: Peeters, 1992.

Gibbon, Edward. *The History of the Decline and Fall of the Roman Empire.* Vol. 5. London: Strahan and Cadell, 1898.

Gibran, Khalil. *Jesus, The Son of Man.* New York: Alfred A. Knopf, 1928.

Gidlow, Elsa. *Elsa I Come With My Songs.* San Francisco: Booklegger, 1986.

Gilbert, Sandra and Susan Gubar. *No Man's Land: The Place of the Woman Writer in the Twentieth Century*. Vol. 1. New Haven: Yale UP, 1988.

Giles, Paul. *Antipodean America: Australasia and the Constitution of U.S. Literature*. Oxford: Oxford UP, 2014.

Gillespie, Abraham. "Textighter Eye-Ploy or Hothouse Bromdick?" *The Syntactic Revolution: Abraham Lincoln* Gillespie. Ed. Richard Milazzo. New York: Out of London, 1980.

Gilman, Charlotte Perkins. *The Man-Made World; or, Our Androcentric Culture*. New York: Charlton, 1914.

---. *Women and Economics*. Vol. 8. Boston: Small, Maynard and Co., 1898.

Gilmore, Mary. "No Foe Shall Gather Our Harvest." *The Australian Women's Weekly* 29 June 1940.

Giovannitti, Arturo. *Arrows in the Gale*. Riverside, CT: Hillacre Bookhouse, 1914.

Glassgold, Peter. *Anarchy! An Anthology of Emma Goldman's Mother Earth*. Berkeley: Counterpoint, 2001.

Gold, Michael. *Change the World!* 1934. Westport, CT: Greenwood, 2000.

---. "A New Program for Writers." *New Masses* Jan. 1930: 21.

---. "Out of the Fascist Unconscious." *The New Republic* 26 July 1933: 295.

Goldman, Emma. "Alexander Berkman's Last Days." *The Vanguard* [New York] Aug./Sept. 1936.

---. *Living My Life*. 1931. New York: Cosimo, 2011.

---. "Suffrage for Women." *Anarchism and Other Essays*. New York: Mother Earth Publishing, 1910.

Gordon, Linda. *The Moral Property of Women: A History of Birth Control Politics in America*. Champaign: U of Illinois P, 2007.

Gordon, Lois and Alan Gordon. *The Columbia Chronicles of American Life*. New York: Columbia UP, 1995.

Gornick, Vivian. *Emma Goldman: Revolution as a Way of Life*. New Haven: Yale UP, 2011.

Graham, Bessie. "Literary Prizes and Their Winners." New York: R. K. Bowker, 1946.

Greaves, C. Desmond. *Liam Mellows and the Irish Revolution*. London: Lawrence and Wishart, 1971.

Gregory, Horace. "The Promethean Symbol." *Saturday Review* 8 Mar. 1935.

Gregory, Horace and Marya Zaturenska. *A History of American Poetry, 1900–1940*. New York: Harcourt Brace, 1946.

Grossman, Mark. *Political Corruption in America: An Encyclopedia of Scandals, Power, and Greed*. 2nd ed. Amenia, NY: Grey House, 2008.

Guest, Barbara. *Herself Defined: The Poet H.D. and Her World*. New York: Doubleday, 1984.

Gurganus, Alan. "The Ghosts of Yaddo: What They Taught." *Yaddo: Making American Culture*. Ed. Micki McGee. New York: Columbia UP, 2008.

Gurko, Miriam. *Restless Spirit: The Life of Edna St. Vincent Millay*. New York: Thomas Y. Crowell, 1962.

Guttmann, Allen. "Ridge, Lola." *Notable American Women 1607–1950: A Biographical Dictionary*. Eds. Edward T. James, Janet Wilson James and Paul S. Boyer. Cambridge: Belknap, 1971.

Hackett, Francis. "Lola Ridge's Poetry." Rev. of *The Ghetto and Other Poems*, by Lola Ridge. *The New Republic* 16 Nov. 1918: 76–77.

Hahn, Emily. *Romantic Rebels: An Informal History of Bohemianism in America*. Boston: Houghton Mifflin, 1966.

Haines, Helen E. "Two Poets of Religious Faith." *All Star News* [Pasadena] 28 Dec. 1929.

Haley, James L. *Wolf: The Lives of Jack London*. New York: Basic Books, 2011.

Halio, Marcia Peoples. "The 'Beast with a Bone in his Throat' Emanuel Carnevali." *Italian Americana* 26.1 (Winter 2008).

Hamalian, Linda. *The Cramoisy Queen: A Life of Caresse Crosby*. Carbondale, IL: Southern Illinois UP, 2009.

---. *A Life of Kenneth Rexroth*. New York: Norton, 1992.

Hammer, Langdon. "Sex and the City." *New York Times* 18 July 1999.

Hanscombe, Gillian and Virginia L. Smyers. *Writing for Their Lives: The Modernist Women, 1910–1940*. Boston: Northeastern UP, 1987.

Hansen, Gladys, Richard Hansen and William Blaisdell. *Earthquake, Fire and Epidemic: Personal Accounts of the 1906 Disaster*. San Francisco: Untreed Reads, 2013

Hapgood, Hutchins. *An Anarchist Woman*. New York: Duffield, 1909.

---. *The Spirit of the Ghetto: Studies of the Jewish Quarter in New York*. New York: Funk and Wagnalls Co., 1902.

---. *A Victorian in the Modern World*. New York: Harcourt, Brace, 1939.

Harford, Lesbia. *The Poems of Lesbia Harford*. Sydney: Angus and Robertson, 1985.

Hartmann, Sadakichi. *Conversations with Walt Whitman*. New York: E. P. Coby, 1895.

Hartsock, Ernest. "Two Epic Crucifixions." *Bozart* Jan./Feb. 1930.

Harvey, R. "Sources of 'Literary' Copy for New Zealand Newspapers." *Bibliographical Society of Australia and New Zealand Bulletin* 27.3/4 (Jan. 2003).

Hastings, David. *Over the Mountains of the Sea: Life on the Migrant Ships, 1870–1885*. Auckland: Auckland UP, 2007.

Haught, James A. *2000 Years of Disbelief: Famous People with the Courage to Doubt*. Amherst, NY: Prometheus Books, 1996.

Hayden, Robert Earl. "The Poet and His Art." *Collected Prose*. Ann Arbor: U of Michigan P, 1984.

Heap, Jane. "Pounding Ezra." *The Little Review*. Oct. 1918: 38.

---. "Pied Piper." *The Little Review*. Oct. 1919.

---. "The Reader Critic: Concerning Else von Freytag-Loringhoven." *The Little Review*. Oct. 1919.

Hemingway, Ernest. "The Lady Poets With Foot Notes." *Der Querschnitt* Nov. 1924.

Henderson, Alice Corbin. "A New School of Poetry." *Poetry* May 1916: 103–105.

Henderson, Jeanne J. "Literary Awards." *Encyclopedia of Library and Information Science*. Vol. 16. Eds. Allen Kent, Harold Lancour and Jay E. Daily. New York: Marcel Dekker, 1975.

Henri, Robert. *The Art Spirit*. 1923. New York: Basic Books, 2007.

Hewitt, Andrew. *Fascist Modernism: Aesthetics, Politics, and the Avant-Garde*. Palo Alto: Stanford UP, 1993.

Hicks, Granville. "Illumination." *The Nation* 12 Mar. 1930: 303–304.

Hills, William Henry and Robert Luce. "The Manuscript Market." *The Writer* 31/32 (Jan./Feb. 1921).

Hively, Evelyn Helmick. *A Private Madness: The Genius of Elinor Wylie*. Kent, OH: Kent State UP, 2003.

Hodson, Janice. *William Floyd Estate Historic Furnishings Report, Volume 1: Historical Data*. Mastic, NY: National Park Service, 2011.

Hoenig, John M. "The Triangle Fire of 1911." *History Magazine* Apr./May 2005.

Hoffman, Frederick J., Charles Allen, and Carolyn F. Ulrich. *The Little Magazine: A History and a Bibliography*. Princeton: Princeton UP, 1947.

Holley, Margaret. *The Poetry of Marianne Moore: A Study in Voice and Value*. New York: Cambridge UP, 2009.

Homberger, Eric. *John Reed*. Manchester: Manchester UP, 1990.

---. *New York City: A Cultural History*. Northampton: Interlink Books, 2007.

Homer, William Innes. *Robert Henri and His Circle*. Ithaca: Cornell UP, 1969.

Hoyt, Helen. Introduction. *Others* Sept. 1916.

Hughes, Langston. "'We Want America to Really Be America for Everybody,' Says Langston Hughes." *The Daily Worker* 5 June 1939: 7.

Huneker, James Gibbons. *Steeplejack*. Vol. 2. New York: Charles Scribner's Sons, 1920.

Hunt, Caroline L. "The 'Amherst Movement.'" *La Follette's Weekly Magazine* 26 Aug. 1911: 6.

Hurt, James. "Sandburg's Lincoln within History." *The Journal of the Abraham Lincoln Association* 20.1 (Winter 1999): 55-65

Hutchinson, Percy. "Religious Fervor and Beauty in Miss Ridge's Poem." *New York Times Book Review* 8 Dec. 1929: 7.

Inge, M. Thomas. "The Dixie Limited: Writers on Faulkner and His Influence." *The Faulkner Journal of Japan* May 1999.

Irvine, Alexander. *Jack London at Yale*. Ed. State Secretary of the Socialist Party of Connecticut. Westwood, MA: Connecticut State Committee, 1906.

James, Henry. *The American Scene*. New York: Charles Scribner's Sons, 1946.

Jankowski, James P. and Israel Gershoni, eds. *Rethinking Nationalism in the Arab Middle East*. New York: Columbia UP, 1997.

Jarrell, Randall. "Fifty Years of American Poetry." *No Other Book: Selected Essays*. New York: Harper Collins, 1999.

Jeffers, Robinson. *Californians*. New York: Macmillan, 1916.

---. *The Collected Poetry of Robinson Jeffers: 1938–1962*. Palo Alto: Stanford UP, 1991.

Jenison, Madge. *Sunwise Turn: A Human Comedy of Bookselling*. New York: E. P. Dutton, 1923.

Jennison, Ruth. *The Zukofsky Era: Modernity, Margins, and the Avant-Garde*. Baltimore: Johns Hopkins UP, 2012.

Johns, Orrick Glenday. *Time of Our Lives: The Story of My Father and Myself*. Mechanicsburg, PA: Stackpole Sons, 1937.

Johnson, Craig. "The Great Hillerman Writing Legacy." *New Mexico Magazine* Dec. 2012.

Jones, Amelia. *Irrational Modernism*. Cambridge: MIT P, 2004.

Jones, Robert B. *Jean Toomer: Selected Essays and Literary Criticism*. Knoxville: U of Tennessee P, 2006.

Jones, Ted. *The French Riviera: A Literary Guide for Travelers*. London: Tauris, 2004.

Josephson, Matthew. *Life Among the Surrealists*. Boston: Holt, Rinehart and Winston, 1962.

---. "Made in America." *Broom* June 1922: 266–270.

Joughin, G. Louis and Edmund M. Morgan. *The Legacy of Sacco and Vanzetti*. New York: Harcourt, Brace, 1948.

Joyce, James. *Ulysses*. 1922. New York: Vintage, 1986.

Julius, Emanuel. "This Summer's Style in Poetry, or the Elimination of Corsets in Versifying." *New York Call* 16 May 1915.

Kahn, Albert E. *High Treason: The Plot Against the People*. New York: Lear, 1950

Karman, James, ed. *The Collected Letters of Robinson Jeffers with Selected Letters of Uma Jeffers*. Palo Alto: Stanford UP, 2009.

Katz, Esther, ed. *The Margaret Sanger Papers Electronic Edition: Margaret Sanger and The Woman Rebel, 1914–1916*. Columbia, SC: Model Editions Partnership, 2000.

Kaye, Jeremy. "The 'Whine' of Jewish Manhood: Re-reading Hemingway's Anti-Semitism, Re-imagining Robert Cohn." *The Hemingway Review* 25.2 (Spring 2006): 44–60.

Kellman, Steven G. Redemption: *The Life of Henry Roth*. New York: W. W. Norton, 2005.

Kelly, C. and J. Hamilton. "What kills patients with rheumatoid arthritis?" *Rheumatology* 46 (2007): 183-184.

Kempton, Murray. *Part of Our Time: Some Ruins and Monuments of the Thirties*. New York: Simon and Schuster, 1955.

Kennedy, David M. *Birth Control in America: The Career of Margaret Sanger*. New Haven, CT: Yale UP, 1971.

Kennedy, X. J. "Edna St. Vincent Millay's doubly burning candles." Rev. of *What My Lips Have Kissed: The Loves and Love Poems of Edna St. Vincent Millay*, by Daniel Mark Epstein, and *Savage Beauty: The Life of Edna St. Vincent Millay*, by Nancy Milford. *The New Criterion* 20 Sept. 2001: 96.

Kenton, Edna. *The Provincetown Players and the Playwrights' Theatre, 1915–1922*. Jefferson, NC: McFarland, 2004.

Kerman, Cynthia Earl. *The Lives of Jean Toomer: A Hunger for Wholeness*. Baton Rouge: Louisiana State UP, 1989.

Kershaw, Ian. *Hitler: A Biography*. New York: W. W. Norton, 2008.

King, Henry. *Society of Artists' Selection Committee, Sydney*. 1907. Photograph. Mitchell Library, State Library of New South Wales, Sydney.

Kinnahan, Linda A. Lola Ridge: Women as Workers and Women as Waste. "Economics and Gender in Mina Loy, Lola Ridge and Marianne Moore." *The Oxford Book of Modern and Contemporary American Poetry*. Ed. Cary Nelson. Oxford: Oxford UP, 2012.

Kirkpatrick, Peter. *The Seacoast of Bohemia: Literary Life in Sydney's Roaring Twenties*. Brisbane: U of Queensland P, 1992.

Kirsch, Adam. "The Mystic Word." *The New Yorker* 9 Oct. 2006.

Kissack, Terence. *Free Comrades: Anarchism and Homosexuality in the United States 1895–1917*. Oakland: AK Press, 2008.

Klehr, Harvey. *The Heyday of American Communism: The Depression Decade*. New York: Basic Books, 1984.

Kondritzer, Jeffry B. *Broom: An International Magazine of the Arts*. Diss. Indiana University, 1983. Ann Arbor: UMI, 1984. AAT 8417204.

Kornhauser, Elizabeth Mankin and Ulrich Kirkmaier. *Marsden Hartley* New Haven: Yale UP, 2002.

Kramer, Aaron. "Long Footnotes to Brief References: A Memoir." *Spring* 3 (1994): 80–86.

Kramer, Michael P. and Nan Goodman, eds. *The Turn Around Religion in America: Literature, Culture and the Works of Sacvan Bercovitch*. Surrey: Ashgate, 2011.

Krebs, Albin. "Malcolm Cowley, Writer, Is Dead at 90" *New York Times*. 29 Mar. 1989.

Kreymborg, Alfred. "An Early Impression of Wallace Stevens." *Trinity Review* 8 (1954): 12.

---. "Gertrude Stein—Hoax and Hoaxtress: A Study of the Woman Whose 'Tender Buttons' Has Furnished New York with a New Kind of Amusement." *The Morning Telegraph* 7 Mar. 1915: 6+.

---. *A History of American Poetry: Our Singing Strength*. New York: Tudor, 1934.

---. ed. *Others for 1919: an anthology of the new verse*. New York: Nicholas L. Brown, 1920.

---. "A Poet in Arms." Rev. of *The Ghetto and Other Poems*, by Lola Ridge. *Poetry* Oct./Mar. 1918/1919: 335–340.

---. "Remembering Genevieve Taggard." *Masses and Mainstream* Jan. 1949: 48–49.

---. *Troubadour: An Autobiography*. New York: Liveright, 1925.

Kropotkin, Pëtr. *Memoirs of a Revolutionist*. Boston and New York: Houghton Mifflin Co., 1899.

Kuersten, Ashlyn K. *Women and the Law: Leaders, Cases and Documents*. Santa Barbara: ABC-CLIO, 2003.

La Botz, Dan. "¡Viva la Revolución!" *Against the Current* July/Aug. 2010.

Laidler, Harry W. "Educating for a New Social Order and the League for Industrial Democracy." *New York Call* 18 June 1922: 6.

Laker, Jane [Alice Musgrave]. *Among the Reeds*. London: Cassel, 1933.

Laurie, Alison J. "Lady-Husbands and Kamp Ladies." Diss. Victoria University of Wellington, 2003.

Lawson, David. *Paul Morphy: Pride and Sorrow of Chess*. 1976. Lafayette: University of Louisiana at Lafayette, 2010.

Lawrence, D. H. *Selected Poems*. New York: New Directions, 1947.

Lawson, Henry. "A Song of Southern Writers." 1892. *The 1890s: Stories, Verse and Essays*. Ed. L. Cantrell. Brisbane: U of Queensland P, 1977.

Leavell, Linda. "'Frightening Disinterestedness': The Personal Circumstances of Marianne Moore's 'Marriage.'" *Journal of Modern Literature* 31.1 (Fall 2007): 64–79.

---. *Holding On Upside Down: The Life and Work of Marianne Moore*. New York: Farrar, Straus and Giroux, 2013.

Lebesque, Morvan. *Chroniques du Canard*. Paris: J. J. Pauvert, 1960.

Lees, William. "Suva, The Capital of the Fiji Islands." *Around the Coasts of Australia and Fiji: A Handbook of Picturesque Travel and General Information*. Australian United Steam Navigation Co. Ltd. Steamers, 1918.

Lefer, Diane. *Emma Lazarus*. NY: Chelsea House, 1988

Leggott, Michele. "The First Life: A Chronology of Ridge's Australasian Years." *BLUFF 06*. Te Rau Aroha Marae, Southland. 22 Apr. 2006. Poetry Symposium.

---. "Verses and Beyond: The Antipodean Poetry of Lola Ridge." *Ka Mate Ka Ora: A New Zealand Journal of Poetry and Poetics* 12 (Mar. 2013).

Leggott, Michele, Terese Svoboda and Fredrika Van Elburg. "Lola Ridge: A Chronology." Forthcoming.

Lehman, David, ed. *The Oxford Book of American Poetry*. Oxford: Oxford UP, 2006.

Leick, Gwendolyn. *A Dictionary of Ancient Near Eastern Mythology*. New York: Routledge, 1991.

Leick, Karen. "Popular Modernism: Little Magazines and the American Daily Press." *PMLA* 123.1 (Jan. 2008).

Lensing, George S. *Wallace Stevens: A Poet's Growth*. Baton Rouge: LSU P, 1991.

Leo, Vince. *Nobody Remembers Everything*. Minneapolis: National Association of Artists' Organizations, 1990.

Leon, Sol J. "Abraham Lincoln Gillespie: 1895-1950." *The Syntactic Revolution: Abraham Lincoln Gillespie*. Ed. Richard Milazzo. Out of London Press, 1980.

Leonard, John William. *Woman's Who's Who of America: A Biographical Dictionary of Contemporary Women of the United States and Canada*. Vol. 1. New York: American Commonwealth Company, 1914/15.

Levin, Joanna. *Bohemia in America, 1858–1920*. Stanford: Stanford UP, 2009.

Levitzke, Shannon. "Modernist Women in Print: Mina Loy, Kay Boyle, Mary Butts, and the Periodical Press." Diss. University of Georgia, 2011.

Lewis, David Lanier. *The Public Image of Henry Ford: An American Folk Hero*. Detroit: Wayne State UP, 1987.

Lewis, Henry Harrison. *Industrial Progress* Dec. 1922: 33.

Liber, Benzion. *A Doctor's Apprenticeship*. New York: Rational Living, 1956

Lifflander, Matthew L. "The Tragedy That Changed New York." *New York Archives* 11.1 (Summer 2011).

Lisella, Julia. "Lola Ridge's Firehead." *How2* 1.8 (Fall 2002).

Livingston, Rebecca. "When an American City Is Destroyed: The U.S. Military as First Responders to the San Francisco Earthquake a Century Ago." *Prologue Magazine* Spring 2006.

Lloyd, James B. "The Odyssey of Elsie Dunn." *The Library Development Review*. Eds. James Lloyd and Laura Simic. Knoxville: University of Tennessee, 1995/1996.

Loeb, Harold. *The Way It Was*. New York: Criterion Books, 1959.

Lombardo, Gian. Afterword. *Arrows in the Gale and Other Poems*. By Arturo Giovannitti. Niantic, CT: Quale, 2004.

London, Jack. *The Cruise of the Snark*. 1911. Washington, D.C.: National Geographic, 2003.

Los Angeles Township. Census Bureau. "Christian Orphanages." *Thirteenth Census of the United States*. 26 Apr. 1910. Sheet 13A.

Lowell, Amy. *Pictures of the Floating World*. New York: Macmillan, 1919.

Loy, Mina. "John Rodker's Frog." *The Little Review* Sept./Dec. 1920[a]: 57.

---. "Summer Night in a Florentine Slum." *Contact* Dec. 1920[b]: 6-7.

Ludington, Townsend, *Marsden Hartley: The Biography of an American Artist*. Cornell UP, 1992.

Ludlow, Fitz Hugh. *The Hasheesh Eater: Being Passages from the Life of a Pythagorean*. New York: Harper, 1857.

Luhan, Mabel Dodge. *Intimate Memories: Movers and Shakers*. New York: Harcourt, Brace, 1936.

Lynn, Kenneth Schuyler. *Hemingway*. Cambridge: Harvard UP, 1995.

M. D. "Sunrise and Red Earth." *The Nation* 9 Feb. 1920: 244.

MacDonald, David. "The Flood: Mesopotamian Archaeological Evidence." *Creation Evolution Journal* 8.2 (Spring 1988): 14-20.

MacFarquar, Neil. "Hussein's Babylon: A Beloved Atrocity." *New York Times* 19 Aug. 2003.

Mack, Louise. *The World is Round*. 1896. Auckland: Collins Angus and Robertson, 1993.

MacLeish, Archibald. *Archibald MacLeish: Reflections.* Eds. Bernard A. Drabeck, Helen E. Ellis and Richard Wilbur. Amherst: U of Massachusetts P, 1986.

---. *Poems.* Boston and New York: Houghton Mifflin, 1933.

Magarey, Susan. *Passions of the First Wave Feminists.* Sydney: UNSW P, 2001.

Mallory, Enid. *Robert Service: Under the Spell of the Yukon.* 2nd ed. Victoria: Heritage House Publishing Co., 2009.

Mander, Jane. *The Story of a New Zealand River.* London: John Lane, 1920.

Mansfield, Katherine. *Journal of Katherine Mansfield.* Ed. John Middleton Murry. London: Constable, 1954.

Mapother, Edward Dillon. "Poorer Districts." *Reports of Dr. Mapother's Papers on Subjects Concerning Public Health.* Fannin and Co., 1864.

Marcantonio, Vito. *I Vote My Conscience: The Debates, Speeches, and Writings of Congressman Vito Marcantonio.* Ed. Annette T. Rubinstein and Associates. New York: Vito Marcantonio Memorial, 1956.

Mariani, Paul. *William Carlos Williams: A New World Naked.* New York: Norton, 1990.

Marinetti, F.T. "The Foundation and Manifesto of Futurism." *Le Figaro* 20 Feb. 1909.

Markham, Edwin. "How I Wrote 'The Man with the Hoe.'" *The Dearborn Independent* 21 Nov. 1925.

Marks, Jeannette. *Genius and Disaster: Studies in Drugs and Genius.* New York: Adelphi Co., 1925.

---. *Thirteen Days.* New York: Albert and Charles Boni, 1929.

Marsh, Margaret S. *Anarchist Women 1870–1920.* Philadelphia: Temple UP, 1981.

Marshall, Bill. *France and the Americas: Culture, Politics, and History.* Vol. 2. Santa Barbara: ABC-CLIO, 2005.

Marshall, Peter. *Demanding the Impossible: A History of Anarchism.* Oakland: PM Press, 2010.

Marshall, Theresia Liemlienio. "New Zealand Literature in the Sydney Bulletin 1880–1930." Diss. University of Auckland, 1995.

Martens, Klaus. *Pioneering North America: Mediators of European Culture and Literature.* Würzburg, Germany: Königshausen and Neumann, 2000.

Maun, Caroline. *Mosaic of Fire.* Columbia: U of South Carolina P, 2012.

Max, Gerry. *Horizon Chasers: The Lives and Adventures of Richard Halliburton and Paul Mooney.* Jefferson, NC: McFarland, 2007.

May, Phillip Ross. *The West Coast Gold Rushes.* Christchurch: Pegasus, 1967.

McAlmon, Robert. *North America: Continent of Conjecture*. Paris: Contact Editions, 1929.

---. *Post-Adolescence*. Paris: Contact Publishing Company, 1923.

---. *Village. As It Happened Through a Fifteen Year Period*. Introduction by Edward N.S. Lorusso. 1924. Albuquerque: U of New Mexico P, 1990.

McAlmon, Robert and Kay Boyle. *Being Geniuses Together, 1920–1930*. Revised ed. San Francisco: North Point, 1984.

McCarron, Paul. *The Prints of Martin Lewis: A Catalogue Raisonné*. Bronxville, New York: M. Hausberg, 1995.

McCarthy, Laurette. *Walter Pach (1883–1958): The Armory Show and the Untold Story of Modern Art in America*. University Park, PA: Pennsylvania State UP, 2011.

McCormick, E. H. *Letters and Art in New Zealand*. Wellington: Dept. of Internal Affairs, 1940.

McDowell, Edwin. "Babar at 50, a Trunkful of Memories." *New York Times* 20 Nov. 1981.

McKenzie, Richard B. *Forgotten Home away from Home: The Forgotten History of Orphanages*. Jackson, TN: Encounter Books, 2009.

McKerrow, Bob. *Ebenezer Teichelmann: Cutting across Continents*. New Delhi: India Research, 2006.

McLintock, A.H., ed. *An Encyclopedia of New Zealand*. Wellington: Government Printer, 1966.

McQueen, Humphrey. *The Black Swan of Trespass: The Emergence of Modernist Painting in Australia to 1944*. Sydney: Alternative Pub. Coop. Ltd., 1979.

McWhirter, Cameron. *Red Summer: The Summer of 1919 and the Awakening of Black America*. London: St. Martin's Griffin, 2012.

Meade, Marion. *Dorothy Parker: What Fresh Hell Is This?* New York: Villard Books, 1989.

Mellen, Joan. *Kay Boyle: Author of Herself*. New York: Farrar, Straus and Giroux, 1994.

Meltzer, Milton. *Dorothea Lange: A Photographer's Life*. Syracuse, New York: Syracuse UP, 2000.

Meriwhether, James B. and Michael Millgate, eds. *Lion in the Garden: Interviews with William Faulkner, 1926–1962*. Lincoln: U of Nebraska P, 1980.

Milford, Nancy. *Savage Beauty: The Life of Edna St. Vincent Millay*. New York: Random House, 2001.

Miller, Arthur. *Timebends: A Life*. New York: Grove, 1987.

Millett, Kate. *Sexual Politics*. Champaign: U of Illinois P, 2000.

Mincham, Carolyn Jean. "A Social and Cultural History of the New Zealand Horse." Diss. Massey University, 2008.

Mirrlees, Hope. *Paris: A Poem*. Richmond: Hogarth, 1919.

Mittelman, Amy. *Brewing Battles: A History of American Beer*. New York: Algora, 2008.

Monroe, Harriet. "A Banner in the Wind." *Poetry* June 1927: 154.

---. "Down East." *Poetry* Apr./Sept. 1916: 86.

---. "A Farewell." *The Century Magazine* Feb. 1899: 578.

---. "The Greatest Living Poet." *Poetry* Mar. 1923: 325.

---. "Men or Women?" *Poetry* June 1920: 146-8.

Moore, Marianne. "The Art of Poetry No. 4." *The Paris Review* Summer/Fall 1961.

---. *Becoming Marianne Moore: Early Poems, 1907-1924*. Ed. Robin G. Schultze. Oakland: U of California P, 2002.

---. "Education of a Poet." *Writer's Digest* Oct. 1963: 35+.

---. *Marianne Moore: Selected Letters*. Ed. Bonnie Costello. New York: Penguin Classics, 1998.

---. "Radical." *Others* Mar. 1919: 15.

Moore, Tony. "Australia's Bohemian Tradition." Diss. University of Sydney, 2007.

---. *Dancing with Empty Pockets: Australia's Bohemians*. Sydney: Pier 9, 2012.

Moore, William. "Art and Artists." *The Brisbane Courier* 21 May 1927: 23.

Mora, Teresa Maria. "Finding Aid to the Thomas J. Mooney Papers." The Bancroft Library, UC Berkeley. Regents of the University of California, 2007.

Morgan. "New Poetic Heights Are Attained in 'Firehead.'" *Wilmington [North Carolina] Star-News* 4 May 1930.

Morris, Adelaide Kirby. *How to Live/What to Do: H.D.'s Cultural Poetics*. Champaign, IL: U of Illinois P, 2008.

Morton, Marian J. *Emma Goldman and the American Left: "Nowhere at Home."* New York: Twayne, 1992.

Mott, Frank Luther. *A History of American Magazines*, Vol. III: 1865–1885. 1938. Cambridge: Harvard UP, 1957.

Mount, Nick. "Expatriate Origins of Canadian Literature." *ReCalling Early Canada: Reading the Political in Literary and Cultural Production*. Ed. Jennifer Blair. Edmonton: U of Alberta P, 2005.

Mudgett, Ida Wright. "The Crying Need for Birth Control." *The Birth Control Review* Aug. 1918: 5.

Mühlberger, Detlef. *Hitler's Voice: Organisation and Development of the Nazi Party*. Bern: Peter Lang, 2004.

Munson, Gorham. *The Awakening Twenties: A Memoir-History of a Literary Period.* Baton Rouge: Louisiana State UP, 1985.

Nairn, Geoffrey and Geoffrey Serle, eds. *Australian Dictionary of Biography.* Vol. 7. Melbourne: Melbourne UP, 1979.

---. *Australian Dictionary of Biography.* Vol. 8. Melbourne: Melbourne UP, 1981.

---. *Australian Dictionary of Biography.* Vol. 9. Melbourne: Melbourne UP, 1983.

---. *Australian Dictionary of Biography.* Vol. 10. Melbourne: Melbourne UP, 1986.

Nash, George H. *The Conservative Intellectual Movement in America Since 1945.* Wilmington, DE: Intercollegiate Studies Inst., 1998.

Nathan, Jean. "Yaddo." *New York Times* 19 Sept. 1993.

Naumann, Francis M. *New York Dada 1915–1923.* New York: Harry N. Abrams, 1994.

Neill, James. *The Origins and Role of Same-Sex Relations in Human Societies.* Jefferson, NC: McFarland, 2011.

Nelson, Cary. Introduction. *Edwin Rolfe: Collected Poems.* By Edwin Rolfe. Champaign: U of Illinois P, 1997.

---. *Repression and Recovery: Modern American Poetry and the Politics of Cultural Memory, 1910–1945.* Madison: U of Wisconsin P, 1989.

---. *Revolutionary Memory: Recovering the Poetry of the American Left.* London: Routledge, 2003.

Neugenbauer, Roger and Debra Hartzell. "The Heroic Beginnings of Child Care." *Exchange* Nov./Dec. 2010.

Neville, John F. *Twentieth Century Cause Célèbre: Sacco, Vanzetti, and the Press, 1920–1927.* Westport, CT: Praeger, 2004.

New Zealand Parliament. House of Rep. *Parliamentary Debates, 19 June 1884.* 8th Parliament, 3rd sess. Wellington: G. Didsbury, 1884.

Newby, Richard, ed. *Kill Now, Talk Forever: Debating Sacco and Vanzetti.* Bloomington: AuthorHouse, 2006.

Newcomb, John Timberman. "The Footprint of the American Century: American Skyscrapers and Modernist Poems." *Modernism/modernity* 10.1 (Jan. 2003): 97–125.

---. *How Did Poetry Survive?* Champaign: U of Illinois P, 2012.

---. "The Woman as Political Poet: Edna St. Vincent Millay and the Mid-Century Canon." *Criticism* 37.2 (Spring 1995): 261–264.

Nielsen, Kim E. Appendix B. *Un-American Womanhood: Antiradicalism, Antifeminism, and the First Red Scare.* Columbus: Ohio State UP, 2001.

---. *The Radical Lives of Helen Keller*. New York: NYU P, 2004.

Niven, Penelope. *Thornton Wilder: A Life*. New York: Harper Perennial, 2013.

Nizer, Louis. *My Life in Court*. Eastford, CT: Martino Fine Books, 2012.

Nochlin, Linda. "Why Have There Been No Great Women Artists?" *ARTnews* Jan. 1971: 22–39+.

Norris, Benjamin Dwight. "An American Troubadour: The Career and Life of Alfred Kreymborg as a Modernist and Beyond." BA thesis. College of William and Mary, 2011.

North, Michael. *The Dialect of Modernism: Race, Language and Twentieth Century Literature*. Oxford: Oxford UP, 1998.

---. "Transatlantic Transfer: Little Magazines and Euro-American Modernism." *Modernist Magazines Conference*. De Montfort University, Leicester, UK. 12 July 2007. Keynote Address.

North Shore Historical Society. "Walk 9: Crow's Nest, Site of Old Mater Hospital to St. Leonard's Park." Pamphlet. Historic North Sydney: North Shore Historical Society, 1994.

Noyce, Diana Christine. "Coffee Palaces in Australia: A Pub With No Beer." *M/C Journal* 15.2 (2012).

O'Dowd, Bernard. "Poetry Militant: An Australian Plea for a Poetry of Purpose." Melbourne: Specialty Press, Art Printers, 1909.

Oja, Carol J. *Making Music Modern: New York in the 1920s*. Oxford: Oxford UP, 2003.

Olson, Stanley. *Elinor Wylie: A Life Apart*. New York: Dial, 1979.

Oppenheim, James. "The Story of the Seven Arts." American Mercury 20 (June 1930).

Orange, Claudia, ed. *Dictionary of New Zealand Biography: Vol. Two: 1870–1900*. Auckland: Auckland UP, 1993.

---. *Dictionary of New Zealand Biography: Vol. Four: 1921–1940*. Auckland: Auckland UP, 1998.

Overell, Richard. *Australian Fiction*. Rare Book Exhibition. *5 June–29 Sept. 2013*. Rare Book Collection, Monash University Library, Melbourne, Australia.

P. H. "A New Book of Poems by Lola Ridge." *The New York Times Book Review* 25 Aug. 1935: 2.

Page, David and Marianne Moore. *Marianne Moore*. Mankato, MN: The Creative Company, 1994.

Parisi, Joseph and Stephen Young. eds. *Dear Editor: A History of Poetry in Letters; The First Fifty Years, 1912–1962*. New York: W.W. Norton, 2002.

Parry, Albert. *Garretts and Pretenders: A History of Bohemianism in America*. New York: Cosimo, 2005.

Payne, Edward B. "The 'Hoe Man' on Trial." *Arena Magazine (Boston)*: July–Sept. 1899: 17–19.

Perlmutter, Ted. *Comparing Fordist Cities: The Logic of Urban Crisis and Union Response in Turin, 1950–1975, and Detroit, 1915–1945*. New York: NYU Working Paper Series, #31.

Pfeiffer, Kathleen. *Brother Mine: The Correspondence of Jean Toomer and Waldo Frank*. Champaign: U of Illinois P, 2010.

Phelan, Nancy. *The Romantic Lives of Louise Mack*. Brisbane: U of Queensland P, 1991.

Pinkerton, Jan and Randolph H. Hudson. *Encyclopedia of the Chicago Literary Renaissance: The Essential Guide to the Lives and Works of the Chicago Renaissance Writers*. New York: Facts on File, 2004.

Pitt, Marie. "Women in Art and Literature." *The Socialist* 11 Aug. 1911: 2.

Platts, Una. "Hughes, Joseph Leonard Wharton." *Nineteenth Century New Zealand Artists: A Guide and Handbook*. Christchurch: Avon Fine Prints, 1980.

Ploog, Randy. "The Double Life of Mitchell Dawson: Attorney and Poet." *Legal Studies Forum* Jan. 2005.

---. "A New Others: The Correspondence between William Carlos Williams and Mitchell Dawson." *William Carlos Williams Review* 30.1/2 2: 121–136.

Polenberg, Richard. *Fighting Faith: The Abrams Case, the Supreme Court, and Free Speech*. New York: Viking, 1987.

Pollack, Howard. *Aaron Copland: The Life and Work of an Uncommon Man*. Champaign, IL: U of Illinois P, 2000.

Pondrom, Cyrena. "Mirrlees, Modernism, and the Holophrase." *Time Present* 74/75 (Summer/Fall 2011): 4–6.

Pound, Ezra. "A Few Don'ts by an Imagiste." *Poetry* Mar. 1913.

---. *Pound/The Little Review: The Letters of Ezra Pound to Margaret Anderson: The Little Review Correspondence*. Ed. Melvin J. Friedman. New York: New Directions, 1989.

---. *The Selected Letters of Ezra Pound 1907–1941*. New York: New Directions, 1971.

---. "Small Magazines" *English Journal* 19.9 Nov 1930.

Powys, John Cowper. *Autobiography*. London: Faber, 2011.

Prince, Rosa. "Apple Founder Steve Jobs took drugs and abandoned his family." *The Telegraph* 10 Feb. 2012.

Pritchard, William H. "For Kay Boyle Nothing Succeeded Like Excess." *New York Times* 1 May 1994.

---. *Frost: A Literary Life Reconsidered*. Oxford: Oxford UP, 1985.

Quartermain, Peter, ed. *Dictionary of Literary Biography: American Poets 1880–1945*. Vol 54. Detroit: Gale, 1987.

Quidnunc. "An Irishman's Diary." *Irish Times* 2 June 1942.

Radner, Hillary, Alistair Fox and Irène Bessière, eds. *Jane Campion: Cinema, Nation, Identity*. Detroit: Wayne State UP, 2009.

Rainey, Lawrence. "Consuming Investments: Joyce's 'Ulysses.'" *James Joyce Quarterly* 33.4 (Summer 1996): 531–567.

---. *Institutions of Modernism: Literary Elites and Public Culture.* New Haven: Yale UP, 1998.

Rampersand, Arnold. "His Own Best Disciple." *New York Times* 30 Aug. 1987.

Ransom, John Crowe. "The Woman as Poet." *The World's Body.* New York: Scribner's Sons, 1938.

Rascoe, Burton. "Books and Writers of Books." *Chicago Daily Tribune* 12 Apr. 1919.

Raviglione, Mario C. and Richard J. O'Brien. "Tuberculosis." *Harrison's Principles of Internal Medicine.* 17th ed. McGraw-Hill Professional, 2008.

Reed, Brian. *Hart Crane: After His Lights.* Tuscaloosa: U of Alabama P, 2006.

---. *Phenomenal Reading: Essays on Modern and Contemporary Poetics.* Tuscaloosa: U of Alabama P, 2012.

Reed, James. *From Private Vice to Public Virtue: The Birth Control Movement and American Society Since 1830.* New York: Basic Books, 1978.

Reichert, William O. *Partisans of Freedom: A Study in American Anarchism.* Bowling Green, OH: Bowling Green UP, 1976.

Reilly, John. *Extracts of the Family Register of the Reillys of Kilnacret, Lergun, and Carrickfergus Branches, Ireland.* Transcript of unpublished notes, 1869.

Reilly, Nancy Hopkins. *Georgia O'Keeffe, A Private Friendship, Part 1: "Walking the Sun Prairie Land."* Santa Fe: Sunstone, 2007.

Rexroth, Kenneth. *American Poetry in the Twentieth Century.* New York: Herder, 1973.

---. "The Influence of French Poetry on American." *Assays: A Book of Essays.* New York: New Directions, 1961.

---. *Kenneth Rexroth and James Laughlin: Selected Letters.* Ed. Lee Bartlett. New York: W.W. Norton, 1991.

Reznikoff, Charles. "Rhythms." *The Poems of Charles Reznikoff: 1918–1975.* Ed. Seamus Cooney. Santa Rosa: Black Sparrow, 1989.

Rice, Philip Blair. "Not Easily Labeled." Rev. of *Dance of Fire*, by Lola Ridge. *The Nation* 5 June 1935: 662.

Rich, Adrienne. "At a Bach Concert." *A Change of World.* New Haven: Yale UP, 1951.

---. *The Fact of a Doorframe: Selected Poems, 1950–2001.* New York: Norton, 2002.

Ridge, Lola. "To Alexander Berkman 'In Solitary.'" *The Modern School* Apr./May 1919: 161–162.

---. "American Sagas." Rev. of *In the American Grain*, by William Carlos Williams. *The New Republic* 24 Mar. 1926: 148.

---. "Blossoms." *Others* Dec. 1918[a]: 4–5.

---. "Child and Wind." *The Bookman Anthology.* Ed. John Farrar. New York: George H. Doran Co., 1922.

---. "Clem o' the Creek." *Gunter's Magazine* Nov. and Dec. 1909: 109–142 and 162–183.

---. "Concerning Else von Freytag-Loringhoven." *The Little Review* Oct. 1919: 56.

---. Cover design. *Patriotism: A Menace to Liberty,* by Emma Goldman. 1908.

---. "Covered Roads." *The New Republic,* 23 June 1920, 131–132.

---. *Dance of Fire.* New York: Smith and Haas, 1935.

---. "The Dream Man." *New Zealand Illustrated Magazine* Dec. 1903: 247.

---. "Easter Dawn." *Others* July 1919: 15.

---. "Effects of Public School Education." *Everyman* Dec. 1914: 25–26.

---. "Evelyn Scott." Rev. of *Precipitations,* by Evelyn Scott. *Poetry* Mar. 1921: 334.

---. *Firehead.* New York: Payson and Clarke, 1929[a].

---. "Freedom." *Mother Earth* June 1911.

---. "Genesis." *New Masses* Mar. 1927[a]: 7.

---. *The Ghetto and Other Poems.* New York: B. W. Huebsch, 1918.

---. "A Heroic Rebel." Rev. of *Barabbas, a Dramatic Narrative,* by Sara Bard Field. *The Saturday Review of Literature* 31 Dec. 1932: 350.

---. "Hospital Nights." *Broom* Nov. 1921[a]: 70–71.

---. "The Insane." *The Bulletin* 11 Jan. 1906: 3.

---. "Kevin Barry." *New Masses* Mar. 1927[b]: 7.

---. "The Ladybird." *Gunter's Magazine* July 1909.

---. "Lake Kanieri." *New Zealand Illustrated Magazine* Nov. 1902: 131.

---. Letter to Jane Heap. *The Little Review* Jan. 1919: 63.

---. "Miss Taggard Encircles the Metaphysical Poets." *New York Evening Post* 5 Apr. 1930: 11.

---. "A Modern Mystic." *Saturday Review of Literature* 1 Sept. 1934, 82.

---. "Modernists." Rev. of *The American Caravan II,* ed. Alfred Kreymborg. *The Saturday Review of Literature* 29 June 1929[b]: 1145.

---. "Moscow Bells, 1917." *New Masses* Mar. 1927[c]: 7.

---. "Paul Strand." *Creative Art* 31 Oct. 1931: 312–316.

---. "The Plays of Alfred Kreymborg." *The Double Dealer* Nov. 1921[b]: 229.

---. "The Reader Critic: Concerning Else von Freytag-Loringhoven." *The Little Review.* Oct. 1919.

---. *Red Flag.* New York: Viking, 1927.

---. Rev. of *The Holy City*, by Selma Lagerlöf. *The American-Scandinavian Review* 6.4 (July/Aug. 1918): 222–223.

---. "Russian Women." *New Masses* Mar. 1927[d]: 7.

---. "Sonnet to Beauty." *Saturday Review* 7 June 1941.

---. "At Sundown." *The Bulletin* 10 Sept. 1903: 16.

---. *Sun-Up and Other Poems.* New York: Huebsch, 1920.

---. "Sweet Out of Hard." Rev. of *Honey Out of the Rock*, by Babette Deutsch. *The Nation* 25 Nov. 1925: 601.

---. "Think of Me Not with Sadness." *The Bulletin* 19 Apr. 1906: 40.

---. "The Trial of Ruth." *New Zealand Illustrated Magazine* May 1903: 343–348.

---. "Verses." Unpublished, 1905. TS item 1, CY reel 2694, frames 144–237. A.G. Stephens Papers, 1855–1933, Mitchell Library, State Library of New South Wales, Sydney.

---. "Woman and the Creative Will." 1919. *Occasional Papers in Women's Studies.* Ed. Elaine Sproat. U of Michigan P, 1981.

---. "The Woman with Jewels." *Others* Dec. 1918[b]: 3.

---. "On Zealanda." *The Canterbury Times* 25 Aug. 1892: 33.

Riis, Jacob. *How the Other Half Lives: Studies among the Tenements of New York.* New York: Scribner's Books, 1890.

Rilke, Ranier Maria. *Auguste Rodin.* New York: Sunwise Turn, 1919.

Rilke, Ranier Maria, Lou Andreas-Salomé. *Rilke and Andreas-Salomé: A Love Story in   Letters.* New York: W. W. Norton and Company. 2008.

Ritchie, John, ed. *Australian Dictionary of Biography.* Vol. 12. Melbourne: Melbourne UP, 1990.

Roba, William. "Marjorie Allen Seiffert, Moline Poet." *Western Illinois Regional Studies* 8.2 (Fall 1985): 5–16.

Roberts, Norma J., ed. *The American Collections.* Columbus Museum of Art, 1988.

Robinson, Roger and Nelson Wattie, eds. *The Oxford Companion to New Zealand Literature.* Oxford UP, 1998.

Robinson, Roxana. *Georgia O'Keeffe: A Life*. Lebanon, NH: UPNE, 1999.

Rodgers, Daniel T. *Atlantic Crossings: Social Politics in a Progressive Age*. Cambridge: Harvard UP, 2000.

Rodker, John. *Hymns*. London: The Ovid, 1920[a].

---. "The *Others* Anthology." *The Little Review* Sept./Dec. 1920[b]: 57.

Rosenthal, M. L. "The Unconsenting Spirit." *The Nation* 10 Nov. 1956: 412–413.

Rothbard, Murray N. *America's Great Depression*. 5th ed. Auburn, AL: Ludwig von Mises Institute, 2000.

Rubin, Joan Shelley. *Songs of Ourselves: The Uses of Poetry in America*. Boston: Belknap, 2010.

Rudnick, Lois Palken. *Mabel Dodge Luhan: New Woman, New Worlds*. Albuquerque:
    U of New Mexico P, 1987.

---. *Utopian Vistas: The Mabel Dodge Luhan House and the American Counterculture*. Albuquerque:
    U of New Mexico P, 1998.

Rudwick, Elliot M. *Race Riot at East St. Louis, July 2, 1917*. Champaign, IL: U of Illinois P, 1982.

Rukeyser, Muriel. "Poem of Childhood." *Dynamo* May/June 1935: 23.

---. "Who in One Lifetime" [renamed]. *Out of Silence: Selected Poems by Muriel Rukeyser*. Ed. Kate
    Daniels. Evanston, IL: Northwestern UP, 1994.

Rusch, Frederick. "Form, Function and Creative Tension in Cane: Jean Toomer and the need for the
    avant-garde." *Melus* 17.4 (1991).

Rydsjo, Delia and AnnKatrin Jonsson. "Published by Us, Written by Us, Read by Us: Little Magazine
    Networks." *Global Review* 1.1 (2013): 39-65.

Salemson, Harold J., ed. *Tambour*. Madison: U of Wisconsin P, 2002.

Salter, Mary Jo. "The Heart is Slow to Learn." *The New Criterion* Apr. 1992.

Samson, Gloria Garrett. *The American Fund for Public Service: Charles Garland and Radical Philanthropy,
    1922–1941*. Westport, CT: Greenwood, 1996.

Sanger, Margaret. "Birth Control in America." *Freedom: A Journal of Anarchist Communism*. July 1915.

---. *Margaret Sanger: An Autobiography*. 1938. Whitefish, MT: Kessinger, 2010

Sarason, Bertram. "Harold Loeb." *Dictionary of Literary Biography*. Vol 4. Ed. Karen Lane Rood. Detroit:
    Gale, 1980.

Saul, Norman E. *The Life and Times of Charles R. Crane, 1858–1939: American Businessman,
    Philanthropist, and a Founder of Russian Studies in America*. Lanham, MD: Lexington Books, 2012.

Scarry, Elaine. *The Body in Pain*. New York: Oxford UP, 1985.

Scates, Bruce. *A New Australia: Citizenship, Radicalism and the First Republic*. Cambridge UP, 1997.

Schaffner, Perdita. "Sketch of H.D.: The Egyptian Cat." In *Hedylus*, by Hilda Doolittle. Redding Ridge, CT: Black Swan Books, 1980.

Schlesinger, Arthur M. Introduction. *The Legacy of Sacco and Vanzetti*. By Louis Joughin and Edmund M. Morgan. Princeton: Princeton UP, 1976.

Scholten, Catherine M. "Field, Sara Bard." *Notable American Women: The Modern Period*. 6th ed. Cambridge: Belknap, 1993.

Schulman, Grace. "With Dearest Love, Marianne." *New York Times* 16 Nov. 1997.

Schulz, William F. *Making the Manifesto: The Birth of Religious Humanism*. Boston: Skinner House Books, 2004.

Scott, Cyril Kay. *Sinbad: A Romance*. New York: Thomas Seltzer, 1923.

Scott, Evelyn. "On Lola Ridge." *Firehead*. By Lola Ridge. New York: Payson and Clarke, 1930.

---. *Precipitations*. New York: N.L. Brown, 1920.

---. *The Wave*. New York: Jonathan Cape and Harrison Smith, 1929.

Scott, William B. and Peter M. Rutkoff. *New York Modern: The Arts and the City*. Baltimore: Johns Hopkins UP, 2001.

Scruggs, Charles and Lee VanDemarr. *Jean Toomer and the Terrors of American History*. Philadelphia: U of Pennsylvania P, 1998.

Scura, Dorothy M. Afterword. *Escapade*. By Evelyn Scott. Charlottesville: UP of Virginia, 1995.

Sedgwick, Charles B. "The Fall of San Francisco." *American Builder's Review* July 1906.

Sehgal, Parul. "Less is Moore." *Book Forum* Sept./Oct./Nov. 2013.

Selzer, Jack. *Kenneth Burke in Greenwich Village: Conversing with the Moderns, 1915–1931*. Madison: U of Wisconsin P, 1996.

Serle, Geoffrey. *Australian Dictionary of Biography*. Vol. 11. Melbourne: Melbourne UP, 1988.

Shone, Steve. *American Anarchism*. Boston and Leiden: Brill, 2014.
Sinclair, Upton. *Boston*. 1928. Cambridge: Robert Bentley, 1978.

---. "A Sculptor of Revolt," *Independent* 16 Oct. 1913: 128.

Sisters of Mercy Westland Centenary Executive Committee. *Mercy in Westland, 1878–1978*. Hokitika: 1978.

Skaggs, Merrill Maguire. *Axes: Willa Cather and William Faulkner*. Lincoln: U of Nebraska P, 2007.

Smethurst, James Edward. *The New Red Negro: The Literary Left and African American Poetry, 1930–1946*. Oxford: Oxford UP, 1999.

Smith, Matthew Hale. *Sunshine and Shadow in New York*. Hartford: J.B Burr, 1869.

Smith-Rosenberg, Carroll. *Disorderly Conduct: Visions of Gender in Victorian America*. New York: Knopf, 1985.

Smoller, Sanford J. *Adrift Among Geniuses: Robert McAlmon, Writer and Publisher of the Twenties*. University Park: Penn State UP, 1974.

Sontag, Susan. *Against Interpretation*. New York: Farrar, Straus and Giroux, 1966.

---. *Illness as Metaphor*. New York: Farrar, Straus and Giroux, 1978.

Spanier, Sandra Whipple. *Kay Boyle: Artist and Activist*. Carbondale, IL: Southern Illinois UP, 1986.

Sparrow, Jeff. "Render it Barely." *Sydney Review of Books* 16 Sept. 2014.

Spears, Timothy B. *Chicago Dreaming: Midwesterners and the City, 1871–1919*. Chicago: U of Chicago P, 2005.

Sproat, Elaine. "Information about Poet." *Sydney Morning Herald* 27 Aug. 1978: 17.

"S. S. Finance Manifest." 20 Mar. 1908. Washington, DC: National Archives. Microfilm, series T 714, roll 1086.

"S. S. Moana List of Alien Passengers." Washington, DC: National Archives. Microfilm, series M 1464, roll 62.

Stafford, R. S. *The Tragedy of the Assyrians*. 1935. Piscataway, NJ: Gorgias, 2006.

Stansell, Christine. *American Moderns: Bohemian New York and the Creation of a New Century*. Princeton: Princeton UP, 2009.

Steed, J. P. "Broom." *Encyclopedia of the Harlem Renaissance*. Eds. Cary D. Wintz and Paul Finkelman. New York: Routledge, 2004.

Steele, Richard W. *Free Speech in the Good War*. Basingstoke: Palgrave Macmillan, 1999.

Stein, Leon. *The Triangle Fire*. New York: A Carroll and Graf/Quicksilver Book, 1962.

Steinitz, William. *The Steinitz Papers: Letters and Documents of the First World Chess Champion*. Ed. Kurt Landsberger. Jefferson, NC: McFarland , 2002.

Stephens, A. G. "Canterbury Bells." *Bulletin* 1 Dec. 1900: Red Page.

Sternlicht, Sanford. *The Tenement Saga: The Lower East Side and Early Jewish American Writers*. Madison: Terrace Books, 2004.

Stevens, Wallace. *Collected Poetry and Prose*. New York: Library of America, 1997.

Stone, Fred F. "Poet Has Perfect Command of a Most Treasured Theme." *Ohio State Journal* 19 Feb. 1930.

Stone, Idella Purnell, Felix Salten and Walt Disney Productions. *Walt Disney's Bambi*. Boston: D.C. Heath, 1944.

Stone, Lee Alexander. *The Story of Phallicism*. Chicago: P. Covici. 1927.

Stringer, Jenny, ed. *Oxford Companion to Twentieth Century Literature in English*. Oxford: Oxford UP, 1996.

Strobel, Marion. "Reviewer Bows to Greatness of 'Dance of Fire.'" Rev. of *Dance of Fire*, by Lola Ridge. *Chicago Tribune* 13 July 1935: 6.

Stubbs, Tara. "'Irish by Descent'? Marianne Moore's American-Irish Inheritance." *Irish Journal of American Studies* 1 (Spring 2009).

Studevant, John U. "Mr. Garland World-Reform Fund Comes Home to Roost Pretty Well Plucked." *San Antonio Light* 3 Aug. 1941: 7.

Swan, Gilbert. "In New York." *Syracuse Herald* 19 Dec. 1929: 8.

Symes, Lillian and Clement Travers. *Rebel America: The Story of Social Revolt in the United States*. New York: Harper, 1934.

Syssoyeva, Kathryn Mederos and Scott Proudfit, eds. *A History of Collective Creation*. Basingstoke: Palgrave Macmillan, 2013.

Szuberla, Guy. "Zangwill's The Melting Pot Plays Chicago." *MELUS* 20.3 (Autumn 1995): 3–20.

Taggard, Genevieve, ed. *Circumference: Varieties of Metaphysical Verse, 1456–1928*. New York: Covici Friede, 1929.

---. *Collected Poems: 1918–1938*. Harper, 1938.

---. "Review of Edna St. Vincent Millay." *Equal Rights* 14 Mar. 1925: 35.

Talbott-Tubbs, H.A. "Introductory." *New Zealand Illustrated Magazine* 1 Oct. 1899.

Tan, Cheryl Lu-Lien. "A Chance to Peek Inside Yaddo," *New York Times* 31 Aug. 2011.

Tante, Dilly. *Living Authors: A Book of Biographies*. New York: Wilson, 1935.

Tate, Allen. "Miss Millay's Sonnets." *New Republic* 6 May 1931: 335-336.

"Taunted to Disaster," *Advertiser and Adelaide*. 18 June 1931.

Taylor, George Augustus. *Those Were The Days*. Sydney: Tyrell's, 1918.

Taylor, Georgina. *H.D. and the Public Sphere of Modernist Women Writers 1913–1946: Talking Women*. Oxford: Oxford UP, 2001.

Thesing, William B., ed. *Robinson Jeffers and a Galaxy of Writers: Essays in Honor of William H. Nolte*. Columbia: U of South Carolina P, 1995.

Thompson, Lawrence and R.H. Winnick. *Robert Frost: The Later Years, 1938–1963*. New York: Holt, Rhinehart and Winston, 1976.

Tietjens, Eunice. *The World at My Shoulder*. New York: MacMillan, 1938.

Tippens, Sherrill. "Genius and Hijinks at 7 Middagh Street." *New York Times* 6 Feb. 2005.

Toomer, Jean. *Cane*. 1923. New York: Norton, 2011.

---. *The Collected Poems of Jean Toomer*. Chapel Hill: U of North Carolina P, 1988.

---. "A Drama of the Southwest." TS. Jean Toomer Papers, Beinecke Rare Book and Manuscript Library, Yale University, New Haven, CT.

---. "Reflections on the Race Riots." *New York Call* 2 Aug. 1919.

Topliss, Helen. *Modernism and Feminism: Australian Women Artists 1900–1940*. Roseville East, NSW, Australia: Craftsman House, 1996.

Trager, James. *The New York Chronology: The Ultimate Compendium of Events, People, and Anecdotes from the Dutch to the Present*. New York: Collins Reference, 2003.

Transactions from the Society of Biblical Archaeology. Vols. 5–6. London: Society of Biblical Archaeology, 1877.

Trent, Lucia and Ralph Cheney. *America Arraigned*. New York: Dean and Co., 1928.

Tuchman, Maurice, ed. *The Spiritual in Art: Abstract Painting 1890–1985*. New York: Abbeville, 1986.

Tucker, Benjamin R. "Must We Pay for Life?" *Liberty* 18 Mar. 1893: 2–3.

---. "State Socialism and Anarchism: How far they agree and wherein they differ." *Liberty* 10 Mar. 1888: 2–3+.

Turner, Catherine. *Marketing Modernism Between the Two World Wars*. Amherst: U of Massachusetts P, 2003.

Turner, Darwin T., ed. *The Wayward and the Seeking: A Collection of Writings by Jean Toomer*. Washington, DC: Howard UP, 1983.

Tyrer, Patricia Jean. "Evelyn Scott: The Forgotten American Modernist." Diss. Texas Tech University, 1998.

United States Census Bureau. Federal Census. 1930. 10th Assembly District of NYC. Washington: GPO, 1930.

United States. Cong. Senate. C.I.O Political Action Committee. *UnAmerican Propaganda Activities*. 78th Cong., 2nd sess. Washington: GPO, 1944.

United States. General Records of the Department of State. *Passport Applications, January 2, 1906 – March 31, 1925*. David Lawson Passport. Washington, DC: National Archives. Microfilm, series M 1490, roll 2627.

United States. Immigration and Naturalization Service. "City of Puebla Passenger List." Washington, DC: National Archives. Microfilm, series M 1412, roll 4.

United States. Immigration and Naturalization Service. "Passenger and Crew Lists of Vessels Arriving at New York, NY, 1897–1957." Washington, DC: National Archives. Microfilm, series T 715, roll 1086.

United States. Selective Service System. "WWI Draft card for David Lawson." 12 Sept. 1918. Washington, DC: National Archives. Microfilm, series FHL 31-9-154 C, roll 1786815.

Unterecker, John. *Voyager: A Life of Hart Crane*. New York: Farrar, Straus, and Giroux, 1969.

Untermeyer, Louis. "Alfred Kreymborg." *Proceedings of the American Academy of Arts and Letters and the National Institute of Arts and Letters*. Second ser. no. 17. New York: American Academy of Arts and Letters Special Collections, 1967.

---. "Arteried with Light." Rev. of *Firehead*, by Lola Ridge. *The Saturday Review of Literature* 28 Dec. 1929: 599.

---. "China, Arabia, and Hester Street." Rev. of *The Ghetto and Other Poems*, by Lola Ridge. *The New York Evening Post* 1 Feb. 1919: sec. 3: 1+.

---. *The New Era in American Poetry*. New York: Henry Holt, 1919.

---. "The New Poetry." *American Mercury* Aug. 1935: 505–506.

Vandereycken, Walter and Ron Van Deth. *From Fasting Saints to Anorexic Girls: The History of Self-Starvation*. New York: NYU P, 1994.

Van Doren, Carl. *Three Worlds*. London: Jonathan Cape, 1937.

Van Doren, Mark. Introduction. *Prize Poems, 1913–1929*. Ed. Charles A. Wagner. New York: Charles Boni, 1930.

Vázquez, Margarita, José L. Olivares, Jesús Fleta, Isaac Lacambra, and Mariano González. "Cardiac Disorders in Young Women With Anorexia Nervosa." *Revista Española de Cardiología* 56.7 (July 2003): 669-73.

Veblen, Thorstein. "Industry and the Captains of Industry." *The Dial* 31 May 1919: 552.

Vendler, Helen. "The Terrible Details of Hart Crane's Life." *New York Times* 20 July 1969.

Vickery, Ann. *Stressing the Modern: Cultural Politics in Australian Women's Poetry*. London: Salt, 2007.

Vickery, Ann and Maryanne Dever. *Australian Women Writers (1900-1950)*. Rare Book Exhibition. 29 Mar. - 31 July 2007. Rare Book Collection, Monash University Library, Melbourne, Australia.

Von Freytag-Loringhoven, Elsa. "The Art of Madness." *The Little Review* Jan. 1920: 28-29.

---. "The Cast-Iron Lover." *The Little Review* Sept. 1919: 3–11.

---. "Thee I call Hamlet of the Wedding Ring." Rev. of *Kora in Hell*, by William Carlos Williams. *The Little Review* Jan./Mar. [Part I] and Autumn [Part II] 1921.

Wald, Alan M. *Exiles From a Future Time: The Forging of the Mid-Twentieth Century Literary Left.* Chapel Hill: U of North Carolina P, 2002.

---. *Writing from the Left: New Essays on Radical Culture and Politics.* New York: Verso, 1994.

Walker, Cheryl. *Masks Outrageous and Austere: Culture, Psyche and Persona in Modern Women Poets.* Bloomington: Indiana UP, 1991.

Wall, O. A. *Sex and Sex Worship (Phallic Worship): A Scientific Treatise on Sex, its Nature and Function, and its Influence on Art, Science, Architecture, and Religion.* St. Louis: C.V. Mosby Co., 1920.

Walton, Eda Lou. "The Poetry of Lola Ridge." *New York Herald Tribune Books* 12 May 1935.

Warne, Catherine. *Pictorial History: Lower North Shore.* Sydney: Kingsclear Books, 2005.

Warren, Robert Penn. *Selected Letters of Robert Penn Warren.* Vol. 1. Baton Rouge: LSU P, 2000.

Watson, Bruce. *Sacco and Vanzetti: The Men, the Murderers, and the Judgment of Mankind.* New York: Penguin, 2008.

Weaver, J.V.A. "Elfin and Child." *The Bookman.* Vol. 53. Mar. 1921. 261.

Weber, Brom. *Hart Crane: A Biographical and Critical Study.* London: Bodley, 1948.

Weimer, David R. "On Edwin Markham's 'The Man with the Hoe.'" *Studies in American Culture: Dominant Ideas and Images.* Ed. Joseph J. Kwiat and Mary C. Turpie. Minneapolis: U of Minnesota P, 1960.

Weir, David. *Anarchy and Culture: The Aesthetic Politics of Modernism.* Amherst: U of Massachusetts P, 1997.

Wells-Barnett, Ida B. *The East St. Louis Massacre: The Greatest Outrage of the Century.* Chicago: Negro Fellowship Herald, 1917.

Westley, F. D. "Straw for Silence." *The Spectator* 8 May 1959.

Westropp, Hodder M. and C. Staniland Wake. *Phallicism in ancient worship in the religions of antiquity.* With an introduction, additional notes, and an appendix, by Alexander Wilder. New York : J. W. Bouton, 1875.

Wetzsteon, Ross. *Republic of Dreams: Greenwich Village: The American Bohemia, 1910–1960.* New York: Simon and Schuster, 2003.

Whalan, Mark, ed. *The Letters of Jean Toomer, 1919–1924.* Knoxville: U of Tennessee P, 2006.

Wheeler, Belinda. "At the Center of American Modernism: Lola Ridge's Politics, Poetics, and Publishing." MA thesis. Indiana University, 2008.

---. "Lola Ridge's Pivotal Editorial Role at Broom." *PMLA* 127.2 (Mar. 2012): 283-91.

Wheeler, Edward J. *Current Literature.* Vol. 47. New York: Current Literature, 1909.

Wheelock, John Hall. *The Last Romantic: A Poet Among Publishers*. Columbia: U of South Carolina P, 2002.

Whisenhunt, Eloise Arnold. "It is a Privilege to See So Much Confusion: Marianne Moore and Revision." Diss. University of Alabama, 2009.

White, Eric. *Transatlantic Avant-Gardes: Little Magazines and Localist Modernism*. Edinburgh: Edinburgh UP, 2013.

White, Hannah. "The Sunwise Turn: The Bookshop Plus." *The Independent* 13 Nov. 1916: 280.

White, Mary Wheeling. *Fighting the Current: The Lifework of Evelyn Scott*. Baton Rouge: Louisiana State UP, 1998.

White, Unk. "My Rendezvous with Reminiscence." *Second Unk White's Laugh Parade*. Sydney: Frank Johnson, 1941.

Whiteford, Peter. "Ursula Bethell, 1874–1945." *Kōtare* 7.3 (2008): 101.

Whitelaw, Nancy. *Margaret Sanger: "Every Child a Wanted Child."* Bloomington, IN: iUniverse, 2001.

Whitman, Walt. *Leaves of Grass*. Philadelphia: David McKay, 1900.

Widdemer, Margaret. *A Tree with a Bird in it: a symposium of contemporary American poets on being shown a pear-tree on which sat a grackle*. New York: Hartcourt Brace, 1922.

Williams, Raymond. *Politics of Modernism: Against the New Conformists*. New York: Verso, 2007.

Williams, Tennessee. 26 May 1936. *Notebooks*. New Haven: Yale UP, 2006.

Williams, Thomas J. *I've Written to Browne, or, A Needless Stratagem: A Comedietta in One Act*. Boston: Charles H. Spencer, 1867.

Williams, William Carlos. "The Art of Poetry No. 6." *The Paris Review* Summer/Fall 1964.

---. *Autobiography of William Carlos Williams*. New York: New Directions, 1951.

---. "Belly Music." *Others* July 1919[a]: 25–32.

---. *The Collected Poems of William Carlos Williams: 1939–1962*. Eds. A. Walton Litz, Christopher MacGowan, and John MacGowan. New York: New Directions, 1991.

---. "Gloria!" *Others* July 1919[b]: 3–4.

---. "The Great Opportunity": *Egoist* 3, Sept. 1916.

---. *The Selected Letters of William Carlos Williams*. Ed. John C. Thirlwall. New York: New Directions, 1985.

Wilson, Edmund. "An Appeal to Progressives" *New Republic* 14 Jan 1931, 238.

---. "The Aesthetic Upheaval in France." *Vanity Fair* Feb. 1922: 49+.

Wood, Clement. "I-Sores is the Modern Substitute for Poetry." *The Kansas City* Star 2 Apr. 1919: 26.

Wood, Ellen Meiksins. *Mind and Politics: An Approach to the Meaning of Liberal and Socialist Individualism.* Oakland: U of California P, 1972.

Woodford, Arthur M. *Tashmoo Park and the Steamer Tashmoo.* Mount Pleasant, SC: Arcadia Publishing, 2012.

Woodson, Jon. *To Make a New Race: Gurdjieff, Toomer, and the Harlem Renaissance.* Jackson, MS: UP of Mississippi. 1999.

Woolf, Virginia. *A Room of One's Own.* Richmond: Hogarth, 1929.

Worth, Richard. *The San Francisco Earthquake.* New York: Facts on File, 2005.

Wright, Franz. "A Conversation with Franz Wright." *Image* Fall 2006.

Young, Art. "He Stirreth Up the People." Cover Illustration. *The Masses* Dec. 1913.

---. *His Life and Times.* New York: Sheridan House, 1939.

Young, William and David E. Kaiser. *Postmortem: New Evidence in the Case of Sacco and Vanzetti.* Amherst: U of Massachusetts P, 1985.

Yousif, Bassam. *Human Development in Iraq, 1950–1990.* New York: Routledge, 2012.

Zaturenska, Marya. *New Selected Poems of Marya Zaturenska.* Syracuse UP, 2002.

Zinn, Howard. "Discovering John Reed." *Howard Zinn on History.* New York: Seven Stories, 2000.

Zmora, Nurith. *Orphanages Reconsidered: Childcare Institutions in Progressive Era Baltimore.* Philadelphia: Temple UP, 1994.

Zweig, Paul. *Walt Whitman: The Making of the Poet.* New York: Basic Books, 1984.

*   *   *

WEB SOURCES

Abbott, Karen. "A Chess Champion's Dominance—and Madness." *Smithsonian Institution.* smithsonianmag.com. 12 Dec. 2011.

"Abraham Lincoln Gillespie." *The PIP (Project for Innovative Poetry) Blog.* Blogger, 20 June 2010.

Aiuto, Russell. "The Profession of Executioner: Robert G. Elliott." *Crime Library.* Turner Entertainment Networks, 2014.

Aliperti, Cliff. "History of the *Saturday Review of Literature* with a look inside 1950's issues." *CollectingOldMagazines.com.* Immortal Ephemera, 2014.

"Anna Morgan (teacher)." *Wikipedia, The Free Encyclopedia*. Wikimedia Foundation, Inc. 1 Feb. 2015.

"Archaeologists and Scholars." *Smithsonian Olmec Legacy*. Smithsonian Institute, 2015.

"Arturo Giovannitti, the 'Bard of Freedom.'" *ItalyHeritage*. 2015. italyheritage.com/great-italians/history/giovannitti-arturo.htm.

Austin, Dan. "Cass Tech." *Historic Detroit*. HistoricDetroit.org, 2015. historicdetroit.org/building/cass-tech-high-school-old/.

"The Back of the Pipes, Dublin." *Wikipedia, The Free Encyclopedia*. Wikimedia Foundation, Inc., 19 Nov. 2013.

"Baptism, Marriage and Burial results for Rose Emily Ridge of Dublin." *IrishGenealogy.ie*. 2015.

"Baroness Elsa Biographical Sketch." *Baroness Elsa von Freytag-Loringhoven Digital Library*. University of Maryland Libraries, 2004.

"Battle of Gettysburg." *Hawkesbury Herald* 31 Oct. 1902.

Bellis, Mary. "The History of 7up - Charles Leiper Grigg." About.com. About.com, 21 Dec. 2013. http://inventors.about.com/library/inventors/bl7up.htm.

Benfey, Christopher. "Emily Dickinson's Secret Lover." Slate Magazine. The Slate Group, 9 Oct. 2008.

"Birth Control: Emma Goldman, 1869–1940." *Women of Valor*. Jewish Women's Archive, 2014.

"Birth Control Organizations Birth Control Review." *Margaret Sanger Papers Project*. New York University.

"Birth Control Pioneer." *The Emma Goldman Papers*. Berkeley Digital SunSite, 2 July 2003.

Bishop, Catherine. "Women of Pitt Street 1858." *Dictionary of Sydney*. dictionaryofsydney.org, 2011.

Brent, Jonathan and Lyudmila Sholokhova. Translators Note. "Cloud in Trousers." By Vladimir Mayakovsky. *Conjunctions Literary Magazine*.

Bright, Kimberly J. "Frida Kahlo's Secret Revenge Affair with Leon Trotsky." dangerousminds.net. 13 Nov. 2013.

Brooks, Mike. "Gallery of Paintings: A Few Small Nips." fridakahlofans.com. Aug. 2005.

Brunner, Edward and Cary Nelson. "Kay Boyle's Life." *Modern American Poetry Site*. University of Illinois at Urbana-Champaign.

Brunton, Warwick. "Mental Health Services: Lunatic Asylums, 1840s to 1900s." *The Encyclopedia of New Zealand*. New Zealand Ministry for Culture and Heritage, 13 July 2012.

Burt, Stephen. "Paper Trail: The true legacy of Marianne Moore, modernist monument." *Slate Magazine*. The Slate Group, 11 Nov. 2003.

Connolly, Karen. "75 years on, executed Reichstag arsonist finally wins pardon." *The Guardian*. theguardian.com. 12 Jan. 2008.

Cowen, Dick. *The Garland Book*. Unpublished TS. Yale Law Documents Online. documents.law.yale.edu/sites/default/files/garland%20unpublished%20bio.pdf.

Coy, Peter. "Lessons from the Credit-Anstalt Collapse." *BloombergBusiness*. 20 Apr. 2011.

Crannell, Linda. "California Poor House History." poorhousestory.com. 2012.

Curdy, Averill. "Poetry: A History of the Magazine." *Poetry Foundation*. poetryfoundation.org. 2013.

D'Attilio, Robert. "La Marcia del Dolore / The March of Sorrow: The Funeral of Sacco and Vanzetti." *The Sacco and Vanzetti Commemoration Society*. saccoandvanzetti.org. Aug. 2013.

"David Lawson." *The History and Culture of Chess*. Sarah's Chess Journal. edochess.ca. Aug. 2005.

"Death of Katherine Mansfield: 9 January 1923." *New Zealand History*. New Zealand Ministry for Culture and Heritage, 17 Nov. 2014.

Derby, Mark. "Ridge, Lola: Anarchist and Poet." libcom.org, 4 Nov. 2009.

Doherty, Sean. "Sean Doherty//Composer." *Sean Doherty Music*. seandohertymusic.co.uk/about/. 2015.

Dunphy, Melissa. "L-O-L-A Lola la-la-la-la Lola; or What is my culture?" *Melissa Dunphy*. July 13, 2014.

Hill, Edie. "Thaw." *Edie Hill Composer*. ediehill.com/works/thaw. 2011.

Ehrlich, Sarah. "When Iraq had its Kristallnacht." *The Jewish Chronicle*. The Jewish Chronicle Online, 26 May 2011.

"Emma Goldman – A Dedicated Anarchist – Jacob Kershner." *Women of Valor*. Jewish Women's Archive, 2014.

Engelman, Peter C., ed. "Margaret Sanger and the Modern School." Newsletter #19. The Margaret Sanger Papers Project. New York University, 1998[a].

---. "Yeânnis Revisited." Newsletter #19. *The Margaret Sanger Papers Project*. New York University, 1998[b].

Engholm, Ginny. "'Blossoms of Hope': Our Cultural History of Pregnancy and Infant Loss and Grief." *Nursing Clio*. nursingclio.org. 19 June 2014.

Falk, Candace. "Emma Goldman: Chronology (1901–1919)." *The Emma Goldman Papers*. Berkeley Digital SunSite, 19 Sept. 1996.

Foster, Jonathan. "Early Wireless Experiments." *The Death Ray: The Secret Life of Harry Grindell Matthews*. harrygrindellmatthews.com. 2008.

Frahm, Frederick. Profile page. *LinkedIn*. linkedin.com/pub/frederick-frahm/16/4b8/410.

Franklin, Miles. *My Brilliant Career*. Australia: William Blackwood, 1901. Project Gutenberg, 2004.

Freeman, Colin. "How Gertrude Bell Caused a Desert Storm." *The Telegraph Online*. Telegraph Media Group Limited, 21 Feb. 2014.

Giovannitti, Arturo. "Arturo Giovannitti's Address to the Jury." Nov. 23, 1912. *History is a Weapon*.

Givner, Joan. "Porter, Katherine Ann." *Handbook of Texas Online*. Texas State Historical Association, 21 Jan. 2014.

"Gold Fever in Hokitika." *Roadside Stories*. New Zealand Ministry for Culture and Heritage. mch.govt. nz/roadside. MP3.

Goldman, Emma. "Emma Goldman's Memorial Tribute to Voltairine de Cleyre (1932), an excerpt." *Commemoration of Voltairine de Cleyre's Death*. voltairine.org, 2014.

Gonzalez, Julieta. "UA Poetry Center Receives Million Dollar Gift." *University of Arizona News*. uanews. org. 30 May 2001.

Goodman, Marty. "Introduction To the New Masses digital archive on Marxists Internet Archive." Riazanov Library, 2015. marxists.org/history/usa/pubs/new-masses/intro.htm.

Gubar, Marah. "The Victorian Child, c. 1837–1901." *Representing Childhood*. University of Pittsburgh, 2005.

Hamel, Mathilde. "Killer Beauty: Corsica, The Most Violent Place in Western Europe." *International Business Times*. ibtimes.com, 10 June 2013.

Hamilton, Carol Vanderveer. "American Writers and the Sacco-Vanzetti Case." *Modern American Poetry Site*. University of Illinois at Urbana-Champaign, 2001.

Hamilton, Stacey. "Reed, John." *American National Biography Online*. Oxford UP, Feb. 2000.

Reagan, Michael. "Harry Bridges: Life and Legacy." *Waterfront Workers History Project*. University of Washington, 2010.

Heather. "Women's History Month: Marya Zaturenska Gregory, poet." Now@MPL. Milwaukee Public Library, 27 Feb. 2014.

"Helen Hoyt." Poetry Foundation. poetryfoundation.org.

"Henry Nicholson Levinge." *Register of Admission to the Middle Temple*. The Honourable Society of the Middle Temple. archive.middletemple.org.uk.

Hill, Myrtle and John Lynch. "Ireland: society and economy, 1870–1914." *Multitext Project in Irish History*. University College of Cork. multitext.ucc.ie.

Hutching, Gerard. "Shipwrecks – Graveyard Harbors." *The Encyclopedia of New Zealand*. New Zealand Ministry for Culture and Heritage, 13 July 2012.

Hyman, Paula E. "Eastern European Immigrants in the United States." *Jewish Women: A Comprehensive Historical Encyclopedia*. Jewish Women's Archive, 1 Mar. 2009.

"Idella Purnell." *Wikipedia, The Free Encyclopedia*. Wikimedia Foundation, Inc., 28 Apr. 2015.

Jagielski, Jennifer. "Redfern, Home to the South Sydney Rabbitohs, is an Eclectic Mix of the Old and New." *The Sunday Telegraph*. dailytelegraph.com, 12 Oct. 2014.

James, Bob. "Chummy Fleming (1863–1950): A Brief Biography." *Radical Tradition*. Takver, 5 Sept. 2002.

Jeannette Marks Papers. "Biographical Note." Mount Holyoke College Archives.

Jones, Robert B. "Toomer, Jean." *American National Biography Online*. Oxford UP, Feb. 2000.

Kangas, Steve. "The Great Depression: Its Causes and Cures." *Liberalism Resurgent: A Response to the Right*. 1996. huppi.com/kangaroo/tenets.htm.

Katz, Esther, ed. *The Margaret Sanger Papers Electronic Edition: Margaret Sanger and The Woman Rebel, 1914–1916*. Columbia, SC: Model Editions Partnership, 2000.

Keel, Amelia. "Elinor Wylie." *The Literary Encyclopedia*. The Literary Dictionary Company Limited, 16 Dec. 2009.

Kissane, Erin. "About Hope Mirlees." *Hope Mirlees on the Web*. 19 July 2009.

Kouidis, Virginia M. "Loy, Mina." *American National Biography Online*. Oxford UP, Feb. 2000.

Kuban, Adam. "Brooklyn Literary Walking Tour." *NYCgo.com*. NYC and Company, Inc., 14 Sept. 2011.

Kukil, Karen. *Unconquered By Flames: The Literary Lights of Yaddo*. Sophia Smith Collection, Smith College, 27 Jan. 2014. smith.edu/libraries/libs/ssc/yaddo/yaddo-home.html.

Lambert, Tim. "A Brief History of Sydney, Australia." *A World History Encyclopedia*. localhistories.org/sydney.

Langness, David. "The Baha'i Influence on Kahlil Gilbran's *The Prophet*." bahaiteachings.org, 24 May 2014.

Leiser, Amy. "A. Mitchell Palmer: Red Scare Infamy." Monroe County Historical Association, Oct. 2007.

"Lesbia Harford – The Rebel Girl." *Radical Tradition: An Australian History Page*. Takver, 14 Aug. 2001. www.takver.com/history/harford.htm.

Levitt, Aimee. "The migration of the hipster." *Chicago Reader* 2 Oct. 2013.

Lewis, Femi. "The Red Summer of 1919." *African American History*. About.com, 2014.

Lewis, Sam. "Q&A: Two New Biographies – Emma Goldman and Margaret Sanger." *MetroFocus*. WNET, 18 Nov. 2011.

Linder, Douglas. "The Trial of Sacco and Vanzetti, 1921." *Famous Trials*. University of Missouri-Kansas City School of Law, 2015.

"List of Earthquakes in New Zealand." *Wikipedia, The Free Encyclopedia*. Wikimedia Foundation, Inc., 3 Apr. 2015.

"List of Guggenheim fellowships awarded in 1926." *Wikipedia, The Free Encyclopedia*. Wikimedia Foundation, Inc., 31 Aug. 2013.

Little Magazine Collection. University of Wisconsin Madison Memorial University Library, 14 Feb 2013. uwlittlemags.tumblr.com/post/43090377015/from-the-vault-palms-a-magazine-of.

Lloyd, Virginia. "For the love of Hart Crane and me." Bookslut.com, May 2011.

London, Charmian. Letter to Dr. Goodhue. 18 June 1907. *The Rodman Collection of the London-Goodhue Papers*. The Jack London Collection by Sarah and Darius Anderson. jacklondoncollection.com.

Mann, Richard G. "McAlmon, Robert (1896–1956)." *glbtq literature*. glbtqarchive.com, 2006.

Marcotte, Amanda. "Why are Feminists so Sarcastic These Days? Because Everyone Is." *Slate Magazine*. The Slate Group, 2 Oct. 2012.

"Margaret Butler: Artist Overview." Auckland Art Gallery Toi o Tomaki. aucklandartgallery.com, 2014.

Mark, Joshua J. "Ur." *Ancient History Encyclopedia*. Ancient History Encyclopedia Limited, 28 Apr. 2011.

Martin, John M. "Hayes Perkins Biography and Diary." *Hayes Here and There*. WordPress, 28 May 2011.

Masses (Mar. 1915), *Tamiment Library and Robert F. Wagner Labor Archives*, New York University. dlib.nyu.edu/themasses.

Mayo, Ashlee. "William Rose Benét." *Pennsylvania Center for the Book*. Penn State University, 2003. pabook.libraries.psu.edu.

McAtee, Sean. "Maxwell Anderson." *Pennsylvania Center for the Book*. Penn State University, Spring 2010. pabook.libraries.psu.edu.

McKerrow, Bob. "Ebenezer Teichelmann." *The Official Ebenezer Teichelmann Blog*. Blogger, 26 June 2007.

McLachlan, Sean. "Ghosts of a Dictatorship: Visiting Saddam Hussein's Palaces." *Gadling.com*, 21 Nov. 2012.

McLaughlin, Rosemary. "From Paterson to P'town: How a Silk Strike in New Jersey Inspired the Provincetown Players." *Laconics* 1 (2006). eOneill.com.

McLaughlin, Trevor. "Lost Children?" *History Ireland*. historyireland.com, 2013.

Medina, Miriam. "Life in the Tenements." *New York City, Tenement Life*. maggieblanck.com, Oct. 2013.

Nathan, Simon. "West Coast Places: Hokitika." *The Encyclopedia of New Zealand*. New Zealand Ministry for Culture and Heritage, 13 July 2012.

"National Anthem." *About Australia*. Australian Government Department of Foreign Affairs and Trade, Feb. 2011. dfat.gov.au.

Navares, Alyssa S. "A Ride Back in Time on the Manoa Trolley." Hawaii Aloha Travel, 2014.

"Ned Kelly Timeline." *Australian Geographic*. australiangeographic.com, 1 Sept. 2011.

"New Zealand Women and the Vote." *New Zealand History*. New Zealand Ministry for Culture and Heritage, 14 Jan. 2013.

NIWA. "New Zealand's Rain Falls Mainly in the Mountains." *Scoop Independent News*. scoop.co.nz, 20 Dec. 2011.

North Sydney Council. History Walk. "Henry Lawson's North Sydney: A Walking tour from McMahon's Point to Balls Head." nsw.gov.

"NZ's Heaviest Ever Gold Nugget Discovered, 7 September 1909." *New Zealand History*. New Zealand Ministry for Culture and Heritage, 14 Oct. 2014.

O'Malley, Michael. "The Palmer Raids." *History 409: Between the Wars*. George Mason University, 1997. chnm.gmu.edu/courses/hist409.

Owens, Joanne M. "Roland Hayes (1887–1977)." *New Georgia Encyclopedia*. Georgia Humanities Council, 14 Nov. 2013.

Patrick, Jon. "Photography of Dorothea Lange: An American Archive – Hard Times." *The Selvedge Yard*. selvedgeyard.com, 6 Dec. 2009.

Patterson, Michael Robert. "Laura Benét, Military Daughter and Author." *Arlington National Cemetery Website*. Arlington Cemetery, 25 Oct. 2007.

"Paul Gorguloff." *Wikipedia The Free Encyclopedia*. Wikimedia Foundation, Inc., 19 Oct. 2015.

Pellicer, Carlos. "Deseos (Desires)." 1921. Trans. Taller. *El Galeón de Acapulco News*. elgaleon.weebly. com

"People: Eugene Debs (1855–1926)." *American Experience: Woodrow Wilson*. PBS, 2001.

"People and Events: Voltairine de Cleyre (1866–1912)." *American Experience: Emma Goldman*. PBS, 11 Mar. 2004.

Pernicone, Nunzio. "About the Sacco-Vanzetti Case." *American National Biography Online*. Oxford UP, Feb 2000.

Perrone, Fernanda. "History of the Modern School of Stelton." Finding aid to Modern School Collection. Special Collections and University Archives. Rutgers University Libraries, 1996.

Pettersson, Morgan. "On This Day: Ned Kelly is Hanged." *Australian Geographic*. Australian Geographic Society, 7 Nov. 2012.

Pinsky, Robert. "Poems by Lola Ridge, an early, great chronicler of New York life." *Slate Magazine*. The Slate Group, 22 Mar. 2011.

Pool, Ian and Tahu Kukutai. *Te Ara – the Encyclopedia of New Zealand*. 17 Dec. 2014.

Porter, Katherine Anne. "The Never-Ending Wrong." *The Atlantic Online*. June 1977. The Atlantic Monthly Group.

Prideaux-Brune, Ellen Jane. "Receipt Book." *Victorian Medicine: Use Of Laudanum and Treatment of the Sick*. The Acorn Archive, 29 Nov. 2007.

"The Provincial and Gold-Rush Years, 1853-70." *New Zealand History*. New Zealand Ministry for Culture and Heritage, 19 Oct. 2012.

Punkerslut. "Francisco Ferrer y Guardia (1859–1909)." *The Anarchists Encyclopedia: A Gallery of Saints and Sinners*. Recollection Used Books.

"Queen Mary of the Claremont." *Sydney Eye*. Blogger, 27 July 2012.

Rada, James, Jr. "Looking Back 1929: Drug Addiction in the 1920s." *Public Opinion*. Chambersburg Public Opinion Online, 18 July 2011.

"Rainer Maria Rilke: Biography" *The Poetry Foundation*.

Reagan, Michael. "Harry Bridges: Life and Legacy." *Waterfront Workers History Project*. University of Washington, 2010.

Reuben, Paul P. "Chapter 7: Early Twentieth Century: Katherine Anne Porter." *Perspectives in American Literature: A Research and Reference Guide*. California State University, Stanislaus, 23 June 2014. "Richard Seddon Becomes Premier." New Zealand History. New Zealand Ministry for Culture and Heritage, 20 Dec. 2012.

Richards, Leann. "Her Majesty's Sydney." *History of Australian Theatre*. HAT Archive. hat-archive.com/ Hermajestyssydney.htm.

Rodwan, John G., Jr. "The Arrested Artistry of Elinor Wylie." *Open Letters Monthly: An Arts and Literature Review*. openlettersmonthly.com.

Schaffner, Val. "Perdita Macpherson Schaffner (1919–2001)." imagists.org, 4 July 2002. imagists.org/ hd/perdita.html.

Schnalle, Andy. "History of Bush Poetry in Australia." *Bush Poetry*. Andy's Media Services, 14 Dec. 2013. andy.com.au.

Schroeder, Theodore. *"Obscene" literature and constitutional law: a forensic defense of freedom of the press*. New York: Priv. print. for forensic uses, 1911. onlinebooks.library.upenn.edu.

Schuesler, Michael K. "Frances Toor and 'Mexican Folkways.'" *Inside Mexico* Mar. 2008.

Schulman, Daniel. "Hellen West Heller." *Modernism in the New City: Chicago Artists, 1920–1950*. chicagomodern.org, 2015.

Scrimgeour, Gray. "Sailing Tables for the Pacific: Canadian Australasian Line – Northbound 1893–1914." Postal History Society of Canada, 2006.

Share, Don. "James Dickey: Falling...in and out of favor." *Squandermania and other Foibles*. Blogger, 22 July 2009.

Shay, Alison. "On This Day: The Chicago Race Riot of 1919." *Publishing the Long Civil Rights Movement*. University of North Carolina at Chapel Hill, 27 July 2012.

"Shops and Businesses in Ur." *Odyssey: Adventures in Archaeology.* odysseyadventures.ca, 24 May 2010.

Simkin, John. "Albert Parsons." *Spartacus Educational.* Spartacus-educational.com, June 2014.

---. "Alien Registration Act." *Spartacus Educational.* Spartacus-educational.com, Aug. 2014.

---. "James Larkin." *Spartacus Educational.* Spartacus-educational.com, Aug. 2014.

---. "Lincoln Steffens." *Spartacus Educational.* Spartacus-educational.com, Aug. 2014.

---. "Mabel Dodge." *Spartacus Educational.* Spartacus-educational.com, May 2013.

---. "The Masses." *Spartacus Educational.* Spartacus-educational.com, June 2014.

---. "Michael Gold." *Spartacus Educational.* Spartacus-educational.com, June 2014.

---. "Tom Mooney." *Spartacus Educational.* Spartacus-educational.com, Aug. 2014.

Sprecher, Paul. "John Haynes Holmes." *Dictionary of Unitarian and Universalist Biography.* Unitarian Universalist History and Heritage Society, 2002.

Stayer, Lindsay. "Laura Benét." *Pennsylvania Center for the Book.* Penn State University, 2007. pabook. libraries.psu.edu.

Stimley, Keith. "Oswald Spengler: An Introduction to His Life and Ideas." *Institute for Historical Review.* ihr.org, 2014.

Swanson, Cecily. "Networked NY Q&A: Cecily Swanson." *NYU Workshop in Archival Practice.* nyuarchiveworkshop.wordpress.com, 27 Apr. 2012.

Swift, Todd. "Eye on Abraham Lincoln Gillespie." *Eyewear Blog.* Blogger, 13 May 2006.

"Sydney's History." *City of Sydney.* cityofsydney.nsw.gov.au, 30 Sept. 2014.

"Sydney's Paddy's Markets History." *Sydney's Paddy's Markets.* Sidney Markets Limited, 2014. http:// paddysmarkets.com/

Tan, Cheryl Lu-Lien. "A Chance to Peek Inside Yaddo." *New York Times.* 31 Aug 2011.

Tucker, Diane. "Brutal Destruction of Iraq's Archaeological Sites Continues." *Huffington Post Online.* thehuffingtonpost.com, Inc., 29 Sept. 2009.

"University of Hawaii." *Campus Heritage Network.* Society for College and University Planning, 2012.

"The Use of Violence: Emma Goldman, 1869–1940." *Women of Valor.* Jewish Women's Archive, 2014.

Vicary, Elizabeth Zoe. "Ridge, Lola." *American National Biography Online.* Oxford UP, Feb. 2000.

Wagner-Martin, Linda. "Williams, William Carlos." *American National Biography Online.* Oxford UP, Feb. 2000.

Walrond, Carl. "Gold and Gold Mining: Methods of Mining." *The Encyclopedia of New Zealand*. New Zealand Ministry for Culture and Heritage, 13 July 2012.

"Walter Arsenberg." *The PIP (Project for Innovative Poetry) Blog*. Blogger, 1 Dec. 2010.

Wehr, Paul and Christiane Griffin-Wehr. *Love's Animation*. wehranimations.com, Oct. 2004.

Whiteford, Peter. "Secrets of Felicity: Letters of Ursula Bethell." *New Zealand Electronic Poetry Center*. University of Auckland, 7 Aug. 2005.

Wichlan, Dan. "Introduction to Foreword for Prison Memoirs of an Anarchist." *Jack London's Nonfiction*. The Dan Wichlan Collection, 2014.

"Wilhemina Bain." *New Zealand History*. New Zealand Ministry for Culture and Heritage, 20 Aug. 2014.

Williams, Suzanne. "Carl Sandburg and the Chicago Race Riots." *Illinois Periodicals Online*. Northern Illinois University Libraries, Apr. 1997.

Willis, Patricia C. "'Voracities and Verities' and Louise Crane." *Marianne Moore: Poetry*. moore123.com, 9 Nov. 2010.

"Women and the Vote: The National Council of Women." *New Zealand History*. New Zealand Ministry for Culture and Heritage, 9 June 2014.

Woolf, Emma. "Did great-aunt Virginia Woolf have anorexia? Her great niece, a former sufferer, investigates." *Mail Online*. dailymail.co.uk, 25 May 2013.

Worden, Darian. "Old Time Libertarian Community: The Ferrer Colony of Stelton, New Jersey." *Center for a Stateless Society*. C4SS.org, 17 Aug. 2013.

Worthen, John. "Biography: Round the World and Back Again." *DH Lawrence*. University of Nottingham. dh-lawrence.org. 2005.

Wray, Ron. "Ron Wray's compositions 'Dreams' and 'I Have Been Dreaming.'" *YouTube*. YouTube, 2 Mar. 2015.

Yezzi, David. "CPR Classic Readings: At Melville's Tomb." *Contemporary Poetry Review*. cprw.com, 29 Mar. 2007.

"The Ziggurat of Ur-Nammu." *Odyssey: Adventures in Archaeology*. odysseyadventures.ca, 16 Dec., 2010.

Notes

Epigraph

"Let anything that burns" Tante 1935, 341.

PART I:
DUBLIN, SYDNEY, HOKITIKA,
SYDNEY, SAN FRANCISCO,
1873–1907

Chapter 1 — "One of Them"

p. 3 "That's Lola Ridge!": Porter 1977.

p. 3 Newspapers announce Ridge's presence: "Plan to Picket Prison," *Lincoln Evening Journal* 10 Aug. 1927.

p. 3 "Get them good and proper": Watson 2008, 160.

p. 3 No re-trial: D'Attilio 1998.

p. 4 "Ought to be a just people": Watson 2008, 184.

p. 4 Ten thousand mourners, footage destroyed: D'Attilio 2013.

p. 4 "Awaiting the falling/Cataract of the hooves": Ridge 1935, 75-76.

p. 4 Monroe and William Rose Benét call Ridge a genius: Dunbar 1948, 192, and 1933, 52.

p. 4 "Early, great chronicler": Pinsky 2011.

p. 5 Likened to the Dickinson's: Kreymborg 1918/1919.

p. 5 Presided over hotshot salons: Hively 2003, 72.

p. 5 Ridge the editor of *Others*: Churchill 2006, 56.

p. 5 Eating, drinking, flirting, planning, reading, and stomping: Mariani 1990, 247.

p. 5 Speech in Chicago: Ridge 1919.

p. 5 "man's natural inferior": Ridge 1981/1919, 18.

p. 5 Editing Sanger's magazine: *The Birth Control Review* May, June, July, Aug., and Sept. of 1918, New York City.

p. 5 Reciting her own poems: Goldman 2011/1931, 710, and Avrich 2012, 293-294.

p. 5 Arrested during demonstration: Marks 1929, 9.

p. 5 Solidarity in Mexico City: Ridge to Lawson, 6 May 1936.

p. 5 Ridge's obituary: *New York Times* 22 May 1941.

p. 6 Elitism of Eliot and Pound: Chevalier 1997, "Pound, Ezra," 671.

p. 6 Two anthologies, work not revived: Berke 2001, 83. The anthologies are *The Women Poets in English* (1972), edited by Ann Stanford, and *The World Split Open* (1974), edited by Louise Bernikow.

p. 6 "The buried history": Bernikow 1974, 45.

p. 6 "Something you feel intensely": Tante 1935, 341.

p. 6 "Even sophisticates...": Rev. of *Modernist Women Poets: An Anthology*, eds. Robert Hass and Paul Ebenkamp, publishersweekly.com.

p. 6 "Irish race of Princes": Stephens, A.G. Mitchell Library. "Autobiographies of 231 Australian and New Zealand Authors and Artists, 1901–1924." 994.

p. 7 Proof of royal descent: Eliza McLennan, personal communication. 5 June 2013. The document was Donovan's *Annals of Ireland*.

p. 7 Verified by the Biographical Society of Ireland: E. McLennan, personal communication. 5 June 2013.

p. 7 "I, John Reilly...": E. McLennan, personal communication. 5 June 2013.

p. 7 Built around Loughrea Lake: "Loughrea," *Slater's Dictionary of Ireland*, 18.

p. 7 Joseph H. Ridge: Pettigrew and *Oulton's Dublin Almanac*, 1842, 515.

p. 7 Famine and decimation: "Portumna Workhouse," irishworkhousecentre.ie, and McLaughlin 2013.

p. 7 Maria Ormsby Reilly, death and survivors: E. McLennan, personal communication. 5 June 2013.

p. 7 John Reilly retired: Leggott 2006.

p. 7 "Back of the Pipes": "The Back of the Pipes, Dublin," *Wikipedia*.

p. 7 Eight times in *Ulysses*: Joyce 1986/1922, 50, 128, 228, 303, 306, 307, 400, 590, 598.

p. 7 "Stone sofa": Quidnunc 1942, 2.

p. 7 Later and fewer marriages: Hill and Lynch, "Ireland: Society and Economy."

p. 7 Maria married an attorney: Ireland Civil Registration of Marriages Index, Drogheda District, Vol. 5, 8, and "Henry Nicholson Levinge."

p. 7 Emma wed Joseph Henry Ridge, 1871: Ireland Civil Registration of Marriages Index, South Dublin, Vol. 17, 669.

p. 8 Same-named attorney: Dublin Street Directory, 1838, 1839, and 1842. Joseph Henry Ridge esq., attorney, at 12 Frederick Street North, and at Loughrea.

p. 8 Ridge born Dec. 12, 1873: Civil Registration of Births, Vol. 3, 663.

p. 8 Ridge's parents separated: Leggott 2006.

p. 8 Horsewhipping an amicable solution: *The Argus* 23 July 1828, 5. Skerret and Ridge made up and signed a petition together for the lighting, cleansing and washing of Loughrea, according to *The Connaught Journal* 15 Oct. 1840.

p. 8 Divorce not legal until 1996: Burckhardt 2010, 535.

p. 8 Emma was living with her father: Ridge's birth certificate.

p. 8 "Fate" keeps them apart: Sproat, Letter to J. Engles, 24 Apr. 1977.

p. 8 Ridge's grandfather died: Reilly 1869.

p. 9 "915 persons who sleep in 294 beds": Mapother 1864, 9.

p. 9 "Mysie": M. Leggott, correspondence with Alison Clarke, 24 Apr. 2011.

p. 9 A second husband: Ireland Civil Registration of Marriages, 1845-1958, Vol. 7, 449.

p. 9 Sailed for Australia around 1876: Penfold's death certificate estimates around 1876. New South Wales Registry of Births, Deaths and Marriages (BDM), 1869.

p. 9 Three Penfolds: NSW Directory for 1867.

p. 9 Uncle William and a Reilly cousin emigrating: M. Leggott, personal communication, and Reilly 1869.

p. 9 Arrival in Australia: LDS Victoria, Australia, Assisted and Unassisted Passenger Lists, 1839-1923, Victoria Public Record Office, VPRS 947.

p. 10 The down from the breast of an albatross: Ridge, Diary, 7 Jan. 1941.

p. 10 "Virgins' cage": Hastings 2007, 173.

p. 10 Factory and office work: Bishop, 2011.

p. 10 Forced to Redfern: Ridge, Diary, 5 Feb. 1941.

p. 10 Mostly immigrants and factories: Jagielski 2014.

p. 10 "Just you and I": Ridge, Diary, 1 Jan. 1941.

p. 10 "A small bare room...": ibid.

p. 11 "A man carried a sewing machine...": Ridge, Diary, 7 Jan. 1941.

p. 11 "Why do you watch me...": ibid.

p. 11 "hear the sunlight singing...": ibid.

p. 11 Memorialized one miserable Christmas: ibid., and Ridge 1920, 7.

p. 11 "An open air affair...": "Sydney's Paddy's Markets History."

p. 11 "But, dear, are you sure...": Ridge, Diary, 7 Jan. 1941.

p. 11 "Just under the ribs...": ibid.

p. 11 "I asked for biscuits...": ibid.

p. 12 "My angel": ibid.

p. 12 "I felt very happy": ibid.

p. 12 Refused Christmas dinner: Ridge, Diary, 5 Feb. 1941.

p. 12 "The Jews are good people": Ridge, Diary, 6 Feb. 1941.

p. 12 "Pretend not to notice the fleas...": ibid.

p. 13 More men than women: Australian Historical Population Statistics, Australian Bureau of Statistics, 2008.

p. 13 Relatives would have known: "Australia in the 1870s," myplace.edu.au.

p. 13 "I took what money I had...": Mander 1920, 245.

p. 13 Similar ruse: Hastings 2007, 175.

p. 13 Ore the size of a man's palm: "Arrival of the Wallaby from Hokitika, with Eleven Thousand Ounces of Gold," *Nelson Examiner and New Zealand Chronicle* 15 Aug. 1865.

p. 13 Rumors of a gold strike: *Timaru Herald* 5 May 1877.

p. 13 "Lakelet thick with masts": Catton 2013.

p. 13 Thirty-two ships: Hutching 2012.

p. 13 Insurance to run aground again: "Gold Fever in Hokitika."

p. 14 Set up the town of Hokitika: ibid., and May 1967, 334-335.

p. 14 Barefoot boys and company miners: Sisters of Mercy 1978.

p. 14 Gold rush finished: May 1967, 299.

p. 14 Dying race: Pool and Tahu Kukutai 2014.

p. 14 Fisherman drowned, cook disappeared, wife and child murdered: *Thames Star* 7, 17, 21, 28 Sept. 1880.

p. 14 Declared herself a widow and remarried: ibid., and Ridge, Diary, 2 May 1940. McFarlane might also be the man mentioned in May (1967, 88). Richard Sherrin's 1863 expedition up the Hokitika in a whaleboat to find gold included a McFarlane, "a young remittance man anxious to avoid some equally anxious creditors," or perhaps he was mixed up with the other member, a runaway sailor from the *Emerald Isle*.

p. 14 Working stake in Kanieri Forks: "Rimu District Miners Prospecting Association." *West Coast Times* 7 July 1893, 2.

p. 14 General shortage of females: "The Provincial and Gold-Rush Years" 2012, and May 1967, 272.

p. 14 "Appalling isolation": Mander 1920, 14.

p. 14 McFarlane's alcoholism: Ridge, Diary, 2 May 1940.

p. 14 Fifteen years by 1880: "List of Government Immigrants." *Press [Canterbury, NZ]* 5 Apr. 1862. See also *Cyclopedia of New Zealand* 1906, and The Seaview Asylum Casebook, 1886-1906, Hokitika Museum. (The Seaview Asylum, in Hokitika, was the name of the mental institution in which McFarlane died.)

p. 14 "He impersonated Macbeth": Ridge, Diary, 2 May 1940.

p. 15 Proud Irish family: Ridge, Guggenheim application. 1935.

p. 15 "Like a touch on my heart": Ridge, Diary, 2 May 1940.

p. 15 "Waters trebling": ibid.

p. 15 "Staring at the log fire": ibid.

p. 15 "Making her [own] sweeten": ibid.

p. 16 "The whistling water": ibid.

p. 16 "Stepfather's gaze" ibid.

p. 16 "I did not answer" ibid.

p. 16 Harness poetic power: I am indebted to Simon Turkel for this insight.

p. 16 "I am a poet": Ridge, Diary, 2 May 1940.

Chapter 2 — Ambition in New Zealand

p. 17 Education at St. Joseph's: Sproat to Engles, 1977. St. Joseph's was the only parochial school in Kanieri at the time. *Cyclopedia of New Zealand* 1906.

p. 17 "In a convent school": Ridge to Content, 18 June 1935.

p. 17 "Tone is much superior": Sisters of Mercy 1978, 25.

p. 17 Schoolwork on slates: Ridge to Content, n.d.

p. 17 "Could not cook a mutton chop": Sisters of Mercy 1978, 27–28.

p. 18 "The rich and the poor": New Zealand Parliament.

p. 18 "Partially civilized": "Richard Seddon becomes Premier" 2012.

p. 18 "London and the Digging": May 1967, 296.

p. 18 "Australasian colonies as examples": Coleman 1987, xi.

p. 18 "Seddon did not support women's suffrage": "Seddon, Richard John" in McLintock 1966.

p. 18 Afraid of women for Prohibition: "Votes for Women." elections.org.nz.

p. 19 "Hit the end wall with a thud": "Women's Suffrage Petition." *Archives New Zealand*, 2013.

p. 19 "The issue passed": "New Zealand Women and the Vote" 2013.

p. 19 First National Council of Women: "Wilhemina Bain" 2014.

p. 19 Demands of the council: "Women and the Vote" 2014.

p. 19 "On Zealanda": Ridge 1892.

p. 19 Newspapers carried poems: Harvey 2003.

p. 20 "Dawning of national pride": Talbott-Tubbs 1899, 5.

p. 20 "Who serve an art more great": McCormick 1940.

p. 20 "Best Literary and Artistic Talent": Talbott-Tubbs 1899.

p. 20 Featuring Ridge's poems: Ridge 1902.

p. 20 "Signs of prematurity": McCormick 1940, 124.

p. 20 Who stayed late had become despondent: May 1967, 296.

p. 20 Physical hardships and drink: May 1967, 291. The medical superintendent of the Hokitika hospital claimed that insanity on the goldfields was largely the result of delirium tremens, or alcohol withdrawal. See also Coleborne 2009.

p. 20 Admitted to Seaview: Seaview Casebook, 221-222.

p. 20 "Shrewd blue glance": Ridge, Diary, 2 May 1940.

p. 20-21 "The Insane": Ridge Jan. 1906.

p. 21 Good food, rest, recreation: Brunton 2012.

p. 21 "Never failing supply of ozone": "Visit to the Seaview Asylum." *West Coast Times* 6 Apr. 1905.

p. 21 Chess, billiards, music: ibid.

p. 21 Janet Frame: janetframe.org.nz/biography.

p. 21 Still contemplating suicide: "Seaview." *Grey River Argus* 15 Feb. 1895, 2.

p. 21 Ridge married Webster: New Zealand BDM, "Marriages in the District of Hokitika," 1895.

p. 21 Occupation "painter": ibid.

p. 21 Webster's photo, "record plain facts": *Cyclopedia of New Zealand* 1906, 26–27.

p. 21 Same goldfield as Ridge's stepfather: "Rimu District Miners Prospecting Association." *West Coast Times* 7 July 1893.

p. 21 A share of a mine and a nearby pub: Alison Clarke, correspondence with M. Leggott, Apr. 2006.

p. 21 "Precious rubies": Bell 1906, 77.

p. 21 Largest chunk of gold: "NZ's Heaviest Ever Gold Nugget" 2014.

p. 22 No longer a tent town: *Cyclopedia of New Zealand* 1906.

p. 22 Yellow birds: May 1967, 152.

p. 22 Wollstonecraft in Hokitika: Susan Asplin, personal communication. 18 Aug. 2013.

p. 23 "On a fork of grassed earth": Ridge 1920, 47.

p. 23 Photo of Webster's claim: *Cyclopedia of New Zealand* 1906, 27.

p. 23 "Strong enough to kill a person": Walrond 2012.

p. 23 Desolate tree stumps: ibid.

p. 23 Visitors in their Victoriana: Untitled photograph #1451, Hokitika Museum Photography Collection, Hokitika.

p. 23 Wettest places on earth: National Institute for Water and Atmospheric Research (NIWA) 2011.

p. 24 Paul Webster born: New Zealand BDM, 1896.

p. 24 Paul Webster dead: ibid.

p. 24 Dead children poetry: Gubar 2005.

p. 24 "The Magic Island" and "The Three Little Children": Ridge 1905.

p. 24 "The Returned Hero": *The Bulletin* 30 June 1904, 36.

p. 24 Regular horse races: "Hokitika Easter Races." *West Coast Times* 27 Apr. 1878, 2. See also Mincham 2008, 79.

p. 24 Psychological effects of high infant mortality: Engholm 2014.

p. 25 Hyde's attempted suicide: M. Leggott, personal communication. 3 Sept. 2014.

p. 25 Price of gold fell: Nathan 2012.

p. 25 Kanieri Forks entertainments: *West Coast Times* 21 Aug. 1885, 2; 5 Nov. 1898, 2.

p. 25 "I've Written to Brown": Williams 1867.

p. 25 Remembered as an actress: Alison Clarke, unpublished notes. 2006.

p. 25 "We sma' hoors": *West Coast Times* 18 Apr. 1898, 2.

p. 25 Keith Webster born: New Zealand BDM, 1900.

p. 25 Ridge's mother: According to the record of Emma McFarlane's 1907 death in the New South Wales BDM, "The deceased lady formerly resided at Kaniri Forks for many years."

p. 26 "At Sundown": Ridge Sept. 1903.

Chapter 3 — *"The Smoking Fuse"*

p. 27 "Plowed a lonely furrow": "MacKay, Jessie" in Robinson 1998.

p. 27 "Thin, grey, fragile woman" and the nationalist movement: "MacKay, Jessie" in McLintock 1966.

p. 27 "The weaker side": Cowan 1937.

p. 27 "The editor": "MacKay, Jessie" in Roberts 1993.

p. 27 *Otago Witness*: paperspast.natlib.govt.nz.

p. 27 Never married, little fame, "under-recognised": Roberts 1993.

p. 27 "Everyone had been blind before": Cresswell 1948.

p. 28 She called off a marriage: Whiteford 2005.

p. 28 "Big, black Essex motor car": "Bethell, Mary Ursula" in Orange 1998.

p. 28 "Religious certainty and everyday experience": ibid.

p. 28 Evelyn Hayes: Charman 1998.

p. 28 As in exile: Whiteford 2008.

p. 28 "Dodged to and fro": Bethell 2005, xxii.

p. 28 Inspired *The Piano*: Radner et al. 2009, 284.

p. 28 Moved twenty-nine times: "Mander, Jane" in Robinson 1998.

p. 28 "Brain-benumbing...": "Mander, Mary Jane" in Orange 1998.

p. 28 "Pupil-teacher": Robinson 1998.

p. 28 Newspaper work: "Mander, Mary Jane" in McLintock 1966.

p. 28 Future Premier, travel to America, fell ill: ibid.

p. 28 Women forbade their daughters, Mander persisted: Robinson 1998.

p. 29 Noted among the literati: "Sheriff Ends Julia's Bookshop in Village." *New York Evening Post* 8 Aug. 1925.

p. 29 Return and death: Orange 1998.

p. 29 "Too enthusiastic": McLintock 1966.

p. 29 "Philistia itself": McCormick 1940, 134.

p. 29 "But at eighteen...": Cather 1988/1936.

p. 29 "Leap into the eyes": Mansfield 1954/1916, 65.

p. 29 "Katherine the Great": "Mansfield, Katherine" in Robinson 1998.

p. 29 Never returned: "Death of Katherine Mansfield" (2014).

p. 29 Turned to mystic, dung: Fromm 1988. The breath of oxen was a traditional cure for consumption. See J.D. Rolleston's "The Folklore of Pulmonary Tuberculosis," *Tubercle* 1941, 55.

p. 29 "A Bush Track, Kanieri River": artvalue.com.

p. 29 Joseph Wharton Hughes: Platts 1980.

p. 30 Butler: "Butler, Margaret Mary" in Orange 1998.

p. 30 Gave up sculpting: "Margaret Butler" 2014.

p. 30 Edith Bendall: Laurie 2003.

p. 30 Return to Europe 1901: "Hodgkins, Frances Mary" in Orange 1993.

p. 30 One of England's leading artists: ibid.

p. 30 Teichelmann: McKerrow 2006.

p. 30 "A sense of intimacy": McKerrow 2007.

p. 30 Moved to Hokitika: ibid.

p. 30 MacFarlane's position as an educator: "Westland Board of Education." *West Coast Times.* 13 Feb. 1890, 2.

p. 30 Witnesses at her wedding: New Zealand BDM, 1895.

p. 30 Monroe would publish Ridge: Curdy 2013.

p. 31 "A Farewell": Monroe 1899.

p. 31 Other signers: *Grey River Argus* 12 Nov. 1901, 27 Feb. 1902, and 29 Jan. 1903. Also *The New Zealand Tablet* 2 Oct. 1902.

p. 31 "The Trial of Ruth": Ridge May 1903.

p. 32 Left for Sydney: Leggott 2006.

p. 32 Husband's reluctant consent: Sproat to Engles, 1977.

p. 32 Husband's company touted: *West Coast Times* 6 Apr. 1901: 2.

p. 32 Boarded ship: New South Wales. Shipping Master's Office. *Passenger Arrivals for the S.S. Mokoia.* Ref X286. Microfilm no. 2015.

Chapter 4 — The Arts in Australia

p. 33 "Australian by sympathy & association": Rose Webster [Lola Ridge] to A.G. Stephens. 27 Jan. 1904.

p. 33 "One of the largest cities": "Sydney's History" 2014.

p. 33 Electric trams on wooden streets: Lambert, n. d..

p. 33 Her Majesty's theater reopened: Richards, n. d..

p. 33 "Masterpiece of Cyclonic Art": "Battle of Gettysburg." *Hawkesbury Herald* 31 Oct. 1902, trove. nla.gov.au.

p. 33 Movies and operas playing: *Sydney Morning Herald* 11 Nov. 1903: 2.

p. 33 "No better teacher in Paris": "History," julianashtonartschool.com.au.

p. 33 Ned Kelly Day: Leggott 2006, with thanks to Michele Leggott for calling this coincidence to my attention.

p. 33 "Jerilderie Letter": A transcript of the letter is available via nma.gov.au.

p. 33 One heist dressed as cops: "Ned Kelly Timeline" 2011.

p. 33 "Articulated a struggle between rich and poor": qtd. in Pettersson 2012.

p. 34 Omitting her married name: Schnalle 2013 and Rose Webster [Lola Ridge] to A.G. Stephens. 27 Jan. 1904.

p. 34 Ridge's prior names: Leggott 2006 and the unpublished notes of Alison Clarke.

p. 34 Christened Rose Emily Ridge: Irishgenealogy.ie.

p. 34 Stone against coverture: DuBois 1998, 88.

p. 34 A generation of name-shifters: Crosby: Hamalian 37; Willela: Gilbert and Gubar,241; H.D. and Bryher: Gilbert and Gubar 242; and Loy: Kouidis, 132.

p. 34 Trinity still examines music candidates in Australia: trinitycollege.com.

p. 35 Passed four exams: Ridge to Louise Adams Floyd, 21 Jan. 1930.

p. 35 Lived at 193 West St.: Sproat 1978.

p. 35 Bullock teams, most houses only two years old: North Shore Historical Society pamphlet.

p. 35 "In New Zealand there is no Bohemia": Morton, Frank, *Triad* Oct. 1908. 121.

p. 35 "A writer or artist should be a bohemian": Moore 2012, 194

p. 35 Under the influence of Ashton and Stephens: Ridge (using the name Rose Webster) gave "North Sydney" as her address in her 27 Jan. 1904 letter to A.G. Stephens, the center of bohemian Australia.

p. 35 Queen Victoria's son: Moore 2012.

p. 35 Ashton the chairman: Moore 2012 and julianashtonartschool.com.au.

p. 35 *Plein air* techniques: "The Founding of the Sydney Art School," julianashtonartschool.com. au.

p. 35 White-haired Ashton: julianashtonartschool.com.au, under the heading "Julian Ashton and students Bradleys Head Mosman 1895."

p. 35 Son of an American, grandson of a count: "Ashton, Julian Rossi" in Nairn 1979.

p. 35 St. Bernard: ibid.

p. 35 "The artist must be content...": Astbury 1987.

p. 35 "Women artists..." qtd. in W. Moore "Art andArtists." *Brisbane Courier* 21 May 1927: 23.

p. 35 Penchant for live models: "The Founding," julianashtonartschool.com.au.

p. 35 With male model in briefs: http://quantumjoss.tumblr.com/post/26596704714.

p. 36 Female models: King 1907, referenced in Moore 1927. The photograph is available electronically via dictionaryofsydney.org, under the heading "A smorgasbord of delights."

p. 36 "Her flesh glistening": Taylor 1918.

p. 36 Beseeching nude: Ridge. Autograph book.

p. 36 She modelled nude: Berke 2010.

p. 36 Regarding Ridge's artistic output: Ridge's executor, Elaine Sproat, revealed in a letter to Michele Leggott (2012) that she found eight drawings from the Australasian period, including a self-portrait, as well as five later works. None of these have been made available for viewing.

p. 36 All pictures strictly naturalistic: Lola Ridge Papers. "Drawings."

p. 36 Ashton denigrated modernism: McQueen 1979, 21.

p. 36 Winckler: "Ruby Winckler," *Design and Art Australia Online* and "Winckler, Ruby," *Manuscripts, Oral History and Pictures*, State Library of New South Wales Online.

p. 36 Henry George Julius: "Harry Julius," *Design and Art Australia Online*.

p. 36 *Art in Australia*: ibid.

p. 36 "Kings Cross Bohemian and drunk": White 1941, 20.

p. 36 Mick Paul: "Paul, Mick," National Library of Australia, trove.nla.gov.au.

p. 36 Howard Ashton: "Ashton, Julian Rossi" in Nairn 1979.

p. 37 "Painted with a strong virility": Topliss 1996.

p. 37 Founding member: "Nelle Marion Rodd," *Design and Art Australia Online.*

p. 37 A thousand submissions a week: Moore 2012.

p. 37 "Ridge's practice is as good…": Leggott 2013.

p. 37 "Rolling stones down the floor": Phelan 1991, 59-60.

p. 37 80,000 subscribers: Moore 2012.

p. 37 It also paid: Schnalle 2013.

p. 37 "First call on almost every Australasian writer": Kirkpatrick 1992.

p. 37 Sometimes between 1902 and 1905: Leggott 2013.

p. 37 Editor of a series of books: "Stephens, Alfred George" in Ritchie 1990. Stephens would eventually publish 40 volumes.

p. 37 "Strongest single force": ibid.

p. 37 Purple ink with a confident hand: ibid.

p. 38 Fond of Louise Mack: According to Phelan (1991), "he [Stephens] was mad about her" (89).

p. 38 "A great deal of Irish charm": Phelan 1991, 92.

p. 38 "I hate your stories…": Mack 1993/1896, 35.

p. 38 Stephens and Ashton socialized: Kirkpatrick 1992, 46-47.

p. 38 Attended Mack's farewell party: Phelan 1991, 101.

p. 38 "Tame and uninspiring": Stephens 1900.

p. 38 She deleted Maoriland: Leggott. 2013.

p. 38 Two lists of Australian writers: "Autobiographies of 231 Australian and New Zealand Authors and Artists," housed in the Mitchell Collection at the State Library of New South Wales.

p. 38 "Lola was too junior": Leggott 2013, 74.

p. 38 Lost much of his power: "Stephens, Alfred George" in Ritchie 1990.

p. 38 A copy was archived at the Mitchell: Guttmann 1971, 158 and Leggott 2013, 8.

p. 39 A typescript with Penfold…lost again: Leggott 2013, 7, 43, 75.

p. 39 "Waltzing Matilda": "National Anthem" 2011.

p. 39 Bush ballads: "Bush Songs and Music," australia.gov.au.

p. 39 Class conflict a common theme: Moore 2007, 210.

p. 39 Over a hundred magazines established: Moore 2012.

p. 39 Paul gave up art for politics: "Emily Letitia Paul," *Design and Art Australia Online,* 2007.

p. 40 O'Dowd became an activist: "O'Dowd, Bernard Patrick" in Serle 1988.

p. 40 "Poetry of purpose": O'Dowd 1909. An electronic copy of the essay is available via marxists.org.

p. 40 "Criticised the press, the Church and the State": "Pitt, Marie Elizabeth Josephine" in Serle 1988.

p. 40 "Community of marionettes": Pitt 1911. qtd. in Vickery 2007, 63.

p. 40 Pitt grew up in the bush: Vickery and Dever 2007.

p. 40 "Contributed his talents to progressive reform...": Scates 1997.

p. 40 "Social art" yields recognition: Moore 2012.

p. 40 Lawson quarreled with his mother: Vickery 2007, 23.

p. 40 Brought out his first book of poems: Dalziell 2004, 121, and "Lawson, Louisa" in Nairn 1986.

p. 40 Eroticism by flower: P. Bennett 2003, 168.

p. 40 Editors removed stanzas: Leggott 2013, 12.

p. 40 "Romantic agony": ibid.

p. 41 "The small boy Jude": Ridge to Marshall, 19 Nov. 1937.

p. 42 Returned to New Zealand, 1905: Leggott 2006.

p. 42 "Mrs. Peter Webster...": "Topics of the Day." *West Coast Times* 20 Jan. 1905.

p. 42 Sellers signed her book: Ridge, Autograph book.

p. 43 Husband threatened to kill her: Bernand-Wehner, correspondence with Michele Leggott, Apr. 2011, and Sproat to Engles, 1977.

p. 43 Ashton's wife spoke against marriage: "Ashton, Julian Rossi" in Nairn 1979.

p. 43 Marriage contract: Magarey 2001, 24.

p. 43 Mack abandoned her husband for Europe: "Mack, Marie Louise" in Nairn, 1986.

p. 43 Webster hauled into court, guilty and fined: "Magistrates Court Hokitika," *West Coast Times* 3 June 1905: 4.

p. 43 House auctioned off: "Sale of Residential Property at Kanieri." *West Coast Times* 11 May 1905.

p. 43 Webster died in 1946: *Hokitika Guardian* 10 June 1946, and New South Wales BDM.

p. 43 No second wife, one of thirteen siblings: Unpublished notes of A. Clarke.

p. 43 "A rather wicked figure": M. Leggott, personal communication. 6 Mar. 2013.

Chapter 5 — Beyond Sydney

p. 44 Lawson traveled between New Zealand and Australia: Edmond 2014.

p. 44 A patron to send him to England: Moore 2007, 222.

p. 44 "Talent goes for little here": Lawson 1977/1892, 18.

p. 44 "The Australian Girl": Castilla 1888.

p. 45 "I was not born a parasite": "Franklin, Stella Maria Sarah Miles" in Nairn 1981.

p. 45 "One of the blood-suckers who loll..." and "Ah, thou cruel fiend": Franklin 2004/1901.

p. 45 Eight-minute walk: Sands New South Wales Directory, 1903/1904, 1041.

p. 45 Future Premier: Warne 2005.

p. 45 Most photographed of the city: North Sydney Council.

p. 45 Home to writers and artists: Moore 2012.

p. 45 Lawson kept a room at Byer's Coffee: North Sydney Council.

p. 45 His daughter's high school: North Shore Historical Society 1994.

p. 45 "Found themselves of more importance": Mack 1993/1896, 42.

p. 45 "Beerhemia": Moore 2012, 231.

p. 46 "The old horse ferry...": qtd. in North Shore Historical Society 1994.

p. 46 Sex speeches in a toga: ibid.

p. 46 "Wowser": See urbandictionary.com/wowser.

p. 46 Mary Gilmore: "Gilmore, Dame Mary Jean" in Nairn 1983.

p. 46 "State funeral: Gilmore 1940.

p. 46 Our women shall walk in honor...": "Queen Mary of the Claremont" (2012).

p. 46 "One of the two finest...": qtd. in Dennis 2014.

p. 46 Father went bankrupt: "Biography of Lesbia Harford," poemhunter.com.

p. 46 Law degree, Wobblies, organizer, ill health: ibid.

p. 46 Affairs with both sexes: "Lesbia Harford – The Rebel Girl" 2001.

p. 47 Cubism and Vorticism: ibid.

p. 47 "Poetry...should not be consciously propagandized": "Biography of Lesbia Harford," poemhunter.com.

p. 47 "I will not rush with great wings gloriously": "Deliverance Through Art" Harford 1915/1985.

p. 47 Harford died in 1927, leaving behind: Sparrow 2014.

p. 47 Stephens opened a failed bookstore: "Stephens, Alfred George" in Ritchie 1990.

p. 47 "Breeders" for "white" Australia: Magarey 2001.

p. 47 "Beloved city, city I love": Ridge, Diary, 1 Jan. 1941.

p. 47 Stepfather died of pneumonia: New Zealand BDM, 1906, and *West Coast Times* 16 Jan. 1906.

p. 47 Mother died shortly thereafter: New South Wales BDM, 1907.

p. 47 Planning to travel to San Francisco: Sproat to Engles, 1977.

p. 47 Still a coffee bar today: The contemporary shop is called Il Centro Espresso Bar, located at 50 King Street in Sydney.

p. 47 Didn't serve liquor: Noyce 2012.

p. 47 Informant on the death certificate: Leggott 2006, 9, and New South Wales BDM.

p. 47 Alderman in Canterbury: *Sydney Morning Herald* 4 Feb. 1904, 2.

p. 48 "Rosa Webster": New South Wales BDM. Her mother was buried 6 Aug. 1907.

p. 48 "Nil": "S.S. Moana List of Alien Passengers."

p. 48 "Fiercely independent girl": Overell 2013.

p. 48 Mother and son set sail: Sproat to Engles, 1977; Brown hair and blue eyes: "S.S. Moana List of Alien Passengers," and Gillian Simpson, ANMM Library, personal communication 6 Sept. 2014.

Chapter 6 — Last Links with Australasia

p. 49 Description of the *Moana*: Brewer 1982, 73-77.

p. 49 "The moneymakers": Phelan 1991, 107.

p. 49 "I came steerage to America": Ridge to Lawson 16 Mar. 1932.

p. 49 First stop Suva: Scrimgeour 2006.

p. 50 "The ever-smiling face": Lees 1918, 175.

p. 50 Docked in Honolulu: Scrimgeour 2006.

p. 50 75 guest rooms: "History of the Moana Hotel," hawaiiforvisitors.com.

p. 50 London spent the year surfing: Charmian London to Dr. Goodhue, 18 June 1907.

p. 50 "We could see the masts and funnels": London 2003/1911, 47.

p. 50 Taro beds: "University of Hawaii" 2012.

p. 50 Electric trolleys: Navares 2014.

p. 51 James and Margaret Webster photograph: *Cyclopedia of New Zealand* 1906, 426, courtesy of Hokitika Museum.

p. 51 Worked as a government valuator: *West Coast Times* 3 Feb. 1906: 2.

p. 51 The children had children: Leggott 2013, 33.

p. 52 Inherited his father's ears: G. Bernand-Wehner, photo in correspondence with M. Leggott, 8 Apr. 2011.

p. 52 Poorhouses in the U.S.: Crannell 2012.

p. 52 Two-year-old died of starvation: "Marina Tsvetaeva Biography," egs.edu.

p. 52 "Motherhood, for the women poets": Drake 1987, 121-122.

p. 52 Broke all the dishes: Barnet 2004, 44.

p. 52 Icy toolshed: Hamalian 2009, 28, and Mellen 1994, 121.

p. 52 Deposited with shepherds: Conover 2001, 62.

p. 53 Never mentioned the son: Drake 1987, 123. Drake theorizes that not mentioning him was the only way Wylie could cope with the guilt.

p. 53 Ridge paid for Boyle's abortion: Berke 2001, 83.

p. 53 Her daughter wore tunics, sandals, punished: Mellen, 1994, 122.

p. 53 Dragged through ménage à trois: Daggy 1996.

p. 53 "Keep herself fresh": Bynner 1951, 188.

p. 53 H.D. abortion and daughter's name: Schaffner 2002.

p. 53 Claimed to have been happy: Schaffner 1980, 143.

Chapter 7 — *"Not Without Fame in Her Own Land"*

p. 54 Record dry spell: "Vancouver sets record for driest Sept.," CBC News, 1 Oct. 2012. cbc.ca/news.

p. 54 Robsons in Canada: "Robson Family Tree," ancestry.ca.

p. 54 Canadian writers emigrated to New York: Mount 2005, 237.

p. 54 Transferred son and luggage: U.S. Immigration and Naturalization Service, "City of Puebla."

p. 54 "Parents to Fight for Custody of Babes": *The San Francisco Call* 30 Sept. 1907.

p. 54 10 years younger: "S.S. Moana List of Alien Passengers."

p. 54 Took years off her age in Australia: Leggott 2013, 6; Rose Webster [Lola Ridge] to A.G. Stephens. 27 Jan. 1904 in "Stephens, A.G. Mitchell Library. "Autobiographies of 231 Australian and New Zealand Authors and Artists", 1901-1924. 994.

p. 55 Her mother lied about her age: Leggott 2013, 1.

p. 55 Declared she was Australian: ibid; "S.S. Moana List of Alien Passengers."

p. 55 Gratitude to cousin Eddie: M. Leggott, personal communication. W. C. Penfold was a prominent stationer and printer and Elaine Sproat suggested that Eddie was particularly beloved in an email to Leggott. "The fact that Eddie had Lola['s] mss. and drawings that were passed down to his daughter is an indication that Eddie and Lola were close," according to Leggott.

p. 55 "Not without fame in her own land": *San Francisco Overland Monthly* Mar. 1908, 295.

p. 55 "Chronicles of Sandy Gully as Kept by Skiting Bill": ibid., 298-9.

p. 56 Service's book had become a bestseller: Mallory 2009, 216.

p. 56 "Western *Atlantic Monthly*": Mott 1957/1938, 403.

p. 56 Cather and Neihardt contributed: ibid., 408.

p. 56 London received 15 cents a word: ibid.

p. 56 Ash and plague: Worth 2005, 60.

p. 56 Kidnapped, dynamited, and shot: Denman 1910; Grossman 2008, 407.

p. 56 Money to the Red Cross: Coate 2010, 3.

p. 56 Armed streetcar conductors: "Strike!" *Market Street Railway*, 20 July 2008, streetcar.org/strike.

p. 57 Living in horse stalls: "1906 Earthquake," mtdavidson.org/1906-earthquake.

p. 57 "Liberated" flour: Davies 2011, 76.

p. 57 Telephones and saloons speedily restored: Livingston 2006, Hansen et al. 2013, 150; Sedgwick 1906.

p. 57 Three major earthquakes: "List of Earthquakes in New Zealand," Wikipedia.

p. 57 "Sydney Valley": Giles 2014, 168.

p. 57 No Penfolds: San Francisco 1907 City Directory.

p. 57 Lewis, a student of Ashton's: "Martin Lewis," britishmuseum.org/research.

p. 57 "Posthole digger and a merchant seaman": "Martin Lewis," oldprintshop.com.

p. 57 Published in *The Bulletin*, New York by 1909: ibid.

p. 57 McKinley campaign: ibid.

p. 57 Sold proto-social realist prints: McCarron 1995, 5, "Martin Lewis," spanierman.com, and "Marin Lewis," britishmuseum.org/research.

p. 57 "Escapee from a tramp steamer": Albert Reese's introduction to McCarron 1995, ix.

p. 58 Lawson's draft card: U.S. Selective Service System.

p. 58 Daycare was five cents: Neugenbauer and Hartzell 2010, 34-35.

p. 58 She and Keith traveled to LA: In a letter to Lawson, 7 Apr. 1936, Ridge writes, "I lived in [California] from Sept. till end of Feb."

p. 58 Asserted her husband had died: Bill Shennum, personal communication. 10 Apr. 2013.

p. 58 Left her son 3 Feb.: G. Bernand-Wehner, correspondence with M. Leggott. 4 Apr. 2011.

p. 58 Cared for "incorrigibles": California Board of Charities and Corrections, 329.

p. 58 Mostly "half-orphans": ibid., 130.

p. 58 "Places they could leave their children temporarily": Zmora 1994.

p. 58 More than 100,000 children: Dabbagh 2011, 32.

p. 58 Scheiderman's children: Hyman 2009.

p. 58 Lange's children: Meltzer 2000, 137.

p. 58 Children not regularly adopted: McKenzie 2009, 247.

p. 58 Terrible overcrowding: California Board of Examiners, 11.

p. 58 $25 aid for two months: ibid.

p. 59 Keith moved to LA: Bill Shennum, personal communication and summary of records for Keith Bernand. See also Los Angeles Census Bureau.

p. 59 Fourteen years old: McKenzie 2009, 68.

p. 59 Dreiser pushes to end orphanages: Dreiser 1909.

p. 59 Orphanages burgeoning with castoffs: Zmore 2008.

p. 59 Rousseau abandoned bastards: Damrosch 2007, 191-195.

p. 59 Steve Jobs and daughter: Prince 2012.

p. 59 Sailed from Panama to New York: "S.S. Finance Manifest."

p. 59 Cheaper than traveling overland: Martin 2011.

p. 59 Arrived at Ellis Island: U.S. Immigration and Naturalization Service, "Vessels Arriving at New York, NY, 1897-1957."

PART II:
NEW YORK CITY AND BEYOND,
1908-1917

Chapter 8 — "Our Gifted Rebel Poet"

p. 63 Most famous anarchist: Reichert 1976, and letters from Goldman to Ridge, 1 and 2 Oct. 1908, 19 Aug. 1911.

p. 63 Goldman's Yiddish lecture series: Falk 1996.

p. 63 Lewis may have introduced them: McCarron 1995, 6.

p. 63 Crowd of five thousand: Falk 1996.

p. 63 Goldman sailing for Australia: Falk 2005, 496.

p. 63 Hoping to live a quieter life: Goldman to Ben Reitman, 18 Sept. 1908, in Falk 2005, 370. See also Falk 1990, 78.

p. 64 Fleming promised her the funds: James 2002.

p. 64 She could never return: ibid.

p. 64 "Anarchism became the favorite doctrine": qtd. in Avrich's obituary, *New York Times* 24 Feb. 2006.

p. 64 Joyce, Shaw, and O'Neill, anarchists and pioneers of social justice: Avrich 2005, 146.

p. 64 "Every good person...an anarchist": Avrich 2005, 147.

p. 64 "Liberty that consists in the full development": Bakunin 1950/1870. Bakunin's text is available via marxists.org. See also Marshall 2010, 292.

p. 64 Anarchists practicing violence: Avrich 1995, 483-504, and Avirch 2005, 84.

p. 64 Berkman's attempted murder: Avrich and Avrich 2012, 106-108.

p. 64 "Red of comradeship": qtd. in Wetzsteon 2003, 304.

p. 64 "An elderly lady in black silk": Bruno 1921, 68.

p. 65 Havel another of her lovers: Communiqué from the Royal Prussian Police to the French Interior Ministry, Berlin, 12 Mar. 1900, qtd. in Ferguson 2011, 178. The communiqué reads, "Mr. Joseph-Hyp Havel...with whom she has lived for some time."

p. 65 Havel practiced free love: Ferguson 2011, 31.

p. 65 Lived on 15th street: Bruno 1929, 69.

p. 65 "No true anarchist could destroy something": ibid.

p. 65 America was in a recession: National Bureau of Economic Research, nber.org/cycles.

p. 65 "All the people on the edge": Stansell 2009, 132.

p. 65 She drew one for Playboy: "I got Playboy and your drawing is beautifully reproduced." Scott to Ridge 3 June [1921].

p. 65 "Hate to hurry you dear": Goldman to Ridge, 1 Oct. 1908.

p. 65 "Patriotism a Menace to Liberty." Ridge 1908, cover design.

p. 65 Goldman admonished her: Goldman to Ridge, 2 Oct. 1908.

p. 65 No ball until May of next year: Falk 2005, 423 fn 3.

p. 66 "Devoted to social science and literature": *Mother Earth*, cover.

p. 66 Admission fee to the masked balls: *Mother Earth* Mar. 1911.

p. 66 "Capitalist press" and "false friends": ibid.

p. 66 "Saturnine and dyspeptic lot": "The Anarchists to Have a Ball," *New York Times*, 19 Dec. 1909.

p. 66 "The Anarchists Slide": Gornick 2011, 65.

p. 66 "A greater literary talent than any" Avrich 1978.

p. 66 "As aspen leaves quiver": De Cleyre et al. 1914, 382.

p. 66 A future without gender: De Cleyre 1908.

p. 66 "Sex Slavery": De Cleyre c.1890, http://praxeology.net/VC-SS.htm.

p. 66 De Cleyre's son: Marsh 1981, 130.

p. 66 Theories about education, but little love: Reichert 1976, 341.

p. 66 Goldman too had a child: Falk 2005, 31.

p. 66 Goldman was critical of prolonged suffering: Ferguson 2011, 119.

p. 66 Parents not responsible for upbringing: Marsh 1981, 95.

p. 67 Child should be subjected to "the boycott": Tucker 1893.

p. 67 Family at the root of inequality: Marsh 1981, 58-64.

p. 67 "Suffrage is an evil": Goldman 1910, 197.

p. 67 Preferred education, espoused violence: "The Use of Violence" 2014.

p. 67 "The ballot hasn't made man free": De Cleyre c.1891 and De Cleyre 1896.

p. 67 Resembled Wollstonecraft: Avrich 1978, 14.

p. 67 "She had the same spirit": qtd. in Avrich 1995, 212.

p. 67 Debilitating migraines: Goldman 2014/1932.

p. 67 "Capacity to conquer physical disability": ibid.

p. 67 Such a meeting was possible: "People and Events: Voltairine de Cleyre" 2004.

p. 67 Job as an artist's model: "Lola Ridge" in Quartermain 1987, 365.

p. 68 "Whitman posing in the nude": Image 115, whitmanarchive.org.

p. 68 Going rate for modeling: Baldwin 2008, 93.

p. 68 $25 in 2014 currency: davemanuel.com/inflation-calculator.php.

p. 68 Published four covers: Albers 2002, 235.

p. 68 Died under suspicious circumstances: "Biography," modotti.com.

p. 68 Heller was beaten unconscious: Schulman 2015.

p. 68 Wrote advertising copy: "Lola Ridge" in Quartermain 1987, 355.

p. 68 Advertising coming into its own: "History 1910-1920," adage.com.

p. 69 "I got so I simply gagged": Hart Crane to Charles Harris, 2 Dec. 1923.

p. 69 Where Goldman lived with Reitman: Falk 2005, 42.

p. 69 Thirty-seven-city tour: Falk 1996.

p. 70 Goldman smuggling contraceptives: "Birth Control: Emma Goldman" (2014).

p. 70 "Not your martyrs anointed of heaven": *Mother Earth* 2 Apr. 1909, 33-34.

p. 70 "Clem o' the Creek": Ridge Nov. and Dec. 1909.

p. 71 "Through many strong climaxes...": "The Magazines," *Evening Chronicle Charlotte* 8 Nov. 1909, 4.

p. 71 Sold thirteen stories in America, seven in *Gunter's* and successor: "The FictionMags Index," philsp.com.

p. 71 Sir Henry Rider Haggard: "H. Rider Haggard," booksforlearning.com.au.

p. 71 "The cities call me with a million lips": Ridge July 1909, 801.

p. 71 Emma had read Ridge's potboiler: Goldman to Ridge, 19 Aug. 1911.

p. 71 "Our gifted rebel poet": Goldman 2011/1931, 706.

p. 71 "Remote and rather conventional themes": Goldman to Ridge, 19 Aug. 1911.

p. 72 David Lawson to forward a note: ibid.

Chapter 9 — David Lawson and the Ferrer Center

p. 73 Met at the Ferrer Center: Avrich 1995, 198.

p. 73 Around five-four: Brady 2011, 64-65.

p. 73 "Always shabbily dressed...": Scott 1923, 8. As a fictional character.

p. 73 Lawson nightly at the Ferrer: Avrich 1995, 199.

p. 73 "Attracted quite a few young Americans": Goldman to Reitman, 27/28 July 1911.

p. 73 "Right by her side all the time": Avrich 1995, 212.

p. 73 Capt. Will Whipple: "Charles William Matthew Howie or David Lawson," genweb.whipple.org.

p. 73 Name given by father and mother: U.S. General Records of the Dept. of State.

p. 74 He settled on David: "David Lawson" (2005); Steinitz 2002, 19.

p. 74 Lawson had just moved to New York: Avrich 1995, 199.

p. 74 Gold tooth in his smile: Ridge to Lawson, 1 Oct. 1931.

p. 74 "An effective foil": Drake 1987, 191.

p. 74 1925 census: New York State Census, 1 June 1925, ancestry.com.

p. 74 Work as an engineer: Berke 2000, 295.

p. 74 A toolmaker in 1918: U.S. Selective Service System.

p. 74 A machine designer in 1924: U.S. General Records of the Dept. of State.

p. 74 "Consulting engineer" in 1929: Thomas Aiello's introduction to Lawson 2010/1976, xv.

p. 74 Took exams but never found a job: Lawson to Ridge, 7 Sept. 1929.

p. 74 Worked for the Board of Water Supply: Lawson to Ridge, 14 and 21 Aug. 1929.

p. 74 Civil engineer for NYC: U.S. Census, NYC, Kings County, Columbia Heights no. 387, 22 Apr. 1940, ancestry.com.

p. 74 In today's money: davemanuel.com/inflation-calculator.php.

p. 74 Ferrer Center's first manager: Avrich 1995, 198.

p. 74 "Long live the Modern School!": Abbott 1910.

p. 74 Prominent figures mourned: Avrich 2005, 31.

p. 75 Response of the Church: Punkerslut.

p. 75 Inspiration of his martyrdom: "The History of the Modern School Movement," modeducation.blogspot.com.

p. 75 Forty in Barcelona: Haught 1996, 223.

p. 75 Ferrer center had no school in June 1910: Worden 2013.

p. 75 Shared a founder but not dogma: "The Rand School, An Institution of Learning How," *New York Call* 25 Jan. 1919: 6.

p. 75 "And talk for hours on end": Avrich 2005, 111, 124.

p. 75 "Seething ocean of thought and activity": Avrich 1995, 220.

p. 75 "The longest period...": Ridge to Loeb, 1 Feb. 1922.

p. 75 "Her tireless energy": Avrich 2005, 83.

p. 75 "Had to fight hostile forces...": ibid.

p. 75 Together with a near aristocratic group: Weir 1997, 144.

p. 76 Lawson fed the hungry: Avrich 1995, 199.

p. 76 Lined up for bread: "Bread Line of Men on New York's City's Bowery 1910," allposters.com.

p. 76 Homeless men sleeping: "Homeless Men Sleeping on a Park Bench in New York City, 1910," allposters.com.

p. 76 Vagrancy had increased by fifty percent: "More Vagrancy Here than Ever Before," *New York Times* 15 May 1911.

p. 77 Henri's free art lessons: Avrich 2005, 36, and Antliff 2007, 27.

p. 77 "Personalities" in the slums: Antliff 2007, 15.

p. 77 Arthur B. Davies: Adrian 2007, 223.

p. 77 Leon Trotsky attended: Homer 1969, 174.

p. 77 Art would "keep government straight": Henri 2007/1923, 189.

p. 77 Hide their identities from the state: "Robert Henri (1865-1929)," Museum of Nebraska Art, monet.unk.edu.

p. 77 "Absolute freedom of consciousness": "Sees Artists Hope in Anarchist Ideas," *New York Times* 18 Mar. 1912.

p. 77 "The Limitation of Offspring," "The Syndicalism and Woman": Avrich 2005, 230.

p. 77 "Everybody except Schroeder": Avrich 2005, 42.

p. 77 Goldman lectured on literature and drama: ibid.

p. 78 "Every symbol in religious history": ibid., 167.

p. 78 "The Man with the Hoe": qtd. in Weimer 1960.

p. 78 "Clergy made the poem their text": Payne 1899.

p. 78 "I am...of the 'Hoemanry'": Markham 1925.

p. 78 Huntington offered $5,000: Nelson 2003, 15.

p. 78 "Laureate of Labor": Abbott 1902.

p. 78 Working for the Poets Guild: Rubin 2010, 187.

p. 79 "The Bird with the Woe": Widdemer 1922.

p. 79 Harry Kemp: Brevda 1986, 81; Buchan 2007, 65; and Alexander 2005, 39.

p. 79 Kemp the son of a candy maker: "Harry Kemp," poemhunter.com.

p. 79 Crane's father invented Lifesavers: Reed 2006, 110.

p. 79 Absconded with Sinclair's wife: ibid.

p. 79 "Poet of the dunes": Brooks 1980.

p. 79 "Fancied wearing capes": ibid.

p. 79 "Yours for the Revolution": Stansell 2009, 152.

p. 79 Rooming with Bellows: Alexander 2005, 29.

p. 79 O'Neill's first poem: Frazer 1979; Avrich 1996, 490 fn 133.

p. 79 Raids on Havel's weekly: Alexander 2005, 30.

p. 79 A character based on Havel: Levin 2009, 345; Avrich 1996, 490 fn 133; and Alexander 2005.

p. 79 Havel worked on the scenery: Avrich 2005, 143.

p. 79 O'Neill won the Pulitzer: "1920 Winners," Pulitzer.org.

p. 79 Reed shared his wife and wrote poetry: Als 2009.

p. 79-80 "Paterson Strike Pageant": Avrich 2005, 133.

p. 80 The audience sang *The Internationale*: McLaughlin 2006; and Leo 1990.

p. 80 Reed's account of the Russian Revolution: Hamilton 2000.

p. 80 Ridge repeatedly attempted Russia: Ridge to Kreymborg, [1921]; and Ridge to Dawson, [1921].

p. 80 *Crimes of Charity*: "Konrad Bercovici on Spain in New York 1924," spanishbenevolentsociety. com.

p. 80 Bercovici's multitudinous occupations: Bercovici 1941, 59, 93.

p. 80 His children attended the Ferrer: Symes and Travers 1934, 278.

p. 80 First stories in English and Yiddish: ibid., 51, 52.

p. 80 "Orphans as Guinea Pigs": Cooter 1992, 1852; and Bercovici 1921.

p. 80 Friends with Hemingway, Chaplin: spanishbenevolentsociety.com.

p. 80 Sued Chaplin: "Bercovici vs. Chaplin: 1947," law.jrank.org.

p. 80 Lawyer proved plagiarism: Nizer 2012, 9-10.

p. 80 Ridge met London: Ridge to Austin, 31 Mar. 1930.

p. 80 London was visiting the Ferrer: Haley 2011, 275-277.

p. 80 Berkman did not use the introduction: Wichlan 2014.

p. 80 London was burnt out: Hahn 1966, 117.

p. 80 Manuel Komroff: Glassgold 2001, xix.

p. 80 Wrote plays: Avrich 2005, 113.

p. 80 Music appreciation: Avrich, 2005, 88.

p. 80 Edited *The Modern Library* and fifty novels: Avrich 1995, 113.

p. 80 Travels of Marco Polo: Manuel Komroff. *Wikipedia.*

p. 81 Durant's books began at the Center: Avrich 2005, 103.

p. 81 Presidential Medal of Freedom: "Personalities," themodernschools.wordpress.com.

p. 81 Sympathetic to anarchism: Avrich 2005, 96.

p. 81 "I looked for long whiskers": Durant 1978, 188.

p. 81 Hapgood was also part of the Center: Avrich 2005, 155.

p. 81 "Everyone ends up kissing": "An Anarchist Woman" in Wheeler 1909.

p. 81 "Large eyes, dark and glowing": Hapgood 1909, 1.

p. 81 *The Story of a Lover:* "Hutchins Hapgood," *The Oxford Encyclopedia of American Literature,* 2004.

p. 81 A series of provocative letters: Stansell 2009, 297.

p. 81 Hapgood was on the bill: Kenton 2004, 93.

p. 81 Values that would transcend society: "The History of the Modern School Movement," modeducation.blogspot.com.

p. 81 163 people attended a banquet: Avrich 2005, 81-82.

p. 82 Lasted only a few weeks: ibid.

p. 82 Lawson invited Durant to head the School: Avrich 2005, 81.

p. 82 "Open-hearted Dawson": Durant 1978, 184.

p. 82 "I stood in amazement": Durant 1978, 184.

p. 82 Love at first sight: Avrich 2005, 83.

p. 82 "To give a libertarian education": Durant 1978, 185-186.

p. 83 Almost converted to anarchism: Avrich 2005, 84.

p. 83 "Try education by happiness": Durant 1978, 183-187, 196.

p. 83 "Bribes of bananas": Avrich 2005, 86.

p. 83 "Frying bananas and telling charming stories": Bercovici 1932, 102.

p. 83 Wrote a letter to his father: Liber, 486.

p. 83 Jan. 1911 protests: Avrich 2005, 88.

p. 83 Durant, lectures and marriage: Avrich 2005, 82.

p. 83 Couldn't sleep with her until she was sixteen: ibid., 100.

p. 83 "No discussions on sex...no excitement": Bercovici 1932, 103.

p. 84 "Let men be free!": Ridge 1911.

p. 84 Six months after the Modern School opened: Perrone 2015.

p. 84 Ridge proposed to publish a magazine: Avrich 2005, 170.

p. 84 6 St. Marks: "Ferrer School (1911-1953)" in Katz 2000.

p. 84 East 12th...MODERN SCHOOL": Ridge to Loeb. 1 Feb. 1922.

p. 84 Lawson designed the cover: ibid., 170.

p. 84 Durant looks dismayed: photograph in ibid., 92.

p. 84 "One of the most beautiful cultural journals": Avrich 2005, 170.

p. 84 Gave Ridge her first experience as an editor: This is despite the fact that she is neither credited as editor nor mentioned in the table of contents.

p. 84 Three died in explosion for Rockefeller: Chertoff 2013.

p. 84 "Real danger lies in suppression": *Mother Earth* July 1914.

p. 84 Alden Freeman: Avrich, 2005, 208.

p. 85 "One of the most radical experiments": Avrich 1995, 256, 507.

p. 85 The Center soon closed: Perrone 2015.

p. 85 She and Lawson left New York to travel: Avrich 2005, 161.

p. 85 "Something of the stern authoritarian in her": Durant 1978, 190.

p. 85 "I was no disciple": Ridge, Diary, 9 June 1940.

p. 85 Scott's son: Scott to Lawson, 17 Mar. 1953.

p. 85 "Each child requires individual attention": Ridge 1914.

p. 86 "We sent for her son": qtd. in Avrich 1995, 198-199.

Chapter 10 — *"Small Towns Crawling Out of Their Green Shirts"*

p. 87 Keith was fourteen: Bill Shennum, personal communication. 10 Apr. 2013.

p. 87 As Gladys Bernand-Wehner suggested: personal communication. Mar. 29, 2013.

p. 88 "Child and Wind": Ridge 1922.

p. 88 "Small house on a side street": Ridge, Diary, 22 Nov. 1940.

p. 88 Traveled to upper NY, PA, OH, MO, TN: Leggott 2006, and Ridge to Lawson 7 Aug. 1931. Ridge writes, "Dear, such a city—you get trapped in it as we did in Knoxville Tennessee once..."

p. 88 Goldman's speaking engagements across the states: Falk 2012.

p. 88 "When I was able to scrub": Ridge to Lawson, 10 July 1935.

p. 89 Tripling its population: Perlmutter, 8.

p. 89 Musicians on steamers to island parks: Woodford 2012, 43-44.

p. 89 Wide avenues, hotels and offices: "Bustling Detroit 1915," shorpy.com.

p. 89 $5 day: Perlmutter, 12.

p. 89 One millionth car: Lewis 1987, 65.

p. 89 "Fighting pacifist": ibid., 78.

p. 89 Ferrer at its height: Avrich 2005, 66.

p. 89 Left Keith never to see him again: G. Bernand-Wehner, correspondence with Leggott. 31 Mar. 2013.

p. 89 Avid reader: G. Bernand-Wehner, correspondence. 17 July 2015.

p. 89 New York Electrical School location: EMF Electrical Year Book, 240.

p. 89 Declarations of love: G. Bernand-Wehner, personal communication, 9 June 2015.

p. 89 He was seventeen: ibid. G. Bernand-Wehner, correspondence with Leggott. 31 Mar. 2013.

p. 89 Cass Tech High School: Austin. historicdetroit.org/building/cass-tech-high-school-old/ 2015.

p. 89 "Staying with people I know": Ridge to Dawson, [Feb. 1919].

p. 90 "Too painful": Ridge to Lawson, 1 Oct. 1935. Ridge writes, "No I would never go back to Los Angeles—too painful...or San Francisco either..."

p. 90 "Recognize his mother in beauty": Scott to Ridge, [Aug.] 1930.

p. 90 "My dead boy": Ridge to Lawson, 8 Mar. 1936.

p. 91 "Frank Little at Calvary": Ridge 1918, 49.

p. 91 "Lullaby": ibid., 71.

p. 91 Forty-five electrocutions: "U.S. Executions: 1917," deathpenaltyusa.org.

p. 91 "Electrocution": Ridge 1927, 65.

p. 92 Mooney began serving, 1917: Mora 2007.

p. 92 Ridge's poem helped free him: "Stone Face," *The Nation* 14 Sept. 1932, 235.

p. 92 50,000 lumber workers, 40,000 copper miners: Flynn 1973, 230.

p. 92 "Disloyal, profane, scurrilous...": U.S. Sedition Act of 1918, Sec. 3.

p. 92 Goldman and Berkman spoke against the draft: Antliff 2007, 155.

p. 92 Bottles, bricks, and catcalls, fighting broke out: ibid.

p. 92-93 "I am an Anarchist": "Meeting of the No-Conscription League," *Emma Goldman Papers*, microfilm roll 48, frames 17-22, University of California, Berkeley.

p. 93 "Induce persons not to register": ibid.

p. 93 Tarred, feathered, and beaten: Flynn 1973, 229.

p. 93 German farmers: Symes and Travers, 301.

p. 93 "Almost suicidal": ibid.

p. 93 Ridge returned alone: Sproat to Burke, 31 Jan. 1978.

p. 93 Lawson returned in Dec.: Leggott 2013.

PART III:
MODERNISM IN NEW YORK,
1918-1928

Chapter 11 — The Ghetto and Other Poems

p. 97 Monroe began publishing modernists: "A Brief Guide to Imagism," poets.org.

p. 97 "Rockets of poetry": Oppenheim 1930, 156-157.

p. 97 Settled with Lawson in Manhattan: Ridge to Harriet Monroe, 20 Apr. 1918.

p. 97 Esta Verez: "Martin Lewis," britishmuseum.org/research.

p. 97 Son of a rabbi: "B. W. Huebsch, Prominent American Publisher, Dead; Was Son of Rabbi," *The Global Jewish News Service* 10 Aug. 1964.

p. 97 "Appealed personally": Munson 1985, 143.

p. 97 Crane wanted to be published by him: ibid.

p. 97-98 Francis Hackett: "Francis Hackett – Introduction," University of Illinois at Chicago, tigger.uic.edu.

p. 98 Hackett made the connection, manuscript accepted: Ridge to Hackett [1918]; Huebsch to Ridge, 4 May 1918.

p. 98 "Refused to degrade literature": Turner 2003, 4.

p. 98 Brought out *The Ghetto*: Ridge to Monroe, 2 July 1918.

p. 98 Advertised alongside H.G. Wells: *The New Republic* 16 Nov. 1918.

p. 98 "Most vivid and sensitive and lovely": Hackett 1918.

p. 98: Left-handed compliment of masculine: Aiken, 1919.

p. 98 Evoked the masculine in praise: Topliss 1996, 16.

p. 99 "Cramped ova": Ridge 1918, 26.

p. 99 "Concern of being powerful": Aiken 1919.

p. 99 "Throb of unrelenting engines": Deutsch 1919.

p. 99 Discovery of the year: Untermeyer 1919.

p. 99 "Nothing is forced or artificialized," "unusual sense of perspective," "thin steel spring": ibid.

p. 99 "She really is a poet": Goldman to Stella Ballantine, 15 Aug. 1919.

p. 99 "Prototype of the artist rebels": Kreymborg 1918/1919.

p. 100 "Reminded of something": Ridge to Lawson, 13 Aug. 1929.

p. 100 Hester Street: "Hester Street," Community Service Society Photographs, Rare Book and Manuscript Library, Columbia University, item 230, photograph 323.

p. 100 "Pig Market": "The Lower East Side: Polish/Russian," *Immigration*, Library of Congress, loc.gov; "Jewtown" in Riis 1890.

p. 100 Roaches and garbage: "New York Tenement Life," thehistorybox.com.

p. 100 Raw oysters and rented dinner plates: "Dish Lender's Shops," *New York Daily Tribune* 5 Nov. 1905.

p. 100 Noisy streets: Medina 2013.

p. 100 Children to fend for themselves: ibid.

p. 100 Portrayed as victims or subhuman: James 1946/1907, 77.

p. 101 "Five by seven room": "Miss Ridge to the Rescue," interview by John Nicholas Beffel, Mitchell Dawson Papers, Newberry Library, Chicago, box 26 Fl 791a.

p. 101 Saw Jews only in 1911, according to Lawson: Avrich 1995, 199.

p. 101 Rough working terms: Lifflander 2011.

p. 101 "Announced to the world...": Cott 1989, 24.

p. 101 "A lot of cattle": qtd. in Stein 1962, 26-28.

p. 102 Two survivors, forty bodies: ibid., 19.

p. 102 Fined $20: Hoenig 2005.

p. 102 "That's a great play": qtd. in Szuberla 1995.

p. 102 "My self is destroyed": "Morris Rosenfeld's Sweatshop Songs," *The Assimilator*, forward. com.

p. 102 "An attempt made by a 'Gentile'": Hapgood 1902, preface.

p. 102 "Turbulent love for man and nature": ibid., 312.

p. 103 Lazarus: Lefer 116.

p. 104 "I hear his lifted praise...": Ridge 1918, 11.

p. 104 "Brilliant and cutting...": ibid, 12.

p. 104 "Appeal of a folk song": ibid., 13.

p. 104 "Vorwaerts": ibid., v, 17.

p. 104 Popular radical paper in Europe: Capper et al. 2008, 18.

p. 104 "Immigration to the metropolis": Williams 2007, 45.

p. 104 "Anything that burns you": qtd. in Tante 1935, 341.

p. 105 Swore she saw his ghost: Cluck 1941.

p. 105 One of the six books: Callard 1986, 13.

p. 105 "Euclid alone": Berke 2001, 19.

p. 105 Enthusiastic free love: "Percy Bysshe Shelley," adnax.com/biogs/pbs.htm.

p. 106 "The best America has produced": Pound 1971, 50.

p. 106 "Resist much, obey little": "Caution." Whitman 1900.

p. 106 "Treasure even its memory": Donaldson 1896, 209, and "Died in Bowery Lodgings: Sad Endings of the Career of George G. Clapp," *New York Times* 10 Apr. 1893, 3.

p. 106 "Nursed controversies": Zweig 1984, 310.

p. 107 Clapp published Whitman: "Clapp, Henry Jr.," The Vault at Pfaff's, Lehigh University, pfaffs.web.lehigh.edu.

p. 107 "Songs of insurrection also": Whitman 1900.

p. 107 Whitman's editors convicted: Avrich 1995, 15.

p. 107 "Poet-Anarchist": "Poet-Anarchist Whitman," *New York Times* 21 July 1907.

p. 107 "Uncouth, elemental, Anarchistic": Avrich 2005, 149.

p. 107 "Personalities": de Cleyre et al 1914, 340.

p. 107 Goldman at the Brevoort: Avrich 2005, 140.

p. 107 Dreiser's speech: ibid., 138.

p. 107 Traubel's contributions: ibid., 149.

p. 107 Hartmann lunched: Hartmann 1895.

p. 107 Hartmann's accomplishments: Avrich 2005, 487. Avrich (1995) writes that Manuel Komroff described Sadakichi "toothless except for two tusks." "He [Sadakichi] played the (Chinese

Magician) main thief in Douglas Fairbanks Senior's *The Thief of Baghdad*, but disappeared near the end of the filming, then demanded more money to finish" (202).

p. 107 Giovannitti: "Arthur Giovannitti, The Bard of Freedom" italyheritage 2015.

p. 107 A fearsome orator: ibid.

p. 108 "The Walker": Giovannitti 1914, 21.

p. 108 Keller's introduction: ibid, 9.

p. 108 Keller's interest in socialism: Nielsen 2004, 32, 44.

p. 108 Workers paid to hear Giovannitti's book: Lombardo 2004, 142.

p. 108 Looked like Pound: Giovannitti's obituary, *New York Times* 1 Jan. 1960.

p. 108 Spent weeks in a cage: *Giovannitti*. 1941.

p. 109 "The Cage": Giovannitti 1914, 44.

p. 109 "And so was a fanatic the Saviour": *Ettor and Giovannitti*.

p. 109 Modern prose poem: Lombardo 2004.

p. 109 Visited the Ferrer Center: Avrich 2005, 142.

p. 109 "Shopgirls leaver their work": Reznikoff 1989, 9.

p. 109 His family supported him: "Charles Reznikoff: Biography," poetryfoundation.org.

p. 110 "Does not know when to go on!": "Charles Reznikoff," *Boston Evening Transcript* 3 July 1927.

p. 110 Louis Zukofsky: Zukofsky published labor poems in New Masses. See Jennison 2012.

p. 110 Identified with the objectivists: "Charles Reznikoff: Biography," poetryfoundation.org.

p. 110 Hulme's Imagism: "T.E. Hulme: Biography," poetryfoundation.org.

p. 110 "A new cadence means a new idea": "A Brief Guide to Imagism," poets.org.

p. 110 Inspired by haiku and tanka: Kei 2006.

p. 110 Promoted H.D.: Aldington 2002, 38.

p. 110 "A Few Don'ts": Pound 1913.

p. 110 *The Glebe*: "The Glebe Description," Index of Modernist Magazines, sites.davidson.edu/littlemagazines.

p. 110 "Amygism": "Ezra Pound," The Modernism Lab at Yale, modernism.research.yale.edu.

p. 110 Believed derived from Keats: "Amy Lowell," poets.org.

p. 110 "Use the language of common speech": "A Brief Guide to Imagism," poets.org, and "Make it Sell!" in Dettmar and Watt 1997.

p. 111 "A Farm Picture": Whitman 93.

p. 111 "Too remote from our lives": "Free Verse Revolt" in Kreymborg 1934.

p. 111 "Achieves a sharp line": Untermeyer 1919, 347.

p. 112 "Records her reflections": Berke 2010, 27. Berke provides a detailed discussion of Ridge as a *flaneuserie*.

p. 112 Monroe founded *Poetry*: "Harriet Monroe: Biography," poetryfoundation.org.

p. 112 Anderson editing *The Little Review*: "Finding Aid of the Margaret C. Anderson Papers, 1930-1973," Archives Department, University Wisconsin-Milwaukee Libraries.

p. 112 Forty percent women: Newcomb 2012, 284 fn 22.

p. 112 "The one goal in life": qtd. in Weir 1997, 179.

p. 112 Became the Egoist: Taylor 2001, 25; and "Views and Comments," *The New Freewoman* June 1913, 3.

p. 112 "More rewarding than the men": qtd. in Drake 1987, 68.

p. 112 "Define oneself as an artist": Stansell 2009, 164.

p. 112 Publishers rushed: Newcomb 2012, 20-21; and "Poets Again Bestsellers," *Literary Digest* Apr. 1914.

p. 112 "Vigorous male note...": Monroe 1920.

p. 113 "Did not think of themselves as rebels": Drake 1987, 145.

p. 113 "Rage...and maternal urgency": Drake 1987, 4.

p. 113 "Uses the maternal role": Allego 1997, 68.

p. 114 "Maternal" friendships: Maun 2012, 62.

Chapter 12 — *"Sex Permeates Everything"*

p. 115 "Sex permeates everything": Ridge, Notebook, [1909].

p. 115 "Discussions of erogenous zones": Symes and Travers 1934, 283.

p. 115 "Weather-Cock Points South": Lowell 1919, 51-52.

p. 115 Two thousand brothels: Lewis 2011.

p. 115 Everyone was having sex: Chesler 2007, 62-64, Lewis 2011.

p. 115 Sex enthusiasts at the Ferrer: Avrich 2005, 81.

p. 115 Abbott's bisexual encounters: Abbott to Thomas H. Bell, 23 Mar. 1935, qtd. in Avrich 2005, 121 fn 21.

p. 116 Goldman's talk: "Emma Goldman: The Unjust Treatment of Homosexuals," angelfire.com/ok/Flack/emma.html.

p. 116 "Modernité": Baudelaire 1972, 403.

p. 116 Goldman smuggled contraceptives: "Birth Control Pioneer" 2003.

p. 116 Lectured since 1908: "Goldman Says Anarchism Will Mean Absolute Equality and Freedom for Women," *St. Louis Post-Dispatch* 1 Nov. 1908, referenced in Falk 2005, 70.

p. 116 "No Gods...": Sanger 1915, 51.

p. 116 "Women were subjugated": *The Woman Rebel*, Mar. 1914.

p. 116 Goldman's support for Sanger: "Birth Control Pioneer" 2003.

p. 116 "Intense rebel from Australia": Sanger 2010/1938, 74.

p. 116 "The Limitation of Offspring": Avrich 2005, 132.

p. 117 University of the liberal arts: Engelman 1998[a].

p. 117 Relationship with Rompapas: Engelman 1998[b].

p. 117 Sanger's eldest son: ibid.

p. 117 Donation of the *Book of Knowledge*: Avrich 2005, 101.

p. 117 "Extraordinarily effective": ibid., 92.

p. 117 "Bertha Watson": Baker 2011, 89.

p. 117 Goldman mustered support: Gordon 2007, 152 fn 106. Goldman's letter of 8 Dec. 1915 can be accessed at sunsite.berkeley.edu/Goldman/Exhibition/sanger.html.

p. 117 Sanger's husband in jail: Engelman 1998[a].

p. 117 Abbott's help with strategy: ibid.

p. 117 "Growing interest in the whole issue": Abbott to Sanger, 1 May 1915.

p. 117 "Inciting murder and assassination": Whitelaw 2001, 51.

p. 117 Sanger criticized Goldman: "Goldman, Emma (1869-1940)" in Katz 2000.

p. 117 Goldman's magazine helped: see, for example, *Mother Earth* Apr. 1915, 25.

p. 117 A book to read in jail: Reed 1978, 87-88.

p. 117 Fifteen day sentence: Marshall 2010, 112.

p. 117 Traveled with Portet: "Portet, Lorenzo (1871-1917)" in Katz 2000.

p. 117 Planning to resettle: ibid.

p. 118 "Only one stove": qtd. in Avrich 1995, 235.

p. 118 Hair frozen to her pillow: Cohen and Ferm 2006, 27-28.

p. 118 Sympathy for loss of daughter: Kuersten 2003, 134.

p. 118 Rosicrucian rituals: Baker 104.

p. 118 "Guilt" and "regret": Baker 2011, 103.

p. 118 "Leave": qtd. in Chesler 2007, 524.

p. 118 "To My Friends and Comrades": ibid., 523-524.

p. 118 Cut ties entirely: Friedman 2004, 267-269.

p. 118 Absconded with everything: Kennedy 1971, 92-93.

p. 118 New York Women's Publishing: ibid., and "Birth Control Organizations Birth Control Review," *The Margaret Sanger Papers Project*, nyu.edu/projects/sanger/aboutms/organization_bcr.php.

p. 119 "Place of expression": Goldman 2011/1931, 377.

p. 119 All deserve contact with the arts: Boyle May 1918.

p. 119 "To the Little Unfortunates": Boyle June 1918.

p. 119 Between the deep sea and the devil: Edgren 1918.

p. 119 "The bitter injustice": Mudgett 1918.

p. 119 Circulation jumped: "Birthday of the Review and Havelock Ellis," *The Birth Control Review*, Feb. 1923, 27-28.

p. 120 Taft's consolation: Olson 1979, 72.

Chapter 13 — Others and Its Editors

p. 121 Kreymborg an American Pound: Untermeyer 1967, 83.

p. 121 "Leading up to the point": Johns 1937, 221-222.

p. 121 Kreymborg's accomplishments: Norris 2011, 2.

p. 121 "Great granddaddy": Archibald MacLeish to Kreymborg, 10 Dec. 1941.

p. 121 Stieglitz circle: Norris 2011, 4, and ronsilliman.blogspot.com, Jan. 2012.

p. 121 *The Glebe*: Newcomb 2012, 271 fn 26.

p. 121 *Others* and *Broom*: Hoffman et al. 1947, 45-46.

p. 121 Moved to Ridgefield shacks: Avrich 2005, 509 fn 377.

p. 121 "First dada sports": Wetzsteon 2003, 351.

p. 121 *Others* began: Kreymborg 1925, 238.

p. 122 Play ball and talk: Mariani 1990, 123.

p. 122 "Condemning the world at large": Kreymborg to Harriet Monroe, 6 June 1915, in Parisi and Young 2002.

p. 122 Skipwith Cannell: Davis et al, 126.

p. 122 Arsenberg provided the funds: "Walter Arsenberg" 2010.

p. 122 Published an annual: Braddock 2013, 59.

p. 122 "Everybody is reading poetry": Benjamin 1919.

p. 122 "Crowds of people": Monroe 1916.

p. 122 "This Summer's Style in Poetry": Julius 1915.

p. 122 "Modernism...really begins": Rexroth 1961, 155.

p. 122 "Devoted pair of friends": Kreymborg 1925, 326; and Churchill 2006, 56.

p. 122 "Kept the movement going": Kreymborg 1925, 257.

p. 123 Ridge and Kreymborg neighbors: Sproat to Burke, 31 Jan. 1978, and length of stay confirmed by personal communication with Christine Colburn at the Special Collections Research Center, University of Chicago Library.

p. 123 Sandburg first read Ridge: Ridge to Carl Zigrosser, [1919].

p. 123 "Feared to be identified with the crowd": Ridge Nov. 1921[b].

p. 123 "Mountainous breasts tremble": Ridge Dec. 1918[b].

p. 123 Kreymborg liked "Song of Iron": Kreymborg 1918/1919.

p. 123 Pulled out by the roots: Ridge to Dawson, 16 July 1919.

p. 124 "Insurgent, heterodox character": Churchill 2006, 13.

p. 124 Three hundred subscribers: Kreymborg, 1925, 12.

p. 124 "There are always others": "Alfred Kreymborg: Biography," poetryfoundation.org.

p. 124 "Like taking out a swallowed fish hook": Robert Frost to Lola Ridge, 24 Apr. 1919.

p. 124 Frost eventually sent a check and three poems: Churchill 2006, 7.

p. 124 "Significant modernist choice": Newcomb 2012, 80.

p. 124 "I-am-it school": Henderson 1916.

p. 124 "Cutting its 'I' teeth": Wood 1919.

p. 124 "Free running sewer": qtd. in Parisi and Young 2002, 124.

p. 124 "Perceptually disjunct and socially heterogeneous": Newcomb 2012, 82.

p. 125 "Broadened the purview": Wheeler 2008, 34.

p. 125 Art and other genres: Hills and Luce 1921.

p.125 "Everything of individual quality": Ridge to an unknown recipient, [spring 1922]. *Broom* correspondence.

p. 125 Aunt of the poet: "Helen Hoyt." Poetry Foundation poetryfoundation.org 2015.

p. 125 "Woman will tell of herself": Hoyt 1916.

p. 125 "Mystery woman": Ridge Mar. 1921.

p. 125 Harrowing year of near starvation: "Evelyn Scott: An Inventory of Her Collection at the Harry Ransom Humanities Research Center," *Texas Archival Resources Online*, Harry Ransom Humanities Research Center, University of Texas at Austin.

p. 125 "Impossible for two women": Scott to Ridge, 1919.

p. 125 "Keep always like a flower": Ridge to Scott, [1919].

p. 125 "My thought reaches out to you...": ibid.

p. 125 "Moulding you with fire": Scott to Ridge, [summer] 1920.

p. 125 Scott's seductions: Scott to Ridge, 7 Jan. 1922, qtd. in Mariani 1990, 215; Newcomb 2012, 287; and Tyrer 1998, 16.

p. 125 Agreed to Rio: Ridge to Dawson, [1919], Scott to Ridge, 1919, and Cyril Kay-Scott to Ridge, 1919.

p. 127 "Lola Ridge!!": Rodker 1920[b].

p. 127 "John Rodker's Frog": Loy 1920[a].

p. 127 "Had we been frogs": Rodker 1920[a], 24.

p. 127 "Impotent neurotics": ibid.

p. 127 "God damn/woman": Rodker 1920[a], 20.

p. 127 Manuscript permanently mislaid: Loeb to Ridge, 7 Sept. 1922 and 19 Feb. 1923.

Chapter 14 — Soirées

p. 128 Weekly soirées: Ridge to Dawson, [1920].

p. 128 "All in that group": Flossie Williams 1964.

p. 128 "Yeast...was tremendously stirring": Williams 1951, 136.

p. 128 "Printed page was not enough": Kreymborg 1925, 240.

p. 128 Becoming a major force: Churchill 2006, 56.

p. 128 "She was charismatic": qtd. in Callard 1986, 58.

p. 129 "Aesthetic merits of salon conversation": Swanson 2012.

p. 129 "No one laughed": Scott 1923, 55.

p. 129 "Well-bred to the point of discomfort": ibid., 8.

p. 129 "Remembered with despair": ibid., 235.

p. 129 "I am a bitter female": ibid., 156.

p. 129 Sanger held soirées: Sanger 2010/1938, 70.

p. 129 Dodge's salons: Scott and Rutkoff 2001, 76, 80.

p. 129 Cather's salons: Skaggs 2007, 42.

p. 129 "Inside of a stomach": Barnet 2004, 46.

p. 129 Toomer's reading group: Woodson, 39.

p. 129 Millay's soirées: ibid., 46, 106.

p. 130 "Keep the flame of literature alive": Kondritzer 1984, 13.

p. 130 "[Ridge] kept the movement going": Kreymborg 1925, 257-258.

p. 130 "Arguments over Cubism": Williams 1951, 135.

p. 130 "Intensified his quest": Wagner-Martin 2000.

p. 130 So new few understood it: Williams 1951, 155.

p. 130 "Rend and pull apart": Ridge 1926.

p. 130 "Vestal of the Arts": Williams 1951, 163.

p. 130 "Flattened her with a stiff punch": ibid., 169.

p. 130 "Marianne was our saint": ibid., 146.

p. 130 "American quality in poetry": Marianne Moore to Ridge, 25 May 1920.

p. 130 Moore's 1915 visit to Kreymborg: Moore 2002, 391.

p. 130 Picnic at the Ridgefield shacks: Stansell 2009, 99.

p. 131 "Pass as a novelty": Moore 1961.

p. 131 "Rapids of an intelligent stream": Kreymborg 1925, 239.

p. 131 Socialism and suffrage: Schulman 1997.

p. 131 "We all are socialists": Moore, letter from college, 1909.

p. 131 "Radical": Moore 1919.

p. 131 "The color of the set-/ting sun": Burt 2003.

p. 131 "Moral force in light blue": Moore 1963.

p. 131 "Sojourn in the Whale": Moore to Ridge, 19 Apr. [1919].

p. 132 Ridge and Colum her main contacts: Stubbs 2009.

p. 132 "Practically recluses": Ridge to Louise Adams Floyd, [subsequent to 1927].

p. 132 Religious mania, amputation: Sehgal 2013.

p. 132 "A little painting for fun": Holley 2009, 7-8.

p. 132 Female identity and Americanness: Erkkila 1992, 120.

p. 132 Encouraged guest participation: Brooker and Thacker 2012.

p. 132 "England" at two a.m.: Kreymborg 1925, 160.

p. 132 "Even Stevens was inspired": ibid.

p. 133 Thayer had rejected the poem: Page and Moore 1994, 36.

p. 133 Tea and walked her home: Holley 2009, 45; and Moore 2002, 425.

p. 133 "Marriage": Leavell 2007, 64.

p. 133 Replaced as editor-in-chief: Hoffman et al. 1946, 200.

p. 133 "My dear Hart Crane": Ridge to Hart Crane, 5 Apr. 1919.

p. 133 Published at sixteen: Lloyd 2011.

p. 133 Pound's demand to *Little Review*: Pound 1989, 185.

p. 133 Crane's rented room: Kondritzer 1984, 15.

p. 133 Williams accepted but never printed: Mariani 1990, 137.

p. 133 At the time of Ridge's first parties: Reed 2006, 31; Unterecker 1969, 137; and "Hart Crane: Biography," poetryfoundation.org.

p. 133 Review of *The Ghetto*: Crane 1919.

p. 133 "Over the black bridge": Ridge 1918, 49.

p. 133 Introduced Loy to Bogan: Burke 1996, 288; and Frank 1986, 43.

p. 134 Bogan's Robin Hood: Frank 1986, 43.

p. 134 Loy's baby, boxer/artist: Hanscombe and Smyers 1987, 112-128; and Kouidis 2000.

p. 134 "Betrothed" and "Young Wife": Frank 1986, 40.

p. 134 "Summer Night in a Florentine Slum": Loy 1920[b].

p. 134 Return to the poor and oppressed: Dunn 1999.

p. 134 Toomer attended in May 1920: Kerman 1989, 72.

p. 134 Introduced by a mutual friend: Whalan 2006, 18.

p. 134 "Studied twenty years hence": Kerman 1989, 106, and Toomer 2011/1923, 229.

p. 134 "Delicately impressionistic...": Ridge to Jean Toomer, 12 Oct. 1920.

p. 135 "Young Indian boy": Ridge to Loeb, 1922.

p. 135 First African American governor: Rampersand 1987.

p. 135 "First American": Turner 1983, 121.

p. 135 Women to support him: Rampersand 1987.

p. 135 "Sharpened knives" East 2009, 26.

p. 135 "A toga about his spare form": Kreymborg 1925, 114.

p. 135 Hartley published in: Ludington 1992, 137, 138, 145.

p. 135 "The Fishmonger": Ludington 1992, 137-138, 145; and Kreymborg 1920, 61.

p. 135 Carnevali, immigrant, labor, prize: Halio 2008, 21.

p. 135 Spirit of a Ridge party: Carnevali 1925, 247.

p. 135 *Post-Adolescence*: McAlmon 1923.

p. 135 "Always so bored...": Moore, Conversation Notebooks, 25 Feb. 1921.

p. 135 "Piggy": Leavell 2013, 187.

p. 135 "Cross and the crown": ibid., 1 Mar. 1921.

p. 135 "He talks just that way": ibid., 7 Oct. 1921.

p. 136 "Isn't Ezra married?": ibid., 8 Feb. 1921.

Chapter 15 — "Woman and the Creative Will"

p. 137 "Never will be a really great woman artist": Ridge 1981/1919, 9.

p. 137 "Why have there been no great woman artists?": Nochlin 1971.

p. 137 "A Room of One's Own": Woolf 1929.

p. 137 "Women in Art and Literature": Pitt 1911.

p.137 "Art is Human": Gilman 1914, "Men and Art."

p. 137 "Quiet as possible": Ridge to Dawson, 1919.

p. 137 Changing the title: Ridge to Dawson, 4 Feb. 1919.

p. 137 The triumvirate: Wood 1972, 6.

p. 137 "A bohemian lifestyle": Bookchin 2001, 8.

p. 138 "Genius": Ridge 1981/1919, 9.

p. 138 "Many gifted [women]": ibid., 6.

p. 138 Positive notice of Lagerlof: Ridge July/Aug. 1918.

p. 138 "Belongs in spirit": Ridge 1981/1919, 6.

p. 138 "Largest share of intuition": ibid., 8.

p. 138 "Must be united in one individual": ibid., 9.

p. 138 "Correlating thought," "grasp truth": ibid.

p. 138 "Easily squandered": ibid.

p. 138 "Quality of the spirit": ibid.

p. 138 "Women of genius are ... men": ibid., 10.

p. 138 "No woman has yet made herself ridiculous...": ibid.

p. 139 "Naturally predatory": ibid., 14.

p. 139 "A girl slave who had the temerity...": ibid., 15.

p. 139 "The so-called courtesans": ibid.

p. 139 "Occupation by women of men's places": ibid., 18.

p. 139 "Task of providing fodder": ibid.

p. 139 "Human rights movement": ibid.

p. 139 "No longer be dictated by governments": ibid.

p. 139 "When with simian": qtd. in Huneker 1920, 192-194.

p. 139 "Great future for women": Ridge 1981/1919, 19.

p. 139 "End to sexual antagonism": Drake 1987, 195.

p. 139 "Woman is not and never has been man's natural inferior": Ridge 1987/1919, 18.

p. 139 "Completely new social and economic fabric": Ridge to Smith and Haas, 7 Dec. 1937.

p. 139 "Woman Renaissance": Ridge 1987/1919, 6.

p. 140 Ridge helped organize the tour: Ploog 2013, 122; and Churchill 2006, 58.

p. 140 In correspondence with Sandburg's lawyer: Ploog 2013, 132; and Kreymborg 1925, 343.

p. 140 Johns felt too humiliated: Kennedy 2001.

p. 140 Not included in the Chicago schedule: Ploog 2013, 123.

p. 140 Frost declined to speak: ibid., 135 fn 3.

p. 140 "Respectable, high-minded persons": Beffel Feb. 1919.

p. 140 The poets delivered their speeches: Stansell 2009, 52.

p. 140 Epicenter of Chicago's bohemian scene: "Further Signs of Spring," *Chicago Evening Post* 21 Feb. 1919; and White 2013, 89. White identifies the location as the private studio of the socialite Anna Morgan, but *Wikipedia* suggests that the studio was part of a school of drama that also hosted readings in literature. See "Anna Morgan (teacher)," *Wikipedia*.

p. 140 "A Provisional Scheme of the Universe": Beffel Apr. 1919; and Mariani 1990, 159.

p. 140 "You could hear them breathe": Williams 1951, 161.

p. 140 "Women Do Not Like His Poems": Rascoe 1919.

p. 140 "To be just a poet": Bernstein 1998.

p. 141 Hot Chicago: Levitt 2013.

p. 141 Columbia Exposition: Spears 2005, 205.

p. 141 Dawson and Kreymborg met during the war: Ploog 2005, 190.

p. 141 Ridgefield Gazook: "The Ridgefield Gazook," *DADA and Modernist Magazines*, dada-companion.com.

p. 141 One issue of TNT: "Biography of Mitchell Dawson," Inventory of the Mitchell Dawson Papers, Newberry Library, Chicago. Available online at mms.newberry.org.

p. 141 Contents of TNT: Baldwin 2000, 64.

p. 141 Work with Saphier: Kreymborg 1925, 260.

p. 141 Stroebel and Taylor: *Others* Mar. 1919, 25.

p. 141 Was to have toured: ibid.

p. 141 Ridge delivered to a good crowd: Orrick Johns to Dawson, 11 Mar. 1919.

p. 141 Frost, Lindsay, Sandburg, Stephens to have lectured: Ridge 1987/1919, 21 fn 9.

p. 141 The first season was the last: Dawson to Max Bodenheim, 6 Apr. 1919.

p. 141 "Sold lots of books": Churchill 2006, 58, and *Others* Apr./May 1919, 33.

p. 141-142 "Individuals working for society along radical lines": Ridge 1987/1919, 3.

p. 142 Expand speech to book length: Sproat's introduction to Ridge 1987/1919, fn 11.

p. 142 "Mistake you for a lamb": Ridge to Dawson, n.d.

p. 142 Viking withdrew its support: Ridge to B. W. Huebsch, 11 May 1929.

p. 142 "Its success was really *all* due to you": Ridge to Dawson, [1920].

p. 142 "Criticize fiercely": Ridge to Dawson, 11 July 1919.

p. 142 "Standing in a trolley": Ridge to Dawson, 11 Mar. 1919.

p. 142 "Deny or destroy something": Ridge to Dawson, n.d.

p. 142 "Nothing...but love and courage": ibid.

p. 142 "Till the room turned around": Mitchell Dawson to George and Eva Dawson, 5 May 1919.

p. 142 "Brilliant conversationalist": McCarron 1995, 8.

p. 143 "Phallic dances in solitude": Ploog 2005, 189-193; and Halio 2008, 21.

p. 143 "This rebellion of hers is pure beauty": Carnevali 1925, 117.

p. 143 "Preoccupation with technique": ibid.

p. 143 "Shrill, half-crazed": Mariani 1990, 169.

p. 143 "Suggestive violentism...": Carnevali 1925, 247.

p. 143 "My friends...I hate you": ibid., 260.

p. 144 "The restlessness that has no direction": ibid., 261.

p. 144 "I am disgusted with your little review talk": ibid., 264.

p. 144 "Then I don't want to be a poet": ibid., 266.

p. 144 "The Great Opportunity": Williams. *Egoist* 3, Sept. 1916, 137.

p. 144 Williams was moved by Carnevali: ibid., 101.

p. 144 "WIDE open": Williams 1919[b], 3.

p. 144 "Inevitably to be a lie": ibid.

p. 144 "BEGINNING of artistic criticism": Williams 1919[a], 28.

p. 145 "The Compromise/New Moon": White 2013.

p. 145 Letters to Dawson from the hospital: Ridge to Dawson, n.d.

p. 145 "Ready to act as a kind of intermediary": Williams to Dawson, 30 Sept. 1919.

p. 145 "A good ally": ibid.

p. 145 "Acetylene torch": Mitchell Dawson to Eva Dawson, 14 July 1919.

p. 145 Carnevali abandoned wife and children: Mariani 1990, 169.

p. 145 "My dear boy": Parisi and Young 2002, 235.

p. 145 Moore did not appreciate her work's placement: Whisenhunt 2009, 94.

p. 145 "Such ROTTEN work": Williams 1985, 44-45.

p. 145 "Easter Dawn": Ridge 1919.

p. 146 *Winged Victory* looming: photograph is in the Lola Ridge Papers at the Sophia Smith Collection, Smith College, Northampton, MA.

p. 146 Futurist manifesto: Marinetti 1909.

p. 146 "Greater as pure Victory": Ridge, Diary, 18 July 1940.

Chapter 16 — Red Summer

p. 147 "Red Summer": Arneson 2011.

p. 147 Johnson published alongside Ridge: Kreymborg 1920.

p. 147 Wave of violence from returning soldiers: Bone and Courage 2011, 78; and loc.gov/exhibits/naacp.

p. 147 Blacks fought back: Toomer 1919.

p. 147 Seventy lynchings: Gordon 1995, 95.

p. 147 Hundreds killed, thousands homeless: Lewis 2014.

p. 147 Police refused to arrest the man: Shay 2012.

p. 147 Vicious prequel in 1917: Rudwick 1982, 44.

p. 147 *It's the whites*: Barnes 2008, 143.

p. 147 Over 100 dead African Americans: Rudwick 1982, 50.

p. 147 "During the East St. Louis riots": Wells-Barnett 1917, 16.

p. 147 Torn apart: ibid, 6.

p. 148 "Baby snatched from its mother": DuBois and Gruening 1917.

p. 148 "Becomes a full poet": Hackett 1918.

p. 149 "Sleep Dolores": Ridge 1905, 33. Thanks to Michele Leggott for calling this to my attention. She also notes that "Dolorias" is a misprint in her manuscript, and that it was correctly spelled when published in the Bulletin.

p. 149 Bomb on Palmer's doorstep: O'Malley 1997.

p. 149 Blacks were susceptible to anarchism: McWhirter 2012, 56.

p. 149 "American Negro...conveying Bolshevism": qtd. in ibid.

p. 149 Predecessor of HUAC: Mittleman 2008, 83; and Polenberg 1987, 170.

p. 150 Norman Hapgood, ambassador to Denmark: Saul 2012, 188.

p. 150 Quotations from the Committee hearings: U.S., Cong., Subcommittee of the Committee on the Judiciary, Serial Set 2754.

p. 150 Reed's summons: Hamilton 2000, and U.S., Cong., Senate, Committee on the Judiciary Bolshevik Propaganda, *Hearings Before a Subcommittee...Pursuant to S. Res.*, 22 Feb., Washington: GPO, 1919.

p. 150 "Trying to get to Russia": Ridge to Dawson, 16 July 1919.

p. 150 Komroff in Russia: Avrich 1995, 202.

p. 150 "I have been over into the future and it works": Simkin 2014, "Lincoln Steffens."

p. 150 "Foremost statesmen of the age": Gordon 1995, 95.

p. 151 A million for Debs despite incarceration: "People: Eugene Debs 1855-1926" 2001.

p. 151 Berkman in solitary confinement: Fellner 2005, xiv.

p. 151 Twice married Kershner: "Emma Goldman – A Dedicated Anarchist – Jacob Kershner" 2014.

p. 151 Hoover convinced the court: ibid., and Leiser 2007. According to Hoover, Goldman and Berkman were "the most dangerous anarchists in this country." See also "She fought the law," *American Experience: Emma Goldman* on pbs.org.

p. 151 Going away party at Brevoort: Goldman 2011/1931, 710; and Editorial, *The Modern School* Jan./Mar. 1920, 78.

p. 151 "Constitution...a dead letter": Avrich and Avrich 2012, 293.

p. 151 "Even Czolgosz should be safeguarded": Goldman 2011/1931, chapter 51.

p. 152 "May be only the beginning": qtd. in Avrich and Avrich 2012, 294.

p. 152 All lists and ledgers confiscated: *New York Times* 16 June 1917.

p. 152 Mass arrests of 7 Nov. 1919: U.S. National Park Service, "Emma Goldman," nps.gov.

p. 152 "Backbone of the radical movment ... is broken": "Emma Goldman," *The American Experience*, PBS.

p. 152 Asserted she was a citizen: "S.S. Finance Manifest."

p. 152 Married Lawson: Guttmann 1971.

Chapter 17 — "We Who Touched Liberty"

p. 153 "Can't let anyone rock *Little Review*": Ridge Jan. 1919, 63. "My stone arm balks at swinging in rhythm with the mobs," she writes with regard to Pound's choices.

p. 153 Lesbian, transvestite, totalitarian: Michele Green, "Making no Compromises with Critical Taste: The War for *The Little Review*," littlereview.com/mca/mcapaper.htm.

p. 153 "Pied Piper": Heap, *The Little Review*, Oct. 1918, 38.

p. 153 "Are you hypnotized?" Ridge, *The Little Review*, Oct. 1919. 56

p. 153 "No one has yet done much": Heap, *The Little Review*, Oct. 1919. 56.

p. 153 "The Cast-Iron Lover": Von Freytag-Loringhoven, *The Little Review*, 1919.

p. 154 Freytag-Loringhoven wandered the Village: Gammel 2003, 182.

p. 154 Sent Duchamp a urinal: McCarthy 2011, 80-81; and Gammel and Zelazo 2011. See also Naumann 1994 for a discussion of her other readymades, including one called "God," a sculpture of a pipe made in collaboration with Morton Schamberg, "who is probably responsible only for taking the photograph" (171).

p. 154 Met Duchamp through Man Ray: "Baroness Elsa Biographical Sketch" 2004.

p. 154 Not necessarily heterosexual: ibid.

p. 154 Punched in the mouth: Mariani 1990, 162.

p. 154 "America personified": qtd. in Martens 2000, 67.

p. 154 Anti-Semitic review: Von Freytag-Loringhoven 1921.

p. 154 "[Madness] was a public custom": Von Freytag-Loringhoven 1920.

p. 154 "The thought of insanity scares me": Ridge to Lawson, 11 Aug. 1931.

p. 154 "The cacophonous clash": A. Jones 2004, 10.

p. 155 "She is the future": qtd. in Rexroth 1973.

p. 155 Use of many voices: Clement 2009, 180.

p. 155 Ridge reversed her stance: Ridge to Loeb, 2 Jan. 1923.

p. 155 Goldman and Berkman's going away party: Avrich 2005, 329.

p. 155 Welcomed by Shatoff: Goldman 2011/1931, 595-596.

p. 156 "Greatest railway builder" disappeared in the Purge: Symes and Travers 1934, 333; and Avrich 1995, 290.

p. 156 Reed's quarrels with Goldman: Homberger 1990, 202.

p. 156 Meeting with Lenin: Falk 1996.

p. 156 Stalled on their new magazine: White 2013, 95, references the Dawson/Williams correspondence in the Dawson Papers at Newberry Library, Chicago.

p. 156 Timidity: McAlmon to Dawson. June [1920].

p. 156 "I won't have it cut": Ridge to Dawson, [1920].

p. 156 "It spoils the friendship": Ridge to Dawson, n.d.

p. 156 "Can't just now": Ridge to Dawson, 24 Sept. [1919].

p. 156 "Rio de Janeiro for a visit": Ridge to Dawson, [1920].

p. 156 Lacking funds for Russia: Ridge to Dawson, n.d.

p. 156 "Please pay it for me": Ridge to Dawson, June 1920.

p. 156 "I shall not accept it": Ridge to Dawson, [1920].

p. 156 "Stomach trouble and nerves": Ridge to Dawson, 27 June 1920.

p. 157 "I don't want to criticize": Ridge to Dawson, [late 1920].

p. 157 Carnevali to an insane asylum: Ploog 2005, 193.

p. 157 "Undesirable to become God": qtd. in Hahn 1966, 228.

p. 157 "Until you send some dough": qtd. in Ploog 2005, 194 fn 35.

p. 157 Meningitis and death: Halio 2008, 21.

Chapter 18 — Sun-up and Other Poems

p. 158 "A foremost place of any American woman": Herman Gorman, *New York Times Book Review*, 9 Jan. 1921.

p. 158 The Bookman: *The Bookman*. Mar. 1921. 261.

p. 158 Published 1920 by Huebsch: Ridge to Jean Toomer, 12 Oct. 1920.

p. 158 "Acidly translated truth": "Briefer Mention." *The Dial* Aug. 1921, 243.

p. 158 "Honesty so quick as to be diabolical": M. D. 1920.

p. 159 "When Nero was a little boy": Ridge 1920, 8.

p. 159 "Little babies getting drowned": Ridge 1920, 9.

p. 159 "You wonder/if God has spoiled Jimmy": ibid., 12.

p. 159 "Not to be patted on the head": Crawford 1921.

p. 161 "Castle has no roofs": ibid., 13.

p. 161 "Floats dim and beautiful": ibid., 14.

p. 161 "Stairs go up into the sky": ibid., 15.

p. 161 "Mama peeps out the window and smiles": ibid., 32.

p. 161 "Jude isn't afraid of shadows": ibid., 31.

p. 162 Bethell, Mansfield and Hyde: I am indebted to Michele Leggott's insights here.

p. 162 "Never forgive them": Ridge 1920, 32.

p. 162 "He is the kind of boy": ibid., 34.

p. 163 "The grass didn't fall down under his feet": ibid., 36.

p. 163 "Like threshing things": ibid., 39.

p. 163 "Hot sweet song": ibid., 41.

p. 163 "Remote hunger": ibid., 44.

p. 163 "What are you to me": ibid., 46.

p. 164 "Scandal-mongers with gum trees": ibid., 48.

p. 164 "Playing virgin": ibid., 51.

p. 164 "Wireless whispers": ibid., 52.

p. 164 "Charged phalluses": ibid., 54.

p. 164 "I know your secrets": ibid., 55.

p. 164 Excitement of the new metropolis: Newcomb 2003.

p. 164 "East River": Ridge 1920, 57.

p. 164 "Wall Street at Night": ibid., 56.

p. 165 "Silence/builds her wall": ibid., 63.

p. 165 "Did you enter my wound": ibid., 64.

p. 165 Freud's *Group Psychology*: Ridge's Boni and Liveright edition is kept at Bryn Mawr College Library's Special Collections.

p. 165 "Man size courage and woman size understanding": Scott to Ridge, 1920.

p. 165 "She is death enjoying Life": "Autumn Night," Scott 1920, 104.

p. 165 "We beat at the door": Ridge 1920, 77.

p. 166 Hypatia flayed alive: Gibbon 1898, 109-110.

p. 166 "Feet that jig on air": Ridge 1920, 79.

p. 166 "Pelvis lifting to the white body of the sun": ibid., 84.

p. 166 Climax in the sweatshop: Lowry 1994, 26. According to an article in the *New Orleans Medical and Surgical Journal* of 1867, foremen were supposed to listen for the sound of runaway sewing machines to discourage the one benefit of treadle sewing (Castellanos 1886/1887).

p. 166 "They think they have tamed you": Ridge 1920, 87.

p. 166 Jim Larkin: Simkin 2014, "James Larkin."

p. 166 "Prejudices with economic logic": Symes and Travers 1934, 290.

p. 167 "Marianne takes great pride": Mary Moore to Ridge, 13 Mar. 1921.

p. 167 "Better work than any": Ridge to B. W. Huebsch, 12 Apr. 1920.

p. 167 A summer stay at the MacDowell colony: Courtney Bethel, personal communication. 15 Oct. 2012.

p. 167 *Our Town* and *Porgy and Bess*: "Artists and Works Supported by MacDowell," macdowellcolony.org.

p. 167 "Unplumbed potentialities": "Far from the Madding Crowd in Peterborough," *New York Times* 15 Jan. 1922.

p. 167 Ill during her stay: Ridge to Marian MacDowell, [May 1934].

p. 167 Two endorsements or an invitation: "Far from the Madding Crowd," New York Times 15 Jan. 1922.

p. 167 Returned every summer: "A Century of Creativity: The MacDowell Colony, 1907-2007," Library of Congress Online Exhibition, loc.gov/exhibits/macdowell.

p. 168 "Grapes/on a ragged corsage": Bynner 1920, 25.

p. 168 Spectra Hoax: "Guide to the Witter Bynner Papers, 1905-1962," Special Collections, University of New Hampshire Library.

p. 168 Seiffert commended, in contrast to women: Churchill 2005, 96.

p. 168 "My own emotions are not feminine": Seiffert to Hoyt, 12 Mar. 1917.

p. 168 *A tree with a bird in it*: Widdemer 1922, 42.

Chapter 19 — *Sunwise Turn and Ridge's* Broom

p. 170 "Rise, triumph and assimilation": Rainey 1998, 65.

p. 170 "Sunwise": *Dwelly's [Scottish] Gaelic Dictionary*, 1911.

p. 170 Stieglitz 291 Gallery: Jenison 1923, 12.

p. 170 "Would close his gallery": Robinson, 182.

p. 170 "So deliriously lovely": Jenison 1923, 84-85.

p. 170 Arthur Davies: Rainey 1996, 551.

p. 170 What the store displayed: Dearborn 2004, 34; and Jenison 1923, 22.

p. 170 Ancillary material supported the store: Rainey 1998, 66-67.

p. 170 Invest in art to prevent war: Dearborn 2004, 35.

p. 171 Clarke's husband: ibid.

p. 171 "Packed into a bit of plaster": Sinclair 1913, 128.

p. 171 Ferrer Center regulars: McCarron 1995, 29 fn 22; and Antliff 2007, 44, 126.

p. 171 Conference of "libertarian education": ibid., 134.

p. 171 "Recent college graduate...missionary": White 1916.

p. 171 "Read all the books before we sell them": ibid.

p. 171 Sold half the store and relocated: Loeb 1959, 53; and Rainey 1996, 553.

p. 171 "Electric light bulbs and tacks": Jenison 1923; and Dearborn 2004, 34.

p. 171 Books for decorative purposes: Dearborn 2004, 35.

p. 171 Ridge's reading: Marianne Moore to Ridge, 11 May 1920, writes, "So sorry I did not know you were going to speak at the Sunwise Turn last Tuesday."

p. 171 Each voyage turned east: My thanks to Michele Leggott for surmising this.

p. 171 Other readers at Sunwise: Rainey 1996, 553.

p. 171 Early performance of *Lima Beans*: Dearborn 2004, 36.

p. 171 Europe might be more interested: Kreymborg 1925, 252-253.

p. 171 Not ill-disposed to Rome: Norris 2011, 39.

p. 172 Hemingway's Cohn based on Loeb: Kaye 2006 44 fn 43.

p. 172 Less caustic portrait that Loeb liked: Loeb 1959, 133.

p. 172 "Squat young man": Cowley 1922, 52.

p. 172 Loeb after Princeton: Sarason 1980, 251.

p. 172 Launched *Broom* with bookshop proceeds: Fedirka 2008, 44.

p. 172 Cheaper abroad: North 2007.

p. 172 "Mother's family and its industrial achievements": Loeb 1959, 44.

p. 172 Harold Content: ibid., 42; and "Harold A. Content" in Katz 2000.

p. 172 Marjorie stayed put: Loeb 1959, 41.

p. 172 Publishing from Rome was difficult: North 2007.

p. 172 Loeb and Kreymborg argued: Loeb 1959, 95, and Loeb to Ridge, 7 Aug. 1922.

p. 172 Loeb bought out Kreymborg: Kondritzer 1984, 40-42.

p. 173 Ridge replaced Kreymborg: Loeb 1959, 87.

p. 173 "Very self-reliant young woman": ibid.

p. 173 Living in Montreal: Ridge 1918/1919, 3.

p. 173 "This ghastly country": Ridge to Scott, [1922].

p. 173 "Russian paralysis of the will": Ridge to Louise Morgan, 3 Jan. 1922.

p. 173 Evelyn Scott in Montreal: Scott to Ridge, [1928].

p. 173 Bercovici and Traubel in Montreal: Bercovici 1941, 96.

p. 173 "$60 of poems the last ten days": Ridge to Dawson, [1920-1].

p. 173 "Let me know when you are preparing": ibid.

p. 173 Musterbook: "Biographical Note," *Guide to the Hi Simons Papers, 1915-1950*, University of Chicago Library, 2006.

p. 173 "The tented autumn gone": Ridge to Dawson, n.d.

p. 173 Dawson asked Williams for work: Dawson to Williams, [1921].

p. 173 $1233.06 in 2014 dollars: davemanuel.com/inflation-calculator.php.

p. 173 An amount she often had to forgo: Ridge to Otto Theis, 21 Feb. 1922.

p. 173 "Full of enthusiasm for BROOM": Ridge to Loeb, 1 Feb. 1922.

p. 173-174 "Will not ever leave you in the lurch": ibid.

p. 174 Operated out of Marjorie's basement: Kondritzer 1984, 9.

p. 174 "Most widely circulated...of its time": Wheeler 2012, 283.

p. 174 Ridge's three conditions: Ridge to Loeb, 1 Feb. 1922.

p. 174 "Quite acceptable": Loeb to Ridge, 6 Feb. 1922.

p. 174 "Meet her half way": Loeb 1959, 103.

p. 174 "I sympathize with the project": Loeb to Ridge 6 Feb. 1922.

p. 174 "Must reserve full veto power": ibid.

p. 174 "You will run into difficulties...": ibid.

p. 174 "Wide-ranging and often discordant": Brooker and Thacker 2012, 644.

p. 174 "I think the French influence": Ridge to Loeb, 25 Mar. 1922.

p. 175 "Don't talk of quitting!": Ridge to Loeb, 28 Feb. 1922.

p. 175 Only $95 in the bank: Ridge to Loeb, 10 Mar. 1922.

p. 175 Secured $5,000 from his mother: Ridge to Loeb, 25 Mar. 1922.

p. 175 "Deeply grateful for the five thousand": Loeb to Ridge, 12 Apr. 1922.

p. 175 "The machine age of America": Ridge to Loeb, 22 Mar. 1922.

p. 175 "One of the moaners": Loeb 1959, 102.

p. 175 "Capitalism was impersonal, its products magnificent": ibid., 121.

p. 176 "Our magnificent slave": Josephson 1922.

p. 176 "The buildings are flattening us": Wilson 1922.

p. 176 "Critics assailed us": Josephson 1962, 191.

p. 176 "Stieglitz could do it": Ridge to Loeb, 25 Mar. 1922.

p. 176 Strand was willing: Ridge to Loeb, 14 Apr. 1922.

p. 176 Striking pictures of the Ghetto: Homberger 2007, 79.

p. 176 Discouraged but hoped Strand would contribute: Loeb to Ridge, 12 Apr. 1922.

p. 176 "Total agreement": Loeb to Ridge, 3 Apr. 1922.

p. 176 "Life-life-life": Ridge to Loeb, 14 Apr. 1922.

p. 176 "Harold would be as proud": Ridge to Stieglitz. 23 Nov. 1922.

p. 176 Stieglitz wanted to be in the American number: Ridge to Loeb. 14 Apr. 1922.

p. 177 "Probably the most important American Artist": Loeb to Ridge, 1 May 1922.

p. 177 Loeb asking for money in Rome: Loeb to Ridge, 20 May 1922.

p. 177 Wanted to live on his mother's gift: Loeb to Ridge, 30 May 1922.

p. 177 Mimeographed 10,000 campaign letters: Ridge to Loeb, 13 July 1922.

p. 177 A sample copy for stamps: Ridge, Postal Campaign Letter, May 1922, *Broom* Correspondence, Princeton University, Princeton, NJ.

p. 177 Subscriptions flooded in: Ridge to an unknown recipient, [spring 1922], *Broom* correspondence.

p. 177 Oscar Williams: Ridge to Loeb, 6 Nov. 1922.

p. 177 "Anything I can for *Musterbook*": Ridge to Dawson, [1922].

p. 177 "Bless your heart for sympathy": Ridge to Dawson, 29 Mar. 1922.

p. 177 Dawson's intensity waned: Ploog 2005, 196.

p. 177 "Send something good": Ridge to Williams, 30 Apr. [1922].

p. 177 "Red Eric": Ridge to Loeb, 4 Oct. 1922.

p. 177 Most significant American work: North 2007, 21.

p. 177 Accepted Williams, Bogan and Wylie: Ridge to Loeb, 30 June 1922.

p. 177 "Lead not follow": Ridge to Loeb, 26 Sept. 1922.

p. 177 "A fraction of its function": Loeb to Ridge, 30 May 1922.

p. 178 Jolas the preferred archetype: Rydsjo and Jonsson 2013.

p. 178 "Let up a little on the financial end": qtd. in Wheeler 2008, 39.

p. 178 "The great unknowns": Ridge to Loeb, 26 Sept. 1922.

Chapter 20 — Broom's Parties and the Making of an American Idiom

p. 179 Pound noted her impact: Ahearn 1987, 12. Pounds writes, "Of the earlier possible lights, there once was a certain Lola Ridge."

p. 179 Cummings' apology: e. e. Cummings to Ridge, n.d.

p. 179 Added one night a week: Hively, 92.

p. 179 Partygoers came in evening dress: Marianne Moore to John Warner Moore, 18 Feb. 1923. Gregory and Zaturenska 1946 write, "Those who remember Lola Ridge also remember the large, barely furnished, wind-swept, cold-water loft where she lived in downtown Manhattan," 445.

p. 179-180 "Jammed with writers, painters, musicians": Loeb 1959, 153.

p. 180 Boyle had replaced Benét: Ridge to Loeb, 6 Nov. 1922.

p. 180 Boyle would become a noted writer: "Kay Boyle: An Inventory of Her Collection," Harry Ransom Humanities Research Center, University of Texas at Austin, Archival Resource Online.

p. 180 "Loved each other instantly": Kay Boyle to Sandra Spanier, 19 Nov. 1984, qtd. in Spanier 1986, 10.

p. 180 $18.00 a week: Spanier 1986, 10.

p. 180 "Mother...exactly my age": McAlmon and Boyle 1984, 18.

p. 180 Taste for the avant-garde, proletariat: Levitzke 2011.

p. 180 "Lola who spoke the vocabulary": McAlmon and Boyle 1984, 22.

p. 180 "Fiery awareness of social injustice": McAlmon and Boyle 1984, 15.

p. 180 Abortion money and dancing together: Mellen 1994, 50-54.

p. 180 "Rarest and most beautiful persons": Boyle to Scott, 12 June 1922.

p. 180 "Flame I held cupped": McAlmon and Boyle 1984, 15.

p. 180 Three months as an assistant: Mellen 1994, 50.

p. 180 Ridge to encourage Scott and Moore: Marianne Moore to Ridge, 27 Nov. 1922, writes, "I shall watch for Kay Boyle."

p. 180 "Too pleasant to be great": Boyle to Ridge, 20 Aug. 1923.

p. 180 Pleasant to Ridge's guests: Maun 2012, 74.

p. 180 Selling *Broom*, cutting cake, etc.: Loeb 1959, 124-125; and Spanier 1986, 11.

p. 181 "A light in that room": Jean Toomer, "On Being American," Toomer Collection, Fisk University Library, Nashville, TN.

p. 181 "Untracked wilderness but dimly blazed": Frank 1919, 9.

p. 181 Three editions in six months: Kirsch 2006.

p. 181 "Racial composition" of no concern: Byrd and Gates 2011.

p. 181 Hoped to be published together: Pfeiffer 2010, 11.

p. 181 Managed to publish on the same day: North 1998, 163.

p. 181 Toomer wrote *Holiday* dialogue: Pfeiffer 2010, 15.

p. 181 Gurdjieff's influence: Jones 2006, xiv; and Weber 1948, 214. Jones writes, "It is a commonly held belief that Toomer's literary artistry devolved into moral pronouncements after the publication of *Cane*, owing to the influence of Gurdjieffian philosophy."

p. 181 Frank suggests Toomer submit to *Broom*: Scruggs and VanDemarr 1998, 106.

p. 181 "The calibre of Lola Ridge": qtd. in Whalan 2006, 36.

p. 181 Toomer's affair with Frank's wife: Whalan 2006, xxxv, and Pfeiffer 2010, 20.

p. 181 Identified as black: Toomer 2011, 234.

p. 181 O'Keeffe and marriage to Content: Scott W. Williams, "A Jean Toomer Biography," University of Buffalo Online.

p. 181 She stayed upstairs: Kerman 1989, 229; and McAlmon and Boyle 1984, 18.

p. 181 "How much you have given to me": Moore to Ridge, 1 Jan. 1927.

p. 181 Ridge's poem: The much anthologized "Reveille," which appeared in *The Dial* 31 May 1919, 551.

p. 181 "Industry and the Captains of Industry": Veblen 1919.

p. 181 "But should you rather not": Moore to Ridge, 25 Jan. 1929.

p. 182 "Diminution of intensity": Moore to Ridge, 3 June 1925.

p. 182 "Be sure your own...": Moore to Ridge, 1 Dec. [1927].

p. 182 Ridge published and recommended Moore's work: Moore to Ridge, 28 Nov. 1920.

p. 182 Moore and mother typed for Ridge: Moore to Ridge, 30 Apr. 1925, 18 Sept. 1924, and 1 Jan. 1921.

p. 182 "Frost typing...Stevens": Drake 1987, 265.

p. 182 "Great liking to Hart Crane": Moore 1961, 42.

p. 182 "In that bemused state": ibid., 41.

p. 182 Benéts were frequent guests: The Marianne Moore Collection Summary, Rosenbach Museum and Library, Philadelphia, PA.

p. 182 Laura Benét as assistant and substitute review editor: Stayer 2007.

p. 182 *Fair Bred*: Patterson 2007.

p. 182 Bill Benét co-founded the *Saturday Review* and won the Pulitzer: Aliperti 2014; and Mayo 2003.

p. 182 Winner of two Pulitzer Prizes: "Stephen Vincent: Biography" poetryfoundation.org.

p. 183 Wylie would appear as Benét's wife: "Elinor Wylie," allpoetry.com.

p. 183 "Lovely, amused formality": Hively 2003, 73.

p. 183 Never pleased Laura: ibid.

p. 183 Chain-link weave: Walker 1991, 74.

p. 183 "Imperious brows...": qtd. in Barnet 2004, 123.

p. 183 "Queen of poets": Rodwan, n.d.

p. 183 Millay's review of Wylie: ibid.

p. 183 Wylie's publications between 1921 and 1928: ibid.

p. 183 Torchlight parade: "Elinor Wylie: Biography," poetryfoundation.org.

p. 183 "Stood between her and living men": ibid.; and Van Doren 1937, 198.

p. 183 "I wish it were Shelley/astride my belly": OUP 31.

p. 183 Wylie haunts MacDowell: Hively 2003, 83.

p. 183 "Did you see how they hate me": qtd. in Hively 2003. See also Tietjens 1938, 192.

p. 184 Distant relative a witch: Hively 2003, 85.

p. 184 "Stood with crimson roses": Ridge, Diary, 29 Mar. 1940.

p. 184 "The greatest American sculptor": Eglington 1935.

p. 184 "You are the Goddess": lachaisefoundation.org/biography.

p. 184 Louis Ginsberg attended: Vicary 2000.

p. 184 Louis Ginsberg and nudist wife: "Commentary on Louis Ginsberg's Waterfalls of Stone," writing.upenn.edu.

p. 184 Mayakovsky's feet on the table: Mariani 1990, 247. William Carlos Williams refers to this in his poem "Russia": "He put one foot up/on the table that night on 14th Street when/he read to us."

p. 184 "Thundered out his tremendous strophes": Deutsch to Ridge, 21 Sept. 1925, qtd. in Mariani 1990, 247.

p. 184 Futurist poems in 1912: Brent and Sholokhova, n.d.

p. 184 Suspicious suicide: "Mayakovsky, Vladimir Vladimirovich," sovietlit.net/bios; and "Vladimir Mayakovsky," poets.org.

p. 184 Stole the idea: "Entry 05: Criticizing the Poet/Critic," barrettwatten.net.

p. 184 "Petrograd": Deutsch's poem is available via allpoetry.com.

p. 184 *A Brittle Heaven*: Bendixen and Serafin 2003.

p. 184 Self-described Michaelangelo: McAlmon. 1990. 3.

p. 184 "Even Robert McAlmon": F. Scott Fitzgerald to Ernest Hemingway, Dec. 1927, qtd. in Bruccoli 1995, 155.

p. 184 "Half assed fairy": Hemingway to Ezra Pound [Dear Herr Gott], 1926.

p. 185 "Office boy's revenge": "*A Scarlet Pansy*: Robert McAlmon's Secret Book," neilpearsonrarebooks.com.

p. 185 Published Fitzgerald...Stein: Mann 2006.

p. 185 Farmhand and cowpuncher: Smoller 1974, 10.

p. 185 Traveled to Chicago: Mariani 1990, 174.

p. 185 Ended up kissing his hand: ibid., 173.

p. 185 Married Bryher, ménage à trois: Guest 1984, 184-185.

p. 185 Gay subculture, classic: "*A Scarlet Pansy*," neilpearsonrarebooks.com.

p. 185 Slept with McAlmon, Oscar Wilde: Mellen 1994, 122.

p. 185 Why Dawson published alone: "Contact" in Chielens 1992, 74.

p. 185 Co-published five issues: Mann 2006.

p. 185 Early summer 1920: White 2013, 95.

p. 185 Hartley and Moore read: Barnet 2004 portrays Loy as a socialite with a voice like "thin glasses" struck "successively at random" (51).

p. 185 "Distrusted people like Ridge": Mariani 1990, 174.

p. 186 *Post-Adolescence*: McAlmon 1923.

p. 186 "We'll have to form a union": ibid. 24.

p. 186 "Even the coffee tastes like vinegar": ibid. 27.

p. 186 "A dead horse on the curb": ibid. 31.

p. 186 "Vera St. Vitus—the jumpy cooey little thing": ibid., 50.

p. 186 "The illegitimate child of industrialization, the city": ibid.

p. 186 Blue door at the top of 7 East 14: Ridge to Marshall, 1 June 1934; Smith to Ridge, 2 Nov. 1934, calls the place "a little Klondike."

p. 186 "Except she had still been pathetic": McAlmon 54-55.

p. 186 "Never do we fete our own worker": ibid.

p. 186 After founding *Contact*, that was his interest too: Mariani 1990, 175, quotes McAlmon as saying, "We will be...American."

p. 186 "One's own place in one's own idiom": Mariani 1990, 174.

p. 186 "Very sensitive": McAlmon 55-56.

p. 187 "Isn't this modern poetry awful?": ibid., 56.

p. 187 "I'd like to take art and drown it in the river": ibid.

p. 187 "Greater poet if he put more social content into his work": McAlmon 56-57.

p. 187 Faun-eared young man: Josephson 1962, 72.

p. 187 "She-ass": Mariani 1990, 172.

p. 187 "I used to like Dora": McAlmon, 54.

p. 187 "It's only ten cents": McAlmon, 61.

p. 187 "Tenderness in intercourse not the same in life": McAlmon 63.

p. 187 "Machine Dance Blues": McAlmon 1929, 36.

p. 188 "The stability of his sentences": Moore 2002, 28.

Chapter 21 — Broom's Demise

p. 189 "Glamour...would carry us over": Loeb 1959, 77.

p. 189 "Who ain't a slave?": The back cover can be viewed at sites.davidson.edu/littlemagazines/broom-gallery.

p. 189 Strikingly Cubist/Futurist: "Medgyes to Comment on European Stage Design." *Vassar Miscellany News* 19 Oct. 1927.

p. 189 Josephson Dadaist, economic history: Marshall 2005, 630.

p. 189 Josephson satirizes "Foreign Exchange": "Made in America." *Broom* June 1922, 266.

p. 190 "Elaborately odd job application": North 2007.

p. 190 "I am further hindered": Ridge to Loeb, 11 July 1922.

p. 190 Loeb rejected and complained: Loeb to Ridge, 15 July 1922.

p. 190 "If you are still a comrade": ibid.

p. 190 Publisher for Rodker: Loeb to Ridge, 29 July 1922.

p. 190 "Thankful that you exist": ibid.

p. 190 "Wiry energy and frail determination": Farrar 1922.

p. 190 "Pitied his inability": Loeb 1959, 121.

p. 190 "No longer a forum": Loeb to Ridge, 3 Oct. 1922.

p. 190 "*I can not*": Ridge to Loeb, 11 July 1922.

p. 191 "Hollow, erudite obscurity": Loeb to Ridge, 12 Apr. 1922.

p. 191 Lost her manuscript: Ridge to Loeb, [1922].

p. 191 Scott admonished Ridge: Scott to Ridge, [late] 1921.

p. 191 "I could just see you": Scott to Ridge, 1924.

p. 191 Collected by Gertrude Stein: "Louis Marcoussis" and "Alice Halicka," ecoledeparis.org.

p. 192 "Why don't you write your mother": Ridge to Loeb, 5 Aug. 1922.

p. 192 Hoping to interest Moody's widow: Ridge to Loeb, 26 Aug. 1922.

p. 192 Anti-Spanish American war poems: Pinkerton and Hudson 2004, 237.

p. 192 Many writers, Robert Frost: Dunbar 1948, 182.

p. 192 "Vachel Lindsay also here": Ridge to Loeb, 5 Aug. 1922.

p. 192 Rodker the unofficial English editor: Loeb to Ridge, 7 Sept. 1922.

p. 193 "Working without pay...the devil": Loeb to Ridge, 11 Sept. 1922.

p. 193 Loeb to Berlin: Josephson 1962 writes, "The somewhat lower costs and superior facilities we would find in Germany, *in my view*, would help prolong Broom's existence" (188, my italics).

p. 193 A month late, losing publicity, ads: Ridge to Loeb, 20 Oct. 1922.

p. 193 Ridge increased the subscription base: Leick 2008, 126.

p. 193 Could ill afford such mishandling: Wheeler 2012, fn 25.

p. 193 A month on copyright: Ridge to Loeb, 27 Sept. 1922.

p. 193 Tin box in Moscow: Ridge to Loeb, 30 June 1922.

p. 193 The work of Marjorie Content: Ridge to Loeb, 4 Oct. 1922.

p. 194 "I was all set to go back to America...": Matthew Josephson to Ridge, 20 Oct. 1922.

p. 194 "Something we have both been dreaming of": ibid.

p. 194 Further asserted his editorship: Josephson 1962, 230.

p. 194 "Pièce de résistance": ibid.

p. 194 Josephson as associate editor: Steed 2004, 187.

p. 194 "The Great American Billposter": Josephson to Ridge, 17 Nov. 1922.

p. 194 Already set in motion: Ridge to Josephson, 1 Dec. 1922.

p. 194 "At loggerheads with Lola Ridge": Josephson 1962, 230.

p. 195 "Like the burning of green roots": Ridge to Loeb, 1922.

p. 195 "Rhythm of peasantry with...machines": Jean Toomer to Ridge, Dec. 1922.

p. 195 Suggested numerous cuts: Whalan 2006, xxxi; and Ridge to Toomer, n.d.

p. 195 "Asked him to hurry with it": Ridge to Loeb, 14 Feb. 1923.

p. 195 "He has not been felt by you": Ridge to Toomer, n.d.

p. 195 Toomer revised it twice more: Scruggs and VanDemarr 1998, 129.

p. 195 "Ridge's diligent championing": Kondritzer 1984, 170.

p. 195 One of the "major forces": Rusch 1991, 16.

p. 195 "I thank you Lola Ridge": qtd. in Whalan 2006, 127.

p. 195 "Planned...a Negro number": Toomer to Ridge, n.d.

p. 195 "People in Hollywood":Toomer to Ridge [late] Jan. 1923.

p. 196 "The great negro sculpture": Loeb to Ridge, 16 Nov. 1922.

p. 196 "Should be our star number": Loeb to Ridge, 17 Nov. 1922.

p. 196 Karl Einstein, "world authority": Loeb 1959, 129; and Loeb to Ridge, 17 Nov. 1922.

p. 196 Central to the aesthetics of African art: "Carl Einstein," trashface.com/carleinstein.html.

p. 196 "Very wonderful" sculpture: Loeb to Ridge, 17 Nov. 1922.

p. 196 "Has Toomer any negroe blood?": ibid.

p. 196 Mongolian number: Loeb to Ridge, 16 Nov. 1922.

p. 196 "Shocking sex-suppression": *Broom* Dec. 1922, 53.

p. 196 "A challenge to America to recognize a national art": *Broom* Dec. 1922, 82.

p. 197 90 percent due to Ridge: Loeb to Ridge, 20 Nov. 1922.

p. 197 "Karintha": *Broom* Jan. 1923, 83.

p. 197 "The Springs of Guilty Song": Kondritzer 1984, 170.

p. 197 "Began reaching a wider audience": Wheeler 2008, 40.

p. 197 "No one...captured the spirit as lyrically": Kondritzer 1984, 171.

p. 197 "Ridge who brokered Moore's post-Kreymborg contributors": Schultze, 386.

p. 197 "He has the fine idea..": Ridge to Loeb, n.d.

p. 197 "Forgo colonial histories": Wheeler 2012, 284.

p. 197 "Her literary taste was retrograde": Josephson 1962, 231.

p. 197 "Much encouraged by your cooperation": Ridge to Josephson, 1 Dec. 1922.

p. 198 "Their brutality": *Broom* Jan.. 138.

p. 198 "Is *Broom* too conservative": *Broom* Jan. 1923, 83.

p. 198 "Any general interest in Stein?": Loeb to Ride, 19 June 1922.

p. 198 "Mostly blah! Blah!": Ridge to Loeb, 11 July 1922.

p. 198 "RESIGN ON INCLUSION OF GERTRUDE STEIN": Loeb 1959, 142.

p. 198 Stein too influential to leave out: Loeb to Ridge, 20 Nov. 1922.

p. 198 "Am rushing everything": Ridge to Loeb, 23 Nov. 1922.

p. 198 "You amaze me": Marianne Moore to Ridge, 27 Nov. 1922.

p. 198 Josephson's "proposition": Josephson to Gorham Munson, 22 Nov. 1922.

p. 199 "Josephson refused to send it": Loeb 1959, 146.

p. 199 Wrestling match in upstate New York: Brooker and Thacker 2012, 636, list the various versions of their fight.

p. 199 Munson eventually showed Ridge: Josephson 1962, 231-2.

p. 199 "The co-operation of Josephson," "flippant cleverness of presentation": Ridge to Loeb, 2 Jan. 1923.

p. 200 "It is not amusing, it is not interesting": qtd. in Bercovitch 2003, 213.

p. 200 "Hoax and Hoaxtress": Kreymborg 1915.

p. 201 "The din...rises relentlessly": *Broom* Jan. 1923.

p. 201-202 "Stein, whom I found so intriguing": Josephson 1962, 231.

p. 201 "Insisted on publishing more of Gertrude Stein": ibid.

p. 201 "The effect is entirely disproportionate": Loeb to Ridge, 20 Nov. 1922.

p. 201 "Last jerk that snapped the string": Ridge to Loeb, 2 Jan. 1923.

p. 201 Not the ideal business partner: Loeb 1959, 132, and Wheeler 2012, 46.

p. 202 Stein's obsolescence: Ridge to Loeb, 2 Jan. 1923.

p. 202 "Lola did not approve ... I didn't either": Loeb 1959, xv–xvi.

p. 202 "Struggling with obscure forces": Ridge to Loeb, 2 Jan. 1923.

p. 202 Thought Boni was complicating the situation: ibid.

p. 202 "Dinner at the *Broom* Tuesday...": Marianne Moore to John Warner Moore, 28 Jan. 1923.

p. 203 "A watchfulness between Lola Ridge and me": Loeb 1959, 152.

p. 203 Coward: Loeb 1959, 155.

p. 203 "Big businessman may think it strange": Ridge to Loeb, 22 Dec. 1922.

p. 203 "For a rich man with a hobby": Loeb 1959, 155.

p. 203 Request to print a long-held poem, comments to Toomer: Ridge to Loeb, 14 Feb. 1923.

p. 203 Boni had withdrawn: Ridge to Loeb, 23 Feb. 1923.

p. 203 "Into a vacuum cleaner": Loeb to Ridge, 28 Feb. 1923.

p. 203 "One thousand in monthly payments": Ridge to Loeb, 28 Feb. 1923.

p. 203 Willard, Loeb's brother: Loeb 1959, 95.

p. 204 "I shall fight along": Ridge to Loeb, 28 Feb. 1923.

p. 204 "Yes" on Mar. 1: Loeb to Ridge, 1 Mar. 1923.

p. 204 "You can edit...better than I": Loeb to Ridge, 1 May 1922.

p. 204 "Second thought, no": Loeb to Ridge, 7 Apr. 1923.

p. 204 "Cable if other plans": Ridge to Loeb, 7 Apr. 1923.

p. 204 Willard, sign over subscribers: ibid.

p. 204 Insisted lists be returned: Josephson 1962, 244.

p. 204 "Josephson's father had bought *Broom*": Ridge to Loeb, 7 Apr. 1923.

p. 204 Whether this was a better deal is not clear: Selzer 1996, 109.

p. 204 Loeb's request to destroy the letter: Loeb to Ridge, 19 Feb. 1923.

p. 204 "I will not withdraw carbon of my letter": Ridge to Loeb, 7 Apr. 1923.

p. 204 "I had thought that it was your health": Loeb to Ridge, 20 Mar. 1923.

p. 204 "Things in a state of confusion": Josephson 1962, 239.

p. 205 "That American poet with a pile of saucers": Lynn 1995, 214.

p. 205 "I reserved absolute veto power": Loeb to Ridge, 20 Mar. 1923.

p. 205 "No mail will be opened": Ridge to Loeb, 23 Mar. 1923.

p. 205 "Not permitted to let go": Ridge to Mary Austin, 31 Mar. 1930.

p. 205 "Salary balance...a personal debt": Loeb to Ridge, 26 May 1923.

p. 205 "Laughed out of any business": Loeb to Ridge, May 1923 [unsent].

p. 205 Withholding truth about his finances: ibid.

p. 205 Toomer had another poem: Ridge to Witter Bynner, [1922].

p. 206 Another piece from Williams: "Red Eric." Ridge to Loeb, 4 Oct. 1922.

p. 206 Carnevali poem: (to Loeb by way of Josephson) Ridge to Josephson, 1 Dec. 1922.

p. 206 "One of the most important collaborators": Kondritzer 1984, 10.

p. 206 "Whole-hearted and unselfish labors": *Broom* Aug. 1923, 61.

p. 206 "Equal voice in editorial matters": Josephson 1962, 241.

p. 206 By September, Loeb complained: Loeb 1959, 187.

p. 206 Malcolm Cowley editor at Viking: "Malcolm Cowley, Writer, Is Dead at 90" *New York Times.* 29 Mar. 1989.

p. 206 Ran *Broom* into the ground: Cowley 1994/1951, 188-190.

p. 206 "In the life of any magazine": ibid.

p. 207 The failure emphasizes Ridge's power: Wheeler 2012, 47.

p. 207 "A snowflake sparkling": Josephson 1962, 246.

p. 207"Dishonest, treacherous, irresponsible": Selzer 1996, 110.

p. 207 "Words couldn't do justice": Marianne Moore to John Warner Moore, 10 May 1923, in Moore 1998, 389.

p. 207 Loeb worked for the government: Josephson 1962, 241.

p. 207 "No longer wanted to meet ES": Loeb 1959, 215.

p. 207 Pushed to review Scott: Loeb to Ridge, 28 June 1922, 15 July 1922; Ridge to Loeb 17 May 1922.

p. 207 Outrageous, tore apart form: Scura 1995, 313-315.

p. 207 Scott catapulted Faulkner to fame: Inge 1999.

p. 207 "Pretty good, for a woman": qtd. in Meriwhether and Millgate 1980, 49.

p. 207 Loeb's reversal of the aesthetic: North 2007. 13-14.

p. 207 "Ridge's work with *Broom*": Wheeler 2012, 283.

p. 208 "Plain American": *Broom* Jan. 1923, 84.

Chapter 22 — Finding the Means: Marie Garland and Louise Adams Floyd

p. 209 Boyle confronted Loeb: Loeb 1959, 124.

p. 209 Roused from his bed: Mellen 1994, 62-63.

p. 209 "Finished by liking him": Kay Boyle to Ridge, 24 July 1923.

p. 209 Kay had his letter: ibid.

p. 209 Sent Loeb a poem: Boyle to Ridge, 8 Nov. 1923.

p. 209 Boyle felt the economic pinch: ibid.

p. 209 Grant from the Garland Fund: Avrich 1995, 511; and Maun 2012, 78.

p. 209 "The artist has been an isolated figure": Ridge to Garland Fund secretary Anna N. Davis, 8 Mar. 1924, qtd. in Boyle, Kay. *Process.* Ed. Sandra Spanier. Chicago: U of Illinois P, 2001, xxvi.

p. 209 Garland helped fund "Woman and the Creative Will": Sproat's introduction to Ridge 1981/1919, 21 fn 12.

p. 209 Dropping off Debs leaflets: Spanier 1986, 9.

p. 209 Did not persuade the fund: Samson 1996, 83.

p. 209 Ridge sent a hundred dollars to Boyle's mother: Berke 2001, 83; and Boyle to Lawson, 18 Feb. 1924.

p. 210 "Write me all you think": Boyle to Ridge, 11 Aug. 1924.

p. 210 "You are not strong": Boyle to Ridge, 20 Aug. 1923.

p. 210 Send anything she finds: ibid.

p. 210 Ridge as associate editor, Boyle as publisher: ibid.

p. 210 Suggested Ridge take her novel to her publisher: Boyle to Ridge, 15 Dec. 1924.

p. 210 Demanding Ridge re-read her novel: Boyle to Ridge, 21 Oct. 1925.

p. 210 Introduced to Evelyn Scott: Maun 2012, 2.

p. 210 Boyle abandoned her husband for Walsh: Brunner and Nelson, n. d.

p. 210 Walsh's magazine and T.B.: Spanier 1986, 17.

p. 210 Please send the subscription lists: Boyle to Ridge, 12 June 1926.

p.210 "Edit and stimulate me": Boyle to Ridge, 29 Nov. 1927.

p. 210 "Had a fine raise": Boyle to Ridge, 12 Mar. 1925.

p. 210 Scott began every letter with sympathy, illness, poverty: for example, Scott to Ridge, 3 Jan. 1921.

p. 210 Introduced Ridge to a patron: This would be Lenore Marshall, Scott to Ridge, 10 Sept. 1931.

p. 210 Ridge's finances: Bank statements are in the Lola Ridge Papers at the Sophia Smith Collection, Smith College, Northampton, MA. See also Ridge to Lawson, 20 Aug. 1933.

p. 210 Scott on a monthly stipend: Scott to Ridge, 3 Jan. 1921.

p. 210 House on Bermuda, piece of land: Scott to Ridge, 1 Dec. 1921.

p. 211 Her stated reason: Ridge to Dawson, [1921-1922].

p. 211 Boyle's new baby: Spanier 1986, 23.

p. 211 $100 prize, other recipients: "Announcement of Awards." *Poetry* Dec. 1923: 161-167.

p. 211 Commemorative ode to Columbus: "Harriet Monroe: Biography," poetryfoundation.org.

p. 211 Began *Poetry* in 1912: ibid.

p. 211 "In a Station of the Metro": *Poetry* Apr. 1913.

p. 211 Those featured in the first two years: Moore 2002, 481.

p. 211 James Joyce soon after: The year 1917 saw the publication of nine of his poems in *Poetry*.

p. 211 Monroe did not confine herself to the elite: Lensing 1991, 245.

p. 211 "The greatest poet is not always the noisiest": Monroe 1923.

p. 211 "It's hard on a man": Ridge 1927, 23.

p. 212 "Between his twitching lips": ibid., 23-24.

p. 212 Fifth floor in "The Ghetto": Ridge 1918, 20.

p. 212 Scott and Ridge at Buzzard's Bay: Scott to Ridge, June 1921.

p. 212 Grounds adequate for inspiration: overbrookhouse.com; and Erin Koh, personal communication.

p. 212 Gilbran drafted *The Prophet*: Langness 2014.

p. 212 Mother of eight and two: "On Refusing a Million," *New York Times* 28 Nov. 1920.

p. 212 Garland at suffragist convention: *Suffragist* Nov. 1920, 278.

p. 212 Supporter of La Follette: Hunt 1911.

p. 212 Served on the Committee of 48 alongside Hale: Bridges 1920; "Swinburne Hale Weds Mrs. M. T. Garland," *New York Times* 3 Mar. 1921; and "Reds Hire Counsel to Regain Freedom," *New York Times* 9 Jan. 1920.

p. 212 "About to take over America": qtd. in Irvine 1906.

p. 212 Yale banned speakers for ten years: Laidler 1922.

p. 213 Original committee members: Lewis 1922.

p. 213 "The home folks on Main Street": Laidler 1922.

p. 213 "System which starves thousands": "Garland Refuses Millions Not His," New York Times 30 Nov. 1920, 11.

p. 213 Friend of John Reed: Cowen, 88.

p. 213 Use the money for social change: "Accept $1,500,000 They Once Refused," *New York Times*, 10 Jan. 1922, 5.

p.213 Essay and three books of poetry: Cowen, 27; and Reilly 2007, 307.

p. 213 Included a poem published in *Poetry*: Marie Garland's "Desert" was published in *Poetry* Oct. 1924.

p. 213 "Shatter it to bits": Garland 1917, 79.

p. 213 "Because I am a woman": ibid., 23.

p. 213 Garland's motherhood: Garland was also a neglectful mother of six and eight adopted children, at least two of whom married one another, according to Cowen.

p. 213 Scott left Bermuda, 1923: Lloyd 1995/1996, 5.

P. 213 Traveling on "Arcadian": "Passengers for Voyage of Arcadian," *EllisIsland.org*, The Statue of Liberty-Ellis Island Foundation, 2010.

p. 213 Marie paid for Ridge's passage: Ridge, Diary, 16 May 1940.

p. 213 Including Georgia O'Keeffe: Robinson 1999.

p. 213 Wrote sonnets every morning: Ridge, Diary, 16 May 1940.

p. 214 "You are too completely creative": Scott to Ridge, 1924.

p. 214 Ridge's only regret: Ridge, Diary, 16 May 1940.

p. 214 "The flowers there burned": ibid.

p. 214 Lawson's travel plans: U.S. General Records of the Dept. of State.

p. 214 "Blue Moon Schooner Yacht to Sail on Adventure Quest in South Seas": *Bridgeport Telegram* 8 Oct. 1924.

p. 214 "Marie Garland Plans Two Year Tropical Cruise": *Portsmouth Herald* 1 Oct. 1924.

p. 214 "One of the finest of her kind": *Bridgeport Telegram* 8 Oct. 1924.

p. 215 "Lola Ridge...and her husband Lawson": ibid.

p. 215 "Contribute to geographical information": ibid.

p. 215 Ridge looking askance: photograph is in the Lola Ridge Papers at the Sophia Smith Collection, Smith College, Northampton, MA.

p. 215 Trip around the world called off: Studevant 1941.

p. 215 Marie Garland decided to marry: ibid.

p. 215 "Very, very sexy": qtd. in Cowen, 33.

p. 215 Fifty-five and twenty-two: ibid., 30.

p. 215 A good friend of Adams: Adams 1978, 174.

p. 215 Rodakiewicz, work with Strand, film on O'Keeffe: Studevant 1941, and "Henwar Rudakiewiez," thenedscottarchive.com.

p. 215 "Of course the trip is off": Ridge to Scott, Oct. 1924.

p. 215 Ridge had met Groat: Ridge to Austin, 31 Mar. 1930.

p. 216 Groat third on the Socialist ticket: City Clerk of Somerville, MA, "Elections," *Annual Reports Somerville* (MA), 1916, 379.

p. 216 "Socialist Theory; Should It Be Revised": *The Intercollegiate Socialist* 6.4 (Apr.-May 1918): 33.

p. 216 "Beautiful women I have met": Young 1939, 445.

p. 216 Groat served on the Committee of 48: *The Committee of Forty-Eight* 1919.

p. 216 Organized the School of Social Science: Gold 2000/1934, 137. Groat supported Eugene Hough, who was involved in the Chicago eight-hour workday movement.

p. 216 Groat would soon marry Floyd: Hodson 2011, 1.

p. 216 "Doubtful speaker," blacklisted: Nielsen 2001.

p. 216 "War Resistance: What Each Individual Can Do For War Prevention": Floyd 1931/1932.

p. 216 "Effort to make civilized people ashamed of war": ibid. Hodson 2011 mentions St. Bernard (54). See also S. Bennett 2003, 41.

p. 216 "Socialists being the middle ground people hated by all": Floyd, Autobiographical MS, 10.

p. 216 Charlotte Perkins Gilman served: Rodgers 2000, 314.

p. 216 "There is no female mind": Gilman 1898, 74.

p. 216 Marriage primarily an economic arrangement: ibid.

p. 216 Gilman at "Old Mastic House": Hodson 2011, 43.

p. 216 Their visits did not overlap: Marcotte 2012; and Louise Adams Floyd Guestbook, William Floyd Estate, Fire Island National Seashore, National Park Service.

p. 216 Ridge one among a number that Louise supported: Gold 2000/1934, 137.

p. 217 Wearing a black model's smock: photograph is in the Lola Ridge Papers at the Sophia Smith Collection, Smith College, Northampton, MA.

p. 217 Worked on a bust of Ridge: Ridge to Louise Adams Floyd, 30 July 1931.

p. 217 "For a perfect peace as for a quarrel": Ridge to Floyd, June 1925.

Chapter 23 — *Politics and* Red Flag

p. 218 "Individuals will always rule": Ridge to Louise Adams Floyd, 10 Aug. 1932, qtd. in Berke 2001, 53.

p. 218 Followed the precepts of Tucker: Shone 2014, 46.

p. 218 "All external government is tyranny": Tucker 1888.

p. 218 Aestheticizing the machine: Hewitt 1993, 144.

p. 218 Refused managing editor at New Masses: Ridge to Martin Becker, Feb. 1925. American Fund for Public Service Records, New York Public Library, New York, NY.

p. 218 One of the first contributing editors: Berke 2001, 87.

p. 218 *New Masses*: "The Masses," *The Modernist Journals Project*, Brown University and The University of Tulsa, modjourn.org. See also Young 1913 and Zinn 2000.

p. 218 "Socialism, sex, poetry": Symes and Clement 1934, 280.

p. 218 "Poetry is something from the soul!": Parry 2005, 291.

p. 218 It attracted illustrators: "The Masses." *The Modernist Journals Project*; Young. Young 1913; and Zinn 2000.

p. 218 Editors on trial: Simkin 2014, "The Masses."

p. 218 Mike Gold became convinced: *The New Masses* prospectus, Dec. 1925, American Fund For Public Service Records, New York. See also Syssoyeva and Proudfit 2013.

p. 218 Past contributor, shot-lived *Liberator*: Simkin 2014, "Michael Gold."

p. 218 Garland's fund, half the launch cost: "Metamorphosis," *New Yorker* "Talk of the Town." 26 Dec. 1925.

p. 218 "The principal organ": Foley 1993, 65.

p. 218 "To make the 'worker-writer' a reality": ibid., 88.

p. 218 "Poetry must become dangerous again.": Berry 2000, 110.

p. 219 Attracting Langston Hughes: ibid.

p. 219 "Gertrude Stein: A Literary Idiot": qtd. in Gold 2000/1934.

p. 219 Proletarian literature rather than literary leftists: Goodman 2015.

p. 219 "Vague, rootless people": Gold 1930.

p. 219 Joining Ridge among the "rootless": Berry 2000, 110.

p. 219 Preeminent author/editor of proletarian literature: Simkin 2014, "Michael Gold."

p. 219 Struggled with ideological upheaval: Ferrari 1985, 185-186.

p. 219 "Bare throat warm to the wishful rope": Ridge Mar. 1927[b].

p. 219 "Re-Birth": Ridge Mar. 1927[a].

p. 219 "Russian Women": Ridge Mar. 1927[d].

p. 219 "Moscow Bells, 1917": Ridge Mar. 1927[c].

p. 219 "Our silence will be more powerful": qtd. in Simkin 2014, "Albert Parsons."

p. 219 Parsons hanged for talk of violence: ibid.

p. 220 "Could not see salvation": Gidlow 1986, 81-82.

p. 220 "Without dogma": Ridge to Leonard Abbott, [1920].

p. 220 Midst of the Red Scare: "Red Scare," ushistory.org.

p. 220 "This is red, and so am I": *Indianapolis Star* 22 Nov. 1922, 6.

p. 220 Two years after Viking's founding: "Viking Books," penguin.com.

p. 220 "Possibility of reconciliation with life": Monroe 1927.

p. 220 "The fire, the earnestness": Deutsch 1927.

p. 220 "Short-story writer gone astray": Aiken 1927.

p. 220 Aiken switching from poetry to prose: "Conrad Aiken," *Encyclopaedia Britannica Online Academic Edition*, 2014.

p. 220 "Misleads the average mind": Scott to Ridge, 8 May 1927.

p. 220 Mo-ti: hyperhistory.com/online_n2/people_n2/persons2_n2/moti.html.

p. 221 "Catch a garbled word...": Ridge 1927, 12.

p. 221 "Only your/words": ibid, 13.

p. 221 "The beauty of a city dawn": Monroe 1927.

p.221 Sell one to the British Air Ministry: Foster 2008.

p. 221 "Spread a curtain of death": "The 'Death Ray' Rivals," *New York Times* 29 May 1924.

p. 221 Americans claimed to have built one: "Denies British Invented 'Death Ray'. E.R. Scott Asserts He and Other Americans Preceded Grindell-Matthews," *New York Times* 5 Sept. 1924.

p. 221 "A bomb no bigger than an orange": Alkon 2006, 156.

p. 221 "Glamorous dim light": Ridge 1927, "Death Ray," 17.

p. 221 "There is that in the air": ibid.

p. 221 "Jesus...Washed as a white goat": ibid.

p. 221 "A stirring at the quick": ibid., 18.

p. 222 Published as "Om": *The New Republic* 2 July 1924, 156.

p. 222 "The Key of Life and Death": Laker 1933, 112. Laker, a feminist, was a pupil of Julian Ashton's around the same time Ridge was his student. Dever, Maryanne and Ann Vickery. "Introduction." *Australian Women Writers 1900-1950: Rare Book Exhibition.* Sir Louis Matheson Library, Monash University. Mar.–31 July 2007. PDF.

p. 222 "This nuclear/Period": Ridge 1927, "Death Ray," 20.

p. 222 "A golden nailhead, burning": ibid.

p. 222 "Rejoiced over the Russian Revolution": qtd. in Avrich 1995, 199.

p. 222 Ridge spoke to the Irish Women's Council: Greaves 1971, 205.

p. 223 Patrick Pearse, Easter Rebellion: "The Poets of the Easter Rising," 1916rising.com.

p. 223 "Written after Ridge resigned": Berke 2000, 297.

p. 223 Lynching of a young Jewish pencil factory manager: "Leo Max Frank Bibliography," leofrank.org/bibliography.

p. 224 "Rapid Transit": "Williams and Duchamp: Artistic Rebels," teachmix.com.

p. 224 Toomer's "Gum": Jones 2000; and Toomer 1988, 18.

p. 224 "After the Recital": Ridge 1927, 79.

p. 225 Hayes' command performance: Owens 2013.

p. 225 "I shall never again even initial a poem": Ridge to Lawson, 7 June 1929.

p. 225 "No bleached white evidence": Ridge 1927, "Obliteration," 97.

p. 225 Sent a copy to Trotsky: Ridge to Louise Adams Floyd, n.d.

p. 226 Eastman and Trotsky: Eastman 1962 offers a very charming description of his relationship with Trotsky.

p. 226 Corrine Wagner: Ridge to Floyd, n.d.

p. 226 Goldwater, iconoclastic bookseller: Dickinson 1998, 78-79.

p. 226 Goldwater, avid chess player: ibid.

p. 226 Trotsky, Turkish exile: "Leon Trotsky: A Virtual Exhibition," Glasgow University Library Special Collections, special.lib.gla.ac.uk/exhibns/trotsky.

p. 226 Williams' "Russia": "William Carlos Williams: Biography," poetryfoundation.org, and Williams 1991, 145.

Chapter 24 — *"Brunhilda of the Sick Bed"*

p. 227 "Ill and in need": Mariani 1990, 258.

p. 227 Seiffert's fifty dollars: ibid.

p. 227 "Take freely what is freely given": Williams to Ridge, 5 July 1927.

p. 227 Tally of Ridge's fund: "Ledger sheets for the Lola Ridge Fund," Evelyn Scott Collection, Harry Ransom Center, University of Texas at Austin.

p. 227 $8,225 in 2015 dollars: davemanuel.com/inflation-calculator.php.

p. 227 "Stultifies the life of another...to deny love": Mary Moore to Ridge, 29 Feb. 1928.

p. 227 "Just in the rough my roses": Mary Moore to Ridge, 29 May 1925.

p. 227 "I hope it gave...indigestion": Ridge to Floyd, Feb. 1927.

p. 227 "Unheralded nerve and extreme vulgarity": Scott to Lawson, 2 Feb. 1928.

p. 228 "Incorrigibly improvident": qtd. in White 1998, 96.

p. 228 "I went one night with Becky": Scott to Ridge, 18 Feb. 1928.

p. 228 "Ravaged by illness": qtd. in Tante 1935, 340.

p. 228 "Invalid most of her life": Swan 1929.

p. 228 "Cannot be denied...cannot be confirmed": Scarry 1985, 4.

p. 228 Nothing that might warrant the life of an invalid: Ridge to Lawson 4 Aug. 1933 or 10 Oct. 1930.

p. 228 Never seasick: Ridge to Lawson, 26 May 1931.

p. 228 "In that Lu. [Louisiana] swamp": Ridge to Lawson, 24 Oct. 1935.

p. 228 Took no precautions regarding food or drink: Ridge to Lawson, [17] Oct. 1935, and 1 Nov. 1931.

p. 228 Hospital stays: Ridge to Marks, June 1920, 26 Jan. 1924; Ridge to Lawson, 4 Mar. 1929, 27 Aug. 1933; Ridge to Marshall 22 Nov. [1936].

p. 228 Surgery in 1924: Ridge to Marks, 26 Jan. 1924.

p. 228 "Ward X": Ridge 1927, 90.

p. 229 "Illness rather than age": Vicary 2000.

p. 229 "The Lady Poets": Hemingway 1924. See also "Ernest Hemingway in His Time," Special Collections, University of Delaware Library, Newark, DE.

p. 229 Ridge's weight: Ridge to Scott, 16 June 1928 (mentions 77 pounds), and Ridge to Lawson, 27 July 1933 ("Now 81 pounds, a gain of 9 pounds").

p. 229 The skinny "new woman": Stansell 2009, 213.

p. 229 Barely matches husband in height: photographs are in the Lola Ridge Papers at the Sophia Smith Collection, Smith College, Northampton, MA. See also Salter 1992 for Millay's height. For a comparison between the two, see Millay and Ridge arrested together at the demonstration: Youtube. youtu.be/1aAVU6VIedg

p. 229 "Blown away like a leaf": McAlmon and Boyle 1984, 19.

p. 229 "Nearer to a skeleton": Marianne Moore to John Warner Moore, 10 July 1929.

p. 229 Moore at seventy-five pounds: Leavell 2013, 189.

p. 229 Wylie was thin: Hively 2003, 170.

p. 229 Gaunt Virginia Woolf: E. Woolf 2013.

p. 229 Ridge's doctors baffled: Louise Adams Floyd to Lawson, 1 Aug. 1935.

p. 229 "Voluntary poverty": Kinnahan 2012, 156; and Vicary 2000.

p. 229 "Devout believer in the humanity of letters": Williams 1951, 163.

p. 229 "She made a religion of it": ibid., 146.

p. 229 "Unworldly presence": Gregory and Zaturenska 1946, 445.

p. 230 *Smart Set*: Munson 1985 writes, "Its rates of payment were low, but decisions were wonderfully prompt. One submitted little fables, epigrams, plays, short stories and within four days one received payment for an acceptance or the returned manuscript" (120).

p. 230 Sixty dollars of poems in ten days: Ridge to Dawson, [1921]. Mitchell Dawson Papers.

p. 230 A thousand dollars in today's money: davemanuel.com/inflation-calculator.php.

p. 230 Pound married well: "Biography of Ezra Pound," poemhunter.com.

p. 230 Loy's wealthy parents: Burke 1996, 18.

p. 230 H.D.'s family and fortune: Morris 2008, 122.

p. 230 Wylie and Seiffert's wealth: Keel 2009; and Roba 1985.

p. 230 Millay married money: "Millay Married Secretly," *New York Times* 19 July 1923.

p. 230 Pay his college tuition and fees: Ridge, Diary, 21 July 1940, Ridge to Lawson 24 Aug. 1933.

p. 230 "If I have to borrow every cent": *Masses* Mar. 1915

p. 230 Asking when he could get a better job: Ridge to Lawson, 20 and 26 Aug. 1930, 27 Mar. 1936, 1 June 1929, and 4 Sept. 1933. Ridge to Marks, Mar. [1920?]: "If only he can hang onto his job...have some money ahead when we leave."

p. 230 Liked to keep a studio: Scott to Lawson, 9 Oct. 1928.

p. 230 "Duty of rich people": qtd. in Hahn 1966, 137.

p. 230 The Twenties and the Renaissance: Oja 2003 writes, "Private patronage experienced a major revival in the 1920s" (203). See also Gilbert and Gubar 1988, 147.

p. 230 Goldman a midwife and masseuse: Falk 2005, 29.

p. 231 Ridge at Bryher and McAlmon's wedding: Guest 1984, 138.

p. 231 "Is it not queer": Ridge to Louise Adams Floyd, 9 Aug. 1935.

p. 231 Robinson's sinecure: "Edward Arlington Robinson," poetryfoundation.org.

p. 231 Pound's from Quinn: Casillo 1993.

p. 231 Crane's from Kahn: Kirsch 2006.

p. 231 Frost supported by Amherst, Dartmouth, Harvard: Bromwich 1977.

p. 231 "To hell with all their pity": Ridge to Lawson, 8 Mar. 1936.

p. 231 "Height of felicity": Smith 1869, 38.

p. 232 "Contemptuous silence of brick and stone": Ridge to Louise Adams Floyd, n.d.

p. 232 Doctor paid for her stays: Ridge to Lawson, 9 Dec. 1931 and 20 July 1929.

p. 232 Dawson helped pay: Ridge to Dawson, [1920].

p. 232 Marks in 1924: Ridge to Marks, 11 Feb. 1924.

p. 232 Compliments of Canby and Crane: Ridge to Henry Seidel Canby, [1929].

p. 232 Marshall paid for a workup: Ridge to Content, 23 Nov. 1937.

p. 232 "Unable to consider things ... materially": Ridge to Lawson, 3 Oct. 1935.

p. 232 "The German chef": Ridge to Lawson, 10 June 1929.

p. 232 "Avoidance of regular meals": Vandereycken and Van Deth 1994, 2.

p. 232 "Playing with an inch of toast": Ridge to Lawson, 24 Aug. 1930.

p. 232 "An occasional buttered part": Ridge to Content, [May 1935].

p. 232 Sick at the Bent Hotel: Ridge to Lawson, 26 May 1935.

p. 232 Ulcerative colitis: connecttoresearch.org/publications/21.

p. 233 Lining of her bowel: Ridge to Louise Adams Floyd, n.d.

p. 233 "Endurance despite emaciation": Vandereycken and Van Deth 1994, 2.

p. 233 127 lines before breakfast: Ridge to Lawson, 18 Aug. 1929.

p. 233 400 lines as a prelude: Ridge to Lawson, 24 Oct. 1935. See also Ridge to Kreymborg, 12 Oct. 1921, in which she brags of having written 900 lines during a short period in Montreal.

p. 233 "See colors not perceptible": Roberts 1988, 68.

p. 233 Anorexia and heart disorders: "Eating Disorders," University of Maryland Medical Center, umm.edu/health/medical.

p. 233 Tried nitroglycerin and complained: Ridge to Lawson, 5 Aug. 1935; and Ridge to Dawson, [1929], which refers to her "old stomach troubles complicated by my heart which every now and then [indiscernible] to stop functioning."

p. 233 Wylie died of heart failure: Milford 2001, 294.

p. 233 "Myocardial degeneration": Vázquez et al. July 2003.

p. 233 Death certificate: under Lola Ridge Lawson, 21 May 1941, File No. 10849, Bureau of Records, Department of Health, Borough of Brooklyn.

p. 233 "How interesting he looks in dying": Sontag 1978, 31.

p. 233 T.B., reputation as the sensitive artist's disease: ibid., 34.

p. 233 Interesting, romantic, ethereal: ibid.

p. 233 Life of spirit instead of body: ibid., 33.

p. 233 Youth, purity, genius, libido: Byrne 2011, 3.

p. 233 Girls swallowed sand: Dormandy 2000, 91.

p. 233 Arsenic to pale their skin: Pirdeaux-Brune 2007.

p. 233 "Vinegar cure": Vandereycken and Van Deth 1994, 215.

p. 234 "Great reservoir of consumption": Dormandy 2000, 240.

p. 234 Dust, dirt, rags, sputum: Brewer 1913.

p. 234 Fatal within five years: Raviglione and O'Brien 2008.

p. 234 "In fact so large": Ridge to Lawson, 11 Mar. 1929.

p. 234 "Awake all night with pains": Ridge to Lawson, 29 Mar. 1929.

p.234 Castor oil abused by anorexics: wellness.com/reference/therapies/eating-disorders.

p. 234 Davy smuggled hard candy: Lawson to Ridge, 16 July 1933.

p. 234 Anorexics use hard candy: Densmore-John 1988, 311.

p. 234 Codeine and veronal: Ridge to Lawson, 13 Sept. 1933 and 4 Aug. 1933.

p. 234 "Beautiful and loyal person": Ridge to Lawson, 11 Mar. 1929.

p. 234-235 "Always taking and seem unable to help": Ridge to Lawson, 5 Aug. 1933.

p. 235 Doctor liked her sonnets: Ridge to Lawson, 27 July 1933.

p. 235 Clean bill of health despite Mexico: Ridge to Marshall, 22 Nov. 1937.

p. 235 "Brunhilda of the sick bed": Scott to Ridge, 11 Aug. 1938.

p. 235 Passionate feeling that caused the illness: Sontag 1978, 22.

p. 235 Floyd retired to her room for years: Hodson 2011, 56.

p. 235 Scott, Boyle, and Wylie, sickly: Walker 1991, 76; and "Elinor Wylie," allpoetry.com.

p. 235 Williams and Lowell, stoic: Walker 1991, 34.

p. 235 Hysteria mimics other ailments: Smith-Rosenberg 1985, 203.

p. 236 "Would take a genius": Scott to Lawson, 30 Apr. 1929.

p. 236 "Sun machine" and radioactive belt: ibid.; and Scott to Ridge, n.d.

p. 236 "Catalyzing belt": Leon Srabian to Ridge, 14 Aug. 1928.

p. 236 "Russian intellectual sickness": Ridge to Jean Toomer, 12 Oct. 1920.

p. 236 "Unless I am very much irritated": Ridge to Lawson, 1 Jan. 1932.

p. 236 "Inhibiting voices that live within": Bennett 1986, 10.

p. 237 Callard and Glick suggested suicide: Sproat to Burke, 19 June 1978; and Callard 1986, 164.

p. 237 One meal a day for nine days: Ridge, Diary, 6 Mar. 1940.

Chapter 25 — Sacco and Vanzetti

p. 238 "Most brilliant piece of work": Jeanette Marks to Ridge, 22 Nov. 1918.

p. 238 "Poetry Shop Talks": ibid.

p. 238 Included Robert Frost and Amy Lowell: Adams, Katherine 85.

p. 238 "I have not touched my woman book": Ridge to Marks, [late 1921].

p. 238 "Have not touched my woman book since July": Ridge to Marks, [1922].

p. 238 Surgery that Marks helped pay for: Ridge to Marks, 26 Jan. 1924 and 11 Feb. 1924.

p. 239 "Enjoying Sappho": Ridge to Marks, 11 Feb. 1924.

p. 239 Woolley...one of Floyd's Peace Patriots: Ford et al. 1930, and Leonard 1914/1915, 904.

p. 239 Death of Salsedo, framing of Sacco and Vanzetti: Marks 1929, 85; and "The Execution of Sacco and Vanzetti," libcom.org/history.

p. 239 "Dubious place in society": Marks 1929.

p. 239 Court appeals six years: Pernicone 2000.

p. 239 The case is still open: Linder 2015; and "Sacco-Vanzetti Case," writing.upenn.edu/~afilreis/88/sacvan.html.

p. 239 Worldwide public feeling: Schlesinger 1976, xi.

p. 239 Shaw, France, and Einstein: Gurko 1962, 182.

p. 239 "I was crazy to come to this country": qtd. in Linder 2015. See also Newby 2006, 345.

p. 239 "Both men...were social militants": Avrich 1995, 174-175.

p. 239 "An imposing number of liberals": "Liberals in a Protest," *The Evening State Journal and Lincoln Daily News* 10 Aug. 1927.

p. 239 "Worked upon...artistic temperaments": Sinclair 1978/1928, 645.

p. 240 "Hangman's Hall": Bradshaw and Munich 2004, 196.

p. 240 Ridge and forty-four others arrested: Marks 1929, 9, and Carr 2004, 227.

p. 240 "Hang the anarchists!": Marks 1929, 9.

p. 240 "Not an anarchist...Communist...Socialist": Marks 1929, 9.

p. 240 Left her estate to King: Meade 1989, 10.

p. 240 Porter's coverage of Mexico: Reuben 2014.

p. 240 "No good to us alive": Porter 1977.

p. 240 Ridge and Millay marched away: "Demonstrations for Sacco and Vanzetti 1925 [sic]." Online film clip. *YouTube*. Google, 1 Aug. 2011. youtu.be/1aAVU6VIedg.

p. 240 "Justice is dead in Massachusetts": Gurko 1962, 185.

p. 240 Three-fourths of Harvard Law: Gordon and Gordon 1995, 171.

p. 240 "The judge...portentously": Porter 1977.

p. 241 Money provided by Edward James: Hamilton 2001.

p. 241 Martial law in Boston: Meade 1989, 180.

p. 241 Planes circled: ibid., 183.

p. 241 Dos Passos covered for the *Worker*: Neville 2004, 135.

p. 241 "Let them out!": Meade 1989, 183.

p. 241 "Quiet in the tense office": Marks 1929, 33.

p. 241 "Two in the Death House": Ridge, in Trent and Cheney 1928, 36-38.

p. 241 Machine guns and search lights, "silent figures against the grim gray": "Sacco and Vanzetti Put to Death Early This Morning," *New York Times* 23 Aug. 1927, 1.

p. 242 Ridge led a group of fifty: Marks 1929, 36.

p. 242 Met by armed mounted police: Porter 1977, 192.

p. 242 Eye-witness account of the assault: Porter 1977.

p. 242 "Lola Ridge slipped under the ropes": Marks 1929, 36.

p. 242 "The beginning of the end": Porter 1977.

p. 243 "Such a weight of pure bitterness": ibid.

p. 243 "Marched the streets alone": Cowley 1994/1951, 221.

p. 243 "Each into his personal isolation": ibid.

p. 243 "Responded with a great sob": Kahn 1950, 101.

p. 243 International rioting: Felix 1965, 230.

p. 243 Procession of fifty thousand: Marks 1929, 58.

p. 243 Tremendous funeral, all footage destroyed: Watson 2008, 349; and Young and Kaiser 1985, 6.

p. 243 "Distributing anarchistic literature": Marks 1929, 59-60

p. 243 Marched until charged by police: ibid.

p. 243 "Prepared to martyr herself": Maun 2012, 24.

p. 244 "Glad to see that our dear Lola Ridge": Goldman to Scott, 3 Sept. 1927.

PART IV:
YADDO, *FIREHEAD*, BAGHDAD, *DANCE OF FIRE*, TAOS, 1929-35

Chapter 26 — Yaddo and the Writing of Firehead

p. 247 "Henry James to MacDowell's Henry David Thoreau": Robert Towers, qtd. in Nathan 1993.

p. 247 Drunken John Cheever: "A Chance to Peek Inside Yaddo," Tan 2011.

p. 247 Gurganus' theory: Gurganus 2008, 59.

p. 247 Arrived at the colony: Kukil 2014.

p. 247 Trask's firm: spencertraskco.com/about/the-legacy.

p. 247 Trask's ill fortune: ibid.

p. 247 Poe had written there: yaddo.org/yaddo/history.shtml.

p. 247 "Creating, creating, creating": ibid.

p. 247 Train wreck: "Spencer Trask Dead in a Train Wreck," *New York Times* 1 Jan. 1910.

p. 247 Katrina survived him thirteen years: yaddo.org/yaddo/history.shtml.

p. 248 Ames hired: ibid.

p. 248 Ames invites Ridge: Ames to Ridge, 20 Feb. 1929.

p. 248 Offered another month: Ames to Ridge, 11 Aug. 1929.

p. 248 "Support of artists at political risk": yaddo.org/yaddo/history.shtml.

p. 248 "The Lowell Affair": ibid.

p. 248 Kreymborg and Lewis Mumford: Kukil 2014.

p. 248 Ridge was criticizing: *Saturday Review of Literature* 29 June 1929, 1145; and Kukil 2014.

p. 248 "Americans are the most malleable": Ridge 1921[b].

p. 248 "Heaven[s] what a job": Ridge to Louise Adams Floyd, [June 1929].

p. 248 Ridge and others reviewed positively: Van Doren 1930.

p. 248 "Too sure of myself": Ridge to Lawson, 1 June 1929.

p. 248 Ames warmed to few: ibid.

p. 248 Single bed in place of double: Nathan 1993.

p. 248 "I admire you with all my heart": Ames to Ridge, 25 June 1929.

p. 249 "I like to be shut in": Ridge to Louise Adams Floyd, [June 1929].

p. 249 "Ames persuaded her to stay": Ames to Ridge, 20 Feb. 1929.

p. 249 "Mrs. Trask's gentle presence": Ridge to Floyd, n.d.

p. 249 *Judas* from Jones: Ridge to Llewellyn Jones, n.d.

p. 249 "Most comprehensive...scholarly": Powys 2011, 518.

p. 249 The books her husband sent: Ridge to Lawson, 10 June 1929.

p. 249 *Jesus, the Son of Man*: Gibran 1928.

p. 249 "Gilbran is more formalized": Ridge to Floyd, [1928].

p. 249 "Poor little circumscribed temperate Jesus": Ridge to Floyd, [1931].

p. 249 Admired Jeffers: Scott to Ridge, 8 May 1927.

p. 249 "Eucalyptus Trees": Jeffers 1916, 153.

p. 250 "That great death-carrier": Ridge 1929[b].

p. 250 "One hour's sleep": Lawson to Ridge, 25 Aug. 1929.

p. 250 Begs for Gynergen: Lawson to Ridge, 31 July–Sept. 1929.

p. 250 Side effects of Gynergen: drugs.com/mmx/gynergen.html.

p. 251 Corax to calm herself: Ridge to Lawson, 1 Sept. 1929, and Lawson to Ridge, 16 Aug. 1930.

p. 251 Constipation and hallucination: rxlist.com/Librium-drug.htm.

p. 251 "I could not concentrate": Ridge to Lawson, 18 June 1929, in which she writes, "I have to take castor oil every third night." See also Ridge to Lawson, 14 June 1929.

p. 251 Over-the-counter narcotics: Rada 2011.

p. 251 Lithium citrate in 7-Up: Bellis 2013.

p. 251 "Some demoniacal logic": Marks 1925, 170.

p. 251 "Power and passion were made greater by tuberculosis": ibid., 182.

p. 251 "Opium taken within bounds": ibid., 184.

p. 251 "Annie Laurie": "Winifred Sweet Black," *Encyclopaedia Britannica Online Academic Edition*, 2014.

p. 252 *The Hasheesh Eater*: Ludlow 1857, 13.

p. 252 "Looking forward to coming up": Lawson to Ridge, 19 June 1929.

p. 252 $28 suit, suggestion that she come to New York: Lawson to Ridge, 4 and 13 July 1929.

p. 252 "Worked til 3 am": Ridge to Lawson, 16 July 1929.

p. 252 "Glad to see you and read your poem": Lawson to Ridge, 29 July 1929.

p. 252 Began to fix up her studio: Lawson to Ridge, 27 July 1929, 25 Aug. 1929, and 28 Aug. 1929.

p. 252 "I feel like a race horse": Ridge to Louise Adams Floyd, 29 Aug. 1929.

p. 252 "Very pleased you've got so much done": Lawson to Ridge, 8 Aug. 1929.

p. 253 "You are creating great literature": ibid.

p. 253 "378 lines in two days": Ridge to Lawson, 12 Aug. 1929.

p. 253 Benét had found her Payson and Clarke: Scott to Ridge, 27 Aug. 1929.

p. 253 Whenever she could produce it: Ridge to Lawson, 25 Sept. 1929.

p. 253 Benét to edit: Ridge to Lawson, 25 Aug. 1929.

p. 253 Seldom went down for dinner: Ridge to Lawson, 10 June 1929.

p. 253 Eisenberg's character sketch: Horoscope for Lola Ridge, 23 July 1929, Lola Ridge Papers, Sophia Smith Collection, Smith College, Northampton, MA.

p. 253 "Made for everyone to worship": Kay Boyle to Joan Boyle, 19 Nov. 1923, qtd. in Mellen 1994, 50.

p. 253 Paul Bowles in attendance, and Dahlberg: Lesley Leduc, personal communication.

p. 253 "The one I like best is Gerald Sykes": Ridge to Louise Adams Floyd, n.d.

p. 253 Couldn't write after talking to Benét: Ridge to Lawson, 19 July 1929.

p. 253 Fitts translating from Latin: "Dudley Fitts," *Encyclopaedia Britannica Online Academic Edition*, 2013.

p. 254 Scott and Metcalfe: Lawson to Ridge, 29 Aug. 1929; and L. Leduc, personal communication containing a list of all guests during Ridge's two stays at Yaddo.

p. 254 Dedication to Ridge: Scott 1929.

p. 254 Eda Lou Walton: Kellman 2005, 103.

p. 254 Mead disapproving of Walton: ibid., 101.

p. 254 "Voyeurs of the 'liberal' persuasion": ibid., 104.

p. 254 Walton on UnAmerican list: U.S. Cong. 1944.

p. 254 Ridge and Walton published together: *Poetry* Apr./Sept. 1920.

p. 254 "I'm seeing no one and it wouldn't help": Lawson to Ridge, 14 Aug. 1929.

p. 254 "Only death will stop me": Ridge to Lawson, 27 Aug. 1929.

p. 254 "It isn't worth it": Lawson to Ridge, 28 Aug. 1929.

p. 254 "The boat at Albany": Lawson to Ridge, 29 Aug. 1929.

p. 254 "Only your personal condition and work": Lawson to Ridge, 1 Sept. 1929.

p. 255 "His will foil any chance of mine selling": Ridge to Lawson, 2 Sept. 1929.

p. 255 Davy met her with roses: Ridge to Ames, 16 Sept. 1929.

Chapter 27 — Firehead's Success

p. 256 "225 copies on rag paper": Kukil 2014.

p. 256 Sixty reviews: The idea of a poem receiving sixty reviews today is laughable. Many excellent books receive a single review, or none, although this has changed somewhat with the Internet.

p. 256 "Ecce Homo": Hutchinson 1929.

p. 256 Society pages: *Kokomo Tribune* 12 Nov. 1930.

p. 256 "Poet Has Perfect Command": Stone 1930.

p. 256 "New Poetic Heights": Morgan 1930.

p. 256 "Mighty Poem of Crucifixion": Bradley 1929.

p. 256 "One of possibly three": "Close Reading of Haskin..." *The Helena Daily Independent* 12 Jan. 1930.

p. 256 "This is magnificent work": Benét 1929.

p. 256 "One of the most impressive creations": Untermeyer 1929.

p. 256 "Proud indeed—and very humble": Ames to Ridge, 16 Dec. 1929.

p. 256 "It was ordained": Ridge to Lawson, 25 Oct. 1931.

p. 256 "Lunch with all my publishers": Ridge to Louise Adams Floyd, 12 Dec. 1929.

p. 257 "A man dangerous to governments": Ridge 1929[a], 203.

p. 257 Some form of inner violence: Lisella 2002.

p. 257 "Deep blaze of tenderness": Ridge 1929[a], 134.

p. 257 "Tits[z]ell...talked me up": Ridge to Louise Adams Floyd, 12 Dec. 1929.

p. 257 Titzell, the man-in-the-know: "The Perennial Bachelor," 1925 by Anne Parrish, Brandeis Best Sellers Database. unsworth.unet.brandeis.edu/courses/bestsellers.

p. 257 "Founded on a complete misconception": Ridge to Floyd, 12 Dec. 1929.

p. 257 "Stung tinglingly awake": Hutchinson 1929.

p. 257 Written in direct response to Sacco and Vanzetti: Vicary 2000; and Sproat to Burke, 19 June 1978.

p. 258 Began writing after their deaths: Quartermain 1987, 359; and Benét 1933, 52.

p. 258 "Most famous victim of institutionalized murder": Berke 2001, 40.

p. 258 *America Arraigned*: Trent and Cheney 1928.

p. 258 Another Pontius Pilate, "Two Crucified": ibid., 52, 57. See also Kramer and Goodman 2011.

p. 258 "Two in the Death House": qtd. in Kramer and Goodman 2011, 273.

p. 258 "He was but eleven then": Ridge 1929, 133.

p. 259 "I did not love him": ibid., 136.

p. 259 Letters stopped coming from her son: Bernand-Wehner personal communication. June 9, 2015.

p. 259 "He is old enough now to have read": Scott to Ridge, [Aug.] 1930.

p. 259 "Ridge has attempted too much": Applegate 1932.

p. 259 "Fiercely maternal urgency": Drake 1987, 4.

p. 259 "Anachronistic poetess-like lyric style": Lisella 2002.

p. 259 "Scalding lavas": Ridge 1929, 95.

p. 259 "O hills": ibid.

p. 260 "Take back thy son": ibid., 98.

p. 260 "*Nice* is...laughable": Ridge to Floyd, 12 Aug. 1932.

p. 260 John Haynes Holmes: Schulz 2004, 95; and Sprecher 2002.

p. 260 Reading at the Park Avenue Community Church: *Columbia Daily Spectator*, 16 Jan. 1931. See also Austin 1979, 118, for the invitation.

p. 260 "Criticism beyond me": Gerald Sykes to Ridge, 2 Jan. 1930.

p. 260 She supported his Guggenheim application: Kukil 2014.

p. 261 "Christ's mystic power": Marianne Moore to Ridge, 19 Sept. 1929.

p. 261 "Reiterated images of light": Gregory and Zaturenska 1946, 446.

p. 261 The two books reviewed together: For example, Ford 1929; Gale 1931; Haines 1929; and Hartsock 1930.

p. 261 Jeffers influenced by Noh plays: "Works by Jeffers," robinsonjeffersassociation.org.

p. 261 Jeffers wasn't interested in Christianity: Thesing 1995, 123.

p. 261 "Jeffers is more subtly and more sophisticated": Hartsock 1930.

p. 261 "Ridge's book is...more momentous": Salemson 2002, 74.

p. 261 "Thinking seriously about our selection...": Robinson Jeffers to Harriet Monroe, 11 Apr. 1932, in Karman 2009.

p. 262 "Jeffers was for me": Ridge to Louise Adams Floyd, n.d.

p. 262 "A great puritan poet": Ridge to Floyd, n.d.

p. 262 Dedicated a poem, recommended him, shared his work: Ridge to Owen Small, 31 Jan. 1931. The ailing Mr. Small of Saranac Lake sent requests for recommendations to Edward Arlington Robinson, Louis Untermeyer, and Canadian writer Constance Lindsay Skinner. These requests can be found in the Edward Arlington Robinson Papers, NYPL; the Library of Congress; and Boutilier and Prentice 1997, 162, respectively. See also Ridge to Floyd, 7 Aug. 1932.

p. 262 "Hang Hitler and Roosevelt in one tree": Jeffers 1991, "Fantasy," 109.

p. 262 Anarchism caused him to fall out of favor: "Robinson Jeffers," poets.org.

p. 262 *Firehead* was to be set in NY: Ridge to B. W. Huebsch, 11 May 1929.

p. 262 *Lightwheel*: Berke 2001, 83.

p. 262 Waterwheels in Kanieri Township: "The Kanieri and Waimea Districts," *West Coast Times* 11 Feb. 1870, 3. And Mary Rooney, personal communication, 10 Feb. 2013.

p. 262 Ever-present threat of fire: "Destruction of the Fire Brigade Hall and Bell Tower," *Grey River Argus* 16 Jan. 1875. This article tells the story of a lightning strike that burned down the firehall while they were celebrating the purchase of a new fire engine. All was destroyed but the fire engine, named "Surprise."

p. 262 "In case I want to make alterations": Ridge to Lawson, 18 July 1929.

p. 263 "The poet does have that authority": Hart Crane to Harriet Monroe, printed in *Poetry* Oct. 1926, 235.

p. 263 "Pope might translate Shakespeare": Deutsch 1935, 23.

p. 264 "Thy Guerdon...Accolade thou dost bestow": Crane 1987, 1.

p. 264 "*The Bridge* does not succeed": Jarrell 1999, 245.

p. 264 "Hardly understand a single line": Williams 2006/1936, 35.

p. 264 "Set above Yeats and Stevens": Bloom 1991.

p. 264 "Greatest contemporary American love poem": Vendler 1969.

p. 264 "Non-rational, connotative connections": Yezzi 2007.

p. 264 Childhood friend of Crane: Fisher 2002, 248.

p. 264 "Concerted effort to promote him": Introduction, *Field* (fall 2006), 9.

p. 265 "Mostly I've loved lines": ibid., 16.

p. 265 "Overly sweeping and mythic": ibid., 38.

p. 265 "Fondness for bombast": ibid., 47.

p. 265 "Institutions of privacy": Dean 1996, 84.

p. 265 "Subverts both the modernism and the Marxism": Daly 2002.

p. 266 "Promotion...plays a role": Nelson 1989, 35.

p. 266 "We were not yet acquainted": qtd. in Pondrom 2011, 4.

p. 266 "A wealthy Scottish family: Kissane 2009.

p. 266 "Verlaine's bed-time...Alchemy": Mirrlees 1919, 22.

p. 266 Joyce's doppelganger: "Abraham Lincoln Gillespie" 2010.

p. 267 Link, groomed for bourgeois life: Leon 1980.

p. 267 Published in *Transition*: "Abraham Lincoln Gillespie" 2010.

p. 267 "Sweettrustmisery-Eyed...": Gillespie 1980.

p. 267 One room stone house: Leon 1980.

p. 267 Gillespie's sonic performances: "Abraham Lincoln Gillespie" 2010.

p. 267 Occupation, "none": Swift 2006.

Chapter 28 — Return to Yaddo: Taggard and Copland

p. 268 Settled in her old room: Ridge to Lawson, 10 July 1930.

p. 268 "In a beastly temper": Ridge to Louise Adams Floyd, [Apr. 1930].

p. 268 Invited for a second stay despite restriction: Kukil 2014.

p. 268 Entertained visitors in her room: ibid.

p. 268 Taggard's visit: Ridge to Lawson, 12 July 1930.

p. 268 "At last you are here": qtd. in Kukil 2014.

p. 268 Formative years in Hawaii: Nancy Berke, "Genevieve Taggard: Biographical Note," *Modern American Poetry*, english.illinois.edu.

p. 268 Helped publicize *Sun-Up*: Berke 2001, 28. Ridge also critiqued a story she sent to Broom. Ridge to Taggard, n.d. NYPL Manuscripts and Archives.

p. 268 Co-founded *The Measure*: Nancy Berke, "Genevieve Taggard: Biographical Note," *Modern American Poetry Site*. See also Berke 2001, 28.

p. 268 "The Alianthus Tree": *The Measure: A Journal of Poetry* Apr. 1921, 16.

p. 269 Dickinson's ordinary life: Benfey 2008.

p. 269 Taggard and Ridge contributed to *New Masses*: Laura Morris, Guide to the Genevieve Taggard Papers, 2011, NYPL.

p. 269 "Hold a wider consciousness": Taggard 1938.

p. 269 "Control and...abandon": Taggard 1925, 35.

p. 269 Taggard to Russia, Ridge to Baghdad: Berke 2001, 97.

p. 269 "Script for collective chants": qtd. in Drake 1987, 89.

p. 269 Interest in African American lyric: Berke 2001.

p. 269 "Dynamo Poets": Wald 1994, 153.

p. 269 Editor died from poverty: Genevieve Taggard, "Sol Funaroff," in Wald 2002.

p. 269 "Not Sappho, Sacco": Rukeyser 1935.

p. 269 Interest in metaphysical poetry: Berke 2001, 112.

p. 269 "Philosophical conception of the universe": Taggard 1929.

p. 270 "Emotion...is in disrepute": Ridge 1930.

p. 270 The notice which appeared: ibid.

p. 270 Copland set "Lark" to music: Laura Morris, Guide to the Genevieve Taggard Papers, 2011, NYPL.

p. 270 Defining what was American in music: "Copland and the American Sound," pbs.org/keepingscore.

p. 270 "Most friendful man in America": Ridge to Lawson, 24 July 1930.

p. 270 "Piano Variations": "Copland and the American Sound," pbs.org/keepingscore.

p. 270 Rewriting "Symphonic Ode": Ridge to Lawson, 10 Sept. 1930.

p. 270 Approved in 1955: Crist 2000, 262.

p. 270 "Only got to work today": Ridge to Lawson, 15 Sept. 1930.

p. 270 Glick's oratorio: Ridge to Louise Adams Floyd, 21 Jan. 1930.

p. 270 "I reading aloud to her": Ridge to Floyd, 21 Jan. 1930.

p. 270 Collaboration with LaViolette: Ames to Ridge, 28 Apr. 1930.

p. 270-271 "You belong definitely with the coming group": qtd. in Pollack 2000, 106.

p. 271 "Essence of contemporary reality": Copland to Ridge, 21 Apr. 1931, qtd. in Copland and Perlis 1984, 183.

p. 271 "We listened to Aaron Copland's Billy the Kid...": Ridge, Diary 10 and 11 Nov. 1940.

p. 271 Strand and Copland friends: Pollack 2000, 257.

p. 271 Reading Frazer, working on Sonnets: Kukil 2014.

p. 271 "White hope": William Rose Benét to Ridge, 9 Aug. 1930.

p. 271 "Second bottle of Gynergen": Ridge to Lawson, 24 July 1930.

p. 272 Another on Aug. 9: Ridge to Lawson, 9 Aug. 1930.

p. 272 "A bottle...to you tonight": Lawson to Ridge, 11 Aug. 1930.

p. 272 "Some time together": Ridge to Lawson, 16 Aug. 1930.

p. 272 "You'll take me to Museum of art": ibid.

p. 272 "Suppose you won't want to": Lawson to Ridge, 27 Aug. 1930.

p. 272 Clock and Gynergen: Lawson to Ridge, 7 Sept. 1930.

p. 272 "Don't forget the Gynergen": Ridge to Lawson, 15 and 22 Sept. 1930.

p. 272 "You called up to me": Kukil 2014.

p. 272 Eight vases of flowers: Ridge to Lawson, 16 Aug. 1930.

p. 272 "If you had more interest in my work": Ridge to Lawson, [Aug.] 1930.

p. 272 "Powwow on the trend of American letters": Ridge to Lawson, 23 Aug. 1930.

p. 272 "Dare to talk to you as an equal": "Stan" to Ridge, [Sept. 1930].

p. 272 Ames asked to meet Lawson: Ridge to Lawson, 17 July 1930.

p. 272 "It won't be possible for me to come up": Lawson to Ridge, 23 Sept. 1930.

p. 273 "Care and attention...should help": ibid.

p. 273 "They seem quite eager": Ridge to Lawson, 25 Sept. 1930.

p. 273 Had to find another publisher: Ridge to Lawson, 12 Oct. 1930.

p. 273 "Frightful headache and ready to scream": Ridge to Lawson, 3 Oct. 1930.

p. 273 Money for teeth: ibid.

p. 273 Once wrote her husband twice a day: Ridge to Lawson, 14 Oct. 1930.

p. 273 "I must have Gynergen": Ridge to Lawson, 21 Oct. 1930.

p. 273 "Trees like evening fountains of gold": Ridge to Lawson, 12 Oct. 1930.

p. 273 Group to select new guests: Ames to Ridge, 24 Jan. 1933. Kukil 2014. All Kukil citations show photographs of the letters at smith.edu/libraries/libs/ssc/yaddo/lola6.html.

Chapter 29 — Europe on Patronage

p. 274 Ridge set sail on the *Tuscania*: Ridge to Louise Adams Floyd, 18 May 1931.

p. 274 "Building a Babylon": McCarron 1995, 22.

p. 274 "Until I lost their dear faces in the dark": Ridge to Louise Adams Floyd, 18 May 1931.

p. 274 "Mrs. Richter...": Ridge to Josephine Boardman Crane, 18 Oct. 1931. According to the address scribbled on Ridge to Lawson, 17 Aug. 1932, Mrs. Richter lived in Warren County, Malverne Lodge.

p. 274 "If only...Palestine": Ridge to Lawson, 29 June 1929.

p. 274 Asked around for additional funding: Ridge to Lawson, 15 June 1931.

p. 274 "Make friends with other women": Ridge to Lawson, 20 May 1931.

p. 275 "This thought troubles me": Ridge to Floyd, 30 July 1931.

p. 275 "Babylonian notes and my *slippers!*": Ridge to Lawson, 24 May 1931.

p. 275 "The sea...thunderous song": ibid.

p. 275 Never getting seasick: Ridge to Lawson, 16 June 1931.

p. 275 "Got a match?": Ridge to Lawson, 24 May 1931.

p. 275 "We've been depending on America": Ridge to Lawson, 26 May 1931.

p. 275 Major European banks: Coy Apr. 20, 2011. bloomberg.com/bw/magazine/content/11_18/b4226012481756.htm

p. 275 17th century country house: Ridge to Lawson, 26 and 30 May 1931.

p. 275 "Enchanted with the English countryside": Ridge to Lawson, 1 June 1931.

p. 275 "Algerian claret": Ridge to Lawson, 2 June 1931.

p. 275 "Ruthless female hate": Ridge to Lawson, 8 June 1931.

p. 275 "He's an old satyr": Ridge to Lawson, 10 June 1931.

p. 275 Richard Hughes: "Richard Hughes," biography.yourdictionary.com.

p. 276 "Sat and talked for two hours": Ridge to Lawson, 16 June 1931.

p. 276 Five hundred drowned: "Taunted to Disaster," *Advertiser and Adelaide* 18 June 1931.

p. 276 Lost baggage, withdrawal: Ridge to Lawson, 15 June 1931.

p. 276 "Stupid self-absorption": Ridge to Lawson, 16 June 1931.

p. 276 Ajaccio reminiscent of New Zealand: ibid.

p. 276 Paintings by Paterson: accessible online at bonhams.com/auctions/17228/lot/12/.

p. 276 Center of European organized crime: Hamel 2013.

p. 276 "As safe here as...New York": Ridge to Lawson, 16 June 1931.

p. 276 French invasion: "Cleaning up Corsica! [1931]," britishpathe.com/video/cleaning-up-corsica. Also reported in "Rival Arguments: Corsican Bandits Fight," *Morning Bulletin* 11 Nov. 1931.

p. 276 "Let him rest, poor chap": Ridge to Lawson, 24 June 1931.

p. 276 No bread money: Ridge to Lawson, [11] July 1931.

p. 277 "Pushed into the position of a parasite": Ridge to Lawson, 21 July 1931.

p. 277 Kennan's activism: Ferguson 2011.

p. 277 Lover of Cyril Kay-Scott: Falk 1996; and Lloyd 1995/1996.

p. 277 "Malicious behavior": Ridge to Lawson, 16 Mar. 1932.

p. 277 Always too poor to return the money: Ridge to Lawson, 23 July 1931.

p. 277 "Did you get your expected raise?" Ridge to Lawson, 5 July 1931.

p. 277 "I shall write to Mrs. W. Murray Crane": Ridge to Lawson, 25 July 1931.

p. 277 Helped found the Met, weekly salon, checks to Ridge: Wheelock 2002, 173; Willis 2010.

p. 277 Checks to Ridge: Ridge to Josephine Crane, 26 Oct. 1928.

p. 277 "Some epidemic on": Ridge to Lawson, 23 July 1931.

p. 277 "Bad form of malaria": Ridge to Lawson, 26 July 1931.

p. 278 "Unboiled for the first month": Ridge to Lawson, 31 July 1931.

p. 278 Bennett's Parisian death: Westley 1959.

p. 278 Suspected Thomson's rumor: Ridge to Lawson, 4 Aug. 1931.

p. 278 "Cost of traveling in Arabia enormous": ibid.

p. 278 "Decrease by train the distance": Ridge to Floyd, 30 July 1931.

p. 278 "I'll die with hatred of this city": Ridge to Lawson, 3 Aug. 1931.

p. 278 "My place is with the outlaws": Ridge to Lawson, 11 Aug. 1931.

p. 278 Avoidance of the poor old Frenchman: Ridge to Lawson, 31 July 1931.

p. 278 He could solicit their friends: Ridge to Lawson, 12 Aug. 1931.

p. 278 Accepted sixty dollars, chided him: Ridge to Lawson, 14 Aug. 1931.

p. 278 "Learned to live cheaply": Ridge to Joseph Brewer, [1931].

p. 278 "All those bourgeois": Ridge to Lawson, 23 Aug. 1931.

p. 278 "Fearful of its cosmopolitan expensiveness": Scott to Ridge, 4 Oct. 1931.

p. 278 Dietrich in *Blue Angel*: "Movie Star Heightens Allure of French Riviera," travelnostalgia.com.

p. 278 Nabokov, Hemingway, Fitzgerald: T. Jones 2004, 71.

p. 279 The wine was cheap: Ridge to Lawson, 23 Aug. 1931.

p. 279 "Do not think I am starving": Ridge to Lawson, 30 Aug. 1931.

p. 279 "Only *one* policeman": Ridge to Lawson, 8 Sept. 1931.

p. 279 "Communism will sweep the entire world": Ridge to Floyd, [1931].

p. 279 16 percent unemployment: Kangas 1996.

p. 279 "I must not let my work spoil yours": Ridge to Lawson, 4 Sept. 1931.

p. 279 "Do not send me any money Oct.": Ridge to Lawson, 8 Sept. 1931.

p. 279 Started her Babylon poem: ibid.

p. 279 "Hunch-backed beauty": Ridge to Lawson, 4 Oct. 1931.

p. 280 Falling markets, bad exchanges: Rothbard 2000, 257-277.

p. 280 "Everywhere whispers of revolution": Ridge to Lawson, 13 Oct. 1931.

p. 280 "Try and save a little": Ridge to Lawson, 19 Oct. 1931.

p. 280 "Most gorgeous sunset": Ridge to Lawson, 25 Oct. 1931.

p. 280 "Huge rats": ibid.

p. 280 "I can't think": Ridge to Lawson, 26 Oct. 1931.

p. 280 "Someone had been murdered a few minutes before": Ridge to Lawson, 31 Oct. 1931.

p. 280 Bird's travels to Baghdad: Bird 1891, 26-45.

p. 280 Bell's travels: Freeman 2014.

p. 280 Ridge travelled with one of Bell's books: Ridge to Lawson, 16 Mar. 1932.

p. 280 "Conceited, gushing, flat-chested": qtd. in Freeman 2014.

p. 280 "Well-spent morning": ibid.

p. 280 Bell died: ibid.

p. 280 Bell appeared as a ghost: Ridge, Diary, 29 Mar. 1941.

p. 280 "I'm in the old mood": Ridge to Lawson, 31 Oct. 1931.

p. 281 28-hour desert crossing: Ridge to Lawson, 28 Oct. 1931.

p. 281 "Hate streamed like a deadly fire": Ridge to Lawson, 2 Nov. 1931.

Chapter 30 — Babylon and Back

p. 282 Largest city in the world: George 1992.

p. 282 "Gate of the Gods," evil, whore, first wheel, agriculture, base-60, writing, Hammurabai: Mark 2011.

p. 282 Site of the ancient Flood: MacDonald 1988.

p. 282 Nebuchadnezzar's Hanging Gardens: Dalley 2013.

p. 282 Tower of Babel, working conditions: MacFarquar 2003.

p. 282 "Disney for a Despot": McLachlan 2012.

p. 282 Babel software: babel.ifarchive.org/program.html.

p. 282 Destruction of the city's history: Tucker 2009.

p. 282 Ritz stationary: Ridge to Lawson, 31 Oct. 1931.

p. 282 "On special request": ibid.

p. 282 Another American writing about Babylon: ibid.

p. 282 "These things are in the air": ibid.

p. 282 "Filled with appalling filth": Ridge to Lawson, 1 Nov. 1931.

p. 283 "Someone will come to the rescue": Ridge to Lawson, 31 Oct. 1931.

p. 283 "I'm without reliable information": Ridge to Lawson, 2 Nov. 1931.

p. 283 Stoned by the locals: Ridge to Lawson, 1 Nov. 1931.

p. 283 "Are they not hated everywhere?": ibid.

p. 283 "Old lung trouble": Ridge to Lawson, 11 Nov. 1931.

p. 283 Two servants: ibid.

p. 283 "Worst climate...in the world": ibid.

p. 283 Death toll of 415/787: "Cholera Epidemic Sweeps Irak," *The Straits Times* 14 Sept. 1931, 12; and "Port Health," *The Singapore Free Press and Mercantile Advertiser* 6 July 1931, 17.

p. 283 "I'm glad I've come": Ridge to Floyd, 12 Nov. 1931.

p. 283 Hillah terrible for tourists: Ridge to Lawson, 1 Nov. 1931.

p. 283 "Very dirty town": Ridge to Lawson, Nov. 1 1931.

p. 283 "You will need the money: Ridge to Lawson, Nov. 17 1931.

p. 283 "A bit like living on my wits": Ridge to Lawson, 11 Nov. 1931.

p. 283 "Ought to get together soon": ibid.

p. 284 Iraq's Kristallnacht: Ehrlich 2011.

p. 284 Arabs educated in Germany: Jankowski and Gershoni 1997, 18.

p. 284 Return to Islamic values: Yousif 2012, 23.

p. 284 "Only death will stop me": Ridge to Lawson, 11 Nov. 1931.

p. 284 "Like an out-raged turkey-hen": Ridge to Floyd, 12 Nov. 1931.

p. 284 Bell's heroic maneuver at Hillah: Bell 1927, chapter 26.

p. 284 Excavations from 1875: *Transactions* 1877.

p. 284 "Intact but for the head": Ridge to Lawson, 17 Nov. 1931.

p. 285 "She peed copiously": ibid.

p. 285 "Very nice Irishman": ibid.

p. 285 Asked for a $100 advance: ibid.

p. 285 "Dear persons and angel-publishers": Ridge to Joseph Brewer, 3 Dec. 1931.

p. 285 "Same with most everyone": Ridge to Lawson, 17 Nov. 1931.

p. 285 "Fifty dollars a month": ibid.

p. 285 "Help you to bear it": ibid.

p. 285 "6 cases of Bubonic plague": ibid. Reports of one case of plague ran in *The Straits Times* on 23 Mar., 13 July, 14 Sept., and 28 Dec. 1931, under the heading "Health in Eastern Ports."

p. 285 "Killed a scorpion tonight": Ridge to Lawson, 17 Nov. 1931.

p. 285 Travelled to Kish: ibid.

p. 286 Ancient bricks and pottery: Gertrude Bell to H. B., 30 June 1923, 28 Nov. 1923, and 22 Jan. 1924, in Bell 1927.

p. 286 Beirut or Jerusalem: 17 Nov. 1931.

p. 286 "Could not get any reduction": Ridge to Lawson, 22 Nov. 1931.

p. 286 "The Great Death Pit": Mark 2011.

p. 286 Complex series of streets: "Shops and Businesses in Ur" 2010.

p. 286 Sumerian ziggurat: "The Ziggurat of Ur-Nammu" 2010.

p. 286 Goddesses important until married off: Leick 1991; and Neill 2011, 85.

p. 286 Woolley gave Ridge a tour: Ridge to Lawson, 2 Dec. 1931.

p. 286 My wonderful friends: ibid.

p. 287 "I'd love to make India": ibid.

p. 287 "Cholera...kept them away": Ridge to Lawson, 18 Nov. 1931.

p. 287 Doctor wanted her hospitalized: Ridge to Lawson, 8 Dec. 1931 [misdated 8 Nov.].

p. 287 "Inadequate covers": ibid.

p. 287 "Your brave clear spirit": ibid.

p. 287 Driver ignored her urgings for speed: Ridge to Lawson, 16 Dec. 1931 [misdated 16 Nov.].

p. 287 "Approach of danger has put me into high spirits": Ridge to Lawson, 19 Dec. 1931.

p. 287 Fortune-telling Englishman: ibid.

p. 287 Funds from her Park Ave. doctor: Ridge to Lawson, 9 Dec. 1931. Her Guggenheim application mentioned his address at 940 Park Avenue.

p. 288 "Starving young men would be trying not to die": Lebesque 1960.

p. 288 Moved to Rue Arago, fancy Hotel Slavia: Ridge to Lawson, 15 Jan. 1932; and "Slavia Hotel," europeana.eu.

p. 288 President assassinated: "Paul Gorguloff" *Wikipedia*.

p. 288 "Surprised at your silence": Ridge to Lawson, 25 Dec. 1931.

p. 288 "Practically suicide": ibid.

p. 288 "Some mysterious force": Ridge to Lawson, 15 Jan. 1932.

p. 288 Changed the wallpaper, breakfast in bed until noon: Ridge to Lawson, 28 Jan. 1932.

p. 288 "Buy a roll and a slice of ham": ibid.

p. 288 "Hitler will make Paris": Ridge to Floyd, 17 Jan. 1932.

p. 288 Half million recruits with six million hungry: Mühlberger 2004, 539.

p. 288 Continuous turmoil: "The Rise of Adolf Hitler: Hitler Runs for President," historyplace.com.

p. 288 France was the archenemy: Kershaw 2008, 151.

p. 288 "Fighting year of peace": Ridge to William Floyd, 17 Jan. 1931.

p. 289 "My work, my work": Ridge to Lawson, 21 Jan. 1932.

p. 289 "Haven't really done any work...": Ridge to Lawson, 21 Feb. 1932 [misdated 1931].

p. 289 "We had not corresponded for years...": Ridge to Floyd, [Paris, 1932].

p. 290 "I have not forgotten you": Alexander Berkman to Ridge, 25 Dec. 1927, qtd. in Avrich 2005, 58.

p. 290 Berkman's suicide: Goldman 1936.

p. 290 "The only thing I am going back for is you": Ridge to Lawson, 8 Feb. 1932.

p. 290 "I'll be able to cook cheaply": Ridge to Lawson, 21 Feb. 1932 [misdated 1931].

p. 290 "Help raise my passage money": ibid.

p. 290 Marquis, artist and photographer: Lawson 2010/1976, xvi.

p. 290 "I won't take advantage of Hyman": Ridge to Lawson, 11 Mar. 1932.

p. 290 Isadora Duncan: Flanner 1927.

p. 291 "I am strangely hardy": Ridge to Lawson, 16 Mar. 1932.

p. 291 "Stately and rather weighty content": ibid.

p. 291 "I think it's good": ibid.

p. 291 "I should die right there": Ridge to Lawson, 22 Mar. 1932.

p. 291 No identification, no contacts, no money: Ridge to Lawson, 30 Mar. 1932.

Chapter 31 — *The Radical Left in the 1930s*

p. 292 Emergency Committee for Southern Political Prisoners: Cohen 2011, 18.

p. 292 Dos Passos and sixteen writers: Carr 2004, 277.

p. 292 "We might possibly make it more humane": qtd. in ibid., 278.

p. 292 "Take Communism away from the Communists": Wilson 1931, 238.

p. 292 Members of the National Defense committee: Dilling 1934, 144; Sherwood Anderson, fundraising letter, Jan. 1932, CUNY Digital Archives; W. E. Woodward, letter to members of the Writers' League Against Lynching, 24 Dec. 1934, University of Florida Digital Collections. In 1938 Grattan proclaimed there were no Australian women poets of note, according to Vickery 2007, 78.

p. 292 Poets promoted conscious participation: Filreis 2008, 314.

p. 292 "Anarcho-individualistic, Freudian": Filreis 2008, fn 126; and Rosenthal 1956.

p. 293 Stein was still getting positive reviews: Filreis 2008, 9. Communist art theorist Sidney Finkelstein (1947) wrote that Stein "stimulat[ed] a sensitivity to the sounds and rhythms of speech [and] a careful examination of each word" (194-198).

p. 293 "Naïve, sentimental and hackneyed": Filreis 2008, 9.

p. 293 "Disgust for institutions": Deutsch 1935, 29.

p. 293 "Some wild incomprehensible": Filreis 2008, 105.

p. 293 *The Left* neglected women: Wald 2002, 256.

p. 293 "I discovered that the John Reed club": Edwin Rolfe to Ridge, 9 June 1932.

p. 293 Poet laureate of the Lincoln Battalion: Nelson 1997.

p. 293 "We were joined by David Lawson": Marianne Moore to John Warner Moore, 19 July 1932, in Moore 1998, 272.

p. 294 Draft about Mooney: Ridge to Lawson, 18 July 1932.

p. 294 Serving time: Georgakas 1998.

p. 294 "Money-making agitation for the Communist Party": Dilling 1934, 200.

p. 294 1932 LA Olympics: Berke 2001, 62.

p. 294 Rolph condoned a lynching: Gladys Hansen, "James Rolph, Jr," *The Virtual Museum of the City of San Francisco*, sfmuseum.org.

p. 294 "I'm very proud of that bust": Ridge to Floyd, 25 July 1932.

p. 294 Ridge worried out loud: Ridge to Lawson, 18 July 1932.

p. 294 Traveled upstate to stay near Yaddo: Ridge to Floyd, 7 Aug. 1932.

p. 294 "Light and air and silence": Ames to Ridge, 5 July 1932.

p. 294 "There is no noise": Ridge to Floyd, 7 Aug. 1932.

p. 295 "It is bad in America now": Frances Rose Benét to Ridge, 25 July 1932.

p. 295 "I tremble to think of the result": Ridge to Floyd, 10 Aug. 1932.

p. 295 Wanted to visit a strike: Ridge to Lawson, 25 Aug. 1932.

p. 295 "My own life as a theme": Ridge to Lawson, 21 Aug. 1932.

p. 295 Three sleepless nights, Gynergen: Ridge to Lawson, 30 Aug. 1932.

p. 295 "I was so weak": Ridge to Floyd, [Aug.] 1932.

p. 295-296 "A whole series—a cycle": Ridge to Joseph H. Brewer, 19 Sept. 1932.

p. 296 "You can't be sick all the time": Scott to Lawson, 27 Jan. 1933.

p. 296 72 pounds: Ridge to Lawson, 27 July 1933.

p. 296 Admitted to Mt. Sinai: Scott to Lawson, 30 June 1933.

p. 296 Moved to the Loeb Home: Ridge to Lawson, 27 July 1933.

p. 296 "A little like Yaddo": Ridge to Floyd, 9 June 1933.

p. 296 "Big hole in the day": Ridge to Lawson, 4 Aug. 1933.

p. 296 Codeine was stopped: Ridge to Lawson, 5 Aug. 1933.

p. 296 Written most of "Via Ignis": Ridge to Floyd, 9 June 1933.

p. 296 Fighting for her life: Ridge to Floyd, 1 Aug. 193[3].

p. 296 "Must have my white silk slip": Ridge to Lawson, 5 Aug. 1933.

p. 296 Simele massacre: Stafford 2006/1935, 171.

p. 296 DuPont and Morgan's plot: Kangas 1996.

p. 296 No one was prosecuted: "The Whitehouse Coup." *Document*. BBC Radio 4. London. 23 July 2007. Radio.

p. 296 Scott's abortion: White 1998, 98.

p. 296-297 "She always asked after you": Scott to Ridge, July 1933.

p. 297 Scott asked Ridge to sign a petition: Scott to Ridge, 23 Nov. 1933.

p. 297 Goldman's tour: Kissack 2008, 157.

p. 297 Thousands are turned away: Falk 1996.

p. 297 "Lyrical left" stayed away: Kissack 2008, 158.

p. 297 "Wrong-headed old woman": qtd. in Morton 1992, 138.

p. 297 "Let me handle the money": Ridge to Lawson, 20 Aug. 1933.

p. 297 Left for the Jersey Shore: Ridge to Floyd, 4 Sept. 1933

p. 297 14 pounds at hospital: Ridge to Floyd, 10 July 1934.

p. 297 "Will try to work out an American theme": Ridge to Floyd, 4 Sept. 1933.

Chapter 32 — Shelley Awards, a Poets Guild Prize, and a Guggenheim

p. 298 "Jiggered if I know": Ridge to Floyd, 3 Jan. 1933.

p. 299 "Bring you the world you don't need on a platter": Scott to Ridge, 4 Apr. 1934.

p. 299 Endowed by Sears: Graham 1946, 67.

p. 299 "Selected with reference to his or her genius and need": "Frost and Shelley Awards," poetrysociety.org.

p. 299 First winner and Aiken's attempted suicide: "Conrad Aiken: Biography," poetryfoundation. org.

p. 299 $1750 during the depression: Henderson 1975, 197.

p. 299 $30,000 in 2014: davemanuel.com/inflation-calculator.php.

p. 299 Splitting the award: "Shelley Winners," poetrysociety.org.

p. 299 "Dare": Frost 1929, 25.

p. 299 "Nothing could comfort her": Edwards 1988.

p. 299 Frost's children's books: Register of the Frances Frost Papers, Special Collections and Archives, UC San Diego.

p. 299 *A History of American Poetry*: Heather 2014.

p. 299-300 Lower East Side female Jew, fantasy: Sternlicht 2004, 122.

p. 300 "Haunted by her white dress": Zaturenska 2002, "White Dress," 45.

p. 300 Brewer and Warren: openlibrary.org/publishers/Brewer_&_Warren_inc.

p. 300 Difficulties after *Firehead*: Firms out of Business, Harry Ransom Center and University of Reading Library, fob-file.com. See also Warren 2000, 158 fn 4.

p. 300 Putnam married Earhart: "Amelia Earhart Weds G. P. Putnam," *New York Times*, 7 Feb. 1931.

p. 300 Scott introduced her to Smith: Scott to Ridge, [1934].

p. 300 Friend of Hart Crane's: Hart Crane to Grace Crane, 30 May 1919, in Crane 1965. See also Yezzi 2007.

p. 300 Smith and Haas, who they published and merger: McDowell 1981.

p. 300 Lenore Marshall became a patron: Ridge to Marshall, 16 Jan. 1934 and 12 Feb. 1934.

p. 300 Helped found S.A.N.E.: "Lenore Marshall Poetry Prize," poets.org.

p. 300 Endowing the $25,000 prize: ibid.

p. 300 Academy of American Poets, establishment: "faq," poets.org/academy-american-poets.

p. 300 Robinson's activities in the Poetry Society: Harriet Monroe, *Poetry* Vol. 16, 232.

p. 300 "Notoriously quarrelsome": Farrar 1922.

p. 300 Betty Kray: author's firsthand experience.

p. 301 Book on living poets: "Lola Ridge," *Living Authors, A Book of Biographies*, ed. Dilly Tante. New York: H. W. Wilson, 1935. 341.

p. 301 "Lofty in thought and universal in feeling": Rubin 2010, 191.

p. 301 "Attainment of social ends by untried means": ibid.

p. 301 The Christadora: Trager 2003, 434.

p. 301 Poets Guild, organizer and original members: Rubin 2010, 240.

p. 301 Poets House awarded Ridge: Ridge to Lawson, [29 or 30] May 1935.

p. 301 Cullen and Deutsch listed among readers: ibid., 191.

p. 301 "Fried eggs and apples": Ridge to Marshall, 1 June 1934.

p. 301 "Emotional as well as an intellectual process": Ridge 1931.

p. 302 Summer in Montauk and Mastic: Ridge to Lawson, 3 and 31 July 1934.

p. 302 "If only Davy could get a job": Ridge to Floyd, 19 July 1934.

p. 302 "People may not understand them": Lawson to Ridge, 22 Aug. 1934.

p. 302 "Disappointed about your work": Lawson to Ridge, 9 Sept. 1934.

p. 302 By the beginning of Nov. 1934: Ridge to Smith, 1 and 2 Nov. 1934; and Ridge to Marshall, 15 Dec. 1934.

p. 302 "I understand about the spring list": Ridge to Smith, 23 Nov. 1934.

p. 302 "His remarks are on the margins": Ridge to Floyd, 19 Dec. 1934.

p. 302 "Interested in Bill Benét's reactions": Ridge to Smith, 7 Dec. 1934.

p. 302 "The spark cannot flash," "an admirer of yours": Smith to Ridge, 10 Dec. 1934.

p. 302-303 MacLeish, friend of Boyle's, triple Pulitzer, "Ars Poetica": "Archibald MacLeish," poets. org.

p. 303 War propaganda and Librarian of Congress: "Archibald MacLeish" in Lehman 2006, 385.

p. 303 "Unconscious fascist": Gold 1933.

p. 303 "Pretty completely negative": MacLeish 1986, 94.

p. 303 "Comrade Edward Remington Ridge": MacLeish 1933, "Background with Revolutionaries," 183.

p. 303 "Twas long before that alack!": Ridge to Lawson, 20 Aug. 1933.

p. 303 Marshall called Moe: Ridge, Guggenheim application, 1935.

p. 303 Copland and Benét: Davis 1978, 222.

p. 303 900 applications a year: Davis 2015, 216.

p. 303 Awarding only 39: "List of Guggenheim fellowships awarded in 1926," *Wikipedia*.

p. 303 "Millay says her poetry is first rate": Ridge, Guggenheim application, 1935.

p. 303-304 Ridge and Hughes won, 1935: gf.org/fellows.

p. 304 "Significant of something coming": Ridge to Lawson, 7 Apr. 1936.

p. 304 "The Passage of Theresa": Ridge, Guggenheim application, 1935.

Chapter 33 — Dance of Fire *from New Mexico*

p. 305 "Without street names or numbers": Ridge to Marshall, 9 Apr. 1935.

p. 305 Lange's photography: Patrick 2009.

p. 305 Settled at Bent House: Ridge to Lawson, 29 Mar. 1935.

p. 305 First territorial governor: Ridge to Lawson, 4 June 1935.

p. 305 "Horribly inconvenient but most attractive little studio": Ridge to Marshall, 4 Apr. 1935.

p. 305 "Transformed itself to larger meaning": Gregory 1935.

p. 305 In a hurry to travel to the Southwest: Ridge to Lawson, 9 May 1935.

p. 306 Accused Smith of letting publicity go cold: ibid.

p. 306 "No ads, no reviews": Ridge to Lawson, 20 May 1935.

p. 306 "Dumb as usual": Scott to Ridge, 12 May 1935.

p. 306 "A world of young writers and poets": Walton 1935, 6.

p. 306 Wehr, trained by Sloan and Weber, sought to convey justice: Wehr and Griffin-Wehr 2004.

p. 306 "Dynasty of fire": Ridge 1935, flap copy.

p.306 "We may come forth": ibid.

p. 306 "Unmistakable stigmata of genius": ibid.

p. 306 "Harrison S. has determined to ruin me": Ridge to Lawson, 20 May 1935.

p. 307 *Fantasy*: Smethurst 1999, 36; and Guide to the Fantasy Magazine Papers, YCAL MSS 55, Yale University Library.

p. 307 "This is to bear, with cleavage and in pain": *Poetry* Oct. 1935, 41; and Ridge 1935, 44.

p. 307 "This is major poetry": Strobel 1935.

p. 307 "Revolutionary in a technical as well as a spiritual sense": Untermeyer 1935.

p. 307 "Revolutionary and metaphysical": Ridge to Lawson, 27 Aug. 1934.

p. 307 "Irish and intense": P. H. 1935.

p. 307 "More mature poetry": Rice 1935.

p. 308 "Unforgettably but without bitterness": Strobel 1935.

p. 308 "Even the former Governor": Rice 1935.

p. 308 Anderson's "Winterset": McAtee 2010.

p. 308 "Living through another crucifixion": Joughin and Morgan 1948, 174.

p. 308 One hundred forty-four: ibid., 382.

p. 308 "Longest...most significant": ibid., 384.

p. 309 "Justice Denied: Massachusetts": Newcomb 1995.

p. 309 "Deserve a permanent place": Joughin and Morgan 1948, 392.

p. 309 "This relative obscurity": ibid., 389.

p. 309 Celestine Madeiros: Aiuto 2014.

p. 309 "Old myth/renews its tenure": Ridge 1935, "Three Men Die," 61.

p. 309 "Drumbeats of the hooves": ibid., 75.

p. 310 "To celebrate the noblest and the bravest": Bogan 1935.

p. 310 "It merely makes me sick": Ridge to Lawson, 12 July 1935.

p. 310 "By which posterity": Scott to Ridge, 5 July 1924.

p. 310 "Arrests the artist's growth by stroking him to sleep": Ridge 1925.

p. 310 "Not the equal of her poems": Kreymborg 1934, 486-488.

p. 310 66,000 copies: Milford 2001, 385.

p. 310 "Epitaph for the Race of Man": "Edna St. Vincent Millay: Biography," poetryfoundation.org.

p. 310 "Not Easily Labeled": Rice 1935, 662.

p. 311 Miriam Allen DeFord: For her poetry see *Poetry* June 1935, 138, and many other issues of that magazine. DeFord was highly critical of incomprehensibility in poetry. See her letter, "Today's Poetry: A Symposium – III," *The Humanist* 15.5 (1955): 227-228. For a discussion of DeFord's radical beliefs: Davin 2005, 378.

p. 311 "Authentic and fine poetry": Floyd to Ridge, enclosure from "Miriam," n.d.

p. 311 "Dividing 'anonymous' to rhyme with 'anon'": This rhyme is in sonnet XVI of Ridge 1935, "I scarce can bear this tone of all but fire/With which thou threadest me, unseen, anon- / Ymous bird, and twice anonymous I" (31).

p. 311 "Disembodied and curiously abstract": Gregory 1935.

p. 311 "Desire to express spiritual...ideals": Tuchman 1986, 17-19.

p. 311 "Impingements of words": Hart Crane to Harriet Monroe, printed in *Poetry* Oct. 1926, 235.

p. 311 "Ridge's poetic maturity began": Gregory and Zaturenska 1946, 445-47.

p. 311 "Premonitory echo": Pinsky 2011.

p. 311 She recalled Crane's suicide: Gregory and Zaturenska 1946.

p. 312 *Phenomenal Reading*: Reed 2012, 95-96.

p. 312 "Again the traffic lights": Crane 1987, "To Brooklyn Bridge," line 34.

p. 312 "Spouting pillars spoor": ibid., line 55.

p. 312 "Ridge's description...would haunt him": Fisher 2002, 74.

p. 312 "Certainly not borrowed": Unterecker 1969, 119. See also Franciosi 1984 for a complete argument regarding the source of Crane's inspiration, including a discussion of his borrowings from Reznikoff.

p. 312 Crane borrowed from Greenberg: "Greenberg and Hart Crane," logopoeia.com/greenberg/crane.html.

p. 312 "Like most men" Ridge, "A Modern Mystic," 1934.

p. 312 "When all people are shaken": Stevens 1997, "A Fading of the Sun," 112.

p. 313 "A body in rags": ibid., "Mozart, 1935," 107.

p. 313 "Labor Day, May Day": Nelson 2003, 51.

p. 313 Mooney one of the most known in Europe: Simikin 2014, "Tom Mooney."

p. 313 "Zola never came": Frost 1968, flap copy.

p. 313 Ridge fulfilled that role: Berke 2001, 61.

p. 313 Best circulated New Zealander poem: Derby 2009.

p. 313 Local politics: Ridge to Lawson, 30 Apr. 1935.

p. 313 Wounded, gassed, an officer killed: Coleman 1935, 9.

p. 313 Ten men arrested: ibid., 11.

p. 313 Daniel Levinson: ibid., 10.

p. 314 "A sign from heaven": Connolly 2008.

p. 314 Used to establish his dictatorship: "75 Years Ago, Reichstag Fire Sped Hitler's Power Grab," dw.de/p/DDSs.

p. 314 "General Wood's son and his hired thugs...": Ridge to Marshall, 12 May 1935.

p. 314 Writes for money to support the cause: Ridge to Floyd, 9 Aug. 1935.

p. 314 "This is the revolution": Ridge to Marshall, 12 May 1935.

p. 314 Levinson and Minor met with a wife of the accused: Marcantonio 1956, speech before the 74th Congress, 4 May 1935. See also Coleman 1935, 2.

p. 314 Minor trained at the Ferrer: Antliff 2007, 27.

p. 314 "Dragged out and thrown on the ground": Marcantonio 1956.

p. 314 Twelve hours through the desert: Coleman 1935, 2.

p. 314-315 "Signs of a world-wide pogrom": Ridge to Lawson, 30 Apr. 1935.

p. 315 "Chances of my...getting down in the mine": Ridge to Floyd, 19 Aug. 1935.

Chapter 34 — Poetry in the Southwest

p. 316 Mabel Dodge: Luhan 1936, 265.

p. 316 Married Tony Luhan: Simikin 2013, "Mabel Dodge."

p. 316 Waves of artists came: Rudnick 1987, 345.

p. 316 Including Ridge's friends: For a complete list of visitors to the Mabel Dodge Luhan house, see Rudnick 1998.

p. 316 Leopold Stokowski: Rudnick 1998, 142.

p. 316 Ridge met Dodge's son: Scott to Ridge, 10 Mar. 1935; and Ridge to Marshall, 4 Apr. 1935.

p. 316 Claire married to Ridge's current publisher: Karman 2009.

p. 316 Alice Oliver Henderson Evans: Ridge to Lawson, 18 July 1935; and Rudnick 1998, 22, 300.

p. 316 "Devoted wife of John Evans": Ridge to Lawson, 17 July 1935.

p. 316 Hosted Toomer: ibid.

p. 316 Toomer and Mabel's affair: Rudnick 1987, 228-229.

p. 316 "A House in Taos": ibid., 352 fn 12.

p. 316 $14,000 in 1926: ibid., 107.

p. 316 "Female fascism": qtd. in ibid., 108.

p. 317 Portrait of Ridge: Marjorie Content, "Lola Ridge," National Gallery of Art, Washington, D.C.

p. 317 "To be their lords and masters": qtd. in Curwood 2010, 78.

p. 317 Slugged her: Rampersand 1987.

p. 317 "The Great Flood of 1935": Johnson 2012.

p. 317 "All night in a chair by the fire": Ridge to Lawson, [2] Aug. 1935.

p. 317 "As if her body were absent-minded": Toomer, "A Drama of the Southwest."

p. 317 Ridge and Johnson's quarrel: Ridge to Lawson, 30 Apr. 1935.

p. 317 "Talons for talent": qtd. in Rudnick 1987, 356 fn 21.

p. 317 "Imagined dead": Rudnick 1987, 302.

p. 317 Lawrence imagined her dead: ibid., 191.

p. 317 Cementing his ashes: ibid.

p. 318 "Suspicion and jealousy": Ridge to Lawson, 8 May 1935.

p. 318 Beck Strand's arrival: Rudnick 1987, 355.

p. 318 Daughter of Buffalo Bill's manager: Reilly 2007, 297.

p. 318 "I cannot have her morning noon and night": Ridge to Lawson, 16 Apr. 1935.

p. 318 "Stopped trying to dominate me": Ridge to Lawson, 26 May 1935.

p. 318 Alice Hunt Bartlett: Stringer 1996, 536.

p. 318 Solicited Cather: Bartlett 1925.

p. 318 Solicited Hillyer: Bohlke 178.

p. 319 Solicited Jeffers: Bartlett 1934.

p. 319 "All life is the domain of poetry": Ridge to Bartlett, 28 May 1935.

p. 319 "Beastly room": Ridge to Lawson, 17 June 1935.

p. 319 Alfredo helped her: Ridge to Lawson, 14 June 1935.

p. 319 Historic and fashionable La Fonda: "History of La Fonda," lafondasantafe.com.

p. 319 Alfredo's further assistance: Ridge to Lawson, 17 and 25 June 1935.

p. 319 Son of a governor: Ridge to Content, 11 Oct. 1936.

p. 319 "One of the loveliest spirits": Ridge to Lawson, 25 June 1935.

p. 319 "Alfau" and "Alfon": Ridge to Lawson, 31 Mar. and 5 Apr. 1935.

p. 319 Working on a novel: Ridge to Lawson, 25 June 1935.

p. 319 "Nothing to do with the emotional attractions": n.d. in the Lenore Marshall Papers. Columbia University Archives.

p. 319 "Boy": Scott to Ridge, 1921. In letters to Lawson, 22 and 26 July 1931, Ridge writes of her liaison in Corsica, "A little man called Owen Merton, about thirty I should judge...an interesting child with real if not stupendous talent." And she was not referring to his son.

p. 319 "The south west is infinitely more bigoted": Ridge to Lawson, 10 July 1935.

p. 319 Alfredo walked to the doctor: Ridge to Lawson, 21 July 1925.

p. 320 "Mis-mated with the industrial world": Ridge to Marshall, n.d.

p. 320 Strand offered to find Davy a job: Ridge to Lawson, 4 June 1935.

p. 320 Ridge discouraged it: Ridge to Lawson, 16 Sept. 1935.

p. 320 Portrait of Ridge destroyed: Ridge to Lawson, 2 June 1936.

p. 320 "Too darn popular": Ridge to Lawson, 10 July 1935.

p. 320 "What a girl you are!": Witter Bynner to Ridge, 26 Nov. 1935.

p. 320 Hoover's invitation: Ridge to Lawson, 14 June 1935.

p. 320 Tea with Henderson: Ridge to Lawson, 30 June 1935.

p. 320 Making a new dress: Ridge to Lawson, 22 June 1935.

p. 320 "Give up" a $27 woven dress: Ridge to Lawson, 10 July 1935.

p. 320 $324 in today's currency: davemanuel.com/inflation-calculator.php.

p. 320 "Blind attack" for nitroglycerin test: Ridge to Lawson, 5 Aug. 1935.

p. 320 Low blood pressure: Ridge to Lawson, 21 July 1935.

p. 320 Sergeant's invitation: Ridge to Floyd, 5 Aug. 1935.

p. 320 Exchanged letters with Frost: Robert Frost to Ridge, 24 Apr. 1919.

p. 320-321 "You of all people": ibid.

p. 321 Reviewed Frost lavishly: Ridge *The New Republic*, 23 June 1920, 131-132.

p. 321 "Beer over Frost's head": Ridge to Lawson, 5 Aug. 1935.

p. 321 "Too young and innocent": Thompson and Winnick, 1976.

p. 321 Her black kimono: Ridge to Lawson, 4 Sept. 1935.

p. 321 "Rather uncommunicative": Ridge to Lawson, 21 Aug. 1935.

p. 321 Ambivalent behavior: Ridge to Lawson, 4 Sept. 1935.

p. 322 "Want[ed] to do Cortez": Ridge to Lawson, 22 Apr. 1935.

p. 322 "Urge to go to Australia": Ridge to Lawson, 5 Aug. 1935.

p. 322 255 lines: Ridge to Lawson, [Aug.] 1935.

p. 322 340 lines: 25 Aug. 1935.

p. 322 "Magnificent prologue": Ridge to Lawson, 10 July 1935.

p. 322 Ten more: Ridge to Lawson, 10 Sept. 1935.

p. 322 Prelude would work for either poem: ibid.

p. 322 "Do only what you wish": Ridge to Lawson, [16 Sept. 1935].

p. 322 "Best I start for Mexico alone": ibid.

p. 323 "You are a self-centered person": Ridge to Lawson, 1 Oct. 1935.

p. 323 The Ouija board: Ridge to Lawson, 11 Oct. 1935.

**PART V:
MEXICO, CALIFORNIA, NEW YORK CITY,
1935-1941**

Chapter 35 — Mexico and Romance

p. 327 "Mexico City teemed with fanatics": Albers 2002, 115.

p. 327 Loy and Cravan in Mexico City: Hanscombe and Smyers 1987, 112-128.

p. 327 Williams over the border: Williams 1951, 74.

p. 327 Lawrence in Mexico: Worthen 2005.

p. 327 MacLeish walked through: "Archibald MacLeish," poets.org.

p. 327 Porter shuttled: Givner 2014.

p. 327 Crane's suicide: "Hart Crane," poets.org.

p. 327 "How emphatically I love [Mexico]": Hart Crane to Lorna Dietz, 12 Apr. 1932.

p. 327 Pre-Columbian art as quintessentially American: *Broom* Jan. 1923, 1.

p. 327 "In self-imposed exile": Sontag 1966, 69-70.

p. 328 "Propinquity and mutual isolation": Williams 2007, 35.

p. 328 Marsden Hartley: "Marsden Hartley: Biography," phillipscollection.org.

p. 328 Monroe/Ridge correspondence: *Poetry* Magazine Papers, Regenstein Library, University of Chicago, IL. Box 20, folder 16.

p. 328 "I need a wilderness": Ridge to Lawson, 24 Sept. 1935.

p. 328 "Room for the night": Ridge to Lawson, 7 Apr. 1936.

p. 328 "I've been to Baghdad!": Ridge to Lawson, 26 May 1935.

p. 328 "Curious holdup": Ridge to Lawson, 12 Oct. 1935.

p. 328-329 "Preaching sedition": Ridge to Lawson, 17 Oct. 1935.

p. 329 Cristero Rebellion: La Botz 2010.

p. 329 Cardenas, nationalization and collectivization: Fox 2010.

p. 329 Outdoor radio, cranial conveyance water: "Mexico City: 'The Land of Montezuma' circa 1935 Rothacker." Online video clip. *YouTube*. Google, 22 Apr. 2013. youtu.be/nI8x2fGp9Fw.

p. 329 Cars and snow-capped mountains: Ridge to Lawson, 17 Oct. 1935.

p. 329 Three days at the Imperial: ibid.

p. 329 "Comfortable Spanish-German home": Ridge to Lawson, [20] Oct. 1935.

p. 329 "Accepted by Mexico": ibid.

p. 329 Wasn't ill for another two months: Ridge to Lawson, 23 Dec. 1935.

p. 329 "Amazed about D. H. Lawrence": Ridge to Lawson, 5 Nov. 1935.

p. 329 Against the Guggenheims: ibid.

p. 329 "A poet hatching a plot!": ibid.

p. 329 Postmaster endorsed her check: Ridge to Lawson, 14 Feb. 1936.

p. 329 Travel permit lost: Ridge to Lawson, 5 Nov. 1935.

p. 329 "Harder for me to remain obscure": Ridge to Lawson, 12 Nov. 1935.

p. 329-330 "Can't even get my mind serene": Ridge to Lawson, 9 Nov. 1935.

p. 330 "Too divided in copying it": Ridge to Lawson, [Nov. 1935].

p. 330 "Prelude": in the Lola Ridge Papers at the Sophia Smith Collection, Smith College, Northampton, MA.

p. 331 Miguel Hidalgo y Costilla: "Guadalajara," *Encyclopaedia Britannica Online Academic Edition*, 2015.

p. 331 Independent University: "University of Guadalajara," *Encyclopaedia Britannica Online Academic Edition*, 2015.

p. 331 Largest colonies of foreigners: "All about Guadalajara," *So You Want to Go to México*, ocf. berkeley.edu.

p. 331 Stone published *Palms* from Guadalajara: "Idella Purnell Stone and Palms: An Inventory of Her Collection at the Harry Ransom Humanities Research Center," *Texas Archival Resources Online*, Harry Ransom Humanities Research Center, University of Texas at Austin.

p. 331 Witter Bynner as teacher: ibid.

p. 331 Lawrence designed cover: Brooker and Thacker 2012, 343.

p. 331 Lawrence offered poem: ibid.

p. 331 Pound deemed it the best: "Small Magazines." *English Journal* 1930, 703.

p. 331 Published poems anonymously: Little Magazine Collection. UW-Madison Memorial University Library 14 Feb. 2013. uwlittlemags.tumblr.com/post/43090377015/from-the-vault-palms-a-magazine-of

p. 331 "Drunk with Old Youth": Ridge 1935, 94.

p. 332 Scientology, gold mine, riveter, books: *Little Magazine Collection* 2013.

p. 332 "Petulant, cranky, rude": qtd. in Brooker and Thacker 2012, 343 fn 65.

p. 332 Mexican menus...Adapting Salten's *Bambi*: "Idella Purnell," *Wikipedia*; and "Walt Disney's Bambi." WorldCat. worldcat.org/title/walt-disneys-bambi/oclc/1004445.

p. 332 "Honorable and utterly impractical": Ridge to Lawson, [Nov. 1935].

p. 332 "Importer of pottery": Ridge to Lawson, 23 Dec. 1935.

p. 332 "Do not worry about me": Ridge to Lawson, [Nov. 1935].

p. 332 "I have crossed the country states...": Ridge to Mr. Moe, enclosed in Ridge to Lawson, 17 Jan. 1936.

p. 332-333 "How different from *our* mine strikes!": Ridge to Lawson, 23 Dec. 1935.

p. 333 "Parades of workers marching": ibid.

p. 333 "The confusion, the intrigue": Ridge to Content, 21 Jan. 1936.

p. 333 Six week delay: Ridge to Lawson, 17 Jan. 1936.

p. 333 "Too unbecoming to me": ibid.

520 ANYTHING THAT BURNS YOU

p. 333 "At least a year to do my book": ibid.

p. 333 "Seems not worthwhile": ibid.

p. 333 Twenty-two typed pages: Ridge to Lawson, 5 Feb. 1936.

p. 333 "The reality I need": Ridge to Content, 21 Jan. 1936.

p. 333 Rockefeller Center masterpiece: Diego Rivera, "Man at the Crossroads," diegorivera.org/man-at-the-crossroads.jsp.

p. 334 "A Few Small Nips": Brooks 2005.

p. 334 "Looks like a Persian": Ridge to Lawson, 28 July 1936.

p. 334 Frida would seduce Trotsky: Bright 2013.

p. 334 Keith dead: Ridge to Lawson, 8 Mar. 1936.

p. 334 "I now know that he is dead": Ridge to Lawson, 8 Mar. 1936.

p. 334 "Strangely secretive": ibid.

p. 334 Lost a fountain pen: Ridge to Lawson, 8 Mar. 1936.

p.334 The mariachis: Ridge to Lawson, 14 Mar. 1936.

p. 334 "Have faith in me": Ridge to Lawson, 20 Mar. 1936.

p. 334 Dr. Alfonso Caso: "Archaeologists and Scholars" Smithsonian Olmec Legacy n.d.

p. 334 "Long before the Toltecs": ibid.

p. 334 Californian engineer's license: Ridge to Lawson, 23 Mar. 1936.

p. 334 "Stimulating and creative": Ridge to Lawson, 27 Mar. 1936.

p. 334 "Rely on Lenore Marshall": Ridge to Lawson, 2 Apr. 1936.

p. 334 Mexican officials waiving the fee: Ridge to Lawson, 4 Apr. 1936.

p. 334 Frances Toor in Mexico City: Ridge to Lawson, 16 Apr. 1936.

p. 334-335 "The Indian...as a complete human being": Schuessler 2008.

p. 335 "No bed...A cell for a room": Ridge to Lawson, 16 Apr. 1936.

p. 335 Refused Stone's offer: Ridge to Lawson, [Apr.] 1936.

p. 335 Tepoztlan, history: frommers.com/destinations/tepoztlan/.

p. 335 1994 golf course uprising: ibid.

p. 335 15 pesos a month: Ridge to Lawson, 21 May 1936.

p. 335 "A major poet": ibid., and Ridge to Marshall, 3 June 1936.

p. 335 Implications of his experience with nature: "Who is Carlos Pellicer?" elgaleon.weebly.com.

p. 335 A museum in his name: "Museo Carlos Pellicer," maya-archaeology.org.

p. 335 "Desires": Pellicer 1921.

p. 335 "Lost almost every trinket": Ridge to Lawson, 4 May 1936.

p. 335 Requested a translated chapter: ibid.

p. 336 Climbed a pyramid: Ridge to Idella Purnell, [1936].

p. 336 "The great strike starts tomorrow": Ridge to Lawson, [30 Apr. 1936].

p. 336 "All shops in the nation shut": Ridge to Lawson, 1 May 1936.

p. 336 1936 "call": Berke 1998.

p. 336-337 "Anti-fascist writers were rescued": finding aid for the League of American Writers Archives [c. 1935-1942], Bancroft Library, University of California Berkeley.

p. 337 Those who joined the "call": Bloom 1987, 400 fn 56.

p. 337 Frank's abdication and Hemingway's speech: U.S. Cong. 1944.

p. 337 "A lie told by bullies": qtd. in Klehr 1984, 355.

p. 337 Blacks and Jews: Hughes 1939.

p. 337 The League was dissolved: Folsom 1994, 265.

p. 337 "Innumerable hovels": Ridge to Lawson, 9 May 1936.

p. 337 "A wonderful peace": ibid.

p. 337 "Great deal of nerve": Ridge to Lawson, 18 June 1936.

p. 337 "Killed a black widow": Ridge to Lawson, 21 May 1936.

p. 338 "More Mexican than anything else": Ridge to Lawson, 19 June 1936.

Chapter 36 — Retreat from Mexico

p. 339 "Hard to see a way out" Ridge to Lawson, 18 June 1936.

p. 339 Davy was downcast: Ridge to Content, 11 Oct. 1936.

p. 339 "It hurts me terribly": ibid.

p. 339 "It does not really interest me": Ridge to Lawson, 2 June 1936.

p. 339 "Had hot words": Ridge to Content, 21 Jan. 1936.

p. 339 "Discontinue writing to you": Ridge to Lawson, 22 July 1936.

p. 339 "In the throes of emotional conflict": Ridge to Marshall 19 July 1936.

p. 340 "Two days after I left": Ridge to Lawson, 5 July 1936.

p. 340 "Hurt me by her jealousy": Ridge to Lawson, 5 July 1936.

p. 340 Not to send more money: Ridge to Lawson, 28 July 1936.

p. 340 "I'm being secret": Ridge to Lawson, 6 Aug. 1936.

p. 341 "I've a right to live completely": Ridge to Content, 11 Oct. 1936.

p. 341 "My life with Davy is broken": ibid.

p. 341 "Not a poem, a novel": ibid.

p. 341 "Something utterly crushed his childhood": ibid.

p. 341 "Don't you want to tell me?": Scott to Ridge, [1937].

p. 341 Sixteen-year-old elopement: Scott to Lawson, 1932 Feb. 14.

p. 342 "A peso": Ridge to Content, 17 Oct. 1936.

p. 342 "Strange letter from Davy": ibid.

p. 342 Lawson moved to a heated basement: Ridge to Lawson, [1936].

p. 342 "Please tell me the truth": Ridge to Lawson, [Nov. 1936].

p. 342 "I hope to be able to give it back": Ridge to Lawson, 28 Nov. 1936.

p. 343 "I shall be utterly stranded": Ridge to Marshall, 14 Nov. 1936.

p. 343 "Forty centavos for a stamp": Ridge to Lawson, 28 Nov. 1936.

p. 343 "Beautiful garden and extensive grounds": ibid.

p. 343 $50 from Lawson, $35 from Marshall: Ridge to Lawson, [1936].

p. 343 "I am too fierce": ibid.

p. 343 "I must try to go on alone": ibid.

p. 344 "What the dickens does she mean?": ibid.

p. 344 Lawson sent five dollars: Ridge to Lawson, 26 Dec. 1936.

p. 344 "Davy I'd die": Ridge to Lawson, 27 Dec. 1936.

p. 344 "Much better as regards my chest": Ridge to Lawson, 19 Jan. 1937.

p. 344 "Three pesos a day": ibid.

p. 344 *Very good* food: ibid.

p. 344 Managed to see Strand and his film: ibid, and Ridge to Rebecca Salisbery Strand, 4 July 1939.

p. 344 Henwar Rodakiewicz: Ridge to Lawson, 19 Jan. 1937, and Rodakiewicz to Ned Scott, 17 Dec. 1933, thenedscottarchive.com/redesfilm/redes-film-letters.

p. 344 "It was corking of you": Ridge to Lawson, 20 Jan. 1937.

p. 344 Owed $350 to Smith: Ridge to Lawson, 1 Feb. 1937.

p. 344 "Angry about everything": ibid.

p. 345 She had wanted to write a serious novel: Scott to Ridge, 28 Aug. 1928.

p. 345 "No more self indulgent than martyrdom": ibid.

p. 345 "I cannot think of another to speak": Ridge to Marshall, 2 Feb. 1937. There are two copies of this letter extant, one with words underlined and one without. I imagine that neither Ridge nor Lawson would have gone back to add the emphases, but rather that a third person must have added them while taking notes.

p. 345 "Too close to my subject matter": Ridge to Marshall, 25 Feb. 1937.

p. 345 "Broken with Alfredo": Ridge to Lawson, [Feb. 1937, Cuernavaca].

p. 345 Robert E. Lee hotel: Ridge to Lawson, 13 Mar. 1937.

p. 345 "Impossible for me to go to N.Y.: Ridge to Lawson, 3 Mar. 1937.

p. 345 Settled in Laguna Beach: Ridge to Lawson, 20 Mar. 1937.

p. 345 "Cook my own food": ibid.

p. 346 "Beastly cold": Ridge to Lawson, 20 Mar. 1937.

p. 346 Low 43, high 86: "Past Monthly Weather Data for Laguna Beach, CA: Mar., 1928-2014," weather-warehouse.com.

p. 346 Plein air: "History of the Festival," *Festival of Arts of Laguna Beach*, foapom.com.

p. 346 First gallery in 1918: ibid.

p. 346 Exhibitions, plays, parade, market...: "Laguna Beach – A History of the Arts," lagunabeacharts.org.

p. 346 Playground for Hollywood stars: "An Overview of Laguna Beach History," savetheboom.com.

p. 346 Bogart and Flynn stayed weekends: "History of Hotel Laguna," hotellaguna.com.

p. 346 "That deathless search": qtd. in Max 2007, 67.

p. 346 "Do not worry about it": Ridge to Marshall, 22 Mar. 1937.

p. 346 "Davy wants me to return": ibid.

p. 346 "To be...like Strand": Ridge to Lawson, 26 Mar. 1937.

p. 346 "T.B. is on me again": ibid.

p. 346 The doctor said her chest was fine: Ridge to Lawson, 14 Nov. 1936.

p. 347 "Should love to be in the same town with you": Ridge to Lawson, 26 Mar. 1937.

p. 347 Two dollars left in the world: Ridge to Lawson, 29 Mar. 1937.

p. 347 "Who has so little": Ridge to Lawson, 3 Apr. 1937.

p. 347 Refused to have Lawson approach Hyman: ibid.

p. 347 California poet Sara Bard Field: Ridge to Lawson, [1937].

p. 347 Review of *Barabbas*: Ridge 1932.

p. 347 Field and Wood: Bingham 1990, 8; and Scholten 1993, 232-4.

p. 347 Friends with Benét: Bingham 1990, 10.

p. 347 "Cap in hand": Ridge to Lawson, [1937].

p. 347 "Downright...reactionaries": Ridge to Lawson, 3 May 1937.

p. 347 "Hurled the book from her": ibid.

p. 347 "Especially not Henrietta!": ibid.

p. 348 Remains of her Mexican sojourn: Ridge to Lawson, 20 Apr. 1937.

p. 348 "The help I've got from others": ibid.

p. 348 Floyd sent $100: Ridge to Lawson, 3 May 1937.

p. 348 Considering the Grand Canyon: Ridge to Lawson, 6 May 1937.

p. 348 Lost glasses, trunk, and pills: Ridge to Lawson, 9 May 1937.

p. 348 "To 17 restaurants": ibid.

p. 348 Midland Club Hotel: ibid.; and Clark 2007, 96.

p. 348 New York by May 10: Ridge to Lawson, 6 May 1937.

Chapter 37 — Anti-Woman, Anti-Experiment, Anti-Radical

p. 349 "House of Rest": Ridge to Lawson, 5 Aug. 1937; and receipt from the "House of Rest," in the Lola Ridge Papers at the Sophia Smith Collection, Smith College, Northampton, MA.

p. 349 Charlotte offered cookies and cake: Wilder to Ridge, 18 Oct. 1937.

p. 349 Introduced to Wilder by Scott: Scott to Ridge, 5 Dec. 1933.

p. 349 Supported Wilder's application: Wilder to Ridge, 22 Oct. 1936.

p. 349 Wilder won the Shelley: "Shelley Winners," poetrysociety.org.

p. 349 "Ever since I left Evelyn's so abruptly": Wilder to Ridge, 10 Aug. 1939.

p. 349 Wilder's lobotomy: Niven 2013, 513.

p. 349 Scott's psychiatric symptoms: Maun 2012, 128.

p. 350 Sugar injections: Ridge to Lawson, [Nov. 1937].

p. 350 "Sensibility, not an intellect": Tate 1931.

p. 350 *Fatal Interview* sold: Milford 2001, 385.

p. 350 "Preoccupation with social justice": Brooks 1935.

p. 350 Conflating women writers with children: Newcomb 1995.

p. 350 "The Woman as Poet": Ransom 1938, 77-8, 103-104.

p. 350 "So thorough was the denigration": Drake 1987, 254.

p. 350 "A too compassionate art is half an art": Rich 1951. See also Rich 2002, 5, for her struggle with feeling and form.

p. 350-351 "A sordid decade": Filreis 2008, 34 fn 36, 125. See also Nash 1998, 87.

p. 351 "Devoid of education": Kempton 1955, 170.

p. 351 "Defy syntax and decency": "Cubists of All Sorts," *New York Times* 16 Mar. 1913.

p. 351 Walton nearly lost her job: Filreis 2008, 144.

p. 351 "Embattled pacifism": Alfred Kreymborg to Henry Rago, 1 Nov. 1956 [misdated 1954].

p. 351 Untermeyer's unmooring: Miller 1987, 263-4.

p. 351 Rukeyser trailed by FBI: Filreis 2008, 146; and U.S. Dept. of Justice, *Muriel Rukeyser* (file no. 77-27812), vault.fbi.gov.

p. 351 "They destroyed me": Kreymborg 1949.

p. 351 Williams red-baited: Filreis 2008, 309-312.

p. 351 "No such idea in his head": Daiches 1956, 57.

p. 351 "Unsullied continuity": Filreis 2008, 51.

p. 351 "Nothing wrong with me": Ridge to Marshall, 22 Nov. 1937.

p. 351-352 "Interested a migraine specialist": Ridge to Content, 23 Nov. 1937.

p. 352 47 Morton Street: ibid.

p. 352 "I'm writing...Tiny crowded apartment": Ridge to Beck Strand, 4 July 1939.

p. 352 "It's like a phallus": ibid.

p. 352 Lawrence and phallic symbolism: Millett 2000, 237-239.

p. 352 "O, the worship of the serpent": Anonymous 1889.

p. 353 "In the likeness of God": Wall 1920, 5, illustrations on 372.

p. 353 "Plato...explained the amatory instincts": Wall 1920, 140.

p. 353 "Rushes into things": Ridge to Marshall, 10 July [1939].

p. 353 "Women are more determined to live": ibid.

p. 353 165 Columbia Heights: Wilder to Ridge, 13 Nov. 1939.

p. 353 "Much work in this large apartment": Ridge, Diary, 29 Mar. 1940.

p. 353 Morphy the world champion: Abbott 2011.

p. 353 Marcel Duchamp: Frank Brady, personal communication, said this: "Duchamp played everyone." I can confirm this as my second husband, not at all renowned as a player, also played with Duchamp in the 60s.

p. 353 Study of French was useful: Ridge to Lawson, 15 Sept. 1935.

p. 353 1940 census: U.S. Census, NYC, Kings County, Columbia Heights no. 387, 22 Apr. 1940, ancestry.com.

p. 353 1930 census: U.S. Census Bureau 1930.

Chapter 38 — "The Fire of the World is Running Through Me"

p. 354 "Under the deepest hell is another": Ridge, Diary, 17 Jan. 1940.

p. 354 "Most intense darkness": Ridge, Diary, 14 Nov. 1940.

p. 354 "Talked in bed this morning": Ridge, Diary, 5 Mar. 1940.

p. 354 One meal a day: Ridge, Diary, 6 Mar. 1940.

p. 355 "Addicted to self-pity": Ridge, Diary, 29 Mar. 1940.

p. 355 "Pampered intellectual gigolo": Dirda 1996.

p. 355 "He was a jerk": Berryman 2007, 3.

p. 355 "The long convalescence which is my life": Rilke 2008, 178.

p. 355 First career move: ibid.

p. 355 Squandered in the most expensive hotels: Dirda. 1996.

p. 355 "The question, L.R.": qtd. in Baer 2014.

p. 355 Monograph on Rodin: Rilke 1919.

p. 356 "You must change your life": Rilke, "Archaic Torso of Apollo," available online via poets.org.

p. 356 "Capitalism is one of the great obstacles": Ridge, Diary, 28 Mar. 1940.

p. 356 "Her friends are very loyal": Ridge, Diary, 3 May 1940.

p. 356 "And never say how or why": Scott to Ridge, 2 May 1940.

p. 356 Scott's increasing paranoia: Ridge, Diary, 2 May 1940. "Though she lived for an additional 22 years Scott was unable to publish her work after 1941, due in part to its controversial nature and her refusal to accept her publishers' suggestions for changes, as well as to her growing paranoia about conspiracies directed against her." From "Evelyn Scott: An Inventory of Her Collection at the Harry Ransom Humanities Research Center," *Texas Archival Resources Online*, Harry Ransom Humanities Research Center, University of Texas at Austin.

p. 356 "Upset over a letter from Evelyn": Ridge, Diary, 3 May 1940.

p. 356 Heart attack: Ridge, Diary, 4 Apr. 1940.

p. 356 "One rage leads to another": ibid.

p. 356 "Frenetic desire for equilibrium": qtd. in Drake 1987, 2.

p. 357 "I love the desert": Ridge, Diary, 6 Apr. 1940.

p. 357 "Blood last night": Ridge, Diary, 8 Apr. 1940.

p. 357 "The imperishable light": ibid.

p. 357 Jung's shadow: Fordham 1985.

p. 357 "An even bolder front": Ridge 1919, 19.

p. 357 "Eyes full of black light": Ridge 1920, 27.

p. 357 "Spirituality in a state of immaturity": Ridge, Diary, 2 Apr. 1940.

p. 357 Apr. 1940: "Historical Events for Apr. 1940," historyorb.com, and "Nazi War Crimes: The Katyn Massacre," jewishvirtuallibrary.org.

p. 357-358 "Appalled by the rigidity of contours": Ridge to Floyd, 24 Apr. 1940.

p. 358 Smith Act against Bridges: Steele 1999, 81.

p. 358 "The constitution must not be expanded": Ridge to Floyd, 24 Apr. 1940.

p. 358 Smith Act became law: Simkin 2014, "Alien Registration Act."

p. 358 "A refusal to face things": Ridge, Diary, 30 Apr. 1940.

p. 358 Executor's discovery in the 1970s: Sproat to Burke, 19 June 1978.

p. 358 "The crowd of me": Ridge, Diary, 3 May 1940.

p. 358 "Continue on one meal a day": ibid.

p. 359 "A column of smoke pillared": Ridge, Diary, 5 May 1940.

p. 359 "My violent reaction": Ridge, Diary, 11 May 1940.

p. 359 "No money even to buy papers": Ridge, Diary, 13 May 1940.

p. 359 "Speech...more clarifying": Ridge, Diary, 19 May 1940.

p. 359 "A record of problems": Ridge, Diary, 9 June 1940.

p. 359 "I felt better for her coming": ibid.

p. 360 She regretted not helping Emma: ibid.

p. 360 About Spengler: Stimley 2014.

p. 360 American's source on Lincoln for decades: Hurt 1999.

p. 360 "A stupendous achievement": Ridge, Diary, 29 June 1940 and 2 May 1940.

p. 360 "Blackout of the mind's light": Ridge, Diary, 12 July 1940.

p. 360 Mixed feelings about 4th of July, happy to celebrate French Revolution: Ridge, Diary, 22 May 1940.

p. 360 "There may be a Woman Dance": Ridge, Diary, 5 July 1940.

p. 361 "Could not even finish dressing": Ridge, Diary, 10 July 1940.

p. 361 "Without underwear": Ridge, Diary, 21 July 1940.

p. 361 "No light in him": Ridge, Diary, 18 Aug. 1940.

p. 361 "Simple and sweet book": Ridge, Diary, 10 July 1940.

p. 361 "Autobiography of a Revolutionist": Kropotkin 1899.

p. 361 Kropotkin's funeral: Avrich 1995, 69.

p. 361 "The Smile": Ridge, Diary, 13 July 1940.

p. 361 "Intelligent businessman": Ridge, Diary, 18 Aug. 1940.

p. 362 Woolley's suggestion: "Iraq's Ancient Past: Ur," penn.museum/sites/iraq.

p. 362 "Abraham the first concept of the male": Ridge, Diary, 8 Aug. 1940.

p. 362 "To go forward, without fear": Ridge, Diary, 26 Aug. 1940.

p. 362 "Fifty minutes to wash the spinach": ibid.

p. 362 "The heart cannot shake itself free": Ridge, Diary, 3 Sept. 1940.

p. 362 "The god of battles": Ridge, Diary, 12 Sept. 1940.

p. 362 Hanna Larsen: Ridge, Diary, 13 Sept. 1940; and "The Hanna Astrup Larsen Collection," luther.edu/anthropology.

p. 363 Lagerlof: Ridge 1919, 6, 11, 13.

p. 363 111 Montague Street: Ridge to Florence Rena Sabin, [1941].

p. 363 It is still garlanded: "The Street Necrology of Downtown Brooklyn," forgotten-ny.com.

p. 363 Auden et al. lived together: Tippens 2005.

p. 363 Wolfe lived a few doors down: Kuban 2011.

p. 363 "She is too complacent": Ridge, Diary, 16 Nov. 1940.

p. 363 "Acres of bad poetry": "Edna St. Vincent Millay: Biography," poetryfoundation.org.

p. 363 "Look droll": Ridge, Diary, 24 Nov. 1940.

p. 363 "Rushing to get in words when I begin to speak": Ridge, Diary, 9 Dec. 1940.

p. 363 "Over some bridgeless space": ibid.

p. 364 "My thought is now a strong current": ibid.

p. 364 "The fire of the world": Ridge to Marshall, [1940].

p. 364 Lawson attended a party for Wright: Ridge, Diary, 12 Dec. 1940.

p. 364 *Native Son*: "Richard Wright: Biography," math.buffalo.edu.

p. 364 "Our bodies must be swarming with this life": Ridge, Diary, 17 Dec. 1940.

p. 364 Rheumatoid arthritis: Ridge, Diary, 31 Jan. 1941.

p. 364 "Through this drying reed of me": Ridge, Diary, 8 Feb. 1941.

p. 365 "When I am angry and disturbed": ibid.

p. 365 "O splendid obituary": Ridge, Diary, 9 Mar. 1941.

p. 365 "The factories had emptied": Ridge, Diary, 12 Mar. 1941.

p. 366 "Heart": Ridge, Diary, 15 Mar. 1941.

p. 366 "If I were only well enough": Ridge, Diary, 8 Apr. 1941.

p. 366 Exchanged poems with Sabin: Ridge to Rena Sabin, [1941].

p. 366 Dr. Sabin: "The Florence R. Sabin Papers: Biographical Information," profiles.nlm.nih.gov.

p. 366 Ridge thanked Floyd: Ridge to Floyd, 26 Mar. 1941.

p. 366 "Davy will have to get his own breakfast": Ridge, Diary, 11 Apr. 1941.

p. 367 "Beauty, beyond all": Ridge 1941.

p. 367 Ridge died: Death Certificate for Lola Ridge Lawson, 21 May 1941, File No. 10849, Bureau of Records, Department of Health, Borough of Brooklyn.

Chapter 39 — Legacy: Fire and Smoke

p. 368 "Capacity to shatter the patriarchal": Drake 1987, 210.

p. 368 "Poor Lola": qtd. in Avrich 2005, 346.

p. 368 Diagnosed with arthritis: Ridge, Diary, 31 Jan. 1941.

p. 368 Death by heart failure: Kelly and Hamilton 2007; and "Interstitial Lung Disease," mayoclinic.org/diseases-conditions.

p. 368 Buried as Lola Ridge Lawson: Death Certificate for Lola Ridge Lawson, 21 May 1941, File No. 10849, Bureau of Records, Department of Health, Borough of Brooklyn.

p. 368 "Dedicated the poem "Still Water": Ridge 1927, 78.

p. 369 "I went to Lola Ridge's funeral": Marianne Moore to Hildegard Watson, 23 May 1941, in Moore 1998, 414.

p. 369 Funeral attendance: Memorial Service for Lola Ridge, 22 May 1941, Rosenbach Museum and Library, Philadelphia, PA.

p. 369 Cox-McCormack: Finding aid to the Nancy Cox-McCormack Papers, Tennessee State Library and Archives.

p. 369 Ridgely Torrence: "Ridgely Torrence," *Encyclopaedia Britannica Online Academic Edition*, 2014.

p. 369 Friends with Moody: "Torrence, Frederic Ridgely," ohiocenterforthebook.org.

p. 369 Romany Marie: "25th Anniversary Committee," *Modern School of Stelton*, New Jersey: Modern School of Stelton, 1940.

p. 369 Candle burning at both ends: Browning 1996; and Wetzsteon 2003, 366.

p. 370 Detroit News: Bernand-Wehner, correspondence with Michele Leggott 8 Apr. 2011.

p. 370 Radio operator: ibid.

p. 370 Three children: Bernand-Wehner, correspondence with Michele Leggott, 3 Aug. 2011; 9 Mar. 2014.

p. 370 "Big depression": Bernand-Wehner, correspondence with author. Mar. 15, 2013.

p. 370 Subscription to *Saturday Review*: Bernand-Wehner, email correspondence with author, 23 Feb. 2015.

p. 370 Appreciation and farewell: Benét 1941.

p. 370 Unpublished poems: Catherine Daly, email correspondence with author, 1 Nov. 2014.

p. 370 "I took the wrong way with him": qtd. in Pritchard 1985, 222.

p. 370 Wylie's son: Drake 1987, 123.

p. 370 Boyles' daughters: Pritchard 1994.

p. 370 "In a class with the greater artists": Drake 1987, 143.

p. 370 "Such as a shark or a crocodile": qtd. in Callard 1986, 81.

p. 370 Plath's son: Bates 2009.

p. 370 "Welcome to hell": Wright 2006.

p. 370 Keith's suicide: Bernand-Wehner, correspondence with author, 15 Mar. 2013.

p. 370 Didn't know his father's name: Bernand-Wehner, personal communication 6 June 2015.

p. 371 "House of a Thousand Bargains": Samuel A. DeWitt to Art Young, 15 Nov. 1934, Art Young Papers, University of Michigan Special Collections Library, Ann Arbor, MI. See also dewitt-tool. com/about-us.aspx.

p. 371 *Idylls of the Ghetto*: Bonner 1946, 49, 255; and Coodley 2013, 17.

p. 371 "Seated Socialists Formally Resign," *New York Times* 24 Sept. 1920.

p. 371 Sinclair based a character on DeWitt: "Sam DeWitt," factualworld.com.

p. 371 "I found the whole group beyond endurance": Kramer 1994.

p. 371 "Energized with ideas and visions": Official Bulletin, *Poetry Society of America* Oct. 1941: 2.

p. 371 Zukofsky and Simpson: Davidson 1950, 22.

p. 371 Jeremy Ingalls: Gonzalez 2001.

p. 371 Killed in a car accident: Sproat to Burke, 31 Jan. 1978.

p. 372 "Harassed by bodily infirmity": Benét 1941.

p. 372 Reviews mentioned her health: Hicks 1930.

p. 372 "Fighting Pain and Death": Bradley 1929.

p. 372 "Intimate terms with death": Official Bulletin, *Poetry Society of America* Oct. 1941: 2.

p. 372 "In terms of a saintliness": Gregory and Zaturenska 1946, 445.

p. 372 "Like mounting Jacob's ladder": enclosure to Ridge, in Scott to Lawson, 6 Aug. [1932].

p. 372 "If religion weren't fear worship": ibid.

p. 372 "Felt by a saint": Kreymborg 1918/19, 337.

p. 373 John Gould Fletcher to James Franklin Lewis, 29 Mar. 1943, in Fletcher 1996, 202.

p. 373 "Who in one lifetime": Rukeyser 1994.

p. 373 "The old men of the world": Ridge 1918, "The Fires."

p. 373 *Theory of Flight*: Benét 1935.

p. 373 "A poet not a propagandist": ibid.

p. 373 Five Rukeyser poems: *Poetry* Oct. 1935.

p. 373 Rexroth recited at the Dill Pickle Club: Hamalian 1992, 16.

p. 374 "These poor people aren't poets": Rexroth 1991, 124.

p. 374 Hayden traced his influences: Hamalian 1992, 16; Wald 1994, 196; and Hayden 1984, 134.

p. 374 "A dubious theme in Western culture": Hayden 1984, 134.

p. 375 "Over-reaching ambition": Lawrence 1947, 15. He continues, "...yet in many ways these are good poets."

p. 375 Glick's obituary: "Henrietta Glick, Secretary and Composer," *Chicago Sun-Times* 2 May 1994, 51.

p. 375 Marsh: Kukil 2014.

p. 375 Gardner: Ridge to Lawson, 19 Sept. 1930.

p. 375 Ned Rorem: Boosey and Hawkes [c1979] and Orchard Enterprises 1983.

p. 375: Edie Hill: Hill 2011.

p. 375 Parallel Octave Chorus: "The First Sound Files of Autumn" *8ve: the parallel octave chorus*, 18 Sept. 2012. paroct.com/2012/09/18/the-first-sound-files-of-autumn-september-9-recordings/.

p. 375 Frederick Frahm: Frahm n.d.

p. 375 Melissa Dunphy: Dunphy 2014.

p. 375 Sean Doherty: Doherty 2015.

p. 375 Ron Wray: Wray 2015.

p. 375 "Wild honey fed her": Benét 1947, 83.

p. 375 "One of the most remarkable long poems": Editorial, *The Saturday Review of Literature* 31 May 1941: 8.

p. 375 "No surprise that worthwhile poets ... discredited": Share 2009.

p. 376 "People felt the necessity": McAlmon and Boyle 1984, 25.

p. 376 "More complete self-expression": Ridge to Scott, n.d.

p. 376 "Anarchy is the philosophy I feel closest to": ibid.

p. 376 "First requisite for a great book": Ridge, Diary, 8 Feb. 1941.

p. 376 "Human rights movement": Ridge 1981/1919, 18.

p. 377 "Anarchism is about responsibility": Critchley 2007, 125.

p. 377 She attended three times: Marianne Moore to Lawson, 16 Dec. 1944, 7 June 1951, and 8 July 1960.

p. 377 Lawson's subsequent marriages: Lawson 2010/1976, xxviii, xxiii fn 25.

p. 377 Friends with Whitaker: ibid., xvi.

p. 377 Dinner with Fischer: Brady 2011, 64-65.

p. 377 Lawson made Brady pay: Frank Brady, personal communication. 9 June 2014.

p. 377 Sold a few copies: ibid.

p. 378 Bohemian Village women: E. Woolf 2013.

p. 378 Goldman portraits: "She looks, if one may approach her with a comparison bordering on levity, like a woman with housecleaning perpetually on her mind," from "Untitled," *New York World* 20 Aug. 1893, 14.

p. 378 "Freedom with responsibility": Scott 1930.

p. 378 Gladys Grant: Grant to Scott, 25 May 1941.

Index

Note: In subentries, Lola Ridge is abbreviated to "LR." All other names in subentries include a first initial unless there is potential for confusion, in which case a full name is given.

Publisher's Note:
Permissions Acknowledgments

Grateful acknowledgment is made to the following for permission to use previously published and unpublished material:

Bancroft Library, University of California, Berkeley, from an unpublished letter by Marjorie Seiffert.

The Estate of William Rose Benét, from the unpublished letters of William Rose Benét and Frances Benét, by permission of Judith Richardson and James Benét, executors.

The Estate of Kay Boyle, from unpublished letters of Kay Boyle, by permission of Ian von Franckenstein, executor.

The Witter Bynner Foundation, from an unpublished letter of Witter Bynner, by permission of Steve Schwartz, executive director.

The Estate of Mitchell Dawson, from the unpublished letters of Mitchell Dawson from the Robert and Julie Baske Dept. of Special Collections at the Newberry Library, by permission of Hilary Schlessiger, executor.

The Estate of Babette Deutsch, from an unpublished letter of Babette Deutsch, by permission of Ben Yarmolinsky, executor.

The Estate of Will and Ariel Durant, from TRANSITION: A SENTIMENTAL STORY OF ONE MIND AND ONE ERA by Will Durant copyright © 1978. Reprinted by permission of Monica Mehill, executor.

The William Floyd Estate, from an unpublished manuscript, courtesy of the Fire Island National Park Service

The Estate of Robert Lee Frost, from an unpublished letter of Robert Frost. Copyright ©2014, printed by permission of Peter A. Gilbert Executor. All rights reserved.

The Ernest Hemingway Society, from the "The Lady Poets" and a letter by Ernest Hemingway. Copyright © 2014. Reprinted by permission of Kirk Curnutt.

The Barbara Hogenson Agency, from an unpublished letter from Charlotte Wilder. Copyright © 2015 printed by permission of Tappan Wilder. All rights reserved.

Houghton Mifflin Harcourt Publishing Company, from *Firehead* by Lola Ridge. Copyright © 1929 by Lola Lawson, Renewed 1944 by David Lawson. Reprinted by permission. All rights reserved.

Jeffers Literary Properties, from the COLLECTED LETTERS OF ROBINSON JEFFERS copyright ©2009 by James Karman. Reprinted by permission of Lindsay Jeffers.

The Estate of Matthew Josephson, from an unpublished letter at the Beinecke Library, Yale University, by permission of Craig Tenney at Harold Ober Associates.

Alfred A. Knopf, from "Mozart 1935" from THE COLLECTED POEMS OF WALLACE STEVENS by Wallace Stevens, © 1954 by Wallace Stevens, and copyright renewed 1982 by Holly Stevens. Used by permission of Alfred A. Knopf, an imprint of the Knopf Doubleday Publishing Group, a division of Penguin Random House LLC. All rights reserved.

The Estate of Aaron Kramer, from LONG FOOTNOTES TO BRIEF REFERENCES: A MEMOIR by Aaron Kramer, by permission of Laura Kramer, executor.

Liveright Publishing Corporation, from "The Bridge" from THE COMPLETE POEMS OF HART CRANE by Hart Crane, edited by Marc Simon. Copyright 1933, 1958, 1966 by Liveright Publishing Corporation. Copyright © 1986 by Marc Simon. Reprinted by permission.

Liveright Publishing Corporation, from an unpublished letter from e.e. cummings. Copyright ©2016 The Cummings Collection at Houghton Library, Harvard University by e.e. cummings. Copyright by the Trustees for e.e. cummings Trust. Reprinted by permission.

The Estate of Harold Loeb, from the unpublished letters from Harold Loeb to Lola Ridge, *Broom* Correspondence of Harold Loeb (C0110); 1920-1956 (mostly 1921-1924), Manuscripts Division, Department of Rare Books and Special Collections, Princeton University Library, by permission of Anah Pytte, executor.

Literary Estate of Marianne Moore from unpublished letters/notes of Marianne C. Moore to Lola Ridge (4-19-19 [V:53:16, Rosenbach Museum], 5-25--20, 3-13-21, 6-3-25, 12-1-25, 1-1-27, 11-22-27, 9-19-29 [V:53:16], letters/Notes from Marianne Moore to John Warner Moore 1-28-23 [V:26:02], 5-10-23, as found in Selected Letters of Marianne Moore, Bonnie Costello, 1998, New York:Penguin, p. 272, 7-10-28 [VI:29:08], 7-19-32, as found in Selected Letters, p. 389, letters/notes from Mary Moore to Lola Ridge 2-29-25 [V:53:16], 2-29-28 [V:53:16], letter/note from Marianne Moore to Mary Moore 2-2-09 [VI:15a:03], letter from Marianne Moore to Hildegarde Watson 5-23-41, as found in Selected Letters, p. 413, and notes from the Conversation Notebooks of Marianne Moore written by Marianne Moore on 2-8--20, 2-25-20 and 10-21 are granted by the Literary Estate of Marianne C. Moore, David M. Moore, Administrator. All rights reserved.

Mt. Holyoke College, from the letters of Jeannette Marks, by permission of Mt. Holyoke Archives and Special Collections, South Hadley, MA.

Newberry Library, Chicago, IL from the unpublished letter of Robert McAlmon to Mitchell Dawson, by permission of the Robert and Julie Baske Dept. of Special Collections.

New Directions Publishing Corp,from William Carlos Williams's unpublished letters to Lola Ridge, copyright ©1990 by William Eric Williams and Paul H. Williams. Reprinted by permission.

New Directions Publishing Corp., from *Others* magazine, copyright ©2016 by the Estates of Paul H. Williams and William Eric Williams. Reprinted by permission.

New Directions Publishing Corp., from three unpublished letters by William Carlos Williams, copyright ©2016 by the Estates of Paul H. Williams and William Eric Williams. Reprinted by permission.

New Directions Publishing Corp., from THE AUTOBIOGRAPHY OF WILLIAM CARLOS WILLIAMS, copyright ©1951 by William Carlos Williams. Reprinted by permission.

New Directions Publishing Corp., from THE SELECTED LETTERS OF WILLIAM CARLOS WILLIAMS, copyright ©1957 by William Carlos Williams. Reprinted by permission.

New Directions Publishing Corp., from unpublished letters from Williams to Mitchell Dawson, copyright ©2016 by the Estates of Paul H. Williams and William Eric Williams. Reprinted by permission.

Katherine Ann Porter Literary Trust, from excerpts of the writing of Katherine Ann Porter © 1977, reprinted by permission of The Permissions Company.

The Estate of Edwin Rolfe, from an unpublished letter of Edwin Rolfe, by permission of Carey Nelson, executor.

The Estate of Evelyn Scott, from the letters of Evelyn Scott, Cyril-Kay Scott and Creighton Scott from the Harry Ransom Center The University of Texas at Austin, by permission of Denise Scott-Fears, executor.

The Estate of Harrison Smith, from the unpublished letters of Harrison Smith from the Manuscripts and Archives Division, New York Public Library, by permission of Sarah Harrison Smith, executor.

The Estate of Jean Toomer from excerpts of "Gum," an unpublished play, and letters to Lola Ridge, courtesy of the Beinecke Library, Yale University, by permission of Nancy Kuhl.

The Corporation of Yaddo, from unpublished letters of Elizabeth Ames from the Manuscripts and Archives Division, New York Public Library, by permission of Elaina Richardson.

The Estate of Mariya Zaturenska and Horace Gregory, from "White Dress" by Mariya Zaturenska. Reprinted by permission of Patrick Gregory, executor.

LIVING AS FORM

KT-377-195

LIVING AS FORM:
SOCIALLY ENGAGED ART
FROM 1991–2011

EDITED BY NATO THOMPSON

CREATIVE TIME BOOKS, NEW YORK
THE MIT PRESS, CAMBRIDGE, MASSACHUSETTS AND LONDON, ENGLAND

UNIVERSITY OF WINCHESTER
LIBRARY

CONTENTS

FOREWORD

Over twenty years ago, artist Peggy Diggs sat in a Western Massachusetts prison and listened as women recounted the abuses they had suffered at the hands of their spouses. She learned that these women were often prisoners in their own homes, unable to tell their stories or get assistance. Many only left their house to conduct basic household errands, such as grocery shopping. Diggs saw an opportunity to help. She enlisted Tuscan Dairy Farms to print a question—"When you argue at home, does it always get out of hand?"—and an abuse hotline number on over one million milk cartons distributed in New York, New Jersey, Connecticut, Delaware, and Pennsylvania. She believed that this message was worth hearing, and that the supermarket was the right forum in which to spread it.

I encountered Diggs' *The Domestic Milk Carton Project*, a Creative Time commission, several years before joining the organization, while I was pouring milk into my coffee. At the time, a friend would call frequently with complaints about her abusive fiancée, and I rarely knew what to say. (It took the murder of O.J. Simpson's wife Nicole Brown in 1994 to lift the veil of shame and secrecy around domestic violence.) So, I called the hotline number. I had no idea that I'd just experienced public art; nor did it matter. What did matter was that

the image, and the message, provoked me to pause, think, learn, and act.

For thirty-seven years, Creative Time has been challenging audiences to expand their views while encouraging artists to broaden and deepen their relationships to the pressing issues of our times and the communities they effect. Projects such as Diggs'; Julian LaVerdiere and Paul Myoda's *Tribute in Light* illuminating Lower Manhattan after 9/11; Gran Fury's famed *Kissing Doesn't Kill* billboards about HIV transmission; Paul Chan's *Waiting for Godot* in Post-Katrina New Orleans; Paul Ramírez Jonas' civic artwork *Key to the City*; Sharon Hayes' *Revolutionary Love* addressing the state of queer desire; and Tania Bruguera's *Immigrant Movement International* have upheld Creative Time's historic belief that artists matter in society and that public spaces are places for their free and creative expression.

In recent years, there has been a rapidly growing movement of artists choosing to engage with timely issues by expanding their practice beyond the safe confines of the studio and right into the complexity of the unpredictable public sphere. This work has many names: "relational aesthetics," "social justice art," "social practice," and "community art," among others. These artists engage in a process that includes careful listening, thoughtful conversation, and community organizing. With antecedents such as the Dada Cabaret Voltaire, Joseph Beuys' notion of Social Sculpture, Allan Kaprow's "happenings," Gordon Matta Clarke's interventions, radical community theater of the 1960s, Lygia Clark's Tropicália movement in Brazil, the community-based public art projects of groundbreaking artists such as Suzanne Lacy, Mierle Laderman Ukeles and Rick Lowe to social movements from the Civil Rights and Feminist Movements to the Green Party, social practice artists create forms of living that activate communities and advance public awareness of pressing social issues. In the process, they expand models of art, advance ways of being an artist, and involve new publics in their efforts.

Despite the growing prevalence of this art practice, and the rise of graduate art programs offering degrees in social practice art, relatively few among the growing masses of art enthusiasts are aware of its existence, let alone its vibrancy. To be fair, this kind of work does not hang well in a museum, and it isn't commercially viable. Furthermore, social practice art has lacked a shared critical language and comprehensive historic documentation. Creative Time's own engagement with the social was often dismissed in an art world that prefers to frame artists as commodity makers rather than change makers, and where many assert that politics and art have no place together. At Creative Time, we have always felt otherwise. So, in 2006 we launched *Who Cares*, a project that brought artists and thinkers together to discuss the role of art and activism. This ultimately led to the creation of The Creative Time Summit, our annual conference on art and social justice, and presentation of The Leonore Annenberg Prize for Art and Social Change.

Living as Form, an exhibition and book that looks at social practice art from around the globe, further extends this legacy. It is, admittedly, a problematic undertaking. After all, how does one present site-specific, community-based work outside of its context? How can a history be written when there are unlimited

and complex social, cultural, economic, political, religious, and class constructs at play? Where does one begin to tell the story? With the manifestos of modern art movements? With the global social protests that ignited the new millennium, or with the impact of microfinancing and small do-it-yourself NGOs in places of need? How does one weave together the diverse narratives of feminist, African-American, and Latino practices that have largely been dismissed as "community art"? How does one deal with differences among local conditions around the world where dictatorial regimes make every act of artistic expression a potential danger that can lead to jail, torture, and even death? (I am reminded in particular of the recent imprisonments and torture of artist Ai Weiwei and the tragic assignation of theater director Juliano Mer-Khamis in the West Bank.) And, perhaps most importantly, what are the ethical implications of this practice?

In light of these questions and the many others surrounding social practice art, Creative Time Chief Curator Nato Thompson took an unusual and difficult path organizing the *Living as Form* project. Rather than attempting an authoritative historical survey or compiling a "best of" list, he conceived of *Living as Form* in order to raise fundamental questions that advance dialogue, ignite conversation, and promote greater understanding of social practice work for the complicated and important field that it is. In this pursuit, Nato turned to twenty-five advising curators, who have guided our understanding of the complexities of the field and exposed us to many new artists working within it. We thank: Caron Atlas, Negar Azimi, Ron Bechet, Claire Bishop, Brett Bloom, Rashida Bumbray, Carolina Caycedo, Ana Paula Cohen, Common Room, Teddy Cruz, Sofía Hernández Chong Cuy, Gridthiya Gaweewong, Hou Hanru, Stephen Hobbs, Marcus Neustetter, Shannon Jackson, Maria Lind, Chus Martínez, Sina Najafi, Marion von Osten, Ted Purves, Raqs Media Collective, Gregory Sholette, SUPERFLEX, Christine Tohme, and Sue Bell Yank.

This book features essays by acclaimed theorists and practitioners Claire Bishop, Teddy

Cruz, Maria Lind, Carol Becker, Shannon Jackson, and Brian Holmes, who each look at the phenomenon of social practice in art from vastly different global, and critical perspectives. Claire Bishop questions the tendency to privilege ethical standards over aesthetic ones, while Brian Holmes provides a four-step process of producing social practice that values both of these standards equally. Carol Becker describes the uniqueness of artist-designed "microutopias" while Maria Lind recounts numerous projects across Europe that demonstrate long-term investment in the messy realities of life outside of the artistic context.

We are deeply grateful to Nato who is a most fervent champion of art and social justice. He is that rare curator and scholar that insists that artists not only create, but also create important change. Research for this project was lead by curatorial fellow Leah Abir, who joined us from Israel thanks to our partnership with Artis, a non-profit that supports Israeli contemporary art around the world.

We applaud Sharmila Venkatasubban, our talented editor who masterfully brought this book to life. It is always a pleasure to work with the designer Garrick Gott, who creates elegant order from chaos. Special thanks goes to our copy editor Clinton Krute and proofreader Ann Holcomb, as well as all the interns and fellows who made this book a reality: Madeline Lieberberg, Winona Packer, Shraddha Borowake, Phillip Griffith, and Rachel Ichniowski.

We cannot say enough just how profoundly grateful we are to the donors who believed in this project and, despite a turbulent global economy, recognized the importance of artists as agents for change and generously invested in this project. Specific funding for *Living as Form* has been provided by the Lily Auchincloss Foundation, Joanne Leonhardt Cassullo, the Nathan Cummings Foundation, the Danish Arts Council Committee for Visual Arts, Stephanie and Tim Ingrassia, the Andrew W. Mellon Foundation, Bella Meyer and Martin Kace, the Mondriaan Foundation, the National Endowment for the Arts, the Panta Rhea Foundation, the Rockefeller Brothers Fund, the Netherlands Foundation for Visual Arts, Design and Architecture, Emily Glasser and William Susman, and the Laurie M. Tisch Illumination Fund. We give special thanks to the Annenberg Foundation for continued support of The Leonore Annenberg Prize for Art and Social Change, a $25,000 award that each year acknowledges an artist who has devoted his or her life's work to promoting social justice.

I'm particularly blessed to work with an incredible team. The Creative Time Board supports our every dream and trusts in us to realize them. That trust is essential as it frees artists to follow their instincts—unencumbered by bureaucracy and fear—without which great art cannot happen. The Creative Time staff is devoted to artists and takes exceptional efforts to make magic happen every day.

Above all, we thank the artists who engage in social practice for their inspiration and for daring to make an impact on our world. We hope through their work, this book will inspire further scholarship and action.

Anne Pasternak, President and Artistic Director, Creative Time

Following pages: Creative Time's *Living as Form* took place at the historic Essex Street Market in Mannhattan's Lower East Side.

LIVING AS FORM

NATO THOMPSON

WHAT STRIKES ME IS THE FACT THAT
IN OUR SOCIETY, ART HAS BECOME
SOMETHING WHICH IS RELATED
ONLY TO OBJECTS AND NOT TO
INDIVIDUALS, OR TO LIFE. THAT ART IS
SOMETHING WHICH IS SPECIALIZED OR
WHICH IS DONE BY EXPERTS WHO ARE
ARTISTS. BUT COULDN'T EVERYONE'S
LIFE BECOME A WORK OF ART? WHY
SHOULD THE LAMP OR HOUSE BE AN
OBJECT, BUT NOT OUR LIFE?

— Michel Foucault

I WENT FROM BEING AN ARTIST
WHO MAKES THINGS,
TO BEING AN ARTIST
WHO MAKES THINGS HAPPEN.

— Jeremy Deller

PART I: LIVING AS FORM

Women on Waves is an activist/art organization founded in 2001 by physician Rebecca Gomperts. The small nonprofit group would sail from the coasts of countries where abortion is illegal in a boat designed by Atelier Van Leishout that housed a functioning abortion clinic. Gomperts and her crew would then anchor in international waters—since the boat was registered in The Netherlands, they operated under Dutch law—to provide abortion services to women, legally and safely. The following quote is from a documentary film about the history of Women on Waves. While reading, bear in mind the almost Homeric qualities this seafaring narrative conjures. It is a drama, and this is no accident.

> "As the ship sails into the Valencia harbor, conservatives dispatch ships bearing banners reading "no" and drumming thunders from the anti-choice protestors leaning on the gates to the port. The dock is mobbed with supporters and aggressive press. As the ship attempts to tie up, a dissenting harbor patrol ship lodges itself between the Women on Waves ship and the dock, securing their lines to the ship and attempting to drag the ship back to sea, while the activists frantically try to untie the line. The authorities seem to be winning the tug of war, when Rebecca, clearly enjoying the moment, emerges from the hole wielding a large knife. The crowd onshore thunderously stomps and cheers as she slices the patrol's rope in half, freeing her ship, bows to the crowd, and tosses the Women on Waves lines to the eager supporters. As the harbor patrol's motorboat circles, baffied and impotent, hundreds of hands pull the ship into dock."

Seven years later, for his project *Palas Por Pistolas,* the artist Pedro Reyes collected 1,527 weapons from residents of Culiacán, a Western Mexican city known for drug trafficking and a high rate of fatal gunfire. Working with local television stations, he invited citizens to donate their firearms in exchange for vouchers that could be redeemed for electronics and appliances from domestic shops. The 1,527 weapons—more than forty percent of which were issued by the military—were publicly steamrolled into a mass of flattened metal, melted down in a local foundry, and recast into 1,527 shovels. Reyes distributed the shovels to local charities and school groups, which used them to plant 1,527 trees in public spaces throughout the city. The spades have been widely exhibited, with labels attached explaining their origins; each time they are shown, they are used to plant more trees.

Here we have before us two socially engaged art projects—both poetic, yet functional and political as well. They engage people and confront a specific issue. While these participatory projects are far removed from what one might call the traditional studio arts—such as sculpture, film, painting, and video—what field they *do* belong to is hard to articulate. Though defined by an active engagement with groups of people in the world, their intentions and disciplines remain elusive. Are these projects geared for the media? Each project flourished among news outlets as these artists created new spin around old stories: a woman's right to choose and the drug wars of Northern Mexico. Women on Waves has performed relatively few abortions over the course of seven years. In fact, the boat has mainly been deployed as a media device intended to bring awareness to the issue. Similarly, Pedro Reyes did remove 1,527 guns from the streets of Culiacán. But, given the actual extent of gun violence there, his gesture seems far more symbolic than practical.

And yet, symbolic gestures can be powerful and effective methods for change. Planting trees does improve quality of life, and using recycled guns to do so speaks directly to those most affected by the violence. Likewise, Women on Waves provided essential services to women in anti-choice countries, regardless of how many were actually able to take advantage of them. While we may not know how to cat-

egorize these projects, they typify a growing array of complex cultural production that continues to garner interest and adherents. Say what one will, socially engaged art is growing and ubiquitous.

The projects in *Living as Form* expose the numerous lines of tension which have surfaced in socially engaged art in the past twenty years, essentially shaking up foundations of art discourse, and sharing techniques and intentions with fields far beyond the arts. Unlike its avant-garde predecessors such as Russian Constructivism, Futurism, Situationism, Tropicalia, Happenings, Fluxus, and Dadaism, socially engaged art is not an art movement. Rather, these cultural practices indicate a new social order—ways of life that emphasize participation, challenge power, and span disciplines ranging from urban planning and community work to theater and the visual arts.

This veritable explosion of work in the arts has been assigned catchphrases, such as "relational aesthetics," coined by French

curator Nicholas Bourriaud, or Danish curator Lars Bang Larsen's term, "social aesthetics." We can also look to artist Suzanne Lacy's "new genre public art," or the commonly known West Coast term "social practice." Other precursors include Critical Art Ensemble's activist approach called "tactical media" and Grant Kester's "dialogic art," which refers to conversation-based projects. We can also go back further to consider Joseph Beuys's "social sculpture." Numerous genres have been deeply intertwined in participation, sociality, conversation, and "the civic." This interconnectivity reveals a peculiar historic moment in which these notions aren't limited to the world of contemporary art, but includes various cultural phenomena which have cropped up across the urban fabric. For example, spontaneous bike rides in cities by the group Critical Mass, guerrilla community gardens, and micro-granting community groups are just a few of the non-discipline-specific cultural projects which share many of the same criteria

Above: The Women on Waves ship prepares to sail to Poland in June 2003 (Courtesy Women on Waves).

as socially engaged artworks.

How do we write such an interdisciplinary, case-specific narrative without producing misleading causal relationships? The desire to merge art and life resonates throughout the avant-garde movements of the twentieth century and then multiplies across the globe at the beginning of the twenty-first. Artists have borrowed from a plethora of histories—from Russian Constructivists, Fluxus, Gutai, Tropicalia, and Happenings to Antonin Artaud's Theater of Cruelty, Boal's Theater of the Oppressed, and the San Francisco Mime Troupe. However, it would be a mistake not to place within that history the seminal pedagogic social movements of the last one hundred years. This includes AIDS activism, the women's movement, the anti-Apartheid movement, Perestroika, the civil rights movement, Paris '68, the Algerian wars, as well as the many leaders and visionaries within those movements who discussed the importance of sociality, methods of resistance and confronting power, and strategies for using media. History itself is a problem when it leads to a false sense of causality. If we follow the trail of this work strictly through the lens of art (which is what most discipline-specific histories do), we could easily imagine a very Western trajectory moving from Dada to Rirkrit Tiravanija in 1991 making Pad Thai—a version of a history in quick strokes. But of course, this kind of highly problematic narrative lacks a true appreciation of the vast complexity of global and local influences, an all-too-common signpost for the contemporary period. Art is no longer the primary influence for culture and because of this, tracing its roots is all the more complex.

Living as Form searches the post-Cold War era, and the dawn of neoliberalism, for cultural works which serve as points of departure for specific regional and historic concerns. However, this book does not offer a singular critical language for evaluating socially engaged art, nor provide a list of best practices, nor offer a linear historic interpretation of a field of practice. Instead, we merely present the temperature in the water in order to raise compelling questions.

WHAT IS MEANT BY LIVING?

Artists have long desired that art enter life. But what do me mean by "life"? In the context of Living as Form, the word conjures certain qualities that I wish to explore, an aggregate of related but different manifestations of the term.

Anti-representational

When artist Tania Bruguera states, "I don't want an art that points at a thing, I want an art that *is* the thing," she emphasizes forms of art that involve being in the world. Yet, she has also said, "It is time to put Duchamp's urinal back in the restroom." Duchamp's "Readymades" are a great place to initiate the conversation about art and life. For some artists, the desire to make art that is living stems from the desire for something breathing, performative, and action-based. Participation, sociality, and the organization of bodies in space play a key feature in much of this work. Perhaps in reaction to the steady state of mediated two-dimensional cultural production, or a reaction to the alienating effects of spectacle, artists, activists, citizens, and advertisers alike are rushing headlong into methods of working that allow genuine interpersonal human relationships to develop. The call for art into life at this particular moment in history implies both an urgency to matter as well as a privileging of the lived experience. These are two different things, but within much of this work, they are blended together.

Participation

In recent years, we have seen increased growth in "participatory art": art that requires some action on behalf of the viewer in order to complete the work. Consider *Tiza* (2002) by artists Jennifer Allora and Guillermo Calzadilla. This public space intervention consisted of twelve enormous pieces of chalk set out in public squares. People used discarded remnants or broke off a chunk to write messages on the ground. Since Allora and Calzadilla generally choose urban environments with politically confrontational histories, the writing tends to reflect political resentment and frustrations.

Opposite: In Pedro Reyes' *Palas por Pistolas*, 1,527 shovels were made from the melted metal of 1,527 guns collected from residents of Culicán, and used to plant 1,527 trees in the community (Courtesy Pedro Reyes and LABOR).

This is just one example of numerous works that enter life by facilitating participation.

Situated in the "real" world

Clearly, an urge to enter the "real" world inherently implies that there is an "un-real" world where actions do not have impact or resonance. Nonetheless, we find in numerous socially engaged artworks that the desire for art to enter life comprises a spatial component as well. Getting out of the museum or gallery and into the public can often come from an artist's belief or concern that the designated space for representation takes the teeth out of a work. For example, Amal Kenawy's *Silence of the Lambs* (2010) focused on a performance in Cairo wherein members of the public were asked to crawl across a congested intersection on their hands and knees; the work critiqued the submissiveness of the general public to the autocratic rule of then-president Hosni Mubarak, and was an ironic precursor to the Arab Spring. Kenawy's performance entered into life by taking place in the public realm. While this is quite literal, it is important to bear in mind the basic semantic difference as well as the potential risk and cost.

Operating in the political sphere

As much as art entering life can have a spatial connotation, it can also possess a judicial and governmental one as well. For many socially engaged artists, there is a continued interest in impact, and often the realm of the political symbolizes these ambitions. Artist Laurie Jo Reynolds's long-term project aims to challenge and overturn harsh practices in southern Illinois's Tamms Supermax Prison. Focusing on the basic political injustice (as she sees it) that this prison uses solitary confinement as a condition of incarceration, and that Tamms meets and exceeds the international definition of torture, Reynolds organized *Tamms Year Ten*, an all-volunteer coalition of prisoners, ex-prisoners, prisoners' families, and concerned citizens. Reynolds has labeled her efforts "legislative art" which reflects the term coined by Brazilian playwright Augusto Boal's "legislative theater." Borrowing from the work of

education theorist Paolo Freire, Augusto Boal produced a new form of living theater in the 1960s whose entire mission was to assist in the politicization and agency of Brazil's most oppressed. In addition to inventing different modes of theatricality that entered into daily life, such as newspaper theater and invisible theater, he developed a form of participatory politics called "legislative theater" when he was a city council member in Rio de Janeiro.

In a world of vast cultural production, the arts have become an instructive space to gain valuable skill sets in the techniques of performativity, representation, aesthetics, and the creation of affect. These skill sets are not secondary to the landscape of political production but, in fact, necessary for its manifestation. If the world is a stage (as both Shakespeare and Guy Debord foretold), then every person on the planet must learn the skill sets of theater. The realm of the political may perhaps be the most appropriate place for the arts, after all.

WHAT IS MEANT BY FORM?

"THE PUBLIC HAS A FORM AND ANY FORM CAN BE ART."

— Paul Ramírez Jonas

Just as video, painting, and clay are types of forms, people coming together possess forms as well. And while it is difficult to categorize socially engaged art by discipline, we can map various affinities based on methodologies. This includes the political issues they address, such as sustainability, the environment, education, housing, labor, gender, race, colonialism, gentrification, immigration, incarceration, war, borders, and on and on.

Focusing on methodologies is also an attempt to shift the conversation away from the arts' typical lens of analysis: aesthetics. This is not to say that the visual holds no place in this work, but instead this approach emphasiz-

Opposite: Jennifer Allora and Guillermo Calzadilla placed twelve enormous pieces of chalk in the Plaza de Armas in Lima, inviting the public to write messages on the surrounding pavement (Courtesy Jennifer Allora and Guillermo Calzadilla).

es the designated forms produced for impact. By focusing on how a work approaches the social, as opposed to simply what it looks like, we can better calibrate a language to unpack its numerous engagements.

Types of gatherings

Consider *Please Love Austria: First Austrian Coalition* by the late artist Christoph Schlingensief. For this work, he invited refugees seeking political asylum to compete for either a cash prize or a residency visa, granted through marriage. He locked twelve participants in a shipping container, equipped with a closed circuit television, for one week. Every day, viewers would vote on their least favorite refugees; two were banished from the container and deported back to their native countries. The container, placed outside the Vienna State Opera House, sported blue flags representing Austria's right-wing party, bearing a sign that read, "Foreigners Out." It was clearly controversial because the project used the technique of over-determination to promote and magnify the nascent xenophobia and racism already existing in Austria. The project took place in a public square, and provided both a physical space for people to come together as well as a mediated space for discussion. This gathering of people wasn't what one would call a space of consensus but one of deep discord and frustration.

Types of media manipulation

I have previously discussed the manner in which Women on Waves and Pedro Reyes used the media as a critical element in their work. One can add to this list most of the socially engaged art in this book, including Bijari, Rwanda Healing Project, the Yes Men, and Mel Chin. As the realm of the political and the realm of media become deeply intertwined, media stunts become an increasingly important part of the realm of politics. This is true for those resisting power and those enforcing it. And it reflects a contemporary condition wherein relationships with mediation are the basic components by which political—and thus social—decisions are made.

Research and its presentation

If politics have become performative, so too, has knowledge—in other words, you have to share what you know. Researchers and scientists who feel a sense of political urgency to disseminate their findings might use the skill sets of symbolic manipulation and performativity in order to get their message out. Similarly, we find numerous artists and collectives who deploy aesthetic strategies to spread their message. For example, Ala Plástica's research-based environmental activism focuses on the damage caused when a Shell Oil tank collided with another cargo ship in the Rio de la Plata. Over 5,300 tons of oil spilled into this major Argentine river. Using photographs and drawings, and working with local residents to conduct surveys, the collaborative deploys techniques of socially engaged art in order to bring this issue to light. One should also mention the work of Decolonizing Architecture Art Residency based in Beit Sahour, Palestine, a group that aims to visualize the future re-use of architecture in occupied territories. In places where war, migration, and mass atrocities have become commonplace—such as Rwanda, Beirut, and Palestine—it is not surprising that many artists focus on archives as a way to document histories now lost.

Structural alternatives

The "Do It Yourself" ethic, as it was termed in the early 1990s, has gained cultural traction, and has spread into the basic composition of urban living. Experiments in alternatives—whether the focus is food production, housing, education, bicycling, or fashion—have become a broad form of self-determined sociality. Once just the modus operandi of anarchists at the fringes of culture, the practice has now entered the mainstream. The food movement, perhaps inspired by increasing fear over genetically modified organisms in food by large-scale corporate agriculture and horror of cruel animal slaughtering practices, has become an integral element of many urban metropolises. Community Sourced Agriculture (CSAs), guerrilla community gardens, and the Slow Food movement, are all forms of new lived civic life that

Opposite: In *Please Love Austria*, Christoph Schlingensief locked 12 refugees seeking political asylum in a shipping container in front of the Vienna State Opera House for one week, and left their fate up to the public. A sign on the container declaring, "Foreigners Out" referenced the pervasive racism in Austria. (Courtesy David Baltzer and Zenit)

takes the work, literally, into one's own hands.

We also find pervasive growth in alternative social programs occurring in response to the evisceration of state-funded social programs by various austerity measures. We find numerous alternative economies and schools at work as well. Fran Illich's *Spacebank* (2005) is just one example of an alternative economy aesthetic/form of living. Launched with just 50 Mexican pesos, *Spacebank* is both an actual and conceptual online bank that offers real investing opportunities, and loans to activists and grassroots organizations. Similarly, Los Angeles-based architect Fritz Haeg offered free classes and workshops in his *Sundown Salons,* which he held in his residence, a geodesic dome. I say "similarly" in so much as these are two art world examples of tendencies reflecting the urge toward a DIY aesthetic that has prevailed for nearly twenty years.

Types of communicating

As group participation increases, the basic skill sets which accompany group process become more useful. Isolated artists must focus on speaking, while groups of people coming together must focus on listening—the art of *not* speaking but hearing. The Los Angeles-based collective Ultra-red writes, "In asserting the priority of organizing herein, Ultra-red, as so often over the years, evokes the procedure so thematic to investigation developed by [Brazilian radical pedagogue] Paulo Freire." Grant Kester has come up with the term "dialogic art" to discuss such methods of art production that emphasize conversation, and certainly many artists privilege conversation as a mode of action. In evoking Freire, Ultra-red also points towards a form of education that must address conditions of power as much as it does culture and politics. The personal is not only political but the interpersonal contains the seeds of political conflict inherently. In reflecting on his work with the sixteen-year-old experimental community housing project/art residency/socially engaged Project Row Houses, Rick Lowe stated in an interview with the *New York Times,* "I was doing big, billboard-size paintings and cutout sculptures dealing with social

issues, and one of the students told me that, sure, the work reflected what was going on in his community, but it wasn't what the community needed. If I was an artist, he said, why didn't I come up with some kind of creative solution to issues instead of just telling people like him what they already knew. That was the defining moment that pushed me out of the studio."

FORMS OF LIFE

Tania Bruguera's call to return Duchamp's urinal to the restroom is a poignant, provocative notion. For once it has been returned, what do we call it? Art or life? Once art begins to look like life, how are we to distinguish between the two? When faced with such complex riddles, often the best route is to rephrase the question. Whether this work can be considered art is a dated debate in the visual arts. I suggest a more interesting question: If this work is *not* art, then what are the methods we can use to understand its effects, affects, and impact? In raising these questions, I would like to quote the former U.S. Defense Secretary responsible for leading the United States into the Iraq War, Donald Rumsfeld: "If you have a problem, make it bigger." Rumsfeld's adage has been taken to heart as we begin to, hopefully, solve the conundrum of art and life by aggregating projects from numerous disciplines whose manifestations in the world reflect a social ecosystem of affinities. By introducing such a broad array of approaches, the tensions nascent in contemporary art exacerbate to the point of rupture. The point is not to destroy the category of art, but—straining against edges where art blurs into the everyday—to take a snapshot of cultural production at the beginning of the 21st century.

An important project that defies easy categorization is Lowe's Project Row Houses. Situated in a low-income, predominately African-American neighborhood in Houston's Northern Third Ward, Project Row Houses was spurred by the artist's interest in the art of John Biggers, who painted scenes of African-American life in row house neighborhoods, as well as his desire to make a profound, long-term commit-

ment to a specific neighborhood. As the community was on the verge of being demolished by the City of Houston, the project began with the purchase of several row houses, which have been transformed into sites of local cultural participation as well as artist residencies. Over the years, many artists have come and gone, more homes have been purchased, and the row houses have undergone rehabilitation. The project initiated a program for the neighborhood's single mothers, providing childcare and housing so that the mothers could attend school. Project Row Houses has built trust and strong relationships with the surrounding neighborhood, offering a sustainable growth model that is perfect for the neighborhood, one created from the ground up.

Project Row Houses is a nonprofit organization initiated by an artist. If it can be included as a socially engaged artwork, why not include more nonprofit organizations as artworks as

well? Many artists and art collectives use a broad range of bureaucratic and administrative skills that typically lie in the domain of larger institutions, such as marketing, fundraising, grant writing, real estate development, investing in start-ups, city planning, and educational programming. As opposed to assuming there is an inherent difference between artist-initiated projects and non-artist-initiated projects, I have opted to simply include them all. Let us call this the "cattle call" method. While it might feel strange to include nonprofit art organizations such as Cemeti Art House and Foundation in Yogyakarta, Indonesia, which has been involved in post-earthquake cultural programming, or the work of the United Indian Health Services located in Northern California, which combines traditional cultural programming with access to health care, consider what they do, not who they say they are. Certainly these projects are not specifically artworks, but their

Above: Artist Sam Durant contributed *We Are the People* to Project Row Houses in 2003 (Courtesy Project Row Houses).

collaborative and participatory spirit, community activism, and deployment of cultural programming as part of their operations makes their work appear close to some projects that arise from an arts background. In fact, there are thousands of other nonprofits whose work could be considered and highlighted as well.

In an even greater stretch of the framework of socially engaged art, some works have been included in *Living as Form* that possess no singular author or organization. For example, the celebrations in Harlem on the night of Barack Obama's election were spontaneous eruptions of joy and street parading in a community that had long thought the election of a black president to be an impossibility. And, in a similar vein, the protests that have erupted across the Middle East—particularly those in Tunisia and Egypt—have become models of spontaneous popular action facilitated across dynamic social networks with the collective desire to

contest power. Does this constitute art? Does this constitute a civic action? Certainly some questions are easier to answer than others.

This book's title borrows from Harald Szeemann's landmark 1969 exhibition at Kunsthall Bern, *When Attitudes Become Form: Live in Your Head*, which featured artists including Joseph Beuys, Barry Flanagan, Eva Hesse, Jannis Kounellis, Walter de Maria, Robert Morris, Bruce Nauman, and Lawrence Weiner, introducing an array of artists whose conceptual works challenged the formal arrangements of what constituted art at the time. The show highlighted a diverse range of tendencies that would later materialize as movements from conceptual art, land art, Minimalism, and Arte Povera. Writing on the exhibition, from Szeemann's catalog, Hans-Joachim Müller stated, "For the first time, the importance of form seemed to be questioned altogether by the conceptualization of form: whatever has a cer-

Above: Artists from all over Indonesia took part in Cemeti Art House's yearlong program, which revitalized the arts in areas traumatized by an earthquake (Photograph by Dwi 'Oblo' Prasetyo, Courtesy Cemeti Art House, Yogyakarta, Indonesia).

tain form can be measured, described, understood, misunderstood. Forms can be criticized, disintegrated, assembled." Such a break is in the air again, but now accompanied by a keen awareness that living itself exists in forms that must be questioned, rearranged, mobilized, and undone. For the first time, the importance of *forms of living* seems to be questioned altogether by the conceptualization of *living as form*. Whatever has a certain form can be measured, described, understood, misunderstood. *Forms of living* can be criticized, disintegrated, assembled.

PART II: NEOLIBERALISM AND THE RISE OF SPECTACULAR LIVING

Why does this book focus on the last twenty years? Since the fall of the Berlin Wall in 1989, a new neoliberal order has emerged. Loosely defined, neoliberalism as a political order privileges free trade and open markets, resulting in maximizing the role of the private sector in determining priorities and deemphasizing the role of the public and the state's function in protecting and supporting them. This pro-capitalist governmentalism has radically shaped the current geopolitical and social map. From the global boosterism of the 1990s to the subsequent hangover and contestation in the 2000s, this vast history includes the growth of capitalism and free-market influence on international governance; formation of the European Union; genocide in Rwanda; the events of September 11, 2001, and ensuing wars in Afghanistan and Iraq; the bellicose efforts of the Bush administration; and flexible labor in the Western world where decentralized businesses hired and fired quickly, and temporary work became a more familiar way of life. As these policies became commonplace, we found a widespread exacerbation of nascent race and class divisions. The prison industry in the United States now booms, and the gap between rich and poor increases. Widespread protests in Europe and Latin America yielded the term "precarity," which gained traction as a description of social life always in jeopardy. Austerity measures forced governments such

as Argentina, Spain, Greece, and Ireland to eliminate their social welfare programs and ignited protest movements. In Latin America, new left governments emerged that redefined the region's relationship to culture, capitalism, and power.

The last twenty years were also accompanied by a global growth of advertising in a more media-rich world—from film to cable television to the explosion of video games to the rapid formation of the Internet and social media. Using the same symbolic manipulation and design methods that have long been the bread and butter of artists, the growth of "creative industries" were undeniably part of the cultural landscape. While in the 1940s, the Frankfurt School philosophers Adorno and Horkheimer warned of an impending wave of capitalist-produced culture that would sweep across the world, the last twenty years has seen that wave become a reality. Guy Debord and the Situationists of Paris 1968 coined the term "spectacle" to refer to the process by which culture, expressions of a society's self-understanding, is produced within the capitalist machine. Typified by the image of an audience at a cinema passively watching television and film, the spectacle can be seen as shorthand for a world condition wherein images are made for the purpose of sales. Certainly when considered from the standpoint of scale, the sheer amount of culture we as a global community consume, as well as produce, indicates a radical break with our relationship to cultures of past eras. Over the last twenty years we find people forced to produce new forms of action in order to account for this radically altered playing field. We find a form of activism and political action that is increasingly media savvy. As opposed to thinking of a war fought with only guns, tanks, and bodies, wars were fought using cameras, the Internet, and staged media stunts.

In 1994, on the same day that NAFTA was signed into office, the Zapatista EZLN Movement emerged in the southern jungles of the Mexican province Chiapas. An indigenous movement demanding autonomy and broadcasting its message via a ski mask-wearing, pipe-smoking Subcommandante Marcos, the Zapatistas were savvy in their early use of cultural symbols and the Internet to rally the international sympathies of the left to their cause. There is no way to conceive of the protest in Seattle in 1999 as anything but inspired by the Zapatistas' use of the carnivalesque, poetics, the Internet, and social networking culture. This is to say that over the last twenty years, we have seen the integration of cultural manipulation into its most poignant social movements and accompanying forms of activism. Certainly the antics of the Yes Men—who poke fun at corporate power through their numerous appearances on television and in print media, posing as executives—is another example of resistance manifesting itself in the media-sphere via the manipulation of cultural symbols.

With that in mind, it should be said that this present spectacular reality is simply the chess board we, as people on the planet, must strategically move across. However, the way in which we choose to produce politics and meaning on it yields different ethical and political ramifications. The September 11th attack and destruction of the World Trade Center Towers by two hijacked planes, and the subsequent media hysteria, were clearly considered by their creators in terms of spectacle, not just casualties. In reflecting on this spectacular political terrain, the theoretical collective Retort wrote, "One of the formative moments in the education of Mohammad Atta, we are told, was when he came to realize the conservation of Islamic Cairo, in which he hoped to participate as a newly trained town planner, was to obey the logic of Disney World."

When considered within the framework of socially engaged art, such events help make sense of the media antics and performativity of hallmark projects such as Women on Waves and *Palas Por Pistolas*. They, too, are meaning-makers in an era of vast spectacle. The same can be said of the aesthetic approaches to research, its presentation, and engaging the political terrain. Who needs to worry about art, when all the world is literally a stage? So rather than thinking of the last twenty years as

the "post-Cold War" era, we might think of it as the moment in which the spectacle became the increasing reality for not only culture-makers, but all people. Reflecting on the fall of the Berlin Wall, Guy Debord wrote, "This driving of the spectacle toward modernization and unification, together with all of the other tendencies toward the simplification of society, what in 1989 led the Russian bureaucracy suddenly, and as one man, to convert to the current *ideology* of democracy—in other words, to the dictatorial freedom of the market, as tempered by the recognition of the rights of homo spectator."

The fall of the Berlin Wall and the crumbling of the Soviet Union can also be seen as a rise of the spectacle behind the veil of democracy. And because the spectacle enjoys its veils and illusions (as a creature of symbolic production), perhaps it can be symbolized by the mass-media phenomenon that we have lived with for the last twenty years: reality television. The format started in 1992 with the launch of MTV's *The Real World*, a supposedly real-life drama about multicultural young people living together, on camera, 24 hours a day. The idea was greeted with paranoiac Orwellian concerns of Big Brother (enjoyably enough, the name of the inspiration for *The Real World* launched in Britain), but over the course of time, what was to stand out about the show was that it not only predicted the largest growth market in television programming, but also foretold the Internet's now-commonplace role in documenting everyday life. Since 1991, contemporary life has become a kind of schizophrenic existence, where we are both on television as well as in the world. We are both being mediated by things as well as experiencing them.

Why mention this in a discussion of socially engaged art? Without understanding that the manipulation of symbols has become a method of production for the dominant powers in contemporary society, we cannot appreciate the forms of resistance to that power that come from numerous artists, activists, and engaged citizens. We find it in the rhetoric of urban cultural economy guru Richard Florida whose quick formulas on the creative class have been accepted and built on by major cities in the United States. A pro-arts, pro-real estate development advocate, Florida's quick fix to economic woes explicitly draws a connection between the arts and the global urban concern of gentrification. While it is not the purview of this book, one could easily write a different one based on the practices of the powerful as well. Take, for example, fast-food chain McDonald's Ronald McDonald House. Here we have a global corporation who offers, "essential medical, dental, and educational services to more than 150,000 children annually." We can also see social programs initiated by most major corporations of the United States as well as the manipulation of cultural symbols in media by right-wing political organizations such as The Tea Party. Socially engaged artworks, perversely enough, are not just the purview of artists, but, in fact, can additionally be deployed by capitalists for the production of their own version of meaning and advertising.

It is upon this stage of vast spectacle that we must attempt to create meaningful relationships and actions. And this is not easy. For as the world of *The Real World* moves from a fiction to a reality, we find ourselves confused by whether things are advertisements or what they say they are. The artist Shepard Fairey's guerrilla wheatpaste poster campaigns across the world have garnered not only great press but also much cynicism as many in the street art community accuse the work of being a corporate-sponsored commercial enterprise. And in an era in which the production of culture is often used as an advertisement, artists too can be guilty of projects wherein the production of art is simply advertising for the ultimate product: themselves. Thus, similar laments might be thrown at some of the work in *Living as Form*. Is an artist genuinely producing a socially engaged artwork to help people, or is it yet another career-climbing maneuver? Does public art in a city serve its current residents, or does it operate as an advertisement for future gentrification?

This paranoia of what cultural producers actually want is an integral part of a global cul-ture caught in decades of spectacular production. It has radically altered not just the arts, but politics in general. Paranoia is the binding global ethos. With that freakish personality trait in mind, many artists have had to reconfigure their methods to account for this lack of transparency. I would like to call this the strategic turn, borrowing from French theorist Michel de Certeau's terms the "tactical" and the "strategic"—notions that explore how aesthetics are produced in space. If the tactical is a temporary, interventionist form of trespass, the strategic is the long-term investment in space.

Throughout the 1990s, the relational aesthetics of contemporary art began to reveal certain political limitations. By being discreet and short-lived, the works often reflected a convenient tendency for quick consumption and exclusivity that garnered favor among museums and galleries. When the artist Rirkrit Tiravanija cooked Pad Thai in a Soho gallery, the work was praised as a radical redefinition of what constituted art. This simple maneuver was heralded by Nicholas Bourriaud as a seminal project in the production of the genre "relational aesthetics." Over time, many in the activist art milieu viewed this kind of discreet performativity as simply digested by the conditions of power. For some, there were too many similarities between a VIP cocktail party and the intimate personal experiences advocated by much of the work gathered under the heading of relational aesthetics. Similarly, suspicions of the global biennial circuit arose; artists who espoused supposed political ambition and content seemed to simply travel the world trading in the symbolic culture of activism. To quote the artist, anarchist, and activist Josh MacPhee, "I am tired of artists fetishizing activist culture and showing it to the world as though it were their invention."

Thus, the strategic turn where we find works that are explicitly local, long-term, and community-based. Rick Lowe's Project Row Houses is certainly an example, as is Laurie Jo Reynolds's *Tamms Year Ten* campaign. The organization Park Fiction combined the efforts of numerous parties, including artists, musicians, filmmakers, and community activists in order to produce a public park in Hamburg by rallying the support and input of numerous community members. What started as a civic campaign in 1994 was finally realized in 2005 after hundreds of meetings, arguments, events, and exhibitions. These are projects that are deeply rooted in community relations and motivated by a commitment to political change. They also gain community traction by committing to an idea over time. As publics become increasingly aware of the hit-and-run style of not only artists, but other industries of spectacle—such as advertising, film, and television—they develop a suspicion of those "helping them." As with many long-term efforts, the longer the project, the more the artist or artists must behave like organizational structures in order to operate efficiently, and combat fatigue and overextension.

At the time of this writing, the protests and occupations of what are being called the Arab Spring, the European Summer, and the American Autumn are moving apace, catching many governments and societies by surprise. In consideration of the strategic turn by artists and activists, we find a similar reflection in the new social movements of the current period. Whereas the protests of the alt-globalization movement possessed a hit-and-run style focusing on various gatherings by large governmental and corporate bodies, including the WTO (World Trade Organization), the GATT (General Agreement on Tariffs and Trade), the G8 (Group of 8), the IMF (International Monetary Fund), et al, the current occupation strategies stay in one place over a longer period of time.

GLITCHES IN THE FORMS
While the language for defining this work is evolving, some criticisms and considerations find their way into most discussions. A constant battle (which is difficult to resolve) is the matter of efficacy and pedagogy between the symbolic, the mediated, and the practical. When is a project working? What are its intentions? Who is the intended audience? When is an artist simply using the idea of social work in order to progress her career? Are these social-

ly engaged works perhaps a little too sympathetic with the prevailing values of our time and, thus, make themselves vulnerable to state instrumentalization? Again, socially engaged art can easily be used as advertising for vast structures of power, from governments to corporations. Determining which forms of social engagement truly lead towards social justice is a constant source of debate. Knowing this, in itself, is useful.

As art enters life, one must consider the powerful role that affect plays in the production of meaning. The concept of affect derives from the understanding that how things make one feel is substantively different than how things make one think. As cultural production is often geared towards emotive impact, understanding how cultural projects function politically and socially would benefit from an understanding of this poorly analyzed concept. In addition, how these projects function and are understood is as varied as the audiences they impact. Unmooring this work from the strict analysis of aesthetics should not only assist in truly appreciating its complexities, but also liberate the dialogue of aesthetics to include knowledge sets of the global public. Moving across racial, cultural, disciplinary, and geographic boundaries provides a complex public to consider. Obviously a person with a contemporary art background appreciates a socially engaged artwork differently than someone who does not. But more important than disciplinary-specific knowledge are the vast differences in approach developed out of geographic, racial, class, gender, and sexuality differences. A form of analysis that can account for this broad spectrum of difference (while obviously difficult) will at least provide a framework for interpreting social phenomena from an honest position based in reality.

Socially engaged art may, in fact, be a misnomer. Defying discursive boundaries, its very flexible nature reflects an interest in producing effects and affects in the world rather than focusing on the form itself. In doing so, this work has produced new forms of living that force a reconsideration and perhaps new language altogether. As navigating cultural symbols becomes a necessary skill set in basic communication and pedagogy, let alone community organizing, the lessons of theater, art, architecture, and design have been incorporated in a complex array of social organizing methodologies. Deep research, media campaigns, dinners, conversations, performances, and online networking are just a few of the numerous techniques deployed in this strategic and tactical playing field.

As Duchamp placed the urinal in the museum at the beginning of the twentieth century, perhaps it should be no surprise to find artists returning it to the real at the dawn of the twenty-first. This maneuver could easily be interpreted as yet another art historical reference. However, I suspect the more important interpretation is that this maneuver reflects a necessary recalibration of the cultural environment surrounding the world today. For, as art enters life, the question that will motivate people far more than What is art? is the much more metaphysically relevant and pressing What is life?

PARTICIPATION AND SPECTACLE: WHERE ARE WE NOW?

CLAIRE BISHOP

1. SPECTACLE TODAY

One of the key words used in artists' self-definitions of their socially engaged practice is "spectacle," so often invoked as the entity that participatory art opposes itself to, both artistically and politically. When examining artists' motivations for turning to social participation as a strategy in their work, one repeatedly encounters the same claim: contemporary capitalism produces passive subjects with very little agency or empowerment. For many artists and curators on the left, Guy Debord's indictment of the alienating and divisive effects of capitalism in *The Society of the Spectacle* (1967) strike to the heart of why participation is important as a project: it re-humanizes a society rendered numb and fragmented by the repressive instrumentality of capitalist production. This position, with more or less Marxist overtones, is put forward by most advocates of socially engaged and activist art. Given the market's near total satu-

ration of our image repertoire—so the argument goes—artistic practice can no longer revolve around the construction of objects to be consumed by a passive bystander. Instead, there must be an art of action, interfacing with reality, taking steps—however small—to repair the social bond. As the French philosopher Jacques Rancière points out, "the 'critique of the spectacle' often remains the alpha and the omega of the 'politics of art'".[1]

But what do we really mean by spectacle in a visual art context? "Spectacle" has a particular, almost unique status within art history and criticism, since it has an incomparable political pedigree (thanks to the Situationist International, or SI) and directly raises the question of visuality. As frequently used by art historians and critics associated with the journal *October*, spectacle denotes a wide range of attributes: for Rosalind Krauss writing on the late capitalist museum, it means the absence of historical positioning and a capitulation to

Above: Eliasson addressed the ubiquitous subject of weather with his vast 2003 installation of *The Weather Project* in Tate Modern's Turbine Hall (Courtesy Olafur Eliasson, neugerriemschneider, Berlin, and Tanya Bonakdar Gallery, New York).

pure presentness; for James Meyer, arguing against Olafur Eliasson's *Weather Project*, it denotes an overwhelming scale that dwarfs viewers and eclipses the human body as a point of reference; for Hal Foster writing on the Bilbao Guggenheim, it denotes the triumph of corporate branding; for Benjamin Buchloh denouncing Bill Viola, it refers to an uncritical use of new technology. In short, spectacle today connotes a wide range of ideas—from size, scale, and sexiness to corporate investment and populism. And yet, for Debord, "spectacle" does not describe the characteristics of a work of art or architecture, but is a definition of social relations under capitalism (but also under totalitarian regimes). Individual subjects experience society as atomized and fragmented because social experience is mediated by images—either the "diffuse" images of consumerism or the "concentrated" images of the leader. As Debord's film, *The Society of the Spectacle* (1971), makes clear, his arguments stem from an anxiety about a nascent consumer culture in the '60s, with its tidal wave of seductive imagery. But the question as to whether or not we still exist in a society of the spectacle was posed by Baudrillard as early as 1981, who dispatches not only Debord but also Foucault in his essay "The Precession of Simulacra":

> We are witnessing the end of perspective and panoptic space... and hence the very abolition of the spectacular.... We are no longer in the society of the spectacle which the situationists talked about, nor in the specific types of alienation and repression which this implied. The medium itself is no longer identifiable as such, and the merging of the medium and the message (McLuhan) is the first great formula of this new age.[2]

More recently, Boris Groys has suggested that in today's culture of self-exhibitionism (in Facebook, YouTube or Twitter, which he provocatively compares to the text/image compositions of conceptual art) we have a "spectacle without spectators":

> the artist needs a spectator who can overlook the immeasurable quantity of artistic production and formulate an aesthetic judgment that would single out this particular artist from the mass of other artists. Now, it is obvious that such a spectator does not exist—it could be God, but we have already been informed of the fact that God is dead.[3]

In other words, one of the central requirements of art is that it is given to be seen, and reflected upon, by a spectator. Participatory art in the strictest sense forecloses the traditional idea of spectatorship and suggests a new understanding of art without audiences, one in which everyone is a producer. At the same time, the existence of an audience is ineliminable, since it is impossible for everyone in the world to participate in every project.

2. HISTORY

Indeed, the dominant narrative of the history of socially engaged, participatory art across the twentieth century is one in which the activation of the audience is positioned against its mythic counterpart, passive spectatorial consumption. Participation thus forms part of a larger narrative that traverses modernity: "art must be directed against contemplation, against spectatorship, against the passivity of the masses paralyzed by the spectacle of modern life".[4] This desire to activate the audience in participatory art is at the same time a drive to emancipate it from a state of alienation induced by the dominant ideological order—be this consumer capitalism, totalitarian socialism, or military dictatorship. Beginning from this premise, participatory art aims to restore and realize a communal, collective space of shared social engagement. But this is achieved in different ways: either through constructivist gestures of social impact, which refute the injustice of the world by proposing an alternative, or through a nihilist redoubling of alienation, which negates the world's injustice and illogicality on its own terms. In both instances, the work seeks to forge a collective, co-authoring, participatory social body, but

Opposite: Democracy in America, a project that took place during the 2008 election season and explored artists' relationship with the American democratic tradition, included a seven-day exhibition at the Park Avenue Armory in New York City (Photograph by Meghan McInnis, Courtesy Creative Time).

one does this affirmatively (through utopian realization), the other indirectly (through the negation of negation).

For example, Futurism and Constructivism both offered gestures of social impact and the invention of a new public sphere—one geared towards fascism, the other to reinforce a new Bolshevik world order. Shortly after this period, Paris Dada "took to the streets" in order to reach a wider audience, annexing the social forms of the guided tour and the trial in order to experiment with a more nihilistic type of artistic practice in the public sphere. It is telling that in the first phase of this orientation towards the social, participation has no given political alignment: it is a strategy that can be equally associated with Italian Fascism, Bolshevik communism, and an anarchic negation of the political.

In the postwar period, we find a similar range of participatory strategies, now more or less tied to leftist politics, and culminating in the theater of 1968. In Paris, the SI developed alternatives to visual art in the "derive and constructed situation"; while the Groupe Recherche d'Art Visuel devised participatory actions, both in the form of installations and street environments. Both of these are affirmative in tenor, but as a critique of consumer capitalism. Jean-Jacques Lebel's anarchic and eroticized Happenings provide a different model—"the negation of negation"—in which the audience and performers are further alienated from an already alienating world, via disturbing and transgressive activities that aimed to produce a group mind or *egregore*. When these artistic strategies were put into play in different ideological contexts (such as South America and Eastern Europe), the aims and intentions of participation yielded different meanings. In Argentina, where a brutal, U.S.-backed military dictatorship was imposed in 1966, it gave rise to aggressive and fragmented modes of social action, with an emphasis on class antagonism, reification, and alienation. In Czechoslovakia, brought into line with Soviet "normalization" after 1968, participatory art had a more escapist tone, with avant-garde actions often masquerading under vernacular forms (weddings, parties, and festivals), often in remote

locations, in order to avoid detection by the secret police. Art was disguised by life in order to sustain itself as a place of nonalienation. The work of Collective Actions Group (CAG), active in Moscow from 1976 onwards, further problematizes contemporary claims that participation is synonymous with collectivism, and thus inherently opposed to capitalism; rather than reinforcing the collectivist dogma of communism, CAG deployed participation as a means to create a privatized sphere of individual expression.

Further analogies to contemporary social practice can be found in the rise of the community arts movement after 1968, whose history provides a cautionary tale for today's artists averse to theorizing the artistic value of their work. Emphasizing process rather than end result, and basing their judgments on ethical criteria (about how and whom they work with) rather than on the character of their artistic outcomes, the community arts movement found itself subject to manipulation—and eventually instrumentalization—by the state. From an agitational force campaigning for social justice (in the early 1970s), it became a harmless branch of the welfare state (by the 1980s): the kindly folk who can be relied upon to mop up wherever the government wishes to absolve itself of responsibility.

And so we find ourselves faced today with an important sector of artists who renounce the vocabularies of contemporary art, claiming to be engaged in more serious, worldly, and political issues. Such anti-aesthetic refusals are not new: just as we have come to recognize Dada cabaret, situationist *détournement*, or dematerialized conceptual and performance art as having their own aesthetics of production and circulation, so too do the often formless-looking photo-documents of participatory art have their own experiential regime. The point is not to regard these anti-aesthetic phenomena as objects of a new formalism (reading areas, parades, demonstrations, discussions, ubiquitous plywood platforms, endless photographs of people), but to analyze how these contribute to the social and artistic experience being generated.

3. TWO CRITIQUES

One of the questions that is continually posed to me is the following: Surely it is better for one art project to improve one person's life than for it not to happen at all? The history of participatory art allows us to get critical distance on this question, and to see it as the latest instantiation of concerns that have dogged this work from its inception: the tension between equality and quality, between participation and spectatorship, and between art and real life. These conflicts indicate that social and artistic judgments do not easily merge; indeed, they seem to demand different criteria. This impasse surfaces in every printed debate and panel discussion on participatory and socially engaged art. For one sector of artists, curators, and critics, a good project appeases a superegoic injunction to ameliorate society; if social agencies have failed, then art is obliged to step in. In this schema, judgments are based on a humanist ethics, often inspired by Christianity. What counts is to offer ameliorative solutions, however short-term, rather than to expose contradictory social truths. For another sector of artists, curators, and critics, judgments are based on a sensible response to the artist's work, both in and beyond its original context. In this schema, ethics are nugatory, because art is understood continually to throw established systems of value into question, including morality; devising new languages with which to represent and question social contradiction is more important. The social discourse accuses the artistic discourse of amorality and inefficacy, because it is insufficient merely to reveal, reduplicate, or reflect upon the world; what matters is social change. The artistic discourse accuses the social discourse of remaining stubbornly attached to existing categories, and focusing on micropolitical gestures at the expense of sensuous immediacy (as a potential locus of disalienation). Either social conscience dominates, or the rights of the individual to question social conscience. Art's relationship to the social is either underpinned by morality or it is underpinned by freedom.[5]

This binary is echoed in Boltanski and Chiapello's perceptive distinction of the difference between artistic and social critiques of capitalism. The artistic critique, rooted in nineteenth-century bohemianism, draws upon two sources of indignation towards capitalism: on the one hand, disenchantment and inauthenticity, and on the other, oppression. The artistic critique, they explain, "foregrounds the loss of meaning and, in particular, the loss of the sense of what is beautiful and valuable, which derives from standardization and generalized commodification, affecting not only everyday objects but also artworks ... and human beings." Against this state of affairs, the artistic critique advocates "the freedom of artists, their rejection of any contamination of aesthetics by ethics, their refusal of any form of subjection in time and space and, in its extreme form, any kind of work".[6] The social critique, by contrast, draws on different sources of indignation towards capitalism: the egoism of private interests, and the growing poverty of the working classes in a society of unprecedented wealth. This social critique necessarily rejects the moral neutrality, individualism, and egotism of artists. The artistic and the social critique are not directly compatible, Boltanski and Chiapello warn us, and exist in continual tension with one another.[7]

The clash between artistic and social critiques recurs most visibly at certain historical moments, and the reappearance of participatory art is symptomatic of this clash. It tends to occur at moments of political transition and upheaval: in the years leading to Italian Fascism, in the aftermath of the 1917 Revolution, in the widespread social dissent that led to 1968, and its aftermath in the 1970s. At each historical moment participatory art takes a different form, because it seeks to negate different artistic and sociopolitical objects. In our own times, its resurgence accompanies the consequences of the collapse of communism in 1989, the apparent absence of a viable left alternative, the emergence of contemporary "post-political" consensus, and the near total marketization of art and education.[8] The paradox of this situation is that participation in

the West now has more to do with the populist agendas of neoliberal governments. Even though participatory artists stand against neoliberal capitalism, the values they impute to their work are understood formally (in terms of opposing individualism and the commodity object), without recognizing that so many other aspects of this art practice dovetail even more perfectly with neoliberalism's recent forms (networks, mobility, project work, affective labor).

As this ground has shifted over the course of the twentieth century, so the identity of participants has been reimagined at each historical moment: from a crowd (1910s), to the masses (1920s), to the people (late 1960s/1970s), to the excluded (1980s), to community (1990s), to today's volunteers whose participation is continuous with a culture of reality television and social networking. From the audience's perspective, we can chart this as a shift from an audience that demands a role (expressed as hostility towards avant-garde artists who keep control of the proscenium), to an audience that enjoys its subordination to strange experiences devised for them by an artist, to an audience that is encouraged to be a co-producer of the work (and who, occasionally, can even get paid for this involvement). This could be seen as a heroic narrative of the increased activation and agency of the audience, but we might also see it as a story of their ever-increasing voluntary subordination to the artist's will, and of the commodification of human bodies in a service economy (since voluntary participation is also unpaid labor).

Arguably, this is a story that runs parallel with the rocky fate of democracy itself, a term to which participation has always been wedded: from a demand for acknowledgement, to representation, to the consensual consumption of one's own image—be this in a work of art, YouTube, Flickr, or reality TV. Consider the media profile accorded to Anthony Gormley's *One and Other* (2009), a project to allow members of the public to continuously occupy the empty "fourth plinth" of Trafalgar Square in London, one hour at a time for one hundred days. Gormley received 34,520 applica-

tions for 2,400 places, and the activities of the plinth's occupants were continually streamed online.[9] Although the artist referred to *One and Other* as "an open space of possibility for many to test their sense of self and how they might communicate this to a wider world," the project was described by *The Guardian*, not unfairly, as "Twitter Art."[10] In a world where everyone can air their views to everyone we are faced not with mass empowerment but with an endless stream of banal egos. Far from being oppositional to spectacle, participation has now entirely merged with it.

This new proximity between spectacle and participation underlines, for me, the necessity of sustaining a tension between artistic and social critiques. The most striking projects that constitute the history of participatory art unseat all of the polarities on which this discourse is founded (individual/collective, author/spectator, active/passive, real life/art) but not with the goal of collapsing them. In so doing, they hold the artistic and social critiques in tension. Félix Guattari's

paradigm of transversality offers one such way of thinking through these artistic operations: he leaves art as a category in its place, but insists upon its constant flight into and across other disciplines, putting both art and the social into question, even while simultaneously reaffirming art as a universe of value. Jacques Rancière offers another: the aesthetic regime is constitutively contradictory, shuttling between autonomy and heteronomy ("the aesthetic experience is effective inasmuch as it is the experience of that *and*"[11]). He argues that in art and education alike, there needs to be a mediating object—a spectacle that stands between the idea of the artist and the feeling and interpretation of the spectator: "This spectacle is a third thing, to which both parts can refer but which prevents any kind of 'equal' or 'undistorted' transmission. It is a mediation between them. [...] The same thing which links them must separate them."[12] In different ways, Rancière and Guattari offer alternative frameworks for thinking the artistic and the social simultaneously; for both, art and the social

Above: At the New Orleans Safehouse, Mel Chin and a panel of experts announce *Operation Paydirt: New Orleans*, a massive art and science project to take on lead pollution in the city (Courtesy Fundred Dollar Bill Project).

are not to be reconciled or collapsed, but sustained in continual tension.

4. THE LADDER AND THE CONTAINER

I am interested in these theoretical models of analysis because they do not reduce art to a question of ethically good or bad examples, nor do they forge a straightforward equation between forms of democracy in art and forms of democracy in society. Most of the contemporary discourse on participatory art implies an evaluative schema akin to that laid out in the classic diagram "The Ladder of Participation," published in an architectural journal in 1969 to accompany an article about forms of citizen involvement.[13] The ladder has eight rungs. The bottom two indicate the least participatory forms of citizen engagement: the non-participation of mere presence in "manipulation" and "therapy." The next three rungs are degrees of tokenism—"informing," "consultation," and "placation"—which gradually increase the attention paid by power to the everyday voice. At the top of the ladder we find "partnership," "delegated power," and the ultimate goal, "citizen control." The diagram provides a useful set of distinctions for thinking about the claims to participation made by those in power, and is frequently cited by architects and planners. It is tempting to make an equation (and many have done so) between the value of a work of art and the degree of participation it involves, turning the Ladder of Participation into a gauge for measuring the efficacy of artistic practice.[14]

But while the Ladder provides us with helpful and nuanced differences between forms of civic participation, it falls short of corresponding to the complexity of artistic gestures. The most challenging works of art do not follow this schema, because models of democracy in art do not have an intrinsic relationship to models of democracy in society. The equation is misleading and does not recognize art's ability to generate other, more paradoxical criteria. The works I have discussed in the preceding chapters do not offer anything like citizen control. The artist relies upon the participants' creative exploitation of the situation that he/she offers, just as participants require the artist's cue and direction. This relationship is a continual play of mutual tension, recognition, and dependency—more akin to the collectively negotiated dynamic of stand-up comedy, or to BDSM sex, than to a ladder of progressively more virtuous political forms.

A case study, now 11 years old, illustrates this argument that art is both grounded in and suspends reality, and does this via a mediating object or third term: *Please Love Austria* (2000) devised and largely performed by the German filmmaker and artist Christoph Schlingensief (1960–2010). Commissioned to produce a work for the Weiner Festwochen, Schlingensief chose to respond directly to the recent electoral success of the far-right nationalist party led by Jörg Haider (*Freiheitliche Partei Österreichs*, or FPÖ). The FPÖ's campaign had included overtly xenophobic slogans and the word *überfremdung* (domination by foreign influences), once employed by the Nazis, to describe a country overrun with foreigners. Schlingensief erected a shipping container outside the Opera House in the center of Vienna, topped with a large banner bearing the phrase *Ausländer Raus* (Foreigners Out). Inside the container, *Big Brother*-style living accommodations were installed for a group of asylum-seekers, relocated from a detention center outside the city. Their activities were broadcast through the internet television station webfreetv.com, and via this station viewers could vote daily for the ejection of their least favorite refugee. At 8 p.m. each day, for six days, the two most unpopular inhabitants were sent back to the deportation center. The winner was purportedly offered a cash prize and the prospect—depending on the availability of volunteers—of Austrian citizenship through marriage. The event is documented by the Austrian filmmaker Paul Poet in an evocative and compelling ninety-minute film, *Ausländer Raus! Schlingensief's Container* (2002).

Please Love Austria is typical Schlingensief in its desire to antagonize the public and stage provocation. His early film work frequently alluded to contemporary taboos: mixing Nazism, obscenities, disabilities, and assorted sexual perversions in films such as

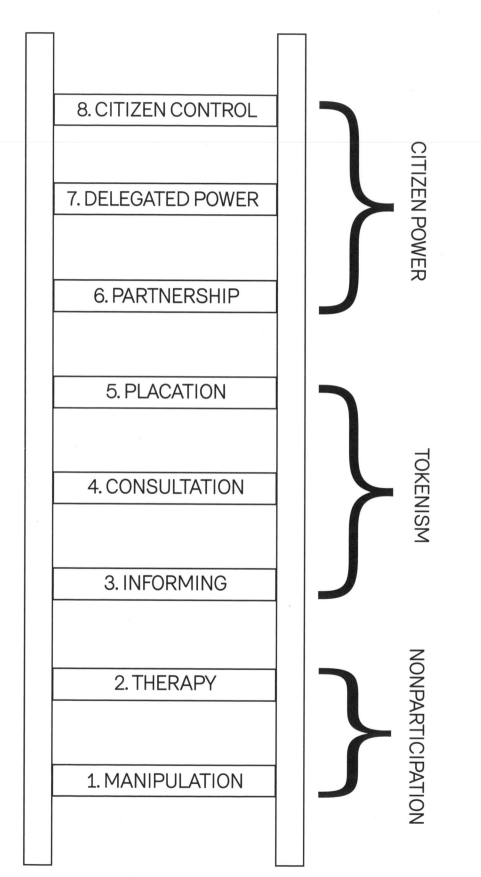

8. CITIZEN CONTROL

7. DELEGATED POWER

6. PARTNERSHIP

CITIZEN POWER

5. PLACATION

4. CONSULTATION

3. INFORMING

TOKENISM

2. THERAPY

1. MANIPULATION

NONPARTICIPATION

Above: Sherry Arnstein's *Ladder of Participation* was originally published in the July 1969 issue of the *Journal of the American Institute of Planners* (Courtesy Sherry Arnstein). *Opposite*: The office of Tania Bruguera's Immigrant Movement International is located in the diverse neighborhood of Corona in Queens, New York, and provides a space for outreach activities for the local immigrant community (Courtesy Tania Bruguera and Creative Time).

German Chainsaw Massacre (1990) and *Terror 2000* (1992), once described as "filth for intellectuals."[15] In the late 1990s Schlingensief began making interventions into public space, including the formation of a political party, *Chance 2000* (1998–2000), which targeted the unemployed, disabled, and other recipients of welfare with the slogan "Vote For Yourself." *Chance 2000* did not hesitate to use the image of Schlingensief's long-term collaborators, many of whom have mental and/or physical handicaps. But in *Please Love Austria*, Schlingensief's refugee participants were barely visible, disguised in assorted wigs, hats, and sunglasses.[16] In the square, the public had only a limited view of the immigrants through peepholes; the bulk of the performance was undertaken by Schlingensief himself, installed on the container's roof beneath the "Foreigners Out!" banner. Speaking through a megaphone, he incited the FPÖ to come and remove the banner (which they didn't), encouraged tourists to take photographs, invited the public to air their views, and made contradictory claims ("This is a performance! This is the absolute truth!"), while parroting the most racist opinions and insults back to the crowd. As the various participants were evicted, Schlingensief provided a running commentary to the mob below: "It is a black man! Once again Austria has evicted a darkie!"

Although in retrospect—and particularly in Poet's film—it is evident that the work is a critique of xenophobia and its institutions, in Vienna the event (and Schlingensief's charismatic role as circus master) was ambiguous enough to receive approval and condemnation from all sides of the political spectrum. An elderly right-wing gentleman covered in medals gleefully found it to be in sympathy with his own ideas, while others claimed that by staging such a shameful spectacle Schlingensief himself was a dirty foreigner who ought to be deported. Left-wing student activists

attempted to sabotage the container and "liberate" the refugees, while assorted left-wing celebrities showed up to support the project, including Daniel Cohn-Bendit (a key figure from May '68), and the Nobel Laureate author Elfriede Jelinek (who wrote and performed a puppet play with the asylum-seekers). In addition, large numbers of the public watched the program on webfreetv.com and voted for the eviction of particular refugees. The container prompted arguments and discussion—in the square surrounding it, in the print media, and on national television. The vehemence of response is palpable throughout the film, no more so than when Poet's camera pans back from a heated argument to reveal the entire square full of agitated people in intense debate. One elderly woman was so infuriated by the project that she could only spit at Schlingensief the insult, "You ... artist!"

A frequently heard criticism of this work is that it did not change anyone's opinion: the right-wing pensioner is still right-wing, the lefty protestors are still lefty, and so on. But this instrumentalized approach to critical judgment misunderstands the artistic force of Schlingensief's intervention. The point is not about "conversion," for this reduces the work of art to a question of propaganda. Rather, Schlingensief's project draws attention to the contradictions of political discourse in Austria at that moment. The shocking fact is that Schlingensief's container caused more public agitation and distress than the presence of a *real* deportation center a few miles outside Vienna. The disturbing lesson of *Please Love Austria* is that an *artistic* representation of detention has more power to attract dissensus than an *actual* institution of detention.[17] In fact, Schlingensief's model of "undemocratic" behavior corresponds precisely to "democracy" as practiced in reality. This contradiction is the core of Schlingensief's artistic efficacy—and it is the reason why political conversion is not the primary goal of art, why artistic representations continue to have a potency that can be harnessed to disruptive ends, and why *Please Love Austria* is not (and should never be seen as) morally exemplary.

5. THE END OF PARTICIPATION

In his essay "The Uses of Democracy" (1992), Jacques Rancière notes that participation in what we normally refer to as democratic regimes is usually reduced to a question of filling up the spaces left empty by power. Genuine participation, he argues, is something different: the invention of an "unpredictable subject" who momentarily occupies the street, the factory, or the museum—rather than a fixed space of allocated participation whose counter-power is dependent on the dominant order.[18] Setting aside the problematic idea of "genuine" participation (which takes us back to modernist oppositions between authentic and false culture), such a statement clearly pertains to *Please Love Austria*, and the better examples of social practice, which have frequently constituted a *critique* of participatory art, rather than upholding an unproblematized equation between artistic and political inclusion.

The fact that the Ladder of Participation culminates in "citizen control" is worth recalling here. At a certain point, art has to hand over to other institutions if social change is to be achieved: it is not enough to keep producing activist *art*. The historic avant-garde was always positioned in relation to an existent party politics (primarily communist) which removed the pressure of art ever being required to effectuate change in and of itself. Later, the postwar avant-gardes claimed open-endedness as a radical refusal of organized politics—be this inter-war totalitarianism or the dogma of a party line. There was the potential to discover the highest artistic intensity in the everyday and the banal, which would serve a larger project of equality and anti-elitism. Since the 1990s, participatory art has often asserted a connection between user-generated content and democracy, but the frequent predictability of its results seem to be the consequence of lacking *both* a social *and* an artistic target; in other words, participatory art today stands without relation to an existing political project (only to a loosely defined anti-capitalism) and presents itself as oppositional to visual art by trying to side-step the question of visuality. As a consequence, these artists have internalized a huge amount of pressure to bear the burden of devising new models of social and political organization—a task that they are not always best equipped to undertake.

My point, again, is not to criticize specific artists but to see the whole rise of social practice since 1989 as symptomatic. That the "political" and "critical" have become shibboleths of advanced art signals a lack of faith *both* in the intrinsic value of art as a de-alienating human endeavor (since art today is so intertwined with market systems globally) *and* in democratic political processes (in whose name so many injustices and barbarities are conducted).[19] But rather than addressing this loss of faith by collapsing art and ethics together, the task today is to produce a viable international alignment of leftist political movements and a reassertion of art's inventive forms of negation as valuable in their own right.[20] We need to recognize art as a form of experimental activity overlapping with the world, whose negativity may lend support towards a political project (without bearing the sole responsibility for devising and implementing it), and—more radically—we need to support the progressive transformation of existing institutions through the transversal encroachment of ideas whose boldness is related to (and at times greater than) that of artistic imagination.[21]

By using people as a medium, participatory art has always had a double ontological status: it is both an event in the world, and also at a remove from it. As such, it has the capacity to communicate on two levels—to participants and to spectators—the paradoxes that are repressed in everyday discourse, and to elicit perverse, disturbing, and pleasurable experiences that enlarge our capacity to imagine the world and our relations anew. But to reach the second level requires a mediating third term—an object, image, story, film, even a spectacle—that permits this experience to have a purchase on the public imaginary. Participatory art is not a privileged political medium, nor a ready-made solution to a society of the spectacle, but is as uncertain and precarious as democracy itself; neither are legitimated in advance but need continually to be performed and tested in every specific context.

ENDNOTES
1 Jacques Rancière, "Aesthetic Separation, Aesthetic Community: Scenes from the Aesthetic Regime of Art," *Art & Research: A Journal of Ideas, Contexts and Methods*, Vol. 2, No. 1, Summer 2008: 7.
2 Jean Baudrillard, "The Precession of Simulacra," in *Simulations*, trans. Paul Foss, Paul Patton and Philip Beitchman (New York: Semiotext(e), 1983): 54.
3 Boris Groys, "Comrades of Time," *e-flux journal*, December 11, 2009, available at www.e-flux.com
4 Boris Groys, "Comrades of Time," *e-flux journal*, December 11, 2009, available at www.e-flux.com (last accessed September 3, 2010).
5 Tony Bennett phrases the same problem differently: art history as a bourgeois, idealist discipline is in permanent conflict with Marxism as an anti-bourgeois, materialist revolution in existing disciplines. There is no possibility of reconciling the two. See Tony Bennett, *Formalism and Marxism* (London: Methuen, 1979): 80–5.
6 Luc Boltanski and Ève Chiapello, *The New Spirit of Capitalism* (London: Verso, 2005): 37–8.
7 The implication of Boltanski and Chiapello's book is that in the third spirit of capitalism, the artistic critique has held sway, resulting in an unsupervised capitalism that lacks the "invisible hand" of constraint that would guarantee protection, security and rights for workers.
8 For a clear summary of "post-politics" see Jodi Dean, *Democracy and Other Neoliberal Fantasies* (Durham, NC: Duke University Press, 2009): 13. She presents two positions: "post-politics as an ideal of consensus, inclusion, and administration that must be rejected" (Chantal Mouffe, Jacques Rancière) and "post-politics as a description of the contemporary exclusion or foreclosure of the political" (Slavoj Žižek).
9 The difference between Gormley's webstreaming and that of Christoph Schlingensief (discussed below) is that the latter is a conscious parody of reality TV's banality, while the former uncritically replicates it. A press shot of Gormley with *American Idol*.
10 Anthony Gormley, www.oneandother.co.uk (last accessed August 23, 2010). Charlotte Higgins, "The Birth of Twitter Art," *Guardian*, July 8, 2009, available at www.guardian.co.uk (last accessed 25 August 2010).
11 Jacques Rancière, "The Aesthetic Revolution and Its Outcomes: Employments of Autonomy and Heteronomy," *New Left Review*, 14, March–April 2002: 133.
12 Rancière, "Emancipated Spectator," lecture in Frankfurt.
13 Sherry Arnstein, "A Ladder of Citizen Participation," *Journal of the American Institute of Planners*, 35:4, July 1969: 216–24. The diagram has recently been the subject of some historical reassessment among architects and planners, reflecting the renewed interest in participation in this sector.
14 See, for example, Dave Beech's distinction between participation and collaboration. For Beech, participants are subject to the parameters of the artist's project, while collaboration involves co-authorship and decisions over key structural features of the work; "collaborators have rights that are withheld from participants." (Beech, "Include Me Out," *Art Monthly*, April 2008: 3.) Although I would agree with his definitions, I would not translate them into a binding set of value judgements to be applied to works of art.
15 Herbert Achternbusch, cited in Marion Löhndorf, "Christoph Schlingensief," *Kunstforum*, 142, October 1998: 94–101, available at www.schlingensief.com (last accessed December 4, 2008).
16 During their evictions, the asylum-seekers covered their faces with a newspaper, inverting the celebratory, attention-seeking exits of contestants from the *Big Brother* house. Rather than viewing this absence of identity as an assault on their subjectivity, we could see this as an artistic device to allow the asylum-seekers to be catalysts for discussion around immigration in general (rather than individual case studies for emotive journalism).
17 Silvija Jestrović has explained this preference for the *performance* of asylum rather than its reality by way of reference to Debord's *Society of the Spectacle*, specifically the epigraph by Feuerbach with which it opens: "But certainly for the present age, which prefers the sign to the thing signified, the copy to the original, representation to reality, the appearance to essence … illusion *only* is sacred, truth *profane*." (Silvija Jestrović, "Performing Like an Asylum Seeker: Paradoxes of Hyper-Authenticity in Schlingensief's *Please Love Austria*," in Claire Bishop and Silvia Tramontana, eds., *Double Agent* (London: ICA, 2009): 61.
18 Rancière argues that participation in democracy is a "mongrel" idea deriving from the conflation of two ideas: "the reformist idea of necessary mediations between the centre and the periphery, and the revolutionary idea of the permanent involvement of citizen-subjects in every domain". (Jacques Rancière, "The Uses of Democracy", in Rancière, *On the Shores of Politics* (London: Verso, 2007): 60.
19 The Slovenian collective IRWIN has recently suggested that "critical" and "political" art are as necessary to neoliberalism as socialist realism was to the Soviet regime.
20 A positive example of new developments is the new left organization Krytyka Polityczna in Poland, a publishing house that produces a magazine, organizes events, and maintains a regular, forceful presence in the media (via its charismatic young leader Sławomir Sierakowski). The artists who have affiliated themselves with this project are as varied as Artur Mijewski and the painter Wilhelm Sasnal.
21 Latin America has been pre-eminent in instituting such solutions. See for example the initiatives introduced by Antanas Mockus, then-mayor of Bogotá, discussed in María Cristina Caballero, "Academic turns city into a social experiment," *Harvard University Gazette*, March 11, 2004, available at http://www.news.harvard.edu.

RETURNING ON BIKES: NOTES ON SOCIAL PRACTICE

MARIA LIND

If you were in Münster, Germany, in summer 1997, near the circular promenade, you likely bumped into people on red bikes, cycling in reverse. Early in the summer it would probably have been a tall young woman and, later on, a group heading down the asphalt trail. Perhaps you even joined them in this unusual activity, pedaling backward on a bicycle that was perfectly ordinary apart from its rear mirror, stabilizer, and extra cogwheels. Riding it required leaving your safety zone to unlearn the most commonplace skill that you probably learned as a child, in order to see the world from an unusual perspective.

This cycle club was Elin Wikström's *Returnity*, produced for Münster's Skulptur Projekte, a high-profile exhibition—international in scope—that marks art's postwar move beyond the walls of the art institution. Skulptur Projekte has occurred every ten years since 1977, filling Münster with both permanent and temporary projects that have peppered the city, primarily outdoors, with public sculpture. However, *Returnity* was unusually non-sculptural within the history and focus of the exhibition... it left no physical trace.[1] Instead, Wikström's cycle club, based on the voluntary participation of exhibition visitors as well as passersby, contributed to the legacy of what is now called "social practice," making an immaterial mark within and beyond the traditional parameters of "contemporary art."

The project did include physical elements, such as the nine bicycles and a circular clubhouse with an adjacent training track where return cyclists could congregate. But most significant was the number of cyclists, which Wikström recorded carefully, as per her practice of combining qualitative with pseudo-bureaucratic, quantitative information. With the help of another artist, Anna Brag, and an assistant, she provided individual instructions to two thousand people who attempted to ride the bikes. Approximately fifty became repeat participants. Some visitors even purchased a *Returnity* kit containing parts that could be mounted onto their own bikes at home.

It was no coincidence that this experiment with bikes took place in Münster: a city of universities which grew around a medieval plan wherein driving a car is a nuisance. As a result, every inhabitant owns, statistically, two and a half bikes. Furthermore, in 1997, the average German was a member of no less than six to eight associations or clubs. *Returnity* alluded to local mobility patterns and social forms of organization, proving that an artwork can actually form a community (albeit temporarily) instead of simply "reaching out" to an existing one. The artist devised a framework within which participants could maneuver either individually or collectively, take part in a behavioral experiment, and—more existentially and ideologically than politically—raise consciousness. *Returnity* was a playful test that referenced lifelong learning, connectivity in a globalized world, and radically rethinking and deliberately disorienting one's naturalized behaviors.[2]

Arguably, *Returnity* was just another art project based on the social—on interaction between people—which provided an entertaining activity for locals and visitors alike. After all, it was commissioned by a body with interest in using art as an instrument to brand the city, generate income, and create new jobs. However, *Returnity* also occurred in a moment when social practice began to be simultaneously acknowledged and instrumentalized in various forms of mainstream exhibitions and other curated projects. Occasional precedents such as *Projet Unité* in Firminy, France (1993–94),[3] *Sonsbeek* (1993)[4] in Arnhem, Germany, *Places with A Past* at the Spoleto Festival in Charleston, South Carolina (1991),[5] and *Culture in Action* in Chicago (1992–93)[6] in the United States paved the way by focusing on site-specific commissions. Many of these can be described as social practice as we know it today.

A little-known curatorial project that stands out as a sensitive and smart predictor of things to come was *Services* (1993), initiated by artist Andrea Fraser and curator Helmut Draxler at the Kunstraum at the University of Lüneburg.[7] *Services* was an activist and discursive project responding to the fact that artists were increasingly asked to

provide new work for specific situations, i.e. "projects," often with little or no pay, ensuing censorship, and unclear rights to the works. An ongoing forum, meetings, and an exhibition called "working-group exhibition" formed the core of the project in which artists such as Mark Dion, Louise Lawler, and Group Material participated. In addition to questioning art's function as a service, *Services* criticized art institutions' conservative views on the nature of exhibitions.

Even a quick glance reveals that social practice is as kaleidoscopic as it is contested as an artistic movement: it is simultaneously a medium, a method, and a genre. As a term, social practice can encompass everything from community art and activism – à la the Art Workers Coalition[8] – to so-called relational aesthetics[9] and kontextkunst.[10] In between lie new genre public art[11] and connective aesthetics[12], dialogical art[13] and participatory practices,[14] as well as hybrids cutting across attempted definitions.[15] They all look, taste, smell, and sound very different from one another. And yet social practice can loosely be described as art that involves more people than objects, whose horizon is social and political change—some would even claim that it is about making another world possible. Social practice concerns works with multiple faces turned in different directions—towards specific groups of people, political questions, policy problems, or artistic concerns; there is an aesthetic to organization, a composition to meetings, and choreography to events, as well as a lot of hands-on work with people. At the core of social practice is the urge to reformulate the traditional relationship between the work and the viewer, between production and consumption, sender and receiver. Furthermore, social practice tends to feel more at home outside traditional art institutions, though is not entirely foreign to them. Another way of phrasing this is to talk in terms of the collaborative turn in art—the genre as an umbrella for various methods such as collective work, cooperation, and collaboration.[16]

The development of social practice can also be understood in light of simultaneous transformations within politics and management. Just as the dematerialization of the art object accompanied the dissolution of economic value through the end of the gold standard, artists also instrumentalized and reflected upon new forms of labor in the Western world post-World War II. Now, artists involved with social practice face the challenge of changing working conditions in a deregulated, post-Fordist job market, affected by an economy radically restructured by financial speculation and abstract values. In service and knowledge sectors, social competence, teamwork, and collaboration are essential, as are self-organization, flexibility and creativity, which all belong to the repertoire of the Romantic artist. In this sense, social practice work is very close to today's ideal of entrepreneurial work. Meanwhile, non-governmental organizations, interventions, and other support structures in the decolonized, developing world have engendered a volunteer sector. In all of this, participation has become a necessary and valued form of engagement, cherished by neoliberalism and Third Way politics alike.[17] Architecture shares this thrust towards participation by underlining methods of participatory consulting and decision-making. In addition, as Western societies become more and more precarious, techniques such as these, used in the developing world, are now applied to projects at home.[18]

The invitation from Creative Time to write this text prompted me to reflect on what it has meant to engage with social practice work as a curator, for the past two decades—not with the intention of privileging this work over other artistic media, methods, or genres—at least not consciously. Rather, I've been interested in projects that relate to the surrounding world, practices that offer the most pertinent and challenging responses to moments, places, and issues, presented by artists I have worked with over time. These responses—both direct and oblique, poetic and agitprop—have had a place in my work alongside documentary, discursive, performative, and spatial practices, as well as abstraction's many incarnations.

An enduring criticism of social practice

Opposite: Part of *Services* was a workshop organized by Fraser and Drexler at the Kunstraum der Universität Lüneburg in early 1994 that allowed the artists and curators involved to develop a framework for their practices and address the socioeconomic conditions of artists. The *Services* exhibition mainly consisted of collected historical and contemporary documents that supported the workshop's conclusions. (Courtesy Michael Schindel and Kunstraum der Universität Lüneburg)

is that it lends to "touch-down" projects that intervene only temporarily in a given situation—not unlike catastrophe relief. But some short-term, commissioned projects have also yielded long-term efforts. *Suggestion for the Day* by Apolonija Šušteršič [19] began as part of a exhibition I curated in 2000 at Stockholm's Moderna Museet, titled *What If: Art on the Verge of Architecture and Design*, which continued for four years with the support of various art and architecture institutions, such as Iaspis in Stockholm and the Architecture Museum of Ljubljana. Šušteršič, trained as both an architect and artist, invited stakeholders in urban development and institutional politics to join in a conversation about the future of Stockholm, a city known for its conservative urban and architectural approach. Like Wikström, Šušteršič stimulated public engagement by providing bicycles for the duration of the exhibition. Participants also received maps with commentary from emerging architects about contested areas in the city's layout and design, and postcards with images of those sites so that visitors could locate them, pedal to them, and view the issues firsthand. Part of the debate on which the exhibition's theme was based was the fact that Moderna Museet itself is located on an island, removed from the urban fabric. Šušteršič then organized a closed, moderated discussion within the exhibition space among commenting architects, city planners, developers, and two prominent local politicians—representatives who don't normally encounter (let alone talk to) one another about urban issues. The audience mix resulted in lively, productive exchanges which could only have occurred within the context of art, primarily because such a diverse group would never have agreed to meet outside of a nonpolitical context. Eventually, the debate focused on the harbor area and its prospected extension.

Moderna Museet's staff initially resisted *Suggestion for the Day* for pragmatic reasons: they simply weren't accustomed to working with living artists, or organizing the production of new work. Another reservation often heard in relation to social practice is that opportunities for direct feedback are limited, outside of the comments generated by the participants—how then should the project be assessed? But even if bigger museums were hesitant to take on social practice projects, at least within their main venues, by year 2000, this kind of work had become a common component of most biennials. This proved especially true in shows that took place outside of the Western world, such as Manifesta 3 in Ljubljana, the Periferic Biennial in Iasi, and the Taipei Biennial. Meanwhile, artists themselves, as well as other non-institutional representatives, began organizing their own initiatives—often long-term, relationship-building efforts designed to contribute significantly to a particular context: *Park Fiction* in Hamburg, a multi-year campaign to transform an empty lot planned for an office development into a public park, as well as Dan Peterman's *Blackstone Bicycle Works*, a youth education bike shop in Chicago, come to mind.

Sustained engagement also characterized Germany-based Schleuser.net (1998–2007). The word "Schleuser" means to transfer or take something through a hindrance like a lock or a border.[20] To that end, Schleuser.net, with artists Farida Heuck, Ralf Homann and Manuela Unverdorben at the helm, focused on border regimes. In 1993, the famous "Budapest Trial" criminalized "escape aid," helping people flee the Eastern Bloc, which had previously been considered a venerable activity, post-WWII. [21] Since then, migration had become a controversial issue in German politics on a local, regional, and national level, as well as across Europe. Modeled after a lobbying organization, Schleuser.net aimed to improve the media portrayal of "the men and women who engage in undocumented cross-border traffic."

With the help of a realistic fiction, Schleuser.net set up an office, organized events, and displayed promotional material, including brochures and gadgets, in various locations, including a municipal administration building. They also employed billboards and exhibitions to communicate their message. The bland, corporate-looking, orange and blue design of their printed matter and website could easily be

SCHLEUSER ▷ .NET
Trade Association for Smuggling People

confused with that of a proper pressure group. This was not by chance: coming out of the German radical Left—Homann co-organized the pioneering "Freie Klasse" (Free Class) at the Munich Academy in the late 1980s—Scheluser.net participated in the widespread theatricalization of activism, while also consciously evoking play and parody.[22] (Another related initiative that Homann co-founded was the activist project *Kein Mensch Ist Illegal*, or *No One Is Illegal*, which, since 1997, has fought for equal rights, regardless of whether or not the persons in question possess legal papers.)

When Schleuser.net was invited to participate in the group exhibition *Exchange & Transform (Arbeitstitel)*, which I curated at Munich's Kunstverein München (2002), it was important to offer the group time and space to carry on their work in a concentrated way.[23] They moved their computers, phones, and files to the exhibition space, furnishing it with the elements of artist duo Bik van der Pol's *Lobby Copy*. Triggered by the Kunstverein's unique location between the historic Hofgarten and the local government building, Schneuser.net produced new promotional material, and organized a month-long series of lectures which targeted politicians and journalists employing incorrect data related to undocumented border crossing. One of the lectures was a hands-on presentation by artist Heath Bunting about how to cross European borders without being documented. In another, historian Anne Klein presented her research on the Emergency Rescue Committee, which in 1940–42 smuggled and saved more than two thousand people from the south of France. Among the rescued were philosopher Hannah Arendt and artist Marc Chagall.[24]

If *Suggestion for the Day* indicated an interest in institutional dilemmas and urban issues, and Schleuser.net exemplified collective endeavors as well as sustained engagement—all increasingly important features of

Above: Founded by a group of German artists, Schleuser.net maintained the appearance of a think tank with its bland corporate logo (Courtesy Bundesverband Schleppen und Schleusen).

social practice—the *Lost Highway Expedition* (2006) testifies to the art world's intensified focus on research-based practices and transversal collaborations. However, these days, research does not necessarily occur in isolation, obscure archives, or remote libraries. Instead, like a flash mob with a clear purpose—to reframe "balkanization" as a window to Europe's future, rather than as an archaic and violent memory of its past—the *Lost Highway Expedition* explored for one month the never completed "Brotherhood and Unity Highway" in ex-Yugoslavia. The expedition also ventured to Albania.

Initiated by the architects Stealth and Kyong Park and the artist Marjetica Potrč, the *Lost Highway Expedition* brought nearly three hundred artists, architects, geographers, critics, and curators to cities along the route of the "Lost Highway" for events hosted by local organizations pertaining to recent urbanization, community politics, and cultural activities. The trip itself was entirely self-organized, with people traveling by car, bus, train, or bike—according to preference and budget. No one was required to commit to the entire journey, although some did. Having worked with Stealth in other contexts, I simply joined them at the first two stops in Ljubljana and Zagreb with my ten-month-old son, opting to take the train as our means of transportation. The expedition culminated in a host of projects, such as the creation of art works, texts, conferences, publications, collaborations, and networks. Among them are artist Kasper Akhöj's *Abstracta*, which relates the geopolitically fascinating story of a flexible display system common in Yugoslavia, as well as the publication of the *Lost Highway Expedition: Photobook*.[25]

The desire and need to work long-term is felt in many corners of the art world, including social practice.[26] To that end, *Time/Bank*, by Julieta Aranda and Anton Vidokle, was designed to operate indefinitely. Based on the classical structure of a nineteenth-century time bank in which units of time are used as currency, this contemporary version allows individuals and groups to pool and trade skills. Different from potlatch and barter, where goods and services are exchanged directly, *Time/Bank* uses an alternate currency, in the fashion of the "Ithaca HOUR" which has been traded in Ithaca, New York, since 1991. So far, *Time/Bank* has primarily concentrated on art world networks; consequently, many of the services on offer relate to what cultural producers do and need. Aranda and Vidokle have opened branches in physical spaces in Basel, den Hague and Frankfurt, accompanied by shops with objects for sale, including bicycles. They asked a number of artists to design prototypes for actual tender, and chose Lawrence Weiner's bill for printing.[27]

As the director of Tensta Konsthall, I have invited Vidokle and Aranda to establish a branch of *Time/Bank* in Tensta, a suburb of Stockholm with approximately twenty thousand inhabitants. It is a geographically distinct neighborhood built in the late 1960s as part of a large late-Modernist housing scheme that was implemented across Sweden. Today, Tensta is a bedroom community with the most diverse concentration of nationalities in the country; because of this, many local business owners are already familiar with parallel economies. Tensta's unemployment rate is high and the average income low. Along with the senior high school, one of the best in the capital, and the local library, Tensta Konsthall serves as a rare stable entity in an otherwise transient area. The challenge here will be to sustain *Time/Bank* in this wide, yet tight, community where money has a different urgency.

Since the days of *Returnity*, social practice has developed its own unique gestures and orthodoxies, tensions and contradictions. In fact, a plethora of new education programs exclusively explore social practice.[28] Bringing the field into light now is neither to crown the genre "king of art," nor to establish a cross-genre alternative canon. Rather, it is to consider projects and practices that do something significant in the moment, in palpable and/or symbolic ways, within a specific set of circumstances. It is obvious that not all social practice projects are interesting and relevant, just as all painting is not uninteresting and irrelevant. And yet, in spite of its increasing visibility,

Opposite, top to bottom: Lost Highway Expedition visited the unfinished Museum of the Revolution and first residential towers built in New Belgrade after World War II. A partially constructed mosque in the Shuto Orizari part of Skopje, Macedonia was abandoned due to lack of funds and the conversion of large parts of the community to Evangelical Christianity. (Photographs by Kyong Park)

social practice still mainly operates within the "minor" strands of the art world—as opposed to the spectacularized and consumption-oriented mainstream institutions of the "major" strand. These minors are self-organized initiatives, artistic and otherwise, as well as small-scale public institutions with precarious economies and they are the source of most of the new ideas in art.[29] Sharing certain features with Gilles Deleuze and Félix Guattari's "minor literature," written by members of a minority but using and corrupting the language of the majority (like Franz Kafka) in order to maintain maximum self-determination, the minors of the art world keep a calculated distance from the "majors."[30]

Being slightly off-center can indeed often be an advantage. Today the minors, in general, and social practice, in particular, benefit from not yet having been subsumed by the majors. This is encouraging, as the work then can still offer the possibility of avoiding preconceptions about art production and direction, even if only for a moment. The questioning is ongoing, the process is rolling, and I keep waiting to one day see someone cycling down the street pedaling forwards, but going backwards.

ENDNOTES
1 *Contemporary Sculpture: Projects in Münster 1997*, Klaus Bussmann, Kasper König, Florian Matzner, eds. (Ostfildern-Ruit: Verlag Gerd Hatje, 1997).
2 "Returnity," text by Elin Wikström in *Moderna Museet Projekt: Elin Wikström*, Maria Lind, ed. (Stockholm: Modern Museet, 2000).
3 Exhibition catalogue: Yves Aupetitallot, *Projet Unité*, (E.G.A. Brighton), 3 vol., 1993.
4 Exhibition catalogue for *Sonsbeek 1993*, Arnhem, curated by Valerie Smith.
5 Exhibition catalogue, Mary Jane Jacob, *Places With A Past: New Site-Specific Art in Charleston* (New York: Rizzoli International, 1991).
6 Exhibition catalogue: Mary Jane Jacob, *Culture in Action: A Public Program of Sculpture Chicago* (Seattle: Bay Press, 1995) and Miwon Kwon, *One Place After Another: Site-Specific Art and Locational Identity* (Cambridge, Mass.: MIT Press, 2004).
7 See Andrea Fraser, *Services: A Working-Group Exhibition*, http://eipcp.net/transversal/0102/fraser/en and Andrea Fraser, "What's Intangible, Transitory, Mediating, Participatory, and Rendered in the Public Sphere?", vol. 80, *October* magazine, 1997.
8 Julia Bryan-Wilson, *Art Workers: Radical Practice in the Vietnam War Era* (Berkeley, Los Angeles, London: University of California Press, 2009).
9 Nicolas Bourriaud, *Relational Aesthetics* (Dijon: Les presses du réel, 2002).
10 Exhibition catalogue: Peter Weibel, *Kontext Kunst* (Köln: DuMont, 1994).
11 Suzanne Lacy, *Mapping the Terrain: New Genre Public Art* (Seattle: Bay Press, 1995).
12 Suzi Gablik, *The Reenchantment of Art* (New York: Thames and Hudson, 1991).
13 Grant Kester, *Conversation Pieces: Community and Communication in Modern Art* (Berkeley and Los Angeles: University of California Press, 2004).
14 *Participation*, Claire Bishop, ed. (London: Whitechapel and Cambridge, Mass.: MIT Press, 2006).
15 *Situation*, Claire Doherty, ed. (London: Whitechapel and Cambridge, Mass.: MIT Press, 2009).
16 See Maria Lind, "The Collaborative Turn" in *Taking the Matter Into Common Hands*, Johanna Billing, Maria Lind, Lars Nilsson, eds. (London: Black Dog Publishing, 2007); and Judith Schwartzbart, "The Social as Medium," in *Meaning and Motivation, Collected Newsletters*, Maria Lind, Sören Grammel, Katharina Schlieben, Judith Schwarzbart, Ana Paula Cohen, Juleinne Lorz, Tessa Praun, eds. (Frankfurt: Kunstverein München and Revolver Archiv für aktuelle Kunst, 2005).
17 See *The Participation Reader*, Andrea Cornwall, ed. (London and New York: Zed Books, 2011).
18 See *Did Someone Say Participate? An Atlas of Spatial Practice*, Markus Miessen
and Shumon Basar, eds. (Cambridge, Mass.: MIT Press, 2006) and Markus Miessen, *The Nightmare of Participation (Crossbench Praxis as a Mode of Criticality)* (Berlin: Sternberg Press, 2010).
19 See Maria Lind, "What If: Art on the Verge of Architecture and Design" in *Selected Maria Lind Writing*, Brian Kuan Wood, ed. (Berlin: Sternberg Press, 2010).
20 See http://www.schleuser.net/en/p1_1.php
21 Maria Lind, "We Support Mobility" in *Symbolproduktion*, eds. Farida Heuck, Ralf Homann, Manuela Unverdorben (Berlin: Goldrausch Künstlerinnenprojekt Art IT, 2004).
22 Lisa Diedrich, "Architecture as an Allusion: Hermann Hiller and the Planet of the Freie Klasse," *Collected Newsletters*, Maria Lind, Sören Grammel, Katharina Schlieben, Judith Schwarzbart, Ana Paula Cohen, Julienne Lorz, Tessa Praun, eds. (Frankfurt: Kunstverein München and Revolver Archiv für aktuelle Kunst, 2005).
23 See Maria Lind, "Exchange & Transform (Arbeitstitel)" in *Selected Maria Lind Writing*, Brian Kuan Wood, ed. (Berlin: Sternberg Press, 2010).
24 Farida Heuck, Ralf Homann, Manuela Unverdorben, "Art Meets the Corporate World; The Bundesverband Schleppen & Schleusen (National Association for Smuggling People) Takes Successful Stock," in *Collected Newsletters*, Maria Lind, Sören Grammel, Katharina Schlieben, Judith Schwartzbart, Ana Paula Cohen, Julienne Lorz, Tessa Praun, eds. (Frankfurt: Kunstverein München and Revolver Archiv für aktuell Kunst, 2005).
25 *Lost Highway Expedition Photobook*, Katherine Carl and Srdjan Jovanovic Weiss, eds. (Rotterdam: Veenman Publishers, 2007).
26 See, for example, Claire Doherty and Paul O'Neill, *Locating the Producers: Durational Approaches to Public Art* (Amsterdam: Antenna Valiz, 2009).
27 See http://www.e-flux.com/timebank/
28 Christina Linden, "En kort lista: Tankar om social praktik" in *Paletten*, no. 1, 2011.
29 Manifesta 8 catalogue: Maria Lind, "Manifesta Murcia," (Milano: Silvana Editoriale, 2010).
30 Gilles Deleuze, Félix Guattari, Robert Brinkley, "What is a Minor Literature?" in *Mississippi Review*, vol. 11, no. 3, Winter/Spring 1983: 13–33.

Opposite, top to bottom: Damir Nikšić delivers his performance on the Miljacka river as part of Lost Highway Expedition in Sarajevo (Photograph by Arnoud Schuurman). In Albania, Peter Lang discusses the editor's introduction of Lonely Planet's guidebook for the Western Balkans, which explains the difficulty for the editors in choosing the book's title over "former Yugoslavia" or "South East Europe" (Photograph by Kyong Park).

DEMOCRATIZING URBANIZATION AND THE SEARCH FOR A NEW CIVIC IMAGINATION

TEDDY CRUZ

THE SHRINKING RELEVANCY OF THE PUBLIC

The obvious is staring us—the public—in the face and, yet, we're ignoring it. We occupy a critical juncture in history, defined by unprecedented socio-economic, political, and environmental crises across any imaginable register. Our institutions of culture, governance, and urban development have atrophied, without knowing how to re-invent themselves, or construct alternative procedures to engage the conditions that have produced the crises in the first place.

How many Wall Street bailouts, foreclosures, superfluous debt ceiling debates, and tea-party zealots—amid the defunding of our public education system, and abandonment of healthcare and energy legislature—will it take to prompt our own spring revolution? The passivity of the American public and its creative sectors, in the context of this renewed return to excessive inequality and ideological polarization, makes clear that protests on par with those that occurred in Cairo's Tahrir Square will never happen in the US. Here, there is no state of emergency. We lack the kind of collective sense of urgency that would prompt us to fundamentally question our own ways of thinking and acting, and form new spaces of operation.

It is also obvious that we learned the best lesson in Democracy 101 from those Middle Eastern societies the American public was lead to believe were turban-wearing terrorists: Democracy is not simply the right to be left alone. Rather it is defined by the co-existence with others in space, a collective ethos, regardless of social media, that unconditionally stands for social rights. I do not mean to naively suggest that those revolutionary instances can be reproduced that easily; each cultural space has its own socio-political complexity. We have witnessed, for example, how specific geo-political configurations and historic power alliances have made it difficult to repeat Egypt's transformation in Syria, Bahrain and Libya. Nonetheless, the uncompromising collective act of seeking transformation of the stagnant status quo resonates, and should encourage our own self-critique.

Sufficient economic analysis of our current dilemma has shown the similarities between late 1920's depression-era conditions and our own situation today. Both socio-economic crises were characterized by the not-so-coincidental meeting of excessive inequality and low marginal tax rates: At these critical points, the income gap between the very wealthy and all other Americans reached record levels. In both 1928 and 2008 the top one percent averaged an income approximately 1,000 times higher than America's bottom 90 percent, while enjoying the lowest taxation available.

While the similarities are clear, there hasn't been enough discussion of the very different outcomes following both periods. In general, the post-depression years were marked by a self-assured consolidation of a collective political will to engage in public participation and public debate. Briefly, the political period following the depression witnessed the emergence of the New Deal and with it a commitment to invest in public infrastructure, education, and services partly enabled by higher marginal tax rates to the wealthy; in the 1950s, the marginal tax rate to the upperclass was 91 percent compared to 35 percent today, ultimately resulting in a few decades of more equitable distribution of economic and civic resources.

The economic and infrastructural growth experienced during that period of committed public spending clearly demonstrates that trickle-down economics, based on de-taxing the rich so that its wealth will eventually touch the rest of Americans, has been the fake democratic façade of neo-liberal models. This falsehood had forced us to believe and defend another one: the mythology of the American Dream as promised by an ownership society, low taxes, and individual freedoms that allow for unchecked economic expansion. Today, as the rich become richer in the middle of soaring unemployment rates, certain socio-economic realities, specific to the United States, reveal themselves. We are the only country in the world where the poor defend the rich, possibly with the belief that someday the American Dream will enable us all to be as wealthy. The public ethos of this period also contradicts the conservative belief that social and economic strength depend on less government. Rather, they require an intelligent one, defined by responsible taxation, progressive public policy, and proactive collective imagination.

Our current period of crisis, then, has been defined by exactly the opposite. The absence of a self-assured political leadership and constructive debate of and about the public has allowed the public to be hijacked by right wing demagogy that turns every socially based effort into a communist coup, co-opted by politics of fear. In fact, the very word "public" has become a liability, and therefore has taken on a negative connotation, even within our 'public,' political institutions; in fact, the way *public option* disappeared from Obama's Health Care Bill reflects this. Therefore, in my mind, different from the post-depression years, which enabled a healthy public debate and general accountability for the re-distribution of resources, our period has been characterized by a shrinking conception of the public and the consolidation of a powerful elite of individual or corporate wealth, which, in fact, has remained unaffected and unaccountable today.

From the time of Margaret Thatcher to Ronald Reagan's re-installment of pre-depression era free-market economic policies based on de-regulation and hyper excessive privatization of resources in the early 1980s, we have once more witnessed the ascendance of income inequality and social disparity that has yielded the current crisis. Equally obvious is that these typical neo-liberal economic models not only enabled a small elite to be in control of economic power but, this time, in control of political power as well, in unprecedented ways. What I am referring to is the philanthropic and lobbying machines sponsored by right wing foundations that have enabled this economic elite to own not only the bulk of resources but also the media and information networks that manipulate public opinion and the electorate. This consolidation of the economic and political power of this wealthy elite to lobby and install an anti-taxes, anti-immigration and anti-public culture in our time is

what makes our period radically different from the post depression era, cementing the final erosion of public participation from the political process and a culture of impunity in the upper echelons of institutional structures.

The ultimate impact of this consolidated economic and political hegemony can be illustrated in what I call the *Three Slaps on the Face of the American Public* since 2008. 1. After the big bubble of economic growth burst in September of 2008, the public unwantedly came to the rescue of the architects of the crisis by bailing out the banking industry (first slap). 2. Following this, the lack of collateral regulation to protect homeowners in the management of loan defaults resulted in millions of foreclosures, producing further insecurity and unprecedented unemployment rates (second slap). 3. Finally, the unfolding of this economic crisis and its political upheaval has recently enabled this conservative wealthy minority to de-fund the public with massive spending cuts on education, health, and social services without raising any taxes to the wealthy (third slap). So, we are now paralyzed, silently witnessing the most blatant politics of unaccountability, shrinking social and public institutions, and not a single proposal or action that suggests a different approach or arrangement.

So, ours is primarily a cultural crisis—rather than an economic or environmental one—resulting in the inability of institutions to question their ways of thinking, or the rigidity of their protocols and silos. It is within this radical context that we must question the role of art and humanities and their contingent cultural institutions of pedagogy, production, display, and distribution. A more functional relationship between art and the everyday is urgently needed, through which artists can act as interlocutors across this polarized territory, intervening in the debate itself and mediating new forms of acting and living.

In fact, one primary site of artistic intervention today is the gap itself that has been produced between cultural institutions and the public, instigating a new civic imagination and political will. It is not enough in our time to only give art the task of metaphorically reveal-

Opposite: Time/Food is a temporary eatery that operates on the Time/Bank economic system—a platform where individuals can pool time and skills, bypassing money as a means of value. Visitors to Time/Food pay for their lunch in exchange for one half-hour of time currency earned by helping others in the Time/Bank community. (Photographs by Sam Horine)

Flood:
A Volunteer Network for Active Participation in Healthcare

Diluvio:
Una Red de Voluntarios para Participacion Activa en el Cuidado de Salud

ing the very socio-economic histories and injustices that have produced these crises, but it is essential that art becomes an instrument to construct specific procedures that can transcend them. The revision of our own artistic procedures is essential today, expanded modes of practice to engage alternative sites of research and pedagogy, new conceptions of cultural and economic production and the re-organization of social relations seem more urgent than ever.

EXPANDING ARTISTIC PRACTICE: FROM CRITICAL DISTANCE TO CRITICAL PROXIMITY

The same ideological divide in politics today permeates art and architecture's current implicit debate. On one hand, we find those who continue to defend these two fields as a self-referential project of apolitical formalism, made of hyper-aesthetics for the sake of aesthetics, which continues to press the notion of the avant-garde as an autonomous project, 'needing' a *critical distance* from the institutions to operate critically in the research of experimental form. On the other hand, we find those who need to step out of this autonomy in order to engage the socio-political and economic domains that have remained peripheral to the specializations of art and architecture, questioning our professions' powerlessness in the context of the world's most pressing current crises.

This need to expand the realm of established artistic practices is a direct result of our creative fields' unconditional love affair, in the last years, with a system of economic excess that was needed to legitimize artistic experimentation. These emerging activist practices seek, instead, for a project of *radical proximity* to the institutions, transforming them in order to produce new aesthetic categories that can problematize the relationship of the social, the

Above: Haha took over a vacated storefront on Greenleaf Street in Chicago, where they planted a hydroponic garden to provide produce for local AIDS and HIV patients (Photograph by Haha, Courtesy Sculpture Chicago).

political, and the formal.

In these practices, artists are responsible for imagining counter spatial procedures, and political and economic structures that can produce new modes of social encounters. Without altering the exclusionary policies that have produced the current crises in the first place, our professions will continue to be subordinated by visionless and homogeneous environments defined by the bottom-line of developers' spreadsheets as well as neo-conservative politics and economics of a hyper-individualistic ownership society. In essence, then, the autonomous role of artists needs to be coupled with the role of the activist. I don't see one as more important than the other because both are necessary today.

NEW SITES OF EXPERIMENTATION: AN URBANISM BEYOND THE PROPERTY LINE

The world's architecture intelligentsia—supported by the pre-2008 glamorous economy—flocked en masse to The Arab Emirates and China to help build dream castles that would catapult these enclaves of wealth as global epicentres of urban development. Yet many of these high-profile projects have only perpetuated the exhausted recipes of an oil hungry, U.S.-style globalization, camouflaging with hyper-aesthetics an architecture of exclusion based on urbanities of surveillance and control. Other than a few isolated architectural interventions whose images have been disseminated widely, no major ideas were advanced to transform existing paradigms of housing, infrastructure, and density.

While the world had been focused on those enclaves of abundance up until our current economic downturn, the most radical ideas advancing new models of urban development were produced in the margins, across Latin American cities. Challenging the neo-liberal urban logic of development, which is founded on top-down privatization, homogeneity and exclusion, visionary mayors in cities such as Porto Alegre, Curitiba, Bogota, and Medellin encouraged new public participation, civic culture, and unorthodox cross-institutional collaborations, rethinking the meaning of infrastructure, housing, and density. I cannot think of any other continental region where we can find this type of collective effort led by municipal and federal governments seeking a new brand of progressive politics.

This suggests the need to reorient our focus to other sites of research and intervention, arguing that some of the most relevant practices and projects forwarding socio-economic sustainability will not emerge from sites of abundance but from sites of scarcity. New experimental practices of research and intervention will emerge from zones of conflict. It is in the periphery where conditions of social emergency are transforming our ways of thinking about urbanization.

RADICALIZING THE PARTICULAR: MOVING FROM THE AMBIGUITY OF THE PUBLIC TO THE SPECIFICITY OF RIGHTS

We need to move beyond the abstraction of the "global" in order to engage with the particularities of the political inscribed within local geographies of conflict. It is within this specificity where contemporary artistic practice needs to reposition itself in order to expose the particularity of hidden institutional histories, revealing the missing information that can allow us to piece together a more accurate anticipatory urban research and intervention. To be political in our field requires that we commit to revealing conditions of conflict and the institutional mechanisms that perpetuate them. What produced the crisis in the first place? Only knowing the specific conditions that produced it can enable us to think politically. In other words, artistic and architectural experimentation in our time should involve the specific re-organization of the political and economic conditions that continue to produce conflict between top-down forces of urbanization and bottom-up social and ecological networks, enclaves of mega wealth and sectors of marginalization. Conflict is a creative tool.

At this moment, it is not buildings, but the fundamental re-organization of socio-economic relations that is the necessary ground for producing new paradigms of democratization and urbanization. Artists and architects

have a role in the conceptualization of such new protocols, infiltrating into existing institutional mechanisms in order to reconstruct politics itself, not simply political art or architecture. It has been said that the Civil Rights movement in the United States began in a bus. At least that is the image that detonated the unfolding of such constitutional transformation. A small act trickling up into the collective's awareness. While public transport at the time was labeled "public," it wasn't actually accessible to all. To that end, it is necessary to move from the generality of the term "public" in our political debate to the specificity of rights to the city, and its neighborhoods. This would expand the idea that architects and artists, besides being producers of buildings and objects, can be designers of political processes, alternative economic models, and collaborations across institutions and jurisdictions. This can be in the form of small, incremental acts of retrofit of existing urban fabrics and regulation, encroaching into the privatization of public domain and infrastructure, as well as the rigidity of institutional thinking.

NEW URBAN PEDAGOGY: THE VISUALIZATION OF A NEW CIVIC IMAGINATION

Fundamental to the rethinking of exclusionary political and economic frameworks that defined the logics of uneven urban development in the last years is the translation and visualization of the socio-cultural and economic entrepreneurial intelligence embedded in many marginal, immigrant neighborhoods. While the global city had become the privileged site of consumption and display, marginal neighborhoods across the world remained sites of cultural production. But the hidden socio-economic value of these immigrant communities' informal transactions across bottom-up cultural production, economies and densities, continues to be off the radar of conventional top-down planning institutions.

If we consider citizenship as a creative act, it is new immigrants in the U.S. today who are pointing at a new conception of civic culture and a more inclusive city. In this context, I see informal urbanization as the site of a new interpretation of community, citizenship, and praxis, where emergent urban configurations

Above: Suzanne Lacy's *The Roof Is On Fire* operated as an outlet for Oakland teens to openly discuss pressing topics while an audience, including the local and national news media, listened in (Courtesy Suzanne Lacy).

produced out of social emergency suggest the performative role of individuals constructing their own spaces. The most radical urban interventions in our time have in fact emerged in marginal neighborhoods, as immigrants have been injecting informal economies and housing additions into mono-use parcels, implicitly proposing the urgent revision of current discriminating land-use policies that have perpetuated zoning as a punitive tool to prevent socialization, instead of a generative tool that organizes activity and economy.

But these immigrant communities' invisible urban praxis needs interpretation and representation; this is the space of intervention institutions of art, culture, and governance need to engage. How do we mobilize this activism into new spatial and economic infrastructures that benefit these 'communities of practice' in the long term, beyond the short-term problem solving of private developers or the institutions of charity?

But, often, just as artists and architects lack awareness of the specific political and social knowledge embedded within these marginal communities, community activists also lack the conceptual devices to enable their own everyday procedures, and how their neighborhood agency can trickle up to produce new institutional transformations. It is in the context of these conditions where a different role for art, architecture, environmental, and community activist practices can emerge. One that goes beyond the metaphorical representation of people, where only the community's symbolic image is amplified (what a community "looks" like) instead of its operative dimension (what a community "does"). New knowledge-exchange corridors can be produced, between the specialized knowledge of institutions and the ethical knowledge of "community," and artists can have a role to facilitate this exchange, occupying the gap between the visible and the invisible.

Questioning new forms of urban pedagogy is one of the most critical sites for artistic investigation and practice today, do we produce new interfaces with the public to raise awareness of the conditions that have pro-duced environmental, economic and social crises? The conventional structures and protocols of academic institutions may be seen to be at odds with activist practices, which are, by their very nature, organic and extra-academic. Should activist practices challenge the pedagogical structures within the institution? Are new modes of teaching and learning called for?

Today, it is essential to reorient our gaze toward the drama embedded in the reality of the everyday and in doing so, engage the shifting socio-political and economic domains that have been ungraspable by art and design. It is not the "image" of the everyday and its metaphorical content that is at stake here, though. More than ever, we must engage the 'praxis' of the everyday, enabling functional relationships between individuals, as collectives, and their environments, as new critical interfaces between research, artistic intervention, and the production of the city.

MICROUTOPIAS: PUBLIC PRACTICE IN THE PUBLIC SPHERE

CAROL BECKER

"THE ESSENTIAL FUNCTION OF UTOPIA," SAYS ERNST BLOCH TO THEODOR ADORNO, "IS A CRITIQUE OF WHAT IS PRESENT."[1]

There used to be a greater distinction between private and public. Private events—enactments of the particulars of personal life—took place in what was understood as the private sphere. Meanwhile, public events—the public engagement of public issues, such as politics—took place in the public sphere. Now, weighty discussions about public issues, as well as minute, private intimacies, are posted daily on social media sites. Those separations, which once seemed basic, clear, and reliable, now appear blurred.

While many have noted these changes, little understanding exists about the societal impact of such implosions and inversions in relationship to democracy. How are political affairs influenced when open engagement with public issues is increasingly missing from public discourse? And what about the effects of celebrity culture, in which topics that would have been considered narcissistic self-absorption at one time are now considered newsworthy, and glut the media? It appears that the private has colonized the public and, in fact, the concept of a "public" has all but disappeared—except perhaps as an epithet used by the right wing to reflect its scorn for what its adherents portray as an outdated, liberal notion of citizenship.

Just as nature most recently unleashed catastrophic earthquakes and tsunamis on our physical landscape, tectonic events have rocked our political one, helping us to reimagine the meaning of public space and even the traditional notion of the public square. As Henri Lefebvre wrote, "Events belie forecasts. To the extent that events are historic, they upset calculations."[2]

We watched transfixed and enthralled by the political upheaval in Egypt—a microutopian moment organized via cell phones and social media, such as Twitter, in an elaborately documented process that took years to manifest, including side trips to Serbia, for example, to learn best practices. But the final transformation occurred in real time and space in Tahrir ("Liberation") Square, a public arena designed by French urban planner Baron Haussmann to simulate the Paris of Napoleon III. The physical reality of those prepared to stay in Tahrir Square until President Hosni Mubarak stepped down—a real-life, choreographed showdown—was so large in scale, duration, and imagination that it not only transformed Egypt, but continues to shake the region (Yemen, Bahrain, Iraq, Iran, Syria, and Libya) to very dramatic, exhilarating, and even devastating effect.

The events in Egypt and elsewhere in the Middle East demonstrated yet again that the Internet is a very effective organizing tool (used for good and bad). But it has not replaced human interaction and the manifestation of real resistance in public space which occurs when bodies are put on the line. No matter how

Previous page: Paul Ramírez Jonas' *Key to the City* bestowed the key to New York City—an honor usually reserved for dignitaries and heroes—to esteemed and everyday citizens alike (Photograph by Paul Ramírez Jonas, Courtesy Creative Time).

many digital petitions we sign, when societal change occurs, it most often happens in a physical *location* where a mass of people congregates for an assignation. Even most voting requires that we physically show up at a designated place to cast our vote with the populace.

Egypt reconfirmed that we humans need the *agora*—the public square—as it existed in ancient Greece, a site where we come together physically, as bodies, in order to hear one another. We show force as a crowd—a purposeful mob, a *res publica*—with an expressed shared desire. In the architecture of traditional cities, one can usually find a place where the collective gathers, whether in Egypt's Tahrir Square, Athens' Syntagma Square, Washington's National Mall, Argentina's Plaza de Mayo, or Madison, Wisconsin's Capitol Square (which usually serves as the site of an excellent outdoor farmers' market when it is not a place of protest).

As social observers and cultural commentators who employ multiple forms and strategies to engage their audiences, artists are uniquely positioned to respond to social transformation and to educate communities about its complexity and implications. But now that more people are employing art forms to communicate, how can artists hope to make an impact in this sphere? And how can we think of such space as local when technology focuses our thoughts so profoundly on the global? Or is public space always local—defined by a particular group, who now affects its meaning from one society to the next in our increasingly interconnected world?

The challenge to navigate the tension between public and private realms is hardly new to artists. After all, museums, as well as other traditional art spaces, can be considered a kind of "public space," since these institutions are partly funded by both cities and states, or sit on park district land. Yet, they are specifically designed to feel private. In fact, we often enter museums expecting to experience something deeply personal—moments that are contrary to the disorder of our daily lives—despite the presence of others, who disrupt our sense of intimacy and ownership of the space.

So even when throngs surrounded Marina Abramović during the run of her piece *The Artist is Present* at the Museum of Modern Art in 2010, those participating in it expected a private moment. For this work, Abramović gave visitors the opportunity to sit facing her, quietly, for as long as they desired, while hundreds of other visitors watched. The performance was recorded on video, under blaring lights, and then posted on the Internet, where it would reside permanently for all to see. So how could this be a private experience? And yet it was. For many, this very public interaction with Abramović—who acted as both the artist and the art piece—was revelatory, contemplative, and emotional.

The more the Museum of Modern Art makes itself available for such encounters, the more the space is transformed into a performative space within which we, as viewers, collaborate with artists to fabricate our public/private experience. In the winter of 2011, Janine Antoni, at both the Hayward Gallery in London and the Haus der Kunst in Munich, surreptitiously placed a letter in visitors' checked bags. Antoni designed the mass-produced letter to look like a personal note, handwritten on a page ripped from a museum program. While some visitors assumed it was a love letter from another person, the notes were actually sent from an unspecified work of art—an imaginary act that generated a real object—extending the experience of the museum beyond the physical building, and highlighting the intimate, relational connection between art and spectator.

A number of artists have used these inversions of public/private to take on a new role and a new line of interrogation appropriate to this historical moment. Because artists often gravitate to what is missing, many have committed themselves to creating events that connect people and ideas in the public sphere because they discern that *what is missing* now is public discourse about the relationship of individuals to society. Artists also reconfigure contemporary physical or psychical elements into an imagined, ideal, hypothetical organization of reality. When they felt that the world was too sanitized and our interior life was not respected, understood, or made visible, they wanted to bring those subjective issues into the public arena. Later, as this interiority became the norm, artists continued to focus on what was still silenced—for example, sexuality, gender, and transgender—the complex emotions and sociology of identity.

Now many artists fear that the world has become too interior-focused and that private space and identity are all there is, even in the public arena. Most significantly, those personal issues are rarely linked to the greater social context that could help frame them, isolate their origins, and catalyze their resolutions. As sociologist Zygmunt Bauman writes, "...Public Space is not much more than a giant screen on which private worries are projected without, in the course of magnification, ceasing to be private."[3] Public confession has become the norm, as we regress to a shame-based society. "And so," adds Bauman, "public space is increasingly empty of public issues."[4] As artists take on these contradictions, their actions are not necessarily intended to challenge the art worlds of galleries and museums but, rather, to help reinvigorate collectivity and connectivity throughout the larger world.

They do this through the creation of microutopic communities—small locations of utopian interaction. Utopia, from the Greek *utopos*, meaning "good place" (as opposed to *outopos*, meaning "no place"), is the creation of imaginary "good places" that do not exist on any map, other than that of the imagination. Such experiments attempt to create physical manifestations of an ideal "humanity" in an inhumane world—interventions in a world overrun by the spectacle. Even if their duration is brief, these interventions reflect the desire to give form to what Ernst Bloch might call "the not yet conscious," that which "anticipates" and "illuminates"[5] what might be possible. And because utopian thinking is always communal, it has always historically implied the coming together of people within an imagined societal situation. (Therefore, you cannot have a utopia of one; an idealized experience with oneself would not qualify as "utopia" in the philosoph-

ical sense with which it has most often been employed.)

By asking her museum audience to sit with her in deep silence, Abramović created such a microutopian moment. Similarly, Tino Seghal, in *This Progress* at the Guggenheim Museum in New York, asked visitors to discuss the concept of "progress" with performers who greeted them as they walked up the ramps. As visitors approached the top of the museum, the age of the performers increased and the nature of the dialogue they initiated became less overtly philosophical and more narrative. These were interventions that engaged audiences in unexpected acts with an unspecified result.

Art is often a kind of dreaming the world into being, a transmutation of thought into material reality, and an affirmation that the physical world begins in the incorporeal—in ideas. Even Marx, the materialist, believed in the uniqueness of humans to imagine their world into being. He wrote that humans were better architects than bees and ants—the great builders of collective living—because they could see the plan before building it.[6] In other words, we humans could "anticipate" what we would create.

Art is the great anticipator. It generates an "interpretation of that which is, in terms of that-which-is-not," as Rousseau might say.[7] If one thinks that what exists is inevitable, then there is no space for art. This is why, in a very pragmatic society like the U.S., art is so often misunderstood. Yet, for that same reason, art is also so essential.

At this time, there is a collective understanding that, as John Muse wrote in an essay about Flash Mobs, "Everybody is an audience all the time."[8] He adds, "Public spaces are more than ever becoming sites for communal isolation."[9] Artists are both attempting to circumvent the spectacle and to reclaim urban space for the coming together of its inhabitants. They embrace diversity and resist the suburbanization of such space. But how *do* you bring people together to truly make a connection between them? Cultural anthropologist Arjun Appadurai asserts that the answer is microutopian. "We need to think of the biggest problems in the world," he has said, "and

come up with the smallest contribution toward their solution." It's a sentiment the artist Paul Ramírez Jonas has alluded to in work that has so often addressed both the interests, and the complexities, of the creation of "public."

What might we think of as the biggest problems and what might be the smallest solutions? Ramírez Jonas' 2010 Creative Time commission, *The Key to the City*, presented the following questions: How can we reclaim the centrality of citizenship as the most important element of society? How can keys to the city be available to all New Yorkers? And can this act of reclaiming the city be done in the most recognized public site of all—Times Square? According to written and spoken testimonies, the piece created a temporary community, as people waited to gift and to receive the keys. And it spread across the city, encouraging citizens to explore and experience greater access to one of the least intimate global cities in the world.

His newest piece, *The Commons*, is a heroic statue modeled after the bronze original of Marcus Aurelius atop his steed, located in the Campidoglio in Rome. But this horse has no rider, and it is made of cork, so that the public can use pushpins to leave notices for others, and watch it erode as the material deteriorates. The piece, which is ephemeral, collective, and historical, immediately reminded me of the *Polygonal Wall* in Delphi, where the ancient Greeks posted public messages in stone—the release of slaves by their owners, the amount of time a slave would stay after the decision of release, an inscription of gratitude to a benefactor, the record of a debt repaid. Private acts were recorded in the public sphere to last forever.

In Ramírez Jonas' act of creating the riderless horse, we have a perfect gesture for this historical moment. The unspecified rider—the completion of the heroic statue—can only be the public itself. Without the rider, the galloping horse has no clear direction, and without the public, the piece is incomplete. As Jacques Rancière would say, "The Spectator also acts..."[10] Engagement is the only antidote to the spectacle. And the reinvention of public space is the only antidote to its disappearance. Like Ramírez Jonas, artists have taken on the task of creating microutopian interventions that allow us to dream back the communities we fear we have lost.

Carol Becker first presented this piece as a lecture at the Museum of Modern Art, New York, April 28, 2011.

ENDNOTES

1 Ernst Bloch, *The Utopian Function of Art and Literature: Selected Essays*, Jack Zipes and Frank Mecklenburg, trans. (Cambridge, Mass.: MIT Press, 1988): 12.
2 Henri Lefebvre, *The Explosion: Marxism and the French Upheaval*, Alfred Ehrenfeld, trans. (New York: Modern Reader Paperbacks,1969): 7.
3 Zygmunt Bauman, *The Individualized Society* (Cambridge, U.K.: Polity, 2001): 107.
4 Ibid.: 108.
5 Jack Zipes, "Introduction: Toward a Realization of Anticipatory Illumination," Bloch, xxxi.
6 David Harvey, *A Companion to Marx's Capital* (London: Verso, 2010): 112.
7 Alain Martineau, *Herbert Marcuse's Utopia* (Montreal: Harvest House, 1986): 35.
8 John H. Muse, "Flash Mobs and the Diffusion of Audience," in *Theater*, 40:3, Tom Seller, ed. (New Haven: Yale School of Drama, 2010): 12.
9 Ibid.
10 Jacques Rancière, *The Emancipated Spectator*, Gregory Elliott, trans. (London: Verso, 2009): 13.

*Opposite:*The cork version of Marcus Aurelius' steed created by Ramírez Jonas displays a variety of messages and pictures pinned on by the public (Photograph by Paul Ramírez Jonas, Courtesy Alexander Gray Associates).

EVENTWORK: THE FOURFOLD MATRIX OF CONTEMPORARY SOCIAL MOVEMENTS

BRIAN HOLMES

Art into life: Is there any more persistent utopia in the history of vanguard expressions? Shedding its external forms, its inherited techniques, its specialized materials, art becomes a living gesture, rippling out across the sensible surface of humanity. It creates an ethos, a mythos, an intensely vibrant presence; it migrates from the pencil, the chisel or the brush into ways of doing and modes of being. From the German Romantics to the Beatnik poets, from the Dadaists to the Living Theater, this story has been told again and again, each time with a startling twist on the same underlying phrase. At stake is more than the search for stylistic renewal: it's about transforming your everyday existence.

Theory into revolution: The fundamental demand of the thinkers and rioters of May '68 was also "change life" (*changer la vie*). But from a revolutionary viewpoint, the consequences of intimate desire should be economic and structural. Situationist theory had no meaning without immediate communization. "Marx, Mao, Marcuse" was a slogan for the streets. The self-overcoming of art was understood as just one part of a program to vanquish class divides, transform labor relations and put alienated individuals back in touch with one another.

The '60s were full of wild fantasies and unrealized potentials; yet significant experiments were undertaken, with consequences extending up to the present. Campus radicalism gave new life to educational alternatives, resulting in large-scale initiatives like the University Without Walls in the United States or the Open University in Britain. The counter-cultural use of hand-held video cameras led to radical media projects like Paper Tiger Television, Deep Dish TV and Indymedia. Politics itself went through a metamorphosis: autonomous Marxism gave rise to self-organized projects all across Europe, while affinity groups based on Quaker conceptions of direct democracy took deep root in the USA, structuring the anti-nuclear movement, becoming professionalized in the NGOs of the '80s, then surging back at full anarchist force in Seattle. From the AIDS movements onwards, activism regained urgency and seriousness, grappling with concrete and progressively more complex issues such as globalization and climate change. Yet society still tends to absorb the transformations, to neutralize the inventions. The question is not how to aestheticize "living as form," in order to display the results for contemplation in a museum. The question is how to change the forms in which we are living.

Social movements are vehicles for this metamorphosis. At times they generate historic events, like the occupation of public squares that unfolded across the world in 2011. Through the stoppage of "business as usual" they alter life-paths, shift labor routines and career horizons along with laws and governments, and contribute to long-lasting philosophical and affective transfigurations. Yet despite their historic dimensions, the sources of social movements are intimate, aspirational: they grow out of small groups, they crystallize around what Guattari called "non-discursive, pathic knowledge."[1] Their capacity for sparking change is widely coveted in our era. Micro-movements in the form of trends, fashions and crazes are continually ignited, channeled and fueled by PR strategists, in order to instrumentalize the upwelling of social desire. Still grassroots groups, vanguard projects and intentional communities continue to take their own lives as raw material, inventing alternate futures and hoping to generate models, possibilities and tools for others.

Absorbing all this historical experience, social movements have expanded to include at least four dimensions. Critical research is fundamental to today's movements, which are always at grips with complex legal, scientific and economic problems. Participatory art is vital to any group taking its issues to the streets, because it stresses a commitment to both representation and lived experience. Networked communications and strategies of mass-media penetration are another characteristic of contemporary movements, because ideas and directly embodied struggles just disappear without a megaphone. Finally, social movement politics consists in the collaborative coordination or "self-organization"

of this whole set of practices, gathering forces, orchestrating efforts and helping to unleash events and to deal with their consequences. These different strands interweave, condense into gestures and events, then disperse again, creating the dynamics of the movement. A fourfold matrix replaces any single, easily definable initiative.

No doubt the complexity of this fourfold process explains the rarity of effective interventionism. But that's the challenge of political engagement. What has to be grasped, if we want to renew our democratic culture, is the convergence of art, theory, media and politics into a mobile force that oversteps the limits of any professional sphere or disciplinary field, while still drawing on their knowledge and technical capacities. This essay tries to develop a concept for the fourfold matrix of contem-

porary social movements. The name I propose for it is *eventwork*.

But wait a minute—if we're talking grassroots activism, why insist on complexity? Why even mention the disciplines and the professions? The reason is that the grassroots has gone urban and suburban and rurban, and it's *us*: the precarious middle-class subjects of contemporary capitalist societies, which are based on knowledge, technology and communication. Our disciplines create these societies. Our professions seem only able to maintain them as they are. The point is to explore how we can *act*, and what role art, theory, media and self-organization can have in effective forms of intervention.

Like the sociologist Ulrich Beck in his book *The Risk Society*, I think the movement outside the modernist institutions has been made necessary by the failure of those institutions to respond to the dangers created by modernization itself.[2] The dangers of modernization grew clearer at the close of the postwar period, when the Keynesian-Fordist mode of capitalist development revealed its inherent links with inequality, war, ecological destruction and the repression of minorities. It became apparent that not only "hard" science, but also the social sciences and humanities were helping to produce the problems; yet nothing in their internal criteria of truth or legitimacy or professional success could restrain them. The most conscious and articulate exponents of each of the separated disciplines then felt the need to develop a critique of their own field, and to merge that critique into an attempt at social transformation. Only in this way could they find an immanent response to the sources of their own alienation.[3]

So there is a paradox of eventwork: it starts from within the disciplines whose limits it seeks to overcome. In this text I'll start with the internal contradictions of avant-garde art in the late '60s, and with the attempt by one group of Latin American artists to go beyond them. With that narrative as a backdrop, I'll sketch out the emergence of an expanded realm of activism in the post-Fordist era, from the '70s up to now. The aim is to discover some basic ideas that could change the way each of us conceives the relations between our daily life, our politics, and our discipline or profession.

In this movement, certain truisms will run up against their shortfalls. What I want to make clear is that despite their rhetorical attractions, the twin formulas of "art into life" and "theory into revolution" are too simplistic to describe the pathways that lead people beyond their professional and institutional limits. The failure to describe those paths with the right mix of urgency and complexity leads to the bromides of "relational art" (intimacy on display in a sterile white cube) or the radical chic of "critical theory" (revolution for sale in an academic bookstore). Through their weakness and emptiness, these failures of cultural critique provoke reactionary calls for a return to the modernist disciplines (as when we are enjoined to restrict artistic practice to some version of "pure form"). The result is a disjunction from the present and a lingering state of collective paralysis: which is the most striking characteristic of left politics today, at least in the United States.

As living conditions deteriorate in the capitalist democracies, one pressing question is how artists, intellectuals, media makers and political organizers can come together to help change the course of collective existence. The answer lies in a move across institutional boundaries and modernist norms. Each of the separated disciplines needs to define the paradox of eventwork—and thereby open up a place for itself, beyond itself, in the fourfold matrix of contemporary social movements.

HISTORY

Let's go straight to the most impressive example of eventwork in the late '60s, which unfolds not in New York or London or Paris, but in Argentina. This was the moment of the country's industrial take-off, when an expanding middle class enjoyed close links to cultural developments in the metropolitan centers. In capitalist societies, utopian longings often accompany periods of economic growth: because the abundance of material and symbolic production promises real use values. But since mid-1966 Argentina was under the grip of a military dictatorship, which repressed individual freedoms and imposed brutal programs of economic rationalization. Under these conditions, a circle of self-consciously "vanguard" artists in Buenos Aires and Rosario began to sense the futility of the rapid cycles of formal innovation that had marked the decade of pop, op, happenings, minimalism, performance and conceptualism. They became keenly aware that inventions designed to shatter bourgeois norms were being used as signs of prestige and intellectual superiority by the elites, to the point where, as León Ferrari wrote, "the culture created by the artist becomes his enemy."[4] Therefore, these artists began an increasingly violent break with the gallery and museum circuits that had formerly sustained their practices, using transgressive works, actions and declarations to curtail their own participation in officially sanctioned shows.

By mid-summer of 1968 they decided to organize an independent congress, the "First National Meeting on Avant-Garde Art." The goal was to define their autonomy from the elite cultural system, to formulate their social ideal—a Guevarist revolution—and to plan the realization of a work that would embody their aims.[5] In this work, the aesthetic material, as Ferrari explained, would no longer be articulated according to formal innovations, but instead with clearly referential and immediately graspable "meanings" (*significados*) which themselves would be subjected to transgressive profanation, in order to generate a powerful denunciation of existing social conditions. Echoing Ferrari's approach in the language of semiotics and information theory, another contributor to the meeting, Nicolás Rosa, insisted that "the work is experimental when it proceeds to the *rupture of the cultural model*." This rupture was, to be frank, direct and irreversible, enacted in a visual, verbal and gestural language that would allow anyone to participate. It would also be disseminated in the mass media. Situated outside the elite institutions and linked to the social context of its realization, the work would "produce an effect similar to that of political action," in the words of the artist Juan Pablo Renzi, who had drafted the framing text for the meeting. And because "ideological statements are easily absorbed," Renzi continued, the revolutionary work "transforms the ideology into a real event from within its own structure." Such was the theoretical program that led to *Tucumán Arde*, or "Tucumán is Burning."

What was meant by the title? The group sought to denounce the process of restructuring that had been imposed on the sugar industry in the province of Tucumán, resulting in widespread unemployment and hunger for the workers. Beyond Tucumán itself, they wanted to reveal the larger program of economic rationalization being carried by the national bourgeoisie under dictatorial command, in line with US and European interests. To do so would require

the production of "counter-information" on the strictly semiotic level, using factual analysis to oppose the government propaganda campaign that surrounded the restructuring. So the artists collaborated with students, professors, filmmakers, photographers, journalists and a left-wing union, engaging in a covert fact-finding mission which they disguised as a traditional cultural project. In the course of two trips they visited fields and factories, circulated questionnaires, interviewed, filmed and photographed workers and their families, putting their preliminary analysis to the test of experience. This on-site research was the first phase of the project, culminating in a press conference where they ripped the veil from their activities and explained the real purpose of their work, hoping—in vain, as it turned out—to raise a scandal and push their messages out into the mass media.

An effective denunciation would also require the production of what the artists called an "over-informational circuit" (*circuito sobreinformacional*) which would operate on the perceptual level, in order to overcome the persuasive power of the official propaganda both quantitatively and qualitatively.[6] For the second phase they formulated a multilayered exhibition strategy, beginning with teaser campaigns that introduced potential publics to the words "Tucumán" and "Tucumán Arde" through posters, playbills, cinema screens and graffiti interventions. They then created two multimedia exhibitions in union halls in Rosario and Buenos Aires, attempting in both cases to use not a single room but the entire building. They deployed press clippings and images from the government propaganda campaign and contrasted these to economic and public-health statistics as well as diagrams indicating the links between industrial interests, local and national officials and foreign capital. They displayed documentary photographs, projected films, delivered speeches and circulated a critical study prepared by the collaborating sociologists. At roughly half-hour intervals the lights were cut, dramatizing the kinds of infrastructural failures that were typically endured by people in the provinces. Bitter coffee was

Opposite: The exhibition, titled both "Tucumán Arde" and "First Avant Garde Art Biennial," took place in the CGT union in Rosario, Argentina, and had an opening night attendance of more than 1,000 people. To market the exhibition, the collective used street publicity in the form of graffiti and posters with the simple slogan "Tucumán Arde." (Courtesy Graciela Carnevale)

served to give the public a taste of the hunger affecting a cane-growing region where food, and sugar itself, was in chronically short supply.

The exhibition strategy was a success. The opening in Rosario on November 3 attracted over a thousand people on the first night, resulting in a prolongation of the show for two weeks instead of one. It was restaged in Buenos Aires on November 25, this time including the covertly produced "Third Cinema" film, *La Hora de los Hornos* (The Hour of the Furnaces, 1968), by Octavio Getino and Fernando Solanas, whose projection was halted every half hour for immediate discussion. The level of courage implied by this process, under conditions of military rule, is difficult to imagine. The show in Buenos Aires was censored on its second day by threats against the union, exposing the repressive character of the regime and inviting a further radicalization of the country's cultural producers.

Because of its collective organization, its experimental nature, its investigatory process, its tight articulation of analytic and aesthetic means, its oppositional stance and its untimely closure, *Tucumán Arde* has become something of a myth in Argentina and abroad. The American critic Lucy Lippard, who would later be active in the Art Workers Coalition, repeatedly claimed that she had been radicalized by her meeting with members of the group on a visit to Argentina in October 1968.[7] The French journal *Robho* devoted a dossier to the work in 1971, emphasizing its break with bourgeois art and its revolutionary potentials. In its more recent reception, which has included a large number of shows and articles from the late 1990s on, the project has been linked to "global conceptualism," and to an interventionist form of media art based on semiotic analysis.[8] This attention from the museum world testifies to an intense public interest in a process that emphasized common speech, direct action and a break with bourgeois cultural forms. But that same attention opens up the questions of absorption, banalization, neutralization. In the most thoroughly documented analysis, the Argentine art historian

Ana Longoni vindicates the aims of the project by asking the obvious disciplinary question: "Where's the vanguard art in *Tucumán Arde*?" She responds: "If *Tucumán Arde* can be confused with a political act, it is because it *was* a political act. The artists had realized a work that extended the limits of art to zones that did not correspond, that were external."[9]

So what was achieved by the move to these zones external to art? At a time when institutional channels were blocked and the modernizing process had become a dictatorial nightmare, the project was able to orchestrate the efforts of a broad division of cultural labor, capable of analyzing complex social phenomena. It then disseminated the results of this labor through the expressive practices of an event, in order to produce awareness and contribute to active resistance. What results is a change in the finality, or indeed the use-value, of cultural production. As one statement indicates, the project was conceived "to help make possible the creation of an *alternative culture* that can form part of the revolutionary process."[10] Or as the *Robho* dossier put it: "The extra imagination found in *Tucumán Arde*, if compared for example to the usual agitation campaign, comes expressly from a practice of, and a preliminary reflection on, the notions of event, participation and proliferation of the aesthetic experience."[11] That's a perfect definition of eventwork.

Its effectiveness comes from a perceptual, analytic and expressive collaboration, which lends an affective charge to the interpretation of a real-world situation. Such work is capable of touching people, of involving them, not through a retreat to the exalted dreamland of a white cube, but instead within the everyday complexity of life in a technocratic society, where the most elusive possibility is that of shared resistance to the vast, encroaching programs of government and industry. My question is how to extend that resistance into the present, how to make it last past each singular event. Graciela Carnevale, who preserved this archive of materials at great risk throughout the Videla dictatorship, said this to me in a conversation: "There is always a great difficulty in how to transmit this experience or make it perceptible, beyond the information about it."[12] Her dilemma is that of everyone who has been involved in a significant social movement: "How to share an experience that produced such great transformations in oneself?"

ACTUALITY

The four vectors of eventwork converge into action beneath the pressure of injustice and the anguishing awareness of risk, in situations where your own discipline, profession or institution proves incapable of responding, so that some other course of action must be taken. "I don't know what to do but I'm gonna do it," as my comrades in the Ne Pas Plier collective used to say. Activism is the making-common of a desire and a resolve to change the forms of living, under uncertain conditions, without any guarantees. When this desire and resolve can be shared, the intensive assemblage of a social movement brings both the agonistic and the utopian dimension into daily experience, into leisure hours, passionate relations, the home, the bed, your dreams. It brings public responsibility into private passion. That's living as political form.

Of course it's not supposed to be that way in modern society, where an institution exists, in theory at least, to address every need or problem. Experts manage risks on government time; artists produce the highest sublimations of entertainment; the media respond faithfully to popular demands for information; and social movements are the disciplined actions of organized laborers seeking higher wages, all beneath the watchful eye of professional politicians. That's the theory, anyway. This functional division of industrial society reached its peak of democratic legitimacy in the decades after WWII, when the Keynesian-Fordist welfare state claimed to achieve stable growth, income equality and social benefits for an expanding "middle class," which included unionized factory laborers alongside a broad range of university-trained technicians, service providers and managers. What revealed itself in 1968 and afterwards, however, was not just the inability of the industrial state to go on delivering the goods for that expanding middle class. What revealed itself, with particular intensity inside the educational and cultural circuits made possible by economic growth, was a shared awareness that the theory doesn't work, and that despite its supposedly corrective institutions, capitalist modernization itself produces conditions of gendered and racialized exploitation, neocolonial expropriation, mental and emotional manipulation and ever-worsening environmental pollution.

The sense of a threat lodged within the utopian promises of Keynesian social democracy and Fordist industrial modernization was a major motivator for the emergence of the so-called "new social movements," which could not be reduced to workplace bargaining demands and which could not be adequately conceived within the frameworks of traditional class analysis. In these movements, to the dismay of an older and more doctrinaire political generation, issues of alienation and therefore of identity began coming ineluctably to the fore.[13] The people involved in the civil rights and antiwar campaigns, and then in a far wider range of struggles, had to bring new causes, arenas and strategies of action into some kind of alignment with thorny questions of perception knowledge, communication, motivation, identity, trust, and even self-analysis, all of which became only more acute as immediate material necessity receded in the consumer societies. Artistic expression now appeared as a necessarily ambiguous mediator between personal conviction and public representation. The intersections of theory and daily life became more dense and entangled, with the result that each movement, or even each campaign, turned into something original and surprising, the momentary public crystallization of a singular group process. The simultaneous inadequacy and necessity of this way of doing politics has come to define the entire period of post-Fordism: it is *our* actuality, our present tense, at least from a progressive-left perspective. If an intervention like *Tucumán Arde* can still appear familiar, in its modes of organization and operation if not in its ideologies and revolutionary horizons, it's because the basic sets of objective and subjective problems underlying it are still very much with us today.

The similarities and the differences will come into focus if we think back on one of the most influential social movements of the post-Fordist period, which is AIDS activism. I wasn't part of that movement and I can't bear witness to its intensities. But what's impressive from a distance is the collective reaction to a situation of extreme risk, where the issue is not so much the technical capacity as the *willingness* of a democratic society to respond to dangers that weigh disproportionately on stigmatized minorities. Rather than widespread police and military repression, as under a dictatorship, it is the perception of an intimate threat that lays the basis for militant action. A totalizing ideological framework like Marxism can no longer be counted on to structure this perception. Instead, subjectivity and daily experience become crucial. The questions of who you are, who others think you are, what rights you are accorded and what rights you are ready to demand, are all life or death issues, felt and spontaneously expressed before being formulated and represented. A recent book called *Moving Politics* makes clear how much these affective dimensions mattered, after a threshold of indignation had been crossed and grief could be transformed into anger.[14] At the micro level, the "event" could be a glance or a tear in private, a gesture or a speech in a meeting, no less than a public action or a media intervention. All these are ways to elicit and modulate affects, which mobilize activist groups while exerting a powerful force on others, whether friends or strangers, elected officials or anonymous spectators.

Yet indignation and rage, along with solidarity and love for fellow human beings, can only be the immediate foundations of a social movement. Critical research, symbolic expression, media and self-organization were the operative vectors for AIDS activism, just as they had been for a vanguard project like *Tucumán Arde*. At first the issues themselves had to be defined, and they were highly complex, involving the social rights to fund or instigate certain lines of research, to legalize or

ingest certain kinds of medications, to receive or dispense certain kinds of publicly supported care. Scientific and legal investigations, often performed by AIDS sufferers, were an essential part of this effort.[15] At the same time it became apparent that the rights to treatment and care were dependent not only on scientific and legal arguments, but also on the ways that risk groups were represented in the media, and on the ways that politicians monitored, solicited or encouraged those representations, so as to advance their own policies and ensure their own re-election.[16] The struggle had to be brought into the fields of education and cultural production, whose influence on the structures of feeling and belief should not be underestimated. But at the same time, it had to reach into the mass media. This breakthrough to the media required the staging of striking events on the ground, often with resources borrowed from visual art and performance. And all that entailed the coordination of a far-flung division of labor under more-or-less anarchic conditions, where there could be no director, no hierarchy, no flow chart, etc. To give some insight into this complex interweave of AIDS activism, I'd like to quote the art critic and activist Douglas Crimp, in an interview with Tina Takemoto:

> *Crimp:* Within ACT UP, there was a sophistication about the uses of representation for activist politics. This awareness came not only from people who knew art theory but also from people who worked in public relations, design, and advertising... So ACT UP was a weird hybrid of traditional leftist politics, innovative postmodern theory, and access to professional resources... One of the most emblematic images associated with ACT UP was the SILENCE=DEATH logo, composed of a simple pink triangle on a black background with white sans serif type. This image was created by a group of gay designers who organized the Silence=Death Project before ACT UP even started. Although they didn't

design the logo for ACT UP, they lent it to the movement, and it was used on T-shirts as an official emblem.[17]

Here again, what lends resonance to the event is the difference of the people involved, and therefore of the techniques and knowledges they are able to bring to bear, whenever they find the inspiration or the need or the courage to overstep their disciplinary boundaries and start to work at odds with the dominant functions. That all of this should only become possible under the menace of illness and the direct threat of death is, I think, of the essence: it's not something one should avoid or shirk away from. Social movements arise and spread in the face of existential threats. What's at issue then, in our blinkered and controlled and self-satisfied societies, is the perception of a threat and the modulation of affect in the face of it—or in other words, the way you rupture a cultural pattern, the way you motivate yourself and others to undertake a course of action. This paradoxical figure of a social solidarity founded on an experience of rupture brings us

back to the larger, trans-generational question of eventwork, exactly as Graciela Carnevale expressed it: "How to share an experience that produced such great transformations in oneself?"

Speaking from my own experience, I've also participated in a large movement, or really a constellation of social movements, the global justice movements opposing financially driven globalization. Starting around 1994 they arose across the earth: in Mexico, India, France, Britain, the US, etc. From the beginning these movements interacted very extensively, first through labor, NGO and anarchist networks, then in counter-summits mounted in the face of the transnational institutions such as the WTO and the IMF, then through the veritable popular universities constituted by the World Social Forums. The people I worked with, mainly in Europe but also in the Americas, were able to twist or subvert some of the utopian energies of the Internet boom, combining them with labor struggles, ecological movements and indigenous demands to create a political response to corporate global-

Above: Members of Philadelphia's chapter of ACT UP protest about the global AIDS epidemic at the U.N. in April 2011 (Photograph by Kaytee Riek).

ization. In the course of these movements, the relations between critical and philosophical investigation, artistic processes, direct action and tactical media opened up a vast new field of practice, more vital than anything I had previously known. The Argentine insurrection of December 2001 was a culminating moment of this global cycle of struggles; and for those involved with art, not only the history but also the actuality of social movements in Argentina seemed to confirm the idea that aesthetic activity could be placed into a new framework, one that was no longer freighted with the strict separations of the modernist institutions.[18] All this convinced me that contemporary art in its most challenging and experimental forms has indeed been suffering from the "cultural confinement" that Robert Smithson diagnosed long ago, and that its real possibilities unfold on more engaging terrains, whose access has mostly been foreclosed by the institutional frameworks of museums, galleries, magazines, university departments, etc.[19] The concept of eventwork is based directly on these experiences with contemporary social movements, which have generated important cooperative and communicational capacities and helped to revitalize left political culture.

It's obvious, however, that the global justice movements were not able to overturn the ruling consensus on capitalist development and economic growth. In fact the recent financial crisis has both vindicated the arguments we began making as much as fifteen years ago, and also shown those arguments to be politically powerless, incapable of contributing to any concrete change. A similar verdict was delivered to environmental activists by the debacle of the Copenhagen climate summit.

All of that fits into a larger pattern. If I had to offer a one-sentence version of what I've learned about society since 1994, it might go like this: "The entire edifice of speculative, computer-managed, gentrifying, militarized, over-polluted, just-in-time, debt-driven neo-liberal globalization has taken form, since the early '80s, as a way to block the institutional changes that were first set into motion by the new social movements of the '60s-'70s."

In other words, cultural confinement does not just affect experimental art, as Smithson seems to have believed. Instead it applies to all egalitarian, emancipatory and ecological aspirations in the post-Fordist period, which now reveals itself to be a period of pure crisis management, one that has not produced any fundamental solutions to the problems of industrial modernization, but has only exported them across the earth. Yet those problems are serious, they have accumulated on every level. What's the use of aesthetics if you don't have eyes to see? It would not be a metaphor to say that the United States, in particular, has been living on credit since the outset of the post-Fordist period; and now, slowly but inexorably, the bill is coming due.

PERSPECTIVES

The question I've tried to raise is this: how do cultural practices become political acts? Or to put it more sharply: how does the operative force of a cultural activity, or indeed of a discipline, somehow break through the normative and legal limits imposed by a profession? How to create an institutional context that offers a chance of mutual recognition and validation for people attempting to give their particular skills and practices a broader meaning and a greater effectiveness?

These questions can be framed, in an inversing mirror, by an image from the wave of protest that swept over the state of Wisconsin in the face of Governor Scott Walker's ultimately successful bid to impose an austerity plan that includes an end to the right of collective bargaining. The image is a protest snap from someone's digital camera, reproduced widely on the web.[20] It shows a middle-class white woman standing in front of an American flag, next to a Beaux-Arts statue. She holds a sign in her hands that says in bold capital letters:

I AM NOT REPLACEABLE
I AM PROFESSIONAL

Who is this woman? An artist? A curator? An art historian? A cultural critic? Why does she proclaim her security in this way? Does

Opposite: The 2011 World Social Forum took place in Dakar, Senegal from February 6-11, and had 75,000 participants from 132 countries. The World Social Forum is an annual meeting of civil society organizations opposed to globalization. (Photographs by Manoel Santos)

she still have a job? Does she still have rights? And how about ourselves? Where do our rights come from? How are they maintained? How are they produced?

It seems to me that in the United States right now, as in other countries, there is a rising feeling of existential threat. Endless warfare, invasive surveillance, economic precariousness, intensified exploitation of the environment, increasing corruption: all these mark the entry into an era of global tension whose like has not been seen since the 1930s. As economic collapse continues and climate change becomes more acute, these dangers will become far more concrete; and we urgently need to prepare for the moments when adherence to a social movement becomes inevitable. Yet it appears that laws, ethical codes and the requirements of professionalism in all-absorbing, highly competitive careers, still make it impossible for most Americans to find the time, the place, the medium, the format, the desire and above all the collective will that would help them to resist the threats. This reminds us of what Thoreau taught in his time, namely that being a citizen of a democratic country means always being on the edge of starting a revolution. Something about our forms of living and working has to change, not just aesthetically and not just in theory, but pragmatically, in terms of the kinds of activity and their modes of organization.[21] Or as Doug Ashford once put it, "Civil disobedience is an art history, too."[22]

This essay was written in the summer of 2011, while major social movements continued to unfold across Europe and the Middle East, and a dead calm weighed on the U.S. As we go to press, the game has changed. Hundreds of thousands of people across the country have taken to the streets, set up encampments in public squares, and are activating all the social, intellectual, and cultural resources at their disposal in order to carry out a deep and searching critique of inequality. Alongside organizers, researchers, and media activists, artists have played a role, which continues to expand as more people overstep the boundaries of their disciplinary identities. Social movements come

in great waves, generating unpredictable consequences: no one knows what this one will leave behind. But the inspiration of Wisconsin has been fulfilled and its paradoxes have been overcome. Floating above crowds across the country, a very different sign could be seen, pointing to what now appears to be a precarious destiny:

LOST A JOB, FOUND AN OCCUPATION

ENDNOTES

1   Félix Guattari, *Chaosmosis: an Ethico-Aesthetic Paradigm* (Indiana University Press, 1995): 25.

2   Ulrich Beck, *Risk Society: Towards a New Modernity* (London: Sage, 1992, 1st German edition 1986).

3   The most striking example of this self-critique in the social sciences is the reaction of anthropologists to their discipline's participation in the Vietnam War; see for example Dell Hymes, ed., *Reinventing Anthropology* (New York: Random House, 1972).

4   León Ferrari, "The Art of Meanings" (1968) in Inés Katzenstein, ed., *Listen Here Now! Argentine Art of the 1960s: Writings of the Avante-Garde* (New York: MoMA, 2004): 312.

5   Four typescripts of texts delivered at this meeting are preserved in the archive of Graciela Carnevale; they are the sorces for this paragraph. Three of them (including the one by León Ferrari quoted above) are translated in *Listen Here Now!* ibid.: 306–18; the fourth, by Nicolás Rosa, is reproduced in Spanish in Ana Longoni and Mariano Mestman, *Del Di Tella a "Tucumán Arde": Vanguardia artística y política en el 68 argentino* (Buenos Aires: Eudeba, 2008): 174–78.

6   See María Teresa Gramuglio and Nicolás Rosa, "Tucumán Arde" (1968), declaration circulated at the Rosario exhibition, reproduced in *Del Di Tella a Tucumán Arde*, ibid.: 233–35. The text is translated under the title "Tucuman Burns" in Alexander Alberro and Blake Stimson, eds., *Conceptual Art: A Critical Anthology* (Cambridge, Mass.: MIT Press, 1999): 76–79; but *circuito sobreinformacional* is rendered as "informational circuit," losing a crucial emphasis.

7   Concerning Lippard's visit to Argentina and her declarations, see Julia Bryan-Wilson, *Art Workers: Radical Practice in the Vietnam War Era* (Berkeley: University of California Press, 2009): 132–38.

8   See Mari Carmen Ramírez, "Tactics for Thriving on Adversity: Conceptualism in Latin America, 1960–1980," in Luis Camnitzer, Jane Farver and Rachel Weiss, eds., *Global Conceptualism: Points of Origin: 1950s–1980s*, (New York: Queens Museum of Modern Art, 1999) and Alex Alberro, "A Media Art: Conceptual Art in Latin America," in Michael Newman and Jon Bird, eds., *Rewriting Conceptual Art* (London: Reaktion Books, 1999). Another important book is Andrea Giunta, *Avant-Garde, Internationalism, and Politics: Argentine Art in the Sixties* (Durham: Duke University Press, 2007). Among major exhibitions featuring the archive of *Tucumán Arde* are *Global Conceptualism* (Queens, 1999) *Ex Argentina* (Berlin, 2003); *Documenta 12* (Kassel, 2007); and *Forms of Resistance* (Van Abbemuseum, Eindhoven, 2007–2008). A copy of the archive of *Tucumán Arde* has been acquired by the MacBa in Barcelona.

9   Ana Longoni and Mariano Mestman, *Del Di Tella a Tucumán Arde*: 216.

10 "Frente a los acontecimientos políticos....," unsigned document in the archive of Graciela Carnevale (2 pages), apparently a sketch for a broadside to be distributed at the Rosario exhibition.

11 "Dossier Argentine: Les fils de Marx et de Mondrian," *Robho* no. 5–6, Paris, 1971: 16.

12 Conversation with Graciela Carnevale, Rosario, Argentina, April 11, 2011.

13 For the concept of "new social movements" and a review of the most prominent theories about them, see Donatella della Porta and Mario Diani, *Social Movements: An Introduction*, 2d edition (London: Blackwell, 2006): chap. 1.

14 Deborah B. Gould, *Moving Politics: Emotion and Act Up's Fight against AIDS* (Chicago: University of Chicago Press, 2009).

15 See Steven Epstein, *Impure Science: AIDS, Activism, and the Politics of Knowledge* (Berkeley: University of California Press, 1996).

16 See Douglas Crimp, ed., *AIDS: Cultural Analysis/Cultural Activism* (Cambridge, Mass.: MIT Press, 1988).

17 Tina Takemoto, "The Melancholia of AIDS: Interview with Douglas Crimp," *Art Journal*, Vol. 62, No. 4 (Winter, 2003): 83.

18 For the role of artists in Argentine social movements, see Brian Holmes, "Remember the Present: Representations of Crisis in Argentina, in *Escape the Overcode: Artistic Activism in the Control Society* (WHW: Van Abbemuseum, Zagreb and Eindhoven, 2009); also available at http://brianholmes.wordpress.com/2007/04/28/remember-the-present. For a book that literally attempts to rewrite the history of contemporary art on the basis of Tucumán Arde, see Luis Camnitzer, *Conceptualism in Latin American Art: Didactics of Liberation* (Texas: University of Texas Press, 2007).

19 Robert Smithson, "Cultural Confinement" (1972), in Nancy Holt, ed. *The Writings of Robert Smithson* (New York: NYU Press, 1979).

20 See among many other blogs and websites, http://thepragmaticprogressive.org/wp/2011/02/19/a-letter-from-a-union-maid-in-wisconsin (accessed 07/11/11).

21 This is exactly the conclusion of Dan S. Wang and Nicolas Lampert, "Wisconsin's Lost Strike Moment," at http://www.justseeds.org/blog/2011/04/wisconsins_lost_strike_moment_1.html.

22 Doug Ashford and 36 others, *Who Cares* (New York: Creative Time Books, 2006): 29.

Opposite: Protesters gathered in Madison, Wisconsin to protest provisions of Governor Walker's Budget Repair Bill that undermine the power of public sector unions (Photograph by Richard Hurd). The Wisconsin Pro-Workers Rally occupied the Capitol Building in Madison, Wisconsin on February 19, 2011 (Photograph by Cynthia Hollenberger).

LIVING TAKES MANY FORMS

SHANNON JACKSON

"THE POWER OF THESE THEATERS SPRINGING UP THROUGHOUT THE COUNTRY LIES IN THE FACT THAT THEY KNOW WHAT THEY WANT . . . . THEY INTEND TO REMAKE A SOCIAL STRUCTURE WITHOUT THE HELP OF MONEY—AND THIS AMBITION ALONE INVESTS THEIR UNDERTAKING WITH A CERTAIN MARLOWESQUE MADNESS."[1]

This was Hallie Flanagan, director of the Federal Theatre Project (FTP), one part of the Works Progress Administration that was so central to implementing Franklin Delano Roosevelt's New Deal. She was recalling her work as the leader of a federally supported theatrical movement charged with responding to the reality of the Great Depression. The Federal Theatre Project addressed timely themes with new plays that dramatized issues of housing, the privatization of utilities, agricultural labor, unemployment, racial and religious intolerance, and more. And the FTP devised innovative theatrical forms—staging newspapers, developing montage stagecraft, and opening the same play simultaneously in several cities at once. The goal was to extend the theatrical event to foreground the systemic connectedness of the issues endured. Social and economic hardships were not singular problems but collective ones; as such, they needed a collective aesthetic. Like other Works Progress Administration (WPA) culture workers—its writers, its mural painters, its photographers—FTP artists used interdependent art forms as vehicles for reimagining the interdependency of social beings. They gave public form to public life.

As we think about the twenty years of work represented in *Living as Form*, we should also remember prior histories of socially engaged art, such as the Federal Theatre Project. To do so is to remember that now is not the first time an international financial crisis threatened to imperil the vitality of civic cultures; it is also to acknowledge that the effects of economic crises and economic prosperity vary, depending upon what global, demographic position one occupies. From Saint Petersburg, Russia to Harare, Zimbabwe, from Los Angeles, California to Glover, Vermont, booms and busts have been socially produced and differentially felt. Accordingly, artists dispersed among different global sites face unique and complex economies as they develop cultural responses to social questions around education, public welfare, urban life, immigration, environmentalism, gender and racial equity, human rights, and democratic governance. Those economies are now distinctively "mixed" in our "post-1989" era, less fueled by the Cold War's capitalism/communism opposition than by Third Way experimentation whose allegiances to public culture are as opaque and variable as its allegiances to public services.[2] As artists reflect upon these and other social transformations, they also reckon with the mixed socioeconomic models that support art itself. Artists based in Europe can still seek national arts funding, but groups such as The Mobile Academy or Free Class Frankfurt might worry about the encroachment of neoliberal models that chip away at the principles behind it. Public sector funding interfaces with other financial models. Some artists seek commissions, and others depend on royalties. Others sell documentation of socially engaged work in galleries, joining the likes of Phil Collins, Thomas Hirschhorn, Paul Chan, or Francis Alÿs whose political practices enjoy art world cachet. Still other artists such as Mierle Laderman Ukeles or Rick Lowe mobilize social sector initiatives in service of the arts, transforming after-school programs, public sanitation, or urban recovery projects into aesthetic acts. Finally, people like Josh Greene sidestep larger systemic processes, choosing to develop micro-DIY networks of shared artistic support instead. But whether you are organizing potlucks to combat the effects of Turkey's Deep State, responding to a coalition government's equivocal faith in the culture industries of the United Kingdom, or celebrating the release from social realism by speculating in China's booming art market, there is no pure position for socially engaged artmaking.

To recall the Federal Theatre Project inside of the WPA is not only to prompt reflection on changing socioeconomic contexts, but also to reflect upon the varied art forms from which social engagement springs. The WPA expanded the practice of photographers, architects, easel painters, actors, designers, dancers, and writers, and the *Living as Form* archive includes practices that measure their expansion from other art forms as well. The installations of Phil Collins sit next to the community theater of Cornerstone. The choreography of Urban Bush Women moves near the expanded photography of Ala Plástica.

But even if the WPA moment is a reminder that socially engaged work develops from a range of art traditions, the willingness to capture the heterogeneity of contemporary work is striking and unfortunately rare. Across the world, artists and institutions celebrate "hybrid" work. However, such hybrid artists still measure their distance from traditional art disciplines, and their conversations and support networks often remain circumscribed by them. In other words, expanded theater artists talk to other expanded theater artists and are presented by an international festival circuit. Post-visual artists talk to other post-visual artists and are represented in the biennial circuit and by the gallery-collector system. The habits of criticism reinforce this inertia, routinely structuring who is cast as post-Brechtian and who is cast as post-Minimalist. It is hard to find contexts that enable conversation across these networks using critical vocabularies. Certainly, the difficulty is due in part to the wide range of skills new art forms require. Not everyone knows how to design a house or produce a film. Not everyone can fabricate a three-story puppet to be graceful or inscribe African diasporic history in a simple rotation of the hips; so it makes sense when architects, videographers, puppeteers, and choreographers seek out conversations with fellow specialists. But the necessity of creating platforms that stitch together the heterogeneous project of socially engaged art remains—and continues to become increasingly urgent. Meanwhile, genuinely cross-disciplinary artists should not to have to cultivate some talents and repress others in order to conform to particular legitimating contexts. It would be nice, for instance, if Theaster Gates did not have to choose between standing in a gospel choir or sitting at his potter's wheel.

Thus, the challenge of *Living as Form* lies in its invitation to contemplate what living means in our contemporary moment, and to reckon with the many kinds of forms that help us to reflect. That challenge is itself embedded in different barometers for gauging aesthetic integrity and social efficacy. The question of art's social role has been a hallmark of Western twentieth-century aesthetic debate—whether sociality is marked by eruptions at Café Voltaire or by the activisms of 1968, whether it is called Constructivist or Situationist, realist or relational, functional or (after Adorno) "committed."[3] Russia's Chto Delat's renewal of Lenin's historic question, "What is to be done?" is both an earnest call and a gesture that renders the question an artifact by asking what "doing" could possibly mean in a twenty-first century global context. Their pursuit resonates with that of choreographer Bill T. Jones who finds himself recalibrating his sense of the role of

politics in art. "I now choose to fire back that 'political' is an exhausted term and most certainly more and more irrelevant in regard to my work. To make a work that says, 'War is bad!' is absurd. I find myself saying with growing confidence that the works that I make now are concerned with moral choice, as in, 'What is the right thing to do, particularly when we seem to have many choices and no real choice at all?'"[4]

Even if ethical and pragmatic questions of "doing" activate contemporary art, modernist legacies of thought and practice carry forward habits of enthusiasm and suspicion. Those habits determine whether work is deemed subversive or instrumentalized—whether it looks efficacious or like "the end of art." Artist groups such as Alternate Roots are quite clear in their desire to craft aesthetic solutions to social problems. Meanwhile, Hannah Hurtzig's The Mobile Academy worries more about the

Above: Workers carry sandwich boards bearing language from Bertolt Brecht's "In Praise of Dialectics" (Courtesy Chto Delat?).

ossification of goal-driven "knowledge," ironically hoping to create "a tool to find problems for already existing solutions."[5] To some, Cornerstone Theater's mission statement provides necessary inspiration: "We value art that is contemporary, community-specific, responsive, multi-lingual, innovative, challenging, and joyful. We value theater that directly reflects the audience. We value the artist in everyone."[6] To others, such a "mission" risks social prescription. These critical tussles depend upon how each receiver understands the place of art. Should art mobilize the world or continually question the reality principles behind its formation? Should art unsettle the bonds of social life or seek to bind social beings to each other? Acts of aesthetic *affirmation* coincide with equally necessary acts of aesthetic *refusal*. But as we come to terms with hybrid forms of socially engaged art, no doubt every citizen will find herself jostled between competing and often contradictory associations that celebrate and reject varied

visions of the "social." This is a matter of what we used to call "taste," a regime of sensibility that we like to pretend we have overcome. Nevertheless, our impulses to describe a work as ironic or earnest, elitist or as literal, critical or sentimental show that many of us have emotional as well as conceptual investments in certain barometers for gauging aesthetic intervention and aesthetic corruption. Such differences will also affect how each of us assesses the role of functionality, utility, and intelligibility in a socially engaged work. Jeremy Deller's reenactments in "The Battle of Orgreave" may look radically functional to some of us and curiously useless to others. On the other hand, Francis Alÿs' works may seem strangely unintelligible to one group but overly didactic to another.

Reactions to socially engaged art thus renew historic questions around the perceived autonomy and heteronomy of art, whether it should be "self-governing" or commit to governance

Above: At Mobile Academy's *Blackmarket for Useful Knowledge and Non- Knowledge No 5: Encyclopedia of Dance Gestures and Applied Movements in Humans, Animals and Matter* at Haus der Kulturen der Welt in Berlin in 2005, up to 100 experts shared their knowledge with participants in half-hour increments (Photograph by Thomas Aurin).

by "external rules." As many have argued, that opposition always cracks under pressure. Arguments in favor of aesthetic autonomy disavow their enmeshment in privatized art markets. Arguments in favor of aesthetic heteronomy backtrack when "the artist's freedom of speech" seems threatened. But as specious as the opposition is, questions of perceived aesthetic autonomy and heteronomy affect our relative tolerance for the goals, skills, and styles of different art forms. The legacy of anti-theatrical discourses in modernist art criticism offers a case in point. Many signature Minimalist gestures purportedly laid the groundwork for contemporary social engagement: for example, the turn to time-based work, the entry of the body of the artist, the explicit relation to the beholder, the avowal of the spatial and institutional conditions of production.[7] Such gestures were criticized in their time for being "theatrical," and arguably the pejorative connotations of that term linger in the many criticisms and defenses of the formal properties of social practice now. However, such a discourse was less potent for artists who actually worked in theater and other performing arts, people for whom time, bodies, space, and audience were already incorporated into the traditions of the medium. Thus, for socially engaged theater producers and choreographers, the effort was not to introduce such properties—they were already there—but to alter the conventions by which such properties were managed. It meant that time might not be narrative, that bodies might not be characters, and that space could exceed the boundaries of the proscenium. It meant that people like Augusto Boal would seek to dynamize the audience relation into a new kind of "spect-actor."[8]

If we then bring work that derives from theatrical, visual, architectural, textual, and filmic art forms under the umbrella of "socially engaged art," it seems important to register their different barometers for gauging skill, goal, style, and innovation. We might call this the "medium-specificity" of social engagement. The performing bodies of political theater may not be traditional characters, but to a sculptor, they still appear to be acting. The installation art piece may exceed the constraints of the picture frame, but to an environmental theater producer, it still appears relatively hermetic. Postdramatic theater may be non-narrative, but to a post-visual artist, it looks exceedingly referential. In other words, our enmeshment in certain art forms will affect how we perceive tradition and innovation in a work. It will also affect how we understand its social reach, its functionality, and its relative intelligibility. What reads as earnest to a Conceptual artist will look snobby to a community organizer. Heteronomous engagement in one art form looks highly autonomous to another. But the harder work comes in a willingness to think past these initial judgment calls. Who is to say that the feminist content of Suzanne Lacy's projects on rape prevents them from getting formal credit for being a "Happening"? Who is to say that there isn't a radical refusal of social convention in Cornerstone's notion that there is "an artist in everyone?" Finally, the cultural location of specific artists will influence their definitions of what qualifies as social. I am reminded of Urban Bush Women founder Jawole Willa Jo Zollar's reflections on the subject: "I don't know that I could make a work that is not about healing. What would that be about? Being? Well, you know, it's interesting, a European director said to me ... you know, your work is old-fashioned because you have this obsession with hope ... and I said, you know the values in my community that I have also internalized are that. So no, it's not about nihilism for me or this train-spotting angst. No, that's not my culture. So it can be corny to you. That's fine."[9]

Once we develop a tolerance for different ways of mixing artistic Forms, however, we can get to the inspiring work of seeing how they each address the problems and possibilities of Living. The Works Progress Administration—like other instances of public, nonprofit, and privately funded efforts at civic culture—knew something about the making of life. At a time of fiscal danger, the arts were not positioned as ornamental and expendable, but as central vehicles for reimagining the social order. Existing economic and social structures did not

remain intact, contracting and expanding with the decrease or increase in financial flows. Instead, it was a time when various social sectors underwent redefinition and engaged in significant cross-training. Sectors in the arts, health care, housing, commerce, urban planning, sanitation, education, science, and child development received joint provisions that required collaboration. It meant health policy, advanced educational policy, and cultural policy, all in the same moment. It meant that citizens were not asked to choose between supporting employment programs or supporting arts programs, as both sectors were reimagined together. In theater, journalists became playwrights, WPA laborers became actors, and public utility companies hung the lights. But this interdependent social imagining was not without its own dangers, especially when such forms of imagining were retroactively cast as politically corrupt. The statement from Hallie

Flanagan that opened this essay was quoted when she was brought before the Dies Committee who argued that her directorship of an arts-based American relief program had been, in fact, un-American. "You are quoting from this Marlowe," noted Dies Committee member Joe Starnes. "Is he a communist?"[10]

The history lesson shows the potential and peril of coordinating public forms of aesthetic inquiry. Funny how acts of citizenship suddenly become unpatriotic once under the rubric of art. In our contemporary moment, we tend to use the word "neoliberal" to describe moral regimes based on highly individuated and market-driven measures for determining value. And the ease with which the privatized financial crisis of 2008 transmogrified into a national and global distrust of public systems shows how robust the psychic as well as financial investment in neoliberalism actually is. I thus find myself emboldened by artists who

Above: For *Touch Sanitation*, Mierle Laderman Ukeles shook hands with 8,500 NYC Sanitation workers (Courtesy Ronald Feldman Fine Arts, New York).

continue to renew our understanding of what cross-sector collaboration can be, even if they also remind us that it is hard to do. Mierle Laderman Ukeles has worked across the domains of art and public sanitation for decades, but her artist-in-residence position remains unpaid. Moreover, as Rick Lowe reminds us, cross-sector collaboration means re-skilling: "I have to keep trying to allow myself the courage to do it, you know, because as we open ourselves up and look around, there are many opportunities to invest that creativity. But it's challenging. Oftentimes, as an artist, you're trespassing into different zones. … Oftentimes … I know nothing. I have to force myself and find courage to trespass. … Artists can license ourselves to explore in any way imaginable. The challenge is having the courage to carry it through."[11] It is of course in that trespassing that art makes different zones of the social available for critical reflection. Cross-sector engagement exposes and complicates our awareness of the systems and processes that coordinate and sustain social life. For my own part, this is where social art becomes rigorous, conceptual, and formal. The non-monumental gestures of such public art works address, mimic, subvert, and redefine public processes, provoking us to reflect upon what kinds of forms—be they aesthetic, social, economic, or governmental—we want to sustain a life worth living. Whether occupying an abandoned building, casting new figures as public sector workers, or rearranging the gestural gait of the street, such aesthetic projects embed and rework the infrastructures of the social. This is where the notion that living has a form gains traction. Living here is not the emptied, convivial party of the relational. Nor is it the romantically unmediated notion of "life" whose generalized spontaneity Boomers still elegize. By reminding us that living is form, these works remind us of the responsibility for creating and recreating the conditions of life. Form here is both socially urgent and a task for an aesthetic imaginary. Living does not just "happen," but is, in fact, actively produced.

In the end, the stakes of maintaining a robust and bracing public culture are too dear for us not to cultivate awareness and respect for the many ways that fellow artists contribute to the effort. Our conceptions of expanded art need to stay expansive. In *Living as Form* we find a tool to help us widen awareness. It is a tool that invites discussion of what form might mean. It is a tool that invites discussion of what living could mean—for future occupants of a world full of potential and in need of repair.

ENDNOTES
1 Roy Rosenzweig and Barbara Melosh, "Government and the Arts: Voices from the New Deal Era," *The Journal of American History* (September 1990): 596.
2 Anthony Giddens, *The Third Way: The Renewal of Social Democracy* (Cambridge, U.K.: Polity Press, 1998).
3 The secondary literature here is vast, but see, for example, RoseLee Goldberg, *Performance Art: From Futurism to the Present*, 2nd edition (New York: Thames & Hudson, 2001); Maria Gough, *The Artist as Producer: Russian Constructivism in Revolution* (Detroit: Thomson Gale, 2006); Tom McDonough, ed., *The Situationists and the City* (London: Verso, 2010). And of course, Theodor W. Adorno, *Aesthetic Theory*, Robert Hullot-Kentor, trans. (Minneapolis: University of Minnesota Press, 1998).
4 Bill T. Jones, "'Political' Work?," (October 4, 2006) at www.billtjones.org/billsblog/2006/10/political_work.htm.
5 Quoted in Bojana Cvejić, "Trickstering, Hallucinating, and Exhausting Production: The Blackmarket for Useful Knowledge and Non-Knowledge," *Knowledge in Motion*, Sabine Gehm, Pirrko Husemann, Katharina vone Wilcke, eds. (Bielefeld: Transcript Verlag, 2007): 54.
6 Cornerstone Theater, Mission and Values, http://www.cornerstonetheater.org/ (July 2011).
7 Once again, the conversation around Minimalism and theatricality is a long one, but see for instance, Michael Fried, "Art and Objecthood," *Artforum* (June 1967); James Meyer, *Minimalism: Art and Polemics in the Sixties* (New Haven: Yale University Press, 2001); Hal Foster, "The Crux of Minimalism," in *The Return of the Real* (Cambridge, Mass.: MIT Press, 1996).
8 Augusto Boal, *Theater of the Oppressed*. Charles A. and Maria-Odilia Leal McBrid, trans. (New York: Theatre Communications Group, 1985).
9 Jawole Willa Jo Zollar quoted in Nadine George-Graves, *Urban Bush Women: Twenty Years of African American Dance Theater, Community Engagement, and Working it Out*, (Madison: University of Wisconsin Press, 2010): 204.
10 This story is oft-recounted. See, for instance, Roy Rosenzweig and Barbara Melosh, "Government and the Arts: Voices from the New Deal Era," *The Journal of American History* (September 1990): 596; Ted Morgan, *Reds: McCarthyism in Twentieth-Century America* (New York: Random House, 2003): 198.
11 Greg Sholette, "Activism as Art: Shotgun Shacks Saved Through Art-Based Revitalization: Interview with Rick Lowe," *Huffington Post* (November 22, 2010).

PROJECTS

AI WEIWEI
FAIRYTALE: 1,001 CHINESE VISITORS
2007

For his contribution to Documenta 12 in Kassel, Germany, artist Ai Weiwei brought to town 1,001 residents of China during the well-known art fair. With $4.14 million from funding sources such as Documenta's sponsors, three Swiss foundations, as well as the German Ministry of Foreign Affairs, Ai arranged all aspects of travel. He paid for airfare, processed visa applications, refurbished an old textile mill into a temporary hostel, transported Chinese chefs to cook meals, designed travel items such as clothing and luggage, and organized tours of Kassel's landmarks. He also installed 1,001 antique chairs throughout the exhibition pavilion to represent the Chinese participants' presence in Kassel. His visitors acted as both tourists and subjects of his art—viewers of a foreign culture, as well as signs of another.

Within three days of advertising the free trip on his blog, Ai received 3,000 applications. He privileged those with limited resources or travel restrictions; for example, women from a farming village, who lacked proper identity cards, were able to obtain government-issued travel documents for the first time. Other participants included laid-off workers, police officers, children, street vendors, students, farmers, and artists. They arrived *en masse*. However, Ai solicited their individual voices through filmed interviews with each traveler, and also a lengthy questionnaire—99 questions—that focused on personal histories, desires, and fantasies.

Kassel is best known as home to the Brothers Grimm, famed collectors of fables from the region. Ai named his project *Fairytale* in reference to their tales, and as a nod to the spirit of the trip, which likely felt mythical to many of the tourists, who had perhaps never before dreamed of leaving China.

Top to bottom: Video stills from Ai's *Fairytale* show the Chinese visitors partaking in Documenta 12 (Courtesy Ai Weiwei).

when a group of 1001 Chinese arrive in
a city with a population of 220,000.

ALA PLÁSTICA
MAGDALENA OIL SPILL
1999–2003

A month after a Shell Oil tank and a German ship collided in Argentina's Rio de la Plata, artists Silvina Babich and Alejandro Meitin began walking along the damaged coast, photographing stained, drenched birds, and pools of indigo liquid collected in buckets and marshes along the riverbank. Over 5,300 tons of oil spilled into the fresh water estuary, which is close to the town Magdelena and the Parque Costero del Sur, a wildlife refuge considered a biosphere reserve by UNESCO. Babich and Meitin collaborate under the name Ala Plástica; working together as environmental activists, they produced photographs, notes, and other documentation—from satellite imagery to maps—to build a case for both repair to the ecosystem and reparations to the community. "We [wanted to] reclaim the strip of land Shell was trying to close down," says Meitin, an artist and lawyer, "and inform people about what was really happening in that place."

Since 1991, Ala Plástica has worked with artists, environmentalists, government agencies, and scientists to study rivers in Argentina. For this project, the group organized a team of researchers that included *junqueros* (reed harvesters), scientists, naturalists, journalists, activists, and other artists to weigh in on the impact, prescribe solutions for aggressive clean-up measures, and present their findings in local and global forums. In 2002, in collaboration with other lobbying groups such as Friends of the Earth and Global Community Monitor, they co-wrote "Failing the Challenge, The Other Shell Report," and presented it to Annual Shareholders Assembly of the company in London. In that same year, the country's Supreme Court ruled in favor of a $35 million cleanup of the river's coastline.

Above: This image, *Last Reed Harvest*, documents the impacts of the oil spill on the human and natural communities of Magdalena, Argentina (Photograph by Rafael Santos).

Top to bottom: Reed harvesters speak to members of the community in Magdalena about the Shell oil spill (Photograph by Thomas Minich). The group surveys damage along Rio de la Plata's coastline caused by the Shell oil spill (Photograph by Fernando Massobrio).

UNIVERSITY OF WINCHESTER
LIBRARY

JENNIFER ALLORA AND GUILLERMO CALZADILLA
TIZA (LIMA)
1998–2006

Jennifer Allora and Guillermo Calzadilla placed twelve five-foot columns of chalk in public squares in Lima, Paris, and New York, ephemeral public monuments that would crumble and dissolve over time into smaller pieces and pools of liquid. The artists then invited people to use the fallen pieces of chalk to write messages on the ground, doodle, or express themselves in any fashion they chose, thereby transforming the material decay into a fleeting opportunity for creative expression. In Lima, Allora and Calzadilla placed the chalk columns directly in front of government offices, which incited passersby to convert the ad-jacent ground into a large, makeshift blackboard overflowing with messages intended to critique the state. This activity evolved into an impromptu, peaceful protest as people gathered in the square, waving banners and hoisting posters above their heads. Eventually, military officers, who were standing by in shields and helmets, confiscated the chalk, and washed away the incendiary political statements.

Puerto Rico-based Allora and Calzadilla represented the United States in this year's Venice Biennale—the first performance artists, and artist collaborative, to do so. Since the late 1990s, the artists have often explored the act of mark making, and the ways in which temporary actions can yield permanent effects. For their *Land Mark* series, the artists worked with activists on the Puerto Rican island Viesques to consider how land is marked, literally and figuratively, and by whom. For decades, the U.S. military practiced bombing and tested chemical warfare technologies in the area, while protesters would break into the range to disrupt activity. Allora and Calzadilla provided them with rubber shoes that would imprint the ground as they ran across the range, thereby leaving behind a reminder of their fleeting act of civil disobedience.

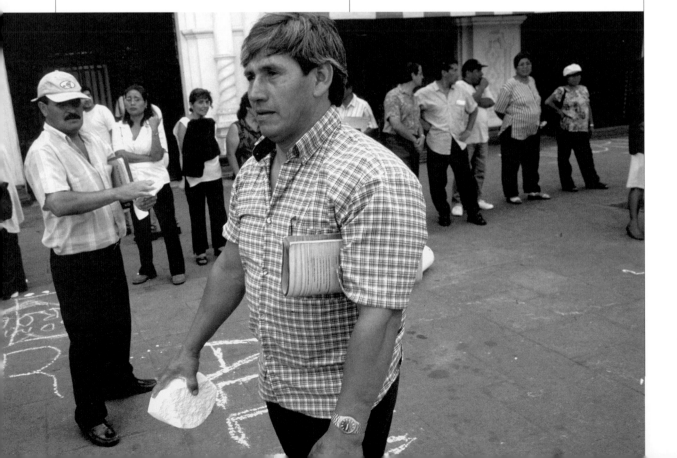

Opposite: As the chalk columns crumbled, participants wrote messages on the nearby pavement (Courtesy Jennifer Allora and Guillermo Calzadilla).

Clockwise from top left: Protesters gather outside the Peruvian Municipal Palace of Lima. Participants write messages in chalk in the Plaza de Armas in Lima. Many of the messages criticized the Peruvian government, and were later washed away by military officers. (Courtesy Jennifer Allora and Guillermo Calzadilla)

LARA ALMARCEGUI AND BEGOÑA MOVELLÁN
HOTEL FUENTES DE EBRO
1997

A national highway runs through Fuentes de Ebro, yet the small, Spanish village rarely receives visitors. In order to draw attention to the area, Lara Almarcegui and Begoña Movellán converted the local train station, which had been abandoned for 20 years, into a free hotel for one week. "The town is not beautiful, and not the kind of village people would likely visit," Almarcegui says. "So, I thought it would be a kind of extreme gesture to propose that people spend a week there."

She used $400 from a small grant to renovate the concrete, two-story building, which—with high ceilings and tiled flooring—was an apt candidate for use as a hotel. Almacegui and Movellán painted the interior walls, brought in furniture donated by the town's residents, installed electricity and plumbing, and advertised the repurposed station in the neighboring city of Zaragoza. Though the hotel was completely booked during the project's run, the effort remained somewhat clandestine, since Almarcegui originally received permission from railway officials to use the station as an exhibition venue, not a residential facility. "They never would have let me create a free hotel, especially since there was no museum" backing the project, she says. "So the event was a secret among the guests. I even asked them to hide their luggage—I was so afraid." Fuentes de Ebro residents continue to use the building as a meeting and event space.

Almarcegui lives in Rotterdam. In preparation for *Hotel Fuentes de Ebro*, she spent one month in Spain researching unused architectural spaces that offer potential solutions to housing and urban dilemmas. Her work often explores different methods for forming relationships to communities, usually through long-term research, interviewing residents, investigating new possibilities for aging infrastructure.

Above: Guests enjoy drinks at the hotel (Courtesy Lara Almarcegui).

Opposite, top to bottom: Maids clean the hotel interior. Almarcegui and Movellán converted the abandoned Fuentes de Ebro train station into a temporary hotel (Courtesy Lara Almarcegui).

Above, top to bottom: Twelve Gulf Coast artists and Alternate ROOTS members affected by Hurricane Katrina participate in The Katrina Project. The performance consisted of a variety of artistic forms, including music, performance, and dance. (Photographs by Carlton Turner)

ALTERNATE ROOTS
UPROOTED: THE KATRINA PROJECT
2006–2008

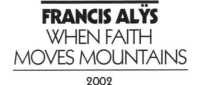

FRANCIS ALŸS
WHEN FAITH MOVES MOUNTAINS
2002

In 2006, Atlanta, Georgia-based nonprofit Alternate ROOTS presented *Uprooted: The Katrina Project*, an experimental theater production, written and performed by twelve artists from Gulf Coast communities, that offered responses to the damages they suffered and witnessed, inflicted by the 2005 hurricane. Using different artistic forms (including dance, hip-hop, and storytelling), the piece reflected the experiences of different populations in the region, based on extensive conversations the artists conducted with current and former residents of New Orleans. The performance and its related community outreach conveyed a message about the way poverty and racism can render communities vulnerable to natural disaster, the complicity of governments and citizens in enabling such destruction, and the need to reframe the tragedy as a social justice crisis.

Uprooted was produced in collaboration with actor and activist John O'Neal, an early member of Alternate ROOTS along with the organization's founder, the late Jo Carsen. Both were artists coming out of the Civil Rights and anti-war movements who wanted to affect social change in their communities through the arts. Since then, Alternate ROOTS has provided artists—particularly those who work with underserved populations in the South—with funding, support, and other forms of assistance. The organization serves communities by bringing the arts to the region, as a way to generate dialogue about the conditions in the region. "A festival can actually begin and create a conversation about the calamity that has happened in a community," says executive director Carlton Turner, "and begin the process of emotional reparation and physical reclamation of the space."

Artist Francis Alÿs provided shovels to 500 volunteers standing at the base of a 1,600-foot sand dune located near an impoverished shantytown outside of Lima. For the next several hours, the volunteers, all dressed in white, climbed the mound in a single, horizontal line, digging in unison until they reach the other side, and had displaced the sand by nearly four inches. Alÿs, who lives and works in Mexico City, often makes work based in single actions, such as pushing a block of ice down a street, or walking home with a punctured paint can, trailing splattered paint behind him. For *Barrenderos*—another group action project—he followed twenty streets sweepers as they pushed garbage through the streets of Mexico City. The sweepers began in the gutters and sidewalks, collecting the debris into the center of the road until the growing heap was too heavy to move—a sculptural form that reflected the environmental costs of urban life as well as the labor of the workers. Alÿs often says that he's less interested in making objects than in making myths or designing collective experiences.

To execute *When Faith Moves Mountains*, Alÿs spent several days enlisting locals to shovel sand under the hot April sun on a cloudless day. "At first I thought it was just silly to move a rock, a stone," one participant noted in Alÿs' video documentation of the project. But interest in the project spread virally, if for no other reason than out of curiosity for how the event might constitute art. Another participant explained that he "got involved because it was about doing something with other people." *When Faith Moves Mountains* was created for the third Bienal Iberoamericana de Lima.

Above, top to bottom: Alÿs' volunteers break ground at the foot of a massive sand dune just outside of Lima, Peru. By the conclusion of the epic project, participants had succeeded in moving the dune four inches from its original location. (Courtesy Francis Alÿs and David Zwirner, New York)

Above, top to bottom: More than 500 volunteer workers lined the base of the 1,600-foot dune. Equipped with shovels, the local volunteers each were asked to push a small quantity of sand. (Courtesy Francis Alÿs and David Zwirner, New York)

APPALSHOP
THOUSAND KITES
1998–

When former DJ Nick Szuberla launched the only hip-hop radio program in the Appalachian region, inmates from the two neighboring SuperMax prisons began writing him letters. Some were very personal, recounting the racism and human rights violations they suffered while incarcerated. He responded by initiating an on-air chess game with the prisoners, a simple gesture that acknowledged, and provided brief respite from, their hardships. Szuberla soon began broadcasting the voices of prisoners themselves via a variety of artistic projects, including poetry segments, rap sessions, and collaborations between hip-hip artists and local mountain musicians. In one episode of the show, an imprisoned man expresses, in verse, a long overdue phone call to his brother, shortly after his mother's passing. In another, titled *Calls from Home*, a mother updates her incarcerated son on family events and describes daily activities like her morning routine.

The radio show has since expanded into *Thousand Kites*, a "national dialogue project" and nonprofit organization based in Whitesburg, Kentucky, that advocates nationally for prison reform, primarily by creating transparency around injustices that occur within the system. Szuberla sits at the helm of the organization, whose name is derived from the phrase "to shoot a kite," which in prison slang means to send a message. At the heart of the *Thousand Kites* project is a comprehensive website that features the stories of prisoners, their families, activists, and artists in the form of video and radio programs, blogs, and letter-writing campaigns. The site also includes news clips, press releases about legislative changes, and accessible educational activities such as "We Can't Pay the Bill," which outlines the rising costs of maintaining prisons.

Thousand Kites operates under the 40-year-old umbrella nonprofit Appalshop, which supports regional arts in the Appalachian region, documents local traditions, and works to abolish stereotypes of the area's residents.

JULIETA ARANDA AND ANTON VIDOKLE
TIME/BANK
2010–

Imagine that you could cook someone dinner in exchange for getting your bike tire replaced, or could teach someone Chinese to have your website redesigned. *Time/Bank* is an alternative economic model that allows a group of people to exchange skills through the use of a time-based currency. Time banking arose in utopian communities during the mid-19th century and has been adapted for contemporary use by projects like Paul Glover's *Ithaca Hours*.

Started by artists Julieta Aranda and Anton Vidokle in September 2010, *Time/Bank* is an international community of more than 1,500 artists, curators, writers, and others in the field of art, who are interested in developing a parallel economy based on time and skills. Using a free website created by the artists, participants request, offer, and

Above: Thousand Kites and the Community Restoration Tour trained over one hundred activists to use flip video cameras (Courtesy Appalshop).

Opposite: The Portikus exhibition hall currently hosts the Frankfurt branch of *Time/Bank* (Photograph by Helena Schlichting, Courtesy of Portikus).

Because I often make the trip on weekends, I am offering transport between Zürich/Basel, Switzerland and Frankfurt am Main, Germany.

Hand-writing
Communication
Brooklyn NY, 2h

—Regine Basha

If for whatever reason you need something ha
(because we are all losing this skill) I can do a pretty
Especially handwriting in small upper-case letters w
more authoritative.

Regine

Choose Y____ ____wn Audi___ook
Communication
Email, 10h

—Dtails

POSTED: 27 SEPT. 2010

I will ____ke an audio book recording of ____ur
____ve____ or something you've been ____ying
____ead ____t couldn't get away fro____the
____uter.

____sy ____nd b____ks are preferable ____and
____ething ____a r____sonable length ____or ____sk
___0 - 300 pa____s).

ve a
ce...

____es tour guide
____ance
____ h

____ardini

____ad habits are writing an
____ound.
____ to -with fair notice
____es.

____ is rather small, limited ____ the cafes in my
____ood, bookstores, and ____ spaces, with a
____e hiking trails and other ____di____

Anything
Gene____l Assistance
Any____here, 2h

POSTED: 15. SEPT. 2010

pay for services in "Hour Notes." Earned Hours may be saved and used at a later date, given to another individual, or pooled with other Hours for larger group projects.

While much of the activity for *Time/Bank* happens online, the artists are consistently working to develop an international network of local branches. These branches can be temporary or long term, and are arranged by the founders and members of the bank. During Creative Time's 2011 exhibition *Living as Form*, *Time/Bank* opened *Time/Food*, a commissioned project and temporary restaurant located inside the by Abrons Art Center, which offered daily lunch in exchange for time credits and time currency that visitors earned by helping others in the *Time/Bank* community. Each day, the restaurant offered a different menu of meals prepared with recipes provided by artists who like to cook, including Martha Rosler, Liam Gillick, Mariana Silva, Judi Werthein, Rirkrit Tiravanija, K8 Hardy, Carlos Motta, and many others.

Opposite: The Frankfurt Time/Bank houses a Time/Store, which offers a range of commodities, groceries, and articles of daily use (Photograph by Helena Schlichting, Courtesy of Portikus).

Above: Aranda and Vidolke presented Time/Food, a temporary restaurant that operated on the Time/Bank currency system, as part of Creative Time's *Living as Form* exhibition (Photograph by Sam Horine, Courtesy Creative Time).

CLAIRE BARCLAY
THE MILLENNIUM HUT
1999

Located in the Govanhill district of Glasgow, Scotland, The Millennium Hut is a community facility designed by artist Claire Barclay in collaboration with the firm Studio KAP Architects. In 1999, five public areas of Glasgow, including Govanhill, were picked for renewal by the Millennium Space Project. With a footprint of just two meters by two meters, the three-story wooden structure enclosed a community garden store, workshop, library, shelves for growing plants, and a "viewing platform." The building was produced from recycled materials and utilized solar panels, reflecting an effort to harness natural resources, and promote sustainable living practices.

Commissioned by the Govanhill Housing Association, The Millenium Hut acted as an entry point to the Govanhill neighborhood, and served as a means of creating community in an ethnically diverse district. The Millenium Space Project, part of Glasgow's Year of Architecture and Design, is a year long program of exhibitions, events, and new commissions to celebrate the city's designation as the "UK City of Architecture 1999." Ultimately, the program and projects like the Millennium Hut generated an economic benefit of 34 million pounds and served as a catalyst for further urban regeneration.

Claire Barclay is a Glasgow-based artist known for her large-scale sculptural installations that combine formal elements with a scattered aesthetic, using platforms, screens, and other structures around which crafted objects lie in carefully gathered constellations. She draws from both craft and industrial processes, ranging from ceramics to straw weaving, often combining metal forms with intricately woven corn dollies or delicately printed fabric. By mixing the familiar with the strange, a sense of precariousness pervades Barclay's architectural installations.

Above: Barclay's *Millennium Hut* was built to provide a much-needed community facility in the Govanhill district of Glasgow (Courtesy Claire Barclay and Chris Platt).

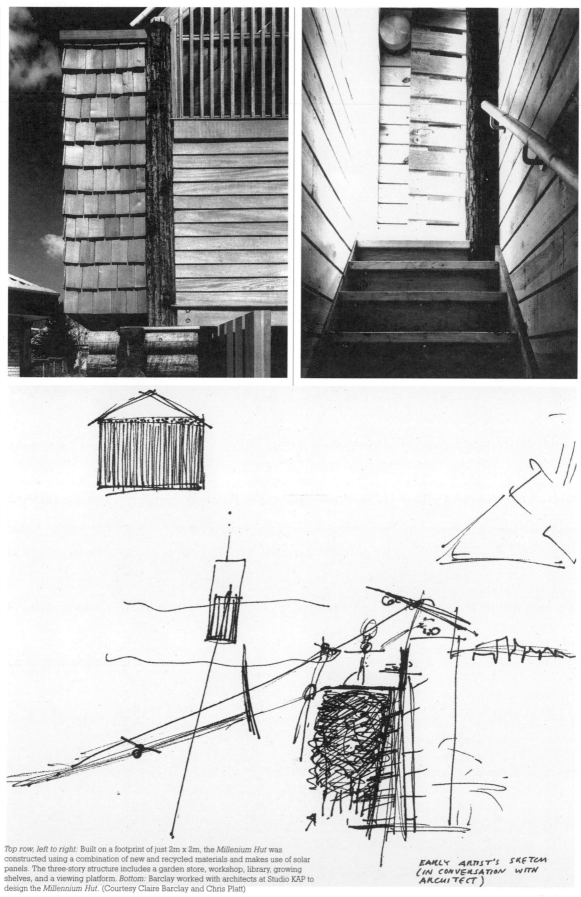

Top row, left to right: Built on a footprint of just 2m x 2m, the *Millenium Hut* was constructed using a combination of new and recycled materials and makes use of solar panels. The three-story structure includes a garden store, workshop, library, growing shelves, and a viewing platform. *Bottom:* Barclay worked with architects at Studio KAP to design the *Millennium Hut*. (Courtesy Claire Barclay and Chris Platt)

EARLY ARTIST'S SKETCH (IN CONVERSATION WITH ARCHITECT)

BAREFOOT ARTISTS
RWANDA HEALING PROJECT
2004—

In 1994, in one of the most brutal moments in the history of genocide, two extremist Hutu militia groups killed over one million people in Rwanda in just 100 days. When Barefoot Artists founder Lily Yeh visited the region of Gisenyi ten years later, she found that mass gravesites were still completely dilapidated and survivors' camps lacked the resources to help families grieve, cope, and ultimately, recover from their losses. With the help of the Red Cross, the Rwandan government, and private foundations, Yeh launched the *Rwanda Healing Project*, a multifaceted program of cultural activities, as well as economic and environmental development efforts, operated by and for village residents.

Barefoot Artists establishes parks, murals, sculptural installations, and other community-based projects in underserved areas by involving residents in the entire process, from making aesthetic decisions to navigating public policy. The Philadelphia-based organization's first project in Rwanda was the realization of the Genocide Memorial Park in Rugerero. As part of the construction of the memorial, village residents worked with a master mason to design and build the central monument's mosaic façade. Since then, the *Rwanda Healing Project* has come to include Saturday morning storytelling sessions, English classes, football games, and visual and performing art instruction. The Rugerero Survivors' Village, where the Genocide Memorial is located, also includes a rain harvest storage system, a campaign to turn corncobs into cooking charcoal, and a women's sewing cooperative, among other initiatives.

More recently, Barefoot Artists has collaborated with residents in the area to build the Pottery Arts Center—by first purchasing property, then building the architecture. Finally, with the help of faculty and students from the University of Florida's Center for the Arts in Healthcare, and volunteers from the U.S. Society for the Arts in Healthcare, the community transformed the structure into a public art project by installing mosaic work and painting a mural of Twa dancers on the façade.

Above: The bone chamber, housed behind the green doors, is one element of the memorial (Photograph by Chris Landy).

Top to bottom: Barefoot Artists erected the Genocide Memorial Park in
Rugerero, Rwanda, in 2007. Flowers lie at the memorial, which was designed
by Barefoot Artists founder Lily Yeh (Photographs by Lily Yeh).

BASURAMA
RESIDUOS URBANOS SÓLIDOS (URBAN SOLID WASTE)
2008

Basurama is a laboratory for considering waste and its reuse launched in 2001 by a group of students at the Madrid School of Architecture. Since then, the group—who now work as professional architects, designers, and other urban planners—has collaborated with communities to explore what trash, and how we treat it, can reveal about the way we consider the world. The group's work often exists in the form of workshops, talks, and other discussion forums. But central to Basurama's practice is the actual collection of detritus, and rebuilding of public spaces, using the leftover material. For example, in Lima, Basurama rehabilitated an abandoned railway by inviting local artists and other community members to create an amusement park along the tracks. They also enlisted school children in Miami to create musical instruments out of old car parts.

Such activities began in 2008, with the series *Residuos Urbanos Sólidos* (Urban Solid Waste), projects Basurama has initiated in numerous cities globally. In the Suf refugee camp in Jerash, Jordan, the group worked with Palestinian refugees to build a children's playground and a shaded area for recreation. And in Buenos Aires, discarded cardboard was used to fashion a makeshift skate park. "We find gaps in these processes of production," Basurama says, "that not only raise questions about the way we manage our resources but also about the way we think, we work, we perceive reality."

Opposite: Recycled car tires were used to construct a climbing wall along an abandoned railway in Lima, Peru (Courtesy Basurama, RUS Lima, 2010).

Above: Community members enjoy the once-derelict public space around the railway (Courtesy Basurama, RUS Lima, 2010).

Top to bottom: Custom carts were built in Mexico City as a way of reclaiming
the streets for community and play (Courtesy Basurama, RUS México, 2008).
The Basurama crew work on a project in Córdoba, Argentina (Courtesy
Basurama, RUS Córdoba, 2009).

BIJARI
TRANSVERSE REALITY
(CHICKEN PROJECTS 1,2)
2001, 2003

Have you ever wondered what happens when the chicken actually does cross the road? According to the Brazilian collective BijaRi, people react in vastly different ways depending on their relative economic and cultural positions. In 2001, BijaRi let a chicken run loose in two São Paulo shopping districts—first near the luxury Iguatemi shopping mall and then in the adjacent Largo da Batata, a bus stop and market generally frequented by lower income residents—and filmed the public's reaction. In the Iguatemi mall, security guards immediately treated the chicken as a criminal suspect (actually referring to it as a "suspicious entity"), carefully scrutinized its behavior, and quickly removed the animal from the property. Meanwhile, patrons of Largo da Batata, likewise suspicious, reacted to the chicken in a much less orderly fashion. They spoke to the chicken reproachfully as if it were a person, followed it *en masse*, and ultimately allowed the bird to remain on the premises. The project was presented in the form of video documentation at the Havana Biennial in 2003.

BijaRi, who work as architects, artists, and activists, explore whether "so-called public spaces are truly accessible to all," says member Mauricio Brandão. "We are interested in the way some of these spaces become almost privatized due to aesthetic, economic, social, and behavioral patterns." They stage confrontational actions and public performances that foster dissent, and present provocative images in urban spaces, including street signs, poster campaigns, and large-scale video projections. Projects such as Transverse Reality aim to disturb the regular flow of life by eliciting unexpected reactions from the public.

Above: A live chicken wanders around Largo da Batata, a bus stop and market generally frequented by low-income Brazilians (Courtesy BijaRi).

BREAD AND PUPPET THEATER
THE INSURRECTION MASS WITH FUNERAL MARCH FOR A ROTTEN IDEA
1962–

"Art should be as basic to life as bread." This is the motto of Bread and Puppet Theater, a 40-year-old nonprofit theater company with roots in the 1960s anti-Vietnam War and Civil Rights movements. Started by German dancer and actor Peter Schumann, Bread and Puppet performed in the streets of Manhattan's Lower East Side before relocating to a farm in Glover, Vermont. The self-financed group still uses its signature giant cardboard and paper mâché puppets—with heads so large and exaggerated that they conjure references to abstract sculpture—to take on a myriad of contemporary issues, including extremist right-wing politics and the Iraq wars. Performances have often been staged outdoors, on grassy fields, while costumed actors bring the gigantic puppets to life by hoisting them into the air, in the fashion of a barn-raising. The puppets, along with the myriad masks, paintings, and other props the company has produced over the years are housed in a one hundred-year-old barn that now serves a museum for the organization.

The Insurrection Mass with Funeral March for a Rotten Idea is a recurring show, part pageantry and part faux-religious ritual, that exorcises "rotten ideas"—political and economic events, policies, and ideologies—after offering a playful critique of them. Modeled after a traditional Catholic mass and historical witch hunts, the performances end with readings, the playing of a fiddle, and hymns; audience members are invited to participate. Bread, a symbol of compassionate, communal living, has been served at every performance since 1962.

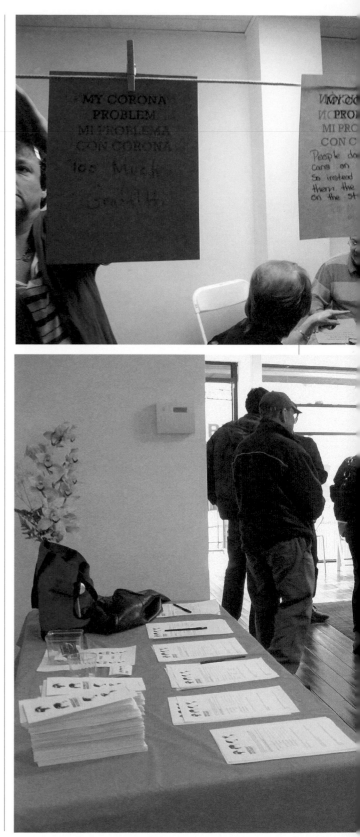

TANIA BRUGUERA
IMMIGRANT MOVEMENT INTERNATIONAL
2011–

Since April 2011, Cuban artist Tania Bruguera has been operating a flexible community space, housed in a storefront on Roosevelt Avenue in Corona, Queens, which serves as the headquarters for *Immigrant Movement International*. Engaging both local and international communities, as well as social service organizations, elected officials, and artists focused on immigration reform, Bruguera has been examining growing concerns about the political representation and conditions facing immigrants. "As migration becomes a more central element of contemporary existence, the status and identity of those who live outside their place of origin starts to become defined not by sharing a common language, class, culture, or race, but instead by their condition as immigrants," Bruguera has said. "This project seeks to embrace this common identity and shared human experience to create new ways for immigrants to achieve social recognition."

IM International, co-presented by Creative Time and the Queens Museum of Art, launched with a "Conversation on Useful Art," an event that featured moderated conversations with artists, representatives from local immigrant community organizations, and local government officials. Since then, *IM International* has opened its offices for use by local community organizations as an essential part of its mission. The Corona Youth Music Project holds weekly lessons at *IM International*, which provide young children with the opportunity learn the basic social and motor skills necessary for playing a stringed instrument. *IM International* has also teamed up with Centro Communitario y Asesoria Legal to provide weekly intakes and workshops on immigrant rights. In addition to these regular events at the *IM International* offices, *IM International* organizes

Clockwise from top left: The office of Bruguera's *Immigrant Movement International* is located in the diverse neighborhood of Corona in Queens, New York. Immigrant Movement International provides a space for outreach activities for the local immigrant community. (Courtesy Tania Bruguera and Creative Time)

group outings and programs, which aim to bring to light the immigrant condition. Most recently, as part of "Make a Movement Sundays," a group participated in the visitor program at the Elizabeth Detention Center in Elizabeth, NJ. Participants met with immigrant detainees to learn about their experiences in order to combat the increased privatization of the detention center system since September 11th.

CEMETI ART HOUSE
TRADITIONAL ART AND CULTURE PROGRAM
2007–2008

CAMP
PAD.MA
2008–

In the age of YouTube, online video archives aren't a novel concept. But *Pad.ma*, short for Public Access Digital Media Archive, offers culturally and politically relevant footage that users can edit, annotate, and distribute for free—transforming notions of authorship, discourse, and digital activism in the process. Co-initiated by the Mumbai-based art space CAMP and other advocacy groups who work in the disciplines of law, information technology, and human rights, *Pad.ma* contains several hundred hours of densely annotated, transcribed, and open-access material, primarily culled from users in Bangalore, Mumbai, and Berlin. Users can view the videos, which include interviews with artists, media criticism, and global healthcare polemic, via an interface that looks similar to video-editing software.

Since the 1990s, changes in video technology, and imaging practices in general, have actually served to limit public access to large archives, particularly historically valuable images. *Pad.ma* offers an experimental approach for creating and sharing video, as well as knowledge, that moves beyond the finite limitations of documentary films and the ubiquitous online video clip.

Cemeti Art House is the oldest art space in Yogyakarta, a city with no established infrastructure for the arts, but with an active, politicized contemporary art scene. In 2007 and 2008, Cemeti partnered with ten Yogyakarta-based NGOs to build a relief program for five villages in the aftermath of the massive earthquake that destroyed regions in South Asia. Called the *Traditional Art and Cultural Program*, this series of carnivals, workshops, and performances mobilized area residents to organize themselves in choreographed parades and lavishly costumed dances in an effort to revitalize traumatized communities. The program resulted in collaborations between local contemporary and traditional artists.

Cemeti was founded in 1988 by artists Mella Jaarsma and Ninditiyo Adipurnomo, who were looking to fill the lack of viable venues for alternative art practices. Since then, the organization has hosted residencies that allow artists to promote their work nationally, and on the international art circuit. In 2010, Cemeti launched "Art and Society," a series with focus on alternate, process-oriented practice, rather than the production of objects intended for gallery exhibition. The organization has also privileged the voices of artists in political discourse. "The days of a common enemy have passed and commenting on the social and political circumstances through revolt or provocation is no longer the only way," says Jaarsma. "Recent art discourse shows us the need to comment sensibly taking into account the perspective of the global market and neo-liberal developments. Artists are taking an active part in the current changes. The motto is: 'If you want change, start with yourself; you can no longer blame the government for everything.'"

Above: The post-earthquake revitalization program spanned five villages in the Bantul area near Yogyakarta. The yearlong Traditional Art and Culture Program included workshops, carnivals, and performances. (Photographs by Dwi 'Oblo' Prasetyo, Courtesy Cemeti Art House, Yogyakarta, Indonesia)

PAUL CHAN
WAITING FOR GODOT IN NEW ORLEANS
2007

When artist Paul Chan visited New Orleans for the first time in November 2006—a little more than a year after Hurricane Katrina—he was struck by the disquieting stillness: no construction crews yelling over clanging drills, no cranes visible on the skyline, no birds singing in the distance. In the ravaged, bleak landscape of the Lower Ninth Ward, Chan recognized the solemn scenery of Samuel Beckett's iconic stage play *Waiting for Godot*. The artist perceived "a terrible symmetry between the reality of New Orleans post-Katrina and the essence of this play, which expresses in stark eloquence the cruel and funny things people do while they wait for help, for food, for tomorrow."

In the artist's words, "seeing gave way to scheming," and Chan began to collect feedback from New Orleanians on the idea of staging a free, outdoor production of the play in the Lower Ninth Ward. One piece of advice that had been given to Chan came to define the artist's approach to the project: "If you want to do this, you gotta spend the dime, and you gotta spend the time." Working closely with director Christopher McElroen of the Classical Theater of Harlem, a cast that included Wendell Pierce and J. Kyle Manzay, and New York-based public art presenter Creative Time, Chan spent the nine months leading up to the production engaging New Orleans artists, activists, and

Opposite: Artists from all over Indonesia took part in Traditional Art and Culture. The program's aim was to revitalize performing and visual arts in the traumatized areas. (Photographs by Dwi 'Oblo' Prasetyo, Courtesy Cemeti Art House, Yogyakarta, Indonesia)

Above: J. Kyle Manzay (Estragon) and Wendell Pierce (Vladimir) perform *Waiting for Godot* in New Orleans in 2007 (Photograph by Donn Young, Courtesy Creative Time).

organizers to help shape the play and broaden the social scope of the project.

The production was ultimately comprised of four outdoor performances in two New Orleans neighborhoods—one in the middle of an inter-section in the Lower Ninth Ward and the other in the front yard of an abandoned house in Gentilly. However, with sustainability and accountability in mind, the project evolved into a larger series of events including free art seminars, educational programs, theater workshops, and conversations with the community. A "shadow" fund was set up to match the production budget and was later distributed to organizations located in the Lower Ninth Ward and Gentilly.

Above: Mark McLaughlin (Lucky) and T. Ryder Smith (Pozzo) perform *Waiting for Godot* in New Orleans. (Photograph by Paul Chan, Courtesy Creative Time).

MEL CHIN ET AL.
OPERATION PAYDIRT/ FUNDRED DOLLAR BILL PROJECT
2006–

When artist Mel Chin traveled to a post-Katrina New Orleans in 2006, he learned that the city's soil contained more than four times the amount of lead deemed safe by the Environmental Protection Agency—a condition that existed long before the hurricane damaged the land. He also learned that they city had no plans to repair it. Chin found that treating lead-contaminated soil, a major contributor in a lead-poisoning epidemic that affected over 30 percent of New Orleans' inner city youth, could cost $300 million. *Operation Paydirt/Fundred Dollar Bill Project* was conceived in New Orleans as a two-fold initiative: to find a solution to the environmental threat through *Operation Paydirt*

and to create a national lead-awareness campaign through the *Fundred Dollar Bill Project*.

The *Project* is a national campaign to raise awareness and support by primarily recruiting schoolchildren (though anyone interested in participating is welcome) to draw "*Fundred*" dollar bills, artistic interpretations of hundred dollar bills on a pre-designed template. The drawings will be delivered, via an armored truck—which has been retrofitted to run on waste vegetable oil—to Congress to garner support of the proposed solution. In 2010, *Fundred's* armored truck set out on an 18,000-mile tour across the country, collecting nearly 400,000 "*Fundred*" dollar bills from thousands of schools.

The solution has also gone national— *Operation Paydirt* is now in collaboration with the EPA in Oakland, California, on the first urban implementation of *Paydirt's* protocol of lead neutralization. *Operation Paydirt* continues HUD-sponsored urban field trials in New Orleans. Chin says, "Awareness is not enough. We are aware that there is lead in the blood and brains of children who can't learn and in the bones of young men in prison. We must move into action with resolve to deliver the voices of the people in opposition to these realities, along with a solution to effectively end this threat to children across America."

Above: The interior walls of the New Orleans Safehouse, which is pictured above, are lined with thousands of hand-drawn Fundred Dollar Bills (Courtesy Endotherm Labs).

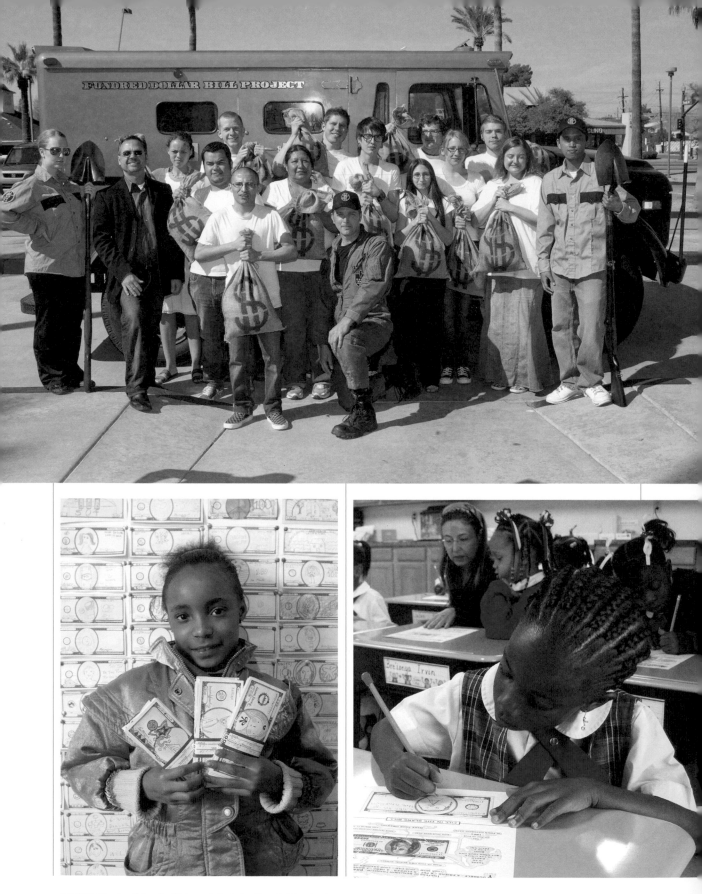

Clockwise from top: University of Arizona students, faculty, and visitors hand over bags full of Fundred Dollar Bills to the armored truck in Tempe, AZ. Schoolchildren from all over the country were asked to draw Fundred Dollar Bills, artistic interpretations of hundred dollar bills on a pre-designed template (Courtesy Fundred Dollar Bill Project).

CHTO DELAT? (WHAT IS TO BE DONE?)
ANGRY SANDWICH PEOPLE OR IN PRAISE OF DIALECTICS
2006

On the hundredth anniversary of the first Russian Revolution, collective *Chto Delat?* (What is to Be Done?) organized activists in protest of contemporary labor inequities on the square at Narva Gate in St. Petersburg, the site of the original uprising in 1905. In this contemporary staging, *Chto Delat?* invited low-income workers who normally wear sandwich boards advertising local businesses to participate by wearing new boards bearing language from Bertolt Brecht's poem, "In Praise of Dialectics", as well as a series of questions: "Are you being exploited? Are you exploiting somebody? Is exploitation inevitable?" The first Russian Revolution was a violent and failed attempt to dislodge government; *Angry Sandwich People* aimed to reflect on the political implications of this failure.

Chto Delat?, which takes its name from Vladimir Lenin's historic political pamphlet, consists of poets, artists, philosophers, singers, set designers, critics, and writers who appropriate the iconography and terminology of Communism in their work. They work as "art soviets," inspired by the councils formed in Russia at the beginning of the 20th century. Relying heavily on political and artistic theory, *Chto Delat?* explores the idea of "participatory democracy," and the history of the word "solidarity," through exhibitions, artworks, and projects in public space.

Above, top to bottom: Low-income workers in St. Petersburg gather at the Narva Gate to commemorate the one-hundredth anniversary of the first Russian Revolution. Workers carry sandwich boards bearing language from Bertolt Brecht's "In Praise of Dialectics." (Courtesy Chto Delat?).

SANTIAGO CIRUGEDA
CASA ROMPECABEZAS
2002–2004

Casa Rompecabezas, or Puzzle House, consists of glass panes, metal beams, and unpainted drywall—a plain, sturdy structure that conjures both Modernist architecture as well as industrial detritus. Designed by architect Santiago Cirugeda to be constructed, deconstructed, and transported quickly, his adaptable building slipped on and off of empty lots in Seville, Spain, for two years, and provided shelter for a range of urban needs. This included safe living space for the homeless as well as for squatters; a performance and exhibition venue for artists; and a multi-use meeting area for community activists.

Since 1996, Cirugeda has developed *Recetas Urbanas*, or "urban prescriptions," like Puzzle House, strategies that sidestep the city's restrictive planning and construction laws enabling anyone to solve housing issues autonomously, without the mediation of architectural specialists. Because Seville, like most cities, requires government-issued permits in order to build permanent structures on public land, Puzzle House was designed as an impermanent structure—located on privately-owned property with permission from the owner. Each installation had a specific purpose and a finite lifespan, at the end of which the inhabitants would disassemble the house in several hours and vacate the lot. The blueprint was equally simple to follow, so new users could replicate it once a new site was located and a new purpose identified. The budget for Seville's Puzzle House included nothing beyond the cost of cheap, readily available materials since there were no permit or rental fees.

Cirugeda's projects promote communal land-use over highly regulated and bureaucratized public ownership. Through his practice of creating affordable solutions that empower individuals to participate in the design of their cities, Cirugeda has often asked, "How can the citizen play an important role in the development and construction of the environment?" Puzzle House proposes one possible answer by separating citizenship and property rights, and dispersing urban planning among those with the least access to the process.

CAMBALACHE COLECTIVO (CAROLINA CAYCEDO, ADRIANA GARCÍA GALÁN, ALONSO GIL, AND FEDERICO GUZMÁN)
MUSEO DE LA CALLE
1999–

El Museo de la Calle, or "The Museum of the Street," is a large wooden cart on wheels—a *carro esferado*—where people can exchange or donate used objects as part of an alternate economy that values recycling and a do-it-yourself ethos above profit. This mobile flea market, which originated in Bogotá, Colombia (a city with no formal recycling program), travels to other locales in order to expand its collection and increase the number of global participants.

El Museo de la Calle was first conceived of by *Colectivo Combalache*, or "Barter Collective," a group of artists that worked in *El Cartucho*, a formerly depressed neighborhood of Bogotá located only seven blocks away from the Presidential Palace that was demolished in order to serve as the site of The Third Millennium Park. After witnessing the bartering practices of homeless people and members of other disadvantaged groups who lived in the area, the artists began swapping goods—including clothing, books, and children's toys—as a way to participate in the community, form relationships with the people they shared the space with, and also to continue the spirit of *El Cartucho* as a site of local culture that no longer exists. Despite its name, *El Museo de la Calle* does not operate in the manner of a traditional museum. Its contents aren't preserved on pedestals or behind glass; instead, they function on the street and in the home, enabling audience interaction.

Clockwise from top right: Two women barter their goods in Plaza Che at the National University in Bogotá. Columbian schoolchildren stand next to El Veloz ("The Swift"), the large wooden cart on wheels containing objects for barter Onlookers view a display of objects available to barter. (Courtesy Cambalache Collective).

PHIL COLLINS
THEY SHOOT HORSES
2004

In 2004, artist Phil Collins recruited teenagers in Ramallah to dance to pop music against a hot pink backdrop, without intermission for an entire day, while he filmed them in a single take. The resulting seven-hour video, *they shoot horses*, captures their sincere, marathon performance, carried out despite power outages, calls to prayer, and technical failures. In sweatbands and jerseys, the teens spun on their backs to Olivia Newton John, moved with slow, deliberate rhythm to Madonna, and scissored their arms to OutKast until finally sliding to the floor in exhaustion as Irene Cara crooned "Fame"—a song about hope, perseverance, and immortality.

Inspired by Horace McCoy's *They Shoot Horses, Don't They?*, a novel about dance marathons that emerged during the Great Depression, Collins' displayed his *horses* in two channels on opposing walls of darkened museum galleries, first in Britain and then internationally. Both his project and its namesake thrived by falsely glamorizing and deeply humanizing ordinary people living amid conflict.

In September 2000, riots at the Al Aqsa mosque in Jerusalem sparked a decade of violence in Palestine, resulting in a death toll of over 6,000. Yet Collins' video, like many of his projects, avoids overtly political messages or lurid accounts of life in contested territories. Instead, he reveals personality and character that come through when people are celebrated, and by turns exploited, in front of a camera by performing uncontroversial acts. He has invited Morrissey fans in Istanbul to record Smiths covers; interviewed former talk show participants who were victimized by unethical production antics; and, on the cusp of the Iraqi war, persuaded Bagdad residents to sit for screen tests for a non-existent Hollywood movie.

Above and opposite: The teenagers danced uninterrupted for eight hours for Collins' video (Courtesy of Shady Lane Productions in Ramallah).

CÉLINE CONDORELLI AND GAVIN WADE
SUPPORT STRUCTURE
2003–2009

Support Structure was an architectural interface, created by architect Céline Condorelli and artist-curator Gavin Wade, that could be continually reinvented by its users for different purposes, such as housing objects or facilitating working environments. In each iteration of the project, the infrastructure allowed the people within it to consider the meaning of the space, as well as the meaning of "support": "While the work of supporting might traditionally appear as subsequent, unessential, and lacking value in itself," Condorelli writes about the project, "[it is also a] neglected, yet crucial mode through which we apprehend and shape the world." *Support Structure* delved into a range of arenas, such as art, politics, urban renewal, and education. Through each iteration, Condorelli and Wade aimed to build a universally adaptable structure that still privileged specific needs over generic, monolithic ones.

Support Structure launched with the project "I Am A Curator," at the Chisenhale Gallery in London, which offered storage, archival, and organizational space for artwork, and provided an interface between the public, the work, curators, and gallery staff. "I Am A Curator" also allowed Chisenhale Gallery's visitors to be a curator for one day, using artworks housed in an architectural environment constructed inside the gallery. Their "music for shopping malls" employed existing commercial icons of the mall—Muzak and shopping bags—to reflect on the components of the space that make this environment tick. "What type of cultural and experiential knowledge does a mall produce?" they asked. "Music for shopping malls" treats malls as both high and low culture, and as choreographed spaces, designed and organized as interior civilizations that are cut off from the outside world, yet completely mired in the global economy and its cultural infrastructure.

Opposite: Phase 9 (Public) of *Support Structure* was the development of Eastside Projects, a new artist-run space and public gallery in Birmingham (Photograph by Stuart Whipps).

Above: Phase 1 (Art) of *Support Structure* took place as part of the exhibition "I am a Curator" at London's Chisenhale Gallery (Photograph by Per Huttner).

CORNERSTONE THEATER COMPANY
LOS ILLEGALS AND TEATRO JORNALEROS SIN FRONTERAS (DAY LABORERS THEATER WITHOUT BORDERS)
2007

For six months, playwright Michael John Garcés spent his days in a Home Depot parking lot in Hollywood and on a street corner in Redondo Beach, two of the most prominent—and controversial—day laborer job sites in Los Angeles. He waited in line with undocumented workers seeking jobs, listened to their stories, and formed relationships with members of this historically voiceless group. Then, as part of his residency at LA's Cornerstone Theater, he wrote the play *Los Illegals*, a fictional account of day laborers caught in the criminal justice system. Since its inception, Cornerstone has embedded professional playwrights and actors in a variety of communities—from small towns to groups organized around social justice issues, like reproductive rights and environmental protection—to produce theater that reflects local concerns, histories, and efforts. Community members are then cast in the production.

Los Illegals, which premiered at Cornerstone in 2007 and then traveled to other cities, evolved into *Teatro Jornaleros Sin Fronteras*, a small touring production that enlists day laborers to engage in dialogue both on and off the stage. Directed by Juan José Magandi, a day laborer who first acted in *Los Illegals*, the company produces two to three plays a year at job sites for approximately 150 audience members. Full-time ensemble members write the scripts, which often convey difficult or painful subject matter in a raucous, rallying, comedic format. For example, on-the-job accidents may be exaggerated for the sake of emphasizing the harsh realities of working without healthcare benefits. Despite the inherent dangers of visibility, few day laborers decline to participate when offered the opportunity, says Garcés, who now serves as Cornerstone's artistic director. "In the social justice movement, it's hard to pin down cause and effect. There's a big difference between being represented in the media, and standing up to represent yourself. To be able to change the meta-narrative; that's empowering."

Opposite, top to bottom: Day laborers perform in *Los Illegals*, which premiered at Cornerstone Theatre in Los Angeles in 2007 (Courtesy John Luker/Cornerstone Theater Company). Day laborers perform in a production of *Teatro Jornaleros Sin Fronteras* (Courtesy Sam Cohen/Cornerstone Theater Company).

Above: Los Illegals evolved into *Teatro Jornaleros Sin Fronteras*, a small touring production that enlists day laborers to engage in dialogue both on and off the stage (Courtesy Sam Cohen/Cornerstone Theater Company).

ALICE CREISCHER AND ANDREAS SIEKMANN
EXARGENTINA
2002–2005

When Berlin-based artists Andreas Siekmann and Alice Creischer began investigating Argentina's 2001 economic collapse and the ensuing public uprisings, they wondered: Why is the crisis always depicted in the media by burning tires and street barricades, rather than corporate buildings and shopping malls? In other words, why were signs of the downfall highlighted in lieu of its causes? And can the use of such stock, iconic images be avoided? The artists moved to Buenos Aires to search for answers. Within the first few weeks of their stay, they joined citizens in street battles, the occupation of factories, and confrontations with police. Siekmann and Creischer then sought ways to accurately depict this political moment by collaborating with artists to produce *ExArgentina*, three years of immersive projects that included a conference in Berlin, an exhibition in Cologne, the publication of a book, and a second exhibition in Buenos Aires.

These events reflected various methods of coping with economic hardship and enacting resistance without relying on stereotypical or disempowering images of struggle or discord. For example, the screen-printed posters of artists/activists used during demonstrations; suits from a now-defunct clothing factory decorated with descriptions of the G8 meetings and also current working conditions in the country; and a vast map of the Argentinian crisis as it related to the global economy.

This page, right: These drawings accompanied the chapter openings of the publication Creischer and Siekmann produced; from the top, the chapter titles are Negation, Militant Investigations, Cartography, and Political Narration (Courtesy Alice Creischer and Andreas Siekmann).

Above, clockwise from top left: Suits from the defunct Brukman textile factory in
Buenos Aires are adorned with ephemera depicting the economic hardship in the
country. A small ribbon on one of the suits describes the current working conditions
in Argentina. Ex-Argentina was exhibited at the Museum Ludwig in Cologne in 2004
and at the Palais de Glace in Buenos Aires in 2006. (Photographs by Sol Arrese)

MINERVA CUEVAS
THE MEJOR VIDA CORP.
(BETTER LIFE CORP.)
1998–

from photography and video to performance and public intervention, based on detailed research, to skewer corporations. For example, her *Del Monte campaign*, critiqued the privatization of natural resources in South America, and more recent work considers the environmental and historical repercussions of the oil industry in Mexico.

Minerva Cuevas' protests against capitalism don't take the form of riots or picket lines. "In Mexico, there are demonstrations every day, but I don't think they work anymore," Cuevas has said. "People are too used to them." Instead, the artist uses her web-based nonprofit corporation, Mejor Vida Corp. ("Better Life Corp.") to distribute products and services—including basic needs such as access to transportation and affordable food—for free. Since 1998, she has offered pre-validated subway tickets, pre-paid envelopes for domestic and international mailing, student ID cards that allow users to receive discounted rates, and barcode stickers that reduce the price of food in supermarkets. Less obviously functional items include so-called "safety pills" for late-night subway rides (so riders don't fall asleep). Participants in the project can also contribute money—not to Cuevas' project, but to others in need. Mejor Vida Corp. redistributes the donated funds to panhandlers and provides documentation of the donation to the donor. Orders for barcodes, subway tickets, and other products can be placed through Mejor Vida Corp.'s website, which is organized much like a commercial business site, except that it advertises institutional critique—"We wonder if in fact the National Lottery helps to finance public assistance...if so, where is it?"—instead of the consumption of goods.

Cuevas' works tweak existing social and economic systems to suggest possibilities for more equitable conditions, often by offering alternatives such as her MVC products, or "S.COOP," a new currency she introduced at London's Petticoat Lane Market. She uses a range of media

DECOLONIZING ARCHITECTURE ART RESIDENCY
OUSH GRAB
(THE CROW'S NEST)
2008

Decolonizing Architecture Art Residency is a Palestinian art and architecture collective and a residency program based in Beit Sahour, Palestine. Organized by architects Sandi Hilal, Alessandro Petti, and Eyal Weizman, DAAR examines the possible re-usage of existing architecture in occupied territories—a process they refer to as "Revolving Door Occupancy."

In 2006, the Israeli army evacuated Oush Grab (literally translated as "The Crow's Nest"), a hilltop military site at the edge of Beit Sahour, Bethlehem, from which colonial regimes had governed Palestine for centuries. When Israeli settlers took control of the abandoned building, Decolonizing Architecture Art Residency (DAAR), along with other Palestinian and international activists, reclaimed Oush Grab as public space and initiated plans to convert it into a multiuse park. To generate interest as well as support for the plan, DAAR hosted bingo games, film

screenings, prayer sessions, and tours of the land
with the help of NGOs and the local municipality.
The Israeli settlers retaliated by marking the old
structure with graffiti, which DAAR responded to
by organizing community cleanup measures. In
addition, after discovering that same hilltop was
also a roosting ground for thousands of migrating
birds, DAAR punctured the structure with holes in
order to transform it into both an observatory and
a nesting place.

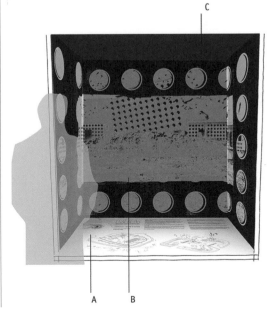

Clockwise from top: The hilltop military site Oush Grab ("The Crow's Nest")
was evacuated in 2006 by the Israeli army. Decolonizing Architecture's rendering of the site illustrates plans for conversion into a multi-use park. (Courtesy
Decolonizing Architecture Art Residency).

JEREMY DELLER
BATTLE OF ORGREAVE
2001–

The memory of labor clashes in working-class neighborhoods often lives on in family folklore and community history. But the 1984 National Union of Mineworkers' strike in South Yorkshire's Orgreave still felt palpable and present to residents of this small village seventeen years later as they gathered for a re-enactment organized by British artist Jeremy Deller. Commissioned by the London-based arts organization Artangel and public television broadcaster Channel 4, Deller enlisted historical re-enactment expert Howard Giles to orchestrate the filmed production. One third of the more than 800 participants were former miners and police officers, many of whom had been involved in the original strike.

Once again, the miners gathered at the local coking plant, then marched to a nearby field when the police arrived. Deller and Giles took pains to match the intensity of the '84 strike, which erupt-

ed into violence, particularly on the part of law enforcement. In preparation for the re-enactment, the artist spent months researching the strike—pouring over court testimonies, oral accounts, contemporary newspaper reports and film footage—in order to reconstruct events as accurately as possible.

London-based Deller acts as curator, producer, and director in his projects, which revolve around his engagement with perceptions and memories. In 2009, he organized *It Is What It Is: Conversations About Iraq*, a collaborative commission of Creative Time, the New Museum and 3M, that culminated in a cross-country road trip and series of conversations about the Iraq War at public sites. In tow was the ultimate conversation starter: a car destroyed in a bombing on Al-Mutanabbi Street, Baghdad in March 2007.

Above: More than 800 people—many of them former miners and police—participated in Deller's re-enactment of 1984's Battle of Orgreave (Photograph by Martin Jenkinson, Courtesy Artangel).

Above: Re-enactors play the role of strikers dodging an unprovoked charge
from the mounted police (Photograph by Martin Jenkinson, Courtesy Artangel).

Above: Strikers from the re-enactment sport yellow badges that identify them as members of the National Union of Mineworkers. (Photograph by Martin Jenkinson, Courtesy Artangel).

MARK DION, J. MORGAN PUETT, AND COLLABORATORS
MILDRED'S LANE
1998–

In 1998, artists J. Morgan Puett and Mark Dion transformed a 92-acre Pennsylvania farm, built in the 1830s, into Mildred's Lane, a mecca for experimental living and art production. The three-building compound serves as a creative retreat at the end of a long dirt road, housing an apiary, tree house, pavilion, and an elaborate, fruitful garden. Puett and Dion invite visitors to inhabit the land as if it were a studio, camp out, and embrace its natural resources as media. Many come to collaborate on performances, films, books, and other projects—particularly those that explore daily life practices, such as eating, shopping, and sleeping.

Each summer, Puett and Dion host themed sessions for three weeks; in 2010 the session Town & Country explored the divisions between urban and rural life through poetry readings, and workshops based on Thoreau's *Walden*. This past summer, a group of artists, engineers, and environmentalists devised a "complete aquatic environment for humans and non-humans" by studying sustainable hydrology, the history of aquariums, and architecture. The original farm-house, now Mildred's Lane Historical Society and Museum, houses an archive of past projects.

Above: Pablo Helguera and Academia de los Nocturnos presented work while guest chefs b in June 2011 (Courtesy Mildred's Lane).

Top to bottom: Participants at Mildred's Lane enjoyed a Social Saturday dinner with artist Fritz Haeg in 2010. For a Social Saturday Supper Club in 2011, a selection of readers, including Robert Fitterman of The Word Shop, read their work. (Courtesy Mildred's Lane).

MARILYN DOUALA-BELL AND DIDIER SCHAUB
DOUAL'ART
1991–

iteration of the SUD festival, addressed the theme "Water and the City." Host to thirty events including public art installations and performances, the festival also offered fourteen short-term (15 days to one month) residencies that allowed guest artists from abroad to participate.

Doual'art is a nonprofit cultural organization and research center founded in 1991 in Douala, Cameroon, by husband and wife team Didier Schaub and Marilyn Douala-Bell. Created to foster new urban practices in African cities, *doual'art* invites contemporary artists to engage with the city of Douala in order to mold its identity and to bridge the gap between the community and contemporary art production. In particular, the organization offers coaching and support to artists whose research and work are centered on urban issues.

The group uses art as an instigator of economic and social change, especially as a means of fighting poverty and indigence. By producing site-specific interventions and hosting exhibitions, lectures, residencies, and workshops *doual'art* works as an intermediary between social and economic actors, local collectives, and the general population. It fosters cultural and artistic initiatives as a tool for bridging divides between different urban populations, in turn promoting social cohesion. *doual'art* implements a participatory approach to cultural practice, negotiating with local communities, NGOs and authorities their specific needs and aspirations and involving artists as facilitators of the development processes.

In 2007, *doual'art* hosted the first Salon Urbain de Douala (SUD 2007), a weeklong public art festival that gave artists free rein to explore urban issues specific to Douala. Proposals addressed contemporary issues like urban mobility, tradition vs. modernity, African continental integration, and the art world and cultural policy, and resulted in performances, temporary installations, happening, concerts and film screenings. Three years in the making, SUD 2010, the second

ELECTION NIGHT
HARLEM, NEW YORK
2008

On November 4, 2008, people across the U.S. celebrated the election of Barack Obama—on streets, at polls, and in bars. Yet, in the predominantly African-American neighborhood of Harlem, New York, the mass, spontaneous eruptions of spirit seemed unified, at times even choreographed, as if residents had been waiting backstage, maybe not for the curtain to lift, but for the glass ceiling to finally shatter. Minutes after Republican nominee John McCain conceded the race to Obama, thousands of people poured out of their homes and businesses onto the intersection of 125th Street and Adam Clayton Powell, Jr., Boulevard waving banners, line dancing, and breaking out in song as they paraded through the neighborhood. Police officers charged with patrolling the scene clasped Obama T-shirts, while people climbed atop cars to record the festivities with their cell phones. With the camera crews' bright lights beaming on them, revelers built ice sculptures, beat drums, painted their faces, and blared music from speakers, which were eventually quieted before the broadcast of the president-

Above: On Nov. 4th, 2008, a massive celebration broke out in Harlem, New York,
after the announcement that Barack Obama had won the presidential election
(Photograph by Spencer Platt, Courtesy Getty Images).

elect's speech—an event that, for many, signified a power shift beyond the usual torch-passing from one political party to the next.

In the 1920s, Harlem incubated a flood of artistic production, the formation of black cultural and political organizations, and an overall collective expression within the community. The post-election demonstrations commemorated the history of the Harlem Renaissance, as well as the energy of grassroots activism that the Democratic campaign had embodied in its last few months. The night also conjured a more typical American phenomenon: the endorphin-induced euphoria of sports fans after a winning game. As one blogger wrote the day after, "Not since the Giants won the Super Bowl has New York come together like this."

FALLEN FRUIT
PUBLIC FRUIT JAM
2006–

In 2004, Fallen Fruit—the artists David Burns, Matias Viegener, and Austin Young—created maps of fruit trees growing on or over properties in Los Angeles within a five-block radius of their homes, and then distributed the maps to the public for free. Property laws regarding the ownership of trees, even those on private land, are ambiguous in Los Angeles: When branches and foliage extend beyond one neighbor's yard to another, maintenance rights extend as well. And when fruit hangs over fences and sidewalks in the urban environment, passersby arguably have the right to pluck it. By making these potentially contested areas in Los Angeles visible, Fallen Fruit encouraged the city's residents to consider their implications and also to explore this car-centric region on foot, thereby socializing with new people under new conditions.

The group's *Public Fruit Jam* project takes this outreach effort one step further: Since 2006, they have invited the public to bring their own home-grown or street-picked fruit to events at museums or galleries in order to make jam. Without working from recipes, they ask people to sit at tables with strangers, negotiate ingredients, and engage in discussion. For example, "If I have lemons and you have figs, we'd make a lemon jam (with lavender)," the artists explain on their website. These "jam sessions" stem from the seeds of Fallen Fruit's practice—a reconsideration of public and private land use, as well as relations between those who have resources and those who don't. "Using fruit as our lens, [we] investigate urban space, ideas of neighborhood and new forms of located citizenship and community," says Burns.

Above: Children carry signs of support for Barack Obama in Harlem on election night, 2008 (Photograph by Spencer Platt, Courtesy Getty Images).

Opposite, clockwise from top left: Fallen Fruit post jam-making instructions for the event attendees to follow. The public brings different kinds of fruit and works without recipes, which results in unique jam flavors. Attendees participate in a Public Fruit Jam at Machine Project, Los Angeles (Courtesy Fallen Fruit).

HOW to JAM

1. BRING TO A BOIL:
   - 5 cups fruit _CHOPPED!! NO SEEDS!!_
   - ½ cup + pectin

2. ADD:
   - 5 cups SUGAR

3. BRING TO A BOIL AGAIN *BRIEFLY*

4. POUR INTO JARS

5. LEAVE A JAR FOR FELLOW JAMMERS

6. SWAP A JAR WITH YOUR NEICHBORING JAMMER!

7. Enjoy

PUBLIC FRUIT JAM – EAT QUICK

Only store this jam in a sealed ____
refrigerator. Or freeze for longer ____
public fruit and sugar with no ____

http://www.fallenfruit.org

BITA FAYYAZI, ATA HASHEMINEJAD, KHOSROW HASSANZADEH, FARID JAHANGIR AND SASSAN NASSIRI
STUDIO
1991

In 1991, five Iranian artists, Farid Jahangir and Sassan Nassiri, Bita Fayyazi, Ata Hasheminejad, and Khosrow Hassanzedeh, took over an abandoned house in Tehran, Iran, and used it as both studio space and found object—a place to collaborate, and also explore the physical and political meaning of urban architectural detritus. They spent two months creating various projects in the house, including paintings, installations, and sculptures. An installation of wallpaper peeled away from the walls in long strips, broken vases spilled over countertops and out of cabinets, and atmospheric projections of images like El Greco's *Burial of Count Orgaz* filled the relatively spare rooms of the house.

At the end of the two-month period, they opened the project to the public, as well as other

Above: In 1991, five Iranian artists took over an abandoned house in Tehran and treated it as an art piece (Photograph by Behnam Monadizadeh).

artist collaborators. During the artists stay, the house maintained its status as abandoned property—no effort to renovate it occurred—while it also evolved into an active, lived space. After the run of the show, the artists demolished the house, carrying out its original, intended fate.

Above and right: Over the course of two months, the artists created installations using various materials in the house (Photograph by Farid Jahangir). After that time, they opened the house up to the public (Photograph by Afshin Najafzadeh). At the end of the exhibition, the house was destroyed (Photograph by Afshin Najafzadeh).

FINISHING SCHOOL
THE PATRIOT LIBRARY
2001–

The Patriot Library is a nomadic collection of books, periodicals, and other media deemed potentially dangerous by the Federal government once The Patriot Act took effect after the acts of terrorism on September 11, 2001. These documents cover aviation training, chemistry, propaganda, tactical manuals, tourist information, and weaponry—general topics that were likely researched by the World Trade Center attackers. "However, we don't believe the pursuit of knowledge is in itself dangerous," says Finishing School's Ed Giardina. "Individuals should be allowed access to all media free of governmental oversight and intimidation." Finishing School conceived of the project after many conversations with librarian Christy Thomas, who witnessed the government's violation of library patrons' right to privacy without judicial oversight. Understanding the American Library Association's privacy standards, *The Patriot Library* doesn't keep records of visitor's personal information or use of materials. The project, co-organized by Thomas and Finishing School, was first installed in Oakland's Lucky Tackle gallery in 2003.

Los Angeles-based Finishing School works with experts from other fields to investigate and take on alternative approaches to activism, particularly environmental, social, and political issues. In 2008, the collective launched *Little Pharma*, which examines alternative medicines and lifestyles as a viable antidote to some of the drug industry's pathologies. *Little Pharma* consists of a series of workshops, roundtable meetings, lectures, weblog, community medicinal garden, and a drug-themed bike ride.

Top: At Oakland's Lucky Tackle gallery, *The Patriot Library*'s reference website could be used to browse the book collection. *Above and opposite:* Posters advertising The Patriot Library. (Courtesy Finishing School and Adam Rompell/ Lucky Tackle)

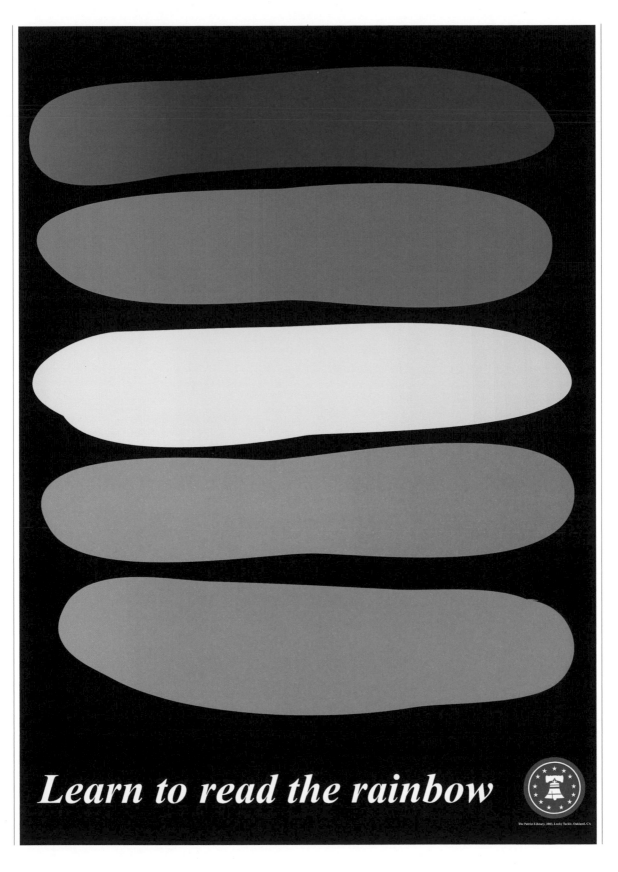

Learn to read the rainbow

The Patriot Library, 2003, Lucky Tackle, Oakland, CA

FREE CLASS FRANKFURT/M
ART WORKERS COUNCIL
2007–

The Art Workers Council is a forum initiated by Free Class Frankfurt, a group that began as a reading club at the art school Staedelschule, and expanded to include members from outside the student body. This self-organized artists' association addresses art and politics via reading groups, seminars, collaborative exhibitions, parties, and public events—all non-academic frameworks that counter economic disparities that result in limited access to the arts and arts education. In April 2010, Art Workers Council staged a demonstration against wage labor to promote "a social revolution that won't be satisfied with formal promises of freedom, but sees communism of the 21st century as the solid self-determination of everybody," according to their manifesto:

"Art is no wage labor. Artistic freedom promises its producers to themselves decide about the means, ways, and content of production. This formal independence from the standards of surplus value production still feeds the contradicting promise of art to allow self-determined production, despite capitalism. This assumed salvation of artistic refusal of wage labor is the humiliating competition for a place among those 5 percent, who at least temporarily can survive from their income as artists. One who is not yet part of those chosen few, is allowed to hope for the slightly better chance of getting a place in the state-funded residency carousel, traveling from one gentrification project to another. This includes free studio-usage and pocket money, but continuities of political commitment and solidarity organization can barely take place in this context."

Above: Posters advertising The Patriot Library (Courtesy Finishing School and Adam Rompell / Lucky Tackle).

nmer in einem Arbeiterklub.

rklub", Aufführung eines Stückes von Meyerhold.[1]

FRENTE 3 DE FEVEREIRO
2004—

On February 3rd, 2004, Brazilian dentist Flávio Sant'Ana was in the wrong place at the wrong time—or, so the story goes. As he made is way down a street in sprawling São Paulo, Sant'Ana—a young black man—was shot in the head and killed by the city's military police. In the aftermath of the tragedy, the police claimed that they had mistaken Sant'Ana for the perpetrator in a robbery and that his death was nothing more than an unfortunate accident. The mainstream media quickly perpetuated this narrative. However, a counter-narrative soon emerged and Sant'Ana's death became a touchstone for racial injustice in Brazil.

For one group, made up of artists and academics, the event revealed "racial democracy as a deliberate attempt to deny perverse social practices punctuated by the legacy of slavery." Adopting the name *Frente 3 de Fevereiro* the self-described "research and intervention group" began creating overtly political projects to challenge the mainstream narrative and bring public awareness to the killing. First, the group fabricated a plaque that was placed at the exact spot where Sant'Ana was murdered. The text on the plaque served as a memorial for Sant'Ana but also made a clear case for what had actually transpired. Later, *Frente* pasted posters throughout the city asking the provocative question, "Who polices the police? Police racism."

Frente 3 de Fevereiro's outreach culminated in the fifty-minute video *Zumbi Somos Nós: Cartografia do Racismo para o Jovem Urbano* (*We are Zumbi: A Cartography of Racism for Urban Youth*), a poetic manifesto on racism that has been screened internationally. The group contin-

Top to bottom: Members use a reading room in a workers' club in Germany. Free Class Frankfurt layers a contemporary image with a vintage photograph of a performance in a typical German worker's club. (Courtesy Free Class Frankfurt)

Above: Frente 3 do Fevereiro created a horizontal monument to commemorate
the death of Flavio Sant'Ana, a young black dentist wrongfully murdered by São
Paulo military police in 2004 (Courtesy of Frente 3 de Fevereiro).

ues to advocate for racial justice by contextualizing information the public receives through mass media and creating new forms of protest pertaining to racial issues.

Top to bottom: During Rio de Janeiro's Carnival in 2010, Frente 3 de Fevereiro's intervention *Haiti Aquí* (Haiti Here), a 3-foot inflatable ball, connected the past and present conditions in Haiti with the conditions in the slums of Rio de Janeiro (Photograph by Cris Ribas). Signs created by Frente 3 de Fevereiro reading, "Save Black Brazil" and "Where are the blacks?" (Courtesy Frente 3 de Fevereiro); "We are zombies" (Photograph by Peetssa).

Above: The "We Are Zumbi" flag hangs outside a Homeless Movement occupation in downtown São Paulo as part of the resistance to keep the building (Photograph by Julia Valiengo).

THEASTER GATES
THE DORCHESTER PROJECT
2009–

Since 2009, artist and urban planner Theaster Gates has purchased three abandoned buildings on Chicago's South Side and refitted them with remnants of the city's urban landscape, including wooden floors that once lined an old bowling alley, and windows that served as doors in a museum. The renovated structures—a former candy store, a single-family home, and a duplex—also house pieces of Chicago's cultural history: In an effort to preserve the collections, Gates acquired 14,000 books from a now-defunct bookstore and 60,000 antique lanternslides from the University of Chicago's archive. Last year, he purchased 8,000 vinyl records when a Hyde Park record shop closed. *The Dorchester Project*, named after the street his buildings occupy, has become an expansive redevelopment effort, with the help of architects, students, and city officials.

What began as a mission to rescue architecture and objects has evolved into a larger mission to bring artistic and social change to the South Side, a historically underserved neighborhood. *The Dorchester Project* serves as an incubator for community artists and as an informal gathering space where the public can meet for dinner, attend performances, and engage in discussions about art, urban blight, and possibilities for renewal. While Gates' project has been largely touted as a positive development, it has also generated criticism—in the form of hate letters.

Above: Remnants from Chicago landmarks were repurposed to create the façade and decorate the interior of the *Dorchester Project* building (Courtesy of the artist and Kavi Gupta Chicago | Berlin).

Above: The building houses a collection of 60,000 antique lanternslides from the University of Chicago (top), 14,000 books Gates acquired from a now-defunct bookstore (middle), and 8,000 vinyl records from a closed Hyde Park record shop (bottom). (Courtesy of the artist and Kavi Gupta Chicago | Berlin)

ALONSO GIL AND FREDERICO GUZMÁN
ARTIFARITI
2007–

For years, the Moroccan government and a local Sahrawi dissident group have been at an impasse over ownership of occupied land in the disputed territory of Western Sahara in North Africa. The conflict has resulted in a myriad of human rights violations in Sahrawi refugee camps along a 2,700-kilometer sand wall, studded with landmines, that divides the Western Sahara territory from Morocco. ARTifariti is an international art festival that was launched in 2007 in response to the violence and repressive conditions that the militarized "Wall of Shame" engenders. This annual event, comprised of exhibitions, workshops, and symposia, takes place in the refugee camps and in the oasis town of Tifariti, part of the so-called "Liberated Territories" or "Buffer Zone" of Western Sahara.

Initiated by artists Federico Guzmán and Alonso Gil, ARTifariti accepts proposals from artists across the globe. A team of curators chooses six projects that generally involve local materials and resources and prompt permanent, structural change in Sahrawi. For example, in 2010, the festival supported a series of children's workshops in a neighboring town. The school-aged participants painted a mural of Western Sahara that was used as a backdrop while they re-enacted bombings, bank robberies, and other events that mark the lives of their Sahrawi peers.

Opposite: Kneita Boudda prints T-shirts at Sahara Libre Wear workshop, a fashion label created by Alonso Gil in collaboration with the Sahrawi community (Photograph by Paula Álvarez, Courtesy ARTifariti)

Above: Artist Robin Kahn bakes a loaf of bread in the desert outside of Tifariti, Western Sahara, as part of *Dining in Refugee Camps: The Art of Sahrawi Cooking* (Courtesy ARTifariti).

PAUL GLOVER
ITHACA HOURS
1991–

In Ithaca, New York, you can mow a lawn to pay for a movie ticket, or change a light bulb for a cup of coffee—not through direct barter, but by using a local alternative currency called *Ithaca HOURS*. Nearly 500 businesses, including banks, contractors, restaurants, hospitals, landlords, farmer's markets, and the local Chamber of Commerce, accept *HOURS*, which are worth 10 dollars, or roughly the average pay in Ithaca. Since its inception, over 110,000 *HOURS* have been issued, and millions of dollars in value have been traded through the system, which is locally referred to as the "Grassroots National Product." The bills are counterfeit-proof, serialized notes, produced in denominations of 2 HRS, 1 HR, 1/2 HR, 1/4 HR, 1/8 HR, and 1/10 HR.

Author and activist Paul Glover created the *Ithaca HOURS* system in 1991 as a way to strengthen the local economy by backing it with community labor, rather than national debt. Since the tender is only valid within a 20-mile radius, trade is limited to residents and businesses within in the region; to that end, the currency promotes local shopping and reduces dependence on transport fuels. "*HOURS* reminds us that wealth comes from labor, and everyone deserves fair pay," Glover writes on his website. "We printed our own money because we watched Federal dollars come to town, shake a few hands, then leave to buy rainforest lumber and fight wars. Ithaca's *HOURS*, by contrast, stay in our region to help us hire each other. While dollars make us increasingly dependent on transnational corporations and bankers, HOURS reinforce community trading and expand commerce which is more accountable to our concerns for ecology and social justice." *Ithaca HOURS* is one of the largest, and oldest, alternative currencies in the United States.

Top to bottom: Ithaca HOURS are printed in five denominations (Courtesy Paul Glover). Glover, along with artist Jim Houghton, created a cartoon that explains the purpose and use of *HOURS* (Designed by Paul Glover, Art by Jim Houghton).

JOSH GREENE
SERVICE-WORKS
2006–

For the past ten years, Josh Greene has been working both as an artist and a waiter in a high-end San Francisco restaurant. One night a month, Greene donates his tips—between $200 and $300—to another artist through his micro-granting project *Service-Works*. Approximately twenty-five applicants a month submit pitches to the program through Greene's website. He underwrites one proposal per round and displays the idea online. Greene is the sole juror, and the application process for *Service-Works*, unlike those of most foundations or government funding agencies, requires only a simple project description sent in the body of an email message, and an itemized budget. While anyone is eligible for a stipend, those awarded grants are typically projects that can be realized with roughly $300, within three weeks, and are in tandem with Greene's personal interests in "exchange, interaction, storytelling, and problem solving."

"I have a particular fondness for projects that grow out of and deal with real-life situations, be they political, personal, or environmental," Greene says. "I also enjoy work that incorporates risk, humor, pathos, and absurdity."

Some of the projects Greene has funded include a mobile replica of a front stoop that fostered impromptu conversations in Nashville, Tennessee; a call for writers requesting impersonations of George W. Bush lamenting his presidency's failures; and a cake party for first graders. Each entry on the *Service-Works* website includes a brief narrative about how Greene earned the money that went toward the project. While the projects he funds are disparate in content and form, each reflects his interest in connecting his labor to an artist's work.

Tina Heringer

A 273 Dollar Project

Tina Heringer bartered two paintings of the Fair Oaks area for the Lind Brothers Mortuary in exchange for the cremation of her father.

The Making of 273 Dollars

I am fairly certain that this new job is not for me. After my first night of training I found myself longing for my old job. I went as far as contacting my former manager and seeing if I could have my old job back. He said he filled my spot.

A few weeks have gone by since that first night of training and there have been moments in which I have felt that everything would be ok. I reason with myself that my discontent has to do with it being a new situation. But in a way, this is the opposite of reason. I have been the new guy a couple of handfuls of times in my service-industry career and usually the beginning stages of jobs are characterized by excitement as opposed to dislike.

This night did not stand out in any particular way except at the end of the shift I told myself that after tomorrow night's shift - my last one before a two-week vacation- I will tell them that it is not working out for me and give my notice.

Above: With Greene's $273 grant, Tina Heringer made paintings to barter with a mortuary in exchange for the cremation of her father (Courtesy Josh Greene).

FRITZ HAEG
SUNDOWN SALON
2001–2006

Los Angeles-based artist and architect Fritz Haeg bridges public and private spheres in his inclusive, community-oriented actions. For his *Edible Estates* project in 2005, he replaced suburban lawns—the ultimate modernist moat—with gardens full of native plants that encouraged neighbors to talk to each other, use their properties communally, and grow the land into an environmentally productive space. Likewise, his *Animal Estates* (2008) were homes for animals that had been displaced by humans, usually situated on the premises of commissioning museums. These makeshift sanctuaries included a beaver pond located in a courtyard and an eagles' nest placed in an outdoor foyer.

From 2001 to 2006, Haeg used his own estate, a geodesic dome on Los Angeles' Sundown Drive, to host semi-public gatherings of artists, neighbors, and other collaborators in which participants gardened, knitted, read poems, played music, organized pageants, performed yoga, showed visual art work, screened films, and simply exchanged ideas. These so-called *Sundown Salons*, which began as a small group of friends, expanded to include a wide range of artists including My Barbarian, Pipilotti Rist, Eve Fowler, Chris Abani, and Assume Vivid Astro Focus, among others. "The salons provided an alternative to the isolated solitary creator in the studio. Instead, the salon celebrated the truly engaged human, responding to their time, environment, community, friends, neighbors, weather, history, place," Haeg writes.

Haeg, via *Sundown Salon,* also staged similar events at the Schindler House in West Hollywood in collaboration with the MAK Center. In September 2006, after thirty events, *Sundown Salon* was converted into *Sundown Schoolhouse,* an alternative art school where "public interaction, physical connectedness, and responsiveness to place are valued above all else."

Above: Sundown Salon #29 (Dancing Convention, July 9, 2006) was a dance workshop that took place in a geodesic dome (Photograph by Fritz Haeg).

Top row: Sundown Salon #11 (February 22, 2004, organized with Sabrina Gschwandtner & Sara Grady) was a celebration of extreme knitting, art, craft, and the handmade, where guests were invited to wear things they made and bring projects to work on (Photograph by Jeaneann Lund).

Bottom: Sundown Salon #28 (*Young Ones*, June 18, 2006) was organized with Joyce Campbell and Iris Regn as an opportunity for local children to participate in salon events and projects, and for parents and children to establish a like-minded local network (Photograph by Fritz Haeg).

HAHA
FLOOD
1992–1995

In 1992, the collective Haha planted a hydroponic garden that grew therapeutic herbs and leafy, green vegetables in an empty Chicago storefront, and distributed the produce on a weekly basis to local AIDS and HIV patients. From the sidewalk, the long rows of small plants, boxed in perforated containers under artificial lights, looked more like a scientific laboratory than a functioning garden. Yet for Laurie Palmer, a founding member of Haha, the interconnected plastic tubes captured the spirit of community, and that of the human body itself—"Complex, intricate networks," she says, "which were at the basis of all of our interventions." Unlike outdoor gardens, hydroponic gardens transport nutrients and minerals through water, not soil. The resulting aseptic conditions have proven to be safer for those with immunodeficiency disorders. The vegetables that Haha grew—including spinach, kale, arugula, and collard greens—also contained anti-oxidants that could possibly enhance the effectiveness of treatments.

With the help of a network of thirty neighborhood volunteers, Haha transformed the garden into a vast resource hub for the AIDS/HIV community, which they intended to hand off to a social service organization at the end of their temporary project, *Flood*. The group held lectures and workshops, provided informational materials, and offered the storefront as a meeting space and public forum for discussion about sex education, contraceptives, nutrition, treatment, healthcare, and questions of personal and collective identity.

Flood was commissioned by Sculpture Chicago's seminal exhibition, *Culture in Action*, a two-year project that helped transform the role of audience in public art from spectator to participant. "We were already interested in creating change through our work as artists," Palmer says. "And believed that incremental change was the fine-grained substrate that would make it happen."

Opposite: Haha took over a vacated storefront on Greenleaf Street, where they planted a hydroponic garden to provide produce for local AIDS and HIV patients (Photograph by Haha, Courtesy Sculpture Chicago).

Above: A school group helps with the storefront community hydroponic garden on Greenleaf Street in Chicago's North Side (Photograph by Haha, Courtesy Sculpture Chicago).

HELENA PRODUCCIONES
FESTIVAL DE PERFORMANCE DE CALI
1997–2008

For eleven years, Helena Producciones' *Festival de Performance de Cali* played a key role in the cultural life of Cali, Colombia, a city with a notable shortage of resources and support networks for the arts. The festival provided a forum for both emerging and established international artists to create performances that were interactive and politically motivated, and defied traditional boundaries between artist and audience. Artists were invited to participate by invitation and through an open call for submissions. The five-day festival would also include workshops, street interventions, and talks held in various cultural centers throughout the city—from public plazas to modest artist-run spaces. Examples of past performances include Spanish artist Santiago Sierra's installation of an enormous American flag on the wall of the Tertulia Museum; French artist Pierre Pinoncelli's amputation of his pinkie finger in protest of the kidnapping of 2002 presidential candidate Ingrid Betancourt; and a concert by Las Malas Amistades, a Casiotone art school band whose independently produced CDs have attained cult status among college students.

Helena Producciones is a nonprofit, multidisciplinary collective that expands definitions of visual art by organizing events that promote local culture and community-initiated activism. The collective, which includes artists Wilson Díaz, Ana María Millán, Andrés Sandoval, Claudia Patricia Sarria, and Juan David Medina, often offers institutional critique through its work, as well as perspectives on local conditions, alternative to the routine social and economic conflict endemic in Colombia. The collective was also responsible for *Loop*, a semi-weekly television program that aired in Cali from 2000-2001 and mimicked the variety show format in order to report on the activities of local artists and punk bands.

Above: Members of the Puerto Tejada school of fencing compete in a match using machetes (Courtesy Helena Producciones).

STEPHEN HOBBS AND MARCUS NEUSTETTER
URBANET – HILLBROW/ DAKAR /HILLBROW
2006

While conducting site research for an urban redevelopment project in Johannesburg, South Africa, Stephen Hobbs and Marcus Neustetter were stopped at the Hillbrow border by two francophone immigrants, who warned the artists against entering the inner-city neighborhood with a camera—suggesting that it might be stolen. Inspired by the exchange, Hobbs and Neustetter asked a group of Senegalese immigrants to draw maps of Dakar, which the artists then used to navigate the city during their two-week residency in May 2006. The project, titled *UrbaNET – Hillbrow/ Dakar/Hillbrow*, became their collective contribution to the Dak'Art Biennale fringe program "Dak'Art OFF." The resulting exhibition, held at the Ker Thiossane residency space, was comprised of wall paintings of the maps and projections of photographic stills that reflected Hobbs' and Neustetter's tour of Dakar on foot and documented their interactions with people they met along the way.

The exhibition was designed as a reflection on racial and ethnic changes in the social fabric of Dakar and in the artists' hometown of Johannesburg. *UrbaNET* was included in Johannesburg's "Sightings/Site-ings of the African City" conference, held at the Wits Institute of Social and Economic Research in June 2006. The project's last iteration was an audio-visual presentation and discussion forum in which Senegalese immigrants were able to examine and compare the findings from Johannesburg and Dakar.

Top to bottom: Attendees enjoy the Seventh *Festival de Performance de Cali* in 2008. For the Coco Show, a market event organized by Helena Producciones, artisans displayed and sold their products in the main street in Cali. (Courtesy Helena Producciones)

FRAN ILICH
SPACEBANK
2005–

Spacebank is a virtual community investment bank that uses traditional capitalist trading structures in tandem with an alternate, fictional currency in order to promote anti-capitalist values. *Spacebank* clients can open functioning bank accounts, invest in established stock exchanges, buy bonds, and trade, all using the Digital Maoist Sunflower network currency, which is backed by the labor of its founder, Fran Ilich, a media artist, writer, and activist. The *Spacebank* network allows participants to "purify their money" by investing in socially conscious projects involving art and activism, including a community farmers market, through a micro-financing program. As *Spacebank*'s mission states, "We help you reach your objectives … without hurting others."

Ilich operates *Spacebank* under his umbrella D.I.Y. media conglomerate Diego de la Vega, which takes its name from the 'true' identity of the fictional pulp character Zorro. Diego de la Vega, a limited liability corporation that Ilich started with fifty pesos, now hosts a web server (Possibleworlds.org), a research and development initiative on narrative media (Ficcion.de), a collective online radio (Radiolatina.am), a community newspaper (elzorro.org), and a think-tank called Collective Intelligence Agency (ci-a.info).

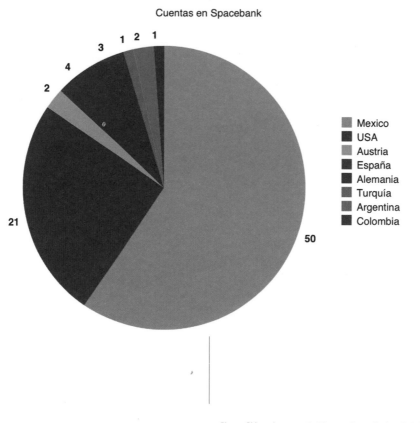

Above: Although account holders are located primarily in Mexico, people from all over the world have opened Spacebank accounts (Courtesy Fran Ilich).

TELLERVO KALLEINEN AND OLIVER KOCHTA-KALLEINEN
COMPLAINTS CHOIR
2005–

As organizers of *Complaints Choir*, Tellervo Kalleinen and Oliver Kochta-Kalleinen have heard it all: "My dreams are boring." "My grandmother is a racist." "My neighbor organizes Hungarian folk dances above my bedroom." "I am fat and lazy and half-old." Since 2005, the artists, who live in Helsinki, Finland, have invited people to sing their gripes in unison, in public, and online. The process is simple. First, invite others. Then, find a good musician. Once complaints are collected, written in verse, and rehearsed, participants are asked to record a public performance and submit it to the *Complaints Choir* website, a warehouse for songs with submissions from Japan to Chicago. Complaints include the overtly political—for example, social injustices in a small, Brazilian town—to the deeply personal, like having too much sex on the brain. "The private, the personal, can be very political," Kalleinen and

Top to bottom: The Complaints Choir of St. Petersburg performing in 2006 (Photograph by Yuriy Rumiantsev). The Complaints Choir of Helsinki rehearses in 2006 (Photograph by Heidi Piiroinen).

Kochta-Kalleinen write on their website. "'I have too much time!' can be seen as a personal tragedy, but also points to a major defect in capitalistic society, which sidelines people because they are of no use in the production cycle." In Cairo, Egypt, a recent complaints choir drew so much interest and such large crowds, that it evolved into the "Choir Project," an ongoing, local version that generates reflections and concerns about political conditions in the region.

Kalleinen and Kochta-Kalleinen make work that often documents daily experiences, such as on-the-job mishaps, and doctor-patient relationships. The artists first got the idea for *Complaints Choir* while living in Finland, where the word for those who complain literally translates to "complaint choir." They compiled their first choir in Birmingham, England, with the help of two arts organizations; since then, over seventy choirs have formed around the world.

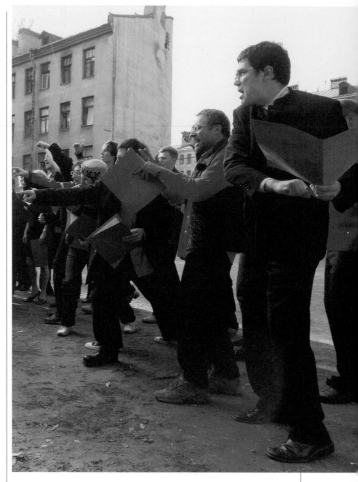

AMAL KENAWY
SILENCE OF THE LAMBS
2010

opening and closing of the exhibition. However, the second iteration was cancelled before the show's end, in fear of inciting further conflict on the street.

SURASI KUSOLWONG
MINIMAL FACTORY/
($1 MARKET)/
RED BULL PARTY (WITH D.J.)
2002

In December 2010, while citizens across the Middle East rose in widespread political unrest, fifteen men and women crawled across a busy Cairo intersection on their hands and knees, at the instruction of Egyptian artist Amal Kenawy. The performers, who included Kenawy's brother, a curator, and a dozen hired day laborers, moved slowly in a single file line, impeding traffic and drawing a large, emotionally charged crowd. Some passersby were annoyed by the halt of midday travel; others protested the potential critique of the state that triggered the act, as well as the submissive behavior of the men in line. Many people filmed and photographed the performance, which took place during the opening of 25th Alexandria Biennale and an international curatorial workshop in Cairo, organized by Tate. The artist and participants were eventually arrested, and briefly imprisoned, once heated tempers turned violent. On the surface, the action seemed to simply jar the daily routine of people on the street; yet, their ensuing reactions reflected an underlying conservatism, and undercurrent of tension rampant in the region.

Kenawy's *Silence of the Lambs* was commissioned for the exhibition *Assume the Position* at Cairo's Townhouse Gallery for Contemporary Art, and included photographs and videos as well as newspaper clippings of the event. The performance was scheduled to occur twice, marking the

Black Friday. Christmas Eve. End-of-season sales. If you've ever visited a shopping mall, a department store, or an outlet center you've experienced the frenzy and emotional high of material consumption that fascinates Thai artist Surasi Kusolwong. Imagine a dimly-lit, factory-like space scattered with long tables in primary colors. Each table is heaped with a seemingly random assortment of goods, like a clandestine rummage sale: washing baskets, soup ladles, footballs, space invader machines, inflatable toys, and footballs. As you peruse the space, a DJ pumps loud, energetic dance music and a counter offers cold cans of Red Bull. Other shoppers swarm over the abundance of goods, piling baskets high with colorful items, all on sale for $1 each.

This is Kusolwong's *Minimal Factory/($1 Market)/Red Bull Party (with D.J.)*, part of his touring *Market* project. Exploring the intersection of art, consumption, and community, Kusolwong

Opposite, top to bottom: The Complaints Choir of St. Petersburg performing in 2006 (Photograph by Yuriy Rumiantsev). The first Complaints Choir was formed in Birmingham in 2005 (Photograph by Springhill Institute).

recreates a typical Thai market with cheap goods purchased *en masse* in Bangkok. As shoppers fawn over the Thai-manufacture goods—made precious by their exotic origin and the gallery setting—Kusolwong intends the thumping music and beverage service to draw out the social interactions inherent to the consumer experience.

Kusolwong's practice navigates between public and private spaces, playing with concepts of both economic and cultural values, and the dialogue between people, art, and consumer products. His interactive installation *Golden Ghost (The Future Belongs To Ghosts)*, which was commissioned for Creative Time's 2011 exhibition *Living as Form*, was composed of large piles of multicolored, tangled thread waste—a byproduct of textile production. Hidden within the thread waste were gold necklaces designed by the artist. Visitors were invited to dig through the sea of delicate knots in search of the jewelry. Every week, the artist added another piece of jewelry to what he called the "economic landscape."

Top to bottom: At the *1 Euro Blinky Market (Dumme Kiste)* in 2006 at Westfaelische Kunstverein, Münster, Germany, over 2,000 everyday objects from Thailand were sold for one euro each. For the Cork Caucus in 2005, Kusolwong invited various local market vendors to take part in *1 Euro BangCork Market*, which took place over three days. (Courtesy of Surasi Kusolwong)

Top to bottom: 1,000 Lire Market (La vita continua), 2001, featured various everyday objects sold for 1,000 Lire in the main square of Casole d'Elsa, Sienna, Italy. The *10 Kronor Market (ohne die Rose tun wir's nicht)* featured Thai goods for sale for ten Kronor each at the Rooseum Center for Contemporary Art, Malmö, Sweden, in 2004. (Courtesy of Surasi Kusolwong)

BRONWYN LACE AND ANTHEA MOYS
EN MASSE
2010–

The first step in solving problems may be learning how to talk about them, and by appreciating what Johannesburg-based artists Anthea Moys and Bronwyn Lace consider to be the vastly underappreciated components of the creative process: "those aspects of becoming inspired, brainstorming, sharing, and debating." In 2010, they launched *En Masse*, a several-year, multi-step effort to suggest working models for environmental activism by first bringing together a group of forty-nine artists, architects, science educators, engineers, and curators at the Bag Factory Artists' Studios, where Lace serves as education director—then implementing their ideas in subsequent phases. Attendees of these initial workshops participated in eight three-hour conversations. Lace and Moys presented the results of the workshop sessions in an exhibition, which included installations, audio recordings of the conversations, drawings, and textual documentation.

The discussions and exhibition in 2010 introduced participants to one another and then encouraged people to develop ideas in collaboration. For example, Metro Mass—a proposed solution to Johannesburg's problematic public transportation—calls for over 5,000 suburbanites from the Greater Johannesburg Metropolitan Area to give up their vehicles on a given day.

Top: Lace and Moys produced a series of workshops, exhibitions, performances, and a book. *Bottom row:* The installation of *En Masse* included linked text and images (Courtesy Bronwyn Lace and Anthea Moys).

SUZANNE LACY

THE ROOF IS ON FIRE
1994

For one afternoon in 1994, two hundred and twenty high school students in Oakland, California, sat in parked cars on a rooftop garage and talked to each other about violence, sex, gender, family, and race. The teens spoke candidly, without any kind of script, while an audience of nearly one thousand people—including numerous reporters and camera crews—walked from car to car, leaning in and bending over, to hear their conversations through rolled-down windows. The resulting footage of the performance, called *The Roof Is On Fire*, was aired locally on multiple networks and nationally on CNN.

Oakland teens were already accustomed to receiving media attention, though largely through negative portrayals of young people involved in riots, violence, and conflicts with police. This event, however, which was organized by artist Suzanne Lacy in conjunction with TEAM (a group of teens, educators, artists, and media workers), was designed as a positive media spectacle, with young people depicted as citizens rather than liabilities. For five months, Lacy met weekly with teachers and teens, including those from a nearby probation program, to discuss issues important to them, and to craft a message for civic leaders about the role of young people in Oakland's future. *The Roof Is On Fire* reflected the crux of those discussions, as well as Lacy's decades-long mission to counter misleading media images with empowered, community-oriented actions. Since the 1970s, she has created performances that offer alternative narratives and interpretations of news coverage. For example, *In Mourning and In Rage* presented a public ritual on the steps of Los Angeles' City Hall in response to coverage of the murders of 10 women in December 1977. While the stories focused on the random nature of the violence, Lacy's collaborative performance was a call to action, and reframing of the killing spree from a feminist perspective.

Above: Four Oakland teens that participated in Lacy's *The Roof Is On Fire* candidly discuss pressing topics while an audience listens in (Courtesy Suzanne Lacy).

Above: The Roof Is On Fire took place on the rooftop of an Oakland parking garage one evening in 1994 (Courtesy Suzanne Lacy).

LAND FOUNDATION
THE LAND
1998–

In 1998, artists Rirkrit Tiravanija and Kamin Lertchaiprasert bought a rice field in Sanpatong, a village 20 minutes outside of Chiang Mai, Thailand. At the time, flooding in the area had rendered rice cultivation difficult; instead, they began cultivating, and experimenting with, notions of utopian, socially responsible living. *The Land* became a testing ground for meditation and ideas, such as ecologically conscious systems that don't rely on the use of electricity or gas, but call for self-sufficiency, sustainable practices, and natural resources. For example, harnessing bio-mass (or fecal matter) to generate power; creating fishing ponds filled with purified water; building kitchens modeled to support communal living; and installing meditation rooms.

Since purchasing the property, they have invited artists from around the world, including SUPERFLEX, Tobias Rehberger, Philippe Parreno and François Roche, to create projects and to build housing structures on *The Land*. They also began growing rice once the ground was viable again, and donated the food to local villages—communities that have been ravaged by the AIDS epidemic in the region.

Tiravanija is best known for cooking and serving Pad Thai to visitors of a Soho gallery (one of the first instances of so-called "relational aesthetics" that engages audiences as participants instead of viewers) while Lertchaiprasert's art often explores the daily rituals, disciplines, and values of Buddhism. Though the artists continue to live on *The Land*, operations are managed by *The Land Foundation*—an independent, anonymous group—in an effort to disperse ownership among the space's users, visitors, and inhabitants.

Top to bottom: American artist Robert Peters and Thai artist Thasnai Sethaseree designed *Asian Provision*. Lin Yilin's *Whose Land? Whose Art?* consisted of two walls, one constructed in the countryside in Chiang Mai, Thailand, and the other in a Bangkok gallery. Farming at the Land Foundation is open to those who wish to learn. (Courtesy The Land Foundation)

Top to bottom: German architect and installation artist Markus Heinsdorff designed the *Living Bamboo Dome*, which will regenerate by means of renewable construction approximately every three years. *Angkrit's House*, a simple structure for one person designed by Thai artist Angkrit Ajchariyasophon, was inspired by housing for Buddhist priests at a monastery in Chiang-Rai, Thailand. (Courtesy The Land Foundation)

Top to bottom: Rice paddy farming is organized in a two-crop annual cycle. *Somyot & Thaivijit's House*, by Thai artists Somyot Hananuntasuk and Thaivijit Poengkasemsom, was conceived as a venue for sharing ideas and designed to accommodate a staging area for performances. A Buddhist farming concept inspires the agricultural layout of the rice paddies—only one quarter of the area is solid ground while the other three are water, similar to the composition of the human body. (Courtesy The Land Foundation)

LONG MARCH PROJECT
HO CHI MINH TRAIL
2008–2011

In 2008, the Beijing-based art collective Long March Project launched an expedition across the Ho Chi Minh Trail, originally a secret system of jungle pathways during the Vietnam War. For this trip, also called *Ho Chi Minh Trail*, Long March invited international and local curators, artists, scholars, and students to re-walk part of the trail while participating in panel discussions, visual art collaborations, and other creative actions in cities on the itinerary. Understanding that history is as complex and branched as the 600-mile path, Long March's program uses the trail as a point of entry into dialogue about Vietnam's past and present. "Though internationally understood as a logistical supply route created during the Second Indochina War, [the trail] formed a vast network of passageways across China, Vietnam, Laos and Cambodia," Long March writes. Their *Ho Chi Minh Trail* was envisioned as a "nomadic residency," in these same countries, as well as their international diasporas, with the goal of exploring interactions the legacy of interactions among the regions: "How can sensitive misgivings between cultural and social communities be creatively engaged so as to create new identifications, and new possibilities of beneficial engagement where … prejudices are laid aside?"

Founded by artist and writer Lu Jie, Long March Project takes its name from the historic military retreat of the Chinese Red Army from nationalist troops in 1945. In 2002, the collective toured the 6,000-mile historical stretch; called *A Walking Visual Display*, Long March brought together 250 artists, curators, writers, theorists, and scholars in public parks, community halls, private living rooms, and government offices to discuss topics such as the "ideological legacy of the Cultural Revolution," and "the birth of Communism." The trip was documented through photography, installations, painting, performances, symposia, and other forums.

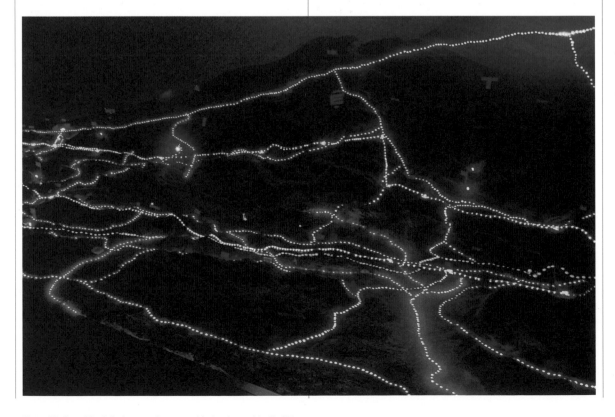

Above: The Long March Project uses the geographical pathway of the Ho Chi Minh trail to reexamine China's socialist and revolutionary past (Courtesy Long March Project).

LOS ANGELES POVERTY DEPARTMENT
AGENTS & ASSETS
2001–

Los Angeles Poverty Department is a 26-year-old theater company that employs homeless actors living on the city's Skid Row, one of the largest homeless populations in the country. In 2001, LAPD produced *Agents & Assets,* a staged performance of the "Report on the Central Intelligence Agency's Alleged Involvement in Crack Cocaine Trafficking in Los Angeles"—transcripts that were presented to the House of Representatives after the *LA Times* launched an investigation into the charges. Though the CIA was eventually acquitted, the LAPD's production explored the implications of high-level profiteering by enlisting homeless actors to perform as Congress members and CIA officials. Each performance was followed by discussions between law-enforcement officials, audience members, and the actors involved.

In 1985, actor John Malpede founded, and still continues to direct, LAPD, the first performance group in the nation comprised primarily of homeless and formerly homeless people, giving this often silent community a voice and platform to speak—not simply about the experience of being homeless, but about the political and civic conditions that create poverty, as well as areas such as Skid Row. Malpede had worked with, and advocated for the rights of, homeless populations in New York. The theater company began as an improvisational group, and now primarily produces scripted works that address injustices within the criminal justice system. LAPD's productions are often site-specific installations, as well as public projects with educational programming.

Above: Agents and Assets being performed in Cochabamba, Bolivia, in 2009. (Photograph by Henriëtte Brouwers).

UNIVERSITY OF WINCHESTER LIBRARY

MAMMALIAN DIVING REFLEX
HAIRCUTS BY CHILDREN
2006

For one day, fifth- and sixth-grade students from Toronto's Parkdale Public School provided haircuts, free of charge, in hair salons across the city. Using the tresses of mannequin heads, they trained for one week with professional stylists, learning how to trim bangs, add color, shave necklines, create long layers, and use a blow dryer. While adults provided supervision during the sessions, most patrons trusted the novice hairdressers, who worked in pairs or groups, to make aesthetic decisions like color choices and hair length, on their own. The project, which later traveled internationally, culminated in a two-day series of performances at the Milk International Children's Festival of the Arts back in Toronto.

Haircuts By Children was organized by Mammalian Diving Reflex, a Toronto-based arts and research group that creates very specific interactions between people in public spaces. For *Out of My League*, participants were asked to approach strangers who they believed were 'out of their league' and engage in conversation with them. *Slow Dance with Teacher* made high-school teachers available for one night to slow dance with their students. The group's name is inspired by a self-preservation technique triggered by extreme physical duress. For example, when the body is suddenly submerged in water or caught in a freezing environment, all major bodily functions slow almost to a halt, minimizing the need for oxygen, and increasing the chances of survival. To that end, *Haircuts* leveraged the image of children per-forming a highly specialized, and personal, form or labor, as well as the often-precocious nature of 10- to 12-year-olds, to convey a larger message: If children can be empowered as creative thinkers and decision makers, shouldn't they be allowed to vote, too?

Above: A woman enjoys a free haircut from students in Parkdale Public School's 5th and 6th grade classes. *Opposite:* Stan Bevington receives a haircut from Amahayes Mulugeta and Dailia Linton. (Photographs by John Lauener)

MARDI GRAS INDIAN COMMUNITY
FUNERAL PROCESSION FOR BIG CHIEF ALLISON "TOOTIE" MONTANA

2005

Since the 1800s, working-class Blacks in New Orleans paid tribute to Native Americans who aided escaped slaves on their routes to safety by "masking Indian": building and donning elaborate costumes for Mardi Gras, fashioned from layers upon layers of feathers, beads, sequins, and billowing fabrics dyed in energetic colors. For 52 years, Allison "Tootie" Montana, a construction worker and chief of the chiefs of these Mardi Gras Indians, lead the parade: His signature, three-dimensional geometric designs often weighed hundreds of pounds, costs thousands of dollars, and earned him a National Endowments for the Arts grant, and was the subject of feature-length documentary. On July 10, 2005, thousands New Orleans residents gathered to march in his funeral procession, out of respect for his art, and his advocacy for this community.

Montana was a long-time, outspoken advocate for Mardi Gras Indians, who often faced discrimination from local law enforcement. On the night of his death, he addressed the City Council, along with other chiefs, to protest police brutality, as well as efforts to squash Mardi Gras Indian parades and other public gatherings. Moments later he collapsed on the floor, and was taken to a nearby hospital, where he was pronounced dead of a heart attack. His funeral procession, which drew both non-Indians and Indians, was one of the largest to trickle down the well-known parade route from the church to the cemetery; participants beat tambourines, chanted, and moved like rhythmic clouds of aqua, orange, red, and yellow smoke.

Above: Members of The Baby Dolls pay their respect to Big Chief Allison "Tootie" Montana (Photograph by Keith Calhoun).

Opposite, top to bottom: Mardi Gras Indians attend the funeral of Big Chief Allison "Tootie" Montana. The funeral took place in Treme, and a large part of the community turned out to pay their respects. (Photographs by Keith Calhoun)

ANGELA MELITOPOULOS AND COLLABORATORS
TIMESCAPES/B-ZONE
2005–2006

For three years, video artists and activists from Germany (Angela Melitopoulos and Hito Steyerl), Serbia (Dragana Zarevac), Greece (Freddy Viannelis), and Turkey (Octay Ince and Videa) worked to build a shared video database called *Timescapes,* which uses non-linear editing to explore collective memory and alternative forms of filmic representation.

Through this experimental, collaborative media, the group explored themes of mobility and migration in "B-Zone territories"—political areas subject to mutations, wars, and conflicts that resulted from the rise of European infrastructure projects and new routes of migration after the fall of the Berlin Wall. These territories exist at the crossroads of three major political regions: Europe, the countries of the former Soviet Union, and the Arab-Islamic World.

Each of the collaborators participating in *Timescapes/B-Zones* hailed from locations along the "old" European axis between Berlin and Istanbul—one so-called B-Zone—and contributed images and visualizations that, combined, suggested a psychological landscape of that territory. Going beyond a simple accumulation of images and facts, the artists manipulate audio and visual content as a means of questioning the supposedly progressive capitalist ideology of integration. The process has yielded two projects: *Behind the Mountain* (70 min., 2005), a video essay on forced migration in Turkey, and *Corridor X* (124 min., 2006), a road movie that travels through the Tenth European Corridor between Germany and Turkey.

Timescapes/B-Zones was conceived of by artist Angela Melitopoulos, who creates time-based work, including experimental single-channel-tapes, video installations, video essays, documentaries, and sound pieces that focus on issues of migration, memory, and narrative.

Above: Timescapes' video database explores "B-Zone territories," which are the political areas affected by the fall of the Berlin Wall (Courtesy Angela Melitopoulos).

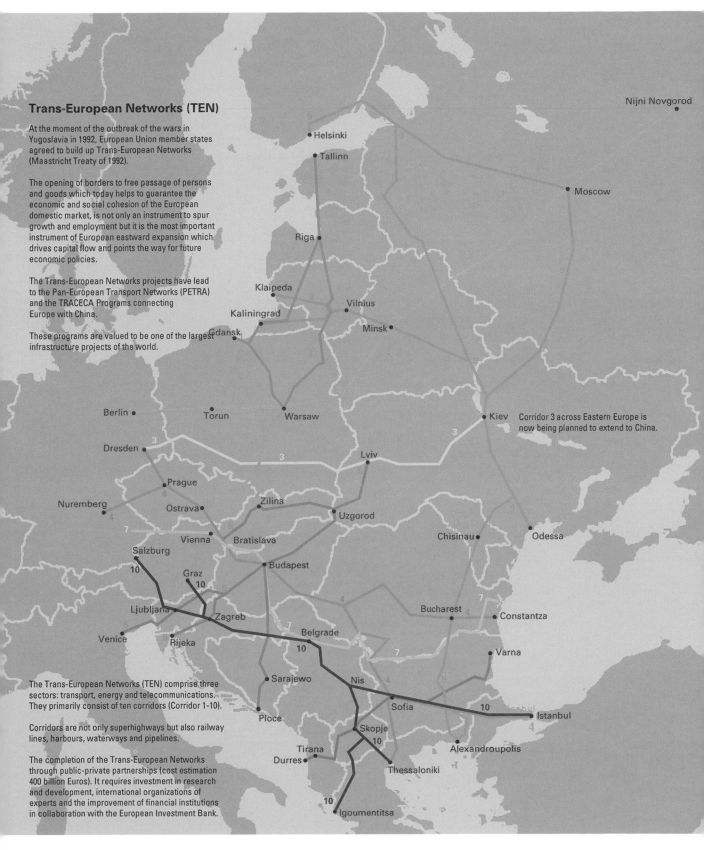

Trans-European Networks (TEN)

At the moment of the outbreak of the wars in Yugoslavia in 1992, European Union member states agreed to build up Trans-European Networks (Maastricht Treaty of 1992).

The opening of borders to free passage of persons and goods which today helps to guarantee the economic and social cohesion of the European domestic market, is not only an instrument to spur growth and employment but it is the most important instrument of European eastward expansion which drives capital flow and points the way for future economic policies.

The Trans-European Networks projects have lead to the Pan-European Transport Networks (PETRA) and the TRACECA Programs connecting Europe with China.

These programs are valued to be one of the largest infrastructure projects of the world.

Corridor 3 across Eastern Europe is now being planned to extend to China.

The Trans-European Networks (TEN) comprise three sectors: transport, energy and telecommunications. They primarily consist of ten corridors (Corridor 1-10).

Corridors are not only superhighways but also railway lines, harbours, waterways and pipelines.

The completion of the Trans-European Networks through public-private partnerships (cost estimation 400 billion Euros). It requires investment in research and development, international organizations of experts and the improvement of financial institutions in collaboration with the European Investment Bank.

Above: The Trans-European Networks consists of ten corridors that connect parts of Eastern European (Courtesy Angela Melitopoulos).

ZAYD MINTY
BLACK ARTS COLLECTIVE
1998–2003

dis**EMPOWERED**

**CHOICE
ASSORTE**

dis**EMPOWERED**

In the late 1990s, South Africa-based cultural planner and researcher Zayd Minty became aware that artists in his home city lacked adequate spaces in which to openly discuss their practices. It was also clear that many black artists still felt invisible in post-Apartheid South Africa. According to one artist, who later worked with Minty, the city lacked "a place where I could feel both safe and intellectually stimulated...[a place] that allowed me to explore the complex and often contradictory race politics of post-1994 South Africa." Drawing inspiration from the Robben Island Artist Residency Program and other successful artist exchange programs, Minty founded the Black Arts Collective (BLAC) in late 1998 with an inaugural seminar held at the Old Granary building in Cape Town.

For five years, BLAC provided a forum for "discourse building" and explored issues of race, power, and identity through workshops, seminars, articles, public art projects, and a website. Intentionally temporary in its duration, BLAC aimed to address specific, local moments and concerns, sidestepping larger "grand narratives" about race relations. The loose collective of artists, working across media, met regularly to dis-

Top row, left to right: Donovan Ward's *Leisure Time* billboard sat opposite Guga S'thebe Multipurpose Centre in Langa, South Africa (Photograph by Nic Aldridge, Courtesy BLAC). Mustafa Maluka's postcard *Choice* was a part of *Returning the Gaze,* an exhibition in Cape Town in 2000 (Art by Mustafa Maluka, Courtesy BLAC).

Bottom row, left to right: A mural on Klipfontein Road was a part of *Returning the Gaze* (Photograph by Nic Aldridge, Courtesy BLAC). The *Leisure Time* billboard by Donovan Ward was designed for *Returning the Gaze* at the 2000 Cape Town One City Festival (Art by Donovan Ward, Courtesy BLAC).

cuss contemporary black identity, even at times questioning the use of the term at all.

The project adopted a three-fold strategy: to create discussions (through the seminar series and commissioning of articles), to document and publish (through the website project Blaconline), and to provide a platform for production. Several specific public exhibitions took place during this period, including the exhibition "Returning the Gaze" at the 2000 Cape Town One City Festival. The organization served as both an investigation into the cultural politics of black identity as it relates to art, and a professional resource for black artists in Cape Town.

THE MOBILE ACADEMY
THE BLACKMARKET FOR USEFUL KNOWLEDGE AND NON-KNOWLEDGE

2005–

Visitors to *The Blackmarket for Useful Knowledge and Non-Knowledge* can book 30-minute sessions with experts on a range of subjects, from sex and politics to esoteric word games and the meaning of life. In the fashion of speed dating, student and teacher sit across from each other, separated by small, dimly lit tables, while crowds of people wander and eavesdrop in an effort to preview the discussions before choosing among the roughly 100 topics. This traveling event usu-

ally takes place in spaces associated with learning or communication, such as theaters or reading rooms—eschewing privileged transfers of knowledge for shared, non-hierarchical exchanges.

Organized by The Mobile Academy's curator Hannah Hurtzig, *Blackmarket* has occurred in Berlin, Istanbul, Liverpool, and Jaffa, among other locations. The Mobile Academy is an umbrella for projects she initiates with a rotating group of collaborators.

Hurtzig founded The Mobile Academy in 1999, after a long career in theater, particularly experimental German productions focused on disturbing the illusions inherent in representation, which influenced both *Blackmarket* and The Mobile Academy. For example, unscripted conversations with non-actors (like call-center workers and politicians); incorporating food in performances; and staging prohibitively long events that forces audiences to notice their own physical presence and responses. She creates public access to educational resources such as sound archives, film archives, and theater installations—projects with an educational, participatory bent.

Above: At the *Blackmarket for Useful Knowledge and Non-Knowledge No. 10* in Vienna in 2008, up to 100 experts shared their knowledge with participants in half-hour increments (Photograph by Dorothea Wimmer).

MUJERES CREANDO
DUEDORAS
2001–

In 2001, over 6,000 people traveled from Bolivia's provinces to its capital La Paz to protest the loss of their businesses and homes, and ensuing bankruptcy, due to crippling interest rates on microcredit loans. Called Duedoras, or "debtors," this group of primarily low-income women occupied the streets while their family members, out of financial desperation, committed suicide back home. By July, the demonstrations, which had generated little response from the government, escalated: the Duedoras began taking hostages in city buildings, and engaged in violent confrontation with the police.

To mitigate the situation, and prompt negotiations, the self-described anarcho-feminist collective Mujeres Creando (Creative Women), began organizing peaceful activities that would allow the Duedoras to be heard publicly, while rebuilding relationships with stakeholders. This included the creation of a public mural bearing the paint-dipped footprints of protesters (which symbolized their long journey); a series of financial management courses; and other non-violent street actions.

Founded in 1992 by activists Julieta Paredes, María Galindo and Mónica Mendoza, Mujeres Creando are best known for their anti-capitalist messages disseminated as elegantly scripted, public graffiti. Since its inception, the collective has also published an independent newspaper, opened a café, and broadcast a public interest television program, while collaborating with universities, unions, and rural workers to devise challenges to corporate and neoliberal activities.

Above, top to bottom: Mujeres Creando intervene in a clash between insolvent Bolivian women and the police. The Mujeres Creando have developed the concept of Estado Proxeneta (Pimp State), as evidenced in this graffiti reading "Pimp State; I do not want prostitution, I want work." (Courtesy Mujeres Creando)

Above: The performance of Virgin Barbie was shown as part of the exhibition
Principio Potosí (Courtesy Mujeres Creando)

VIK MUNIZ
PICTURES OF GARBAGE
2008

"What I want to be able to do is change the lives of people with the same materials they deal with every day," says artist Vik Muniz in *Wasteland*, a documentary film that follows the production of his photographic series *Pictures of Garbage*. In 2008, Muniz traveled to Brazil, where he was born and raised, to work with garbage pickers from Jardim Gramacho, a 321-acre, open-air dump, the largest in South America, located just outside of Rio. An informal and marginalized labor source, these workers scavenge the garbage that arrives daily, searching for recyclable items to sell. Muniz enlisted them to help him design, and then pose for, massive portraits composed of the collected detritus. The resulting works conjure classical portraiture in which his collaborators are elevated to mythical status amid the trash that looks deceptively like precious material, or thick, glimmering paint.

Muniz lifted more than just the workers' image through his art. He paid all participants for their time and contributed materials. He also auctioned off the works, and donated his share of the sales to the Garbage Pickers Association of Jardim Gramacho, the workers' representative body. Most significantly, he continued to collaborate with them to help enact a formal recycling program in Brazil, bring awareness of their labor to a wider public, and bolster a sense of dignity in this historically underrepresented community and more. In the past few years, plans to close Jardim Gramacho—and implement the first widespread, national recycling program in the country—have surfaced.

Pictures of Garbage typifies much of Muniz's work—near *trompe l'oeil* in his use of lay materials from syrup to peanut butter to figurines. To produce these photographs, which have been exhibited globally, he spent two years at the land-

Top: Muniz used material from a dump in Rio de Janeiro to create this enormous portrait of a *carlao*, a garbage picker, inspired by the *Farnese Atlas* sculpture (Courtesy Vik Muniz).

fill, a common practice for the Brooklyn-based artist who has been invested in supporting non-profit organizations in Brazil, particularly those that offer training and education to underserved children.

NAVIN PRODUCTION STUDIO
MAHĀKĀD ART FESTIVAL: EPIC ARTS IN THE MARKET

2010–2011

Chiang Mai's Warorot Market, which dates back to the 19th century, is best characterized by the word "epic": The densely packed stalls and stores feature inexhaustible rows of wares, from vegetables and chickens to brightly dyed textiles and plastic knick-knacks. Likewise, the market's population has become an equally diverse cross-section of religious and ethnic identities over the years. Artist Navin Rawanchaikul grew up working in his family's fabric store amid the complex, cultural mélange. To celebrate the market's centennial anniversary, he organized an arts festival, called *Mahākād*, inspired by the market's history, that included site-specific installations and events as well as two-dimensional works such as historical photographs; portraits of its current inhabitants; and a vast, monochromatic mural depicting 200 community members. In reference to the international scope of the market, visitors were given maps of the space, and leaflets designed to look like "passports," which could be stamped at each art station. After receiving ten stamps, visitors were eligible to receive a free magazine that recounts *Mahākād's* history. Directed by Rawanchaikul's Navin Production Studio, and in collaboration with several community groups, the festival's accompanying activities

Bottom: Rawanchaikul created a large-format panoramic photograph depicting more than 200 members of the Chiang Mai community—some living, some long dead (Courtesy Navin Rawanchaikul)

included workshops, a tour of the project sites led by Rawanchaikul and a panel discussion about community engagement in contemporary art practices. The festival's title references the ancient Indian text *Mahābhārata*—a complex, network of characters and plots that reflects the interwoven relationships embedded in the market.

Rawanchaikul uses the realm of the everyday as both the subject and venue of his art. He often creates his work under the banner of Navin Production Co., Ltd., his production company that he founded in 1994 and launched by producing bottled, polluted water from a canal in Chiang Mai. In 1995, he initiated "Navin Gallery Bangkok," his taxicab-turned-mobile art gallery.

NEUE SLOWENISCHE KUNST (NSK) EMBASSY IN MOSCOW

1992

Since 1984, Ljubljana, Slovenia-based art collective Neue Slowenische Kunst (NSK) has been creating paintings, posters, music, and manifestos designed to critique governments through incisive, satirical jabs. For example, NSK won a Yugoslavian youth poster contest by slyly alluding to a famous Nazi painting in its entry; tweaked Slovenia's national anthem by singing it in German while wearing military boots; and have repeatedly adopted the kitschy imagery and language of totalitarianism, from hammer-wielding workers to heavy-antlered deer, in their diverse works. In doing so, NSK—which consists of the band Laibach, visual art collective IRWIN, performers Noordung, and graphic designers New Collectivism—tries to dismantle these symbols

Top to bottom: NSK members and guests attend a gathering at the Moscow Embassy, which was established in a private apartment in 1992. In addition to hosting lectures and public discussions, the Moscow Embassy presented paintings, posters, design work, and videos. (Photographs by Jože Suhadolnik)

and the power structures they represent.

Yet NSK's subversive projects have also been sincere, political acts: In 1992, after Yugoslavia collapsed, the group virtually seceded from Slovenia to form "State in Time," its own utopian micronation. NSK produced national postage stamps, wrote an anthem, and issued passports seemingly authentic enough that hundreds of people used them to cross the border out of Sarajevo. The group also set up embassies in cities across Europe, beginning with its *Embassy in Moscow*, an event that launched the "State in Time" project. The *Embassy in Moscow* was modeled after an exhibition series titled *Apartment Art (or APT ART)*, which was first organized in the 1980s by underground Russian artists looking to escape official censorship by hosting events in private spaces. NSK revived this history in its own version—a month-long, live installation in a private apartment, bearing the emblem of a faux state embassy on the building's façade. The event featured lectures, talks, and visual works (primarily produced by members of IRWIN) meant to ignite public discussion about pressing social issues in Eastern Europe.

NUTS SOCIETY
1998–

Nuts Society, in Bangkok, Thailand, employs the language of marketing and consumerism—for example, selling clothing, creating window signage, and packaging products—to foster social consciousness and responsibility in daily practices. In 2002, the group printed the Thai alphabet on large sheets of paper and hung the posters in street-level windows. Called *A Page From Exercising Thai: A Learning Reform*, the project, commissioned by Art in General, aimed to teach passersby how to read the Thai alphabet, using words that represent basic values of social justice, such as "shared," "respect," and "tolerance." Infiltrating spaces in which one would expect to find advertising and eschewing the consumer maxim of "more," signage encouraged viewers to "be adequate, be sufficient, be enough." The poster design was eventually printed on t-shirts, which were sold in the storefront of a Cincinnati art gallery.

For *Nuts Society Tattoo Station*, Nuts Society built a tattoo parlor at the Alliance Française Center in Bangkok, through which they critiqued global consumerism's lack of moral values using uniquely designed tattoos. Other projects, like the Pandora Cookie Project, which fosters child development through the making of educational cookies, and *The New ABC of Learning* promote positive education through creative, direct engagement with language. Since forming in 1998, Nuts Society has worked anonymously and collectively in both public spaces and arts institutions with the mission of delivering earnest messages about civic and global life through humorous and playful images.

JOHN O'NEAL
JUNEBUG PRODUCTIONS/ FREE SOUTHERN THEATER
1980–

In 1963 actor, director, and playwright John O'Neal, a former member of the Student Non-violent Coordinating Committee, founded the Free Southern Theater (FST), which introduced theater to rural, Southern communities through live performances, professional training opportunities, and audience engagement programs with the goal of exposing social injustices in African-American communities. Since then, O'Neal has been a leading advocate of the view that "politics" and "art" are complementary, not opposing terms. When the company dissolved in 1980, after decades of involvement in the social justice and Black Arts movements, Free Southern Theater's last production became the first of its successor, Junebug Productions.

A New Orleans-based nonprofit, Junebug continues FST's tradition of developing theater, dance, music, and other performing arts that reflect the experiences of African Americans in the South by working with educators and organizers to produce community projects, and by supporting residencies with high-school students. The company, which was named after a character created by the SNCC, Junebug Jabbo Jones—a mythic storyteller who narrates the experience of life in the Deep South—continues to use the history of the Civil Rights Movement to explore contemporary issues addressing equality and justice, such as the disastrous social and economic conditions that took root after Hurricane Katrina ravaged the Gulf Coast in 2005. To that end, Junebug's plays are informed by O'Neal's longstanding belief that the work of artists can help the public better understand the notion of a "social conscience."

Top: O'Neal in a performance at Junebug Productions, which he founded in 1963 as a cultural arm of the Civil Rights Movement (Courtesy John O'Neal).

ODA PROJESI
APARTMENT PROJECT
2000–2005

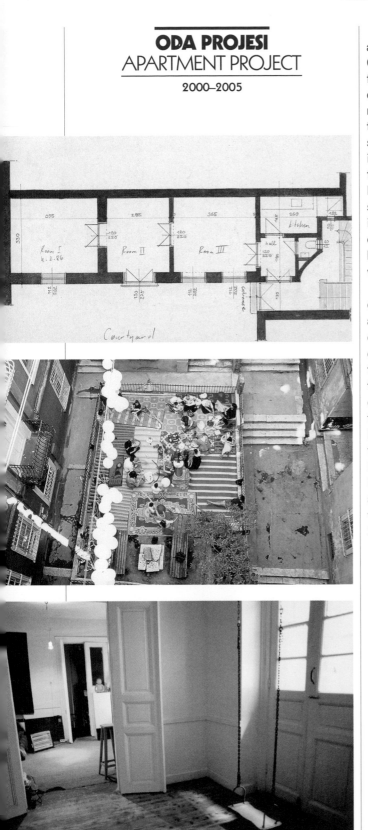

In 2000, artists Özge Acıkkol, Günes Savas, and Secil Yersel, working as the artist collective Oda Projesi (Room Project), rented a three-room flat in Galata, a historic urban district in Istanbul characterized by the mixed income levels of its residents, and the Istiklal, a well-known pedestrian stroll that runs through it. The area also serves as an entertainment district where many immigrants from Eastern Turkey gather when they first arrive in the city. *Apartment Project* was Oda Projesi's organic transformation of the private space into a multipurpose public one, where artists, architects, musicians, neighbors, and children would congregate informally to plan projects, hold get-togethers, and exist communally both within and outside of the context of art.

Each room was equipped and designed to encourage creative, communal interaction—for example, drawing materials for children, an archive of art books, and free meeting space. During the collective's five-year occupation of the apartment they hosted nearly thirty projects, including youth theater workshops, and picnics in the courtyard; exercises in building long-term relationships in the neighborhood, rather than making objects, hosting exhibitions, or marketing the production of art. Since its inception, Oda Projesi has been interested in what space can mean when it borders both public and private. To that end, the artists, who self-financed the space, never advertised their programs, or held "open hours." In 2005, they were evicted due to a rent increase.

Top to bottom: The architectural plan of the three-room flat in Galata, Istanbul, rented by Oda Projesi from 2000–2005 for the *Apartment Project*. The space was host to nearly 30 projects between 2000 and 2005, including Erik Göngrich's *Picnic* in 2001. Artist Seçil Yersel installed *Swing* in the apartment from April 22 until May 19, 2000. (Courtesy Oda Projesi)

PARK FICTION AND THE RIGHT TO THE CITY NETWORK HAMBURG

1994

Above: A "planning container" moved around the St. Pauli neighborhood of Hamburg collecting residents' wishes for the development of the area (Photograph by Sven Barske, Courtesy Park Fiction).

When developers bid on a prestigious river-bank property in St. Pauli, a poor neighborhood in Hamburg, Germany, residents faced losing the only land in the area available for public use. But instead of protesting, they began picnicking and pretending that the contested site would soon house a public park rather than a high-rise office building. The project—dubbed Park Fiction—was initiated by the local residents' association and artist Christoph Schäfer, and emerged as a viable alternate to the city's plan, which favored commercial interests over the community' desire for recreational space.

The group rallied community residents to put the park to use for festivals, exhibitions, and talks—activities that demonstrated local culture and encouraged citizens to take control of the urban planning process themselves, rather than

seek the city's permission first. Inspired by theorists Gilles Deleuze and Félix Guattari's concept,
"the production of desires," Park Fiction coined
the phrase "Desires will leave the house and take
to the streets," to stress the residents' imaginative
transformation of the area.

They built a mobile "planning container"—
equipped with a telephone hotline, questionnaires, maps, and an instant camera—that became
a tool enabling members of the community to travel throughout the neighborhood to solicit input.
The container, as well as documentation of the
efforts that took place inside of it, was exhibited
at art events, including Documenta 11 in 2002.
This strategy of accumulating cultural capital,
then leveraging it to obtain government support
in the form of funding from the city's Art in Public
Space program, proved successful. In 2005, the
city abandoned plans to sell the property. A few
months later, residents installed the first of their
enhancements to the park: fake, plastic palm trees
and rolling AstroTurf.

Top to bottom: Nearly 1,000 spectators congregated at Park Fiction in July 2009
for a screening of *Empire St. Pauli,* a documentary about gentrification in the St.
Pauli neighborhood of Hamburg (Photograph by Antje Mohr, Courtesy Park Fiction). In 2005, a dog park complete with a poodle-shaped boxtree was created
in the park (Photograph by Hinrich Schulze, Courtesy Park Fiction).

PASE USTED
2008–

In 2010, Mexico celebrated the bicentennial of its independence movement, fostering a range of events and activities intended to, according the country's bicentennial homepage, "revive the values and ideals that shaped the nation." In anticipation of the bicentennial events, nine young people—from a range of disciplines, committed to the sharing of ideas and creation of an open community—founded Pase Usted in 2008.

The Mexico City-based nonprofit group promotes civic change and development through conferences that emphasize open dialogue and community building. Bringing together experts in various fields—civic engineering, architecture, art, city planning, design—the platform is unified by a shared agenda to address the most pressing needs facing the city. While community outreach is essential to each project, Pase Usted often enlists specialists to offer solutions where other options fail. While their activities vary—ranging from workshops to salons to exhibitions to public interventions—Pase Usted operates as an open source network, providing individuals with the technological tools needed to promote their ideas.

On April 23, 2011, Pase Usted, represented by Jorge Munguia, participated in a "Conversation on Useful Art," in Corona, Queens, hosted by Cuban artist Tania Bruguera at the headquarters of her project, *Immigrant Movement International*. The event, which also included artists Rick Lowe, Mel Chin, and Not An Alternative, asked participants

Above: Mexican artist Raúl Cárdenas (Torolab) discusses health care issues at a Pase Usted event (Photograph by Ariette Armella).

to share their work in the field of so-called "Useful Art." Pase Usted presented their work in Mexico City, focusing on the project "Genera," for which they made a "call for entries" to anyone with ideas on how to better the quality of life in Mexico City. The ten-week program gives funding to ten selected projects as a way of giving individual people the resources to actualize their ideas.

PIRATBYRÅN (THE BUREAU OF PIRACY)
THE PIRATE BAY
2003–

Launched in 2003 by the Swedish anti-copyright organization Piratbyrån, *Pirate Bay* is a large bittorrent tracking website that has reshaped the technical and legal parameters around file sharing. Key to this shift is a technology called "peer-to-peer," which deviates from standard downloading protocol. Traditional downloads transfer files from a single server. However, in "peer-to-peer" transfers, no centralized server exists; rather, file transfers occur between multiple clients, who send and receive only segments of files. *Pirate Bay* tracks files called "torrents" that in conjunction with "torrent" programs, can find users who share a given file. In doing so, file sharing can occur more quickly: Since multiple locations distribute the data, no single server can delay or interrupt file transfers. Likewise, since no single server can claim responsibility for the distribution of the file, copyright laws become harder to enforce. For example, record labels, film production companies, and software producers are less likely to sue multiple individuals for sharing files intended to be used only for personal use.

Above: Harvard education specialist Dr. Gabriel Cámara speaks to an engaged audience about the education revolution at a Pase Usted event (Photographs by Ariette Armella).

PLATFORMA 9.81

1999–

Platforma 9.81 is a Croatian group of architects, theorists, designers and urban planners. Founded in 1999 as an NGO, its aim has been to generate interdisciplinary debate on the culture of urban spaces, digitalization of the environment, effects of globalization, and shift in architectural practices. They have examined, for example, the layers in the urban fabric of Zagreb and its recent building projects, which reveal shifts in power structures induced by the transition from communism to capitalism.

Part of the group has concentrated on the Croatian coast and islands. For the project *Tourist Transformation,* Platforma members Dinko Peračić and Miranda Veljačić researched the rapid changes marked by global capital and tourism during the past decade. Their work has been driven by an interest in transformations in the built environment, such as the differing expectations, desires, and experiences of residents versus tourists, or the seasonal fluctuations. To that end, their practice traces the precarious balance between the environment and its habitants. They consider what the landscape might look like tomorrow, and the potential cultural implications that occur when relatively untouched regions undergo development.

Peračić and Veljačić have previously worked in another island location, the Lofoten Islands in Northern Norway. Their *The Weather Project* focused on the weather's effects on residents and visitors. They collected proposals from the public

Top to bottom: For their *Invisible Zagreb* project, the group spent two years mapping abandoned spaces in Croatia's capital city (Courtesy Platforma 9.81). Platforma 9.81 has hosted a variety of activities since its inception in 1999 (Photographs by Josip Ostojić and Dinko Peračić).

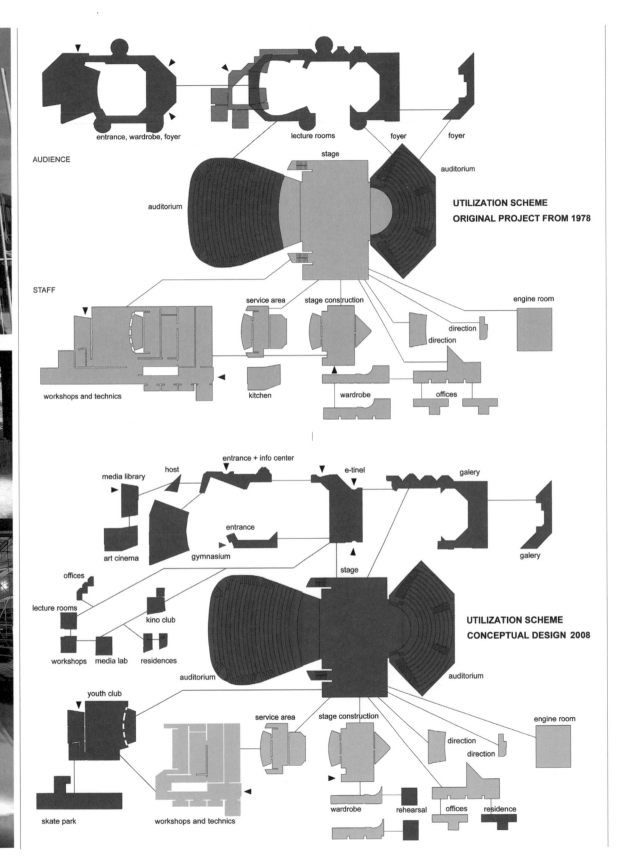

Above: Technical drawings showing a Croatian building's original utilization scheme from 1978 (top) and Platform 9.81's 2008 scheme illustrating proposed utilization (bottom). (Courtesy Platforma 9.81)

for ways of communicating and sharing these experiences, such as the building of a lighthouse or creation of a line of pocket-sized souvenirs.

PUBLIC MOVEMENT
FIRST OF MAY RIOTS
2010

The recurring May Day demonstrations in West Berlin's working class Kreuzberg neighborhood first turned violent as a way to challenge the city's efforts to silence labor protests during the late 1980s. However, the riots have now become less provocative, drawing audiences, as well as anti-capitalist protesters, from far-reaching locales across Europe.

Last year, Israeli artists Dana Yahalomi and Omer Krieger, who work together under the name Public Movement, marked May 1 by creating five radio channels of commentary and music as a soundtrack for the riots, and loaning visitors free mobile headsets during the event. Listeners could choose among the following tracks: two sociologists discussing the demonstration while observing it; a live musical performance; a pre-recorded talk by a philosopher; archival material from a past May 1 riot; and a DJ playing dance music. The project, which was commissioned by Berlin's Hebbel-Am-Ufer theater, allowed participants to consider the staged protest as a kind of performance, and to examine its position within the history of leftwing resistance to the state in this region. In doing so, Public Movement reframes the protest as a demonstration about demonstrations, rather than a reaction against specific issues.

Yahalomi and Kreiger stage performances in public space that test the possibilities for collective political action. Since 2006, the artists have organized what they call "manifestations of presence, fictional acts of hatred, new folk dances, synchronized procedures of movement, spectacles, marches, and re-enactments of specific moments in the lives of individuals, communities, social institutions, peoples, states, and of humanity."

Above, top to bottom: Platforma 9.81 ran a graffiti contest for artists to decorate the outside of the building (Courtesy Platforma 9.81). Images of Croatian buildings whose use has been examined and debated by Platforma 9.81. (Photographs by Sandro Lendler and Dinko Peračić)

PUBLIC MOVEMENT

PERFORMING POLITICS FOR GERMANY.

Above. clockwise from top left: Public Movement is a performative research body that investigates and stages political actions in public spaces. Members of Public Movement take part in the performance *Also Thus!*. (Courtesy Public Movement)

PULSKA GRUPA
KATARINA
2009

Pulska Grupa is a group of architects and urban planners based in Pula, Croatia, who focus on reclamation of public land, and "self-organized urbanism" in Pula and along the Adriatic coastline. After the end of World War II, the Katarina-Monumenti region of Pula—a restricted military zone—became the private residence of former Yugoslovian Communist leader, Josip Broz Tito. After one hundred years of occupation, the area was recently demilitarized and opened for potential new uses. Pulska Grupa organized student workshops to generate ideas for public use and to discuss ways to integrate the military infrastructure into civilian space. Workshops took place in renovated former barracks. Proposals included galleries and art studios, as well as a university center, post offices, and restaurants. A map of the area—imagined as a park—was produced to introduce the local population to the city's expanded space. More recently, Pulska Grupa initiated cultural programming in the Monumenti infrastructure, such as music festivals, in order to generate awareness of the debate over the compound, and to garner support of their plans to implement non-privatized plans for its future. The group's eight members, Ivana Debeljuh, Vjekoslav Gašparović,

Above: When a formerly restricted military zone became open to the public in 2006, Pulska Grupa organized workshops to generate ideas for its use (Courtesy Pulska Grupa).

Emil Jurcan, Jerolim Mladinov, Marko Perčić, Sara Perović, Helena Sterpin and Edna Strenja, actively challenge municipal and state plans for Katarina by producing publications, demonstrations, and exhibitions. "We imagine the city as a collective space which belongs to all those who live in it," they write in the group's manifesto, "They have the right to experience the conditions for their political, social, economic and ecological fulfillment while assuming duties of solidarity."

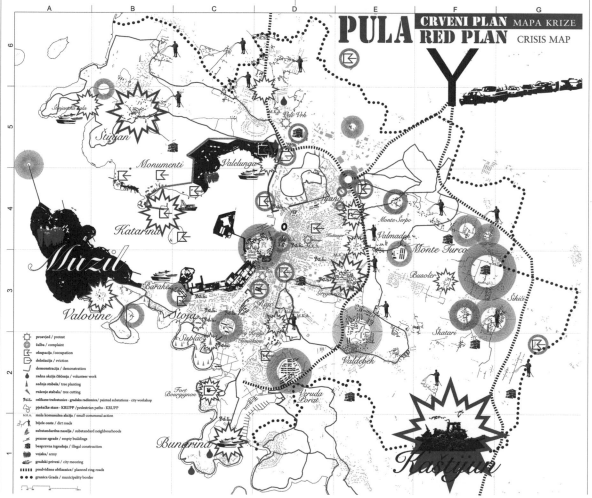

Top to bottom: Pulska Grupa hosted the Post-capitalist City Conference in 2009 (Photograph by Dejan Štifani). A map of the area was produced by Pulska Grupa to introduce the local population to Pula's expanded space (Courtesy Pulska Grupa).

PEDRO REYES
PALAS POR PISTOLAS
(PISTOLS INTO SPADES)

2008

In 2008, artist Pedro Reyes collected 1,527 firearms from residents of Culiacán, a western Mexican city known for drug trafficking and a high rate of fatal gunfire. Almost every resident knows someone who has been killed in a drug war. The weapons were steamrolled into a mass of flattened metal on a military base, melted at a foundry, then recast as shovels, which were used to plant trees on public school grounds. Reyes solicited gun donations by broadcasting announcements on a local television station, and, in exchange, offered vouchers for discounted electronics and appliances that could be redeemed in domestic shops. From the metal, Reyes created 1,527 shovels, and planted 1,527 trees across the city. Called *Palas Por Pistolas*, the project was originally commissioned by the Botanical Garden in Culiacán. Since then, the shovels, which bear labels explaining the history of the material used to produce them, have been installed in numerous exhibitions, and continue to be used to plant trees in locales across the globe. "This ritual has a pedagogical purpose of showing how an agent of death can become an agent of life," Reyes has said.

Trained as an architect, Reyes is known for his architectural structures and his performance and video work from the early 2000s. Some of his public projects include the penetrable sculptures also known as *capulas* (2001 to 2009); and *Baby Marx*, a television show that started through his work with Japanese puppet makers and grew into a commercial TV series. Through his expanded notion of sculpture, he aims to create solutions to social problems by creating room for individual and collective agency in the process.

Above: Residents of Culiacán exchanged guns for vouchers that could be used to purchase domestic appliances and electronics (Courtesy Pedro Reyes and LABOR).

Opposite: During Reyes' campaign, 1,527 guns were collected from residents of Culiacán. Shovels molded from melted-down gun metal were ultimately used to plant trees in Culiacán (Courtesy Pedro Reyes and LABOR).

LAURIE JO REYNOLDS
TAMMS YEAR TEN
2008–

Tamms C-MAX is a supermax prison in southern Illinois designed for the solitary confinement and sensory deprivation of men who have been violent or disruptive in other Illinois prisons. For at least 23 hours a day, men sit alone in seven-by twelve-foot cells. Meals are delivered through a slot in the door. There are no phone calls, jobs, programming, or scheduled activities. Before seeing visitors, men are strip-searched and chained to concrete stools. When the prison opened in 1998, prisoners were told they would be there for one year, yet one-third were still there after a decade. In an international human rights framework, indefinite long-term isolation is considered cruel, inhumane, and degrading treatment.

The Tamms Poetry Committee was a group of artists who started a poetry exchange with men at Tamms to provide them with social contact, and spread awareness about the harm caused by solitary confinement. At the urging of the prisoners, the group began to implement what organizer and artist Laurie Jo Reynolds called "legislative art" in order to establish oversight and end the worst abuses at the supermax. Thus, the Tamms Year Ten campaign, which was launched at the ten-year anniversary of the opening of the prison. This volunteer, grassroots coalition of prisoners, former prisoners, families, friends, attorneys, artists, and concerned citizens organized hearings before the Illinois House Prison Reform Committee, introduced legislation, and held dozens of public events and demonstrations. Their work resulted in the creation of a promising Ten-Point Plan for reform, which has still not been fully implemented. Tamms Year Ten also supports cultural projects. Supermax Subscriptions allows people to order magazine subscriptions for men at Tamms. The new Photos for Prisoners project invites prisoners to request a picture of anything—real or imagined—and then finds an artist to fill the request.

Above: A *Tamms Year Ten* mud stencil designed by Matthias Tegan outside the Museum of Contemporary Art, Chicago (Photograph by Sam Barnett).

ATHI-PATRA RUGA
MISS CONGO
2007

Above: Stills from the artist's three-channel video *Miss Congo* (2007) show him weaving and reworking found tapestry in various locations (Courtesy Whatiftheworld Gallery and Athi Patra Ruga).

Johannesburg-based artist Athi-Patra Ruga has a habit of inserting himself into challenging situations. He once sat in the middle of a basketball court, mid-game, wearing Jane Fonda-era aerobics gear. He also teetered in stiletto heels and a black sheep costume atop a hill in Switzerland, while corralled in a pen with actual, white sheep. In each case, Ruga—whose work spans performance, video, and fashion—confronts prevailing racial, sexual and cultural stereotypes by creating characters that embody extreme manifestations of those same stereotypes.

In 2006, he conceived of *Miss Congo*, a character dressed in drag and born out of the racial and gender inequities the artist witnessed while in Senegal. "[Miss Congo] represented ideas of displacement, of not belonging," he says. For one year, Ruga, in character as Miss Congo, traveled to public spaces and wove tapestries while passersby observed him. The character eventually became the subject of a three-channel video documentary, *Miss Congo*, in 2007. The film depicts three of Ruga's performances—solemn and lonely, but with a distinct undercurrent of humor and sensuality—that were carried out in Kinshasa, Democratic Republic of Congo. The artist stitches a tapestry while sitting or lying in anonymous locations on the outskirts of the city, performing a traditionally domestic task far outside the domestic sphere.

Ruga has called these performances "craft meditations"—interventions into public spaces that draw upon his practice of working with textiles and cross-dressing to express complex, layered notions of cultural and individual identity. The Miss Congo character also allows the artist to explore themes of place and belonging, exercising autonomy by choosing isolation and distance.

THE SAN FRANCISCO CACOPHONY SOCIETY
KILL YOUR TV
1994

Years before the television show *Jackass* entered the popular imagination, The San Francisco Cacophony Society began subverting mainstream behavior through public pranks: for example, passing pre-lit cigarettes to runners during a city marathon, and pretending to take a group shower in a hotel elevator. The twenty-five-year-old club has altered billboards, infiltrated city buses in clown costumes, and held formal dress parties in laundromats—all in the name of "apolitical, nonsensical non-conformity," according to the group's manifesto. On October 22, 1994, two Cacophonists, Kevin Evans and John Law, organized the event Kill Your TV, during which 500 fully-functioning televisions were smashed, burned, and dropped from a three-story rooftop.

The San Francisco Cacophony Society, which has often been described as a second-wave Dada movement, began as an offshoot of "The Suicide Club," an underground event series launched in 1977 that aimed to get people to experience new things, generally in private. Cacophonists, on the other hand, perform in public, with chapters in numerous national cities, including Los Angeles, Ann Arbor, Baltimore, Pittsburgh, and Chicago. The original San Francisco branch of the Cacophony Society was involved early on in the annual Burning Man festival, and is credited with launching the first SantaCon—a non-religious "Santa Claus" convention for those who dress in holiday gear year-round. The group also served as inspiration for Chuck Palahniuk's "Project Mayhem," the fictional organization in his 1996 novel *Fight Club*.

SARAI AND ANKUR
CYBERMOHALLA ENSEMBLE
2001–

Cybermohalla Ensemble is a collective of practitioners and writers that emerged from the project called Cybermohalla, a network of dispersed labs for experimentation and exploration among young people in different neighborhoods of the city. Cybermohalla was launched in 2001 by two Delhi-based think tanks, Ankur: Society for Alternatives in Education and Sarai-CSDS. Over the years, the collective has produced a very wide range of materials, practices, works and structures. Their work has circulated and been shown in online journals, radio broadcasts, publications, neighborhood gatherings, contemporary and new media art exhibitions. Cybermohalla Ensemble's significant publications include *Bahurupiya Shehr* and *Trickster City*. Their forthcoming publication, in collaboration with Frankfurt-based architects Nikolaus Hirsch and Michel Muller, is a consolidation of the conversations, designs, and efforts over the last few years to carve out a language and a practice for imagining and animating structures of cultural spaces in contemporary cities. Cybermohalla Ensemble use verse to describe their project:

"To Stand Before Change"

At times lava, at times water, at times petrol: it melts, it courses, it burns.
A shadow we chase because of our sense of connectedness.
A cunning battle with the measure of things.
A collision of forms of life.
Movement without a fixed shore.
That which does not bend according to you.
It becomes your own, but you cannot own it.
That which relentlessly takes on different masks.

CHRISTOPH SCHLINGENSIEF
PLEASE LOVE AUSTRIA
2000

After the Austrian People's Party coalesced with the right-wing, anti-immigration Freedom Party of Austria, artist, filmmaker, and theater producer Christoph Schlingensief staged a performance/reality TV show that allowed the Austrian public to vote on the fate of asylum seekers. He corralled twelve participants in a shipping container placed next to the Vienna Opera House for one week, with webcams streaming footage to a website. Unlike Big Brother, in which participants vote their least favorite character out of the show, Austrians were voting the asylum seekers out of the country; Austrian citizens were asked to vote two of the asylum seekers out of the country each day, either by phoning in or cast their ballot online. The remaining contestant would receive a cash prize and the possibility of Austrian citizenship through marriage.

As the performance began, Schlingensief unfurled a flag that read, "Foreigners Out" atop the container, along with a logo of Austria's best selling tabloid, *Kronenzeitung*; the flag referenced the familiar right-wing slogan of "Germany for Germans, Foreigners Out." In the end, left-wing groups who were protesting against the Freedom Party's Jurg Haider intervened in the performance, surrounding the containers and demanding that the asylum seekers be let free. They climbed on top of the, and trashed the "Foreigners Out" slogan, eventually evacuating the asylum seekers. In response to this disruption, Schlingensief raised another banner, an SS slogan that had been used by the Freedom Party, "Loyalty is Our Honour." While his work shocked people, the artist claimed that he was only repeating Haider's own slogans. Schlingensief died in 2010.

Above: A sign on the container declaring, "Foreigners Out" referenced the pervasive racism in Austria (Courtesy David Baltzer and Zenit).

FLORIAN SCHNEIDER
KEIN MENSCH IST ILLEGAL (NO ONE IS ILLEGAL)
1997–

In German, the article "kein" roughly translates as none, or the negation of a preceding noun. "Kein" can also mean to withdraw or reject, as in a set of ideas. For media artist, filmmaker, and activist Florian Schneider, the word acts as a tool, for understanding how national borders are maintained in the digital era—and for contesting those borders: as citizenship status is increasingly monitored through databases and other digital information systems, protests against the civil rights abuses caused by such immigration controls are becoming equally ubiquitous. In response to these abuses, Schneider launched *Kein Mensch Ist Illegal*, or *No One Is Illegal* at the art fair Documenta X in Kassel, Germany. This conference brought together 30 international anti-racism groups, artists, and other activists, and marked the beginning of a loose, "borderless" network in support of reformed labor conditions for undocumented workers, as well as fair access to healthcare, education, and housing. The network soon acquired a virtual presence, with international chapters organized via email and the Internet, still an emerging platform at the time.

Kein Mensch Ist Illegal served as the precursor to kein.org, Schneider's ongoing, open source website that facilitates cross-cultural, -disciplinary, and -geographic collaborations aimed at dismantling boundaries drawn along those same lines.

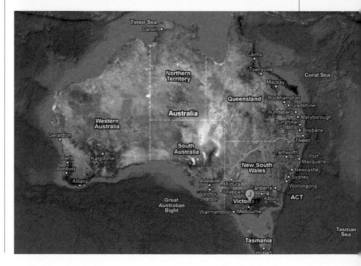

Above: Electronic maps depict locations of refugee rights advocacy groups that make up the international *No One Is Illegal* network (Courtesy Florian Schneider).

KATERINA ŠEDÁ
THERE IS NOTHING THERE
2003

One Saturday morning in 2003, the mayor of a small, Czechoslovakian village, Ponetovice, broadcast a message to all 350 residents: He asked them to go shopping—at the same time. For the rest of the day, the people continued to synchronize their routine according to a schedule that was posted on the village bulletin board. They simultaneously opened windows, swept porches, ate dumplings, met for beers, and finally all retired to bed at 10 pm. Though the regimen, created by artist Katerina Šedá, was strict, members of the community felt liberated by the shared activities, an experience many Europeans perhaps associated—somewhat nostalgically—with their lives before the fall of the Soviet Union in 1989.

Šedá, who lives and works in Brno, named the project after a common saying in Czech provinces: "There is nothing there." "They feel that everything important happens in cities or somewhere beyond our borders," Šedá has said. For one year, she conducted interviews, distributed surveys, and observed life in the village, which was once the site of major military battles in the 19th century, but was now largely disconnected from the socio-political fabric of Europe.

Šedá often asks her projects' participants to recount personal information that she then represents in order to encourage new reflection on what their lives can mean. When the artist's grandmother fell into a deep depression after her husband's death, refusing to leave her armchair to perform even basic, hygienic tasks, Šedá encouraged the elderly woman to draw, from memory, every item sold in the hardware store where she worked as a bookkeeper for 30 years. The activity, which yielded hundreds of images, allowed Šedá's grandmother to engage with the past, in order to re-enter her life in the present. Similarly, by performing their minute, daily tasks *en masse*, Ponetovice residents were empowered to reconsider the larger terms of their citizenship.

Above: Residents of the Czech village Ponetovice participate simultaneously in everyday actions as part of Šedá's 2003 performance (Courtesy the Essl Collection, Klosterneuburg/Vienna, Austria and the Museum of Modern Art in Warsaw).

The houses of Naranjito, located outside of San Juan, Puerto Rico, follow the contour of the mountain beneath them, rising and falling along the ridges. This is the first thing Chemi Rosado Seijo noticed from the foot of the hillside; not the boarded windows or trash-lined streets—signs of a declining economy in what was once a thriving community founded by coffee-plantation workers. And so, in an effort to draw attention to the uniquely organic shape of this small town—and to instill a sense of civic pride among residents who were increasingly disillusioned with their economic situation—he began to paint all of Naranjito's houses green.

During the project, Rosado-Seijo asked homeowners for permission to paint their homes a shade of green of their choosing. Many declined at first, primarily because the color is associated with the *independistas,* a local group that sought secession from the United States. But gradually, as the color popped out of the terrain and complemented the hues of the surrounding trees, they began to agree on condition that he also repaint other parts of the property such as chimneys, stoops, and fences in different colors. He enlisted local youth to help him paint, and held workshops, conferences and other events that brought positive press coverage to a community inundated daily with reports of the endemic unemployment and crime that had overtaken the village.

Throughout his practice, Rosado Seijo transforms public perception by presenting new approaches to the urban experience. In 2005, he was commissioned by the New York-based organization Art in General to explore Manhattan on skateboard. He then created a map of the best skate sites and routes he located during his travels; his

15-foot diagram proposed an alternate transportation option as well as a new aesthetic understanding of the city. *El Cerro* was presented at the 2002 Whitney Biennial.

Above: Locals gather in a public park in Naranjuto, previously known for its heavy crime (Photograph by Edwin Medina, Courtesy Chemi Room).

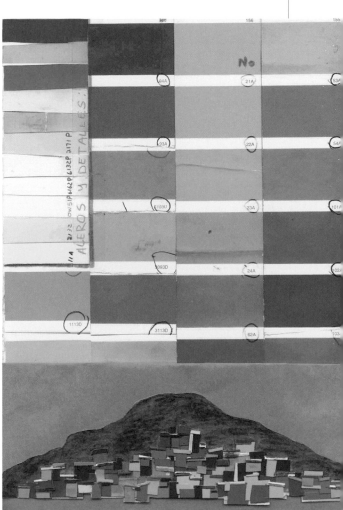

Clockwise from top: The painted houses in the Puerto Rican village of Naranjuto now echo the colors of the nearby mountainside. Swatches show the different shades of green that were used to paint structures. Visitors entering Naranjuto. (Photographs by Edwin Medina, Courtesy Chemi Room)

MICHIHIRO SHIMABUKU
MEMORY OF FUTURE
1996

Japanese artist Michihiro Shimabuku's 1996 installation *Memory of Future* took place in the car-oriented, decentralized city of Iwakura, Japan. Given the city's bustling layout, pedestrians are scarce and communal spaces are often under-used, even in commercial districts. Shimabuku filled an empty plaza with a variety of props, including a papier mâché bird's head, flowers, and a pineapple—intentionally incongruous objects meant to provoke passersby to stop, enter the space, and reflect on their relationship to the city. In drawing attention to previously ignored public land, Shimabuku asked Iwakura's citizens to consider new possibilities for activating it.

Shimabuku often tweaks routine experiences by performing absurdist acts in public passage-ways. For example, he shaved off an eyebrow in the London Underground, and then engaged in discussion with shocked and amused witnesses. He also carried an octopus down a Tokyo street, and afterward returned the animal to sea. In each instance, the strange act forced an often-oblivious public to re-connect with their familiar surroundings and participate in new exchanges.

In addition to engaging the public directly by creating interactive situations, Shimabuku's inventive, playful art practice often involves travel and transformation. He has made pickles while traveling by canal from London to Birmingham. He has also biked across specific regions in Japan looking for deer where none are known to exist—and, as with all of his projects, meeting passersby, making friends, and dispersing stories along the way.

Above, top and bottom: Shimabuku installed a handmade sculpture in an unused public plaza in Iwakura, Japan (Courtesy Shimabuku). *Opposite:* Residents of Iwakura engage with props included in Shimabuku's public installation (Courtesy Shimabuku).

BUSTER SIMPSON
BELLTOWN, P-PATCH, COTTAGE PARK, AND GROWING VINE STREET
1993–

"Get in early, make no assumptions, and treat your taxpayer as you would your patron." So says artist and environmental activist Buster Simpson, who has been initiating community-based interventions in the Seattle neighborhood Belltown since 1993. The area is densely populated; over the years, Simpson's sculptures have operated as civic improvements, and functioning solutions to urban problems. Simpson's sculptures can often be seen on the tops of buildings, integrated into downspouts, temporarily placed on street corners, protecting trees from cars, and in other locations.

His more extensive projects include P-Patch—a city-owned but community-run garden—occupying a spread of land next to Cottage Park, a development of three cottages used as a community center and a space for writers' residencies. Projects developing the community space in Belltown address urban sustainability, pollution, and bio-filtration of urban runoff water.

In the mid-1990s, a diverse group of Belltown residents organized the Growing Vine Street project, turning the Vine Street area into a street park that cleans the environment while providing open space for the neighborhood. Over the years, the project has developed into a laboratory for green solutions designed as temporary prototypes for sustainable improvements.

Skyway Luggage Seed Bank

Situated on the roof of the old Skyway Luggage Manufacturing Building (about to be renovated as a dot-com complex,) a volunteer landscape has been allowed to nurture itself atop an old water tower platform. Sod from this volunteer landscape has been harvested and replanted in suitcase planters fixed to pallets. These portable landscapes will initiate an urban re-seeding strategy for future "green roof" landscapes. They could provide a tolerant and diverse seed bank for urban roof landscapes. Launch date: Spring 2001.

skeasy.org/~bsimpson 901 Yakima Avenue S., Seattle, WA 98144 206.328.6212 voice & fax bsimpson@speakeasy.net

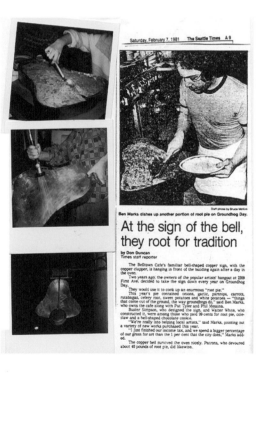

Opposite: The Beckoning Cistern, part of the Growing Vine Street project, is a water cistern that receives roof runoff from the 81 Vine Street building. (Courtesy Buster Simpson). *Above:* Fabrication of the Belltown Pan, a bell-shaped pan created and used by the Belltown Café on Groundhog Day to cook a symbolic, communal dish (Courtesy Buster Simpson and the Seattle Times).

Clockwise from top left: A rooftop garden and seed bank was created using old suitcases from the Skyway Luggage Manufacturing company. A pedestrian walks across the hand-carved *Poem to Be Worn*, located in the First Avenue Urban Arboretum. In *Shared Clothesline*, Simpson installed nine clotheslines across an alley in the Pike Place Market District of Seattle as a simple gesture toward reconnecting the gentrifying neighborhood. (Courtesy Buster Simpson)

SLANGUAGE
2002–

The 1992 riots in Los Angeles left many lots in the city's center empty, and chain-linked off from public use. Yet, the chains themselves became canvases for public expression, when city residents started hanging signs for their businesses, and posting messages, on them. Years later, artists Juan Capistan and Mario Ybarra, Jr., considered these re-uses, and their history, when they began making art together, devising actions and music performances in the lots—"slanguage," as they coined it. The word, as well as their practice of collaborating, repurposing, and creating a new vocabulary around the urban environment, inspired them to launch Slanguage, a shared studio space and gallery in Wilmington, California, outside of Los Angeles, that took advantage of the lacunae that arose in the abandoned region. Since then, the collective, with Capistan, Ybarra, as well as artist Karla Diaz at the helm, has become a community resource for artists in Southern California that offers a residency program, workshops for teenagers, public events, and international exhibitions. The collective's work ranges from local poetry readings and summer art camps to major museum exhibitions and commissioned projects.

In line the with organization's origins, Slanguage members continue to explore the visual vernacular of street art, as well as its stereotypes, in their practice. For example, last year Capistan, Ybarra, and Diaz co-curated "Defiant Chronicles" at the Museum of Latin American Art, a group show that challenged graffiti as a male-dominated art form. More recently, Diaz organized "Laced Souls," an exhibition of artist-designed athletic shoes produced in collaboration with a local custom sneaker shop. The first "Slangfest," which took place in Long Beach this past summer, featured break-dancing lessons and recycled art workshops presented by the group's teen council. Such endeavors combine Slanguage's mission of connecting street artists to contemporary art institutions and the general public to the history of art in the urban environment.

Top row: Slanguage is a Los Angeles-area artist group that hosts exhibitions, leads art-education workshops, and coordinates events (Courtesy Slanguage).

Bottom row, left to right: As part of the 2008 Whitney Biennial, teenagers were invited to work on a mural in Manhattan's Meatpacking District with Slanguage co-founders. As part of their three-month residency at MOCA Los Angeles in 2009, members of Slanguage presented a performance titled *Dislexicon* which included a headdress workshop. The Slanguage base is located in Wilmington, CA. (Courtesy Slanguage)

SUPERFLEX
GUARANÁ POWER
2004

Guaraná is a berry grown in the Amazon that holds high concentrations of caffeine. In 2000, the main multinational companies that sell drinks produced from the berry merged to form a cartel. This created a monopoly on guaraná seeds, which drove prices down by 80 percent, jeopardizing the livelihood of Brazilian farmers who cultivate it. Beginning in 2004, SUPERFLEX worked with a farmers' cooperative to counter the local economic effects of the merger by creating an alternative product—called *Guaraná Power*—that would compete with the corporate brands.

The artists and farmers collaborated to develop the drink, determine ways to affordably produce it, and create marketing campaigns in the form of commercials featuring the farmers own narratives about the project. In 2006, the *Guaraná Power* soft drink was banned from the 27th Sao Paulo Biennial by the president of the Biennial's foundation. In response, SUPERFLEX blacked out the label, and all references to the project in the exhibition materials. Since then, the project has also served as a reflection on copyright, trademark, intellectual property, and free speech. *Guaraná Power* has been exhibited in other exhibitions, in various forms, to bring attention to the Brazilian farmers' struggles and their attempt to find working solutions.

SUPERFLEX, founded in 1993 and based in Copenhagen, create projects that engage economic forces, explorations of the democratic production of materials, and self-organization. They describe their projects as tools for spectators to actively participate in the development of experimental models that alter the prevailing model of economic production. For *Living as Form*, SUPERFLEX was commissioned to create a life-sized, detailed, and functional copy of the JPMorgan Chase executives' restroom inside the Olympic Restaurant. The installation, open to the public, provided an essential service and also asked visitors to contemplate the structures of power that become imbued in even the most unassuming architectural spaces.

Above: Guaraná Power was bottled and sold at a production bar at the 2003 Venice Biennale (Photograph by SUPERFLEX).

Opposite: SUPERFLEX developed the drink *Guaraná Power* with local farmers in Maués, Brazil to compete with similar corporate products (Photograph by Jeppe Gudmundsen Holmgreen).

APOLONIJA ŠUŠTERŠIČ
BONNEVOIE? JUICE BAR
1998

The art fair Manifesta 2 took place in the Centre de Production et de Création Artistique (CPCA)—a former fruit and vegetable warehouse in the Luxembourg neighborhood Bonnevoie that was converted into an exhibition venue. For her contribution to the show, the Ljubljana- and Amsterdam-based artist Apolonija Šušteršič built a juice bar outside of the building in homage to the history of the space, and to attract attention to historic architecture's new role as an experimental art center in the area. Her installation included a long, black counter covered in fruits, and a seating area, where visitors could congregate before entering, or after exiting, the exhibition. By placing the bar directly in the entryway, Šušteršič was able to draw both art patrons as well as neighborhood residents into the space—and into a dialogue—about its future in Bonnevoie. The project included video documentation that recounted the neighborhood's history.

With formal training as an architect, Šušteršič designs forums for conversation about urban infrastructure, and its effectiveness. For example, *Suggestion for a Day*, at the Moderna Museet in Stockholm, Sweden, offered museum visitors bike tours of contested architectural sites; an overview of the urban planning and policy debates those sites have sparked; and finally, an opportunity to discuss those issues with experts and municipal officials. In *Video Home Video Exchange* at the Kunstverein Muenster, Germany, she screened films that address the social function of suburban architecture (think: Ang Lee's *Ice Storm* and David Lynch's *Blue Velvet*). Then she asked viewers to produce their own videos about homes and gardens, and submit them for review, in exchange for a copy of a screened film.

Top to bottom: The *Juice Bar* was presented as part of Manifesta 2 in Luxembourg, and took place inside a former fruit market. In order to entice a local audience, the *Juice Bar* was open to the street. (Photographs by Apolonija Šušteršič)

Top to bottom: Still from a video titled *How to make your own juice?* which was shown at the exhibition space (Courtesy Apolonija Šušteršič). Šušteršič's *Juice Bar* acted as an in-between zone for the community to explore the contemporary art exhibition that was taking place inside the building (Photograph by Roman Mensing).

TAHRIR SQUARE
CAIRO, EGYPT
2011

For one month in January 2011, Cairo, Egypt, reverberated as thousands of citizens flooded Tahrir Square in mass protest of former president Hosni Mubarak's 30-year-rule, which was marked by human rights abuses, corruption, economic depression, and food shortages across the region. The protests transpired for a mere 18 days, yet the during that time the energy of the crowd, which consisted of student coalitions, Islamic women and labor groups, as well as other historically underrepresented constituents, escalated, due in part to the sheer number of people in the Square, as well as the new media-savvy tactics they used.

Since then, the so-called "Arab Spring" has been celebrated as a political and social media revolution, with Tweets, YouTube videos, and Facebook pages garnering as much attention as the vast on-site demonstrations. While the actual impact of this technology is still up for debate, these websites were inarguably an important communication tool for protest organizers, and Egyptian media outlets, who labored to disseminate images of the protests, and the ensuing crackdown, to the broader public imagination. Likewise, the active commemoration of the event—the production of poetry, T-shirts, and slogans—was reflective of the new communication channels. In February, Mubarak lost the support of his military, the international community, and the United States, and was forced to step down.

TALLER POPULAR DE SERIGRAFIA (POPULAR SILKSCREEN WORKSHOP)

2002–2007

Taller Popular de Serigrafia, or *Popular Silkscreen Workshop*, was a collective of artists and designers that formed during the protests following Argentina's 2001 economic collapse. Drawing on Latin America's long history of weaving political activism and graphic arts, the group used silk-screen printing, a quick, inexpensive process, to create materials inspired by, and as instruments for, political events. *Taller Popular*'s members would stand amid mobs of demonstrators pulling ink across screens to print images on t-shirts, and create posters and leaflets, to be used on site during protests, and as advertisements in train stations and other public corridors.

In 2004, the group silk-screened tank tops in collaboration with the sewing workshop La Juanita, a fair labor project by Movimiento de Trabajadores Desocupados de La Matanza (Matanza Neighborhood Unemployed Workers' Movement). *Taller Popular*'s designs, often monochromatic, iconic images appropriated from sports marketing and political propaganda, have been exhibited in international art exhibitions, including the Brussels Biennial and the 27th São Paulo Biennial.

Opposite: Egyptian protestors focused on political issues, and demanded the overthrow of President Mubarak (Photograph by Pedro Ugarte, Courtesy of AFP and Getty Images). *Above:* Demonstrations in Tahrir Square began in January 2011 (Photograph by Mahmud Hams, Courtesy of AFP and Getty Images).

TEMPORARY SERVICES
PRISONERS' INVENTIONS

2001–

Prisoners' Inventions was a collaboration between art collective Temporary Services and Angelo, an incarcerated artist in California, who illustrated the inventions of fellow prisoners that were designed to fill needs often repressed by the restrictive environment of the prison. The inventions range from homemade sex dolls and condoms to battery cigarette lighters and contraband radios. Angelo created drawings, recreated inventions, and worked with Temporary Services to build a life-size replica of his cell that would give visitors a sense of where the inventions were designed and produced. His work has been pub-

lished in a book, installed in exhibitions, and represented in other ongoing iterations of the project.

"If some of what's presented here seems unimpressive, keep in mind that deprivation is a way of life in prison," Angelo has written. "Even the simplest of innovations presents unusual challenges, not just to make an object but in some instances to create the tools to make it and find the materials to make it from."

Temporary Services is an art collective including Brett Bloom, Salem Collo-Julin, and Marc Fischer. They produce exhibitions, publications, events, and projects that explore the social context and the potential of creative work as a service provided to communities. The group started as an experimental exhibition space in a working class neighborhood of Chicago and went on to produce projects including *Prisoners' Inventions* and the nationally-distributed newspaper *Art Work: A National Conversation About Art, Labor, and Economics*.

To investigate the intersection of art, labor, economics, and the production of social experiences, Temporary Services invited over forty organizations and businesses from the Lower East Side to operate stalls in a section of the historic Essex Street Market during *Living as Form*. *MARKET* returns the space to its original function as a marketplace, but one that is free to use, non-competitive, and particularly diverse in its offerings.

Above: One of artist and prisoner Angelo's inventions, a battery cigarette lighter (Courtesy Temporary Services).

TOROLAB
SURVIVAL UNITS/
TRANSBORDER TROUSERS
2004–2005

In *The Region of the Transborder Trousers* (La región de los pantalones transfronterizos), Torolab, a Tijuana-based collective of architects, artists, designers, and musicians, use GPS transmitters to explore daily life in the border cities Tijuana and San Diego. For five days, the collective carried GPS transmitters, wore Torolab-designed garments including a skirt, a vest, two pairs of pants, and sleeves that could be worn with t-shirts, each with a hidden pocket for a Mexican passport. They also kept records of their cars' fuel consumption. The GPS and fuel data was then fed into a computer and visualized (using software reprogrammed by Torolab) as an animated map. Each tracked Torolab member appeared as a colored dot on an urban grid surrounded by a circle whose diameter indicated the amount of fuel left in his or her tank.

Torolab has also produced the Transborder pant, wide-legged, denim trousers that serve as part of a Survival Suit for border crossing. The pants are designed with a series of flat, interior pockets to protect important documents from the trials of a long journey through rough terrain. One pocket is intended specifically to hold a Mexican passport; another accommodates a laser-read visa card. However, the pants are not intended exclusively for use by Mexican immigrants. For Americans, who often don't need to show any form of identification to cross the border, the pockets can be used for money, credit cards and pharmaceuticals purchased cheaply south of the border.

Torolab was founded by Raúl Cárdenas Osuna in 1995 as a "socially engaged workshop committed to examining and elevating the quality of life for residents of Tijuana and the transborder region through a culture of ideologically advanced design."

MIERLE LADERMAN UKELES
THE BEGINNING
OF MY ARCHIVE
1976–

"The sourball of every revolution: *After* the revolution, who's going to pick up the garbage on Monday morning?" Over forty years ago, Mierle Laderman Ukeles wrote these lines in her *Manifesto for Maintenance Art, 1969!*, a treatise on work, service, home, life, and art that called upon service workers, of all kinds, to change the world through routine maintenance and preservation, rather than commercial development. Eight years later, Ukeles was appointed the first artist-in-residence with the New York City Department of Sanitation, a position she still holds and uses to explore the social and ecological implications of waste management. Her work has largely been exercises in outreach—sometimes literally: In 1977, Ukeles began interviewing New York City sanitation workers for her *Touch Sanitation Performance*. This multivalenced work included *Handshake and Thanking Ritual*, in which the artist shook hands and personally thanked each of the city's 8,500 sanitation workers over an eleven-month period, and *Follow in Your Footsteps*, where Ukeles, working eight- to sixteen-hour shifts, followed sanitation workers on their routes in every district throughout the city and mirrored their motions as a street dance. In 1985, she built *Flow City*, a visitor center at the 59th Street Marine Transfer Station where the public could view used and recyclable materials as they moved through the sanitation system. Most recently, she has launched plans to reclaim the Fresh Kills Landfill, a 2,200-acre landfill on Staten Island that houses the World Trade Center debris that accumulated after the buildings' destruction.

Ukeles' projects mark her longstanding belief that "art should impinge on the daily life of everyone and should be injected into daily prime-time work-time." *The Beginning of my Archive* tracks another characteristic of Ukeles' practice—her detailed correspondence with workers, bureaucrats, and other stakeholders, as well as her own articulation of her so-called "Maintenance Art."

Top and bottom: For *Touch Sanitation*, Ukeles shook hands with 8,500 NYC Sanitation workers (Courtesy Ronald Feldman Fine Arts, New York).

ULTRA-RED
WAR ON THE POOR
2007

"What is the sound of the war on the poor?" In 2007, the self-described militant sound collective Ultra-red asked fifteen international artists and activists to record a one-minute audio piece in response to this question, which they compiled for the first volume of an ongoing series. The results ranged from field recordings, re-appropriated sounds, mini-symphonies, and spoken rants—both literal and abstract. For example, a reading of words taken from prisoners' intake cards at a Philadelphia penitentiary; sounds captured when squatters took over the offices of a fruit and vegetable factory; a silent hiss.

Ultra-red was founded by two AIDS activists, Marco Larsen and Dont Rhine, who first collaborated to counter police harassment during Los Angeles' inaugural syringe exchange program. Realizing that video documentation would deter users from participating in the exchange, Larsen and Rhine began recording sounds as a way of monitoring law enforcement, a practice the blossomed into a series of installations and performances. Since then, Ultra-red has expanded into an international group that explores acoustic space, social relations, and political struggle though so-called "Militant Sound Investigations," as well as radio broadcasts, texts, and actions in public space.

Above and right: Sound interventions produced by Ultra-red included artists' responses to the question, "What is the sound of the war on the poor?" (Courtesy Ultra-red).

UNITED INDIAN HEALTH SERVICES
POTAWOT HEALTH VILLAGE
1994–

URBAN BUSH WOMEN
SUMMER LEADERSHIP INSTITUTE
1997–

"Good health goes beyond the individual. It must include the health of the entire community including its culture, language, art and traditions, as well as the environment in which it exists." These are the words of Jerry Simone, chief executive officer of United Indian Health Services, a 50-year-old healthcare organization that emphasizes the role of art, and sustainable practices, alongside allopathic medicine in its facilities. In 1994, the UIHS broke ground for Potawot Health Village in northern California, now a 40-acre farm with an outpatient medical clinic, community food garden, orchard, children's camp, and a wildlife reserve.

The wildlife reserve, called Ku'wah-dah-wilth ("Comes back to life" in the native Wiyot language), spans twenty acres of restored wetlands devoted to preservation of natural habitats, parks, and traditional agricultural and spiritual programs. Produce from the garden is distributed through a bi-weekly produce stand or a subscription member service between June and December. Another two acres are dedicated for growing medicinal herbs. And an additional one-acre garden, the Ishtook Basket and Textile Demonstration Garden, provides a workspace for traditional basketry as well as information on the negative effects of pesticides and chemicals on weavers and gatherers of fibrous plants.

The Summer Leadership Institute is the feminist dance troupe Urban Bush Women's ten-day intensive training program that melds the performing arts with community activism in movement classes, workshops, field trips, community renewal events, and the development of new choreographies. Each day begins with a dance class followed by discussions groups on topics such as "undoing racism," and understanding cultural difference through storytelling. The Institute, which began in Tallahassee, now takes place in New Orleans to mobilize city performers in the ongoing recovery of Hurricane Katrina.

Choreographer and founding artistic director Jawole Willa Jo Zollar formed the seven-woman ensemble in 1984 to develop a "woman-centric perspective" on social justice issues. The troupe takes inspiration from both contemporary dance practice and traditions from the African Diaspora; often, Urban Bush Women performances consist of bold, powerful movements and intimate, narrative gestures—a vocabulary that offers alternate notions of femininity, politics, and personal history. The troupe has also collaborated with numerous artists working in a range disciplines from jazz musicians, poets, and visual artists.

This year, the troupe produced "Resistance and Power," a series of works that typify the approach of Urban Bush Women to exploring history: Though the choreography is rarely literal, the messages—stories that take on issues surrounding race, inequity, and the process of empowerment—are clear. "The arts are very powerful in addressing social change, and it's not where people often look first," Zollar has said. "But the arts connect people not to how they think about social issues, but to how they feel about them. Once you're clear about how you feel, then action becomes more of a possibility."

Above: Urban Bush Women perform "Scales of Memory" at the Next Wave Festival at the Brooklyn Academy of Music in 2008 (Courtesy Urban Bush Women).

US SOCIAL FORUM
2007–

The U.S. Social Forum gathers tens of thousands of activists over several days with the goal of building a unified, national social justice movement across the country. Since its inception, two forums have taken place, in Atlanta in 2007 and in Detroit in 2010. Each forum drew over 15,000 activists, and offered a multitude of programs, including workshops, arts and culture performances, activities for children and youth, direct actions, tours, and fundraising initiatives. The event has attracted organizers—a younger, ethnically diverse crowd from a range of fields—interested in developing new "solutions to economic and ecological crises."

Inspired by the World Social Forum—which, starting in 2001 brought together international activists fighting against neoliberal globalization—the U.S. Social Forum began to take shape in 2005. The planning committee was formed by the group Grassroots Global Justice and was comprised of over forty-five organizations, including Amnesty International USA, the AFL-CIO, and the U.S. Human Rights Network. Despite the breadth of the event, and vast attendance, the USSF, has received little press coverage in the mainstream media.

Detroit was a particularly apt host city for the USSF because of its persistently declining economy, lack of jobs, and other inequitable conditions that have come into central focus in recent years. The tagline for the event, "Another U.S. Is Necessary," marks the spirit of the USSF, and the desire to overhaul economic systems and government practices—also reflected in the recent "Occupy Wall Street" movement, as well as other protests cropping up in municipal plazas across the globe. Over 1,000 USSF workshops took place, which veered away from standard meeting formats toward more collaborative efforts.

BIK VAN DER POL
ABSOLUT STOCKHOLM: LABEL OR LIFE, CITY ON A PLATFORM?
2000–2001

Imaging walking into a museum gallery and seeing your favorite POANG chair from IKEA. Your BJURSTA table is there as well, and balanced on top of it is your AROD lamp. It's an entire room composed of IKEA products, laid out as it might be in your own home. But there's one critical distinction: the whole familiar living room set up is affixed directly to the museum wall. In 2001, Rotterdam-based Bik van der Pol—the collaborative practice of Liesbeth Bik and Jos Van der Pol—created a three dimensional, life-size billboard at the Moderna Museet in Stockholm,

Sweden. Mounting actual pieces of IKEA furniture within the outline of Absolut's iconic bottle shape, *Absolute Stockholm* constituted a cheeky mash-up of two global Swedish corporations.

Using the billboard as a springboard, Bik Van der Pol explored relations between ideas, ideals, propaganda, and personal investment in the past. To build on the themes of the project, the pair selected a number of public spaces in Stockholm that had played a significant role in Sweden's past and the development of the "Swedish model." These spaces were then host to public meetings, small events, and interventions intended to foster connections between residents and visitors. In particular, participants were asked to interrogate the idea of "publicness," and the meaning of public space in a city where public places often disappear in favor of pragmatic capitalist developments.

Since Bik and Van der Pol began working together in 1995, their installations, videos, and drawings have interrogated physical, and cultural, time and space. For example, in 2007, they designed a screening format and guidebook for the Istanbul Biennale's *Nightcomers* video program throughout the city that broadened public access to the "high culture" event, as opposed to the traditional design of an exclusive screening structure.

Above: Absolut Stockholm took place all over the city of Stockholm and is a search for the life 'behind the labels' (Photograph by JN van der Pol).

Above, top to bottom: Absolut Stockholm took place all over the city of Stockholm and is a search for the life 'behind the labels'. *Absolut Stockholm* combined a New York Absolut Vodka billboard with IKEA furniture. (Photographs by Jos van der Pol)

Above: Bik van der Pol installed *Absolut Stockholm*, a life-sized reproduction
of a New York ad for Absolut Vodka, at the Moderna Museet in Stockholm
(Photograph by JN van der Pol).

WENDELIEN VAN OLDENBORGH
MAURITS SCRIPT
2006

The renowned art institution the Mauritshuis, in The Hague, was once home to Johann Maurits van Nassau, the former governor of colonial North East Brazil (1637–44), who was considered to have exercised a more enlightened, tolerant rule than many other colonial governors. For the third part of Dutch artist Wendelien van Oldenborgh's ongoing collaborative project, *A Certain Brazilianness*, she invited people from diverse ethnic backgrounds, including second- and third-generation immigrants from the former colonies, to the Mauritshuis to read a scripted multiple-voice dialogue compiled from official and unofficial historical accounts of Maurits' governorship. Two participants read each character, while others, including audience members, engaged in discussion about the historical issues raised by the script relative to contemporary culture. The live, staged event was recorded as a 67-minute film, called *Maurits Script*.

Rotterdam-based van Oldenborgh employs diverse voices in her investigation of the public sphere. She often uses the format of an open film shoot, collaborating with participants in different scenarios, to co-produce a script and orient the work towards its final outcome, which can be film or other forms of projection.

Above: A performer recites from van Oldenborgh's script at Johan Maurits van Nassau's residence in The Hague (Photograph by Wendelien van Oldenborgh, Courtesy Wilfried Lentz Rotterdam).

EDUARDO VÁZQUEZ MARTIN
FARO DE ORIENTE
2000–

VOINA
2007–

FARO de Oriente, or East Lighthouse, is a government-funded cultural center, and arts and crafts school in Mexico City intended to serve areas of the city that lack access to cultural services. Founded by poet and educator Eduardo Vázquez Martín, the space is located in the city's Iztapalapa borough, one of most densely populated and underprivileged communities in Mexico. All classes and workshops offered at FARO are free, and range from theater and music to jump rope and fabric printing.

In 2000, architect Alberto Kalach discovered a 24,500 square meter abandoned building, and divided the space into galleries, workshops, a library, an outdoor forum, gardens, and parkland. Designed as both cultural resource and civic outreach, the school serves as a forum for community meetings, and a social service information hub. FARO, which also hosts a pirate radio and television station as well as a print magazine, was the first such community center to open in the city; three more have been erected since then. The three-building space also houses a library, computer lab, gym, childcare facility, welding room, and carpentry workshop.

Conceived as a cultural center and space for artistic production, FARO follows a pedagogical model that emphasizes dialogue and seeks to create a space for diverse expression. Through these services, the center fosters community development as well as the improved use of urban spaces and city infrastructure for culture and art.

Eduardo Vazquez Martin was born in Mexico City in 1962. He has been involved in a number of Mexico City's cultural projects and publications, and is currently the Director of the city's Museum of Natural History and Environmental Cultura (Museo de Historia Natural y de Cultura Ambiental).

For the past year, the irreverent Russian art collective Voina has been laying low, on the run from the police thanks to their incendiary street actions that have ranged from absurdist pranks that suggest institutional critique—throwing live cats at McDonald's cashiers—to illegal, overtly politicized acts—flipping over parked police cars. In 2008, on the eve of Dmitri Medvedev's election, Voina staged perhaps their most notorious performance, *Fuck for the heir Puppy Bear!,* a three-part action carried out over the course of two days for which five couples, including a pregnant woman, had public sex in Moscow's Timirayzev State Museum of Biology.

Two years later, on the anniversary of Che Guevara's birthday, members of the group painted a 65-meter-tall, 27-meter-wide phallus on a drawbridge in an action outside the Federal Security Service in Saint Petersburg. Two of the group's members, Oleg Vorotnikov and Leonid Nikolayev, have been arrested for "hooliganism motivated by hatred or hostility toward a social group." Though they have been released on bail, they artists face up to seven years in prison. Since its inception, membership in the collective has expanded, somewhat virally, to more than 200 participants.

Though the collective's actions often read like high-concept pranks, they're motivated by a serious desire to call out corruption and complacency in modern-day Russia. Speaking to the *New York Times* in January, 2011, about the drawbridge action, Voina member Alexey Pluster-Sarno said, "It is monumental, heroic, romantic, left-radical, an act of protest. I like it as a piece of work, not just because it is a penis."

Top to bottom: Voina's action *Dick captured by KGB* was performed on June 14, 2010. In less than a minute, members of the group painted a 65-meter-tall, 27-meter-wide phallus on a drawbridge outside the Federal Security Service in Saint Petersburg. (Courtesy Voina, in partnership with the Brooklyn House of Kulture)

MARION VON OSTEN
MONEYNATIONS
1998, 2000

When the Berlin Wall fell in 1989, new nations emerged. So did border policies that limited migration from Central and Southeastern Europe into the West, and labor practices that exploited workers and propagated new cultural stereotypes. MoneyNations—a network of artists, theorists, and media activists—formed in 1998 to create public discussion around the racist and discriminatory practices that developed across Europe in the decade after Communism fell. The group, which convened twice within a two-year period, also questioned outdated assumptions about difference, the "center," and the "margin," as well as left-wing criticism that often affirmed these ideas. "Even anti-racist campaigns tend to depict migrants as victims who have been criminalized for the purpose of achieving certain political goals," wrote artist and key organizer Marion von Osten in "Euroland and the Economy of the Borderline," an essay she published in 2000 describing the political climate that prompted MoneyNations to form. She creates collaborative forums—exhibitions, independently published books, and films—to challenge capitalism, sometimes by using capitalist practices to do so.

MoneyNations launched by inviting cultural producers from contested regions to develop communication platforms that didn't simply include "non-Western voices" within Western institutions, but allowed those voices to lead the conversation. Their three-day event and media workshop at Zürich's Shedhalle in 1998 yielded a webzine, video exchange, photographs, installations, and a print publication. Alternatives to top-down panel discussions, which often limit discourse to scripts, and stunt audience participation. In this arena, participants focused on the new collective and individual identities formed in post-1989 Europe by considering cultural production and activism initiated by artists, over official legislative or economic policies.

The second MoneyNations event occurred in 2000 at Vienna's Kunsthalle Exnergasse. This time, participants aimed to challenge existing power structures in Europe by experimenting with so-called grassroots broadcast media. The network launched mnFM, an on-air and online audio database and exchange platform, and MoneyNations TV, an open video-exchange between middle, central, and southeastern European producers.

Above: MoneyNations arranged collaborative forums (top), exhibitions, and events (middle) and invited cultural producers to launch communication platforms for non-Western voices (bottom). (Courtesy Marion von Osten)

Top to bottom: MoneyNations was organized by Marion von Osten
to discuss the discrimination that developed across Europe after
the fall of Communism. Exhibitions and events took place in Zürich
and Vienna. (Courtesy Marion von Osten)

PETER WATKINS
LA COMMUNE
(PARIS, 1871)
1999

Game (1965), for which Watkins used a Vietnam-era newsreel style to capture scenes from an 18th-century battle, point to the critique of modern media and community involvement evident in *La Commune*.

WIKILEAKS
2007–

La Commune (Paris, 1871) is a 375-minute docudrama reconstructing the events of the Paris Commune in its 1871 struggle against the Versaillais French forces. The filming took place in an abandoned factory on the outskirts of Paris that was outfitted to resemble the 11th Arrondissement, one of the poorest working-class districts at the time of the Commune's suppression, and the scene of some of the conflict's bloodiest fighting.

The cast included 220 people from Paris and the provinces, most of them lacking prior acting experience. People with conservative political views were deliberately recruited to act in roles opposed to the Commune. The cast members were encouraged to do their own research into the historical events, as well as to improvise and to discuss the events during the filming process. Even after the shooting was over, the cast's involvement with its ideas continued in different ways; for example, a weekend of public talks organized by one of the actors, featuring presentations and debates on the Paris Commune.

English director Peter Watkins has been experimenting with the "newsreel style" seen in *La Commune* since the 1950s. He is particularly interested in the play between reality and artificiality that the medium of documentary film calls up—the "high-key" Hollywood lighting tempered by the emotions and faces of real people. Earlier films like *The Forgotten Faces* (1960), a recreation of the 1956 Hungarian uprising, and *The War*

In April 2010, a shocking video of an American helicopter firing upon a group of Iraqi journalists on the ground in Bagdad stunned mainstream media and the diplomatic world, and inspired a global debate about the relationship between news outlets and the governments they report on. The video, titled *Collateral Murder*, was released by WikiLeaks, a whistle-blowing non-profit organization that, since its inception, has aimed to shine light on the operations of governments and corporations around the world. Founded by former computer hacker Julian Assange, as well as a group of technologists, dissidents, and activists, WikiLeaks is guided by the premise that democracy works best when citizens are aware of state and military operations, and can hold governments accountable to their actions.

Historically, large media groups consult with government sources before releasing potentially sensitive information, in order to leverage these relationships for greater access to information. WikiLeaks has challenged this process by eschewing such negotiations and releasing classified memos, diplomatic cables, videos, and other materials directly to the public via its website. "Publishing improves transparency, and this transparency creates a better society for all people," states WikiLeaks' mission. "Better scrutiny

Opposite: Wikström repeated her original performance in 2009 at the ICA Maxi supermarket in Kalmar, Sweden (Photograph by Oscar Guermouche).

leads to reduced corruption and stronger democracies in all society's institutions, including government, corporations and other organizations. A healthy, vibrant, and inquisitive journalistic media plays a vital role in achieving these goals. We are part of that media." WikiLeaks' critics, with the U.S. government at the helm, have countered that the organization's practices have endangered military and intelligence personnel as well as their civilian sources.

WikiLeaks operates with a small, all-volunteer staff as well as a network of 800 to 1,000 experts who advise on issues such as encryption, vetting information, and programming. Its material is housed on servers around the globe, outside of the jurisdiction of any single institution or government.

ELIN WIKSTRÖM
WHAT WOUILD HAPPEN IF EVERYBODY DID THIS?
1993

For her contribution to a group exhibition in Malmö, Sweden, Elin Wikström moved a bed into a grocery store, and lay silently under the covers every day, from morning until close, during the three-week run of the show. She installed an electronic display sign overhead that read, "One day, I woke up feeling sleepy, sluggish, and sour. I drew the bedcovers over my head because I didn't want to get up, look around or talk to anyone. Under the covers I said to myself, I'll lie like this, completely still, without saying a word, as long as I want. I'm

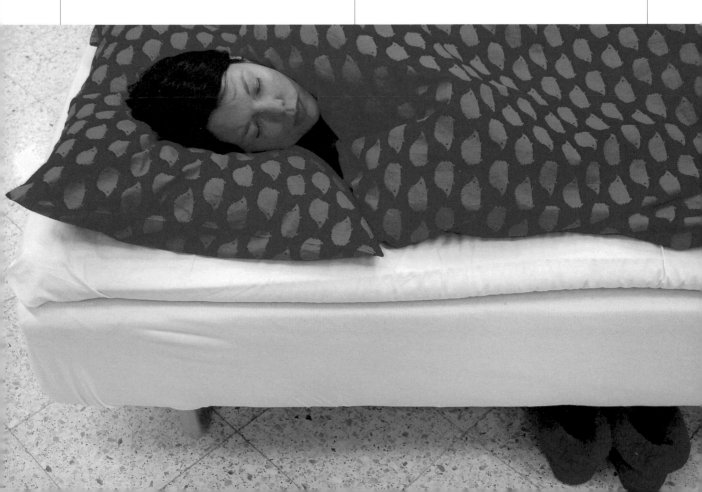

Above: Wikström lay on a bed in the middle of the store in Kalmar during business hours for seven days (Photograph by Oscar Guermouche).

not going to do anything, just close my eyes, and let the thoughts come and go. Now, what would happen if everyone did this?"

Wikström's presence drew mixed reactions from shoppers, as well as a range of discussions in the store—a place where otherwise nothing unpredictable happens, according to the artist. An elderly woman stood by the bed daily, and read passages from the Bible, while a young man pulled up a stool and read his poems to her. Another pinched Wikström's toe. "What is this? A real person or a mannequin?" he asked. "It's a work of art," his companion responded.

Within the art world, the acronym ICA generally refers to "Institute of Contemporary Art." In Sweden, the letters also represent the name of one of the largest supermarket chains. By hosting the exhibition in a grocery store, local artists were granted a new venue amid the closing of many of the city's exhibition spaces. Meanwhile, the show also brought performative works, such as Wikström's piece, to a wider public.

WOCHENKLAUSUR
MEDICAL CARE FOR THE HOMELESS
1993–

Austrians are insured under their country's universal health coverage. Yet, the homeless often go without treatment due to a highly bureaucratic system that favors those with proof of residency. When the Vienna-based collective WochenKlausur was invited to present work at the contemporary art space Vienna Succession, they organized a free mobile clinic in the Karlsplatz, a plaza near the gallery generally populated by many homeless people. The clinic, which was run out of a van and equipped to facilitate basic medical treatment, was initially designed as a prototype intended to operate for 11 weeks. This was

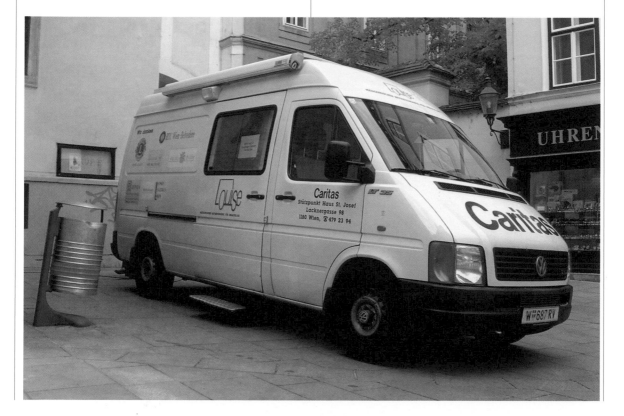

Above: The clinic's van, now run by Caritas, travels to public spaces around Vienna and provides health care for homeless people (Courtesy WochenKlausur).

1993. The van still travels daily to public spaces throughout Vienna, providing medical care to over 600 people per month.

The collective—a group of eight artists—raised 70,000 Euros from commercial sponsors in order to purchase the van, medical equipment, supplies, and licensing required to operate the facility on public property. However, paying physicians' salaries proved to be a larger obstacle, since the only viable funding source—the city government—refused to participate. But after WochenKlausur enlisted a German reporter to interview Vienna's chancellor, the city acquiesced to the request, and continues to support two full-time positions.

Medical Care for the Homeless was the first of nearly 30 endeavors WochenKlausur has launched in the past 17 years, each designed to create immediate impact on a pressing local issue. The collective travels to different cities upon invitation by arts institutions, reads local papers, talks to residents, and then identifies precise actions that can be carried out within a given timeframe, in order to institute sustainable change. The projects have ranged from establishing a pension for sex workers in Zurich to recycling materials from museums into objects useful to homeless shelters, soup kitchens, and clothing distribution centers.

WOMEN ON WAVES

2001–

Women on Waves rocked the boat well before setting sail in 2001. Lead by physician Rebecca Gomperts, this women's healthcare advocacy group aimed to provide abortion services in countries where the procedure is illegal. They built a seafaring abortion clinic registered in The Netherlands,

Top: The Women on Waves ship Aurora prepares to sail to Ireland (Courtesy Women on Waves). *Above:* The first Latin American abortion hotline was officially launched in 2008 in Ecuador when a banner was hung on the Virgen del Panecillo in Quito (Photograph by Mrova, Courtesy Women on Waves).

anchored it 12 miles away from harbors in international waters, where they could operate under Dutch law, and attempted to safely bring women on board. Yet, media buzz resulted in strong resistance including military intervention as the ship approached Portugal and pelts from fake blood and eggs in Poland. No surgical abortions were performed at sea, and only fifty women received abortions of any kind on the vessel. "But the boat created a lot of controversy, which has always been important to the campaign," says Kinja Manders, project manager for Women on Waves. "Our goal has always been to stir public debate, and to send the message that abortion is not simply a public health issue—it's a social justice issue."

The small team, a mix of healthcare specialists and activists, provided contraceptives, pregnancy testing, information about STDs, and prescribed the abortion pill (RU-486) aboard until 2008. While the sea voyages have ended, Women on Waves has exhibited the boat in international exhibitions, in homage to the organization's roots in the arts: early funding was provided by the Mondriaan Foundation, and Gomperts earned a degree in art before attending med school. "We've always been interested in the link between activism and art," Manders says, "and in finding creative and conceptual solutions that are on the edge." The organization now exists online and educates women on safe, self-induced abortions, a medically uncontroversial, but politically charged practice; how to obtain abortion pills; and where to seek accurate information and counseling before and after an abortion.

Above: The Portuguese Navy blocks the Women on Waves ship from entering Portugal (Photograph by Nadya Peek, Courtesy Women on Waves).

THE LEONORE ANNENBERG PRIZE FOR ART AND SOCIAL CHANGE

Starting in 2008, Creative Time has had the honor of bestowing The Leonore Annenberg Prize for Art and Social Change to three distinguished artists who have committed their life's work to promoting social justice in surprising and profound ways. The $25,000 prize is presented annually at the Creative Time Summit and has been generously supported by the Annenberg Foundation.

The prize is directly in line with the achievements of Mrs. Annenberg's generous spirit, passion for humanitarian efforts, and devotion to the public good. The award also furthers Creative Time's long commitment to commissioning and presenting groundbreaking, historically important artwork, and fostering a culture of experimentation and change.

Founded by self-described "impostors" Andy Bichlbaum and Mike Bonanno, The Yes Men work to raise awareness around pressing social issues, specifically targeting "leaders and big corporations who put profits ahead of everything else." Known for their public pranks and parodies, the duo agree their way into the fortified compounds of commerce and politics and share their stories to provide the public with a glimpse at the inner workings of corporate and political America. An early project took the form of a satirical website, www.gwbush.com, which drew attention to alleged hypocrisies and false information on President G. W. Bush's actual site. On December 3, 2004, the twentieth anniversary of Bhopal disaster in India, Bichlbaum posed as a spokesperson from Dow Chemical—the company responsible for the chemical disaster—for an interview with the BBC. Announcing on live television that the company intended to liquidate $12 billion in assets to assist victims of the Bhopal incident, Bichlbaum started an international rumor resulting in a loss of $2 billion for Dow.

In their most notorious prank to date, The Yes Men, the 2009 recipients of The Leonore Annenberg Prize for Art and Social Change, designed and distributed fake editions of three world newspapers. On November 12, 2008, they distributed a fake edition of *The New York Times* in NYC and LA. The lead headline proclaimed, "Iraq War Ends." Their fake edition of *The International Herald Tribune*, on which Greenpeace collaborated and which was distributed in Brussels, NYC, and Beijing, coincided with an international climate change summit in Brussels. It declared, "Heads of State Agree on Historic Climate-Saving Deal." When the summit failed to produce a solid agreement, The Yes Men updated the online edition to read, "World Actually Not Saved." On September 21, 2009, a bogus *New York Post* distributed in New York City read "We're Screwed," again commenting on worldwide climate change.

Over the years the group has also launched some very unconventional products—from the Dow Acceptable Risk calculator, a new industry standard for determining how many deaths are acceptable when achieving large profits, to Vivoleum, a new renewable fuel sourced from the victims of climate change. The gonzo political activists have produced two documentary films, *The Yes Men* (2003) and *The Yes Men Fix the World* (2009), which was awarded the prestigious audience award at the Berlin International Film Festival.

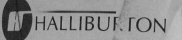

Opposite: A New Yorker takes in the shocking news from the Yes Men's faux *New York Times* cover (Courtesy Steve Lambert).

Above, top to bottom: The inflatable costume SurvivaBall claims to be a self contained living system for corporate managers for surviving disasters caused by global warming. The Yes Men pose as corporate executives. (Courtesy Steve Lambert)

RICK LOWE
PROJECT ROW HOUSES
1993–

In 1993, artist Rick Lowe purchased a row of abandoned shotgun-style houses in Houston, Texas', Northern Third Ward district, a low-income African-American neighborhood that was slotted for demolition. He galvanized hundreds of volunteers to help preserve the buildings, first by sweeping streets, rebuilding facades, and renovating the old housing's interiors. Then, with funding from the National Endowment for the Arts and private foundations, the growing group of activists transformed the blight-ridden strip into a vibrant campus that hosts visiting artists, galleries, a park, commercial spaces, gardens, and as well as subsidized housing for young mothers, ages 18-26, looking to get back on their feet. Called *Project Row Houses*, the effort has restored the architecture and history of the community, while providing essential social services to residents. Now functioning as a non-profit organization, the project continues to be emblematic of long-term, community-engaged programs, and has been exhibited around in world in museums, and other art venues.

Since Project Row Houses' inception, Lowe—the 2010 recipient of The Leonore Annenberg Prize for Art and Social Change—has privileged art as a catalyst for change, a word that he has considered carefully. "It used to be that you could assume a progressive agenda when you heard the word 'change,'" he says. "But language is shifting. Clarity is missing." The project first took root after a conversation he had with a high school student who questioned the efficacy of making art objects in the quest for social justice. Inspired, Lowe looked to the work of artist John Biggers, who believed that art holds the capacity to uplift tangible social conditions, before intervening in the Northern Third Ward.

Project Row Houses has grown from 22 houses to 40, and includes exhibition spaces, a literary center, a multimedia performance art space, offices, low-income housing, and other amenities. In 2003, the organization established the Row House Community Development Corporation, a low-income rental-housing agency.

Opposite: The white clapboard duplex structures were built to provide housing for low-income families (Photograph by Eric Hester, courtesy Project Row Houses).

Clockwise from top: Lowe discovered this abandoned block and a half of row houses in Houston's Northern Third Ward in 1993. Visitors attend the opening of Project Row Houses Round 33 in October 2010. Artist Andrea Bowers contributed *Hope in Hindsight* as part of Round 33 at Project Row Houses. (Photographs by Eric Hester, courtesy Project Row Houses).

JEANNE VAN HEESWIJK

1993–

"If you really want to contribute to changes in social structures, you need time." Jeanne van Heeswijk took this ethos to heart in *Valley Vibes*, her effort to gather the voices of East London's residents, who in 1998 began witnessing gentrification—or the replacement of local culture for corporate business—in their neighborhood. As part of the project, van Heeswijk built a "Vibe Detector," a simple aluminum storage container on wheels that functions as a mobile karaoke machine, radio station, and recording studio, equipped with a professional sound kit and DAT recorder.

At the project's launch, van Heeswijk enlisted members of the architecture and urban-planning research group CHORA to occupy sidewalks (à la street food vendors) and ask residents to use the available equipment to record their stories, music, performances, or any other signifier of local culture that countered the regeneration taking place in the neighborhood. The Vibe Detector traveled to private parties, the local hairdresser's salon, shops, nightclubs, poetry readings, school events, municipal meetings, and festivals—wherever residents would gather to discuss issues important to them. CHORA still operates the Vibe Detector by offering the equipment for use free of charge, as well as technical assistance and marketing advice.

Van Heeswijk is the 2011 recipient of The Leonore Annenberg Prize for Art and Social Change. Since 1993, she has created public art that mediates relationships among neighborhood residents by initiating different modes of communication around pressing issues. For one of her first projects, she organized a joint exhibition between Amsterdam's Buers van Berlage art museum and the Red Cross that addressed notions of human dignity in an age of violence. In 2008, she revitalized the Afrikaander market in South Rotterdam by bringing artists, vendors, and consumers together to rebuild stalls, rethink the selection of wares for sale, and create a new economy within this struggling neighborhood.

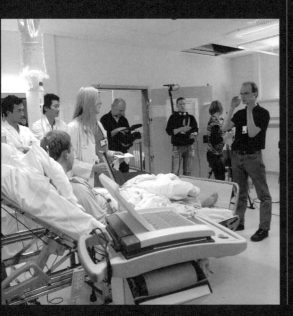

Above: Van Heeswijk created Norway's first hospital soap opera with *It Runs in the Neighbourhood* at the Stavanger University Hospital in 2008, when Stavanger was the European Capital of Culture (Photograph by Jeanne van Heeswijk).

Above: Valley Vibes took place in parts of East London designated for regeneration, like this section near Deptford (Courtesy of Jeanne van Heeswijk and Amy Plant).

Top row, left to right: The Blue House, one of the buildings in a planned development in Amsterdam, was turned into a place for research into the history, development, and evolution of experimental communities. *Tomorrows Market* is a project based on cultural production as a means of economic growth for the redeveloping Afrikaanderwijk neighborhood of Rotterdam. (Photographs by Ramon Mosterd)

Bottom: Van Heeswijk, with architect Dennis Kaspori, offered children a collective learning environment with the project *Face Your World, Urban Lab Slotervaart* in Amsterdam in 2005 (Photograph by Dennis Kaspori).

THANK YOU VERY MUCH

Living as Form: Socially Engaged Art from 1991—2011
was generously made possible by:

The Andrew W. Mellon Foundation

PROJECT SUPPORTERS

Living as Form was made possible by:

The Lily Auchincloss Foundation
Joanne Leonhardt Cassullo
The Danish Arts Council Committee for Visual Arts
Stephanie & Tim Ingrassia
The Andrew W. Mellon Foundation
Bella Meyer & Martin Kace
The Mondriaan Foundation
The National Endowment for the Arts
The Netherlands Foundation for Visual Arts,
    Design and Architecture
The Rockefeller Brothers Fund
Emily Glasser & Billy Susman

ART WORKS.
arts.gov

Living as Form (the Abridged, Nomadic Version) is curated by Nato
Thompson and co-organized by Creative Time and Independent
Curators International (ICI), New York.

CREDITS

Living as Form: Socially Engaged Art from 1991–2011:

Nato Thompson, Editor
Sharmila Venkatasubban, Managing Editor
Garrick Gott, Designer
Clinton Krute, Copyeditor
Ann Holcomb, Proofreader
Cynthia Pringle, Proofreader
Sadia Shirazi, Fact Checker
Merrell Hambleton, Editorial Assistant
Phillip Griffith, Intern
Madeline Lieberburg, Intern
Rachel Ichniowski, Intern
Winona Packer, Intern

Curatorial Advisors:

Caron Atlas, Negar Azimi, Ron Bechet, Claire Bishop, Brett
Bloom, Rashida Bumbray, Carolina Caycedo, Ana Paula Cohen,
Common Room, Teddy Cruz, Sofía Hernández, Chong Cuy,
Gridthiya Gaweewong, Hou Hanru, Stephen Hobbs, Marcus
Neustetter, Shannon Jackson, Maria Lind, Chus Martínez,
Sina Najafi, Marion von Osten, Ted Purves, Raqs Media
Collective, Gregory Sholette, SUPERFLEX, Christine Tohme,
and Sue Bell Yank

Creative Time Board of Directors:

Amanda Weil (Board Chair), Philip E. Aarons, Steven Alden,
Peggy Jacobs Bader, Jill Brienza, Joanne Leonhardt Cassullo,
Suzanne Cochran, Beth Rudin DeWoody, Marie Douglas, Dana
Farouki, Thelma Golden, Michael Gruenglas, Sharon Hayes,
Tom Healy, Stephanie Ingrassia, Liz Kabler, Stephen Kramarsky,
Patrick Li, Bella Meyer, Vik Muniz, Shirin Neshat, Amy Phelan,
Paul Ramírez Jonas, William Susman, Elizabeth Swig, Felicia
Taylor, Jed Walentas

Creative Time Staff:

Anne Pasternak, President and Artistic Director

Jay Buim, Leonhardt Cassullo Video Fellow
Merrell Hambleton, Development Associate
Katie Hollander, Deputy Director
Marisa Mazria Katz, Artists on the News Editor
Christopher Kissock, Digital Marketing and
    Communications Associate
Zoe Larkins, Executive Assistant
Cynthia Pringle, Director of Operations
Lydia Ross, Foundation and Individual Giving Associate
Danielle Schmidt, Associate Director of Events
    and Membership
Justin Sloane, Designer
Jessica Shaefer, Interim Director of Communications
Kevin Stanton, Production Assistant
Leila Tamari, Programming Assistant
Nato Thompson, Chief Curator
Sharmila Venkatasubban, Curatorial/Editorial Fellow

Additional thanks to former Creative Time staff who were
involved with the project:

Leah Abir, Artis Curatorial Fellow
Aliya Bonar
Shane Brennan
Anna Dinces
Rachel Ford
Dina Pugh
Sally Szwed

UNIVERSITY OF WINCHESTER
LIBRARY

COLOPHON

LIving as Form: Socially Engaged Art From 1991–2011

© 2012 Creative Time

Foreword © 2012 Anne Pasternak

Living as Form © 2012 Nato Thompson

Participation And Spectacle: Where Are We Now?
© 2012 Claire Bishop

Returning On Bikes: Notes On Social Practice
© 2012 Maria Lind

Democratizing Urbanization and the Search for
a New Civic Imagination © 2012 Teddy Cruz

Microutopias: Public Practice In The Public Sphere
© 2012 Carol Becker

Eventwork: The Fourfold Matrix of Contemporary
Social Movements © 2012 Brian Holmes

Living Takes Many Forms © 2012 Shannon Jackson

All rights reserved. No part of this book may be reproduced in any form by any electronic or mechanical means (including photocopying, recording, or information storage and retrieval) without permission in writing from the publisher.

Designed by Garrick Gott

Design assistant: Maggie Bryan
Typefaces: Geometric 213 and 712 by Bitstream
and Mercury by Radim Pesko

Printed and bound in Hong Kong by Paramount

Production supervision: The Production Department,
Sue Medlicott and Nerissa Dominguez Vales

Co-published by:

Creative Time Books
59 East 4th Street, 6th floor
New York NY 10003
www.creativetime.org

Creative Time Books is the publishing arm of Creative Time, Inc., a public arts organization that has been commissioning adventurous public art in New York City and beyond since 1972.

The MIT Press
55 Hayward Street
Cambridge, MA 02142
www. mitpress.mit.edu

MIT Press books may be purchased at special quantity discounts for business or sales promotional use. For information, please email special_sales@mitpress.mit.edu or write to Special Sales Department, The MIT Press, 55 Hayward Street, Cambridge, MA 02142.

First edition, 2012

ISBN 978-0-262-01734-3

Library of Congress Control Number: 2011941569

10 9 8 7 6 5 4 3 2

UNIVERSITY OF WINCHESTER